MARKETING DYNAMICS

Theory and Practice

MARKETING DYNAMICS

Theory and Practice

Rajagopal, *Ph.D. FRSA*

Monterrey Institute of Technology and Higher Education
(Instituto Technologico y de Estudios Superiores de Monterrey - ITESM)
Mexico City Campus
Mexico

PUBLISHING FOR ONE WORLD

NEW AGE INTERNATIONAL (P) LIMITED, PUBLISHERS

(formerly Wiley Eastern Limited)

New Delhi • Bangalore • Chennai • Cochin • Guwahati • Hyderabad
Jalandhar • Kolkata • Lucknow • Mumbai • Ranchi

Visit us at **www.newagepublishers.com**

Published by New Age International (P) Ltd., Publishers
First Edition: 2007
Reprint: 2013

BRANCHES

- **Bangalore** 37/10, 8th Cross (Near Hanuman Temple), Azad Nagar, Chamarajpet, Bangalore-560 018
Tel.: (080) 26756823, Telefax: 26756820, E-mail: bangalore@newagepublishers.com
- **Chennai** 26, Damodaran Street, T. Nagar, Chennai-600 017
Tel.: (044) 24353401, Telefax: 24351463, E-mail: chennai@newagepublishers.com
- **Cochin** CC-39/1016, Carrier Station Road, Ernakulam South, Cochin-682 016
Tel.: (0484) 2377004, Telefax: 4051303, E-mail: cochin@newagepublishers.com
- **Guwahati** Hemsen Complex, Mohd. Shah Road, Paltan Bazar, Near Starline Hotel, Guwahati-781 008
Tel.: (0361) 2513881, Telefax: 2543669, E-mail: guwahati@newagepublishers.com
- **Hyderabad** 105, 1st Floor, Madhiray Kaveri Tower, 3-2-19, Azam Jahi Road, Nimboliadda, Hyderabad-500 027
Tel.: (040) 24652456, Telefax: 24652457, E-mail: hyderabad@newagepublishers.com
- **Kolkata** RDB Chambers (Formerly Lotus Cinema) 106A, 1st Floor, S.N. Banerjee Road, Kolkata-700 014
Tel.: (033) 22273773, Telefax: 22275247, E-mail: kolkata@newagepublishers.com
- **Lucknow** 16-A, Jopling Road, Lucknow-226 001
Tel.: (0522) 2209578, 4045297, Telefax: 2204098, E-mail: lucknow@newagepublishers.com
- **Mumbai** 142C, Victor House, Ground Floor, N.M. Joshi Marg, Lower Parel, Mumbai-400 013
Tel.: (022) 24927869, Telefax: 24915415, E-mail: mumbai@newagepublishers.com
- **New Delhi** 22, Golden House, Daryaganj, New Delhi-110 002
Tel.: (011) 23262368, 23262370, Telefax: 43551305, E-mail: sales@newagepublishers.com

ISBN : 978-81-224-1942-9

₹ 299.00

C-12-10-6628

Printed in India at Glorious Printers, Delhi.
Typeset at In-house.

PUBLISHING FOR ONE WORLD
NEW AGE INTERNATIONAL (P) LIMITED, PUBLISHERS
7/30 A, Darya Ganj, New Delhi-110002
Visit us at **www.newagepublishers.com**

PREFACE

In the highly competitive and global marketplace of today, the pressure on organizations to find new ways to create and deliver value to customers grows ever stronger. The growing internationalization of business induces changes in the positioning of competitors and appropriate competitive strategies. As the companies attain gradual success in geographically expanding their business and effectively performing international operations, they reach at critical point and would be able to synchronize the proximity to the overseas markets and customer needs. Global companies at this point blue print their successful business systems in the emerging markets by creating relatively decentralized operations in production, marketing and sales. The largest and powerful multinational business houses prefer to be aggressive to dominate over the most demanding and emerging sectors. General Motors, for example is offering credit cards and supermarket groups routinely now offer gasoline, banking, pensions and saving plans apart from the manufacturing and marketing of automobiles. Companies that are capable of managing appropriate diffusion of technology and adaptation process among the customer segments are found to be highly successful. Competition among multinationals these days is likely to be a three-dimensional strategic game wherein the moves of an organization in one market are designed to achieve goals in another market in ways that aren't immediately apparent to rivals[1].

Successful business strategies are those which are cohesive with the marketing in action. Once such strategy is synchronized, the firm may be involved in every stage in the life cycles related to products, services and markets. It is not a easy task to identify strategies for entering new markets or to decide which segments to do business with. Many firms simply rush to the marketplace with limited business insights and fall far short of their goals. It is often difficult to draw a precise and powerful strategy for many companies to compete in reference to financial and technological resources, the seasoned management, and the powerful competing brands. However, local companies often have more options than they might think.

In the changing business scenario marked by rapid globalization, intensive competition in the

---

1 Ian C. MacMillan, Alexander B. van Putten and Rita Gunther McGrath : Global Competition— What is the First Move, *HBS Working Knowledge,* Harvard Business School, June 23, 2003

products and services segment, fast moving technology and changing consumer preference, it is essential for the companies to develop the strategic marketing skills for both survival and sustenance in business. The new school of business and contemporary researchers have emphasized that, towards maximizing the lifetime value of customers, a firm must manage customer relationships for the long term. In a disagreement to this notion, a study demonstrates that firm profits in competitive environments are maximized when managers focus on the short term with respect to their customers[2].

The strategic marketing skills provide a shield to the companies to play defensive during rival attacks and to go aggressive when they foresee an opportunity in the given business environment. However, success will depend on the ability of the companies to understand the markets unfolding around them and develop a rational strategy for long term gains. One of the significant aspects of the marketing strategy in the contemporary sense may be the convergence of customer focus with corporate goals for holding the larger share of competitive advantages. Marketing strategy may be conceived as an innovative mindset and tool for digging deeper into competitive arena of the business in order to derive optimal solutions for the problems. The most critical aspect of strategy implementation process in marketing is towards ensuring creation of sustained customer value. The key internal process for managing implementation and control of marketing strategy includes operations management, customer relationships, innovation, regulatory and social processes. While critically examining the business environment we may find complex interplay between consumer and marketer's strategy which determines the scope of every product and services in a given market. Such a strategic move may be understood as the *mind of the market*. Most of the companies are transforming their business strategies facing to the customers value chain and an intriguing look at how the mind, company, and environment interact to drive corporate decisions, this book is a welcome addition to the existing resources.

This book highlights the most recent trends and developments emerged in marketing theory with an emphasis on integrated application of strategies between marketing and all the other functions of the business. It introduces new perspectives in successful strategic market planning, and presents additional company examples of creative, market-focused, and customer-driven action. Coverage includes a focus on competitor analysis, brand strategy, sales management, marketing-mix and marketing research. Chapter topics discuss building customer satisfaction, market-oriented strategic planning, analyzing consumer markets and buyer behavior, dealing with the competition, designing pricing strategies and programs, and managing the sales force. Strategy applications and best practices have been discussed in the book for marketing managers who want to increase their understanding of the major issues of strategic, tactical, and administrative marketing-along with the opportunities and needs of the marketplace in the years ahead. This book would benefit largely the undergraduate and graduate management students who study international marketing course as a core or elective subject. This book has been written keeping in view the international coverage and contents of the subject that is commonly adapted in most of the Latin merican and sian universities including management schools in India.

2 Villanueva Julian, Bharadwaj Pradeep, Chen Yuxin and Balasubramanian Shridhar, *Managing Customer Relationships- Should Managers Really Focus on Long Term*, IESE Business School, Working Paper # D/560, May, 2004, pp 1-37

I express my thanks to my daughter Ananya for being instrumental in drawing the Tables and Charts in this book. My son Amritanshu always stood by with me in the hectic times of revising the draft which helped me in de-stressing and regaining the energy back to work. Finally, I express my deep gratitude to my wife Arati Rajagopal who copy edited the first draft of the manuscript and stayed in touch till the final proofs were cross checked. She has been the light of the spirit in carrying this comprehensive work.

Rajagopal

CONTENTS

1. UNDERSTANDING COMPETITORS AND COMPETITION 1-64

Understanding Competition • Theoretical Framework of Competition • Competitor Learning • Competitor Learning Models • Playing in the Competition • Competitor Strategies • Market Place Strategy • Competitor Analysis: Capabilities and Competency • Analyzing Competitor's Signals • Re-engineering Business for Competitive Advantage • Customer Value and Reengineering Process • Corporate Concepts of Re-engineering Business • Competitive Focus • References.

Case 1.1

Case of EID-Parry (India) Ltd. – Product- Mix – Product Performance – Competitive Business Process – Strategic Moves: Alliances and Mergers – IT in Corporate Business: A Challenge in Competition – Discussion Issues.

Case 1.2

Retail Expansion in Global Arena: Strategies of Wal-Mart to Sustain Competition – The Wal-Mart Culture – Respect the Individual – Service to Our Customers – Strive for Excellence – Wal-Mart International Operations – Development Opportunities – Pricing Philosophy – Retail Divisions of Wal-Mart – Super-centers – SAM'S Club – Neighborhood Market – WAL-MART.COM – External and Internal Threats.

2. PRODUCT STRATEGY 65-101

Levels of Product • Product Hierarchy • International Product-line Analysis • Product Design Strategy • Product Life Cycle Management • New Product Development • Product Planning Matrix • Product Portfolio Matrix • Dimensions of Product Strategies • Product Repositioning Strategy • Product Strategy Perspectives • Selected Readings.

Case 2.1

L'oreal Netherlands: Product Marketing Strategy in Europe – The Dutch Market – Synergie – Skin Care Market – Competition – Consumer Behaviour – Product Manager's Review.

3. BRAND STRATEGY **103-141**

Brand Categories • Brand Drivers In International Markets • Brand Architecture • Brand Hierarchy • Brand Architecture Process • Brand Architecture Audit • Brand Drivers • Reach of the Brand • Communication Sensitivity and Brand Personality • Cognitive Dimensions in Branding • Brand Portfolio and Advertising • Selected Readings.

Case 3.1

BMW: Building Brand through Relationship Networking – Customer Prospecting and Retaining Trends – BMW Milestones (1916-2001) – Market Performance of BMW-2003 – Conceiving Customer Delight: The Value Chain – Customer Relationship Tracking.

4. PRICING STRATEGY **143-192**

Value and Skimming Pricing • Pricing With Demand Curve • Penetration Pricing • Geographical Pricing • Conspicuous Pricing • Psychological Pricing • Value-added Pricing • Complementary Product Pricing • Price Discounts • Discriminate Pricing • Promotional Pricing • Mark-up Pricing • Pricing Fundamentals • Cost-Plus Pricing • Customer Expectation-based Pricing • Pricing Models • Price-Market Relationship • Pricing Strategies Management • Price Control • Building Pricing Strategies • Other Pricing Modalities • Strategy for Price Leadership • Non-price Factors • An Overview on Pricing Strategy • References.

Case 4.1

The Air Cargo Competition.

Case 4.2

'Crimson Nectar' Blows-up in Boardroom : A Case of Building Marketing Policy of a New Generation Product – Consumption Trends of Non-Alcoholic Beverages – Exotic Fruit Nectars- Industry Dimensions – Idea Chain Management – Board Room Discussions – Expert Voice in Board Room – Customer Value and Re-engineering Process – Adjournment.

Case 4.3

Blockbuster Entertainment Corporation: Cross Promotion and Pricing Strategy.

5. DISTRIBUTION STRATEGY **193-227**

Profile of Principal Distribution Strategies • Distribution Strategies • International Channel Selection • Distribution in Gray Market • Logistics Management • Channel Management • Developing Logistics Strategy • Physical Distribution • Distribution Planning • Functional Excellence in Distribution Planning • Seclected Readings.

Case 5.1

Domino's Pizza Distribution Plan – Leadership Strategy – The Information Technology Solution – Re-engineering for Cross-Functional Excellence – Phased Approach to

Implementation – Team-Development Initiatives – Achieving the Vision – Domino's Mission: Global Leadership.

6. **PROMOTION STRATEGIES** 229-283

Developing Advertising Strategy • Advertising Environment • The Advertising Process • Advertising Categories • Advertising and Buyer Perception • Strategies in Advertising • Advertising styles • Developing a Media Plan • Media Scheduling • Direct Response Advertising • Display Advertising • Brand Positioning and Advertising Evaluation • Positioning Methods • Concept of Promotion Mix • Advertising Objectives • Advertising Styles • Message Strategy • Creative-Mix • Strategies to Develop Word-of-Mouth Advertising • Copywriting • Developing Media Plan • Direct Response Advertising • Advertising Campaign • Institutional Advertising • Advertising Appropriation • Advertising Research • Effectiveness in Advertising • Web Advertising and Promotion • References.

Case 6.1

Penetrating Media Market across the Boundaries: The Strategy of Azteca America – International Trend of Television Industry – Company Background and Time Line – Hispanic Market in the US – Expansion in Hispanic American Regions – Advertising Issues – Sales Force Deployment of the Company – Performance in Hispanic American Market – Strategy Perspectives for Future • References.

7. **MARKETING RESEARCH** 285-308

Scope of Marketing Research • Marketing Research Process • Sampling Techniques • Tools of Data Collection • Data Preparation • Data Analysis Approaches • Market Information Management • Monitoring and Evaluation Research in Marketing • SWOT Analysis • Qualitative Market Research • Selected Readings.

Case 7.1

Cadbury Schweppes: Positioning in Latin America – The Product Line – Modes of Entry – Brand Management – Corporate Growth – Brand Promotion – Business Threats – Issues of Concern.

8. **SALES MANAGEMENT** 309-338

Consultative Sales • Technical Sales • Commercial Sales and Direct Sales • Organizing the Sales Force • Retailing • Departmental Store • Exclusive Retail Stores • Super Markets • Convenience Stores • Discount Stores • Catalogue Showroom • Non-store Retailing • Decision Making in Retailing • Tools of Retailing • Distribution • Information on Sales • Selling and Buying Process • Measuring Sales Performance • Sales Compensation • Selected Readings.

Case 8.1

Canon in Mexican Business Environment – Corporate Philosophy – Key Areas of Canon in Mexican Market – Buyer Behaviour and Distribution – Product Distribution and Sales – Organizational Restructuring – Compensation Program – Future Perspectives: Beyond Customer Satisfaction • References.

9. STRATEGIC MARKETING 341-364

Focus of Strategic Marketing • Strategic Marketing Screening Process • Strategic Directions • Strategic Management • Growth Strategies • Strategic Marketing Planning • Developing Activity Schedule • References.

Case 9.1

Tropicana Fruit Beverage in India.

10. INNOVATIVE MARKETING STRATEGIES 364-412

Economic Value-Added (EVA) Concept • Market Entry Strategies • Developing Entry Plan • Control Management • Profit Impact on Marketing Strategy • Marketplace Standing • Market Uncertainties and Entry Decisions • Managing Social Marketing • Comprehensive Branding • Selected Readings.

Case 10.1

Dell Takes a Different Tack in China.

Case 10.2

Consumer Preferences on Buying Automobiles – Chronology of Growth – Recent Performance – PT Cruiser : Performance Appraisal – Slump in Chrysler's Market – The Time Ahead.

CHAPTER 1

UNDERSTANDING COMPETITORS AND COMPETITION

CHAPTER FOCUS

- *To understand and analyze the competitor moves in the market,*
- *To acquaint skills in competitor learning models, market place strategy and theory of competitive advantage, and*
- *To learn competitor signals, moves, strategies and approaches to win the rival attacks in the competitive business arena*
- *To gain knowledge about the business re-engineering strategies and competitive forces.*

Productivity differs across individual, monopolistically competitive firms in each country. Firms face some initial uncertainty concerning their future productivity when making an irreversible investment to enter the domestic market. In addition to the sunken entry cost, firms face both fixed and per-unit export costs. Only a subset of relatively more productive firms export, while the remaining, less productive firms only serve their domestic market. This microeconomic structure endogenously determines the extent of the traded sector and the composition of consumption baskets in both countries. Exogenous shocks to aggregate productivity, sunken entry costs, and trade costs induce firms to enter and exit both their domestic and export markets, thus altering the composition of consumption baskets across countries over time[1]. The microeconomic features have important consequences for macroeconomic variables. Macroeconomic dynamics, in turn, feed back into firm level decisions, further altering the pattern of trade over time. The aggregate picture of world economic growth shows a remarkable diversity in

1 Fabio Ghironi and Marc Melitz : International Trade and Macroeconomic Dynamics with Heterogeneous Firms, *Society for Economic Dynamics,* Annual Meeting Papers, 2004.

growth performance, both geographically and across time. There exist high growth countries and low growth countries on the panorama of global economy. Some countries have grown rapidly over time while others have experienced growth spurts for a decade or two. What is the role of policy in this diversity? How can policy help transform this picture? However the increasing globalization tries to answer these questions in terms of catalyzing the economic growth and institutional innovations in the developing countries. Analysis of the success story of China, with an astonishing annual growth rate of 8.0 percent since the late 1970s, together with other well-known East Asian experiences that have taken place in countries such as South Korea and Taiwan, provide the basis to build some stylized facts about the take-off and the process of sustaining economic growth. On the other hand, the experience of liberalization, deregulation and privatization in countries such as Mexico, Argentina, Brazil, Colombia, Bolivia, and Peru have offered substantial evidence that allows us to question the standard formulae used to propel and maintain economic growth.[2]

UNDERSTANDING COMPETITION

Competition may be defined as an object centered process in business performance. Competition may be semantically described as a combination of two distinct Latin words - *com* (together) and *petere* (to seek). Similarly conflict is derived from *com* (together) and *fligere* (to strike). This distinction between the quest and the blow, to strive or to strike seems precisely the pertinent one for clarity and efficiency in social science.[3] Competition may be characterized as striving together to win the race not to destroy the other competitors from the point of view of the supporters of globalization. The local market competition is targeted towards the customers and the competitors strive to win the customer, temporarily or permanently. However, in business-to-business process, the competition may turn more tactical and strategic in order to outperform the rivals firms. In this way competition can be seen as regulated struggle. There are rules of economic competition and they do not generally include the destruction of competitors. The technology of marketing research is devoted to the difficult tasks of discovering customer needs, and the sub-disciplines of consumer and organizational buying behavior attempt to provide theoretical bases for the results. In this process the emphasis is on determination to win customers where competitors turn tactical towards brand or product positioning.

Emergence of virtual shopping, liberalization of economic policies in the developing countries all over the world competition has become like a traditional derby in which many companies participate for neck-to-neck race. In this business game the rules are subject to change without notice, the prize money may change in short notice, the route and finish line is also likely to change after the race begins, new entrants may join at any time during the race, the racers may form strong alliances, all creative strategies are allowed in the game and the governmental laws may change without notice and sometimes with retrospective effect. Hence, to win the race any company should acquire the strategies of outwitting,

2 Pessoa Argentino: Institutional Innovations, Growth Performance and Policy, *Conference Paper, European Regional Science Association,* 2004.

3 Mack R F: The Components of Social Conflicts, *Social Problems*, 22 (4), 1965, 388-397.

outmaneuvering and outperforming the competitors. In this process a company must understand thoroughly all the moves of the rival firms from various sources. The locales of the business rivalry have to be spotted to assess their strengths. An intriguing aspect of the marketplace is that the nature of competition can change over time. A technology, company, or product does not need to remain prey to another forever. Competitive roles can be radically altered with technological advances or with the right marketing decisions. External light meters, used for accurate diaphragm and speed setting on photographic cameras, enjoyed a stable, symbiotic (win–win) relationship with cameras for decades. As camera sales grew, so did light-meter sales. But eventually, technological developments enabled camera companies to incorporate light meters into their own boxes. Soon, the whole light-meter industry became prey to the camera industry. Sales of external light meters diminished while sales of cameras enjoyed a boost, and the relationship passed from win–win to *predator–prey*.[4] Table 1.1 exhibits the competitors' arena, which has to be studied comprehensively, and strategies to be build accordingly.

Table 1.1 Possible Arena of Business Rivalry

Business factors	*Customer locale*	*Geography*	*Channels*	*Institutions and patrons*
• Supply Chain • Promotion • Investment	• Market Place • Segments • Individual	• Spread • Regional	• C&F Agents • Retailers • Wholesalers • Franchisees • Mailers	• Government agencies • Co-operatives

The access to the infrastructure, raw material, the process, supplies and the other vital business factors is the most vulnerable to the competition. The competing firms pay more attention to the sources of factors, quality thereof, cost and management of the factors in order to prove better over each other. Customer, the end user, is the ultimate target of competitor for building aggressive and defensive strategies in business. The competing firms try to attract the customers by various means to polarize business and earn confidence in the market place. It is necessary for the successful business companies to look for such a place of business that provides them more location advantage and hold the customers for their goods and services. The business cordoning or securing the trade boundaries is an essential decision to be taken for building competitive strategies to attack rivals across regions. Even small business company can compete globally with the firms of all sizes through the Internet. The distribution channels, franchisees, carrying and forwarding agents, retailers and mailers with value added services represent an increasingly intense business rivalry or competition in all markets or competitive domains. Many firms like Godrej (Diversified Products), Proctor and Gamble (Consumer Goods), Compaq (Computers) reward their managers handsomely for winning the business battles in their channel wars. In succeeding to the market competition, the institutional and political patronage provides long run support to the companies.

4 Modis Theodore: *Conquering Uncertainty,* McGraw-Hill, New York, 1998.

The wining in product, channel and factor market place in many instances may not last long in building relationships with the customers. Many business firms have found themselves outmaneuvered in various functional aspects of business by the adept actions of rivals in the institutional arena. An intriguing aspect of the marketplace is that the nature of competition can change over time. A technology, company, or product does not need to remain prey to another forever. Competitive roles can be radically altered with technological advances or with the right marketing decisions. The need of the hour is to apply scientific methods to manage competition. Only then could modern corporations withstand the pressures of intense competition of a dynamic business era. The paper examines issues involved in the scientific approach of managing competition

> Struggle between fountain pens and ballpoint pens had a different ending. The substitution of ballpoint pens for fountain pens as writing instruments went through three distinct stages. Before the appearance of ballpoint pens, fountain pen sales grew undisturbed to fill the writing- instrument market. They were following an S-shaped curve when the ballpoint technology appeared in 1951. As ballpoint sales picked up, those of fountain pens declined in the period 1951 to 1973. Fountain pens staged a counterattack by radically dropping prices. But that effort failed. Fountain pens kept losing market share and embarked on an extinction course. By 1973, their average price had dropped to as low as 72 cents, to no avail. Eventually, however, the prices of fountain pens began rising. The fountain pen underwent what Darwin would have described as a character displacement to the luxury niche of the executive pen market. In the early 1970s, the strategy of fountain pens became a retreat into non-competition. By 1988, the price of some fountain pens in the United States had climbed to $400. The Volterra-Lotka model indicates that today the two species no longer interact but each follows a simple S-shaped growth pattern. As a consequence, fountain pens have secured a healthy and profitable market niche. Had they persisted in their competition with ballpoint pens, they would have perished.[5]

Many factors determine the nature of competition, including not only rivals, but also the economics of particular industries, new entrants, the bargaining power of customers and suppliers, and the threat of substitute services or products. A strategic plan of action based on this might include positioning the company so that its capabilities provide the best defense against the competitive forces, influencing the balance of forces through strategic moves and anticipating shifts in the factors underlying competitive forces.[6] In outwitting the competitors the companies must detect the changes in the strategy game in reference to the market players' status in gaining more knowledge, networking, entrepreneurship and increasing ambitions. The changes that are taking place in all the arenas as discussed in Table 1.1 have to be considered. The driving forces of competing firms, their organization and micro-economic environment need to be studied carefully by the company planning to overtake competitors in the business. Further in the process of winning the battle of rivals it would be helpful for a company to understand the changing stakes of the competitors and the forces after such developments. A company can outmaneuver the rival by being more skillful in particular tasks and reshaping the stakes in one or more business arenas. Outmaneuvering the rivals is the

5 Modis Theodore: A Scientific Approach to Managing Competition, *The Industrial Physicist,* 9 (1), 25-27, 2003
6 Porter Michael E: How Competitive Forces Shape Strategy? *Harvard Business Review,* March, 1979.

core of changing the rules of market place. The strategy for outperforming the competitor is largely based on two basic issues- the performance parameters and assessment criteria of the performance. However the critical parameters may include probe for the following information as *who is*:

- Creating new customer needs that do not exist
- Developing and establishing the new attributes of the product
- Establishing new channels to reach all the existing and potential customers
- Reinventing stakes to make others confined to play catch-up roles
- Creating new capabilities as the source of new products and customer needs
- Creating knowledge base for driving the capabilities for the new goods and services
- Establishing new relationships with the channels, institutions and customers
- Winning or loosing in the business battle
- Establishing new chain of customer delight
- Leading the product
- Dominating the price-value relationship

Parameters and assessments of the above actions would help in focusing both the thinking and strategy building process for sailing through the competition successfully. The current and future strategy of competitors must be considered by any company planning to outwit, outmaneuver and outperform them.

THEORETICAL FRAMEWORK OF COMPETITION

Philosophy of free enterprise system has been laid on the basics of competition. Competition is found in all marketing functions which include the prices at which products are exchanged, the attributes and qualities of products manufactured, the volume of products exchanged, the methods of distribution and promotion. The school of thought, which has constructed the competition related theories, may be categorized in two groups - economic theory and industrial organization perspective. The economists of former group have discussed many different models of competition. The focus of their work is the model of perfect competition, which is based on the premise that, when a large number of buyers and sellers in the market are dealing in homogeneous products, there is complete freedom to enter or exit the market and everyone has complete and accurate knowledge about everyone else. The latter group of the school of thought on competition in reference to industrial organizations postulates that a firm's position in the marketplace depends critically on the characteristics of the industry environment in which it competes. The industry environment comprises structure, conduct, and performance. Structure refers to the economic and technical perspectives of the industry in the context in which firms compete. It includes concentration in the industry such as the number and size distribution of firms, barriers to entry and product differentiation. The competition theories have further laid emphasis also on the market competition on functional dimensions, which include non-price competitions towards the product differentiation and quality competition. Products are differentiated when the products of different firms are not perfect substitutes and companies may compete by changing the characteristics of the product they sell. Such strategy may not be necessarily to make a product better than the competitor, but just to differentiate it in order to create an appeal to a different *market niche*.

Niche strategies provide a classic instance of such situations. No market is entirely homogeneous. There are always groups of customers which differ in terms of their needs. The environment thus created may well be fragmented; at the very least it will be structured. There exists the possibility of the occurrence of niches which individual competitors may occupy. Niches are unlikely to be complete, separate and well-defined. There will always be overlap. However, if such niches are rather subtly defined they may not always be obvious to all the players. Thus niche players may appear to compete but in practice do not do so or at least not fully. The competitive strategy of product differentiation helps the company in enhancing the product-mix by introducing many varieties, which increase the range of consumer choice. However, it divides up the market, leading to higher prices and costs for the firm. From an economist's point of view this definition of competition most closely resembles the category of monopolistic competition. In this case it is assumed that a large number of buyers and sellers exist, with each seller producing a variety of the essentially differentiated product which characterizes the product group. The distinctive features of each attribute yield the firms to gain small but nevertheless positive monopolistic advantage. This in turn accords the firms in question some of the features of the monopoly described earlier, but at a more modest level. The precise level of monopoly power enjoyed by each of the firms depends crucially upon the number of competing varieties in the market, and the distribution of consumers' preferences.

Modern economic theories on functioning of a firm have been developed since 1960. These have examined, why firms grow at different rates and tried to model the normal life cycle of a company, from fast-growing start-up to lumbering mature business. The more competition there is, the more likely are firms to be efficient and prices to be low. Economists have identified several different sorts of competition. In perfect competition every firm is competitive and plays in the market as a price taker. Where there is a monopoly, or firms have some market power, the seller has some control over the price, which will probably be higher than in a perfectly competitive market. By how much more will depend on how much market power there is, and on whether the firm(s) with the market power are committed to profit maximization. Firms earn only normal profits, the bare minimum profit necessary to keep them in business. If firms earn more than this (excess profits) other firms will enter the market and drive the price level down until there are only normal profits to be made. The market power may be stated as when one buyer or seller in a market has the ability to exert significant influence over the quantity of goods and services traded or the price at which they are sold. Market power does not exist when there is perfect competition, but it does when there is a monopoly, *monopsony*[7] or oligopoly. The basic attributes of the monopolistic competition include:

- Many buyers and sellers
- Differentiated products
- Sufficient knowledge
- Free entry

7 Monopsony may be described as the market dominated by a single buyer unlike monopoly wherein there exists a single seller.

Hair dressing industry may be a good example to understand monopolistic competition. There are many hairdressers in the country, and most hairdressing firms are quite small. There is free entry and it is at least possible that people know enough about their hairdressing options so that the "sufficient knowledge" condition is fulfilled. But the products of different hairdressers are not perfect substitutes. At the very least, their services are differentiated by location. A hairdresser in the downtown of Mexico may not be a perfect substitute for a hairdresser in the suburbs, although they may be good substitutes from the point of view of a customer who lives in the suburbs but works in downtown. Hairdressers services may be differentiated in other ways as well. Their styles may be different; the decor of the salon may be different, and that may make a difference for some customers; and even the quality of the conversation may make a difference. A very customer of a hair dressing firm may change hairdressers because an old hairdresser was an outspoken market protectionist.

In the contemporary analysis of competition and related strategies thereof, it is observed that the competitive firms intend to ascertain a continuous organizational learning process with respect to the value creation chain and measure performance of the new products introduced in the market. In the growing competitive markets the large and reputed firms are developing strategies to move into the provision of innovative combinations of products and services as 'high-value integrated solutions' tailored to each customer's needs than simply 'moving downstream' into services. Such firms are developing innovative combinations of service capabilities such as operations, business consultancy and finance required to provide complete solutions to each customer's needs

Strategy Focus 1.1: Organizational Competencies and Competitive Efficiency of Multinational Companies

The high-performing companies like Barclays, Cisco, Dow Chemical, 3M, and Roche drive to establish some basic rules for setting and delivering strategy which include simple executable strategy, realistic, short-run result oriented and transparency in process of strategy implementation. The above companies work on debating over the assumptions, and do not construct strategic frameworks on forecasts. The high performing companies create cross-functional teams drawn from strategy, marketing, and finance to ensure the assumptions underlying your long-term plans which reflect both the real economics of the company's markets and its actual performance relative to competitors. It has been observed that rigorous analytic framework is used by the high performing companies. Such companies as above ensure that the dialogue between the corporate office and the business units about market trends and assumptions is conducted within a rigorous framework, such as that of *profit pools*. These companies manage the resources deployments early to support the scheduled production and marketing activities. Proper resources management would in turn help the company create more realistic forecasts and more executable plans by discussing up-front the level and timing of critical deployments. The companies like Barclays, Cisco, Dow Chemical, 3M, and Roche clearly identify priorities and prioritize tactics so that employees have a clear sense of where to direct their efforts and continuously monitor performance. Tracking resource deployment, monitoring and evaluating results against plans, using continuous feedback to reset assumptions and reallocate resources have been principal activities performed by the business monitoring centers of these companies. The monitoring and evaluation reports are directly reported to the top management periodically. The Reward is set for the best strategy, product, brand and sales managers who achieve the targets and non-planned market shares in the up-stream markets. These companies also develop execution capabilities and motivational tools for the staff. Following these rules strictly the high performing companies narrow the strategy-to-performance gap and achieve sustainable growth among the competitors.

Source: Euro Monitor Online www.euromonitor.com
For more comprehension on the functional efficiencies of high performing companies see Mankins Michael C and Steele Richmond: Turning great strategies into great performance, *Harvard Business Review*, July 2005

in order to augment the customer value towards the innovative or new products. It has been argued that the provision of integrated solutions is attracting firms traditionally based in manufacturing and services to occupy a new base in the value stream centered on *systems integration* using internal or external sources of product designing, supply and customer focused promotion.[8] Besides the organizational perspectives of enhancing the customer value, the functional variables like pricing play a significant role in developing the customer perceptions towards the new products.

Most markets exhibit some form of imperfect or monopolistic competition. There are fewer firms than in a perfectly competitive market and each can create barriers to entry to some degree. A firm may own a crucial resource, such as an oil well, power generation, or it may have an exclusive operating license, which restricts other competitors to enter in the business. Operating on economies of scale for a large firm may also have a significant competitive advantage as it may enjoy a large volume of production at lower costs which may further lead to the price leadership with low retail prices. Such strategy would also prevent the potential competitors to enter in the business. An incumbent firm may make it hard for a would-be entrant by incurring huge sunk costs with high budget advertising. In view of such strategy any new entrant may match to compete effectively but may lose the market share, if the attempt to compete would fail. The sunk costs are costs that have been incurred and cannot be reversed such as spending on advertising or researching a product idea. They can be a barrier to entry. If potential entrants would have to incur similar costs, which would not be recoverable, if the entry failed, they may be scared off. Another radical strategy may be used by the powerful firms to discourage entry by raising exit costs, for example, by making it an industry norm to hire workers on long-term contracts, which would build the escalated cost barriers for rival companies. Thus firms can earn some excess profits without a new entrant being able to compete to bring prices

Least competitive market is a monopoly, dominated by a single firm that can earn substantial excess profit by controlling either the amount of output in the market or the price but not both. In this sense it is a price setter. When there are few firms in a market (oligopoly) they have the opportunity to behave as a as cartel. A cartel may be described as an agreement among two or more firms in the same industry to co-operate in fixing prices and/or carving up the market and restricting the volume of production they handle. A market dominated by a single firm does not necessarily have monopoly power, if it is a contestable market. In such a market, a single firm can dominate only, if it produces as efficiently its competitors and does not earn excess profits. If it becomes in-efficient or earns excess profits, another more efficient or less profitable firm will enter the market and dominate it instead.

An environment surrounding a specific product or market concerning the competition rather than a country's overall economic environment refers to the microeconomic environment. A careful analysis of a microenvironment indicates whether a company can successfully enter a

8 Davies Andrew (2004), Moving Base into High-value Integrated Solutions: A Value Stream Approach, *Industrial and Corporate Change*, 13(5), October, pp 727-756.

specific market. It may be hypothesized that rising prosperity of a nation depends on the productivity with which it uses its human, capital and natural resources. This is manifested in the way in which a nation's firms compete. Productivity, in turn, is a function of the interplay of many factors including political, legal and macroeconomic context; the quality of the microeconomic business environment; and the sophistication of company operations and strategy. Together they determine the capacity of a nation to produce internationally competitive firms and support rising prosperity. A context that creates pressure for firms continuously to upgrade the source and sophistication of their advantage and at the same time supports the upgrading process is a favorable micro-economic context. Pressure for upgrading is supplied by *demand conditions* featuring sophisticated and demanding customers, whose demands spur the local firms to innovate in order to upgrade their product/service offerings. Particularly valuable is pressure from local customers that anticipate the nature of demand elsewhere in the world. Different competitors, however, might aim to satisfy different types of demand: existing, latent, or incipient. *Existing demand* refers to a product bought to satisfy a recognized need. *Latent demand* applies in a situation where a particular need has been recognized, but no products have been offered. *Incipient demand* describes a projected need that will emerge when customers become aware of it, sometime in the future.

Competition may be analyzed in reference to the characteristics of products as breakthrough, competitive, and improved. A *breakthrough product* is a unique innovation that is mainly technical in nature, such as the digital watch, VCR, and personal computer. A *competitive product* is one of many brands currently available in the market and has no special advantage over the competing products. An *improved product* is not unique but is generally superior to many existing brands. For example, let us assume Aubrey Organics is interested in manufacturing shampoo for tender hair in Turkey and seeks entry into the emerging market in the middle-eastern countries. The company finds that in addition to a number of local brands, Johnson & Johnson's baby shampoo and Helene Curtis Industries' Suave Shampoo are the competitive products in the market. Proctor and Gamble has recently entered the market with its Pantene Pro-V brand, which is considered as an improved product. Most of the competition appears to be addressing the existing demand. However, no attempts have been made to satisfy latent demand or incipient demand. After reviewing various considerations, Aubrey Organics may decide to fulfill latent demand with an improved offering through its Camomile Luxurious brand. Based on market information, the company reasons that a hair problem most consumers face in that part of the world is dandruff. No brand has addressed itself to that problem. Even Proctor & Gamble's new entry mainly emphasizes health of hair. Thus, analysis of the competition with reference to product offerings and demand enables Aubrey Organics to determine its entry point into the market of middle-eastern countries.

Contemporary ideology on the competition emphasizes largely on the competitive environment which contribute to various dimensions of rivalries. It has been observed that the low-end competitor indulging a company in offering much lower prices for a seemingly similar product, has been the common fear of each industry leader managing his business among competitors. The vast majority of such low-end companies fall into one of the four broad categories which include strippers, predators, reformers, or transformers.[9] Each of these is defined by the functionality of product and the convenience of purchase. Strippers, for instance, typically enter a market with a bare-bones offering, reduced in function and usually in convenience. Industry leaders have significant advantages for combating low-end competition, but they often hesitate because they're afraid their actions will adversely affect their current profit margins. The solution then may be to find the response that is most likely to restore market calm in the least disruptive way. An industry leader could choose to ride out the challenge by ignoring, blocking, or acquiring the low-end competitor or it could decide to strengthen its own value proposition by adding new price points, increasing its level of benefits, or dropping its prices. Such tactics can be effective in the short term, but the industry leader also needs to consider strategic retreat, particularly when certain conditions make future low-end challenges inevitable.

COMPETITOR LEARNING

There are many ways of competitor learning process. Comparative learning occurs when two or more competitors are compared and contrasted. It especially entails analysis of outputs which is necessary frequently to compare and contrast the projections of two or more competitors' future strategies as a means of anticipating which competitors are likely to do what and when. It is also often necessary to compare and contrast how competitors are responding to the focal firm's own initiatives. The process of descriptive learning of competitors involves learning about the individual competitors at the basic level in reference to capturing the processing data and information about the competitor to identify the facts and features. This learning tool supports the inputs to comparative learning. Many of the concepts and analysis tools such as marketplace strategic activity, value chain, assumptions, resources, and competency facilitate comparisons across two or more competitors. The comparative learning process generates insights and inferences that cannot be derived by examining individual competitors in isolation. Learning is a cognitive process as customer decisions make sense of the world around them. They select and array the information, permeate data with meaning, draw inferences from incomplete data and portray the results. Thus, the wide variety of analysis tools and techniques

Competitor analysis learning model

- **Stage 1**
  Assessment: Current, previous, need for knowledge base
  Decisions and Actions: Situation based, action plan, strength
- **Stage 2**
  Capturing: Building information base
- **Stage 3**
  Processing: Information analysis and interpreting Results
- **Stage 4**
  Crafting: Shaping output, reviewing, communicating output

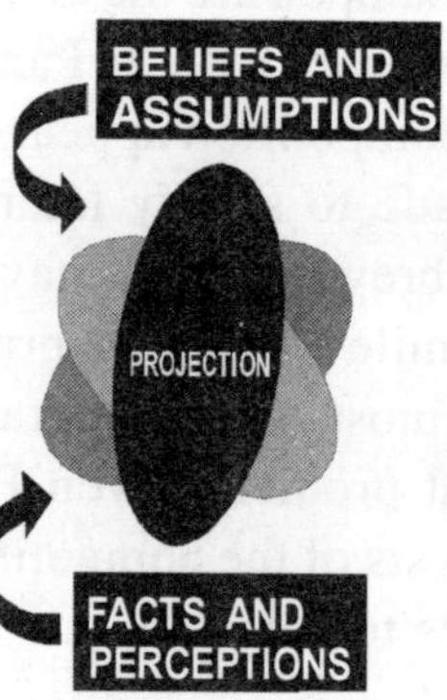

Figure 1.1

9 Potter Don: Confronting Low-end Competition, *Harvard Business Review*, July, 2004

Strategy Focus 1.2: Race of Cosmetics Companies in China

The Chinese cosmetics and toiletries industry certainly presents an attractive proposition for any business, valued at US$7.9 billion. It is the world's eighth largest market for the industry and second largest of Asia which has registered 12 percent growth in 2004. Increased disposable income has meant that more consumers can afford higher value products and so, are increasingly buying into the growing 'upper mass' sector or are trading up from mass brands to premium ones. Distribution has been affected by chained retailers, such as Wal-Mart, Carrefour and Hong Kong based Sa Sa, extending their retail networks in China. Skin care is the most valuable cosmetics and toiletries sector in China, accounting for 38 percent of all industry sales during and demonstrating significant potential for further expansion. Key to the growth of skin care was a rise in the up take of anti-ageing or nourishing facial care products, which form part of a the emerging 'upper-mass' segment. Such brands command higher prices as they adopt attributes that were once confined to premium products therefore offering consumers added value above their usual moisture products.

With dynamism and high value, skin care was the sector that presented the maximum opportunity for brands to establish themselves in China. This sector attracts western brands which are keen to make their presence, particularly when local markets are proving to be stagnant. However, cultural differences can often make it harder for them to establish themselves. Chinese skin care draws inspiration from the abundance of herbs and plant life in the country and this is one way in which companies have tried to become closer to understanding the market. Multinationals are quick to establish partnerships with local scientists and doctors so as to increase their understanding of the medicinal properties of skin care in native herbs and plants and their effects on the skin. The improving situation in China has led companies like Procter & Gamble (P&G) and L'Oréal to step up their investment in the market. Procter & Gamble's Olay brand has a strong established presence in China, which is maintained through an extensive product range, affordable pricing and strong national advertising, often endorsed with celebrities. Procter & Gamble launched, Olay brand in China during April 2005 as a test market for their make up brands while Max Factor and Cover Girl also set to fortify their dominant presence in the market by using the channels established on the strength of the Olay brand of P&G. During 2004 L'Oreal made two acquisitions in the Chinese cosmetics and toiletries market, firstly with Mininurse, a well loved domestic skin care brand, and then Yue-Sai. L'Oréal will benefit from the strong and extensive distribution channels these brands hold and is challenging Olay's dominance in the market through development of the *Mininurse* brand image. L'Oréal has already introduced the Garnier Naturals range under the *Mininurse* name, which has proved popular with young and trendy consumers and their market share, particularly in the skin care sector, is building rapidly. Procter & Gamble and L'Oréal's increased presence in China has helped the expansion of the 'upper-mass' segment in skin care too, which creates higher value sales for their products.

Source: *Euro-monitor International On line, September 2005*

presented throughout the remaining chapters are intended as aids to interpretation. Learning also is a collective process though transforming individual learning into organizational learning is a difficult task. Learning truly occurs when individuals share their knowledge, challenge each other, and reflect on each other's judgments and assessments.

Understanding and analyzing each move of the competitor and using the output to developing counter strategy may be defined as the process of the competitor learning. This integrates the process of knowledge management through four stages as exhibited in the Figure 1.1. The company must make assessment of the existing needs, historical perspectives and develop the knowledge bank accordingly to help in decision making and scheduling the actions. The actions need to be taken by the company as required to project the facts and beliefs more effectively among the customers. The learning exercises may take place with individuals and groups who are engaged in decision-making. It is necessary to build-up strong, comprehensive and reliable database for capturing the activities of any business rival or competitor. Data is thus the basic input for competitor learning. In the process of capturing the competitor's moves the first task is to determine the data requirement and issue clear instructionsthe data base managers (DBM). The DBMs have to first identify the data sources, prepare checklist of information, collect data and submit it for analysis to the competent department or agency. The information collection is a very vulnerable issue and there may be many companies looking for the similar sets of information. Hence taking the opportunity first is always advantageous in the business. The major task in processing the data is proper interpretation of results. There should be no biases and the results of the analysis should be able to detect some signals. The crafting of the information outputs is one of the important tasks which should give a shape to the output. The outputs are crafted to inform the decision makers and influence decision-making in the interest of the business.

Two core concepts of the competitor learning process are *efficient and effective* learning. The former refers to the learning input-output ratio. The input for the learning process is the competitor data and the output includes the change in knowledge level. The effective competitor learning addresses the output-decision relationship. In the process of competitor learning both efficiency and effectiveness need attention and require data, information and intelligence. Data constitute the basic input in the process of competitor learning. The data about any competitor may be put into three broad categories *viz.* behavioral pattern of the competitor, statements pertaining to the competitor, and organization change. The individual actions of competitors or the patterns displayed thereof are referred as the competitor behavior. The actions may be analyzed in reference to the market place strategy, customer relationship, brand management, sales and promotion of the products and services in the region. The statements of the competitors may be of various types such as the performance data, announcements, annual reports and the like. These constitute formal business communications made in the public periodically. The informal communications on the other hand are largely oral comments delivered by the channels, competitors' personnel and high profile rivals, though these statements are not authentic. However, such informal information may be very useful to build strategies down to reality for outwitting the competitors in the market. The changes in the business strategies, financial status, business credentials and production and sales data represent the data on organizational change. Such information plays significant role in understanding the latest moves of the competitor in the market and allows the new entrants to build shield for their business as well as develop strategies to overcome the competitive blockades. It is essential that the data on the competitor's strategies should have following attributes for efficient and effective analysis:

- Quantification
- Temporal values *i.e.* time series data
- Precision, and
- Description and opinion

It is necessary to look into some of the information errors that may occur during the data collection process. The fallacy of misplaced facts is most common among various problems in data collection. The information on the projections of the cash flows, sales and production levels are more vulnerable for the competitors as well as the customers and investors in business. The information error also constitutes the misconstrue pattern or underlying structure in a set of information or data. Such information errors are based on the assumptions drawn by the information collectors and disseminators. However, the exaggerated information provided to the strategy builder or decision-makers is also one of the common information errors that occur often in the process of outwitting the competitor from the market. Evidence for the success of relationship marketing remains contradictory, with practitioners reporting that most relationship marketing efforts fail, and academic researchers suggesting that further exploration of the boundary conditions of relationship marketing are needed. A number of researchers have identified changes in the competitive environment as the basis for the adoption of relationship marketing, although recent research suggests a more complex, contingent view.[10]

> At the turn of the twentieth century, American and Chinese millers were locked in a fiercely contested battle for control of China's flour market. Imported American flour had dominated Chinese urban markets since the early 1880s, but the founding of a modern native milling industry in 1900 had initiated a commercial war that pitted the great flour corporations of the Pacific Coast against the independent mill owners near Shanghai. Although the anti-American boycott of 1905 had boosted sales for Chinese mills and sparked growth in the native industry, the period between 1905 and 1909 severely tested the ability of the young industry to survive foreign competition. A high silver/gold rate, low transpacific shipping rates, and bumper wheat harvests in the Pacific Northwest lowered the relative cost and enhanced the market appeal of American flour to Chinese brokers. Conversely, severe flooding in China's wheat-producing regions forced curtailment or even cessation of production for some native mills. Facing catastrophic reductions in their wheat supplies and markets saturated with American flour, Chinese millers devised alternative business strategies and implemented collaborative measures to ensure the solvency of their mills. A study[11] examines the details and dynamics of the competition between native and imported flour and highlights the decisive measures Chinese mill owners employed to assure the survivability of the modern milling industry in China. If there were any question or doubt about the Chinese becoming a flour-eating people to a considerable extent, the building of a mill by the Fou Foong Flour Mills Co. at Shanghai would dispel it. It is not in the nature of things for Chinese businessmen to act hastily, so that the erection of this mill may be regarded as an index of the future.

A common mistake, which many firms make is to start by collecting information without thinking how the information will be used such junk data has no value and it will be just shelved. The information needs to be comprehensive and adequate to help analysis of the strategic or tactical decisions on the role of competitors and vita indicators. If a firm is planning a new product, information on the status

10 Beverland Michael and Lindgreen Adam: Relationship Use and Market Dynamism-A Model of Relationship Evolution, *Journal of Marketing Management*, 20 (7-8), August 2004, 825-858.

11 Meissner, Daniel J : The Business of Survival- Competition and Cooperation in the Shenghai Flour Milling Industry, *Enterprise and Society,* 6(3), September,2005, 364-394.

of the competitors in the area will help in the decision processes and plans for this new product. Alternatively, the firm may review how the industry will develop in future towards the market leadership, potential merger, and acquisition or business partnership. The information requirements for each of these business decisions will be completely different and so the information that should be sought will also be different. Thus before starting to search for information, the competitor analyst needs to sit back and define what the firm is looking for and why. It is important to identify the key areas of concern for the business decision makers requesting the information, and aim to satisfy these. The supplementary information may be interesting, but unless it helps the decision process it should be viewed as superfluous, and should be stored for use at another time or even ignored, if it is unlikely to ever have value. Hence, a firm may streamline its search needs towards better planned and focused strategies which would help in answering various intelligence requirements of the business.

> Asian product and services industry has posed a major competitive threat to the western countries. The principal concern for many firms is the impact of low-cost Chinese manufacturing and Indian services on global pricing. Focusing on this concern alone represents a profound misunderstanding of the nature of the competitive threat. Emerging markets might seem an implausible wellspring of innovation. Certainly, most of the companies must overcome significant obstacles to threaten those in developed ones. Yet the challenge remains of serving the harder-to-reach and more cost-conscious consumers of developing countries who are also typically less loyal to established brands. Such challenge may force companies to design and deliver products comparable to the offerings of developed nations for as little as one-fifth the price in order to stand competitive in the price sensitive markets. Doing so requires big changes to the design of products and processes, and these changes may soon affect developed markets dramatically to reconcile their competitive strategies. The spread of Chinese products as low priced mass market drivers may be described as the case of extreme competition wherein, an oversupply of labor, infrastructure, production, and capital has weakened the performance of whole industry while helping upstarts to challenge their established positions in global markets.

Many multinational companies are now advertising their services and some specialize in offering information that can be used for competitor research. Some of them include *Dun & Bradstreet* (D&B) with a database of over 30 million companies world wide. The information on patents can be obtained from companies such as *Derwent Information* or from local patent offices. And global press information is available from databases made available by companies such as *Dialog, Lexis-Nexis and Factiva*. There are numerous other web-sources which include discussion forums, web-logs (blogs), protest groups, customer and governmental sites and so on.

COMPETITOR LEARNING MODELS

It is essential that any company planning for competitive strategies should possess high learning skills in order to collect right information, analyze and interpret the results. The organization's knowledge about competitor and his moves broadly consists of perceptions, beliefs, assumptions and projections. Learning as the detection and correction process has varied implications for outwitting, outmaneuvering and outperforming competitors. The Figure 1.2 exhibits the single and double loop learning methods. The single loop learning may occur when the organization detects and corrects the knowledge base without changing thrust on its strategies and actions. This is closed and confined learning method that do not allow reviewing or re-engineering the information spool. On the contrary, in the double loop learning process the organizational knowledge, information base and strategies in addition to its action plans are open for review and re-engineering in the long-term interest of the company.

There are three levels of competitor analysis - a system, an individual competitor and specific components of the competitor. The framework of competitor analysis includes the infrastructure and culture of an organization and value chain, networks and relationships representing the environment of the company. The entire analysis must focus on the current strategy of the competitor firm and its future steps. Besides the assumptions in business risks and prospects, it is also important to analyze the assets, capabilities, competence levels and technology usage of the competing firm. In all these exercises, the data must be reliable and comprehensive to make the competitor learning process stronger. Signals are perhaps the most important core concept in competitor learning. A signal is an inference drawn by an individual in some specific context from the data and information about a competitor pertaining to the past, current and future strategies. The core components of the signal are indicators of the data and information. The inferences on signals received from the competitors on the basis of data need to be drawn to derive strategies for implementation.

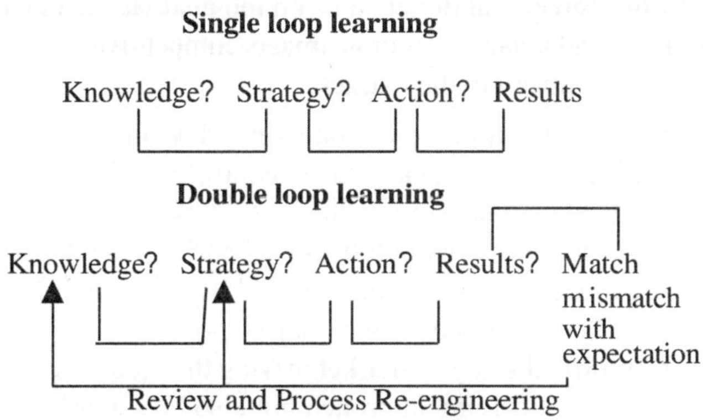

Figure 1.2 Competitor learning models

A competitor signal is difficult to interpret and assess, if there is no proper database and the indicators are not relevant. The ambiguity about indicators may occur by words, actions, unclear strategies of the organization and biased information. The signals from the competitor may be direct or indirect. The analyst needs logical aptitude and strong reasoning to use the indirect signals appropriately for building strategies. The competitors send signal in the market about all the vital indicators of business like product, services, advertisement, prices, channels etc. in a distorted fashion to weaken the business rivals. It is thus, necessary to capture the signals well in time and draw inferences. Late attention to the signal may lead to detection lag, caused due to the extended length of time between the availability of the information and its capture by the analyst. The competitors' signaling is very volatile and needs to be attended immediately to avoid any time lag or delay in drawing the inferences out of the available information. Knowledge is an important component in the process of competitor learning. Knowledge in the business activities is an outcome of intellectual efforts performed by the individuals with an objective of providing vital information on the move of the rivals in the market. There are some companies who provide information services as consultancy. However, the large companies, which have narrow objective of only production, have realized the importance of building knowledge base for sustaining competition and heading towards continuous growth. The business players of product and services need to replenish their knowledge continuously on the consumer behavior, competitor moves, technology development and future market dynamics. The linkages outside the company in the form of alliances, informal business partnership, and networking also are contemporary sources to the knowledge on the competitor learning. It may be observed on the present business platforms that the large corporations and MNCs have been acting with ever greater ingenuity by crafting linkages with rivals, channels, customers, suppliers and technology sources. The competing television channels may be one of the examples of such strategies, which develop variety of contacts for getting information from the customers and the reaction of the rivals in the market. The customer behavior towards the products and services of any company is analyzed on the basis of the perceptual dimensions on the qualitative parameters. The perceptual indicators may broadly include brand loyalty, corporate image, competitive standing and the extent of business credibility earned by the company in the market.

Analysis of the information for learning the competitor movements should be aimed at knowing who is winning and loosing the business game in each arena, who is controlling the majority of business stakes in the market and which company is redefining its business strategies in a modified way convenient to its customers and suppliers on the win-win platform. Theorists have highlighted the issue of 'market driving' wherein, in contrast to focusing on being close and listening to the market/customer (market driven), the firm 'leads the customer' or reshapes the markets to their own requirements. This study aims to present an empirical study of market driving that generates insights into not only what factors lead a firm into a market driving approach but also how market driving occurs in practice. A review of existing literature reveals that while a range of contributions have considerably advanced our understanding of both market driven and more recently, of market driving organizations, few empirical studies have been presented. An exploratory discussion has been presented in the case study of De Beers in China as a potentially valuable source of insights, complemented by a propositional inventory. The case of De Beers proposes that two factors lead to the adoption of a market driving approach, namely; customer familiarity and preconceptions of product characteristics, and the extent of market control. This study also contributes insights into the nature and dynamics of market driving. In particular, four tenets of market driving are identified which include market sensing, changing customer preferences, channel control through relationship formation, and local sensitivity.[12]

Competitive intelligence also contributes to the learning process of a growing firm. Competitive intelligence is the information available to the competitors for free access on the public resources, which is periodically updated to present the current contents and potential strategic information. The information acquired by the competitors through public sources serves as an important input in formulating marketing strategy. A firm must be aware of the perspectives of its competitors before deciding which competitive moves to make. The competitive intelligence includes information beyond industry statistics and trade gossip. It involves close observation of competitors to learn what they do best and why and where they are weak. There exist three types of competitive intelligence - defensive, passive, and offensive. The defensive intelligence is the information gathered, analyzed and used to avoid being caught off-balance. In this process a deliberate attempt is made by the competing firm to

12 Harris L C and Cai K Y: Exploring Market Driving-A Case Study of DeBeers in China, *Journal of Market-Focused Management,* 5 (3), September, 2002, 171.196

gather information on the prevailing competition in a structured fashion and to keep track of moves of the rivals that are relevant to the firm's business. The passive intelligence is the temporary information gathered for a specific decision. A company may, for example, seek information on a competitor's sales compensation plan when devising its own compensation plan. An offensive intelligence is the information gathered by the firms to identify new opportunities and from a strategic perspective; such intelligence is most relevant for a growing firm amidst competition.

PLAYING IN THE COMPETITION

Organizations that seek to win the market by modeling their strategy in a suitable way should build their energy on two platforms. First, they need to endeavor to model the competitive game in view of the various entities involved such as organizational players, market arenas, information builders and scorers. Second, the company should get acquainted to the market place rules as how the customers, channels, factors and institutions are attracted, won and retained in the business. The competitors strive to attract, obtain, and retain the support, commitment, and involvement of end customers, channel members, factor suppliers, and institutions within the context or conditions of strategy games. Such elements include the structure of the game combatants, the arenas, and the nature of the stakes they hold and the entire composition of the business domain. The marketplace rules pertaining to how best to package and distribute products, create image and reputation, deliver service, build relationships emerge over time are the basic challenge for the firms. Many firms may intend to redefine or rescale the customer satisfaction from narrow product functionality to include all aspects of interactions with customers, for example, the Japanese automobile manufacturers redefined *quality* for many consumers to distinguish their quality, services and customer values against the competing overseas brands. In the competitive marketplace some firms may look for introducing frequently the product upgrades cope up with pace of market competition. Besides, some firms may initiate major efforts to develop new capabilities and competency and monitor their progress in doing so against specific competitors as one element their to determine who will reserve their plans to win to in the future marketplace.

Many companies try to alter the number of players by creating situation for deposing them from the market or change their own position relative to other players. The strategies such as alliances, mergers and acquisitions are the direct means of reducing the competition or deposing the existing rivals from the market. The Hindustan Lever Ltd., the giant in the FMCG segment in India, through a series of acquisitions largely reduced the number of players in the consumer goods segment. The development of networks, linking suppliers, manufacturers and consumers is another popular strategy to discourage competition in the particular segment of goods and services. The quick implementation of research and development, new products development and brand extensions indirectly break the existing competition in the market and allow the new company to re-deploy its marketing strategies. The pace of rivalry is such that no firm can now afford to take its resources for granted. Some firms may perceive to be in the low-tech business segment such as textiles, shoes etc. Furniture, paint, and books, are feverishly pursuing new knowledge that might radically reshape established products or traditional ways of manufacturing and distributing them. In high-tech businesses such as electronics, firms that include IBM, Apple, Motorola, Intel, and Microsoft have formed multiple alliances with entities all across the activity/value chain and share innovative knowledge, skills and capabilities. Several modes of competition can be employed within the end-customer and channel arenas to get and keep customers. Although rivals compete in many distinct ways, firms can make eight key choices to distinguish and differentiate themselves in the eyes of customers and channels which may be described as product-mix, product features, functionality, service, distribution or availability, image and reputation, selling and relationships, and price.[13]

> Examination of the policy determinants of economic growth by exploiting a new firm level database for ten OECD countries shows that the contribution to productivity growth from firm level dynamic processes should not be overlooked, most notably in high-tech industries where new firms tend to boost overall productivity. There is evidence that burdensome regulations on entrepreneurial activity as well as high costs of adjusting the workforce negatively affect the entry of new small firms. Overall, there are a number of different features of entrant and exiting firms across countries. In particular, in the United States entrant firms tend to be smaller and with lower than average productivity, but those surviving the initial years expand rapidly. By contrast, in Europe firms tend to enter with a relatively higher size and productivity, but subsequently do not expand significantly. These findings tend to support the hypothesis of greater market experimentation in the United States, compared to many continental European countries, which is likely to be the result of differences in regulatory settings across the Atlantic.[14] As the world economy becomes increasingly integrated and globalized, U.S. companies face an unprecedented opportunity and challenge. In the global marketplace, China has made great strides in economic and commercial developments. China is becoming a manufacturing base for the world in providing quality products at low prices. As more businesspeople turn their attention to China's progress also need to review the business trends in its neighboring country, India. In spite of its problems, the Indian government and people are determined to increase India's contribution to the world economy.[15]

Companies also maneuver the arena of customers, channels, institutions and the geographical coverage in order to reconfigure their competitive strategy. The software companies like Intel, Microsoft and 3M always keep extending the product line implementing the R&D results and never let the competition stagnate in the end-customer arena. The healthy companies feel that greater the competition higher will be challenge to establish the brand in the market. The Suzuki collaboration with Maruti Udyog Limited in India has changed the dominance of the popular brand holder Premier Automobiles Ltd and created new competitive context of small city cars. The channels of supply for any company are always vulnerable to the competition. The common practice followed by the competitors is breaking the supply chain by offering more perks and margins than the leading brand. However, if the

13 For detailed discussion on the corporate key choices to withstand competition, see Peter Senge: *The Fifth Discipline*, New York, Doubleday/Currency, 1990

14 OECD: Sources of Economic Growth in OECD Countries, Firm Dynamics, Productivity and Policy Settings, *The Sources of Economic Growth in OECD Countries*, OECD, pp. 210-262 (53)

15 Anshu Saran and Guo Chiquan: Competing in Global Marketplace: The Case of India and China, *Business Horizon*, March 2005

channels are favorably treated with long-term advantages, the endeavor to build the linkages with them would withstand any competitive rivalry. The collaboration between the Proctor and Gamble and Wal-Mart involving strong integration of the product ordering, inventory control and logistic may be a classic example in this context.[16] The factor advantage in the competition may be defined as the relationship of the manufacturing or marketing company with the service providers who develop loyalty towards them. The service providers may be the suppliers of raw materials, packaging services, hiring of machines and the like. Many companies use the legal support, government patronage etc to shape the competitive conditions to their advantage while building the institutional arena in the business.

> Premium automobiles segment has been dominated by two capital and hi-tech giants-BMW and Mercedes. While BMW's plants run at 95% of capacity, Mercedes' German factories operate at around 80%, say analysts. One reason is declining sales of the E-Class and C-Class models, both of which have suffered quality problems. A face-lift for the E-Class in 2006 and a new C-Class expected in late 2007 should help buoy weak sales. But union contracts that make Mercedes workers' work rules less flexible than rivals' are also to blame for the relatively low output. At BMW, employees work less during periods of slow demand and then bank the unused hours, paying them back during peak periods, thus eliminating a lot of overtime pay. Mercedes recently instituted more flexible schedules and got union agreement to shuttle workers among plants, long a practice at BMW. Improving quality is also vital. The drive to lead in new technologies has resulted in cars packed with different electronic systems, which all must be integrated into a core system that functions harmoniously, a devilishly hard task. By contrast, BMW has sought to install common electronics backbones across many model lines. It also saves money by sharing more components among models. However, some business analysts feel that the Mercedes has been over invested in the wrong things. When the competition figured out that the company does not have to design an entirely new car to offer, Mercedes is still working with offer something new with its cars. Mercedes insists its cars use the same electronic architecture but admits that many components vary across the wide array of models. The crux of the problem lies in designing less complex cars and improving test procedures before a model launches. Redesigning and reengineering all Mercedes models for better quality could take two years. The major issue that remains at the bottom line of the business is whether any brand can hold competition for its projected gains?[17]

Stakes in the business may be understood as the benefits of winning the game and the cost of losing the business in the market. Many companies in the market place intend to escalate the stakes in the business as one of their competitive strategies in various arenas as discussed in the previous sections. The companies also redefine their market place strategies for gaining the win-win situation in the market. Table II exhibits the parameters that are used

---

16 Fahe Liam : *Competitors : Outwitting, Outmaneuvering and Outperforming*, John Wiley and Sons, Canada, 1999

17 Gail Edmondson: Mercedes' New Boss Rolls up his Sleeves, *Business Week (Online Edition)*, October 17, 2005.

for redefining the marketplace rules by many companies in order to sustain in the market competition. There are many competitive strategies used by the companies to get and retain the customers and the channels. The companies desired to strengthen themselves against the competitive threats in the market need to develop different modes of entering in the market. The companies also re-focus their strategies to attract the customers and retain them for the long-term benefits. Table 1.2 discusses the major issues related with redefining market place. Many organizations are driven by one or a few overarching, long-run goals that imbue the organization with a collective challenge, shared vision and sense of mission or purpose. Such goals have been designated by others as strategic intent or vision and super ordinate goals. Among goals set by many companies, a few may include as reorientation towards R&D to products that are new to the marketplace; extend product lines to attract new segments of customers; use alliances to build a significant marketplace position in leading Asian or European countries; build new manufacturing facilities for new product development and introduction; and develop new marketing capabilities to outmaneuver specific competitors across major customer segments.

Market place strategies also determine the mergers and acquisitions of the companies for competitive advantage. Acquisitions and alliances are two pillars of growth strategy. But most businesses don't treat the two as alternative mechanisms for attaining goals. Consequently, companies take over firms they should have collaborated with, and vice versa, and make a mess of both acquisitions and alliances. It's easy to see why companies don't weigh the relative merits and demerits of acquisitions and alliances before choosing horses for courses. The two strategies differ in many ways: Acquisition deals are competitive, based on market prices, and risky; alliances are co-operative, negotiated, and not so risky. Companies habitually deploy acquisitions to increase scale or cut costs and use partnerships to enter new markets, customer segments, and regions. Moreover, a company's initial experiences often turn into blinders. If the firm pulls off an alliance or two, it tends to enter into alliances even when circumstances demand acquisitions. Organizational barriers also stand in the way. In many companies, the mergers and acquisitions group reports to the finance head and handles acquisitions, whereas a separate business development unit looks after alliances. The two teams work out of different locations, jealously guard turf and, in effect, prevent companies from comparing the advantages and disadvantages of the strategies. But companies could improve their results, the authors argue, if they compared the two strategies to determine which is best suited to the situation at hand.[18] Firms, such as Cisco, which use acquisitions and alliances appropriately, grow faster than rivals do.

18 Dyer Jaffrey H. Kale Prashant and Singh Harpreet: When to Ally and When to Acquire, *Harvard Business Review*, July, 2004

Table 1.2 Redefining the Marketplace Rules

Redefining parameters	*Attributes of parameters*
Modes of Competition	• Product line and width • Logistics and supply chain aspects • Price, sales and customer relation • Corporate and brand image
Focus	• Attracting, winning, retaining customers and channels
Levels	• Aggregate • Segment • Local
Trends	• Product –service-value differentiation· • Customized solutions • Price, communication and delivery of goods and services.

Marketplace rules can be changed at three distinct but related levels such as the aggregate marketplace or, more narrowly, a competitive domain; a product-customer segment such as a niche within a competitive domain; and local channel member. The marketplace rules have been discussed in Table 1.2. All rivalry ultimately is acted out at the local or micro level. Each individual customer selects among rivals' offerings. At this level, the game is typically zero-sum: purchasing one rival's offering means lost opportunity for other competitors. The firms generally make the choices which have been experience in the past by the competitors to accomplish three distinct, though related, tasks which include attracting, winning, and retaining customers and channels. Attracting customers is a prelude to winning or acquiring them. The brand name and long standing image of the product influence and attracts customers to try a product.

Dell Computer Corporation has plans to enter the competition in the Indian market with its subsidiary. Dell is one of the most globally preferred computers among the business class customers. The company finds that India is growing fast in sales of personal computers and there exists room for Dell to become a major player in the market. Its mode of entry will be through direct selling to its clients with total product customization as a global strategy. The company has plans to offer services to its international clients in the country and then follow it up with large corporate units, the Government and potential institutions in future. This is one of strategies to select the customer segment and operate safely in the market outwitting the competitors. The company is also having alliance with a leading brand in the country - Tata InfoTech Ltd. and plans to launch on a joint platform. The customer support is a major thrust of the company and it is setting up customer call center to redress their needs more efficiently, take orders from the clients as well as provide services to customers. Ever since, the incorporation of the company in 1984 by Michael Dell, it has positioned itself in the top five of the computer sales category across the countries in the world and hopes to replicate the same in Indian market. The company has an idea of offering software solutions instead of boxes and continues the relationship over the long term.[19] The company is looking for local outsourcing for the effective delivery of the products and service and the Indian outfit will be supported by Penang, the Malaysia production base. The company has chosen e-commerce as one of the contemporary strategies to reduce load on the physical channels. The deliveries are promised in a week that may turn to be a major attraction for the clients and a tall task for the service providers. The plans of the company seems to be complex but Dell being a big brand that has proved itself the world over and with a high brand loyalty and image, it has all hopes to succeed in the Indian market penetrating the competition in the computers business. Chip Sunders, the Vice President of the company says, *"Though there are successful players, we will be the winners"*.

Satisfying buyer needs may be a prerequisite for industry profitability. One of the underlying issues in developing the competitive strategy is to address the profitability in reference to the capability of the firm whether it can capture the value in the process for retaining the buyers, or whether this value is competed away to others. The buying power of customers determines the extent to which they retain most of the value created for themselves. The threat of substitutes determines the extent to which some other product can meet the same buyer needs, and thus places a ceiling on the amount a buyer is willing to pay for an industry's product. The power of suppliers determines the extent to which value created for buyers will be appropriated by suppliers rather than by firms in an industry. The intensity of rivalry acts similar to the threat of entry. It determines the extent to which firms already in an industry will compete away the value they create for buyers among themselves, passing it on to buyers in lower prices or dissipating it in higher costs of competing. Some companies engaged in manufacturing automobiles and heavy trucks, create enormous value for their buyers but, on average, capture proportionately less of it for themselves through profits. On the contrary in the services industries such as bond rating services, medical equipment hiring, and oil field services and equipment, firms also create high value for their buyers but have historically captured a good proportion of it. The intensity of rivalry plays a major role in determining whether existing firms will expand capacity aggressively or choose to maintain profitability. Industry structure also determines how rapidly competitors will retire excess supply. Exit barriers keep firms from leaving an industry when there is too much capacity, and prolonged periods of excess capacity.

P&G has a variety of leading brands in the Indian market such as Ariel, Tide, Head and Shoulders, Pantene and Pringle. One more new idea, which is on schedule of the P&G portfolio, is *Febreze*. This product belongs to the P&G Home Products Division which include hair care and fabric care segment. This product has created a niche and holds a monopoly in the fabric odor cleanser category of products across the regions in India. This product was first taken off in the US markets in 1997 and now is available in 20 countries across the world. P&G has launched *Febreze* in Chennai, Coimbatore and Madurai in mid 2000 with a turnover of over Rs 6500 Million. The R&D of the company is confident to attract customers and enjoy the monopoly in the market for a time, as the company does not foresee any competition to come up in the near future. The product attributes are very close to the customer needs, as it is the first cleaning spray that safely and permanently eliminates odours trapped in the household and other fabrics. This product helps in reaching the

19 Reviewed from the Peoples and Products, *Advertising and Marketing,* August 31, 2000, pp 8-12

> difficult-to-clean fabrics, upholstery, carpets, and curtains, mattresses and car seats, which are largely unmanageable and remain unattended. This product is an outcome of the research carried out by the company. The target customers for this product are segmented as per the need parameters and largely constitute the car owners, housewives, hotels and airlines. The Febreze is not a perfume and hence does not compete with perfumes of room-deodorant brands in the market. To stand unique in the market the promotional and advertising strategies have been developed on the conclusions drawn on the research. The product has also been advertised on the net, print and electronic media. The strength of the brand, quality, positioning and the promotional formulae blended with the customer needs may open up an entire new segment depending on how its use values are perceived by the customers.

Results of an imbalance between supply and demand for industry profitability also differ widely depending on industry structure. In some industries, a small amount of excess capacity triggers price wars and low profitability. In view of the key role of competitive advantage in superior performance, the centerpiece of a firm's strategic plan should be its generic strategy. The generic strategy specifies the fundamental approach to competitive advantage a firm is pursuing, and provides the context for the actions to be taken in each functional area. In practice, however, many strategic plans are lists of action steps without a clear articulation of what competitive advantage the firm has or seeks to achieve and how. A firm's strategy is the route to competitive advantage that will determine its performance. Build, hold, and harvest are the results of a generic strategy, or recognition of the inability to achieve any generic strategy and hence of the need to harvest. The multinational firms largely practice strategic planning in reference to the market share to describe a competitive position of the firm. Market share *per se* is not important competitively; competitive advantage is. The strategic mandate to business units should be to achieve competitive advantage. Pursuit of leadership for its own sake may guarantee that a firm never achieves a competitive advantage or that it loses the one it has.

Conceptual framework of competitive forces in the marketplace has been provided by Porter as a five-force model for industry analysis is shown in Figure 1.3. These five forces of competition interact to determine the attractiveness of an industry. The strongest forces become the dominant factors in determining industry profitability and the focal points of strategy formulation. The model identifies the key structural features that determine the strength of the competitive forces within an industry in reference to profitability. It may be explained through the model that the degree of rivalry among different firms is a function of the number of competitors, industry growth, asset intensity, product differentiation, and exit barriers. Among these the most influential variables may be identified as the number of competitors and industry growth. The industries with high fixed costs tend to be more competitive because competing firms are forced to cut price to enable them to operate at the economies of scale. However, with the differentiation strategy the rivalry is reduced among the products and services offered by the competitors, in both real and perceived senses. Another significant concept which may be explained through this model is associated difficulty of exit from an industry, which may result into struggle for survival among the firms and intensified competition. Further, there remains the threat of entry into the industry by new firms which may enhance competition. Several barriers, however, make it difficult to enter an industry. Two cost-related entry barriers are economies of scale and absolute cost advantage. In this process of competition, the new entrants face an up-hill challenge of scaling at a high level of production or to accept a cost advantage. However, absolute cost advantage remains with the long standing firms in the market which possess technological and brand advantages for their products and services. The substitute products in the market affect the industry potential adversely as well as pose threat to the customer preferences. Bargaining power of buyers refers to the direct or indirect pressure tactics to force the industry to reduce prices or increase product features, in view to optimize the customer value. Buyers gain power when they have choices-when their needs can be met by a substitute product or by the same product offered by another supplier. In addition, high buyer concentration, the threat of back-ward integration, and low switching costs add to buyer power. Similarly the bargaining power of suppliers refers to their ability to force the industry to accept higher margins or reduced services, in the interest of augmenting or securing their profits. The factors influencing supplier power are the same as that of buyer power. In this case, however, industry members act as buyers.

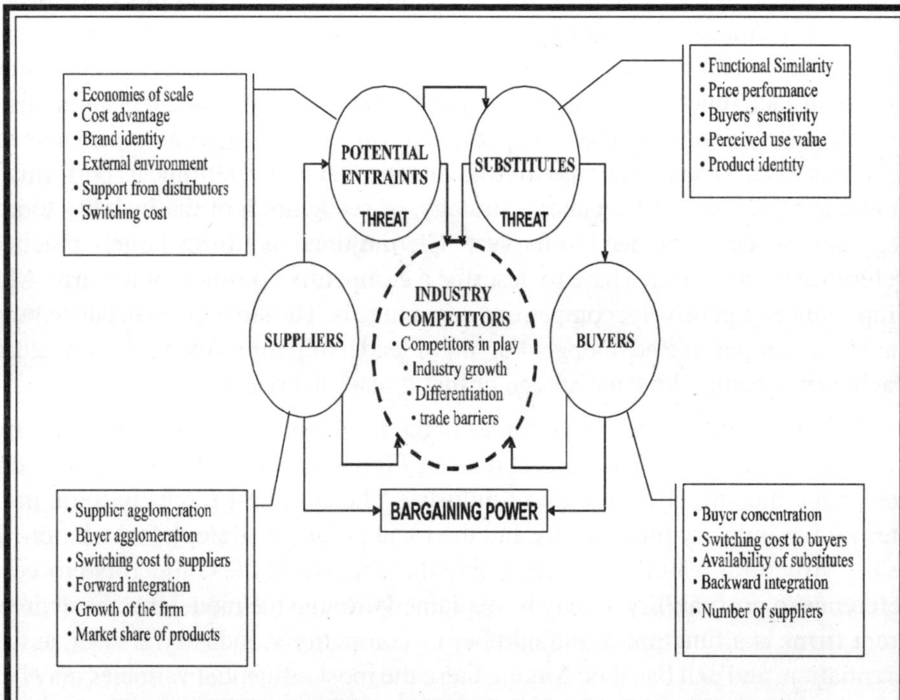

Figure 1.3 Competitive strategy: network of market forces

COMPETITOR STRATEGIES

Companies engaged in competitive business should aim at conducting the competitor analysis to build competitive advantage and this cannot be done in isolation from the market and the rest of the industry, because being better than a competitor will not guarantee success, if what is offered gives little value to the customer. Hence, it should be understood by the firms that any inferences which might be drawn from competitor analysis must be considered in conjunction with the other environmental factors. Every company has strategic options, although this does not mean that all options are sensible for every company. It may choose to operate within the rules of the industry, without major change to what it offers. The options may include a stronger focus on a niche strategy, seeking to identify and exploit segments where its products would have an advantage, or what might be termed improvement strategies. A competing firm may be attacked various ways by a new and prospecting business firm in a given territory in order to optimize the market advantage. The most effective way for a firm to attack may be through implementing a creative and entrepreneurial strategy on a sound knowledge analysis in view of the changes the competitive arena. Alternatively, a firm may attempt to pre-empt a competitor by getting into market first with a new product, in an area of strategic importance. However attacking the strategy of a competitor can leave the firm in a weaker position. The prospecting firm may also attack on the competitor's alliance instead of direct attack on the target. An example of this was the acquisition of Rover by BMW. There were undoubtedly many reasons for this acquisition, but one of them was to cause Honda to withdraw from the alliance it had operated for many years with Rover, and its predecessor British Leyland. Similar patterns of alliances changing allegiance have been observed in the airlines industry. The basic rule of any attack strategy is to know the industry, the market, and the competitors being attacked. If the weak points of the competitors are known, and their likely reactions predicted, the attacker is more likely to arrive at a successful strategy. It is this rational analysis which enables a decision to be made about whether the rewards of success outweigh the costs, and whether the chances of success are high enough to justify the move.

In a competitive business arena the competitors as players may be categorized as hard and soft players. The hard competitive players in business single-mindedly pursue competitive advantage and the benefits it includes a leading market share, great margins, and rapid growth. They pick their shots, seek out competitive encounters, set the pace of innovation, and test the edges of the possible success of their products and services in the market. Soft players, by contrast, may look good, but they are not intensely serious about winning. They do not accept that you must sometimes hurt your rivals, and risk being hurt, to get what you want. The commonly employed methods in taking up the hard competitor strategies in bursts of ruthless intensity may include devastating rivals' profit sanctuaries, deceive the competition, unleash massive and overwhelming force, and raise competitors' costs.[20] The soft players do not play to win; they just participate in the business and try to survive. This approach envelops the issues such as leadership, corporate culture, knowledge management, talent management, and employee empowerment for analysis to the soft players. Every firm is risk averse in facing the business competition as it is a fact of business life, but many companies fail to manage it well. Good risk management not only protects companies from adverse risk but also confers a competitive advantage, enabling them to be more entrepreneurial and, in the end, to make bigger profits. Companies should clearly articulate their risk strategies, understand the risks they are taking, and build an effective risk-management organization that helps foster a responsible risk culture.

20 For detailed discussion on the hard and soft core competitor strategies see Stalk George Jr. and Lachenauer Rob: Hardball-Five Killer Strategies for Trouncing the Competition, *Harvard Business Review*, April, 2004.

> Changing aircraft technology, big capital investments and the shifting priorities of governments have repeatedly forced airline operators to scramble to stay air borne. Consequently, a swing of new low-cost airlines is attacking big incumbent network carriers, some of whom will probably not survive. Such aviation companies sparked meteoric growth by exploiting latent demand for cheap travel, but they can't create profitable markets indefinitely. Major sources of traffic in Northern and Central Europe will soon be saturated. However, interestingly, the differences go deeper as America's budget airlines are starting to move up-market in service quality, whereas Europe's give every impression of moving relentlessly down-market. They emphasize dirt-cheap tickets, yet they are also expanding as they try to fend off start-up competitors. The competition from low-cost carriers has increased the customer's price sensitivity, undermining the ability of the incumbents to charge a premium not only on routes where they compete with these carriers. In order to cope, scheduled carriers must choose their battles carefully and revise their business designs. The adaptation might be subtle for stronger players; for others, it might resemble the radical transformation *Aer Lingus* has begun. Most of the expansion in America has come from *JetBlue, Frontier and AirTran; Southwest*, which accounts for nearly half the sector, has been obliged by the wider air-travel recession to check its expansion, although it is now returning to its former growth path of 10% a year. While in Europe after the liberalization of Europe's domestic airline market was completed in 1997, *Ryanair and EasyJet*, the pioneers, explicitly and expertly mimicked American budget airlines such as Southwest and ValuJet (now *AirTran*). The Indian skies are also experiencing the boom of low-cost airlines like *Air Deccan*. The low-cost carriers find success by stimulating and exploiting pent-up demand for cheap travel. Their entry into a market brings out people who would otherwise travel by train or car, if at all. In 2002, low-cost carriers and network carriers went head-to-head on 80 routes in Europe and America; since then, the former have increased their capacity on those routes by 15 percent, while the incumbents' capacity has shrunk by 4 percent. The biggest difference between low-cost carriers in America and Europe is that they have existed in Europe for less than ten years. In many markets, growth has stagnated after an initial spurt in demand. On these more established routes, growth for low-cost carriers (as for incumbents) now ranges from 4 to 6 percent. However, as they move up-market in America to fill the void left by big network carriers, and as they move to more expensive airports in Europe, the risk is that low-cost carriers everywhere will start to acquire the very same high costs that made their network competitors so vulnerable.[21]

Markets involve many competitors, are compromised of *active terrain* in the way of customers and offer the opportunity of access to alternative resources by means of supply market mechanisms. Perhaps this is why IBM have been attempting to change the warfare metaphor they have been using to one of gardening, where customers are to be cultivated.

There are four major competitor attack strategies which are implemented by the companies at international, national and regional levels. These strategies include the frontal attack, flanking attack,

21 For details see Urs Binggeli and Lucio Pompeo: The Battle for Europe's Low-fare Flyers, *McKinsey Quarterly* (Online edition), August 2005. Also refer *The Economist*: Turbulent Skies, July 08, 2004.

encirclement and guerilla attack. The following fundamental principles are involved in planning and implementation of competitor attacks:

1. Competing company needs to assess the strength of the target competitor and consider the amount of support that the target might congregate from allies. It would be appropriate to choose only one target at a time.
2. Competing company should explore weaknesses in the target's position and launch attack on the core of weakness.
3. It is necessary to work out the time-span as how long it will take for the target to realign their resources so as to reinforce this weak spot.
4. Competitor may then launch the attack on as narrow a front (frame of weaknesses) as possible. Whereas a defender must defend all their borders, an attacker has the advantage of being able to concentrate their strategic and tactical tools at one place.

Frontal attack implies a head-on confrontation where the defense is at its strongest. Some such attacks mirror the defendant's marketing strategy, and hope to achieve results through sheer perseverance. Others have only one point of difference on price. By cutting price for what is otherwise a matched offering, the attacker hopes to be able to persuade customers to switch. Only in markets where there are many niches is it possible to use the full-frontal attack selectively. In markets where the products are nearer each other, an attack on one competitor is really an attack on all of them. In full-frontal attacks, the victory usually goes to the strongest. However, a dominant competitor is less likely to make a full-frontal attack on a competitor, unless it is a niche operator where the effects of the warfare can be isolated. The main consideration in the frontal attack is the strength of the leader's position and a company entering into such warfare may find a weakness in the leader's strength and attack at that point. The company may launch the attack on as narrow a front as possible. The frontal attacks may be strategically fit and lead to an advantage in the business situations as described below:

- Market is relatively homogeneous
- Brand equity is low
- Customer loyalty is low
- Products are poorly differentiated
- Target competitor has relatively limited resources
- Attacker has relatively strong resources

Frontal attacks have appeal in industries where very large cost reductions can be gained from increases in volume, and where price reductions may stimulate growth in the market as well as stealing share from competitors. However, frontal attacks are often unsuccessful. If defenders are able to re-deploy their resources in time, the attacker's strategic advantage is lost. The frontal attacks are very expensive and risky for the companies of any status.

On the contrary to the frontal attacks, where company goes for attacking at the strongest zone, the *flanking attack* goes for areas of weakness. This may be to find geographical areas where the competitor is not performing as well as elsewhere, or to identify segments of the market which have not been spotted by the competitor. If the product has been specifically designed for the segment, it may be some time before the defender can respond. A good flanking move must be made into an uncontested area and the tactical surprise ought to be considered as an important element of the plan. The disadvantage with a flanking attack is that it can draw resources away from your center defense, making you vulnerable to a head-on attack. In business terms, a flanking attack involves competing in a market segment that the target competitor does not consider mission critical. The target competitor will not show his concern about activities of other firm if they occur in market niches. It usually involves subtle advertising campaigns and other discrete promotional measures, like personal selling and public relations. It often entails customizing a product for that particular niche. Rather than finding uncontested market niches, the attacker could also look for uncontested geographical areas. The strategy is suitable when:

- the market is segmented
- there are some segments that are not well served by the existing competitors
- the target competitor has relatively strong resources and is well able to withstand a head-on attack
- the attacker has moderately strong resources, enough to successfully defend several niches

Geographical flanking attacks may be described in reference to the strategy of the retail supermarket which erects its new store in an area where its rivals are weakest. Another is First Direct which established a telephone retail banking operation, which not only avoided the need for branch offices but also enabled the company to accept only the business it wanted, thus cherry picking the more profitable ones. Product flanking is a competitive marketing strategy in which a company produces its brands in a variety of sizes and styles to gain shelf space and inhibit competitors. The defender companies may need to add extensions to an existing product line by introducing new products in the same product category in order to give customers greater choice and help to protect the company from a flanking attack by a competitor.

> U.S. market leader, Marlboro has been hitting all-time highs this year. Despite the sharp advertising restrictions agreed to by cigarette marketers in 1998 and a dramatic rise in state excise taxes since 2002, Marlboro is galloping ahead of the competition. The brand, which commands an average $3.28 per pack, now owns more than 40% of the market. That surge has driven a broader gain for Philip Morris overall, which also makes Virginia Slims, Parliament, and other brands, and added significantly to the company's profits, possibly more than $200 million a year. Marlboro became one of the world's most valuable brands capturing the traditional mass marketing through the strong impact of advertising in print media and billboards. In 2003, more than $15 billion was spent on marketing cigarettes in the U.S., according to the most recent data from the Federal Trade Commission, a 21% jump over 2002. The company has passed through setback during the past and later has become a more deft and efficient marketer as a result of the legal settlement that sought to hobble the cigarette

makers. Back in 1998 the Master Settlement Agreement (MSA) with the state attorneys general ended tobacco advertising in most of its traditional forms. But by forcing Marlboro to go viral, be aggressive in retail stores, and be more creative in its media plan, it put the company on a successful path now being followed by every marketer from General Motors and Audi to AXE deodorant. Today, all kinds of companies are pursuing similar viral marketing campaigns that draw consumers into brand communities. Contests and rewards keep smokers loyal, but to add new followers, marketing experts are of view that some low-tech means of persuasion are also important such as in-store promotions, price cuts, and other deals. The rivals are unhappy and complain that the advertising restrictions leave them with little chance of closing Marlboro's lead. One hot spot in Marlboro's marketing is a growing database of 26 million smokers to whom it sends everything from birthday coupons to the chance to attend events like November's birthday concerts. Indeed, Marlboro isn't just a brand; it is an exclusive club of loyalists.[22]

Companies which attack the competitors in several ways such as branding, pricing, advertising and promotions, value additions, sales in up-markets, product featuring and the like in a given time may be described as *encirclement attack*. The successful encirclement strategies usually attempt to identify and exploit new niches, and to beat the offer made to the customer by competitors. The encirclement strategy is a much broader but subtle offensive strategy and is commonly planned in two ways. A company could introduce a range of products that are similar to product-mix of the target competitor. Each product will liberate some market share from the target competitor's product, leaving it weakened, demoralized, and in a state of siege. Alternatively, the encirclement can be based on market niches rather than products. The attacker expands the market niches that surround and encroach on the target competitor's market. This encroachment liberates market share from the target. The encirclement strategy can be implemented successfully under the following conditions:

- Market is loosely segmented
- Some segments are relatively free of well endowed competitors
- Attacker has strong product development resources
- Attacker has enough resources to operate in multiple segments simultaneously
- Attacker has a decentralized organizational structure

An example of *Sears Roebuck,* a chain retail store of US, may be stated to explain the encirclement strategy. The attempt by US retailers Sears Roebuck to change the financial services industry in the USA was an encirclement attack on competitors from several different industries at the same time. The in-store credit card was converted to Discovery, a full credit card by the company. All state Insurance had been part of the Sears Roebuck group for many years. The new niche the company hoped to conquer was the private consumer who wanted one-stop shopping: to buy a house, furnish it, obtain all necessary loan facilities, and insure everything in any Sears store. The strategy failed, because the niche was not large enough. The acquisitions therefore did not upset the competitive situation in their industries, and the Discovery credit card became a frontal attack on

22 For details on the competitive edge of Marlboro's marketing strategies see *Business Week* (Online edition): Leader of the Packs, October 31, 2005.

existing credit card competitors. At one time Sears were reported to have secured the record for signing up the largest number of defaulting clients in the shortest time.[23] The electronics industry has been transformed due largely to the personal computer segment. For decades, the electronics industry's primary objective for personal computer products was to offer the maximum power and functionality for the lowest possible price. This focus resulted in tremendous innovation and a proliferation of products at prices that virtually everyone could afford. It also began to erode profit margins for electronics companies. Led by the personal computer segment, the electronics industry built a model supply chain that is tightly linked and highly competitive. Vertically integrated companies became outmoded, replaced by companies which specialized in standardized components and software and did business with each other companies. Though swift at capturing and extending cost reductions and efficiencies, this evolved supply chain model led to product commoditization and standardization. Any innovation that a company produced could be copied quickly and usually at a lower cost. Therefore, competitive advantage was fleeting. Rapid technology change and short product lifecycles contributed to the further erosion of profit margins.[24]

Guerrilla marketing warfare strategies are a type of marketing warfare strategy designed to wear-down the enemy by a long series of minor attacks rather than engage in major battles. A guerrilla task force of a competitor firm is divided into small groups that selectively attack the target at its weak points. To be effective, guerrilla teams of the competitor set themselves underground between the strikes. The guerrilla marketing strategies of competitors involve in targeted legal attacks on the competition, product comparison advertising, short-term alliances, selective price cuts and orchestrating negative publicity for a competitor.

MARKET PLACE STRATEGY

Market place strategy includes elements of product and customer segments, competitive posture, goals and moves and directions of the firm. The products and customers are categorized in different ways. The products and services may be classified as per the product line matrix - length and width (type and

Table 1.3 Core Elements of Market Place Strategy

Scope	*Competitive posture*	*Goals*	*Moves and directions*
Customer and product segments	Product line Features Functionality Services Brand and sales CRM*	Type of Strategy	Influence Positioning Marketing-mix Vision

* Customer Relationship Management

23 Hussey David and Jenster Per: *Competitor Intelligence-Turning Analysis into Success*, John Wiley, West Sussex, 1999

24 Brody Paul, Wenzek Hagen and Osterday Tom : *Product Styling-The New Competitive Differentiator in Electronics*, IBM Institute for Business Value, February, 2004.

items). The core elements of market place strategy are exhibited in Table 1.3. The customers are segmented on the basis of the products and services they use at any point of time. The customer demographics are also considered to a large extent in segmenting the customers. The needs of customers relate more directly than any of the demographic profiles. The distributing channels better know the competitor's position and direction of the competitor than any other external agency. The tapping of right information taking the distribution channels into confidence would be more appropriate than any other means to the company. Rival business firms often choose distinctly different channels to reach the end users. The competitive posture reveals how a competitor competes in the market place to attract the customers win and retain them. The customer is the kingpin in determining the competitive posture. The competitive posture of the company consists of product line, attributes of the product, functionality, service, availability, image, sales relationship and pricing pattern. The product line broadly refers to the range of products available with the competitor. The distributors and retailers are more concerned with the width (item under product range). Some companies focus on narrow range of products and build high image among the customers. The product attributes vary in terms of shape, design, style, color and added advantages. Further, the customers may view the functionality of the product as the satisfaction derived from the products. The dimensions of the functionality are highly product specific.

In the competitive markets, the efficiency of the services discharged and extended to the buyers also contributes in building or breaking the market place strategy. Products, in the same market or competitive domain, largely vary in their availability may be due to weak or faulty supply chain management. The competing firms must study this situation and develop strategies accordingly. Beside all, price game played by the mercantile and service sector companies is very sensitive and may carry enough strength to destroy the rivals business. Such market tactics among the companies dealing with fast moving consumer goods (FMCGs) and services have been observed time and again. The example of price war may be cited appropriately of the airlines - Jet Airways, Sahara India and Indian Airlines for attracting more passengers on the domestic trunk routs by slashing the prices. The position and direction of the market place may be assesses by measuring the coverage of product-customer segments and changes that are taking place thereof. The types of strategies that can be adopted in market place is exhibited in Figure 1.4.

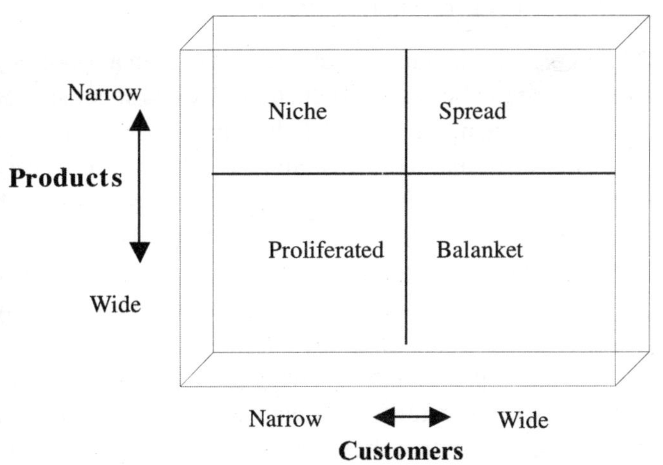

Figure. 1.4 Types of market place strategy

A niche domain involves a narrow product line and customer segment. A competing company must take a note that the rival is always expert in terms of product and customers. The spread domain entails narrow products range targeted at a large segment of customers. Such firms invest more time and resources in building brand and securing the customer segments (eg. Bata Ltd. has narrow product-mix but has wide customer segment). The proliferated domain involves a wide range of products aimed at narrow customer segments (Say class market buyers). Many companies offer a wide range of products in the restricted region. A blanket domain is attained when the competitor has positioned the products and services in all the available segments (*e.g.* Bajaj Scooters Ltd. in automobile sector). In general, if the entry into an industry is relatively easy, many firms, including some marginal ones, are attracted to it. The long-standing, committed members of the industry, however, do not want new entrants to break into their territory. Therefore existing firms discourage potential entrants by adopting strategies that enhance competition. However, if the products offered by different competitors are perceived by customer to be more or less similar, firms are forced into price and, to a lesser degree, service competition. Such competition can be really severe. The marketplace rules may sometimes lay the exit barriers on the rationale of the cost-benefit adjustment. The exit barriers implant deterrence and such strategy may be described as to:

- Persuade new entrants that the market is not worth entering, because of the way you will react, or
- Try to stop encroachments into a segment of the market which is important to you, or
- Attempt to keep a competitor from increasing its market share.

Best deterrence is a strong position, which makes it difficult for an attacker to gain a foothold in an economic way. This is not achieved just by having the largest market share. Indeed sheer size and past success often breeds complacency, despite the achievements of the past. For a variety of reasons, it may be difficult for a firm to get out of a particular business. Some of the possible reasons include the relationship of the business to other businesses of the firm, high investment in assets for which there may not be a beneficial alternative use, high cost that may incur towards discharging commitments etc. Successful companies like Wal-Mart and Intel have devised innovative responses to these threats and have outperformed their competition. A strong competitive position for a firm has market share as a component, and this may be most important when the learning curve effect means that high volumes give lower costs, which in turn allow prices to be set which other competitors find difficult to meet. But it is also about technological foresight, adequate levels of research and development, and giving customers value in all respects so that they have little incentive to change.

Many organizations feel that in growing competition establishing strategic alliances would better check the competitor's penetration in the market. They recognize that alliances and relationships with other companies of repute are fundamental to outwit, outmaneuver and outperform the competitors by ways of better branding, better service and tagging global brands for assuring the quality of goods and services. Alliances and relationships thus transform the concept of competitor. The strategic alliances may be in various forms like branding, logistics, research and development, productions and operations management, packaging, services, sales and customers. The tie-up relationship of any computer firm with Compaq drives the customer demand for both the brands - the mother brand and the aligned brand. The business alliances have to be identified by doing an exercise scientifically. The company has to list all alliances that it is planning to have to outperform the competitor, categorize all available alliances by activity, value chain and resources and identify the key alliances as which alliance will have the cutting edge on the market place strategy of the competitor. It is essential to identify the alliance partner and know about their marketplace strategies. The purpose of the alliance has to be made transparent at the very beginning of the deal. The type of alliance and context of alliance are the relevant competitive conditions, leadership and motivations for the partners. The company has to draft the terms of alliance clearly for striking the final deal. The terms of alliance must delineate the resources contribution of each partner, roles and responsibilities of either of the alliance partners, duration of alliance and the benchmarks. The company proposing to have alliances must assess the evolution date of the alliance, alliance attributes, signals of the market place and consequences for the competitor in terms of changes in the market places strategy. The company should also identify the indicators to monitor the terms of alliance with a view to reorient the business needs, mutual interest and commitment. Marketing environment for a competitive environment is a combination of factors that the customers use as tools for pursuing its marketing objectives in the identified markets for achieving targets. These factors have to be strategically mixed in marketing planning for offering quality services and optimizing customer value. It is an integrated approach for promoting the services with a view to expand the area under services market. The traditional components of marketing-mix including product, pricing, place andpromotion are further supplemented by another set of 5Ps consisting of participants, people, pace, process and physical evidence in marketing of services

A company trying to outwit, outmaneuver and outperform the competitors must also keep a constant watch on its future movements and should draw valuable projection for building the counter strategies to check or defuse its moves. The company must assess the market place strategy alternatives being considered by the competitor firm. The analysis of strategy plots need to be examined carefully. The options of some of the following alternatives of the competitor firm may be examined:

- Aggressive penetration of high-price market
- Low price market entry
- Maintaining the present strategy

Multiple signals typically emerge out of the projected strategy of the competitor and have to be interpreted appropriately. The signals must be assessed in reference to the supporting logics, competitive consequences and the implications thereof.

COMPETITOR ANALYSIS: CAPABILITIES AND COMPETENCY

Degree of competition in a market is largely affected by the moves and countermoves of various firms activity participating in the market. Generally, it begins with a firm trying to achieve a favorable position by pursuing appropriate strategies as what is advantageous for this firm may be harmful to rival firms and in response the rival firms may move counter strategies to protect their interests. The competition attracts the firms seeking to capitalize on an available business opportunity. As the number of firms get involved in the process of sharing the pie, the degree of competition increases. When the entire market represents one large homogeneous unit, the intensity of competition is much greater than segmented market However, if a market is not appropriate for segmentation, firms may compete to serve it homogeneously, thus intensifying competition. Hence, in either of the market situation the intensity of competition is unavoidable for the participating firms. Understanding the capabilities and competency (C&C) of the rival and developing the company's own are the most important tasks in sailing through the marketing competition. This is essential for winning the market place in future, sustain and get the circumstantial leverage .The capabilities in general address as how well an organization performs or executes some of the vital activities like, customer relationship management, services, supply chain management etc. The competency may be stated as what an organization does well across the region and subsidiary units or customer segments. In all, the C&C involve action, the focus and emphasis on what the competitor does in the market to outperform his business rival. The common competenceis that can be judged in reference to the competitor are as following:

- Quick movement of the products to the marketplace from R&D unit
- Faster response to the market opportunities
- Providing convincing and unique solutions to the customer problems
- Hire, train and retain best personnel
- Develop, nurture and extend the best relationship with customers and alliance partners

There are four key tasks in the management of core competency which include selecting core competency, building core competency, deploying core competency, and protecting core competency. Companies are likely to differ in terms of their abilities to select, build, deploy and protect core competency. These differences are, in turn, likely to yield differences in corporate performance. Building core competency requires the accumulation and integration of knowledge, residing both within the firm and without. For example the core competence of a telecom company may reflect in managing billing systems, an insurance company's core competence in claims processing, and Sony's core competence in miniaturization are each a tapestry of many individual technologies and skills. The core competencies of the companies are those that push down the competitors' products in all the business domains. These strategies are central to the customers, channels and alliance advantage. There are many attributes of C&C, however, the following may be defined as the key attributes of the C&C:

- Dynamism
- Span
- Robustness
- Security against imitations
- Ability to expand

Dynamism of the C&C refers to continuous change for the betterment of the policies and execution of the strategies. The organization must be able to identify the new markets continuously and never be static at any point of time. An organization must have a wide span to discharge their competency without specifying the boundaries of time and area. It is essential for a company to retain its C&C for a longer duration and unrestricted to any areas of change. C&C also vary in their acceptability to the current and future business domains. A competitor cannot always leverage a competence for the new products or services development in changing business domains. The companies must secure that their C&C strategies are not replicated by other firms or used in any distorted manner. Indeed, any C&C of any company should be able to enhance continuously so that it adds to the sustainable advantages. In practice, today's global competition is more dynamic and multidimensional than those models suggest. The mature industry paradox is that leadership demands differentiation, yet differences are quickly copied. Single-factor innovations tap one competency, and capable competitors can usually match it. Multiple competency strengthen several dimensions and in effect redefine the basis of competition. The "shadow strategy task force" is offered as a method to force managers to relinquish the comfort of the firm's accepted view of itself. This approach begins with the objective of identifying the strategies and competency that, in the hands of competitors, might be used to attack the firm's competitive position successfully. Especially critical on the task force are individuals with insight into how customers, suppliers, and competitors view the firm's products and services. Developing new competency requires constant experimentation. The innovation-imitation-equilibrium cycle suggests that industry leaders teach customers what to demand by defining the current state of the art in performance, price, service, and other dimensions; customers learn to judge competitive offerings against these standards, and the learning effect is cumulative.[25]

> LG Electronics India and Samsung in India have entered the electronics market as rivals and are getting along in the business with the same spirit and surviving the market competition. Both the companies are of Korean origin and are into almost identical product segments in the market. Their pricing strategies are similar and they follow largely identical business models to compete with each other in the Indian market. In the marketplace these companies are the most spirited rivals and use throwing punches figuratively on each other's performance to prove their capabilities and build customer loyalty. These two companies fight for each piece of consumer electronic goods in the market. In early July 2000 Samsung came-up with an advertisement proclaiming itself the leader on the 310-litre and above frost-free refrigerators segment, LG responded by challenging both the Samsung and ORG-GFK, which provided the market share data to the advertiser for making it a public claim.[26] Growth in an adjacent market is tougher than it looks; three-quarters of the time, the effort fails. But companies can change those odds dramatically. Results from a five-year study of corporate growth conducted by Bain & Co. reveal that adjacency expansion succeeds only when built around strong core businesses that have the potential to become market leaders. And the best place to look for adjacency opportunities is inside a company's strongest customers. A research study revealed that the most successful companies were able to outgrow their rivals consistently and profitably by developing a

25 Werther William B and Kerr Jaffrey L : The Shifting Sands of Competitive Advantage, *Business Horizons*, May, 1995

26 *Business Today,* September 21, 2000 p. 22

formula for pushing out the boundaries of their core businesses in predictable, repeatable ways. Companies use their repeatability formulas to expand into any number of adjacencies. Some companies make repeated geographic moves, whereas others apply a superior business model to new segments. In other cases, companies develop hybrid approaches. The successful repeaters in the study had two common characteristics: they were extraordinarily disciplined, applying rigorous screens before they made an adjacency move, and in almost all cases, they developed their repeatable formulas by carefully studying their customers and their customers' economics.[27] The strategies of Japanese firms have often emphasized its conflicting nature, at least in international markets. It is certainly clear that Japanese firms have more systematic and formal procedures for identifying competitors and analyzing their behavior. It is tempting to conclude that their success is the success of conflict-based strategies. In practice it is almost impossible to come to such judgments. While they are aware of competitors and their weaknesses, they are also keen students of both markets and technology. It is certain that a combination of factors, many of them subtle and difficult to comprehend, leads to the success, in some markets, of Japanese companies. Such success cannot be attributed solely, if at all, to a policy of competitor elimination.[28]

There are many ways to categorize core competency. However, broadly these may distinguish as market-access competency, integrity related competency and functionality related competency. The market access competency includes management of brand development, sales and marketing, distribution and logistics, technical support, etc. All these skills help to put a firm in close proximity to its customers. The attributes associated with competency like quality, cycle time management, just-in-time inventory management and so on which allow a company to do things more quickly, flexibly or with a higher degree of reliability than competitors constitute the integrity related competency of a firm. The functionality related competency lead to the skills which enable the company to invest its services or products with unique functionality, benefit to the customer). Comparative analysis examines the specific advantages of competitors within a given market and offers structural and response advantages. Structural advantages are those built into the business e.g. a manufacturing plant in Mexico may, because of low labor costs, have a built-in advantage over another firm. Responsive advantages refer to positions of comparative advantage that have accrued to a business over time as a result of certain decisions. This type of advantage is based on leveraging the strategic phenomena at work in the business. Besides, the examination of the business system operating in an industry is useful in analyzing competitors and in searching out innovative options for gaining a sustainable competitive advantage. The business-system framework enables a firm to discover the sources of greatest economic leverage, that is, stages in the system where it may build cost or investment barriers against competitors.[29] The framework may also be used to analyze a competitor's costs and to

27 Zook Chirs and Allen James: Growth Outside the Core, *Harvard Business Review*, December, 2003.

28 For details on the competitive behavior of Japanese companies see Easton G *et.al.*, *Managers and Competition*, Blackwell, Oxford, UK, 1993, 246-281.

29 Normann Richard and Ramirez Rafael: From Value Chain to Value Constellation-Designing Interactive Strategy, *Harvard Business Review*, July-August, 1993.

Starategy Focus 1.3: Moving Revlon in Up–markets with Flanking Attack on Competitors

Charles Revson and his brother Joseph had good foresight and entrepreneurship skills. They created a brand of cosmetics in association with Charles Lachman, a nail polish supplier in 1932 and named it Revlon. It has crossed all barriers to become the most popular brand of cosmetics today.

The company was started with an initial capital of $300, and they used pigments instead of dye. The colors were designed in a distinct gradation, to match seasonal fashion. Within six years of its introduction, Revlon became a household name in America. The long lasting nail polish was placed in beauty salons, departmental stores and select drugstores through the country. Towards the end of the 1930s matching lip and nail colors were introduced. During the war period, Revlon manufactured first aid kits and dye markers for the navy and after the war was over, it launched manicure and pedicure instruments, followed be eye make-up. n 1950 it diversified into skin care, took to television sponsorship and went public. In December 1955, it was enlisted in the New York Stock Exchange. In the sixties, Revlon started global business and also introduced Revlon Flex - A "Corrective Treatment for Hair", and Norell - a designer fragrance.

The biggest success of 1970s for the company was the *Charlie* range of perfumes for the young working women. With the death of Charles Revson, its glamour faded somewhat in the 1980s. The new Chairman of executive committee, Ronald O Perelman, had a style of working just opposite to that Revson's. Instead of focusing on product creation, he diverted his resource towards buying and selling business and in 1985; Revlon was sold to a subsidiary of Mac Andrews & Forbes Holdings. The Almay brand of hypoallergenic cosmetics was added to Revlon Hamper but it still went on to lose its popularity. Revlon signed on celebrities like Oprah Winfrey and Audrey Hepburn to gain momentum but on the contrary it put off young consumers. In the 1990s Revlon introduced two "Revolutionary products-Matte-finish *colorstay* lipstick and Age defying make-up, targeted at the 35 plus age group. The *colorstay* lipstick uses transfer-resistance technology enabling an all-day wear and the Age defying complex conceals fine facial lines without setting in to the skin. In 1995, the *colorstay* became the best selling lipstick in US, generating some 14 per cent share in the US self-select distribution channel network. Subsequently, the Revlon *Colorstay* range was extended. Supermodels Cindy Crawford and Claudia Schiffer brought Revlon back into, reckoning. "The most unforgettable women in the world wear Revlon" and "Never met a scoundrel I didn't like" became very attractive *ad lines* for Revlon. Later, Revlon dedicated support and financial resource to cancer, AIDS, infertility and many issues related to woman's health.

Source:

gain insights into the sources of a competitor's current advantage in either cost or economic value to the customer.

In the developed markets both the brands are perceived as low profile and are paying high cost for changing such perception. However, the Indian market has opened up the opportunity for these brands to position at a premium scale at relatively low costs. Both the companies play as high profile rivals in the Indian market as their business strategies closely cut across each other to achieve their business goals. Most companies focus on matching and beating their rivals. As a result, their strategies tend to take on similar dimensions. What ensues is head-to-head competition based largely on incremental improvements in cost, quality, or both. The multinational companies which are dynamic in strategy experimentation and innovative companies break free from the competitive pack by staking out fundamentally new market space by creating products or services for which there are no direct competitors. This path to value innovation requires a different competitive mind-set and a systematic way of looking for opportunities. Instead of looking within the conventional boundaries that define how an industry competes, managers can look methodically across them. By doing so, they can find unoccupied territory that represents real value innovation. Rather than looking at competitors within their own industry, for example, managers can ask why customers make the trade-off between substitute products or services. For example, *Home Depot*- a US chain retail store on construction materials and services, looked across the substitutes serving home improvement needs. Intuit looked across the substitutes available to individuals managing their personal finances. In both cases, powerful insights were derived from looking at familiar data from a new perspective.[30]

ANALYZING COMPETITOR'S SIGNALS

Signals coming out of the business moves of the competitor are the important source of data and information at the market place. As stated in the pretext that the behavior, statements and the organizational information are the major sources of learning the competitors' moves, the signals emerging from the competitor show the magnitude and direction of the information flow. The market place indicators are the principal sources of information for analyzing the signals in reference to the behavioral patterns, statements and the organizational culture of the competitor.

The indicators of organizational change include market place strategies, customer value chain, alliances, relationships, networks, assumptions, assets, capabilities and competency, technology, infrastructure of the company and the like. The business credentials, credit worthiness of the company in the market and its financial status also provide important indications to the competitors for learning their respective moves in the market. It may be understood that an increase in the competitors' credit intakes with any financial institution may generate a signal of its intent to implement a major strategic initiative to expand its business such as an acquisition or planning for capital investment for augmenting its production or marketing activities. The change in the values, beliefs and behavior of the customers, suppliers and business facilitators also indicates the intensity of signals of the competitors. The signals, which indicate the history of the company, current moves and future strategy, may be broadly categorized as below:

- Prospective signals
- Retrospective signals
- Current signals, and
- Anticipated signals
- Alerting signals
- Refuting signals

Prospective signals indicate the future change in the competitor's strategy while retrospective signals indicate significant competitor change that has been resulting into his strategies since long and such information may give strong base to the competing firms to outwit the competitors from the roots. The concurrent signals of the competitor indicate the on going moves thereof in the market place and sometimes indicate the probable future action of the competitor. Such signals are anticipatory and show a way to the future business moves of the competitor. The alerting signals need to be

30 Chan Kim W and Mauborgne Renee A: Creating New Market Space, *Harvard Business Review*, January 1999.

studied carefully and should not be ignored at any level, as these may become fatal for the competing firms at times. The alerting signals reflect the product line shifts, alliances, customer relationships, pricing and promotional strategies of goods and services and new product launch in the market. It is also possible that in the process of analyzing the signals of the competitor some signals may be contradictory to each other and may refute. The analyst should carefully examine such signals and look at their re-conformity.

In 1995, Lakmé Limited, a Tata group company and Hindustan Lever Limited (HLL) formed 50:50 venture as Lakmé Lever to market and distribute Lakme's cosmetic products and in 1998. Lakmé sold its brands to HLL, renamed itself Trent and entered into the retail business. The HLL has entered into the cosmetics market when there is gatecrash of MNCs like Revlon, Maybelline and others and has to build strong market place strategies to outwit the competitors. The corporate statement of HLL after acquisition of Lakmé delineates that by taking on the fashion and glamour platform, the company is not just leading the market over other competitors but has also got a virtual ownership of this plank.[31] It will be very difficult for any other brand to adopt a similar approach. This statement gives a strong prospective signal of its strategies to the new entrants. Lakmé is at the forefront of product innovation and the most preferred brand in the cosmetics. The positioning of the Lakmé products for the HLL seemed a bit complex but a clear strategy was drawn for the same. Lakmé cosmetic products have been positioned as its *aspiration colour cosmetics brand* to cater to the upper-mass customer segment of the company which desires both colours, glamour and skin care. The HLL played safe to protect its primary brand Ponds in the exclusive skincare segment of the customer. The value addition of colors has made the Lakme position itself into a broader spectrum of customer needs and competes with the MNC brands in the product segment. The new-designed aspiration led strategy of HLL for Lakme products has made a dent in the move by the competitors, more prominently Revlon and Maybelline, which have also targeted the same consumer segment. The HLL has a strong product strategy and market intelligence to build suitable strategies to be the market leader. Some of the strategies in reference to Lakme cosmetics is synchronized as below:

- The non-transfer lipstick colors have a long range
- The above product has been launched in wake of the similar range from Maybelline company
- Lakme's nail enamel colours have been launched soon after the launch of Maybelline and Revlon launched their nail-enamel range

Company (HLL) has currently three brands in the cosmetics segment. Firstly, Lakmé itself which is positioned as a fashion brand, Secondly, *Elle 18* which has enjoyed as a teen brand and has captured the largest market share among the female consumers of the age group among 15-25. The third brand of HLL is *Orchid,* a super premium that has not seen really much excitement since, its re-launch in 1999 in the upper consumer segment. The company also plans at aiming the rural markets after exploring the potential carefully. However, by appropriating the fashion platform Lakmé has positioned itself at the glamour end.

---

31 *Business Today,* September 21, 2000, p 48.

It may be necessary for a firm to determine the business cluster for its operations as they foster high levels of productivity, innovation and lay out the implications for competitive strategy. The territorial surroundings of business of a firm also contribute to the competitor vision and analytical dimensions though conventionally, economic geography towards global competition poses a paradox. Conceptually, location should no longer be a source of competitive advantage. Open global markets, rapid transportation, and high-speed communications should allow any company to source any thing from any place at any time. But in applied business sense, location remains core to competition.[32] The contemporary global business paradigm is characterized by distinctive clusters which may be described as critical masses in one place of linked industries and institutions varying from suppliers to universities to government agencies, which enjoy unusual competitive success in a particular field. The business clusters affect competition in three broad ways of :

- Increasing the productivity of companies based in the area
- Driving the direction and pace of innovation, and
- Stimulating the formation of new businesses within the cluster

However, the territorial, cultural, and institutional proximity provides companies with special access, closer relationships, better information, powerful incentives, and other advantages that are difficult to tap from a distance. The competitive advantage lies increasingly in micro resources which include knowledge, relationships, and motivation that distant rivals cannot replicate. For example, as the economy of China is under transition which is growing manifold and opening further, the opportunity it presents to multinationals is changing. Foreign companies are moving to country development and new strategic choices. Now, foreign firms can actually go after the Chinese domestic market, and it's worth going after. Improvements in China's infrastructure, workforce, and regulatory environment are making it possible for companies to lower their costs to reap new competitive advantages. However, in order to optimize the benefits and sustain the international competition in the Chinese playground of business, the multinational companies must properly nest their effort into overall organization, show "one face to China" at the national level but also tailor local strategies, be wary of joint ventures, and mitigate risk, in particular the theft of intellectual property.[33]

RE-ENGINEERING BUSINESS FOR COMPETITIVE ADVANTAGE

Business performance of a company matters a lot for customer to orient himself towards its brand, product or services. A company providing aviation or health services to the customer is rated by its efficiency in delivery and recognized by the certification that the company carries to testify its quality of services. Similarly the companies manufacturing and marketing the fast moving consumer goods (FMCG) also get an advantage in gaining large customer response over their rivals on achieving the certification

32 Porter Michael E: Cluster and the New Economics of Competition, *Harvard Business Review*, November-December, 1998.

33 Lieberthal Kenneth and Lieberthal Geoffrey: The Great Transition, *Harvard Business Review*, October 2003.

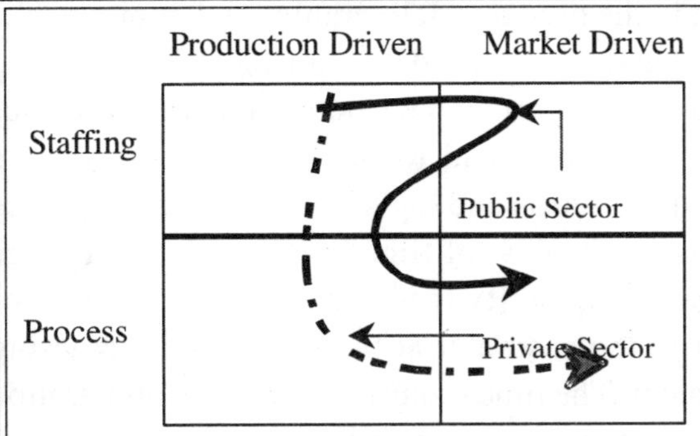

Figure 1.5 Re-engineering typology in business

from an international organization for their process, quality and services. The companies operating on the competitive edge should periodically re-engineer their business strategies by adopting various measures. The companies in the developing countries which are open to global trade have started realizing the importance of re-engineering for process improvement in order to acquire competitive strength. The public sector undertakings (PSU) in India have also realized the need for process re-engineering in business while the private sector companies had thought of such change long back. The process orientated production has been leveraging corporate expertise in the market place for over a decade. The business re-engineering typology in Indian context may be seen as exhibited in Figure 1.5. Initially the PSUs attempted on re-engineering by way of restructuring production and marketing functions and lately some of the PSUs like Bharat Heavy Engineering Corporation, National Thermal Power Corporation, Public Sector Banks, Power Grid, etc. are thriving on process oriented re-engineering to make their stand more competitive in the market. The private sector has re-engineered its business process since long on the line of process change for implementing better product and market driven strategies. The process driven dynamics has been proved to be effective to build the competitive strategies and sustain amidst market competition.

CUSTOMER VALUE AND REENGINEERING PROCESS

In the era of global competition, regardless of whether the company operates in FMCG, industrial goods or services, leading organizations around the world are being driven to rethink their business strategies and reorient them towards process change for reaching higher efficiency levels. In order to engineer their process change it is essential to consider the customer value criteria based on the attributes of four major business determinants - quality, service, cost and time . The customer value metrics is detailed in Table 1.4 among various attributes of quality the

Table 1.4 : Re-engineering Customer Value

Quality	*Service*	*Cost*	*Cycle Time*
• Customer relationship • Useful applications • Minimum variance • Process integrity • Minimizing waste • Regular improvement	• Customer support • Flexibility in meeting customer demands • Delivery and service • Information flow • Value assessment	• Innovation • Quality assurance • Logistics • Staffing • Materials management	• Market preparation • Lead time • Ordering and delivery • Response analysis

companies must look for continuous improvement in the products deliverables and minimize the variances. The customer support in terms of product and price should be prioritized for achieving competitive excellence. The cost factors may need very important consideration in the processes re-engineering as the quality improvement efforts would lead to price rise due to design improvement, quality assurance, restructuring the distribution and logistics strategies, inventory and staffing. The customer value largely depends on the cost of time involved in the change process. Doing re-engineering forces the companies to quantify the business efforts by way of quality, service and cycle time reducing the cost to the customer at the same time increasing the speed of innovation and new-product development. The time required for market preparation includes the concept selling, pre-positioning advertising and information for market initialization. The lead time is the time taken for stabilizing the sales and customer response to the changes engineered in order to outwit, out maneuver and out perform the competitors in the market. In the process of re-engineering the business strategies it is essential for the companies to analyze the customer response to the innovation and modify the entire the process accordingly before finally setting the changes in the market. In all, reengineering the customer value may be expressed in the simple notation as:

$$\text{Customer Value} = \frac{\text{Quality} * \text{Service}}{\text{Cost} * \text{Time}}$$

Process reengineering concept broadly include the philosophies of *just-in-time* (JIT), *total quality management* (TQM), *break even point analysis* and most recently introduced application of *enterprise resource planning* (ERP). These applications and strategies generate pull and push effects in the market releasing signals to the competitors.

CORPORATE CONCEPTS OF REENGINEERING BUSINESS

Re-engineering business strategies for competitive advantage necessarily makes a company redefine its corporate objectives and bring some differentiation in terms of quality of the products, services offered and the customer governance in the process. A company has to define the following corporate objectives while doing the process of production and marketing re-engineered:

- Customer satisfaction and service
- Business safety from the new entrants and existing competitors
- Production efficiency, quality assurance and innovation
- Financial performance and growth
- Customer relationship management and grievances solving
- Creativity in marketing
- Organizational development and human resources

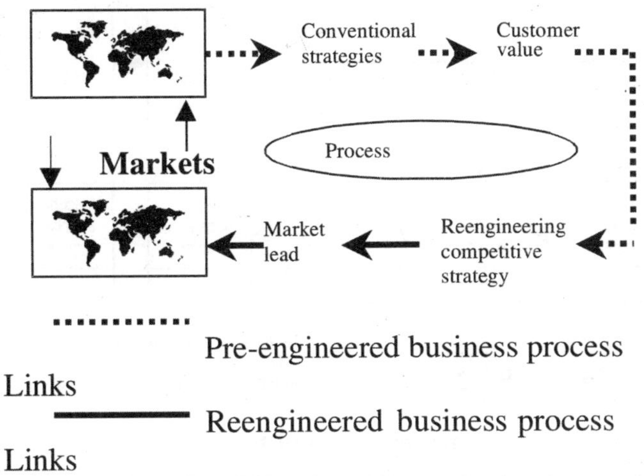

Figure 1.6 Engineering market interplay

It is possible for a company to take advantage of implementing the process improvements either to enhance its lead in the existing market or to enter new markets, once the company successfully implements the re-engineered process along with the value chain elements. The enablers in the process change in a company are people, management, leadership skills, organizational culture, expertise, market place stimuli and the performance measurements. The companies getting prepared to reengineer the business process and sustain in the competition have to give away the bureaucratic way of thinking and must put efforts to shift to the new market driven paradigms. The Figure 1.6 exhibits the market interplay engineering path for the companies looking to adopt process change strategy for regaining the competitive strength. In this process, it is necessary for a company to reorient its team leaders with new paradigm elements and process oriented operations to stand ahead in the competition and outperform the business rivals. Such reorientation must be towards creating vision, articulating and sharing values, transparency in the team work, and relationship management at all levels - customers and channel managers. The company has to develop corporate core team for building functional expertise among the managers implementing the competitive strategies. The company has to establish direct contacts between the market place and customers to have direct control over the flow of goods and services and customer reactions.

Companies open to global trading must accept the challenge of competition. The competitive pressures drive the companies to look at their process and determine that they can become competitive or even leapfrog the competition by focusing on the process, lead attribute and quality. For example, the *Baskin Robbins* Ice Cream Company in its logo writes *31*, the number indicates their distinguished 31 flavors (one flavor a day) which adds to its performance and lead in the market. The Hewlett Packard computers in the early 90's thoroughly redesigned its printers and re-engineered by simplifying the process and are now leading in Indian markets. In many instances, competition goes hand in hand with the customer service as the competition is also related to the customer needs. Hence, the companies need to re-define their process to connect to the customers and subsequently re-engineer them.

Re-engineering business process for a company is a systematic approach for gaining strength in three basic areas comprising optimization of cost, handling renewed competitiveness and building competitive dominance in the market. Of many competitive dimensions the product performance, market reach, rate of new product development and innovation, resource leverage and customer

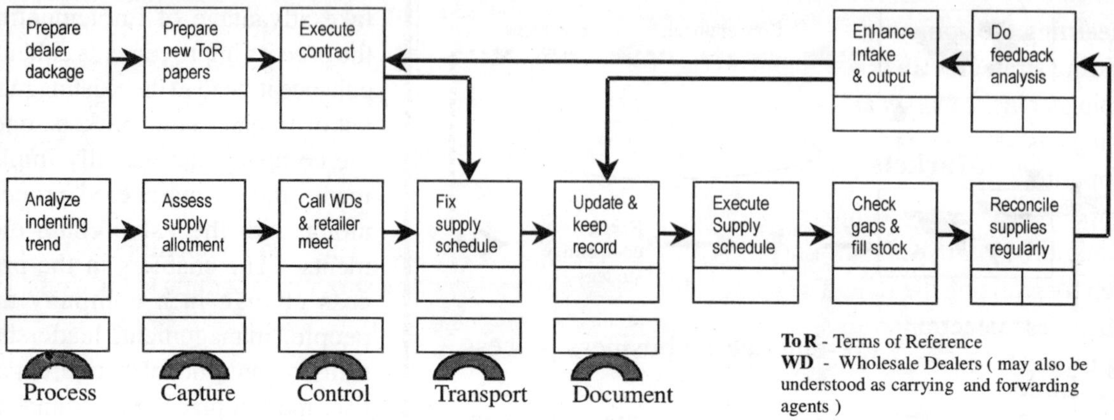

Figure 1.7 Re-engineering supply chain mangement function

loyalty are major ones which need to be emphasized by the company for achieving competitive advantage. The re-engineering strategy gives an opportunity to the company to reduce their cost to the optimal level by process improvement and provided competitive focus in achieving best in the market or to be a class brand. The process improvement is fundamentally an approach to clean-up the redundant activities in the business and set up swift process to reach the market. The supply chain management as a function of re-engineering process has been exhibited in Figure 1.7.

COMPETITIVE FOCUS

Company planning to take lead in the market should develop a strategic vision for dominance in the market place. It should also plan to achieve the output by implementing the strategy successfully. This phase may be viewed as ***discovering*** the competitive strength of the company. Later on the basis of results of discovery the business process need to be ***re-engineered*** and ***executed***. These are the three important phases in the re-engineering the business function with competitive focus, a company has to be prepared for planning to out-wit, out-maneuver and out-perform the competitor. There are various factors associated with these phases of change in business strategy for a company to be one of the best companies surviving in the market. The Table 1.5 exhibits the factors associated with the business reengineering phases of dominance redesign and realize.

Table 1.5: Framework of Re-engineering Business Process

Dominance	*Re-design*	*Realize*
• Learn and unlearn new ideas • Assess suitability • Make appropriate selection • Apply against competitors	• Learn and unlearn new ideas • Analyze suitability • Re-define and engineer strategy • Commit	• Mobilize people/ staff • Communicate and PR • Execute re-designed packages • Measure performance • Sustain

A company making efforts to become the market leader has to put substantial energy and resources in learning the competitor's move and later unlearn the same among the core team responsible for building strategies. In this process it is necessary to generate new ideas and assess their suitability to administer in the market and adaptability in the work environment of the company. Once the appropriate strategy is selected the core team has to take all steps to apply the same against the move of the competitors. These steps will help the company to play its dominance in the market against the competing forces. The dominance will also help the company to re-define the engineered strategy to its suitability in the market and commitment to apply the same against the competitors. The time taken for realizing the re-engineered strategy results against competitors vary according to the intensity of business penetration and customer relationship. However, to get a quick realization to the re-engineered business efforts a company has to build teams, plan execution of strategy in detail, confirm investment (if any), assess and recognize the impact. The company, during such market intervention operations has to handle the communications very carefully among the staff members and channel managers to avert any fowl interpretations and actions thereby. Communications to the staff members and channels should be comprehensive in the context of strategy re-engineering, the vision of work has to be made known to the concerned, explain rationale and assess the impact. The core team has to be trained to execute the task, control strategic points of the plan and to provide continuous inflow of the impact information to the top management of the company. Any business strategy implemented in the market should have strict measures against the task, time and target. Nevertheless, the cost-benefit assessment is important to evaluate the success of the interventions moved against competitors and re-define the next moves. The on-going management reviews and key indicators analysis are essential for a company to count its sustainability amidst competition in the market. The company must prepare a checklist of strength, weakness, opportunities and threats of in reference to the moves of the competitor. Some of the variable of the SWOT is illustrated in Table 1.6. The company has to prepare for the opportunities and build strategies to overcome the threats from the competitors. There are some factors like advertising and communication where equal opportunities exist for both the potential and rival business companies. This is an innovative sector where higher the creativity and reach larger is the impact on market.

Table 1.6 Competitor Learning - SWOT Analysis

Indicators	*Strong*	*Weak*	*Opportunity*	*Posing threat*
Process Technology				
Quality				
Cost				
Lead time				
Delivery time				
Delivery system				

Contd...

Indicators	***Strong***	***Weak***	***Opportunity***	***Posing Threat***
Information management				
Work Team				
Product support/services				
Merchandising				
Marketing and sales				
R&D				
Customer price				
Advertising				
Robustness				
Flexibility				
Differentiation Policy				
Customer response				
Customer relationship				
Correctness to customers				
Channel management				
Profit and performance				
- Competitor Firm				- Your Company

A company should acquire the strategies of outwitting, outmaneuvering and outperforming the competitors to win the race. It is necessary for the successful business companies to look for such a place of business that provides them more location advantage and hold the customers for their goods and services. The driving forces of competing firms, their organization and micro-economic environment need to be studied carefully by the company planning to overtake competitors in the business. Further in the process of winning the battle of rivals, it would be helpful for a company to understand the changing stakes of the competitors and forces after such developments. It is necessary to build-up strong, comprehensive and reliable database for capturing the activities of any business rival or competitor. Data is thus the basic input for competitor learning. In the competitive markets, the efficiency of the services discharged and extended to the buyers also contributes in building or breaking the market place strategy. Products, in the same market or competitive domain, largely vary in their availability may be due to weak or faulty supply chain management. An increase in the competitors' credit intakes with any financial institution may generate a signal of its intent to implement a major strategic initiative to expand its business such as an acquisition or planning for capital investment for augmenting its production or marketing activities. Hence, strategy building against the competitor is a very careful exercise that needs to be done by the practicing managers.

SELECT READINGS

Evans, Philip B. Wurster, Thomas S.: Strategy and the New Economics of Information, *Harvard Business Review,* Sept.-Oct. 1997, pp.71-82

Williamson, Peter J.: Asia's New Competitive Game, *Harvard Business Review,* Sept.-Oct. 1997, pp. 55-67

Drucker, Peter F.: Looking Ahead: Implications of the Present, *Harvard Business Review*, Sept.-Oct. 1997, pp.18-32.

Kenny David and Marshall John F.: Contextual Marketing, *Harvard Business Review*, November-December, 2000, pp 119-125

Leong, G. Keong.; Ward, Peter T.: The Six Ps of Manufacturing Strategy, *International Journal of Operations & Production Management,* Vol.15, No.12, 1995, pp. 32-45.

Belohlav, James A.: Quality, Strategy, and Competitiveness, *California Management Review,* Vol. 35, No. 3, Spring 1993, pp. 55-67

Fahe Liam: *Competitors: Outwitting, Outmaneuvering and Outperforming,* John Wiley and Sons, Canada, 1999

Peter Singe: *The Fifth Discipline, Doubleday/Currency,* New York, 1990

John J McGonagle *et.al.*: *A New Archetype for Competitive Intelligence*, Quorum Books, Westport, CT, 1996

Porter, Michael E.: *Competitive Strategy: Techniques for Analyzing Industry and Competitors,* The Free Press, New York, 1980

Rajagopal: *Marketing: Strategy, Implementation and Control*, Rawat, New Delhi, 2004

Warren Kim : *Competitive Strategy Dynamics*, Wiley, New York, 2002

Boyatzis, R: *The Competent Manager: A Mode for Effective Performance,* John Wiley & Sons: New York, 1982

Case 1.1

Case of EID-Parry (India) Ltd.

Thomas Parry, a young Welsh trader who came to Madras (now renamed Chennai) in 1788, founded Parry & Company. Now called EID Parry India Ltd., the company is well diversified with interests in fertilizers, pesticides, sugar and ceramics. The fertilizer and sugar businesses comprise 70 per cent of turnover. EID Parry belongs to the south based Murugappa group. He was the force behind the company until his death in 1824. The company started its sugar operations in 1803 with a cane sugar plantation near Chidambaram. The first sugar distillery at Nellikuppam in Tamilnadu came up in 1845. In 1906, it set up the Presidency Manure Works to manufacture super phosphates in Ranipet. It got into ceramics when it began making acid jars in 1908 for the sulphuric acid produced in the super phosphate factory. In 1975, the company was registered under the Companies Act as EID Parry (India) Ltd. From the late sixties onwards, the company started showing signs of decline.

Product- Mix

EID - Parry (India) is a diversified company with interests in various business activities such as fertilizers, pesticides, sugar and ceramics. The fertilizer division has two manufacturing units at Ennore and Ranipet (both in Tamilnadu); the pesticides division has units in Ranipet (Maharashtra) and Thane (Maharashtra); the bio-pesticides division has units in Thyagavalli and Nellikuppam (both in Tamilnadu) and the sugar division has manufacturing units at Nellikuppam and Pugalur (both in Tamilnadu). The ceramics division manufactures sanitaryware (Ranipet in Tamilnadu and Alwar in Rajasthan) and wall tiles (Karaikal in Tamilnadu). The fertilizer and sugar businesses constitute 72 per cent of the company's turnover. The installed capacities are as follows:[34] Sugar (8000 cane MT per day - Actual production of 117482 during 1997-98); Ammonium Phosphate Sulphate (170000 MTPA); Super Phosphate (132000 MTPA); Sanitaryware (19000 MTPA) and Tiles (16,00,500 square metres per annum)

Company's size has grown considerably over the past four years between 1993-94 and 1997-98. Turnover (net sales) rose from Rs 4360 Milion[35] in 1993-94 to Rs 8570 Million in 1997-98. Similarly, over the same period, gross block rose 4.4 times to Rs 570 Million. The net profit of Rs 290.95 Million in 1997-98 was 3.35 times higher than that reported for 1993-94. Equity capital has also risen from Rs 100.20 Million to Rs 17.81 crore. The rate of dividend paid has been steadily increasing from 33 percent (1994-95) to 36 percent (1995-96) to 40 percent (1996-97) and then to 50 percent in 1997-98. EID Parry faced labour problems when its employees at its Ennore factory struck work in April 1998.

Product Performance

Sugar

India has been known as the original home of sugar and sugarcane. Indian mythology supports the above fact as it contains legends showing the origin of sugarcane. The Indian sugar industry

34 MT = Metric Ton, MTPA = Metric Ton Per Annum

35 Exchange Rate US $ 1 = 46.85 INR (Peak rate in Last week of July 2001)

banks on the sweet tooth of the country's citizens as sweets and savories favor every occasion. Almost 75% of the sugar available in the open market is consumed by bulk consumers like bakeries, candy makers, sweet makers and soft drink manufacturers. Greater urbanization and rising standard of living have sparked a rising trend in usage of sugar. The quantum of sugar produced by a sugar factory is determined by the factors like daily crushing capacity, duration of crushing season and percentage of sugar recovery from the cane crushed. Sugar prices in the country can be classified into two broad categories at the user end as free market prices and prices of sugar through public distribution system. However, substantial increase in the volume of free international trade in sugar presents an excellent opportunity to the Indian sugar industry to embark on a regular plan for sugar exports.

Sugar making in E.I.D Parry's history dates back to 1842. It was then that the company pioneered the production of sugar by establishing the country's first sugar factory at Nellikuppam. This factory also holds the distinction of being the first ever integrated sugar complex in India. Today, like in the past, the company continues to set standards in the sugar industry. Parry's sugar has been initially launched in Tamil Nadu in one-kg refill packs and pet bottles. Every grain of Parry's pure refined sugar is a product of a superior refining process and is processed hygienically from first grade cane. In addition, Parry's pure refined sugar has a longer shelf life of over 18 months and is absolutely pure and free of all impurities.

There are several *by–products* of sugar that add value to the industry. *Molasses* is used for production of rectified spirit, which is used as a feedstock for production of chemicals as well as potable liquor. The country has been producing about 1.7 billion liters of alcohol utilizing 75-80% molasses production in the country. The surplus molasses is either exported or carried forward to the next sugar season resulting in quality deterioration. *Ethanol* is used as a blend fuel with gasoline in the transport sector. The ethanol program is bound to bring an assured market at a better price than what they get from alcohol. It is widely anticipated that the Government will move in line with happenings in markets like Brazil. It is quite possible that it may increase the quantum of ethanol mix in petrol from the current five percent to 10 percent. *Bagasse*, another by-product of the sugar industry, which constitutes about 30% of cane processed for production of sugar, is used as a fuel for generation of steam and power to meet the process requirements. Co-generated power apart from being a renewable source of energy is also most eco-friendly. The Government of India has a vision plan to increase the share of renewable energy to 10% by the year 2010.

Sanitary Ware

Parryware, from the house of EID Parry is the largest manufacturer of sanitary ware in the country which is aimed at developing cleaner, hygienic sanitary solutions for the customers. The company has introduced the touch and feel concept where products are shown in live bathroom settings, in such a manner that the customer can see how it looks, and also observe how it works, in order to augment the customer value and stand as customer preferred brand in he competitive markets. Parryware has set-up Customer Care Centres across India and is setting a new trend in the sanitary ware industry. The centres are located at Delhi, Chennai, Mumbai, Kolkatta, Cochin, Hyderabad, Bangalore, Pune & Lucknow and provide the following services:

- Complaint handling
- Products installation
- Bathroom renovation
- Annual maintenance of bathrooms
- Selling spare parts.

These centers are equipped with factory-trained personnel, latest tool kits and original spares. The customer is ensured of quality service at a reasonable price. Parryware has the distinction of being the first Company in the Industry to offer comprehensive bathroom solutions to Customer.

Competitive Business Process

EID Parry forged and facilitated partnerships among a wide range of organizations, including Tamil Nadu Agriculture University (TNAU) and its research stations, Tamil Nadu University for Veterinary and Animal Sciences (TANUVAS), National Horticulture Board, AMM Foundation, and Murugappa Chettiar Research Center, to create the agriportal Indiagriline. The agriportal (*www.indiagriline.com*) was developed by using in-house expertise (EID Parry's Sugar and Farm Inputs Division and Corporate Research & Development Lab). So far, EID Parry has set up Internet kiosks in 26 villages around its Nellikuppam factory in the Cuddalore district in Tamil Nadu on a pilot scale. It fashioned a franchise-based business model to meet the demand for information and connectivity. These kiosks are owned and operated by franchisees trained to operate the system.

EID Parry allows the franchisees to use its brand, procure commodities on its behalf, and sell its products or services and by adapting this model the company has been able to keep its fixed costs low. Although EID Parry covers the cost of establishing the infrastructure for voice and data connectivity, each franchisee invests approximately Rs. 60,000 to cover the cost of the computer and all related equipment. The operating costs of running the kiosks, such as electricity and connectivity charges, are covered by the franchisees. For EID Parry, franchising is a cost-effective way to build a chain of many kiosks all operating under their banner. This cooperative relationship builds a win–win situation for both parties involved. It provides the incentives each party needs to contribute to the other's potential success.

Strategic Moves: Alliances and Mergers

In the sanitary ware business, EID Parry has a strategic alliance with Espiem Plastics. In December 1998, the company announced that its seeds division would be transferred to a separate company called Parry Monsanto Seeds Private Ltd. This company is a joint venture between EID Parry and Monsanto Chemicals. It was then stated that Monsanto's stake of 35 percent would rise to 51 percent over a period of time. The company has made exposure to Group Companies as ten percent of EID Parry 's total assets comprise Investments and almost all of the investments (98.16 percent) pertaining to group company investments. These figures are, as of 31st March 1998. The market value of the company's quoted investments as on that day was Rs 260.62 Million as against their cost of Rs 510.35 Million

In June 1998, EID Parry took over Cauvery Sugars & Chemicals, a south India based sugar company. This company turned sick in 1996 and was referred to the BIFR. It has a 40 year old sugar plant with a crushing capacity of 2500 tones of cane per day, located at Trichy in Tamilnadu. By this takeover, EID Parry has acquired control over crushing capacity of 10,500 tonnes of cane per day. It has become the largest sugar-manufacturing group in southern India. In November 1998, EID Parry consolidated its holding in Coromandel Fertilizers by acquiring a 29 percent stake from Mallinckrodt Inc, a co-promoter of Coromandel fertilizers. Purchased at Rs 35.97 per share, the acquisition increased EID Parry's stake in the company to 63 percent. Attempts at taking over another Sugar Company, Kothari Sugars & Chemicals, failed as the negotiators could not agree on the consideration for the deal. Beside EID Parry company owns *The Mofussil Warehouse Trading Company Ltd, Dhanyalakshmi Investments Ltd,* and *Parry Chemicals Ltd.* as wholly owned subsidiaries

IT in Corporate Business: A Challenge in Competition

Recognizing the significance of information and communication technology (ICT) as a powerful tool for bridging the infrastructure gaps in rural India, EID Parry regarded the Internet as the next logical medium for delivering its farm extension services. *Indiagriline* is an effort to provide an end-to-end solution addressing the needs of the farming community in South India. EID Parry launched this project in early 2001 by setting up Internet kiosks in 16 villages around its sugar factory in Nellikuppam. These kiosks were called Parry's Corners, named after a famous landmark in Chennai and were intended to be business hubs of their respective villages-a one-stop shop that acted as a storefront for buying farm inputs, a market for selling goods, and an Internet café for communication and information services.

Indiagriline: The Vision

Strategic goal of the Murugappa Group was to ultimately develop the following capabilities:

Distribution infrastructure: This infrastructure would be capable of supporting bidirectional distribution of products and services into and out of rural India. Therefore, developing a low-cost channel for rural distribution was a key goal.

Trading infrastructure: This would serve as the foundation to a platform for trading agricultural commodities and rural industry manufactured goods.

Towards achieving these ends, EID Parry forged and facilitated partnerships among a wide range of organizations, including Tamil Nadu Agriculture University (TNAU) and its research stations, Tamil Nadu University for Veterinary and Animal Sciences (TANUVAS), National Horticulture Board, AMM Foundation, and Murugappa Chettiar Research Center, to create the agro-portal Indiagriline. www.indiagriline.com was developed by using in-house expertise. It fashioned a franchise-based business model to meet the demand for information and connectivity. These kiosks are owned and operated by franchisees trained to operate the system. Although EID Parry covers the cost of establishing the infrastructure for voice and data connectivity, the franchisee also contributes his portion and attends to the operational expenditure of the kiosk. This cooperative relationship builds a win-win situation for both parties involved. Each Kiosk has a CorDECT-WLL[36] set, a PC, printer,

36 corDECT is the major Indian Innovation in the area of broadband wireless communication, it is the only Wireless Local Loop system that provides simultaneous Voice Telephone and Internet at 35/70 kbps to every subscriber . It has the lowest capital investment and operational cost amongst all the Wireless Local Loop systems.

telephone, furniture and a power source with a back up. The franchisees can leverage the EID Parry brand name to attract customers to their location for selling products or services. They also benefit from a wealth of knowledge transferred to them by EID Parry on how to successfully manage and operate the Parry's Corners. EID Parry also offers assistance in financing the franchisees through arrangements with third-party lending institutions such as Indian Bank. In a rural setting where literacy rates are low and fear of and resistance to technology are high, this facility is slowly changing the life of the farmers, who, instead of traveling to the company or other places to get their business done, now walk into the neighborhood for information.

Discussion Issues

1. What are the advantages of diversification strategy of a company to gain competitive advantage? Review this issue in reference to the EID Parry company.
2. How can EID Parry establish the competitive advantage through high technology to expand its markets in rural areas and enhances the customer value? Discuss

Case 1.2

Retail Expansion in Global Arena: Strategies of Wal-Mart to Sustain Competition

"We're all working together; that's the secret. And we'll lower the cost of living for everyone, not just in America, but we'll give the world an opportunity to see what it's like to save and have a better lifestyle, a better life for all. We're proud of what we've accomplished; we've just begun."

Sam Walton (1918-1992)

Though once a small-town outfit itself, created by home-spun, Arkansas entrepreneur Sam Walton who never lost the opportunity to extol small-town "values", the "super-store" Wal-Mart has succeeded in transforming the face of small towns around the world. At one time welcomed, whole-heartedly, by towns that considered the coming of Wal-Mart to be a sign of revitalization and modernization, more and more communities these days are very skeptical or downright hostile toward the prospect of the arrival of Wal-Mart. Over the past few years the retail titan has suffered through an avalanche of negative publicity — pertaining to a wide variety of issues, and Wal-Mart has become one of the leading symbols of urban sprawl and small-town downtown decay. The world's largest retailer, with 3,562 Wal-Mart stores and another 500-odd Sam's Club stores in 7 countries racked up over $137 billion in sales in fiscal 1998. The corporation is presently positioning itself so aggressively that a new Wal-Mart or Sam's Club opens every 3 days!

Corporation employed 910,000 employees at the start of 1999. Wal-Mart store sizes continue to increase, with emphasis on the regional "superstore", 150,000 square-feet or larger with a full-fledged retail grocery store an integral part. (For comparison, 150,000 sq. ft. is equivalent to 3-1/3 football fields). The corporation typically seeks market areas where there is a customer base of at least 40,000 and targets small to medium-sized towns in particular. Historically, the corporation avoids big city markets where land prices may be too high and competition from other large retailers much stiffer. Instead, Wal-Mart's strategy has been to locate in peripheral, semi-rural areas or city outskirts where it may draw from a regional clientele.

The Wal-Mart Culture

Sam Walton's dream was simple to be stated as giving people high value at low prices and a warm welcome. Today, Wal-Mart Stores, Inc., employs more than 1.2 million associates worldwide. The company has more than 3,000 stores and offices across the United States and more than 1,000 stores internationally. It has also expanded online with Walmart.com, which is dedicated to bringing Sam Walton's dream to the Internet. Low prices have been the retail culture of the company that kept the consumers loyal to the retail brand. It's also because of the Wal-Mart staff starting with the friendly greeters at the front of every store. Prompt, friendly service is a serious matter at Wal-Mart. Sam Walton said "The secret of successful retailing is to give your customers what they want. And really, if you think about it from your point of view as a customer, you want everything: a wide assortment of good quality merchandise; the lowest possible prices; guaranteed satisfaction with what you buy; friendly, knowledgeable service; convenient hours; free parking; a pleasant shopping experience."

"As Wal-Mart continues to grow into new areas and new mediums our success will always be attributed to our culture. Whether you walk into a Wal-Mart store in your hometown or one across the country while you're on vacation, you can always be assured you're getting low prices and that genuine customer service you've come to expect from us. You'll feel at home in any department of any store..." Sam Walton built Wal-Mart on the revolutionary philosophies of excellence in the workplace, customer service and always having the lowest prices. They have always stayed true to the Three Basic Beliefs Mr. Sam established in 1962:

- Respect for the Individual
- Service to Customers
- Strive for Excellence

Respect the Individual

"Our people make the difference' is not a meaningless slogan - it's a reality at Wal-Mart. We are a group of dedicated, hardworking, ordinary people who have teamed together to accomplish extraordinary things. We have very different backgrounds, different colors and different beliefs, but we do believe that every individual deserves to be treated with respect and dignity." Says Don Soderquist, Senior Vice Chairman of Wal-Mart Stores, Inc. (Retired)

Service to Our Customers

Wal-Mart wants that customers trust in its pricing philosophy and to always be able to find the lowest prices with the best possible service. "We're nothing without our customers...Wal-Mart's culture has always stressed the importance of Customer Service. Our associate base across the country is as diverse as the communities in which we have Wal-Mart stores. This allows us to provide the Customer Service expected by each individual customer that walks into our stores." Tom Coughlin, President and chief executive officer, Wal-Mart Stores division

Strive for Excellence

New ideas and goals make them reach further than ever before. They try to find new and innovative ways to push their boundaries and constantly improve. "Sam was never satisfied that prices were as low as they needed to be or that our product's quality was as high a they deserved - he believed in the concept of striving for excellence before it became a fashionable concept." The customers are so important for the company, Wal-Mart, receives letters daily from customers praising individual associates for giving exceptional service. Sometimes they write to express their appreciation for services as simple as a smile, an associate remembering their name or someone carrying out their purchases for them. Other times they write of incidents that seem almost heroic. Years ago, Sam Walton challenged all Wal-Mart associates to practice what he called "aggressive hospitality." He said "Let's be more friendly- offer a smile of welcome and assistance to all who do us a favor by entering our stores. Give better service - over and beyond what our customers expect. Why not? You wonderful, caring associates can do it and do it better than any other retailing company in the world . . . exceed your customers' expectations. If you do, they'll come back over and over again." As Wal-Mart associates know that it is not good enough to simply be grateful to the customers for shopping Wal-Mart stores - they want to demonstrate their gratitude in every way they can and they believe that doing so is what keeps their customers coming back to Wal-Mart again and again. One of Wal-Mart's secrets to customer service is their "10-foot attitude," handed down to us by Wal-Mart Founder, Sam Walton. During his many store visits, he encouraged associates to take a pledge with him: "... I want you to promise that whenever you come within 10 feet of a customer, you will look him in the eye, greet him and ask him, if you can help him."

This pledge is what we now call our "10-foot attitude," and it was something Sam had practiced since childhood. He was always ambitious and competitive, and by the time he reached college at the University of Missouri in Columbia, Sam decided, he wanted to be president of the university student body. In his words, "I learned early on that one of the secrets to campus leadership was the simplest thing of all: speak to people coming down the sidewalk before they speak to you ... I would always look ahead and speak to the person coming toward me. "If I knew them, I would call them by name, but even if I didn't I would still speak to them. Before long, I probably knew more students than anybody in the university, and they recognized me and considered me their friend. I ran for every office that came along." Not only was Sam elected to just about all of those offices, but he also carried that philosophy into the world of retail, where you can see it practiced every day by Wal-Mart associates throughout the world.

Wal-Mart succeeds on two counts: Being such a huge buyer, it can negotiate the best wholesale prices. And it is such a huge seller that it can offer customers the lowest prices and make up the difference in volume. All this explains why many investors are bullish on Wal-Mart. At around $53, shares are down about 6.5% year-to-date, but that's considerably less than the 15.5% hit the shares of retailers as a group have endured. In part, Wal-Mart has fared better because of the outfit's reliable performance, no matter the health of the economy. Wal-Mart targets of opportunity are likely to be apparel and consumer electronics. Consumer electronics is in for similar treatment. Wal-Mart has been taking sales away from consumer electronics retailers for years — mainly on lower-priced products. Wal-Mart's aggressive adoption of information technology to improve logistics and back-office efficiency has also been a major driver of productivity. While suppliers scrambled to meet Wal-Mart's demands, big and small competitors followed the retailer's lead and ratcheted up productivity by 28% from 1995 to 1999. But because of its early adoption, Wal-Mart reaped the most gains and continues to enjoy an edge over competitors.

Company's small-town values drive its relationship with staff and suppliers. Despite its enormous workforce, there is a paternal feel to Wal-Mart. It is as if everybody were still working for some strict, though ultimately benign, uncle. Employees are called "associates". Most own shares and are on profit-share. They also enjoy a large degree of autonomy. Ken Schroader, store manager at Wal-Mart's Super centre in Siloam Springs, Arkansas, proudly demonstrates the scanners that tell his department managers precisely how well products are selling—sales compared with last year, mark-ups, how much is in stock or in transit. Such details allow a department head to become a small shopkeeper, running his section like an independent store and moving stock faster (Wal-Mart shifts inventory twice as fast as the industry average). Every humble store worker has the power to lower the price on any Wal-Mart product, if he spots it cheaper elsewhere. That sort of delegation is apparent outside the stores too. Michael Duke, head of logistics, uses his 6,000 truck drivers (most of whom own Wal-Mart shares) to keep tabs on inventory problems at stores. Involvement breeds loyalty: driver turnover is only 5% a year, compared with an industry average of 125%. George Tracy, head of personnel at a Bentonville distribution centre, cracks down on whatever raises costs and rewards whatever lowers them. For instance, Laura Blumenstein, one of his workers, will get dinner for two and a parking spot near the entrance (this is Wal-Mart, after all) for logging inventory fast and accurately. To raise flagging spirits, weird stunts—such as pig-kissing contests and quasi-evangelical weekend get-togethers—are laid on (see article). In America, at least, this works.

Suppliers are treated as part of the family, once they have proved their worth. Nervous newcomers are shown to "the row", a long corridor of drab rooms, each adorned with a notice explaining that Wal-Mart's buyers do not accept bribes. It is like a scene from a bazaar: sweaters spill out of suitcases and haggling over prices continues all day. Angel Burgos, from Puerto Rico, wants to sell computers to Wal-Mart: "We were grapes," he sighs, "but now we are raisins. They suck you dry." Proven suppliers, though, feel differently. Through Wal-Mart's proprietary systems, they are given full and free access to real-time data on how their products are selling, store by store. By sharing information that other retailers jealously guard, Wal-Mart allows suppliers to plan production runs earlier and so offer better prices. Procter & Gamble's $6 billion-a-year business with Wal-Mart is so important that the maker of Crest toothpaste has a 150-strong Bentonville office dedicated to it. Andy Jett, a director there, says Europe's retailers are still blind to the competitive edge that partnering with suppliers gives Wal-Mart. "Wal-Mart treats suppliers as an extension of its company. All retailers will eventually work this way," he predicts.

Wal-Mart International Operations

Wal-Mart became an international company in 1991 when a SAM'S CLUB opened near Mexico City. Just two years later, the Wal-Mart International Division was created to oversee growing opportunities worldwide. Today, customers at more than 1,200 units in nine countries prove that Wal-Mart's Every Day Low Price promise is a message clearly understood in any language. Wal-Mart, however, continues to experiment more successfully, with analysts speculating that it may add convenience stores to its retailing repertoire. And unlike McDonald's, Wal-Mart regularly embraces products that strike a chord with consumers. Already the leading U.S. consumer source of groceries, apparel, toys, jewelry, DVDs, CDs, sporting goods, and bedding, analysts say Wal-Mart is mulling expansions into new lines like gasoline, insurance, and banking services. "They're really attuned to changes in the marketplace," says Szymanski. "They don't just follow customers, but lead them." Wal-Mart also has room to expand overseas, considering that "there are still a lot of places in the world where it doesn't do business," says Carl Steidtman, chief economist at Deloitte Consulting. "Their growth potential," he adds, "is tied to the rise of the global middle class." This year, in addition to those it plans in the U.S., Wal-Mart will open 120 to 130 stores in countries such as Mexico and Japan.

Development Opportunities

Wal-Mart has experienced success internationally because of its ability to transport the company's unique culture and effective retailing concepts to each new country. Associates get involved in the local communities and adapt to local cultures. They respond to customer needs, merchandise preferences and local suppliers. By serving each hometown in its own unique way, Wal-Mart International has realized significant growth with potential for much greater development worldwide.

Wal-Mart International has achieved global expansion through a combination of new store construction and acquisitions. This strategy has given the company excellent market penetration and positioned it for future development. The company sees its development throughout North America, Latin America, Asia and Europe as a good beginning with many promising areas for further expansion.

Division has posted impressive financial results. Fiscal 2002 sales reached $35.4 billion, a 10.5 percent increase over the previous year, and operating profit rose to $1.4 billion, an increase of 31.1 percent. This year, Wal-Mart International plans to open 120 to 130 units in existing markets. Projects are scheduled to open in each country in which the company operates, and will include new stores and clubs as well as relocations of a few existing units. These announced units also include several restaurants, department stores and supermarkets in Mexico. In addition, Germany will continue with the remodeling of the acquired hypermarkets.

Pricing Philosophy

Sam Walton always knew he wanted to be in the retailing business. He started his career by running a Ben Frankling franchise store and learned about buying, pricing and passing good deals on to customers. He credits a manufacturer's agent from New York, Harry Weiner, with his first real lesson about pricing: "Harry was selling ladies' panties for $2 a dozen. We'd been buying similar panties from Ben Franklin for $2.50 a dozen and selling them at three for $1. Well, at Harry's price of $2, we could put them out at four for $1 and make a great promotion for our store. "Here's the simple lesson we learned ... say I bought an item for 80 cents. I found that by pricing it at $1.00, I could sell three times more of it than by pricing it at $1.20. I might make only half the profit per item, but because I was selling three times as many, the overall profit was much greater. But this is really the essence of discounting: by cutting your price, you can boost your sales to a point where you earn far more at the cheaper retail than you would have by selling the item at the higher price. In retailer language, you can lower your markup but earn more because of the increased volume."

Sam's adherence to this pricing philosophy was unshakable, as one of Wal-Mart's first store managers recalls: "Sam wouldn't let us hedge on a price at all. Say the list price was $1.98, but we had paid only 50 cents. Initially, I would say, 'Well, it's originally $1.98, so why don't we sell it for $1.25?' And, he'd say, 'No. We paid 50 cents for it. Mark it up 30 percent, and that's it. No matter what you pay for it, if we get a great deal, pass it on to the customer.' And of course that's what we did." And that's what we continue to do - work diligently to find great deals to pass on to our customers. Thanks to the legacy of Sam Walton, Wal-Mart is a store you can count on every day to bring you value for your dollar. And that's why at Wal-Mart, you never have to wait for a sale to get your money's worth!

Analysts think the Bentonville (Ark.) discounter can grow at its current pace for years to come, as it expands in the U.S. and beyond. Within the next decade, if you buy this scenario, Wal-Mart's revenues could exceed the gross domestic product of the Philippines, whose $350 billion economy grew 4.6% in 2002. In large part, that's because Wal-Mart has pulled off a difficult balancing act: it continues to woo large numbers of customers who respond to new concepts, things like Sam's Club and the chain's Super centres. At the same time, while avoiding market saturation, it has been improving and expanding its roster of core Wal-Mart stores. Even though Sam Walton's creation seems omnipresent, it isn't. The

U.S. has "only" 2,826 Wal-Mart discount or combined grocery and general merchandise Super centres, plus 525 Sam's Club warehouse stores. While these are some awesome numbers, Wal-Mart has plenty of room for expansion. Current plans see an additional 245 domestic outlets by January, 2004 at least 200 of which will be Super centres. That should still leave a potential for 2,000 more stores in the U.S. by 2011, figures Mark Miller, an analyst at William Blair & Co. Miller thinks Wal-Mart can hit $660 billion in sales by then, an expectation that's evident in Wal-Mart's stock price: It has dropped over the past 12 months, but by only about 12%, to around $54.

Wal-Mart can still expand largely because it has come up with successful variations on its discount model. When its core business began to mature in the 1990s, Wal-Mart started to build combined grocery and general-merchandise superstores-180,000-square-foot behemoths that now account for 54% of revenues from Wal-Mart-branded locations in the U.S., according to Emme Kozloff, an analyst at Bernstein Research. As the growth of superstores slows over the next several years, Wal-Mart will look to its much smaller Neighbourhood Markets for the next wave of expansion. It now has 50 such stores, which represent very little of total revenues. Miller expects to see a further 1,350 by 2011, when he believes they should account for 5% of revenues. The major pricing strategies of Wal-Mart are delineated as below:

Every Day Low Price (EDLP)

Because you work hard for every dollar, you deserve the lowest price we can offer every time you make a purchase. You deserve our Every Day Low Price. It's not a sale; it's a great price you can count on every day to make your dollar go further at Wal-Mart.

Rollback

This is our ongoing commitment to pass even more savings on to you by lowering our Every Day Low Prices whenever we can. When our costs get rolled back, it allows us to lower our prices for you. Just look for the Rollback smiley face throughout the store. You'll smile too.

Special Buy

When you see items with the Special Buy logo, you'll know you're getting an exceptional value. It may be an item we carry every day that includes an additional amount of the same product or another product for a limited time. Or, it could be an item we carry while supplies last, at a very special price. The Wal-Mart's success secret can be resumed in ten key factors made by Sam Walton known as "Sam's Rules for Building a Business." He says:

Rule 1

Commit to your business. Believe in it more than anybody else. I think, I overcame every single one of my personal shortcomings by the sheer passion I brought to my work. I don't know if you're born with this kind of passion, or if you can learn it. But I do know you need it. If you love your work, you'll be out there every day trying to do it the best you possibly can, and pretty soon everybody around will catch the passion from you - like a fever.

Rule 2

Share your profits with all your Associates, and treat them as partners. In turn, they will treat you as a partner, and together you will all perform beyond your wildest expectations. Remain a corporation and retain control if you like, but behave as a servant leader in a partnership. Encourage your Associates to hold a stake in the company. Offer discounted stock, and grant them stock for their retirement. It's the single best thing we ever did.

Rule 3

Motivate your partners. Money and ownership alone aren't enough. Constantly, day-by-day, think of new and more interesting ways to motivate and challenge your partners. Set high goals, encourage competition, and then keep score. Make bets with outrageous payoffs. If things get stale, cross-pollinate; have managers switch jobs with one another to stay challenged. Keep everybody guessing as to what your next trick is going to be. Don't become too predictable.

Rule 4

Communicate everything you possibly can to your partners. The more they know, the more they'll understand. The more they understand, the more they'll care. Once they care, there's no stopping them. If you don't trust your Associates to know what's going on, they'll know you don't really consider them partners. Information is power, and the gain you get from empowering your associates more than offsets the risk of informing your competitors.

Rule 5

Appreciate everything your Associates do for the business. A paycheck and a stock option will buy one kind of loyalty. But all of us like to be told how much somebody appreciates what we do for them. We like to hear it often, and especially when we have done something we're really proud of. Nothing else can quite substitute for a few well-chosen, well-timed, sincere words of praise. They're absolutely free - and worth a fortune.

Rule 6

Celebrate your successes. Find some humor in your failures. Don't take yourself so seriously. Loosen up, and everybody around you will loosen up. Have fun. Show enthusiasm - always. When all else fails, put on a costum0e and sing a silly song. Then make everybody else sing with you. Don't do a hula on Wall Street. It's been done. Think up your own stunt. All of this is more important, and more fun, than you think, and it really fools the competition. "Why should we take those cornballs at Wal-Mart seriously?"

Rule 7

Listen to everyone in your company. And figure out ways to get them talking. The folks on the front lines - the ones who actually talk to the customer - are the only ones who really know what's going on out there. You'd better find out what they know. This really is what total quality is all about. To push responsibility down in your organization, and to force good ideas to bubble up within it, you must listen to what your Associates are trying to tell you.

Rule 8

Exceed your customers' expectations. If you do, they'll come back over and over. Give them what they want - and a little more. Let them know you appreciate them. Make good on all your mistakes, and don't make excuses - apologize. Stand behind everything you do. The two most important words I ever wrote were on that first Wal-Mart sign, "Satisfaction Guaranteed." They're still up there, and they have made all the difference.

Rule 9

Control your expenses better than your competition. This is where you can always find the competitive advantage. For 25 years running - long before Wal-Mart was known as the nation's largest retailer - we ranked No. 1 in our industry for the lowest ratio of expenses to sales. You can make a lot of different mistakes and still recover if you run an efficient operation. Or you can be brilliant and still go out of business, if you're too inefficient.

Rule 10

Swim upstream. Go the other way. Ignore the conventional wisdom. If everybody else is doing it one way, there's a good chance you can find your niche by going in exactly the opposite direction. But be prepared for a lot of folks to wave you down and tell you you're headed the wrong way. I guess in all my years, what I heard more often than anything was: "a town of less than 50,000 populations cannot support a discount store for very long."

Retail Divisions of Wal-Mart

Wal-Mart Stores

Wal-Mart stores are the flagship retail division of Wal-Mart Stores, Inc. They are a national discount retailer offering a wide variety of general merchandise. Wal-Mart stores offer pleasant and convenient shopping in 36 departments including family apparel, health & beauty aids, household needs, electronics, toys, fabrics & crafts, lawn & garden, jewelry and shoes. In addition, some Wal-Mart stores offer a Pharmacy Department, Tire & Lube Express, Garden Centre, Snack Bar or Restaurant, Vision Centre and One-Hour Photo Processing for customer convenience. Wal-Mart stores operate on an "Every Day Low Price" philosophy and are able to maintain their low price structure through conscientious expense control. While other major competitors typically run 50 to 100 advertised circulars per year, Wal-Mart produces only 12-13 major annual circulars. The cost savings associated with fewer circulars are passed on to the customer through lower shelf prices every day. Wal-Mart Associates strive to provide exceptional customer service, a characteristic unique to their chain. They do everything possible to make shopping at Wal-Mart a friendly experience.

Super-centers

Wal-Mart Super centre provides one-stop family shopping convenience. The store combines a full-line of groceries and a general merchandise department under one roof. The growing demand for one-stop shopping led to Wal-Mart's decision to build full-line grocery department into many of its new stores. Referred to as Super centers, Wal-Mart stores with grocery departments offer the ultimate in convenience - grocery shopping and 36 departments of discount general merchandise under one roof.

Super centre feature 36 general merchandise departments including a complete apparel department with accessories, an extensive fine jewelry department, a lawn & garden centre, a large health & beauty aids department, a full line of electronics and a pharmacy department. In addition, grocery areas generally feature a bakery, delicatessen, frozen food section, meat & dairy and fresh produce departments. Super centers also often include, Wal-Mart Specialty Shops such as our Vision Centre, Tire & Lube Express and One-Hour Photo Processing. The Super center is designed to provide a pleasant and hassle-free shopping experience, Wal-Mart Super centers are enhanced with wide aisles, helpful signing throughout the store, departmental directories and 24-hour service. Super centers are also equipped with a customer service desk and scanning registers for fast, efficient checkout service. Super centers average between 100,000 and 210,000 square feet of retail space. Depending on size and customer needs, they employ between 200 and 550 Associates, each dedicated to exceptional customer service. As in all Wal-Mart stores, checks, Master Card, Visa, Discover and American Express cards are accepted. "...As Wal-Mart Associates, we know it is not good enough to simply be grateful to our customers for shopping at our stores - we want to demonstrate our gratitude in every way we can! We believe that doing so is what keeps our customers coming back to Wal-Mart again and again..." - Sam Walton

SAM'S Club

SAM'S Club is the nation's leading members-only warehouse club with locations across the country. SAM'S Club depends on high volume to compensate for very narrow profit margins on merchandise, resulting in extremely low prices for member-customers. To meet the needs of its business members, SAM'S Club limits its merchandise mix to 3,500 items local businesses use most. This includes a complete line of food products & frozen foods; janitorial products; tires, batteries, and auto supplies; small building equipment & hardware; candy & snack items; and office supplies, computers & equipment. Merchandise typically is in larger institutional sizes or multi-packs of like or assorted items. SAM'S Club also offers televisions, VCRs & camcorders, large & small appliances, home furnishings, designer clothing, watches & jewelry and sheets & towels.

Neighborhood Market

Neighborhood Markets offer a convenient shopping experience for customers who need groceries, pharmaceuticals and general merchandise. The neighborhood markets offer a convenient shopping experience for customers who need groceries, pharmaceuticals and general merchandise. Generally, they are located in markets with Wal-Mart Super centers, supplementing a strong food distribution network and providing added convenience while maintaining Wal-Mart's Every Day Low Prices. First opened in 1998, Neighborhood Markets range from 42,000 to 55,000 square feet and feature a wide variety of products, including fresh produce, processed foods, fresh meat and dairy items, health and beauty aids, one-hour photo and traditional photo developing services, drive-through pharmacies, stationery and paper goods, pet supplies, and household chemicals. Neighborhood Markets employ 80-100 associates and offer about 28,000 items

WAL-MART.COM

Wal-mart.com is a mostly like Wal-Mart store. It features a great selection, high-quality merchandise, friendly service and, of course, Every Day Low Prices. Their goal is striving to bring to the customers the best shopping experience on the Internet Their office is located near California's Silicon Valley, their heart and spirit are still in Bentonville, Ark., the corporate home of Wal-Mart Stores, Inc., and the town where Sam Walton opened Walton's Five and Dime in 1950. From humble beginnings in north-western Arkansas, Wal-Mart has grown to become a familiar name in households all over the world. At the heart of Wal-Mart's growth is the unique culture that "Mr. Sam" has built. His business philosophy was based on the simple idea of making the customer No. 1. He believed that by serving the customer's needs first, his business would also serve its associates, shareholders, communities and other stakeholders. The goal of Wal-mart.com is to bring Mr. Sam's culture and philosophy from Wal-Mart stores to the Internet.

External and Internal Threats

Giant retailer has been criticized for everything from labour practices to contributing to urban sprawl. It has been the target of some 40 lawsuits by employees who claim they were forced to work overtime for no extra pay. The stores and product line-ups of the company are so standardized, that if it stops clicking with customers, the effects could ripple quickly through the entire chain. Perhaps more likely is the possibility that a variety of backlashes against Wal-Mart's marketplace muscle could slow down the momentum. Some competitors have tried to make the case that Wal-Mart's sharply lower pricing caused them to lose profits over a substantial period of time.

But Wal-Mart's biggest problem is its lack of "human capital", says Coleman Peterson, head of personnel. The group has been at pains to replace expatriates with locals, and a non-American now leads every overseas country team except China's. It is expanding faster than it can train people internally, and has lost high-quality local managers to rivals. This leads to another problem: that the international division still lacks scale. To exploit savings from sourcing globally, Wal-Mart needs to make more acquisitions. Buying Carrefour would be the boldest move. However, Wal-Mart is more likely to buy the hypermarket businesses of Germany's Metro, worth $4 billion. The two sides talked last year, and insiders say that Metro, controlled by three families, is ready to sell. Buying even part of Metro, which controls a third of Germany's retail space, would bring Wal-Mart huge clout with European suppliers, and also some more experienced European managers.

But Wal-Mart has another problem: its image. In America, its giant stores are symbols of "big retail", blamed for the destruction of entire community. To avoid future growth being constrained by political barriers, Wal-Mart may have to raise its head from Bentonville and worry more about how it is perceived. Unpopularity is hard for Wal-Mart executives to understand. After all, everyday low prices have been good for consumers. And a recent study by McKinsey, a consultancy, credited efficiencies in retailing (mainly Wal-Mart's) to more of America's recent productivity spurt than technology investment. Ultimately, few doubt that Wal-Mart has both the patience and the resources to stay on top. "Never underestimate them," advises Richard Hyman of Verdict, a consultancy. "They foster an image as country hicks. It makes the kill more of a surprise." Certainly, Wal-Mart has made mistakes, but it has also got more things right than its rivals, who mistake its small-town simplicity for naivety at their peril. "...Just because we are simple, doesn't mean we are unintelligent..." as Mr Scott puts it

Most of Wal-Mart's overseas problems were avoidable. In the 1990s it made the mistake of taking out its organizational culture across the countries, rather than adapting to local markets. When it moved into Indonesia, it shipped in an entire warehouse on a barge. In Germany, its biggest headache, Wal-Mart was ready neither for the entrenched position of such discounters as Aldi, nor for the inflexibility of suppliers and the strength of trade unions. It had little feel for German shoppers, who care more about price than having their bags packed, or German staff, who hid in the toilets to escape the morning Wal-Mart cheer.

The strategy could be difficult to pull off, since the stronger, lower-price retailers are expanding in a long-term effort to take a bigger share of the retail pie. Having less inventory can certainly help profits, but it's no sure bet. While too much can hurt gross margins, due to added markdowns, too little can limit selection and hurt overall sales. Because expenses are being spread over less revenue, retailers risk hurting operating margins. Of course, the discount retailers that are expanding aggressively could easily overplay their hand. But retailing is much like a zero-sum game, with one player taking share at the expense of another. With consumers running out of steam, they're more likely to choose lower-price formats, to save money. That could translate into a sluggish second half for all but a few retailers.

Issue for Discussion

1. How are the consumer values defined at Wal-Mart and how is client support built in their retail management strategy?
2. How does Wal-Mart integrate its supply chain activities with purchase network of the company?
3. How can Wal-Mart utilize the growing human resources in the company as this largest retail chain store has automated its all important functions of retailing?
4. What will be the long terms impact on the consumer behaviour and competitive environment on the 'every day low price' strategy of the Wal-Mart and in your view which way price discounting as an organizational policy would lead the marketing organization?

REFERENCES

Bliss Christopher : A Theory of Retail Pricing, *Journal of Industrial Economics*, 36 (4), 1988, 375-391

Business Week Online

Internet Site : www.walmartmexico.com.mx , www.walmart.com

John Campbell : Time to Shop : The Geography of Retailing, *Regional Review*, Summer, 1996, 6-13

Leonard L Berry : The Old Pillars of New Retailing, *Harvard Business Review*, April 2001, 5-11

Lester Kwong : Coupons and 'Every Low Prices' : Price Competition with Multiple Instruments, *Canadian Journal of Economics*, 36 (2), 2003, 443-462

Luciano Catini *et.al* : Global Retailing : Trends and Management perspectives, *The McKinsey Quarterly*, No. 3, 2002, 1-7

Scott Munroe : Retail Structural Dynamics and the Forces Behind Big-Box Retailing, *The Annals of Regional Science*, 35 (3), 2001, 357-373

Tucker K A. : Economics of Scale in Retailing : A Note, *Journal of Industrial Economics*, 20 (3), July 1972, 291-294

CHAPTER 2

PRODUCT STRATEGY

CHAPTER FOCUS

- *To understand the concepts of managing the product*
- *To learn the management issues associated with new product development*
- *To know the product strategies in the contemporary situations and*
- *To discuss the product planning theories and their application in strategic marketing.*

A product is a good, a service, or an idea consisting of a bundle of tangible and intangible attributes that satisfies consumers and is received in exchange for money or some other unit of value. Each product includes a bundle of attributes capable of exchange and use. Product Planning refers to the systematic decision making related to all aspects of the development and management of the products of a company including branding and packaging. One of the important requirements for marketing efficiency is a proper product planning. It is essential for a firm to sell the products, which is the choice of potential consumers, who decide the marketing range or production range of the product. In fact, it is an ambiguous state of affairs. In a practical sense, the scope of production and marketing of products are decided by the marketer, based on its profitability and consumer recognition. However, the consumers influence the products that stay in the range of marketing. The decision of products on a marketing range of a company is complex, difficult and always risk averse. It is observed that introducing such products that customers do not buy soon and those products that the customers buy only in small amounts incur financial losses. Therefore, it is essential to plan for products in the market in a way to optimise the profit of the firm and the efficiency too.

Companies in United States engaged in manufacturing household cleaning products are developing new generation products. As US consumers are working longer hours and leading increasingly busy lives, with less time to devote to cleaning, especially unpleasant tasks such as toilet and floor cleaning, the new generation products aim to make cleaning effortless and eco-friendly. The introduction of "bucket less" mopping systems, designed to replace the mop-and-bucket approach to floor cleaning, has been a key development in the household care market. Consumers, who despised the spill-prone heavy bucket and the less-than sanitary mop head, have happily traded up to these new systems. In consequence, more traditional floor cleaning products experienced a 6.8 percent decline in sales between 2003 and 2004. In late 2003, Prestige Brands introduced the Comet Clean & Flush Flushable Toilet Cleaning System – a wand with a disposable head, which comes pre-loaded with toilet cleaner and can be thrown away after use. Following the success of this product, other companies, including SC Johnson, 3M Home Care and Clorox Co, quickly followed suit with similar products. As a result, toilet cleaning systems experienced a remarkable 5,880 percent increase in value sales between 2003 and 2004, which helped boost the overall toilet cleaning sector by 16 percent.[1] With the aim of reducing the unpleasantness of cleaning, manufacturers are expected to continue innovating in the bathroom-cleaning category. Despite a dismal outlook for the overall surface care market in the US, emerging forecasts reveal that the one bright spot will be the bathroom cleaners sector, which is expected to grow by 12% between 2004 and 2009.

Process of product planning in the international context consists of finding an appropriate match of host country objectives with the corporate objectives to determine conducting a business in the host country. The product objectives of a company should flow from the definition of its business. The firm sets the product objectives accordingly and decides on the type of products to be offered in the host country. The product offering should provide satisfaction to the customer, which will be reflected in the realization of the goals of both the corporation and the host country. The marketing-mix factors comprising product, price, place, promotion, packaging, pace (market dynamics), people (sales force), performance and psycho-dynamics (buying appeals) are developed inter-linking each factor. Product objectives emerge from host country and corporate objectives ultimately gives the business definition to a foreign firm. The common goals of the foreign firms, seeking business in the host country are oriented towards stability, growth, profits, and returns on investment.

LEVELS OF PRODUCT

A product is closely associated with the need and level of satisfaction of the customers. It may be defined as an article introduced in the market, that seeks attention, desire for acquisition and image for use to get satisfaction of a want or need of a customer. Obviously, the hierarchy of products is based on their utility and intensity of customer satisfaction. In developing a useful product, a planner has to look upon its levels. They are core products, tangible products or augmented products. A core product or service that meets the basic need or service may be defined as the product that provides a core benefit to a customer. Such a product may be cloth, a food item or a drinking subsistence, irrespective of its taste, colour, attraction, beauty consciousness etc. A core product is just a substance that satisfies the basic need of a user and does not allow him any comparison. Thus, a product planner has to make the core product tangible to introduce it in the competitive market allowing the customer to exercise his franchise rationally, considering comparative advantages. Table 2.1 exhibits the nature and levels of the product.

1 Euromonitor: New Products Make Household Cleaning Easier, *Euromonitor Archive,* January 05, 2006

Table 2.1 Product Levels and Associated Attributes

Levels of product	Marketing variables	Orientation
Core product	Basic need Basic service Core benefits	Customer
Tangible product	Quality features style, Design Brand Packaging	Market & Customer
Augmented product	Delivery & service Incentives, Warranty, Post-sales, relationship	Company & Customer

Product augmentation is a set of approaches followed by a company in promoting its product through effective delivery and service, incentives to customers and dealers, warranty to seek customers' confidence on product and maintain a product-oriented relationship of customers with the company. This level of products largely draws "company-customer" oriented relationship in the market. The product levels also determine the selling process to a large extent. The core products play an important role in product planning while the tangible products initiate the sales management process. The augmented products drive the concept of extended sales mechanism for marketing expansion and product diversification.

PRODUCT HIERARCHY

Product hierarchy is the intra-level characteristics of the three broad levels of products-core, tangible and augmented. In order to recognise the core product marketers must first define what core benefits the product will provide to the customer. The actual product must be built around the core product. Product has as many as four characteristics as below:

- Quality level
- Features
- Brand name
- Packaging

All these attributes combined together carefully deliver the core benefit(s) of the product. The augmented product offers additional consumer benefits and service such as warranty and customer training. Marketers must first identify the core consumer needs (develop core product), then design the actual product and find ways to augment it in order to create the bundle of benefits that will best satisfy the customer. The product hierarchy stretches from the initial stage of the product i.e. need at the basic level for a particular item of franchise in the process of product planning. There are seven levels of product hierarchy. The products have to be classified under a product-line in accordance with their length and width. The product hierarchy is exhibited in Table 2.2 in reference to its attributes.

INTERNATIONAL PRODUCT-LINE ANALYSIS

It is an essential dimension in evolving a product plan. Product-line is a component of product-mix which a company offers to the customers exhibiting the length and width of the range of products. The analysis of product-line depends on two important information sources. They are (i) volume of sales and profit on each item and (ii) competitors' product-line in the same market or segment. The product-line manager of a company should be aware that each item of the product-line contributes considerably in gross sales and profit. The manager has to collect the item contribution record of product line. The vulnerability of product-line can be identified, if the volume of sales in a few items is very high as compared to the other items of the line. These items need to be mentioned carefully and protected from competing items. It mav be appropriate for a manager to shorten the product-line to reduce marketing expenditure on non-profit items. The analysis of the product-line also requires awareness on the market profile to plan the positioning of the product in a competitive environment. Skill needs to be acquired in positioning the product against the competitors' product and to perform this task, the product line mapping is an important planning exercise. Such an effort would be beneficial also in

Strategy Focus 2.1: Samsung Bio-Refrigerator

Core Product - The ability to efficient cooling at low energy consumption

Tangible Product – Samsung SilverNano (brand name), is designed to offer quality services towards health and hygiene that provide the desired benefits, high quality etc.

Augmented Product – Offer more than just a cooling devise. Give buyers a warranty on parts and workmanship.

Technology- Sophisticated nano-technology has enabled Samsung to apply a SilverNano™ coating in its refrigerators for an overall anti-bacterial and anti-fungal effect. The spread of fungi and bacteria inside refrigerators is prevented thereby providing with the freshest, cleanest and healthiest food to enjoy. The coated nano particles come in contact with bacteria; they suppress the respiration of bacteria. This, in turn, adversely affects bacteria's cellular metabolism and inhibits cell growth. Since, the propagation of fungi and bacteria inside the bio-refrigerator is prevented, this allows circulating fresh odour free air to keep the food fresher for longer period.

Table 2.2 Product Hierarchy and Nature

Product hierarchy	*Nature*
Need family	Basic need that contributes product family.
Product family	All the product classes that satisfy the basic need with a varied degree of satisfaction.
Product class	A group of products within the product family having utility advantages.
Product-line	Type of products in product-class and number of items pertaining to specific size, colour, quality etc. in each type
Product type	Different forms of the product in terms of quality and usage
Brand	i) An associated name of items in product-line for ineforidentification of particular items and quality. ii) A certification of federation or group of companies manufacturing similar products to certify quality.
Item	A particular product passed through all above hierarchical stages.

identifying the market segments according to the customer preferences. Table 2.3 presents the different components of the product-line analysis and task involved thereof.

Table 2.3 Product-line Analysis: Task & Approaches

Analysis components	*Task*	*Approach*
Sales and profit	Identifying vulnerable items on product-line.	Quantitative and time-series data on variables.
Market profile	Product positioning.	Competitive product profiles analysis- physical & monetary.
Line length	Optimal length comprising a number of items.	Analysis of stretching and filling options.
Stretching	Increasing product-line.	Downward/Upward.
Filling	Adding new/missing items.	Lowering the product price or new launching.
Featuring	Increasing profit and volume of sales.	Customer orientation to be made at high end of line with a matching price.
Pruning	Scanning items on the product-line to optimise profit and reduce marketing expenditure.	Cost-effective decision-making, eliminating low sales items.
Modernisation	Product diversification and new product-line.	Market-segmentation, demand analysis and pricing strategies.

Product-line length in a company may be required to stretch downwards or otherwise to optimise the line length. In other words, it is the responsibility of the product-line manager to establish a positive correlation between the number of items and the sale-profit targets of the company. The Product-line should not be constant. It has to be lengthened over time, systematically in two ways - by stretching or filing. The line can be stretched either downward or upward or both ways depending upon the range of competitors and simultaneous product-lines existing in the market. The downward stretch results in selling the upper end products initially at cheaper rates on the product-line. This strategy has to be used very carefully, as losses may pile up through a volume of out-fashioned stock. However, the item image largely depends on the brand name. The upward stretching of the product-line is risk averse. Such an approach allows selling the product-line items at a high price, as the managers are attracted by higher growth rates and profit margins. However, there always remains a threat from the higher end competitors in terms of price 'fall-out' and lower end competitors to introduce a substitute at a lower price. Finally, the sales personnel of the company and distributors have to manage the crisis. The company, at the stage of 'maturity' of its growth cycle, may use both the upward and downward stretching of the product line in different market segments. Adding new items or missing items on the sales stream of the market can also stretch the product-line. The featuring of the product-line items indicates that a few of them have been selected and are being set at a high price and sales target. It may be observed that during Christmas all consumer goods and durables are sold at relatively higher prices as the sales managers motivate the customers to buy the goods located at the higher end of the product-line. However, in the product-line analysis pruning is also essential to identify the low-sales items on the product-line and drop them out of the marketing programme and diversify items on the line to modernise the efforts. Product planning is done not only for the consumer products but also in many other segments of marketing such as the financial markets, social markets and the like.

Corporate objectives may be defined in terms of activities (the manufacture of a specific product, or export to a particular market), financial indicators (to achieve a targeted return on investment), desired market positioning (to gain market share and relative market leadership), and all these in combination with each other. For example, the typical goals of a firm seeking business entry in the less developed country would be to seek faster economic growth, to build a balanced industrial sector, to create employment opportunities, and earn foreign-exchange. On the contrary, the objectives of a developed country might be to provide a modern living standard to its masses in a short time without disrupting the cultural structure of its society and/or to diversify its economy over the long-term.

Adding New Product Line

An international firm should develop country specific product lines for achieving success in the overseas market. To achieve this viability, the composition of the product line needs to be periodically reviewed and changed. Such environmental changes as customer preferences, competitors' tactics, host country legal requirements, and a firm's own perspectives including its objectives, cost structure, and spill over of demand from one product to another, can all render a product line inadequate. Thus, it may become necessary to add new products or eliminate existing products from the product line to customize the product line specific to each country. Alternatively, certain specific products may be for a particular foreign country, either locally abroad or in the home country. The extension of domestic products to foreign markets follows the logic of the concept the international product life cycle. Such product extension into the market of host country is generally adopted through a process, wherein the products are developed first for the home market, that may prove success and lead to induce some export orders. As the exports grow, the firm may consider setting up a warehouse, a sales branch, or a service centre in the foreign locale. Ultimately, the firm finds it more economical to assemble or manufacture the product in the country selected for entry. The firms operating in the overseas market may also choose to add new products to the line in order to serve an unfulfilled customer need in a particular market overseas or to optimize the existing marketing capacity of the firm in a given market. For example, a dairy firm selling different categories of liquid milk and milk products overseas in developing countries may discover a dire need for cattle feed and veterinary products for the dairy farmers to augment the procurement of liquid milk. Hence the firm may add such items in its product line. Alternatively, the same company may establish a good distribution network to serve semi-urban and rural milk producers, though such products may not be directly related to the firm's business.

> Indian disposable paper products market grew by almost 11 percent in current value terms in 2004, with value sales amounting to just under Rs 7.1 billion with predominated urban sales. The rural markets contributed only 6 percent to the total sales of the product line. Higher levels of disposable income, heightened hygiene awareness, as well as the overall upgrading of lifestyles among educated urbanites drove growth in this extremely nascent market. Procter & Gamble made a transition from the premium to the economy price segment, further stimulating demand by encouraging non-users to try sanitary towels for the first time, and existing users to upgrade to more premium varieties. Whisper's excellent brand equity has enabled Procter & Gamble to surpass Johnson & Johnson to command the largest value share in sanitary protection. The entry of multinational players throughout the disposable paper products market beyond the most lucrative sanitary protection products and nappies/diapers/pants, and investments in educational and marketing activities to create brand and product awareness, are likely to remain key to increasing usage among the urban consumers in coming years. Besides promotional activities, affordable pricing will also be essential to stimulate consumption: disposable paper products tend to be perceived as luxury items in India, in contrast to their positioning in Western countries as basic necessities. However, in view of the enormous potential India holds it may be stated that the disposable paper products market has just about started its development.[2]

2 Euromonitor: Disposable Paper Products in India, *Euromonitor Product Report,* June, 2005

Firm's decision to add a product to the line is influenced by its compatibility with reference to marketing, finances, and environment. *Marketing competitiveness* involves the match between the new addition and the current and potential marketing compatibilities of the parent company and its foreign subsidiary in matters such as product, price, promotion, and distribution. The firm needs to analyse the risks pertaining to financial operations and opportunities related to the addition of a new product line, which the firm is looking for. The common criteria in determining the *financial compatibility* of the proposed addition may be the profitability and cash flow implications. Besides, to ensure that the newly added product-line would not encounter any legal and political problems, it is required for the firm to analyze the factors of *environmental compatibility,* which includes concern for the customer, competitive action, and legal or political problems. The inclusion of a product in the line should not pose any problem for either existing or potential customers.

PRODUCT DESIGN STRATEGY

Product and business strategies of a foreign firm should be developed in reference to the macroeconomic conditions of the host country. The definition of the product objectives should emerge from the business definitions developed in accordance with the macro-economic requirements of the host country. The foreign firms need to analyse whether the success of their product or product line can be replicated in a new market destination abroad and explore the factors that may lead the product approach in the host country success. In other words, a decision must be made about which is the more appropriate of two product design strategies - standardization or customization. *Standardization* refers to offering a common product on a national, regional, or worldwide basis while *customization* signifies adopting a product, which is, making appropriate changes in it, to match local perspectives. The trade off for a firm to decide whether product customization or adaptation largely depends on the size of the market for the identified product and off take of the product over the short and long run. The customization of the product may be chosen over standardization in order to cater to the unique situation in each country. Yet, there are potential gains to consider in product standardization. International marketers must examine all the criteria in order to decide the extent to which products should vary from country to country.[3] If there are no new needs to be catered to make the product offering ready for any market, resulting in a significant cost saving, the firm may decide to standardize its products. Though product standardization may turn a risky proposition in the long run, as the consumer behaviour is flexible and tends to change over time. However, some international companies have succeeded in standardization of products for offering in many countries. The General Electric Company's debacles in the small-appliances field in Germany and Polaroid's difficulties with the Swinger camera in France are classic examples of product standardization. At the same time, Volkswagen's success worldwide with Beetle supports standardization.

Excessive concern with local customization can be troublesome, too. Philips Electronics, Netherlands learned the hard lesson that it cannot afford to customize television sets for each European

3 Aaker David A. and Joachimsthaler Eric: The Lure of Global Branding, *Harvard Business Review,* November-December, 1999, pp 137-146

market separately. This internationally popular Dutch company offers its electrical products according to regional standardization based on the power supply categories (In North and Latin America the power distribution for the domestic use is 110 volts while in England it is 120 volts and in India in ranges further high to 220 volts). However, greater extent of standardization may be feasible in the case of industrial goods than consumer goods. Among consumer goods, non-durables require greater customization than durables, because such consumer goods appeal to tastes, habits, and customs pertaining to host countries. The international markets are not always homogeneous and markets in different countries for a given product hold different stages of development at the same time. This phenomenon may be explained through the product life cycle concept wherein products go through several life cycle stages over a period of time, and in each stage different marketing strategies are appropriate. There are four stages usually identified as introduction, growth, maturity, and decline even for the products distributed in markets overseas.

> Traditionally, foods that are rich in carbohydrates have been a staple in North American diets. Until very recently foods such as cereals and breads were typically viewed by many US consumers as a necessary part of a balanced diet. However, the introduction of low carb diets such as Atkins and South Beach has radically changed Americans' attitudes towards healthy eating. The latest research shows that growth in reduced carbohydrate or *low carb* bakery products surged between 2003 and 2004, with a growth rate of nearly 84%. During this period, low carbohydrate biscuits and cereals were the key market drivers, with impressive growth rates of 310% and 110%, respectively. The boom of *carbohydrate conscious* brand extensions from late 2003 onwards has been instrumental in the rapid growth of the *low carb* bakery sector in the US. Instead of creating new brands, US manufacturers have leveraged popular existing brands to create new reduced carb versions. For example, in July 2004, Kellogg launched "Kellogg Special K". for the *low carbohydrate* linking consumers, while its subsidiary keebler introduced keebler chips" a deluxe carbohydrate sensible Cookies. The summer of 2004, also saw Kraft Foods launch the "CarbWell" range, which offers low carb versions of popular brands like Post breakfast cereal and Snack Wells biscuits. In response to the changing consumer awareness about the diet food products and taste for low calorie bakery preparations, a number of speciality brands have emerged in USA and Canada, in addition to the entry of large global brand manufacturers into the reduced carb products market. Atkins Nutritionals Inc, for example, now manufactures bakery products including breakfast cereals, wraps and bagels.[4]

In developing market environment, the firms should develop the product policies in accordance with the requirements of the local markets. If the customer needs tend to be the basic ones and the alternatives for the customers in the home market are found to be weak, it would be appropriate for a firm to offer standardized products from the existing product line. Under such circumstances, a firm may decide to offer a narrow range of choice in product selection at a local market level. This would help in confirming the cost effective and high profitability product offerings in the developing markets. General Motors uses this strategy. The company has developed a special automobile for use in rural areas in Southeast Asian countries such as Philippines, where roads are rough and weary. The chassis can be constructed from steel bars that come in a kit and require only simple

4 Leonie Tait: Boom for Low Carb Bakery in the USA, Euro Monitor International, *Internet Edition,* December 14, 2004. For details see http://www.euromonitor.com/article.asp?id=4251

tools for assembly. The engine and transmission are then mounted on the frame together with two seats and a canopy. The vehicle comes from global brand leaders in automobiles which is cheap, runs high off the ground, and is easy to repair. Such product policy is developed specific to the requirement of the region keeping in view the customer preferences in terms of use value, affordability and convenience.[5] However the product adaptation to match local conditions involves consideration of many cost factors and it is necessary for a foreign firm to undertake the *cost benefit analysis* prior to making firm decisions on product policy. These costs may relate to R&D; physical alteration of the product's design, style, features or changes in packaging, co-branding, performance guarantee, and the like. In contrast with standardization no R&D is required in the process of customization, since manufacturing technology and quality control procedures have been established, and performance has been tested and improved. Hence, standardization brings certain cost savings. Among various cost factors-direct and indirect, it would be difficult for a firm to quantify the opportunity cost. If a product is customized presumably, it will have greater appeal to the mass market in the host country. A cost benefit analysis would help in determining the cost to customize and realizing its benefit. The results of cost-benefit analysis on product customization should be compared with the same analysis applied to standardization. The net difference indicates the relative desirability of the two strategies.

PRODUCT LIFE CYCLE MANAGEMENT

It is important to understand the Product Life Cycle (PLC) as it provides insights on the competitive dynamics of the product being marketed. The PLC also exhibits the distinct stages in the sales history of a product. The PLC comprises four stages known as introduction, growth, maturity and decline. At the *introduction* stage the product in the segmented market the profit remains almost non-existent and product sales also remain slow. However, the expenditure in pushing the product into the market is found heavy for the marketing firm. The product passes into the next stage of PLC- *growth*, with improved sales and profit conditions observing the rapid acceptance of the product in the market. The product remains in the growth stage till the competition increases and pulls back the sales of the existing product. At this juncture the product moves into the stage of *maturity* where it faces setback on the volume of sales but succeeds in sustaining the profit level. While passing into the stage of *decline* the product faces downward trend in both the volume of sales and profit.

Hypothetically all the products in the market move through these stages of life cycle but there could always be some exceptions. Some of the products get out of the market in the stage of introduction itself while few are thrown out of competition at the growth stage. At the stage of maturity the strategy for product diversification begins and some products fall out of the main stream of the product categories in the market. Thus the marketer should develop sustainable marketing strategies to survive his products at each stage of the PLC. The Diagram 2.1 exhibits the possible ways to develop marketing strategy in the stage of introduction of the product. The product requires high promotion at the time of introduction but the price of the product should be kept low as compared

5 For further reference see "General Motor's Asian Alliances" *Harvard Business School Cases,* Reference no. 9-388-094

to its competing brands. Such strategy is known as high penetration strategy. The product later may be moved to either of the segments of the matrix shown in the Figure. Once the brand becomes popular in the market, the expenditure on the promotion may be reduced and the product can be pulled to high price-low promotion bracket following the low skimming strategy.

	Promotion: High	Promotion: Low
Price High	High skimming strategy	Low skimming strategy
Price Low	High penetration strategy	Low penetration strategy

Figure 2.1 Price-promotion matrix

A marketer has to make more crucial decisions at the growth stage of the product. The major strategies drawn at this stage to provide adequate support to the product in the market are as under:

- Rationalising the product line and width
- Innovative promotional approaches
- Identifying new market segments
- Evolving comprehensive distribution policy
- Changing the strategy of product awareness, advertising to the product preference and launching advertising campaigns accordingly

It is essential at this stage of PLC to rationalise the product portfolio in the company and develop strategies to promote only such categories of product, which had gained considerable response from the consumers. Such product categories need to be promoted through innovative promotion approaches and giving more emphasis on the product preference based advertisements and advertising campaigns. However, the possibilities of exploring new market segments and comprehensive coverage of distribution also need to be worked out in the same stage of PLC.

Stage of maturity is the sustainable stage in the PLC. As there will not be encouraging growth in the profit through the product marketing, there exists enormous scope for developing the business relationships and renovating the product attributes. At the last stage of PLC - stage of decline, the strategies need to be built to re-launch the product in the same or new market segments. The more important need at this stage of PLC is to sustain the brand image and rebuild the same through product and institutional advertising.

NEW PRODUCT DEVELOPMENT

New product has to be developed by the companies with great care. It is necessary to understand the need of the consumers, competitive threats, and availability of post sales services and cost of marketing of the product. However, in the contemporary era of competitions new product development is essential for the companies to make continuous efforts to develop new product, though there remains the risk.

> Moen Inc. has designed and developed non-convention shower for the modern bathrooms, desiring to enter the consumer showerhead market, which has many competitive advantages. In order to successfully meet this challenge, the designers developed a research process that would enable a creative team to gain a deep understanding of what people experienced in a shower, a process that would ultimately lead to the successful Revolution Showerhead. This product has unique ergonomic design, easy to adjust with one hand and with eyes closed, rubber spray tips allow easy cleaning and easy to install on a standard shower arm. Operational design of the shower enables simultaneous spinning of each oversized droplet and twirling the entire shower stream using patented revolutionary technology.[6] This research enabled designers to have a deeper understanding of the many aspects of the showering experience, including extensive observations of people showering, the physiology of the showering experience, people's perceptions about showering and point of purchase decisions made about showerheads. Within eight weeks of its introduction at Lowe's, the Revolution Showerhead became the number one selling showerhead (despite it being the most expensive showerhead they sell), and sales volume continues to climb.

New product failure rates in the packed products are about 80 percent in USA according to some studies. Among the services marketing the failure of new services is as high as 75 percent in the States. These products largely include credit cards, insurance schemes, hire purchase schemes, investment plans and the like. These results largely depend on the methodology adopted in the survey. The major factors that obstruct the process of new product development are:

- Limited creativity and paucity of new product ideas
- Fragmented markets
- Social and economic limitations
- Government policies and restrictions
- Cost effectiveness of the process of new product development
- Resource crisis at various levels in the process of product development to launching the market
- Product development and launching time, and
- Short product life cycle

The companies should strengthen their marketing network simultaneously while launching the new products. It has been observed that the failure of new products is often due to the lack of organizational teamwork. Thus it is required to inculcate the team behavior in developing the new products and popularizing them in the test market segments. The results of the test markets may be further carried out in the larger segments. The process of new product development is exhibited in the Diagram 2.2. It is essential that company should conduct brainstorming exercise for understanding the basic and secondary needs for the product, listing the product attributes, and identifying the forced relationship of other goods and services with the new product. Idea generation in the process of new product development is a major exercise. This technique calls for listing of

6 Corporate web site of Moen Inc.

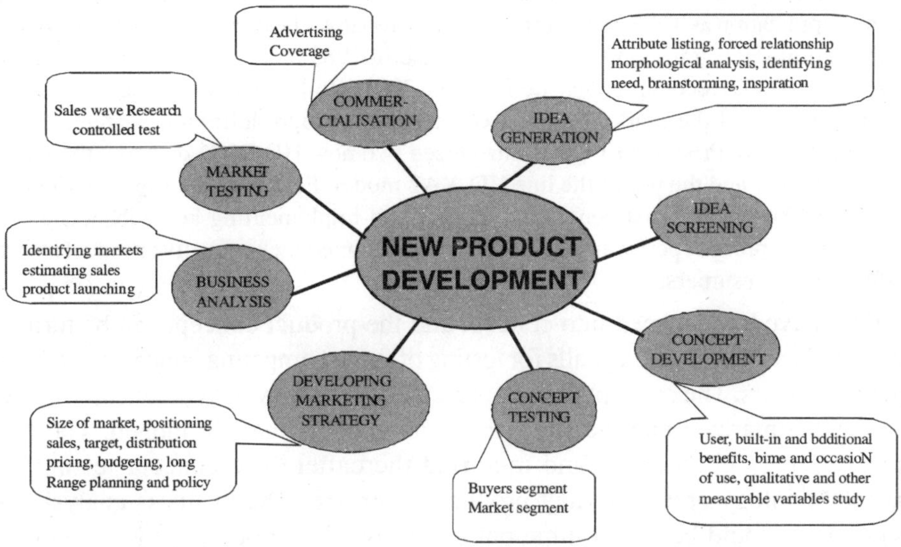

Figure 2.2 New product development process

all major attributes of the existing product and the needed attributes in order to improve the same product. The forced relationship of the new product with the existing accessories also needs to be studies *e.g.* developing a new television set may be related with the consumer need of clock, multi-channel viewing on one screen, microphone attachment and a built-in video game. Such forced relationship has to be identified by the company before launching the product. The morphological analysis calls for identifying the structural dimensions of a problem and examining the relationships among them. The need identification can be done by interacting with the potential and existing customers in a focus group meet. The industrial marketers can identify new product ideas working in association with the lead users of the product. However, the brainstorming exercise is also an important tool, which stimulates the group creativity. In brainstorming exercise the following process is prescribed by Osborn[2]:

- Negative comments in the process may be the stimuli for discussion during the process
- Welcome freewheeling and wilder ideas for better steering
- Encourage more number of ideas and categorize its utility , and
- Establish inter-relation of the ideas for an overall synergy approach.

Basic purpose of this exercise is to generate large number of ideas. These ideas need to be carefully screened in the interest of the consumer satisfaction as well as the company's profit. In this process the company should avoid the *Drop* and *Go* errors. The former attempts dismiss the good idea while the latter attempts allow the poor ideas to move into the process of commercialization. Hence the purpose of screening the idea needs to be understood carefully. It is advised that company should develop an idea-rating matrix on the basis of the emerging ideas and their usefulness.

Toshiba has 130 years of history in electrical and electronic equipment manufacturing for consumer application as Tokyo Shibaura Electric Company. The company has first developed high definition (HD) transceiver television devise in 1985 and commercialized its digital video display (DVD) recorder of high definition in 2001. Building upon the success of its first generation units and the market's increased demand for high definition content, Toshiba America Consumer Products LLC has introduced two new HD DVD players - the HD-A2 entry level model and the top of the line HD-XA2 model. Featuring the superior video and audio capabilities of the first generation models and implementing key enhancements to further improve product performance. Toshiba has designed the innovative products to fit to the lifestyle of consumers.

Product ideas have to be turned into concept and the product concept can be turned later in to the brand concept. The concept testing calls for testing of these competing concepts with an appropriate group of target consumers. The concepts can be presented physically or symbolically. The consumers' response may be summarized and the strength of the concept may be judged. The need gap and product gap levels may be checked and modified thereafter. The concept testing and product development methodology applies to any product or service. The business analysis includes the estimating sales as it would be of one-time purchase, frequently purchasing product or at regular interval purchase product. The estimates should also be made in relation to the tendency of first purchase, replacement purchase or repeat sales. Besides, the company should also assess the estimating marketing costs and the profits from commercialization of this product. The statement of such estimates may be made across the regions and years of sales (spatial and temporal) on the following variables:

- Sales revenue
- Cost of the goods
- Gross margin
- Development costs
- Marketing costs
- Allocated overheads
- Gross contribution
- Supplementary contribution
- Net contribution
- Gross contribution
- Discount contribution
- Cumulative discounted cash flow

Sales projection may be set on the basis of the market assumption; market share of the company and the factory realized price. The cost the goods sold may be found by estimating the average cost of labor, product constituents, logistics and packaging. The difference between the sales, revenue and cost of production would reveal the gross margin of the product. The development cost consists of the expenditure incurred on product development, research cost and operational cost including the development of new equipment, inventory and designs. The marketing cost comprises the cost of product distribution, advertisement and other costs. The overhead cost of this new product covers the share of its cost of executive salaries and infrastructure. The gross contribution may be found by subtracting by the preceding tree costs from the gross margin. The supplementary contribution is used to list any change in income from the other company product caused by introduction of the new product. The discounted contribution may be of some sales incentives or any introductory offers given by the company to promote the product. The cumulative discount cash flow shows the progressive annual contribution of the discounted products. The companies also use other methods to evaluate the good reason for introducing the new product in the market.

Table 2.4 Consumer Preference Measurement Scale

Preferences	*Weight*	*Product1*	*Product 2*	*Product 3*
Like Intensely	7			
Like	6			
Like Somewhat	5			
Can't Say	4			
Dislike Somewhat	3			
Dislike	2			
Dislike Intensely	1			
Preferance Score				

Product development at this stage is designing the prototypes on the lines of the derived concept that has passed through technical tests. The consumer testing of the product may be taken up in two forms – laboratory testing and home testing. The American home durable company Du Pont developed new synthetic carpets and installed then in several homes free of cost in exchange for old ones. Consumer preference testing may be done through variety of techniques such as ranking, paired comparisons, rating scales and focus group discussions. However, while analyzing the consumer preferences the company has to take into account the advantages and limitations of each method. The consumer preferences may be measured by constructing the matrix as exhibited in Table 2.4. The number of responses in each category of preference of the products needs to be multiplied by the respective weights of the preferences and the sum has to be divided by the total number of responses to get the preference score. The cut off score has to be decided by the company and viewed as the cutting edge generally. It should be at a reasonable margin above the break-even point.

According to Godrej Pillsbury, India is a country where cake is the third most popular dessert, but where only 3 percent of urban households own ovens. So Cooker Cake Mix, a global rival to Betty Crocker, is bound to click. This product allows the Indian homemaker to make a cake at home in her pressure cooker. Available in a 150-gm pack which makes a 300-gm cake for just Rs 25, it comes in two flavours - chocolate and sponge. With this product, Godrej Pillsbury also launched its national single-number toll-free helpline: 'Namaste Pillsbury'. Though the company claims that the product is practically foolproof, customers are bound to have queries (some complain that the dough doesn't 'rise' and the cake remains much too gooey). Beginning with the top 25 cities, Godrej has rolled out the product to all major towns having population over 100 thousand and will complete its distribution coverage this month. Godrej Pillsbury is a Joint Venture (JV) between the Godrej group and The Pillsbury Co (which is part of the $21-billion global food and drinks giant, Diageo, that also owns Burger King, Green Giant, Johnny Walker, Smirnoff and Bailey's, amongst others). In India, the JV has already launched Pillsbury *Chakki Fresh Atta* (instant wheat flour) . According to a company spokesperson, The launch of traditional oven cake mixes in late 1998 had met with lukewarm response. While consumers loved cake, few had ovens - resulting in a niche business opportunity. Pillsbury Cooker Cake Mix was designed to explode the category. The product is targeted at the urban Indian homemaker (SEC[7]-ABC), who has consciously passed up the chance of a career to look after her family. Cooking becomes a form of self-expression and development, but most of her innovations revolve around conventional modes of cooking. Baking is alien to her and associated with 'modern, Western-style cooking', an aspiration art."

Apart from the usual ad campaign for the print and electronic media, the brand will also go online with a special channel on Rediff.com. The creative account is with Leo Burnett, while media is with Carat. Design Motive Alla (DMA) has created the packaging. An extensive sampling drive has already been launched with Filmfare (a popular cinema magazine of India), reaching out to about 200,000 households. Retailers have been provided with a special 'display shipper' stocking nine pouches of the mix for better in-store visibility. Pillsbury wants to be seen as being part of India's 'modern tradition', helping the Indian homemaker fulfil traditional roles using modern means. This is why the company has begun right with the basic symbols of Indian nutrition - the chakki (wheat grinder) and the pressure cooker. And it hopes 'The Pillsbury Doughboy' becomes every Indian homemaker's 'teacher, helper, friend'. Pillsbury looks at this as a 'market creation' project. The proposition 'Bring the Bakery Home' expects more than a 10-percent share of the overall instant mixes market in India, which currently includes traditional items such as *gulab jamuns* (an Indian sweet) and *idlis* (a variety of popular snack in India). The primary challenge is assumed on getting trials. However, the long-term challenge is to become a part of Indian food habits. The Indian housewife is probably open to convenience food so long as it is not seen to compromise the diligence of her role as family feeder-in-chief.

Consumer foods marketing testing can be done by using the sales-wave research and controlled test marketing method. The sales wave research enables the company to estimate the repeat purchase rate where consumers spend their own money and choose this product among other competing brands. The controlled test marketing is conducted in a given territory of consumers and segment. The retailers and consumers in the vicinity thereof are identified and the consulting firm conducting research delivers the product to the selected outlets with total package of promotion. The responses of the consumers at the outlets can be collected in a structured questionnaire or fed directly in the computer. The controlled test marketing allows the company to test the impact of retail response as well as the buying behavior of the consumers. Commercialization of the product is a strategic decision in which the company should look into the appropriate time, market and consumer segment to launch the product. The company has to derive the geographical strategy with the logistics administration approaches. The time of launch of the product may be considered looking into three common choice

7 Socio-economic consumer segment (SEC) has been identified considering the levels of gross and disposable income in the region. The high profile consumers are categorised as SEC-A followed by lower profile consumers.

– *maiden entry* or first look in the market, *parallel entry* with the similar or identical product of the competing brand and *late entry* when the firm delays positioning its product in the selected segment. The commercialisation process of the product also prompts the adoption behaviour of the consumers. There are five stages in the adoption process – awareness about the product, interest generated in using or adopting the product, evaluation of the product, trial of the product from the point of perceived use value and perceived price and final adoption of the product for use.

PRODUCT PLANNING MATRIX

It is normally accepted that a product has achieved success when all investments made for its commercialization and development have been recovered and still the product is capable of providing satisfaction to the consumers. The product must be capable of earning substantial revenue to recover the full investment that the company has put into it. The investments broadly include the cost of design, manufacturing and inventory, market research, sampling and logistics and physical distribution. The product manager has to ensure that the marketing programs are designed to attain faster recovery of investments. It is rather impossible to enter the global market in the existing era of competition without proper product planning. The launch of product must be carried out in an energetic and creative style with effective promotional package. In planning for the product markets, it is essential to understand clearly the combinations of the expected margins and turnover in volume of the product. Quite often, it is required to operate on volumes than looking for the higher margins. This may provide the marketer, opportunity for wide coverage of market at low margins and helps to be the market leader as none of competitors may be able to stand at such low margin due to scale of economic problems. It is necessary to position the new products in the new segments carefully by building image of the brand. The competitive pricing strategy would help in penetrating the product against the competing brands in the new segment. At the same time it is required to refresh the consumer behavior periodically and reorient brand image in the existing consumer segment by building better communication strategies. The success stories of the product would help reasonably in carrying such process. The Figure 2.3 exhibits the product planning strategy in the new and existing consumer segments.

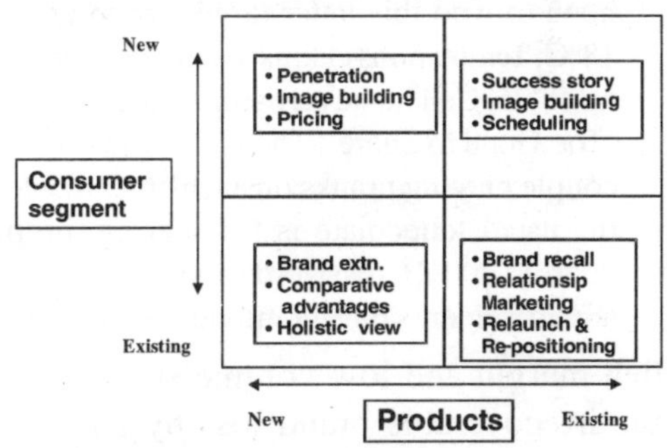

Figure 2.3 Product planning

> Over US$ 10 million, Cadbury India company has launched a premium range of chocolates, Temptations, Roast Almond, Coffee, Old Jamaica, Honey Apricot, Mint Crunch and Black Forest flavours in the Indian market. As a part of the product strategy of the company to launch one major brand every year, the new product range aims to offer the consumer an exotic and international chocolate experience. Temptations is being retailed through Cadbury's existing distribution network, reaching out to 250,000 retailers, with the emphasis on larger

retail stores. Cadbury's already claims a 70-percent share in value terms of the Indian chocolates market, pegged at around US$100 million (22,000 tonnes per annum in volume terms), of which 5 percent is the premium segment. Why launch in the midst of an FMCG slowdown? The management of the company feels that one way to beat the slowdown is to keep track of evolving consumer needs and bring out a product to meet those needs. What market research showed was a definite need for a premium chocolate. The taste profile needed was adult and it needed to be an indulgence product." The research apparently also revealed that the consumer seeks variety from indulgence products and has been buying imported chocolates (such as Ferrero Rocher, Lindt et al). In the larger metro markets in India, it has been noticed that while our current premium range (Fruit & Nut and Roast Almond) was doing well, our presence in this top-end segment had reduced in favour of imported chocolates, which offered greater variety to the consumer. Research further revealed two sets of chocolate consumers in India: those who are exposed to international chocolates and are active consumers of the same, and those who would love to have the 'Differentiated Chocolate Taste' but find international chocolate prices prohibitive. Temptations of taste hope to woo this latter target group of consumers. The foreign chocolates tend to melt at 18°C, Temptations claims to have been specially formulated to stay solid in tropical temperatures up to 26°C. The advertising, handled by Contract, revolves around the brand proposition, 'Too Good to Share'. The TV commercial shows a mischievous 30-something modern, urban couple playing pranks on each other to avoid sharing their Temptations, which is a shift from the usual 'chocolate is for sharing' proposition. Cadbury has also launched ATM kiosk doors in 2001, Crosswords bookstores, sampling at premium restaurants in metros and playing advertisements during movies, all aimed at targeting the consumer in privacy.

High margin and low volume strategy will put the company into distribution crisis and may generate irrecoverable brand loss by allowing the consumer to switch to other brands that may provide satisfaction as the close substitutes. It would be difficult for the company to survive the competition, if it decides to sell its products at low margin to gain the brand acceptance but is unable to meet the supply requirements in the market. Hence, while introducing the new products in existing consumer segment, the company needs to take a holistic view and offer competitive price and quality advantages to gain the consumer preference for the brand. Product planning and control measures that a company should choose in the product planning and management process are listed as below:

- Transfer the Product to Inventory
- Item coding, special classified Goods
- Personnel code, personnel first name and family name of each workshop
- Product order, Product Qty, Material requirement for making piece, Structure of Products
- Material Inventory in Product Process, Transfer product sheet
- Available Machines specification in workshop

High profile companies enjoy the premium market of their product selling high volumes at higher margins. The companies looking for the market leader and believing in operating with large volumes of product or product line should plat at low margins and high volumes while the star companies may adopt the policy of high margin-high volume segment. To achieve a sustainable market share in the existing market the large companies build consumer relations, brand recall strategies and reposition their product and brand periodically.

PRODUCT PORTFOLIO MATRIX

A good planning system must guide the development of strategic alternatives for the current businesses and new business possibilities of the company. It must also provide for management's review of these strategic alternatives and for the corresponding resource allocation decisions. The result is a set of approved business plans that represent the direction of the firm. This process starts with, and its success is largely determined by, the creation of sound strategic alternatives. The top management of a multi-business firm cannot generate these strategic alternatives. It must rely on the managers of its business ventures and on its corporate development personnel. However, top management can and should establish a conceptual framework within which these alternatives can be developed. One such framework is the portfolio matrix associated with the Boston Consulting Group (BCG). Briefly, the portfolio matrix is used to establish the best mix of businesses in order to maximize the long-term earnings growth of the firm. The portfolio matrix represents a real advance in strategic planning in several ways:

- It encourages top management to evaluate the prospects of each of the company's, businesses individually and to set tailored objectives for each business based on the contribution, it can realistically make to corporate goals.
- It stimulates the use of externally focused empirical data to supplement managerial judgment in evaluating the potential of a particular business.
- It explicitly raises the issue of cash flow balancing as management plans for expansion and growth.
- It gives managers a potent new tool for analysing competitors and for predicting competitive responses to strategic moves.
- It provides not only a financial but also a strategic context for evaluating acquisitions and divestitures.

As a consequence of these benefits, the widespread application of the portfolio matrix approach to corporate planning has sounded the death knell for planning by exhortation, the kind of strategic planning that sets uniform financial performance goals across an entire company-15 percent growth in earnings or 15 percent return on equity-and then expects each business to meet those goals year in and year out. The portfolio matrix approach has given the top management the tools to evaluate each business in context of its environment and its unique contribution to the goals of the company as a whole. It has enabled them to weigh the entire array of business opportunities available to the company against the financial resources required to support them. The portfolio matrix concept addresses the issue of the potential value of a particular business for the firm. This value has two variables: the potential for generating attractive earnings levels now and second, the potential for growth or, in other words, for significantly increased earnings levels in the future. The portfolio matrix concept holds that these two variables can be quantified. Current earnings potential is measured by comparing the market position of the business to that of its competitors. Empirical studies have shown that profitability is directly determined by relative market share. The concept of portfolio matrix is exhibited in Figure 2.4.

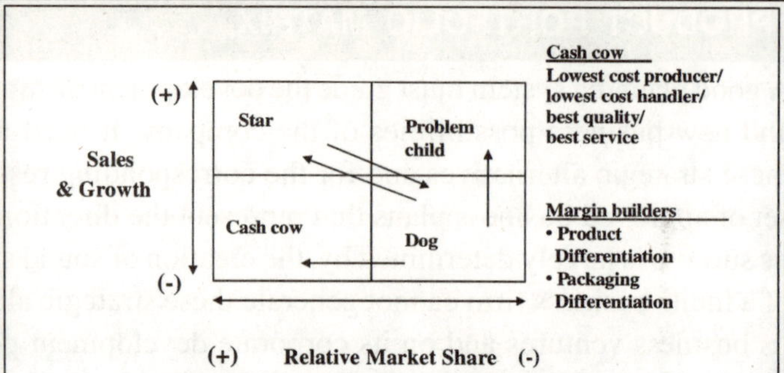

Figure 2.4 Product portfolio matrix

Star: High-growth market leaders are called stars. They generate large amounts of cash. The Star companies represent probably the best profit opportunity available to a company, and their competitive position must be maintained. If a star's share is allowed to slip because the star has been used to provide large amounts of cash in the short run or because of cutbacks in investment and rising prices (creating an umbrella for competitors), the star will ultimately become a dog. The ultimate value of any product or service is reflected in the stream of cash, it generates net of its own re-investment. For a star company, this stream of cash lies in the future growth to obtain the real value, the stream of cash must be discounted back to the present at a rate equal to the return on alternative opportunities. It is the future payoff of the star that counts, not the present reported profit. For GE, the plastics business is a star in which it keeps investing. As a matter of fact, the company has even acquired Thomson's plastics operations (a French company) to further strengthen its position in the business.

Cash Cow: Cash cows are characterized by low growth and high market share. They are net providers of cash. Their high earnings, coupled with their depreciation, represent high cash inflows, and they need very little in the way of reinvestment. Thus, these companies generate large cash surpluses that help to pay dividends and interest, provide debt capacity, supply funds for research and development, meet overheads, and also make cash available for investment in other products. Thus, cash cows are the foundations on which everything else depends in the business. Technically, a cash cow has a return on assets that exceeds its growth rate. Only if this is true will the cash cow generate more cash than it uses. For example, the tyre business can be categorized as a cash cow for Goodyear Tyre and Rubber Company. The tyre industry is characterized by slow market growth, and Goodyear has a major share of the market.

Problem Child: Products in a market with a low share are categorized as problem child. Because of growth, these products require more cash than they are able to generate on their own. If nothing is done to increase market share, a problem child will simply absorb large amounts of cash in the short run and later, as the growth slows down, become a dog. Thus, unless something is done to change its perspective, a problem child remains a cash loser throughout its existence and ultimately becomes a cash trap. What can be done to make a problem child more viable? One alternative is to gain share increases for it. Because the business is growing, it can be funded to dominance. It may then become a star and later, when growth slows down, a cash cow. This strategy is an expensive one in the short run. An abundance of cash must be poured into a question mark in order for it to win a major share of the market, but in the long run, this strategy is the only way to develop a sound business from the question mark stage. Another strategy is to divest the business. Outright sale is the most desirable alternative. But, if this does not work out, a firm decision must be made not to invest further in the business. The business must simply be allowed to generate whatever cash it can while none is reinvested.

Dogs: Products with low market share positioned in low-growth situation, are called dogs. Their poor competitive position condemns them to poor profits. Because growth is low, dogs have little potential for gaining sufficient share to achieve viable cost positions. Usually they are net users of cash. Their earnings are low, and the reinvestment required just to keep the business together eats cash inflow. The business, therefore, becomes a cash trap that is likely to regularly absorb cash unless further investment is rigorously avoided. An alternative is to convert dogs into cash, if there is an opportunity to do so. GE's consumer electronics business had been in the dog category, maintaining only a small percentage of the available market in a period of slow growth, when the company decided to unload the business (including the RCA brand acquired in late 1985) to Thomson, France's state-owned, leading electronics manufacturer.

DIMENSIONS OF PRODUCT STRATEGIES

Product strategies specify market needs that may be served by different product offerings. The product strategies of the company are duly related to market strategies that eventually come to dominate both the overall strategy and the spirit of the company. Product strategies deal with matters such as number and diversity of products, product innovations, product scope, and product design. In this chapter, different dimensions of product strategies are expanded for their essence, significance, limitations, if any, and their contributions to objectives and goals.

Implementations of product strategies require cooperation among different groups: finance, research and development, the corporate staff, and marketing. This level of integration makes product strategies difficult to develop and implement. In many companies, to achieve proper coordination among diverse business units, product strategy decisions are made by top management. In some companies, the overall scope of product strategy is laid out at the corporate level, whereas actual design is left to business units. Such alternative is more desirable than other arrangements because it is difficult for top management to deal with the details of product strategy in a diverse company. The different product strategies that a company should develop at an appropriate time are as below:

- Product-positioning strategy
- Product-repositioning strategy
- Product overlap strategy
- Product-scope strategy
- Product-design strategy
- Product-elimination strategy
- New-product strategy
- Diversification strategy
- Value-marketing strategy

Each strategy is examined from the point of view of a business unit or profit centre. The term positioning refers to placing a brand in that part of the market where it will receive a favourable reception compared to competing products. Because the market is heterogeneous, one brand cannot make an impact on the entire market. As a matter of strategy, therefore, a product should be matched with the consumer segment of the market in which it is most likely to succeed. The product should be positioned, so that it stands apart from competing brands. Positioning tells what the product stands for, what it is, and how customers should evaluate it. Positioning is achieved by using marketing mix variables, especially design and communication. Although differentiation through positioning is more visible in consumer goods, it is equally true of industrial goods. With some products, positioning can be achieved on the basis of tangible differences (e.g., product features); with many others, intangibles are used to differentiate and position products.

Fabricators of consumer and industrial goods seek competitive distinction through product features-some visually or measurably identifiable, some cosmetically implied, and some rhetorically claimed by reference to real or suggested hidden attributes that promise results or values different from those of competitors' products. The offered product is differentiated, though the generic product is identical. The desired position for a product may be determined using the following procedure:

- Analyse product attributes that are salient to customers.
- Examine the distribution of these attributes among different market segments.
- Determine the optimal position for the product in regard to each attribute, taking into consideration the positions occupied by existing brands.
- Choose an overall position for the product (based on the overall match between product attributes and their distribution in the population and the positions of existing brands).

Positioning of beer may be considered to explain this concept. Two positioning decisions for beer that a company may choose are light versus heavy and bitter versus mild. The desired position for a new brand of beer can be determined by discovering its rating on the attributes and by considering the size of the beer market. The beer market is divided into segments according to these attributes and the positions of other brands. It may be found that the heavy and mild beer market is large and there are many companies in the business competition. The light and mild beer market has another big segment dominated by Miller and Anheuser Busch in United States of America. In view of the existing market competition the management of a new entering company may decide to position a new brand in competition with Miller Lite and Bud Light.

Disney stores demonstrate how adequate positioning can lead to instant success in the USA. Disney stores earn more than three times, what other specialty stores earn per square foot of floor space. Disney has created retail environments with entertainment as their principal objective. As a customer enters the store, he/she sees the Magic Kingdom, a land of bright lights and merry sounds packed full of Mickey Mouse merchandise. From a phone at the front of each store, a customer can get the Disney channel or book a room in a Disney World Hotel. Disney designers got down on their hands and knees when they laid out the stores to be sure that their sight lines would work for a three-year-old. The back wall, normally a prime display area, is given over to a large video screen that continuously plays clips from Disney's animated movies and cartoons. Below the screen, at kid level, sit tiers of stuffed animals that toddlers are encouraged to play with. Adult apparel hangs at the front of the stores to announce that they are for shoppers of all ages. Floor fixtures that hold the merchandise angle inward to steer shoppers deeper into this flashy money trap. Managers spend six weeks in intensive preparatory classes and training before being assigned to a store. Decorated with attractive illumination and elaborate ceiling displays, the stores have relatively high start-up and fixed costs, but once up and running, they earn high margins. There are different approaches to positioning distinguished as in Table 2.5.

Table 2.5: Product Positioning Strategies

Product positioning strategies	*Features of the strategy*
Positioning by attributes	Associating a product with an attribute or end user benefit
Positioning by functional variable like price and quality of the product	The price /quality attribute is so pervasive that it can be considered a separate approach to promotion
Positioning with respect to use or application	Associating the product with a use or application
Positioning by the product user	Associating a product with a user or a class of users
Positioning with respect to a product class	Positioning Caress soap as a bath oil product rather than as soap
Positioning with respect to a competitor	Making a reference to competition as in Avis´s now-famous campaign: "We're number two, so we try harder."

Two types of positioning strategies may be identified as single-brand strategy and multiple-brand strategy. A company may have just one brand that it may, place in one or more chosen market segments, or, alternatively, it may have several brands positioned in different segments, simultaneously.

To maximize the benefits on the product with a single brand, a company must try to associate itself with a core segment in a market, where it can play a dominant role. In addition, it may attract customers from other segments outside its core positing area. BMW does very well with such product positioning strategy. The company positions its cars mainly in a limited segment to high-income young professionals. However, if 20 percent of the sales of this brand were susceptible to a competitor's entry (assuming a fairly high probability that the competitor would have indeed positioned its new brand in that open spot), the actual level of cannibalism shouldbe set at 30 percent. This is because 20 percent of the revenue from sales of the existing brand would have been lost to a competitive brand had there been no new brands. Multiple brands can be positioned in the market either as head-on with the leading brand or with an idea of unique sales proposition (USP). The product positioning strategies have been illustrated in Figure 2.5.

Relative strengths of the new entry and the established brand dictate which of the two positioning routes is more desirable. Although head-on positioning usually appears risky, some companies have successfully carried it out. IBM's personal computer was positioned in head-on competition with Apple's. Datril, a Bristol-Myers painkiller, was introduced to compete directly with Tylenol. The product positioning with an idea, however, can prove to be a better alternative, especially- the leading brand that is well established. In addition, if a company already has a dominant position, its attempt to increase its market share by introducing an additional brand may invite antitrust action. Such an eventuality should be guarded against. On the other hand, there is also a defensive, or share-maintenance, issue to be considered here even if one has the dominant entry. A product with high market share may not remain in this position forever, if competitors are permitted to chip away at its lead with unchallenged positions. As a strategy, the positioning of multiple brands, if properly implemented, can lead to increases in growth, market share and profitability.

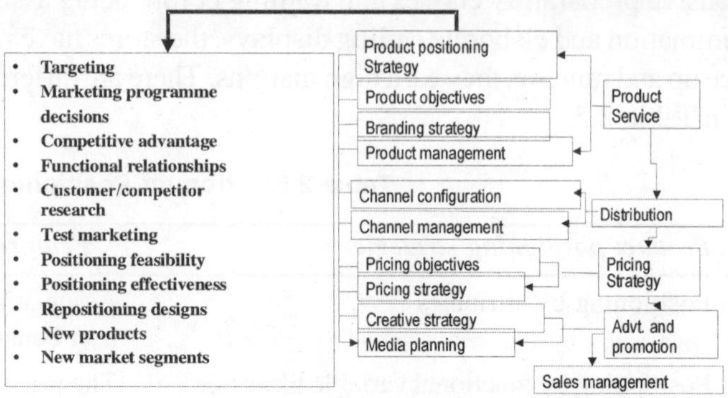

Figure 2.5 Product positioning strategy

PRODUCT REPOSITIONING STRATEGY

Often a product may require repositioning. This can happen, if (a) a competitive entry is positioned next to the brand, creating an adverse effect on its share of the market; (b) consumer preferences change; (c) new customer preference clusters with promising opportunities are discovered; or (d) a mistake is made in the original positioning. Citations from the marketing literature serve to illustrate how repositioning becomes desirable under different circumstances. When A & W went national in 1989 with its cream soda, it failed to clearly articulate the position. As a result, research showed that consumers perceived cream soda as an extension of the root beer family. To correct this, the company repositioned the brand as a separate soda category by emphasizing the vanilla flavour through advertising and packaging. Following the repositioning, cream soda's sales increased rapidly. Over the years, Coca-Cola's position has shifted to keep up with the changing mood of the market. In recent years, the theme of Coca-Cola's advertising has evolved from "Things go better with Coke" to "It's the real thing" to "Coke is it" to "Can't beat the feeling" to "Catch the Wave" to "Always new, always real, always you, always Coke." The current perspective of Coca-Cola's positioning is to reach the generation of young people and those young at heart. The risks involved in positioning or repositioning a product or service are high. The technique of perceptual mapping may be used gainfully to substantially reduce those risks. Perceptual mapping helps in examining the position of a product relative to competing products. There are following advantages of the perceptual mapping:

- To understand how various consumer groups perceive competing products or services in terms of strengths and weaknesses.
- To understand the similarities and dissimilarities between competing products and services.
- To know how to reposition a current product in the perceptual space of consumer segments.
- To position a new product or service in an established marketplace.
- To track the progress of a promotional or marketing campaign on the perceptions of targeted consumer segments.

Use of perceptual mapping may be illustrated with reference to the automobile industry. The map helps the marketing strategist in calculating whether company's cars are on par with the requirements of target consumers. The concentration of dots, which represent competing models, shows how much opposition there is likely to be in a specific territory on the map. Presumably, cars higher up on the graph fetch a higher price than models ranked toward the bottom where the stress is on economy and practicality After looking at the map, General Motors might find that its Chevrolet division, traditionally geared to entry-level buyers, ought to move down in practicality and more to the right in youthfulness. Another problem for General Motors, which the map so clearly demonstrates, is the close proximity of its Buick and Oldsmobile divisions. This close proximity suggests that the two divisions are waging a marketing war more against each other than against the competition. Basically, there are three ways to reposition a product: among existing users, among new users, and for new uses.

PRODUCT STRATEGY PERSPECTIVES

Product positioning strategy is an essential strategy to avoid competitive threats to a single brand. The product positioning strategy requires the analysis of all marketing variables, particularly the design and communication approaches. Successful management of a single brand needs positioning the brand in the market, so that it can stand competition from the toughest rival and maintaining its unique position by creating the aura of a distinctive product. Successful management of multiple brands requires careful positioning in the market so that multiple brands do not compete with each other. Thus, it is important to be careful in segmenting the market and to position an individual product as uniquely suited to a particular segment through design and promotion. Such strategies of product positioning should be implemented in view to meet the needs of specific segments of the market as much as possible, limiting sudden changes in sales and making customers faithful to the brands.

Product strategy helps in reviewing the current positioning of the product and its marketing-mix and seeking a new position for it that seems more appropriate to increase the life of the product and to correct an original positioning mistake. If this strategy is directed toward existing customers, repositioning is sought through promotion of more varied uses of the product. In case the business unit wants to reach new users, this strategy requires that the product be presented with a different twist to the people Who have not been favourably inclined toward it. In doing so, care should be taken to see that the current ones are not alienated. This strategy may also be aimed at presenting new uses of the product; it requires searching for latent uses of the product, if any. Although, all products may not have latent uses, there are products that may be used for purposes not originally intended. The effective implementation of this product strategy results in increase in the sales growth and profitability among existing customers and enlargement of the overall market among the new users. The new product uses as an outcome of such product strategy may be seen in augmented sales, market share, and profitability among the new consumer segments.

India has an installed base of 1 million ink-jet printers under the brand HP Desk-Jet. Hewlett-Packard India (HP) currently rules the market, selling more than two-thirds of all ink-jet printers in India. The success of HP Desk-Jet is the result of a meticulously calibrated strategy. The product was created by HP, one of America's best-known computer firms, in the mid-1980s as a replacement for dot-matrix printers which, apart from giving dotty print-outs, were intolerably slow and noisy. In

1989, HP unveiled its Desk-Jet, meant for office use. By the end of the 1980s, HP was already famous for its laser printers, which offered sharp quality, but were very expensive. Desk-Jet was meant to bridge the price gap between laser printers and dot-matrix ones. It offered a resolution as high as 300 dpi (dots per inch), and could almost match laser-quality printouts of plain text. But high custom duties (300 percent) made Desk-Jet uncompetitive. In 1989, HP imported five Desk-Jet printers, for trial runs (price: Rs 50,000). Local PC-maker PCL got 20 units. But the market gave a thumbs-down to the product. In 1992, one year after the opening of the Indian economy, HP revived the idea of marketing Desk-Jet. But this time, it was cautious. Godrej was appointed as its distributor. Yet, the product didn't get beyond sales of 5-10 units a month. In contrast, HP's LaserJet - 4, launched at the end of 1992, was an instant success. The market's polarization defied logic. People ought to have been excited by modern clarity at a price that did not break them away from the traditional virtue of thrift. Yet, it took a market study in April-May 1993 to reveal the reasons for the failure of DeskJet. The main market inhibitor, it turned out, was price. It was so much above the austere dot-matrix that it did not qualify as a thrifty purchase. Then there were perceptual blocks. Channel partners had reservations about the Desk-Jet's ability to handle 132-column printing. It was also seen as something only for graphics.

In response, in June 1993, HP came up with price points that were only slightly higher than dot-matrix printers. Yet, people were too accustomed to the buzz of these old-fashioned printers to bother replacing them. And everyone had dot-matrix, so why complain? The company knew that it had to shake people out of their sense of conformism. HP was on the lookout for a disruptive market programme, which would make people sit up and take notice. But the big challenge was to convince the trade that the dot-matrix era would end soon. In July 1993, Godrej organized a reseller meet in Goa, which brought together top 100 dealers the distribution firm. National Panasonic and HP, two of Godrej's partners, were invited to address the conference. Sensing its big chance, HP got a creative pitch worked out with MAA Bozell, its ad agency. The first presentation by National Panasonic was a damp squib. The Japanese team reinforced old thinking - that the Indian market was primarily dot-matrix. HP opened its show with an action sequence from the movie Star Trek VI-The Last Frontier. The sequence showed the Starship Enterprise battling an invisible star-ship and destroying it. It ends with Captain Kirk remarking 'It is all about change, madam chancellor.' On this cue, the HP team projected the future market as an undiscovered entity, where change was inevitable. It projected itself as a change agent, committed to delivering better value to customers, even if that meant busting the comfortable old paradigm. Next, HP addressed the channel inhibitors that it had identified earlier. Desk-Jet print-outs with 136 columns were distributed, and HP promised to meet price points that were acceptable to the trade. It also promised advertising support. That did it. Resellers flocked to the HP counter, and for once, the company felt buoyant about DeskJet's prospects. HP decided to focus on the West and North markets, and the product was re-launched in August, 1993. It sold 500 units that month. HP was back in business. By the end of the year, the product was selling across India, with volumes up.

In December 1993, whispers of Canon's imminent entry to the market were doing the rounds. Sensing a threat, HP drew up a contingency plan. In February 1994, HP swung into action. The new Desk-Jet 520 C of HP, a 600 dpi machine, to counter Canon's 360 dpi machine was launched in the Indian market. HP got a boost. By early 1994, HP was using a 50-60 member team to give demonstrations of DeskJet, with some 20,000 trial printers installed across the country. It paid off. By 1995, DeskJet was selling 3,300 units a month. February 1995 saw the launch of Epson, with a 1,440 dpi printer. This was another serious challenge. An ad war ensued between Epson and HP DeskJet. However, the mass market was still with dot-matrix printers, and HP realized that leadership meant converting these customers, not retaliating against Epson. 'The end of dot-matrix' pitch was backed by a trade-in scheme for people to exchange their old printers for new. It worked wonders. Monthly sales jumped to 9,000 units in the first quarter of 1997. By now, corporate letters on dot-matrix were coming to be seen as distinctly downmarket. The need for clarity had risen from 'latent' to 'felt' status in India, at least amongst those in the loop of modern advancements. Yet, there was no room for complacency. A new ad, titled 'Epson's bluff' was put out to counter all the claims of the rival. HP kept the excitement level high; any dormancy could risk a loss of leadership. In August 1997, it launched a series of new printers under Freedom Printers, to celebrate 50 years of India's independence. HP followed this with a series of imaginative package deals. By December 1997, HP was ready to broaden its viewfinder and assume a wider sort of leadership of the Indian printers market. Its communication made a strategic shift from technical aspects to the emotive feel of the brand. In February 1998, HP created an advertisement based on the movie *Mannequin*. It was about 'What happens when a man falls in love with an HP printer', and showed a Desk-Jet transforming into a girl and dancing away to eternal happiness with a man. Roses and heart-shaped chocolates were given out with every DeskJet purchase with a inscription *'I love my HP Desk-Jet'*.

On the retail front, HP opened exclusive stores in Delhi and Mumbai. By the end of 1998, it was selling 18,000 printers a month. Towards the end of 1998, FCB-Ulka replaced MAA Bozell as the brand's ad agency. In 1999, Canon and Epson both turned aggressive. HP DeskJet's market share dipped from 72 to 59 percent that year. But the market was growing so fast that its monthly numbers rose. By mid 2000, HP had managed to stave off the attacks of Epson and Canon, and reached 31,000 units per month – which took its market share back above two-thirds of the market. HP also brought in some innovations in logistics. With the help of advanced computer systems, it introduced end-to-end stock management. This speeded up the distribution while also ensuring that there were no gaps. Now that the dot-matrix printers have been overtaken as a technology, HP has decided to penetrate India as deep as possible. To tap the upcountry market, HP has introduced the DeskJet 630 series at a reasonable price bargain. Today, India is the second largest printer market for HP in the Asia-Pacific region, after South Korea. Yet, the market still needs plenty of expansion. The PC-printer 'connect rate' is still only 40-45 percent in India. Hardware costs are still too high here. For example, a printer that sells for $110 in India, would sell in China for around $70. Globally, colour photo realistic printing is now in vogue. Not so in India. Presently, 80 percent of the printing is black & white. Another global trend is towards multi-functional products, which roll the benefits of a printer, scanner, fax machine and copier into one machine. In the US, such all-in-one machines constitute 16 percent of the printers market. In India, they make up a minuscule 0.5 percent.

Product overlap strategy may be understood as competing against one's own brand through introduction of competing products, use of private labelling, and selling to original-equipment manufacturers. Such product overlap strategy is developed and implemented by the companies to attract more customers to the product and thereby increase the overall market and to work at full capacity and spread overhead. This strategy also supports to sell to competitors; to realize economics of scale and cost reduction. Each competing product must have its own marketing organization to compete in the market for making the product overlap strategy a success. It is also necessary to this strategy that private brands should not become profit drains and each brand should find its special niche in the market. If that doesn't happen, it will create confusion among customers and sales will be hurt. However, in the long run, one of the brands may be withdrawn, yielding its position to the other brand. The successful planning and implementation of product overlap strategy would result in increasing the market share and growth.

> Colgate-Palmolive Canada (CPC) manufactures a range of household, health, and personal care products. Among CPC's major brands are ABC, Arctic Power, and Fab (laundry detergents), Palmolive (dishwashing liquid), Ajax (cleanser), Irish Spring (bar soap), Ultra Brite and Colgate (toothpastes), Halo (shampoo), and Baggies (food wrap). ABC brand of the company had made strong gains in the past four years, moving from sixth to second place in market share based on its value position. ABC was positioned as the low-priced, good-quality cleaning detergent. Arctic Power had been positioned as the superior cleaning laundry detergent specially formulated for cold water washing. Though Arctic Power had been positioned as a product for cold water washing segment of consumers where ABC was also in use by the consumers as an economy product, had overlapped with the existing consumer segment of ABC. The positioning strategies of these brands reflected the benefit segmentation approach used to market laundry detergents but still had entangled competition. The overall objective of Arctic Power was to continue profit development by maintaining modest unit volume growth in Québec and the Maritimes while developing the Alberta British Columbia regions.[8]

Product scope strategy (PSS) deals with the perspectives of the product mix of a company. The product scope strategy is determined by taking into account the overall mission of the business unit. The company may adopt a single-product strategy, a multiple-product strategy, or a system-of-products strategy. To increase economics of scale by developing specialization for the single product a company may focus the PSS. This strategy may be aimed for multiple products to cover the risk of potential obsolescence of the single product by adding additional products. The PSS would also be aimed to increase the dependence of the customer on the company's products as well as to prevent competitors from moving into the market in reference to the system of products. The company must keep updated information on the product and even become the technology leader to avoid obsolescence in case of the single products whereas products must complement one another in a portfolio of products for building the strategy for multiple products. The company should have a close understanding of consumer needs and uses of the products for effective implementation of the strategy. The implementation of this strategy would yield results of increased growth, market share, and profits with all strategies discussed. With system-of-products strategy, the company achieves monopolistic control over the market, which may lead to some problems with the Department, and enlarges the concept of its product/market opportunities.

Product-design strategy deals with the degree of standardization of a product. The company has a choice among the following strategic options viz. standard product, customized product, and

8 Cravens David: *Strategic Marketing,* Boston. McGraw Hill, 2000

standard product with modifications. To develop the standard product the company should aim to increase economics of scale while the company should focus the strategy for customized product to compete against mass producers of standard products through product design flexibility. The company needs to do a close analysis of product/market perspectives and environmental changes, especially technological changes. The implementation of this strategy would benefit the company to increase in growth, market share, and profits. On the contrary the product elimination strategy aims at shaping the best possible mix of products balancing the total business This strategy would help to eliminate undesirable products because their contribution cost and profit is too low and they do not fit in the overall business strategy. No special resources are required to eliminate a product. However, it is impossible to reverse the decision once the elimination has been implemented. An in-depth analysis must be done to determine (a) the causes of current problems; (b) the possible alternatives, other than elimination, that may solve problems (e.g., Are any improvements in the marketing mix possible?); and (c) the repercussions that elimination may have on remaining products or units (e,g., Is the product being considered for elimination complementary to another product in the portfolio? What are the side effects on the company's image? What are the social costs of elimination?). In the short run, cost savings from production runs, reduced inventories, and in some cases an improved return on investment can be expected by implementing this strategy. However, in the long run, the sales of the remaining products may increase because more efforts are now concentrated on them.

A *new-product strategy* is difficult to implement, if a "new product development system" does not exist within a company. Five components of this system should be assessed: (a) corporate aspirations towards new products, (b) organizational openness to creativity (c) environmental favour towards creativity, (d) screening method for new ideas, and (e) evaluation process. The new product strategy is required to meet new needs and to sustain competitive pressures on existing products. In the first case, the new-product strategy is an offensive one; in the second case, it is a defensive one.

Product diversification strategy is developed for developing unfamiliar products and markets through (a) concentric diversification (products introduced are related to existing ones in terms of marketing or technology) (b) horizontal diversification (new products are unrelated to existing ones but are sold to the same customers), and (c) conglomerate diversification (products are entirely new). The example may be cited of Nestlé milk products like milk powder, chocolates, yoghurts etc. that exhibit the concentric diversification whereas the unrelated products of Gillette Company such as men's toiletries, batteries (Duracell) and dental care products (Oral-B) establish the example of horizontal diversification. The Tata group of companies in India which are involved in fully unrelated and new products like steel, telecommunication, textiles and consumer goods may be considered as the example of conglomerate diversification. Diversification strategies respond to the desire for growth when current products /markets have reached maturity and stability by spreading the risks of fluctuations in earnings. The diversification strategies would also be required for the business security when the company may fear backward integration from one of its major customers, and credibility to have more weight in capital markets. In order to reduce the risks inherent in a diversification strategy, a business unit should consider the following parameters:

- Diversify its activities only, if current product/market opportunities are limited,
- Build good knowledge of the area in which it diversifies,

- Provide the products introduced with adequate support, and
- Forecast the effects of diversification on existing lines of products.

Effective implementation of product diversification strategy would benefit the company in terms of increase in the sales and greater profitability and flexibility.

Value-marketing strategy concerns delivering on promises made for the product or service. These promises involve product quality, consumer service, and meeting time commitments. Value-marketing strategies are directed toward seeking total consumer satisfaction. It means striving for excellence to meet customer expectations. To implement value-marketing strategy a company should check the following requirements:

- Examine customer value perspective,
- Design programmes to meet customer quality, service, and time requirements, and
- Offer training to the employees and distributors to deliver on promises.

This strategy enhances customer satisfaction, which leads to customer loyalty and, hence, to higher market share. This strategy makes the company less vulnerable to price wars, permitting the firm to charge higher prices that may help in earning higher profits.

SELECTED READINGS

Aaker, David A., and Erich Joachimsthaler: *Brand Leadership.* NewYork: Free Press, 2000.

Alden, Dana L. Jan-Benedict E. M. Steenkamp; and Rajeev Batra: Brand Positioning through Advertising in Asia, North America and Europe: The Role of Global Consumer Culture, *Journal of Marketing*, 63 January 1999, pp. 75-87.

Cooper, Robert G.: Selecting New Product Projects: Using the NewProd System, *Journal of' Product Innovation Management,* Vol. 2, No.1, March, 1985, pp. 34-44.

Craven David W.: *Strategic Marketing,* 7th Edition, McGraw Hill, New York, 1999

Ganesh, Jaishankar, V. Kumar and Velavan Subramaniam: "Learning Effects in Multinational Diffusion of Consumer Durables: An Exploratory Investigation, *Journal of the Academy of ,Marketing Science*, 25, Summer 1997, pp. 214-228.

Featherstone, Mike : Global Culture: An Introduction, in *Global Culture: Nationalism, Globalization and Modernism*, Featherstone, Mike (ed.), London: Sage Publications,1990.

Hassan, Salah S. and Lea Katsanis: Global Market Segmentation Strategies and Trends, in *Globalization of Consumer Markets: Structures and Strategies*, Salah S. Hassan and Erdner Kaynak (eds.), New York: *International Business Press,* 1994, 47-62.

Jain Subhash C. : *Marketing Planning and Strategy,* 6th Edition, Thomson Learning, Ohio, 2000.

John Quelch and David Kenny: Extend Profit, Not Product Lines, *Harvard Business Review*, September-October, 1994.

Kotlar Philip : *Marketing Management,* 6th Edition, Prentice Hall, Englewood Cliffs, NJ 1998

Olins, W : *Corporate Identity*, London: Thames and Hudson,1989.

Parsons, Andrew : Nestlé: The Visions of Local Managers, *McKinsey Quarterly*, No. 2, 1996,5-29.

Samu, S., Krishnan, H. S., and Smith, R. E. : Using Advertising Alliances for New Product Introduction: Interactions Between Product Complementarity and Promotional Strategies, *Journal of Marketing*, Vol. 63 (1), 57-74.

Case 2.1

L'OREAL NETHERLANDS: PRODUCT MARKETING STRATEGY IN EUROPE

In 1992, the L'Oreal's Group was the largest cosmetics manufacturer in the world having its headquarters in Paris. It had subsidiaries in over 100 countries. In 1992, its sales were $6.8 billion (a 12 percent increase over 1991) and net profits were 417 million dollars (a 14 percent increase). France contributed 24 percent of total worldwide sales, Europe (both western and eastern countries excluding France provided 42 percent, and the United States and Canada together accounted for 20 percent. The rest of the world accounted for the remaining 14 percent. L'Oreal's European subsidiaries were in one of two groups.

- Major countries - England, France, Germany, and Italy
- Minor countries - The Netherlands and nine others

Company believed that innovation was its critical success factor. It thus invested heavily in research and development and recovered its investment through global introductions of new products. All research activities were centred in France. As finished products were developed, they were offered to subsidiaries around the world. As brand life cycles for cosmetics could be very short, L' Oréal tried to introduce one or two new products per year in each of its worldwide markets. International subsidiaries could make continue or withdraw decisions on products, but they generally did not have direct input into the R&D process. In established markets, such as the

Netherlands, any new product line introduction had to be financed by the current operations in that country.

L'Oréal marketed products under its own name as well as under a number of other individual and family brand names. In the 1970s, it acquired Laboratories Garnier, and this group was one of the largest divisions of L' Oréal. In France, with a population of about 60 million people, Gamier was a completely separate division, and its sales force competed against the L'Oréal division. In the Netherlands, however, the market was much smaller (about 15 million people), and Garnier and L'Oréal products would be marketed by the same sales force.

Dutch consumers had little, if any, awareness or knowledge of Gamier and had not formed a brand image. The Gamier sunscreen was a new product and few Dutch women knew of the brand. It was, therefore, very important that any new Gamier products launched in the Netherlands had a strong concept and high market potential. To accomplish this, the products needed to offer unique, desired, and identifiable differential advantages to Dutch consumers. Products without such an edge were at a competitive disadvantage, and could fail and create a negative association with the Garnier´s name, causing potential problems for future Gamier product introductions.

THE DUTCH MARKET

In the late 1980s, 40 percent of the Dutch population (about the same percentage as in France) was under 23 years old. Consumers in this age group were the heaviest users of cosmetics and toiletries. However, like the rest of Europe, the Dutch population was aging and the fastest-growing population segments were the 25 or older groups.

Other demographic trends included the increasing number of Dutch women working outside of the home. The labor force participation rate of women in the Netherlands was 29 percent. This was much lower than the 50 percent or above in the United Kingdom or United States, but the number of women working outside the home was increasing faster in the Netherlands than it was in the United Kingdom or the United States. Dutch women were also delaying childbirth. As a result of these trends, women in the Netherlands were exhibiting greater self-confidence and independence; women had more disposable income and more of them were using it to buy cosmetics for use on a daily basis.

Despite their rising incomes, Dutch women still shopped for value, especially in cosmetics and toiletries. In the European Union (EU), the Netherlands ranked fourth in per capita income; but it was only sixth in per capita spending on cosmetics and toiletries. Thus, the Dutch per capita spending on personal care products was only 60 percent of the amount spent per capita in France or Germany. As a result of both a small population (13 million Dutch to 350 million EU residents) and lower per capita consumption, the Dutch market accounted for only 4 percent of total EU sales of cosmetics and toiletries.

SYNERGIE

Synergie was a line of facial skin care products consisting of moisturizing cream, anti- ageing day cream, anti-wrinkle cream, cleansing milk, mask, and cleansing gel. It was made with natural ingredients, and its advertising slogan in France was "The alliance of science and nature to prolong the youth of your skin."

SKIN CARE MARKET

Skin care market was the second largest sector of the Dutch cosmetics and toiletries market. For the past five quarters, unit volume had been growing at an annual rate of 12 percent and dollar sales at a rate of 16 percent. This category consisted of hand creams, body lotions, all-purpose creams, and facial products. Products within this category were classified by price and product type. Skin care products produced by institutes such as Shisedo or Estée Lauder were targeted at the high end of the market. These lines were expensive and were sold through personal service perfumeries that specialized in custom sales of cosmetics and toiletries. At the other end of the price scale were mass market products like Ponds, which were sold in drugstores and supermarkets. In the last couple of years, a number of companies, including L'Oréal had begun to offer products in the mid price range.

Skin care products could also be divided into care and cleansing products. Care products consisted of day and night creams; cleansing products were milks and tonics. The current trend in the industry was to stretch the lines by adding specific products targeted at skin types such as sensitive, greasy, or dry. An especially fast growing category consisted of anti-aging and anti-wrinkling creams. Complementing this trend was the emphasis on scientific development and natural ingredients. Almost 50 percent of the 5 million Dutch women between the ages of 15 and 65 used traditional skin care products.

Table 1 exhibits that the newer specialized products had a much lower penetration.

Table 1: Usage of Skin Care Products by Dutch Women

Product	*Percentage of users*
Day Cream	46
Cleansers	40
Mask	30
Tonic	26
Anti-ageing Cream	03

Table 2 : Sales Break-up by Retail Outlets for Skin Care Products

Type of stores	*Unit sales(%)*
Supermarkets	18
Drugstores	82

COMPETITION

There were numerous competitors, Some product lines, such as Oil of Olaz (Oil of Olay in the United States) by Procter & Gamble and Plenitude by L'Oréal, were offered by large multinational companies other brands, were offered by regional companies. Some companies offered a complete line, while others, like Oil of Olaz, offered one or two products. The break-up sales across the retail stores for the mid-lower priced brands are shown in Table 2. The Table 3 lists a few of the available lines with the price ranges and positioning statements. The Dutch market was especially competitive for new brands. The rule of thumb in the industry was that share of voice for a brand (the percent of total industry advertising spent by the company) should be about the same as its market share. Thus, a company with 10 percent market share should have had advertising expenditures around 10 percent of total industry advertising expenditures. However, there were deviations from this rule. Ponds, an established and well-known company with loyal customers, had about 9 percent share of the market (units) but onIy accounted for about 2.5 percent of total industry ad expenditures.

Table 3: Competitive Product Lines of Cosmetics

Consumer class	*Brand*	*Price range (Guilders)**	*Positioning*
Lower	Nivea	9.50-11.50	Mild, modest price, Complete line
	Ponds	5.95-12.95	Anti-wrinkle
Middle	Oil & Olaz (P & G)	12 (day cream only)	Moisturizing, antiaging Delay the signs of aging
	Plentitude (L'Oreal) Synergie	10.95-19.95	The alliance of science and nature to prolong the youth of your skin
		11.95-21.95	
Upper End	Yves Rocher	10-26.95	Different products for different skins, natural ingredients
	Ellen Betrix (Estee Lauder)	12-95-43.50	Institute line with reasonable prices, luxury products at non luxury prices

Alternatively, new brands like Oil of Olaz (10 percent market share, 26 percent share of voice) spent much more. The higher ad spending for these brands was necessary to develop brand awareness and, ideally, brand preference. Any innovative products or new product variations in a line could be quickly copied. Retailers could develop and introduce their own private Labels in 4 months; manufacturers could develop a competing product and advertising campaign in 6 months. Manufacturers looked for new product areas in other countries and then transferred the Product concept or positioning strategy across national borders. They also monitored competitors' test markets since a test market typically lasted 9 months, a competitor could introduce a product before test market was completed.

CONSUMER BEHAVIOUR

Consumers tended to be loyal to their current brands. This loyalty resulted from the possible allergic reaction to a new product. Also, facial care products were heavily advertised and sold on the basis of brand image. Thus, users linked self-concept with a brand image, and this increased the resistance to switching. While all consumers had some loyalty, the strength of this attachment to a brand increased with the age of the user. Finally, establishing a new brand was especially difficult since, Dutch women typically purchased facial creams only once or twice a year. Dutch women were showing an increasing interest in products with "natural" ingredients, but they were not as familiar as the French with technical product descriptions and terms.

PRODUCT MANAGER'S REVIEW

L'oréal division in Holland has a very different problem from other L'Oréal divisions since they aren't big enough to justify an own sales force for the Garnier lines. This causes a need for some customized solutions for the Dutch market. When it comes to positioning the product they have chosen to place the product as natural but still scientific and sort of high-tech, which will ensure the customers about the company and the products. The products are focused on certain benefits, as has been the trend recently e.g. anti-wrinkle and other problem solving products. The products will be positioned similar to Plénitude, one of L'Oréals big and successful product lines.

They will mainly be sold in drugstores, drugstore-outlets and big supermarkets i.e. a product sold off the shelf and without sales representatives. For this kind of products, the stores usually require well-known products with brand awareness and brand preference. This can be difficult to obtain with a completely new product so large marketing efforts will be required to create this brand awareness and to make the consumers switch brand. Since skin-care products consumers are usually more cautious in buying new products and switching brands due to the risk of allergic reactions, it is more likely to be a success if the product is promoted as a high quality, higher priced but still mass-market product, just as with the Plénitude line. Even though Dutch women have had rising incomes for the last year they still look for good value products. Therefore one has to take that in to consideration while setting the price. Not too low not too high, that's the trick to find the right price in order to attract the largest potential group of buyers. It is impossible to attract them all. If you have a low range product you will attract the low range consumers and the same with mid-range and high range. One has to decide which group one wants to target in order to make large sales. High range consumers wont buy a mid range product even though it's a good one since, they can afford high range products and don't want the same products as everyone else.

Marketing plan suggested by the Product Manager for improving its efficiency is given below:

Product: Product should be marketed as an upper mid range product. The products of the company are mainly focusing on corrective care, such as anti wrinkle and problem skin. This will put it in a niche of its own, competing with other brands as well as developing its own exclusive features, in order to persuade customers to switch brand.

Price: Since it will be competing with upper mid range products the price has to be slightly higher than the general for midrange products. Around 13-25 guilders depending on the product would be a suitable level. However special introduction promotion prices can be applied for a certain time, to facilitate the consumers to switch brand. However, it has to be emphasised that this is only temporary so that the consumers still get the feeling of buying a high quality product.

Place: Since it will be a competing brand to other L'Oréal products is has to be sold on similar locations. There is off course a problem with competing with its own brands but the products are so similar that it will be very difficult to positioning, it different in order not to without destroying the brand. So drugstores, drug outlets and department stores supermarkets are the main distribution channels to focus on.

Promotion: As mentioned before the skincare market is difficult to enter due to the high brand loyalty among its customers. Therefore, it will need lots of efforts put into marketing in the initial phase of the introduction. The ads should focus on the scientific products with the natural ingredients, which are the main strengths of the product line. Since, the product will be sold off the shelf in stores where there will be no advisors, beauty consultants can be hired to make presentations of the product in these stores. This will create higher product awareness and people will have more faith in the product and thereby more inclined to buy it.

Market for skin care products is quite hard to penetrate in order to gain market shares, therefore, large marketing efforts and a good attractive campaign is necessary. Another problem for the producers of skin care products is that the developing and production time is very short so they have to be quick and efficient, if they don't want the competitors to beat them to the finish line and launch new products ahead of them. They performed tests on Dutch consumers in order to determine their strategy and these were more or less successful. They got similar ratings as the competitors but not significantly better. Also the response after knowing the price and having tested the products was slightly lower than before and was not entirely positive.

CHAPTER 3

BRAND STRATEGY

Brand is largely associated with the attributes of the product, benefits, use values, user culture, and personality and user behaviour. Hence the branding decisions are very important for the company. In this process the company should first take a decision on developing the brand name and its need. Branding is necessary to get the identification of the product and supplier, process supply orders, gain legal protection and good corporate image. The process of branding decision making in a company is exhibited in Figure 3.1. The branding also helps in building loyal customers for the product and organising the seller segments for better operational efficiency.

Company has to assess the strength and weaknesses of the existing brands in the market before taking the branding decision for their product. The manufacturing company may have several options on brand sponsorship. The product may be launched in the market as the brand of manufacturer, which is also known as national brand, a distributor brand as happens in case of edible oils, sugar, processed grains and in many products which needs re-packing, or licensed brand name. The brand category may be chosen from the brand sponsorship in terms of national brand, private brand or licensed brand. Deciding upon the category of brand an appropriate brand name may be selected. The brand names may reflect individual, blanket family name for all products, separate family names for all products or company trademark. The brand name should be easy to pronounce, short and convey proper meaning in the language of the country/region. The brand name should be such that it

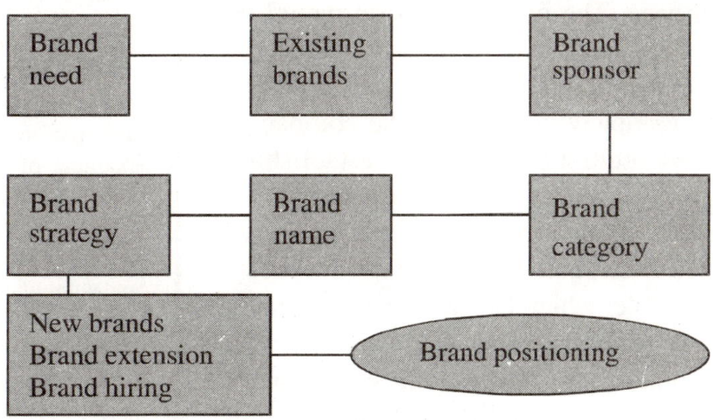

Figure 3.1 Branding decision

suggests some use value or attribute of the product and is distinct from the existing market brands. The brand extension in the same company can be explained as *product line.* It has been observed that the majority of new product activities consist of line extension. The company may have four basic options in brand strategy – *line extension* in which the existing brand can be extended to new attributes in the existing product category, *brand extension* which enables the company to introduce new brand names to new product categories, *multi-brands* may be used, if new brand names are provided to the same category of products and finally the *new brands* are those where new brand names are used for the new product categories.

A company may decide to use an existing brand name to launch a product in a new category. The Honda uses its brand name for two wheelers, four wheeler and stroke engines. Likewise the Hyatt practices the brand extension strategy by using its brand name in every hotel variation such as Hyatt's Resorts, Hyatt's Suits and Park Hyatt etc. This strategy makes the customers understand the reputation of the company and the quality of services. The brand extension would be more beneficial, if it serves to increase the sales of existing as well as the new products of the company. Sometimes the companies feel that multi–brands help in establishing different features to generate appeal to different buying motives. The example may be cited of the multi-brand strategy of Proctor and Gamble, which has introduced as many as nine different brands of detergents. The multi-brands may always gain small market share as compared to the solo brands and in particular these brands may not be able to generate sustainable sales revenue. In the market a strong brand will be considered to

Strategy Focus 3.1: Ice Cream Brand Race in Europe

In France, Cogesal Miko expanded in 2004 its range of bulk ice cream Carte d'Or by adding four new mixed fruit flavours, including pieces of biscuit, with recipes endorsed by the well-known food catering company Lenôtre. Fruit-flavoured dairy-based ice cream is also growing in popularity in Germany. Movenpick's ice of the year Creme Ricotta Pfirsich, introduced in 2004, is a combination of conventional peach flavour with cream cheese. In the Netherlands, a new Orange Fresh flavour of the brand, Solero was launched the same year, aimed at those people willing to eat more fruit as the formula contains 50 percent fruit and less fat. The former variant Solero Exotic was also improved with more emphasis on fruit and health, as the ice cream is enriched with 35 percent fruit and contains only 4 percent fat. According to a recent survey conducted by the Italian Ice Cream Trade Association (AIG), relatively unusual flavours, such as pink pepper, chilli and nutmeg, are increasing in popularity, with nuts and chocolate also being confirmed among the most in-demand. However, some exotic flavours introduced just a few years ago such as kiwi, papaya and coconut, are reportedly declining. The latter exemplifies a current trend in the industry, where recently introduced exotic flavours are tending to be short-lived and replaced immediately by new, more fashionable ones. The brand positioning of ice creams in Europe is a fashion driven exercise as they grow on the basis of moods and trends of celebrities and consumer preferences.

However, market sensations help to create a feeling of 'mystery' in the product, which adds to the pleasure of its consumption. Cornetto Love Passion, introduced in the Spanish market by Frigo in mid 2004 is a clear example of this. This line offers versions such as hazelnut-stracciatella and tiramisú-cinnamon, combining nut and herbal flavours with traditional Italian ingredients used in ice cream. Combinations of familiar and unfamiliar flavours are a growing trend in Germany as well. One of the most recent examples in 2004 is Nestle Schöller's new ice cream creation Schokolade Orange, a chocolate and orange ice cream refined with spices for a unique exotic taste

Source: Francisco R (2005), Ice cream-Differentiation through flavour, *Euromonitor*, August

have high brand equity. The brand equity will be higher, if the brand loyalty, awareness, perceived quality; strong channel relationships and association of trademarks and patents are higher. High brand equity provides many competitive advantages to the company. The brand equity may be understood as the highest value paid for the brand names during buy-outs and mergers. This concept may be defined as the incremental value of a business above the value of its physical assets due to the market positioning achieved by its brand and the extension potential of the brand.[1]

> Latest simplicity concepts have resulted from intensive consumer research, blending traditional design skills with psychology, anthropology, and ethnography. The research showed that an aging population, which caused a rise in health-care costs, will shift the focus of clinical health care from curing to prevention, with individuals taking increasing responsibility for their own health. Philips has reinforced its brand focus on consumer value by demonstrating the high technology aimed at gaining consumer satisfaction. Philips brands now sow human values towards anthropography designs and use values. The brand demonstrations - "Listen to your body" displayed a series of health monitoring devices while "Care for your body" used sensory therapies such as light to rejuvenate and energize. "Move your body" looked at interactive ways to stimulate play for kids and an exercise system to keep in shape for adults. "Relax your mind" used light and music to change the atmosphere of a room and your moods, while "Share experiences" explored innovative and interactive ways to share photos and communicate with family and friends. Philips' Look Good uses light as an integrated skin-care tool. The concept uses a base, bowl, skin analyzer, and cleansing stick to diagnose and improve skin tone and condition. The analyzer stick is shined on the skin to assess the treatment. Shine a blue light with the cleansing stick to heal breakouts or simply look into the bowl, which glows red to rejuvenate and soothe skin. Further, Drag & Draw turns the entire home into a virtual canvas for children. The digital light painting kit enables the user to paint via laser beams. Simply wave the wand over the laser projection bucket, and then use it to draw on any wall or surface. Draw a bus on a road, for instance, and then with another flick of the wand that image is suddenly surrounded by a colourful backdrop. Getting feedback counts as a major goal of the event, too and will be used by the company to make improvements and move the concepts toward actual products in future with refining the brand perceptions among consumers in world markets.[2]

Company may have low price and high consumer loyalty and also more trade leverage. It would be difficult to measure the brand equity of various brands in the market as the parameters are very subjective and the whole exercise may turn out to be arbitrary.[3] The brand equity has four major variable *viz.* awareness, acceptability, preference and brand loyalty and the integration of all these variables offer the high brand equity for the company. The brand equity further leads to brand personality of the company. The company may decide the brand personality strategy after analyzing the strength and weakness of the existing brands in the market. The research on assessing

---

1 Tauber, Edward M: Brand Leverage: Strategy for Growth in a Cost-control World, *Journal of Advertising Research,* August-September, 1998.

2 Capell Kerry : Philips goes fabulous, *Business Week,* October 6, 2006

3 Aaker, David A : *Managing Brand Equity,* The Free Press, New York , 1991, pp 20-46

the brand personality may be conducted by using the brand rating method to get quantitative measures. The methods of photo sorting (trademark), phrase writing and simulation games may be used for assessing the brand personality. The sample consumers for this purpose should be self-directed, principled, externally directed, status oriented action-oriented, consumers and non-driven consumers. The effective strategy for implementing the brand personality measures would be to go for aggressive advertising using the consumer reviews and comparative product advantages. However, the consistency in the message should be taken care of properly.

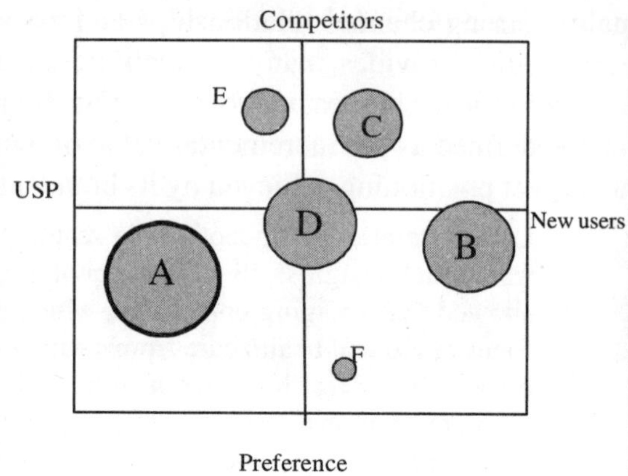

Figure 3.2 Brand positioninng map

Brand once positioned by the company in the market may have to be repositioned over a period of time as the competitor may launch a brand close to the company's and cut into its market share. The shift in consumer preference may also cause the repositioning of the brand in the market. The repositioning of brand has to be carefully done analysing the age and sex response to the company's brand, packaging and advertising response, revenue generation in the new market/consumer segment and strength of the competitors. The brand positioning map is exhibited in Figure 3.2 which shows that positioning the brand at A would be the most profitable where the consumer preference is good and is matched to the USP. On the contrary the repositioning of the brand at E would not be favourable due to high marketing cost to overcome the competitors and re-orient the consumer preference for the brand. The brand promotion for the new users may generate good response for the product sales but may also pose threats of competitors entering in the new segment. Hence, the decision on the brand re-positioning should be made comparing the likely revenues and cost of each repositioning alternatives. It is a must for the company to identify the best preference cluster and the USP for positioning the brand and building image thereof. Hence, the most ideal brand positioning would be at A with reasonably good USP and preference cluster for the product. However, the company may aim at repositioning the brand at B and C over a period of time.

> Procter & Gamble's (P & G) ***Febreze Auto*™** is the second car-care product which carries the *Motor Trend* seal of approval, an endorsement from the world's number one automotive products quality administration authority. This product has appeared as a brand extension of the successful previous product of the company- Mr. Clean Auto Dry™ **car cleaning system.** *Febreze Auto*™ is specially designed for use on the fabric surfaces of car interiors. Its unique formula contains low levels of scent, making it perfect to use on fabric surfaces in your trunk or on infant seats, car seats, and floor mats. The new brand extension in the car-care product category of P&G appears to have come mainly from cost-savings, and high customer value brand portfolios of the company. However, efforts of the company on revamping its distribution chain, making it more cost-effective and streamlining the distribution

channels to focus on the promising markets alone would hold high anticipations of success of the product. A successful brand can be used as a platform to launch related products. The benefits of brand extensions are the leveraging of existing brand awareness thus reducing advertising expenditures, and a lower risk from the perspective of the consumer.[4]

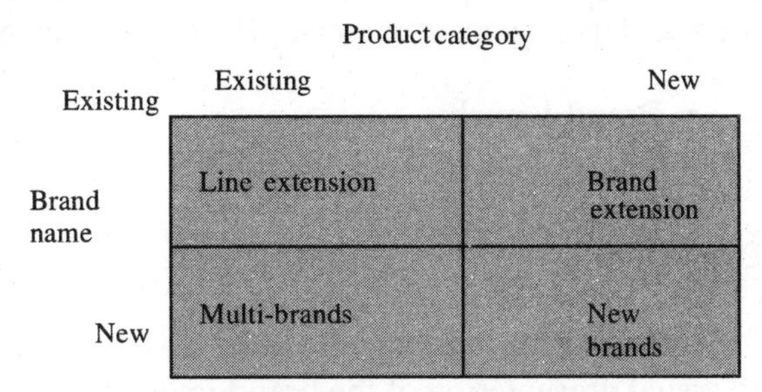

Figure 3.3 Brand strategy matrix

Brand extension in the same company can be explained as *product line.* It has been observed that majority of new product activities consists of line extension. The company may have four basic options in brand strategy – *line extension* in which the existing brand can be extended to new attributes in the existing product category, *brand extension* which enables the company to introduce new brand names to new product categories, *multi-brands* may be used, if new brand names are provided to the same category of products and finally the *new brands* are those where new brand names are used for the new product categories. The branding strategy can be viewed clearly as exhibited in the Figure 3.3. A Company may decide to use an existing brand name to launch a product in a new category. The Honda uses its brand name for two wheelers, four wheeler and stroke engines. Likewise the Hyatt practices the brand extension strategy by using its brand name in every hotel variation such as Hyatt's Resorts, Hyatt's Suits and Park Hyatt etc. This strategy makes the customers understand the reputation of the company and the quality of services. The brand extension would be more beneficial if it serves to increase the sales of existing as well as the new products of the company. Sometimes the companies feel that multi–brands help in establishing different features to generate appeal to different buying motives. The example may be cited of the multi-brand strategy of Proctor and Gamble, which has introduced as many as nine different brands of detergents. The multi-brands may always gain small market share as compared to the solo brands and in particular these brands may not be able to generate sustainable sales revenue.

Brand equity may be understood as the highest value paid for the brand names during buy-outs and mergers. This concept may be defined as the incremental value of a business above the value of its physical assets due to the market positioning achieved by its brand and the extension potential of the brand.[5] In the market a strong brand will be considered to have high brand equity. The brand equity will be higher if the brand loyalty, awareness, perceived quality; strong channel relationships and association of trademarks and patents are higher. High brand equity provides many competitive advantages to the company.

4 http://primedia.com/highlights/febrezeauto

5 Tauber, Edward M.: Brand Leverage: Strategy for Growth in a Cost-control World, *Journal of Advertising Research,* August-September, 1998.

BRAND CATEGORIES

Strategically the brands are managed separately and independently. On some occasions, the brands are introduced in the market on *adhoc* basis. This strategy requires decision making to allocate appropriately the resources to the identified brands. The brand personality is the core-measuring tool of the brand management exercise. The brand management broadly consists of the following activities:

- Brand launch
- Brand leverage
- Brand equity and
- Brand loyalty

A strong brand is a valuable asset and its management should include proper positioning along with visual presentation of the brand image through the trade mark and trade dress. A trade dress of the brand is its nomenclature symbol style and colours put together on the product package. The trade dress of the brand need to be registered to protect imitations. The brand management strategy consists of five major constituents as exhibited in figure 3.4. The brand equity consists of the strength of the brand along with the brand presentation strategy and its association with the user groups. The brand equity is largely reflected in the market behaviour comprising market share, price, perceived quality, distribution efficiency, and consumer loyalty and promotion strategy. The brand leveraging may be defined as an exercise using an existing brand name to enter a new product category. Brand leveraging is potentially very attractive. It makes use of the existing consumer awareness, good will and loyalty. Such exercise of brand positioning is cost effective and reflects greater emphasis on brand. The Procter and Gamble adopted a brand leveraging strategy in the introduction of its sanitary hygiene product *Always.* The P&G adopted similar strategy for introducing the liquid detergent *Tide* as a new category of product. In order to implement an effective brand strategy, it is necessary to identify an appropriate category of branding. Multinational companies in a competitive environment adopt the following brand strategies.

- Specific product branding
- Product line branding
- Corporate branding
- Combination branding
- Private branding

Brand leveraging strategy by a company may be adapted through extending the product line category. The new product line can be formed by stretching it to cater the mass or class market consumers. Sometimes the companies prefer to form a new product line instead of stretching the existing product line vertically or horizontally. The co-banding or brand hiring strategies also provide the brand leverage which may give opportunities for more franchising and better sales promotion of the products and services. Whenever a new product line of the company is developed, it should be decided whether a new brand name has to be given the products thereof or use an existing names. The example may be cited of Coca-Cola Company when it first developed the diet cola drink; it chose to use a new name tag instead of capitalizing on its existing consumer brand to promote franchise by using the Diet Coke. However, later in competition to Diet Pepsi the Coca-Cola Company countered its rival by using Diet Coke which is one of the best seller products now in the market. On the other extreme the company could have introduced a new brand in a new category, and presented it in the market as a solely new product. The *family brands* are group of products sold under one label by a single company. Heinz, Del Monte and General Electric (GE) endorse a wide array of products with their own corporate name while the consumer goods companies like Proctor and Gamble (P&G) and Nestle prefer to use separate brand names for each product. The P&G has eleven brands in the heavy-duty detergent category in the United States of which two brands Tide and Ariel are best sellers in India. The US brands of P&G in this category are Cheer, Bold, Gain, Era, Dash, Oxydol, Solo, Dreft and Ivory Snow including Tide and Ariel. The family brands have the advantage that advertising for one brand promotes the sales of all products carrying that particular label or attributes. The family brands also make it easier to introduce new products to the distribution channels and consumers. However, the family brands offer a narrow distinction among the products of the same category and it is difficult for the product manager to create and maintain an identity for each product and then tie them together with a unifying trade name. This strategy is used by the General Motors as their cars are promoted under their own names and the GM symbol is used as common point of reference in marketing the products.

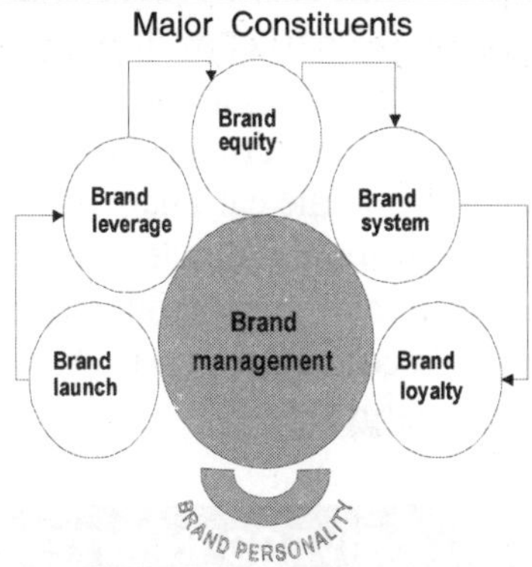

Figure 3.4 Strategic brand management

> A brand may help in gaining competitive advantage but need to be carefully architected. Wal-Mart has emerged as a strong retail brand with emphasis on everyday low prices. The strategy could be difficult to pull off, since the stronger, lower-price retailers are expanding in a long-term effort to take a bigger share of the retail pie. Having less inventory can certainly help profits, but it's no sure bet. While too much can hurt gross margins, due to added markdowns, too little can limit selection and hurt overall sales. Because expenses are being spread over less revenue, retailers risk hurting operating margins. Of course, the discount retailers that are expanding aggressively could easily overplay their hand. But retailing is much like a zero-sum game, with one player taking share at the expense of another. With consumers running out of steam, they're more likely to choose lower-price formats, to save money. Retailing was once a stay-at-home sector. Most of the companies including Wal-Mart were content to grow at home. Universally appealing product assortments are difficult to create, and far-flung, people-intensive retail operations are tricky to run. Since the mid-1990s, however, retailers have come under intense pressure from their shareholders to grow farther and faster, expressed in high share prices. How brand can be used a strategic tool to gain competitive advantage, the question remains for a secured growth?

National brands are identified as long standing in the competitive markets and wide spread distribution over the spatial and temporal market segments. The national brands are not very sensitive to the price gaps and the private labels. When a firm markets another brand in the existing category and protects its market positioning, the product is defined as flanker brand. The flanker brand is also known as fighting brand. Such brand has low investment on advertising and the product is offered on cost price. The American Express sells its premium priced products as green, gold and platinum credit cards and the card named as Optima was brought to the market by the company as a fighting brand. Such brands outwit the competing brands in a cost effective way. The *private brands* are more sensitive to the personal income and most of the retail stores set such brands for selling their grocery and consumer goods. The store based private labels or brand offer a number of advantages with high margins.

BRAND DRIVERS IN INTERNATIONAL MARKETS

Brand Timing

This refers to the creation of a marketing opportunity. Equally it can be the ability to recognise and exploit a shift of some kind. Shifts may result from a number of factors such as technology, consumer changes, etc. International brands look to implement central developments very quickly. As a result of the acceleration of the product development cycle, marketers must maintain competitive advantage for their brands with a rapid roll-out of new developments. The importance of strategic innovation is highlighted. Examples of this strategy are McDonald's vegetable burger, Adidas' *Feet You Wear* communications or Levi's Dockers. The use of global communications media facilitates the rapid roll-out of initiatives across countries.

Positioning

Consistency of positioning appears to be an essential criterion for success in this area. Some of the more successful brands are able to translate and adapt a central guiding theme such as *Just Do It* or *Always Coca-Cola*. The central theme allows the brand values to be maintained and updated or refreshed regularly. In this way, they act as a guide for the brand. Nevertheless, there is still the possibility to express the positioning locally but within the framework of a central strategy. A brand such as Levi's or Nike is able to set the tone for the category. A challenger brand will either have to accept this vocabulary or compete in a new field. An example of the latter is Diesel, a brand that is defining itself rather than mimicking the brand leader. However, even leader brands have to be refreshed and updated. Both Nike and Adidas have been in this position in recent years. In both cases, they were revived by a return, not just to the core sporting values but with a premier sports positioning.

Localization

In the past, brands were often global through a central strategy or they were very decentralised. The former was more efficient but insensitive to local conditions, the latter far more sensitive but less able to take advantage of economies of scale. In the 1990s, we can observe a greater degree of localisation whereby a brand conforms to a central strategy but one that can be adapted locally. This tends to be more efficient and responds to local market opportunities and needs. Brand consumption tends to be local. This strategy is particularly evident for Coca-Cola, MTV and McDonald's. In these cases, the principal offer remains the same but is more tailored to local tastes. McDonald's, for example, may offer different menu items, Coca-Cola's advertising will be more appropriate to the market or it will offer different ranges of soft drinks according to country. For example, Coca-Cola recently launched Smart, the first carbonated soft drink from an international company specifically designed for the Chinese market. MTV offers local or regional programming that will appeal more to viewers. Sports brands such as Nike and Adidas are in a strong position to market locally. This is most visible through the sponsorship of local athletes and events. Adidas' Street-ball events are very much targeted and developed at a local level. This behaviour can be enhanced through its adoption in regional or global communications. In this way a local initiative can become magnified.

Communications and Distribution Channel Diversity

Brands analysed in international markets tend to use a wide spectrum of communications channels. Aside from above-the-line advertising, this may include event marketing, on-line presence, database marketing, institutional marketing, etc. This varied media mix is a result of the greater media fragmentation. Furthermore, it also enables the brand values to be communicated to a more diverse audience with appropriate messages. A halo effect will be integrated with specific, narrow initiatives. The best practices in the area of communication may be describes as below:

- Target audience understanding,
- Segmentation,
- Communications programmes direct to the consumer developing retail presence exploiting opportunistic shifts consistency of positioning,
- Utilising local expression more holistic use of varied communications channels

There are also indications of brands looking to develop additional distribution channels. Diesel, Nike and Levi's have a retail presence. This acts as not only a distribution channel but also a way in which the brand values can be enhanced. McDonald's has looked to develop specific types of stores such as drive-through and on ferries or in hospitals.

The Shortening of the Product & Brand Life Cycle

There is considerable evidence of the shortening of the product and brand life cycle. To some extent this is a factor of the intense competition in the marketplace which means that new products have to prove themselves very quickly or be deleted. We are already seeing the launch of products that are promoted as limited editions and are designed for a short shelf life. This is particularly important in the impulse market where new product development and associated promotional activity are crucial in driving visibility at point-of-sale. Short life-cycle products will also require quick payback. Successful brands of this sort will make profits and then disappear or be quickly updated and reinvented.

Hyper-Segmentation

As we move from mass marketing to mass customisation we move through hyper-segmentation. This refers to many brand variants, each targeted at small, distinct groups of consumers. The brand remains constant representing an endorsement of the product through its associated values. This goes beyond straight demographics. Which variant of the product is right for your lifestyle, occasion or mood at the time? Brand extension will enable the brand equity to be leveraged within the product category. The brand provides the frame of reference for the consumer. However, it should not be at the expense of true innovation and cross-category opportunism. Developing genuinely innovative products and services where the innovation can be sustained will become increasingly important.

The Brand Experience

A brand represents an experience for consumers and, as such, becomes less associated with an individual product or service than the brand values. Under this scenario, a company's manufacturing competencies become less relevant than its ability to understand consumers and to manage a brand. Production can always be outsourced. In practice, it means that a brand can be extended across seemingly unrelated product and service categories, if it maintains its core brand values. The most obvious example of this is the Virgin brand that started with retailing music and gradually moved into the associated areas like films and videos before the launch of Virgin Atlantic aviation service. Since then, the brand has been extended into soft drinks, vodka, television and radio, financial services, rail travel, clothing and cosmetics. One of the pioneers in the development of the cross-category brand is Disney where the brand has been moved from films into theme parks, video, retail, television and, through partnerships and merchandising agreements, food and drink, toys, etc.

> Consumers are becoming increasingly obsessed with personal appearance and well-being. People are now prepared to invest significant amounts of money in order to improve the way they look and extend their lives, and this is having a growing impact on the health and beauty industries. Seeing an opportunity, cosmetics and toiletries companies have tapped into this growth by extending their brands into the beauty supplements niche, with vitamin and mineral cocktails that are said to promote healthy eyes, teeth, skin and nails. Beauty supplements are marketed mainly to women in their 20s and 30s – a group that previously rarely took multivitamins. They differ from regular multivitamins only in that they tend to have particularly large amounts of vitamins A, C and E, omega-3 and omega-6 fatty acids and copper. The vitamins are believed to help prevent oxidative damage to skin cells, while the fatty acids are said to help support blood flow to the skin. L'Oréal, Procter & Gamble, Kanebo, Shiseido and Avon have all made moves into the dietary supplements environment, some in conjunction with celebrity doctors such as Howard Murad and Nicholas Perricone. In July 2005, Japanese-based Kanebo developed skin-whitening supplements, capitalising on continued demand for products that help lighten skin tone in countries where a pale complexion is desirable.[6]

Within the media market there has been a sustained shift away from media owners working within individual channels towards the development of such brands that can run across the different forms of communications or product and service categories. This is a clear response to the fragmentation of media channels and allows the brand owner to develop a brand or brands for these different channels as well as develop products and services that can exploit the brand values. The experience

1 Loenie Tait: *Aesthetics drive health and beauty,* Euromonitor, November 8, 2006

brand becomes more important than the channel. One feature of this development is that a media brand may be extended into channels which are not traditional or "new" media, e.g. events, cafés, etc. This will provide new opportunities for advertisers to have their brand displayed within a new environment but with a familiar media brand name. Within products and services, Cosmopolitan in the UK, for example, has extended its brand beyond the printed page and the Web site into clothing retailing, confectionery and soft drinks. In the UK this development was aided by a relaxation in laws covering cross-media ownership. Marketers now have to question their own brand values to see, if they are applicable to other categories. Brand equity should be carefully measured and managed to evaluate current positioning as well as identify and leverage new opportunities.

Alternative Distribution and Communications Channels

There is a development of a number of products and brands that are choosing to avoid traditional retail and promotional channels in favour of a new approach. This is due to the increasing difficulty of selling through traditional channels in the mass-market where competition is intense and, in some markets the retailers push certain low profile brands in the market to gain high profit. At the same time, marketers are looking for greater efficiency and accountability in their communications and so are moving towards communications channels, where effectiveness can be more accurately demonstrated. Hence, the new generation of brands do not rely on channels of mass distribution or heavy weight advertising campaigns.. More recently,

Strategy Focus 3.2 Cadbury's Chocolates-Brand Positioning Strategy

Over 500 Million rupees Cadbury India company has launched a premium range of chocolates, Temptations, in Roast Almond Coffee, Old Jamaica, Honey Apricot, Mint Crunch and Black Forest flavours, in the Indian market. As a part of the product strategy of he company to launch one major brand every year, the new product range aims to offer the consumer an 'exotic and international chocolate experience. Temptations are being retailed through Cadbury's existing distribution network, reaching out to 250,000 retailers, with the emphasis on larger retail stores.

Cadbury's already claims a 70-percent share in value terms of the Indian chocolates market, pegged at around Rs 500 crore (22,000 tonnes per annum in volume terms), of which 5 percent is the premium segment. Why launch in the midst of an FMCG slowdown? The management of the company feels that one way to beat the slowdown is to keep track of evolving consumer needs and bring out a product to meet those needs. What market research showed was a definite need for a premium chocolate. The taste profile needed was adult and it needed to be an indulgence product." The research apparently also revealed that the consumer seeks variety from indulgence products and has been buying imported chocolates (such as Ferrero Rocher, Lindt et al). In the larger metro markets in India, it has been noticed that while our current premium range (Fruit & Nut and Roast Almond) was doing well, our presence in this top-end segment had reduced in favour of imported chocolates, which offered greater variety to the consumer. Research further revealed two sets of chocolate consumers in India- those who are exposed to international chocolates and are active consumers of the same, and those who would love to have the 'Differentiated Chocolate Taste' but find international chocolate prices prohibitive. European chocolates tend to melt at 18°C, Temptations claims to have been specially formulated to stay solid in tropical temperatures up to 26°C.

The advertising, handled by Contract, revolves around the brand proposition, 'Too Good to Share'. The TVC shows a mischievous 30-something modern, urban couple playing pranks on each other to avoid sharing their Temptations, which is a shift from the usual 'chocolate is for sharing' proposition. Cadbury is also working with self-vending kiosk doors, Crosswords bookstores, sampling at premium restaurants in metros, playing advertisements during movies, all aimed at targeting the consumer in privacy.

Source: Rajagopal: *Marketing: Strategy, Implementation and Control*, Rawat, New Delhi, 2004

Christian Dior promoted a perfume called Dune with a Web site which allows it to capture consumer data. There are number of brands, for example Durex, where the Web represents the lead communication channel as a part of the global strategy of the company. Consumers' acceptance of home shopping offers the potential for many manufacturers to offer a direct service avoiding retail outlets altogether. This is witnessed by the pioneering brands First Direct and Direct Line Insurance. These two brands have provided a model for future customer relationships in the financial services sector. The Internet is a global communications and distribution medium and has the potential to have a substantial impact not just on communications but also on the distribution of many goods and services.

The Differentiated Brand

Different brands will need to use different forms of differentiation and for different consumers. There will also be a trade-off between short-term competitive advantage and long-term differentiation. Service aspects will be the key to securing brand differentiation in the future. The commodity nature of the petrol retailing market, for example, clearly needs an initiative that makes one brand stand apart from the rest. This could be checking the oil or washing the car windows or employing a customer representative to help drivers with directions, avoiding road works and other traffic problems that day. Branding is about providing a means of differentiation. This wills become increasingly vital as the market and, in particular, the competitive situation evolves. Sustained differentiation will also enable a strong defence against me-too products. Information about pricing will be more easily available, even automated through intelligent agents. A low price policy contradicts brand building. Companies that opt for a low price strategy will find that short-term volume gains will be at the expense of longer-term profitability. Furthermore, not only will there be fewer funds available for investment but the brand will be devalued in the longer term. For a market leader this is especially so. Negative marketing will have an adverse impact on the brand.

However, this does not mean that pricing is not important. A company must continually review its pricing and evaluate the price/value equation. If a brand is charging a price premium over own label, the "value" of this must be justified. Sudden and deep changes are less advisable than continuous evaluation and adjustment. Nevertheless, pricing can be still used to differentiate. For example, there may be tiered pricing for different consumers or for different service levels. This may be a subscription TV channel where the cost of the subscription is dependent on the amount of advertising received.

The Consumer-Focused Brand

Marketing has always been about focusing on consumers. However, while marketing has previously only been able to use mass-marketing techniques to reach large groups of consumers, the current and evolving market scenario requires reaching individual consumers. Their different needs and aspirations must be recognised. The brand that is most successful will be the one that is most accurately able to satisfy the needs of individual consumers, meet and even surpass consumers' expectations. This will enable it to rise above those brands that do not have a genuine consumer orientation.

> Amul (Anand Milk Union Limited) has certainly come a long way since, its first product, Amul Butter, was launched in 1945. But it was only in the mid-1960s that the brand started

gaining prominence, after the introduction of the 'Utterly Butterly Delicious' Amul girl with the catchy lines. The concept was an instant hit and Amul was able to counter Polson Butter's position in the market. There has been no looking back since then. This has ensured that Amul re-mains amongst the top brands in India over the years. In 1992, Amul entered to an all-time high rank among the dairy products brands in India. Diversification of the product and brand portfolios has contributed to greater success of Amul. He range of diversified product range to include food stuffs such as Ketchup, Jam, Ice-cream, Mithai Mate (brand of condensed milk), Cheese, Shrikhand (a type of flavour yoghurt with dressing of fruits and nuts) and much more. Such brand extensions have been very successful in Indian markets as well in the markets of south and middle-eastern countries. Amul launched its own range of Ice-creams in 1997 after Hindustan Lever's acquisition of Kwality, Milkfood and Dollop's. The product was positioned as the 'Real Ice-cream'.

Consumer has become marketing-literate. The role of mass media advertising is changing but will still exist alongside evolving communications channels. Under this scenario, consumers will respond to a company which is genuinely interested in them and will take part in a dialogue. A company and brand's response to the consumer must be instant and appropriate. Companies will need to develop systems that enable them to learn about individual consumers and communications tools that allow them to communicate on an individual basis. A retailer should understand a consumer's shopping habits and then tailor its offer. A manufacturer may wish to open a direct consumer dialogue rather than relying on the retailer as the consumer point of contact. We are moving from the four Ps of mass marketing to the one C, the consumer, of relationship marketing.

More Local Marketing

While there has clearly been a desire by many companies to market their products and services globally, we are experiencing a paradox whereby many marketers have moved towards a strategy which is still global but which has increasingly a local execution. Examples of such companies include Coca-Cola, MTV and McDonald's, all well-known for their global presence. While MTV has launched more localised versions of its channel, other satellite broadcasters have taken advantage of technology to offer country-specific windows for their advertisers. This will be accentuated even more with the introduction of digital television technology. Even the world-wide web is seeing a more localised approach by companies. Many of the Web search engines, for example, have launched local versions. This is intended to benefit both users and attract advertisers.

Branding is currently at a crucial phase. The core principles of branding will remain the same but the actual execution of brand strategy will evolve to suit the changing consumer and the changing marketplace. This may involve re-evaluating the brand across all its different aspects. A brand will have to be benchmarked against the needs of the consumer within the framework of the marketplace. Brands will continue to add value, expanding the offer well beyond products and services. They will need to be managed more closely than before. Brand equity, its limitations and opportunities, will have to be fully understood. The value proposition will become all the more important at a time of immense retail own label pressure. Most of all, brands will have to focus on consumer needs and desires. Consistent quality, understood value and closeness to the consumer are the key attributes for the successful brand.

Strategy Focus 3.3 ACER-Building Consumer Centric Brand

The computer industry is one of the most competitive in the world, having always been dominated by the giants such as IBM. So, how has a Taiwanese company become the third largest manufacturer of personal computers in the world, creating a respected, and sometimes feared, brand? How has the company managed to break away from the "Made in Taiwan" image, which like many countries in Asia has been associated with sub-standard products? The answer is, of course, the careful construction of a strong brand positioned his products more at the higher end of the market than any other Taiwanese products had been previously. For example, when entering the Japanese market, he priced his products the same as theirs to avoid the poor-quality image associated with lower-priced products. This was an important signal emitted by the brand which Acer-branded products were not to be classified as commodities.

Acer Computer has always spent huge sums of money on research and development, and in this respect, tends to follow the Japanese technology companies. The company believes in "innovative value" by using innovation to create value in the design and production of cutting-edge products-and leading the industry. Company has positioned personal computers as an aesthetically pleasing home appliance, and this philosophy is summed up in the new corporate mission statement *Fresh Technology Enjoyed by Everyone, Everywhere*. Acer Computer has a long history of innovation, and continues to add to this brand strength at every opportunity.

Acer Computer's aim is to become more consumer-oriented, as it believes that PCs will become consumer-electronic products with a wider range of uses and applications in the areas of communications, entertainment, and education. Acer Computer, therefore, has to become an expert in consumer electronics as well as personal computing. Shih refers to this as a shift from being 'technology-centric" to "consumer-centric." The computer industry has always been the former-emphasizing products more than people. Acer Computer is, thus, repositioning itself to become a customer-centric intellectual-property and service company, as signified by its new slogan *Acer, Bringing People and Technology Together*. Acer adds value by enhancing consumer perceptions of the benefit or value of a product, based on know-how, packaging, design, accessibility, comfort, user-friendliness, and niche solutions-the tangible qualities of its products. This is how Acer Computer is building on its already strong international brand, into a global brand.

Source: Rajagopal: *Marketing: Strategy, Implementation and Control*, Rawat, New Delhi, 2004

BRAND ARCHITECTURE

Brand architecture is an organizing structure of the brand portfolio that specifies brand roles and the nature of relationships between brands. The brand architecture schemes have been referred to brand equity charter, leverages, brand profitability and the new rules of brand management leading to efficacy of the attributes, derived advantages and brand system emerging in relation to the buying power of the customers. The first step in establishing a brand equity management system may be focused towards finalizing brand equity into a document, the brand charter that provides relevant guidelines to the marketing managers. Such documentation strategy requires defining the firm's view on the significance of the equity concept, describing key brands in terms of associated products or names and the manner by which they have been branded and marketed the second step in establishing a successful brand equity management is to integrate the results of the brand track survey performed periodically. Mapping of the market information on the critical indicators of the key brands would also be a guiding tool for the brand architecture and developing the brand value chain. While architecting the brand strategy, it is important to understand that the preliminary definition of the brand equity is not the same for the firm named brands that have their own names. In case of firm owned brands, the brand becomes the principal spokesperson for the firm and often that works as the pivot of the brand architecture process in the domestic and internationally segmented markets.[7]

David Aaker[8] constructed an innovating framework for illustrating brand systems and characterized brand roles as drivers, endorsers and fighter brands and silver bullets. In pursuit of further improving the concept of brand architecture, the concept of brand portfolio strategies has been discussed. It is believed that the brand portfolio strategies will help in searching for the efficient frontier for the brand set, the boundary where brand managers can maximize their returns for any level of portfolio risk. However, the scope of brand portfolio does not restrict membership to the brands owned by the firm. The brand portfolio on the contrary, includes every brand that plays in the consumers' decision to buy. Such distinction is necessary to make in the brand architecture approach for overcoming any conflicts in defining the role and level of the brands. The categories of brands play significant role in the process of brand architecture for a firm in the following ways:

- Creating coherence and effectiveness
- Allowing brands to stretch across the products and markets
- To stimulate the purchase decisions by brand drivers, and
- Targeting market niches and benefit positioning

BRAND HIERARCHY

Sub-brands and *endorsed brands* can play a key role in creating coherent and effective brand architecture. The sub-brands and endorsed brands allow brands to stretch across products and markets, address conflicting brand strategy needs, conserve brand-building resources in part by leveraging existing brand equity, protect brands from being diluted by over- stretching, and signal that an offering is new and different. The brand relationship is related to the driver role that brands play. The driver role reflects the degree to which a brand drives the purchase decision and use experience. A branded house uses a single master brand to span a set of offerings that operate with only descriptive sub-brands. On the contrary, the house of brands strategy, in contrast, involves an independent set of stand-alone brands, each maximizing the impact on a market. The house of brands strategy, however, clearly positions brands on functional benefits and to dominate niche segments. Targeting niche markets with functional benefit positions is the main reason for using a house of brands strategy.

> After extensive research, it was determined that the Danone, a French brand captured the three best attributes. Danone is a French dairy company and leader in dairy products. Among many, the yogurt brand enjoyed brand equity in over 30 countries and contributed to one-quarter of the company's total revenue. The name also tied into company history in that

7 Keller, L Kevin: *Strategic Brand Management – Building, Measuring and Managing Brand Equity*, New Jersey: Prentice Hall, 2003, 409-411

8 David Aaker (1996). *Building Strong Brands*, New York, The Free Press

the dairy product was originally named after the founder's son, meaning Danny or "little Dan." (The brand is referred to as Dannon in the US.) It was decided that products in the portfolio that captured the trinity of values would carry a primary endorsement of the Danone name and the little boy visual mark, serving as a verbal and visual link between all of the product lines, the corporate brand and its associated values. In the case of Bledina, a natural baby food that is so well known in France, The name had become synonymous with "baby food," another strategy was devised. To leverage the brand and associate its "natural" equity with the corporate brand, a migration plan was put into place to slowly transfer the name to "Bledina by Danone" and then to "Danone Bledina," as it is currently known. Hence brand creation and brand endorsement are delicate strategies and need to be handled carefully by the brand managers.[9]

A *shadow endorser brand* is not connected visibly to the endorsed brand, but many consumers know about the link. This subcategory in the house of brands strategy provides some of the advantages of having a known organization backing the brand, while minimizing any association contamination. Brands are not visibly linked makes a statement about each brand, even when the link is discovered. It communicates that the organization realizes that the shadow-endorsed brand represents a totally different product and market segment. The principal attributes of he endorsed brands may be delineated as below:[10]

- It incorporates the shadow brands
- Generates indirect market impact with mother brands
- Represents distinct product and market segments, and
- Endorsed brands operate independently of the mother brands in the market

In the *house of brands strategy*, the brands are independent. Endorsed brands are still independent, but they are also endorsed by another brand, usually an organizational brand. An endorsement by an established brand provides credibility and substance to the offering and usually plays only a minor driver role. The token endorser is one of the variants of the endorser strategy. In this approach, usually a master brand is involved in several product-market contexts that are substantially less prominent than the endorsed brand. The token endorser can be indicated by a logo such as the GE light bulb. The role of the token endorser is to provide some reassurance and credibility while still allowing the endorsed brands' maximum freedom to create their own associations. Another endorsement variant is a linked brand name, where a name with common elements creates a family of brands with an implicit or implied endorser. McDonald's, for example, has McPotato. A linked name provides the benefits of a separate name without having to establish a second name from scratch and link it to a master brand. Sub-brands are brands connected to a mother brand and augment or modify the associations of that mother brand.

---

9 Alycia de Mesa (2004), Your product name: Fame or shame? *Brand Channel,* July 12. For details about the paper please see web site http://www.brandchannel.com/features effect.asp?pf id=218#more

10 Rajagopal and Sanchez R. (2004), Conceptual Analysis of Brand Architecture and Relations within Product Categories, *Journal of Brand Management,* 11 (3), pp 233-247

Mother brand is the primary frame of reference, which is stretched by sub-brands that add attribute associations, application associations, a signal of breakthrough newness and a brand personality. When both the mother brand and the sub-brand have major driver roles, it is considered a co-driver situation. The master brand is performing more than an endorser role-for example, customers are buying and using both Gillette and Match3; one does not markedly dominate the other. In a branded house strategy, a master brand moves from being a primary driver to a dominant driver role across a multiple offerings. The sub-brand goes from having a modest driver role to being a descriptor with little or no driver role. The shadow endorsement and strong endorsement of the brands have greater impact on various attributes of the constituents of the brand architecture.

At one end of the spectrum, international expansion and consumer needs for reassurance about product quality and reliability are resulting in a shift toward corporate endorsement of product brands. This helps to forge a global corporate identity for the firm and gathers its products under a global umbrella, thus generating potential cost savings through promotion of the global corporate brand rather than multiple independent product brands. At the same time, endorsement by the corporate brand provides reassurance for the customer of a reliable corporate image and enhances visibility. The advantages of the corporate endorsement of the product brands include:

- Building umbrella brands
- Establishing global corporate identity
- Developing customer confidence
- Monitoring key strategic brands, and
- Enhancing the brand value in the new segments.

Corporate endorsement of product level brands is increasingly used as a mechanism to integrate brand structure across country markets, providing a unifying element across product offerings. For example, Cadbury uses the Cadbury name on all its confectionery products, in conjunction with product brands such as *Dairy Milk*. Equally, a house brand is sometimes used on a product business worldwide. For example, Akzo Nobel places the Sikkens name on all its paint products. At the other end of the spectrum, rising media costs, coupled with the importance of building high visibility and the need to obtain cost economies, create pressures to extend strong brands across product lines and country borders. Increasingly, new products and variants are launched under existing brand names to take advantage of their strength and consumer awareness. Mars, for example, has launched an ice-cream line as well as a soft drink under the Mars brand name. Cadbury's Milk Tray brand has been extended to desserts, leveraging the brand's association with creaminess. Strong international brands often have high visibility and are prime candidates for brand extensions, especially for entry into new and emerging markets such as Eastern Europe or China. In some cases, a well-known brand name is used on a product line which is marketed under another brand name elsewhere. For example, Danone uses the Danone name to market biscuits in Eastern Europe, in order to leverage customer familiarity with the name. Similarly, Nestlé's Maggi brand, used on sauces and seasonings, had high recognition in Eastern Europe and so was extended to frozen foods rather than the Findus brand used elsewhere in Europe.[11]

Growing prevalence of corporate endorsement and brand extensions, coupled with a focus on building a limited number of strong brands in international markets, has led firms to develop procedures to manage and monitor key strategic brands. A key objective is to maintain their identity and value in international markets. Two important aspects need to be considered; (i) the consistency of brand positioning in different countries and across product lines, and (ii) the value and/or risks of brand extensions in international markets. Widely different approaches have been adopted for managing strategic brands in international markets and assigning custody for them. Typically these vary depending on the organizational structure of the firm and the desired degree of control, and range from having no explicit custody strategy to highly centralized tight control by corporate headquarters.

Firms with strong country management also operate in the product markets where brands are not important and purchase cues may have no explicit custody strategy. Attention is centered around trademark issues and their infringement in different markets. In cases where product markets are becoming more integrated and there is concern to improve brand harmonization across countries, specific brand positioning may be negotiated between corporate headquarters and country managers. This approach may, however, be somewhat cumbersome where there are multiple brands to manage. An approach that appears to be becoming increasingly popular is to appoint a brand champion. The brand champion is typically given responsibility for building and managing the brand worldwide. This includes monitoring the consistency of the brand positioning in international markets, as well as authorizing use of the brand on other products or other product businesses. The brand champion can either be a senior manager at corporate headquarters or a country manager or product development group. For example, a lead country or one with major market share for the brand can be given responsibility for the brand.

In examining consistency in brand positioning in the competitive market environment, often there is recognition that some adjustment to local market conditions will be needed, especially for mature brands. Typically, it is considered desirable that the core positioning should be maintained, though execution may vary. The extent to which some deviation is permitted typically varies considerably from firm to firm, and from one product business to another. The brand custodian is also often responsible for authorizing or providing an opinion on brand extensions. An important issue with brand extensions is to avoid over-extension or stretching of the brand and dilution of its equity and image. Criteria for sanctioning brand extensions vary considerably depending largely on the firm's organizational structure, the diversity of its product lines and businesses and management philosophy. Often, a proposed extension has to be consistent with the core brand's positioning and reinforce or sustain the existing brand concept. For example, extension of a confectionery brand to ice cream or dessert should emphasize the same core attributes. In many cases, proposed extensions of strategic brands are also required to have market potential. Procedures for resolving conflicts in relation to brand extensions also vary considerably depending on custody management principles and the firm's organizational structure.

11 Rajagopal (2006), Brand Architecture - Foundations and Frameworks, *Brand Strategy*, Vol. 206, 47-49

BRAND ARCHITECTURE PROCESS

A firm may choose to develop *brand as reference* at the first stage of brand architecture process as competitive pressures kindle differentiation of their goods from the other producers. The brands should be architected in the consumer space, working with the consumer and achieve differentiation primarily through changes in physical product attributes and augmented consumer perceptions on its use value. Consumers extended memory networks help consumers to use brand names based on their image of the brand though many consumers primarily value brands for their utilitarian value. Utilitarian values may be described as instrumental in making buying decisions because they enable consumers to reach higher levels of satisfaction derived from owning or using the object.

In the following stage marketers may labor to shape their *brand's personalities*. The personality idea responds to the tendency in contemporary society to value personal relationships. It also refers to the idea that relationships are important in social life. In terms of Maslow's hierarchy of needs, it tries to lift products to higher levels of need satisfaction, like belongingness, love and esteem. Brand personalities are created in different ways and with different tools. However, the creation always involves active communications on the side of the firm: the personality has to be disseminated to be alive. An example may be cited of the *Escudo* anti-bacterial soap, a Latin American brand of Procter & Gamble, which has been established by creating the personality of the caring mother; the firm has injected emotion into the consumer's learning and valuing process. The brand, through such personality appeal, pulls it closer to the consumer through an emotional bond (as caring the child), use *Escudo*. In the previous two stages, there was a distinction between the consumer and the brand. Incorporation of personal characteristics into the brand makes, it more appealing to consumers who are more likely to affiliate with brands possessing desirable personalities. While carving the brand personality a firm may try to keep the balance between the personalities of the consumer and the brand when they begin to merge and the value of the brand becomes self-expression. The cultural and ethnic values also influence the products and brands and establish their categorical preferences among the consumer segments. The companies may attempt to classify the users on the basis of brands *viz.,* the affluent drive Rolls Royce and the less affluent drive Fords. However, in a cross-cultural market environment confusion may result in buying behavior of consumers as goods may not be valued for the same reasons in other cultures. So, the values communicated by products and brands must be consistent within the group and the culture.

Subsequent to the association of an appealing personality to the brand, the firm may develop the *brand as icon* to hold as a top of the mind perception. At this stage of brand architecture, the brand may be conceived by the consumer endorsed by their self reference criterion and the firm may be confident of the brand being "owned by customers". An example may be cited of Marlboro cigarettes where the rugged cowboy representing a man standing against odds is a symbol or a brand icon enveloped with a set of values. Similarly, Nike shoes and sports apparel have primary associations with Michael Jordan's athletic prowess and secondary associations with the Chicago Bulls and winning that place the brand as icon. Hence, more associations a brand has, greater becomes its network in the consumer's brand recall process and management of such brands strengthen the iconic stature of the brands of the firm. There are many stages ahead in architecting a successful brand which are exhibited in Figure 3.5 as process control.

In the fourth stage brand may be described as synonym to the firm and it is a complex stage to run thorough wherein, *brand equals the company* as all stakeholders may also perceive the brand (as a constituent of the firm) in the same fashion. The firm must be integrated communications throughout all of their operations. However, communication may not be unidirectional as it flows from the consumer to the firm as well as from the firm to the consumer so that a dialogue is established between the two. The delivery of Ford cars seeking collaborative customization in the process, wherein customers involve in designing the interior of the cars may be an appropriate example wherein customer identifies the brand as a company. Such interaction strengthens the relationship that consumers feel with the firm. A brand is said to have positive (or negative) customer-based brand equity when consumers react more (or less) favorably to marketing mix activity for the brand, as compared to when the same marketing activity is attributed to a hypothetical or unnamed version of the product or service. Consumer response to marketing activity for competitive brands or an

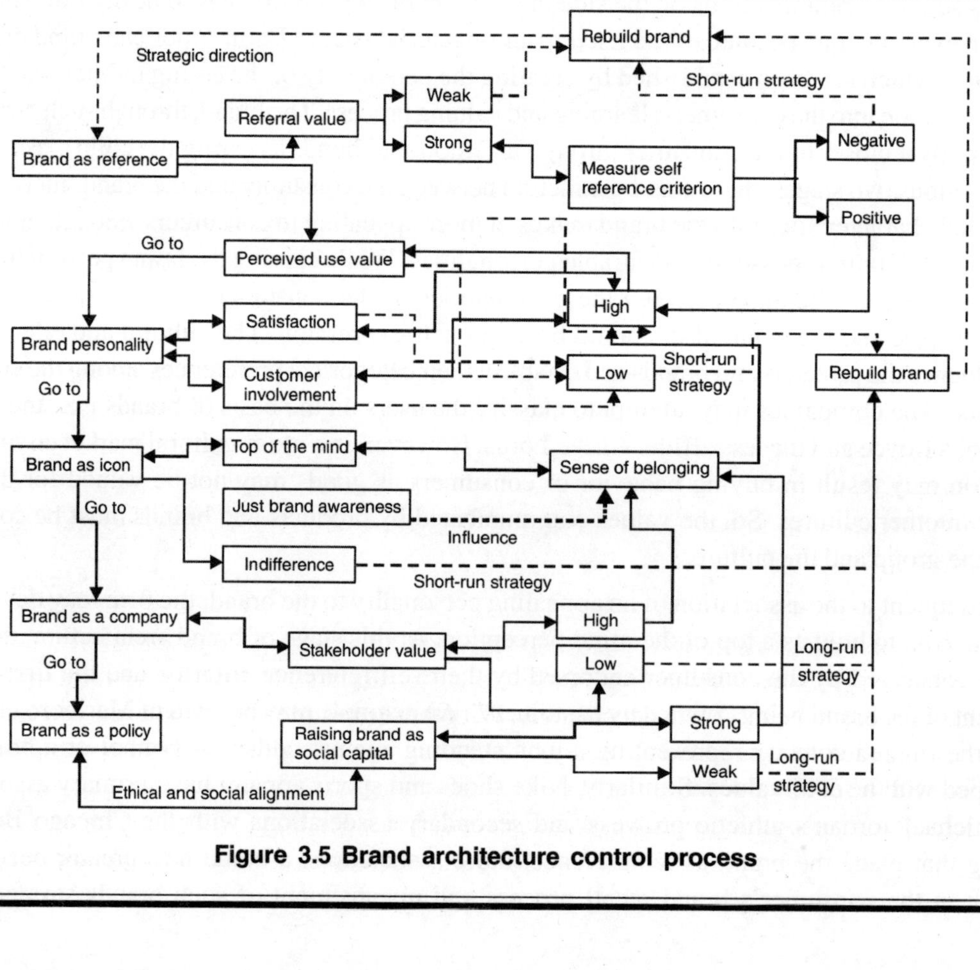

Figure 3.5 Brand architecture control process

alternatively named version of the product or service can also be useful benchmarks (i.e., for determining the uniqueness of brand associations and the opportunity cost of brand extensions, respectively).

Few firms reach the stage five of the brand architecture, which is distinguished by an alignment of firm with ethical, social and political causes. Before moving into this stage, firms have to consider both the risks and their credibility of brand as company. New brands can enter the market at any stage of development so long as other brands have laid groundwork of consumer understanding to support the understanding of the new brand. The brand image at the end of the evolutionary process is similar to Kapferer's conceptual model of the brand. He indicates that brands have a physique, personality, culture, relationship, reflection and consumer's self image. It is necessary for the managers of a firm to know that no brand can incorporate all of these facets without having traveled through the six stages.

BRAND ARCHITECTURE AUDIT

Brand architecture is not a static framework, but one that needs to be monitored and modified continually. The mechanisms established for brand custody help insure that an individual brand is managed in a consistent fashion across multiple countries. However, given the dynamic nature of international markets and the changing competitive realities, the structure must be reviewed, at least annually. A brand architecture audit should be performed to ensure compliance with established procedures and to determine, whether the structure of the architecture should be changed. This needs to take place on two levels. First, the degree to which individual strategic brands have adhered to established guidelines needs to be assessed. Second, the entire portfolio of brands has to be examined in terms of whether the overall brand architecture requires modification.

Compliance audit may be defined as a bottoms-up audit of the individual brands that allows an assessment of how well each functions as part of the overall brand architecture of the firm. The key steps of this phase are:

- Collection of information that establishes how the brand has been used in each country where it is marketed
- Assessment of deviations from its established position in the structure and reasons, and
- Evaluation of the brand's performance.

Deviations are particularly diagnostic. They may suggest poor management of the brand globally or, more importantly, fundamental changes in the underlying market dynamics. If the underlying market dynamics or product market structure has changed, then the brand's position in the overall architecture needs to be modified accordingly. With these preliminaries conducted, the audit should culminate in a face-to-face meeting of key participants, including the brand custodian, to establish guidelines for the coming year.

Strategic audit begins in the second phase as the top down audit conducted on multiple levels. First, logical groupings of strategic brands need to be assessed in terms of their compliance with established guidelines. Once this has been accomplished, senior management needs to evaluate the overall structure of international brand architecture to determine the fit at different levels across multiple countries. Again, a key factor here, is how the underlying drivers of brand architecture have changed. In addition to market dynamics and the product market structure, an important consideration is how the firm itself has evolved, particularly with respect to acquisitions or market expansion initiatives. If the end-result of the strategic audit is that the firm's brand architecture no longer fits underlying drivers, steps should be taken to revise the firm's architecture so that it reflects the new realities of the marketplace.

Product markets continue to change rapidly. Craig and Douglas evolved that as markets evolve, firms need to consider how to modify their brand architecture and look for opportunities to reduce the number of brands and improve efficiency as well as to harmonize brand strategy across product lines and country markets. Focus on a limited number of strategic brands in international markets enables the firm to consolidate and strengthen its position and enhance brand power. Effective management of international brand architecture in the light of changing market conditions and the firm's market expansion is, however, crucial to maintaining its position and strengthening key strategic brands in international markets.

Brand architecture should incorporate the entire firm's existing brands, whether developed internally or acquired. It should provide a framework for consolidation in order to reduce the number of brands and strengthen the role of individual brands. Brands that are acquired need to be merged into the existing structure, especially where these brands occupy similar market positions to those of existing brands. Equally, when the same or similar products are sold under different brand names or have different positioning in each market, ways to harmonize these should be examined. Another important element of brand architecture is its consistency relative to the number and diversity of products and product lines within the company. A balance needs to be struck between the extent to which brand names serve to differentiate product lines, or alternatively, establish a common identity across different products. Establishment of strong and distinctive brand images for different product lines helps to establish their separate identities and diversify risk of negative associations (for example between food and chemicals). Conversely, use of a common brand name consolidates effort and can produce synergies.

Value of corporate brand endorsement across different products and product lines, and at lower levels of the brand hierarchy also needs to be assessed. Use of corporate brand endorsement either as a name identifier or logo identifies the product with the company, and provides reassurance for the customer. In international markets, corporate brand endorsement acts an integrative force unifying different brand identities across national boundaries. At the same time, corporate endorsement of a highly diverse range of product lines can result in dilution of image. Equally, negative effects or associations can harm and have long-lasting effects across multiple product lines. Thus, both aspects need to be weighed in determining the role of corporate brand endorsement in brand architecture.

It may be stated that the brand endorsement with strong and associated name would be helpful in the market penetration for the new brands and extended brands. The presence of the co-drivers would also provide an added impact on the endorsed brands where competition is intensive. The independent brands may be able to make high impact in the niche market by putting inordinate stress on the attributes and application advantages over the closely competing brands. The conceptual synthesis of work on the dynamics of business relationships and the dynamics of brand relationships, with particular attention to new business environments, an area that is becoming more significant with the increasing importance of the Internet as a medium for business and have proposed a taxonomy for a better understanding of the relationships and linkages between brands. It will be of critical importance for future researchers and practitioners to understand the increasingly complex variety of factors underlying and influencing the linkages between brands. Future work will concentrate on the operational implications of the taxonomy proposed here. The research on assessing the brand personality is suggested by using the brand rating method to get quantitative measures. The manufacturing companies may have to exercise several options on brand sponsorship. The product may be launched in the market as the brand of manufacturer which is also known as national brand, a distributor brand as happens in case of edible oils, sugar, processed grains and in many products which needs re-packing, or licensed brand name.

BRAND DRIVERS

Brand personality refers to the emotional side of a brand image. It is created by all experiences of consumers with a brand, but advertising plays a dominant role in personality creation. Successful brands eventually have the opportunity to take on brand leadership positions. This is often expressed in advertising as a product superiority driver; and it works as consumers often prefer the market leader because they assume, it is *better*. Strong brand positions can be built on anything enduring, including images or simply *the biggest selling*. The message must be presented consistently in all marketing initiatives. There are two central elements to brand personalities: the type of benefits offered by the brand and the type of consumer who will value them. Advertisements which show nothing but product features trying to appeal to consumers rationally. Usually the focus would be the unique sales proposition (USP) or a selling idea which can differentiate the brand from its competitors. It has been observed that the consumers will come up with the descriptions like "fun-loving, enjoyable, American style" while people will think of "rebellious and younger generation oriented" when talking about the product. Furthermore, everyone wants something that can reflect or further improve his/her self-portrayal; brand personality which is created and perceived through advertising becomes a vital concern in our purchasing decisions. Advertising builds the emotional image of the brand and the brand personality associated, thereof provides depth, feelings and liking to the relationship. A brand personality thus can make a brand more interesting and memorable and become a vehicle to express a customer's identity. In view of the above discussion, it may be delineated that advertisements or market communications help building the brand personality of the product when consumer correlates the human qualities to the products that is advertised.

REACH OF THE BRAND

"Voice of a Brand" is part of the promise and experience of a brand. Customers hear the voice in automated service systems, at retail, in the media and elsewhere. The tone, content and nuances of that voice are critical. The meaning or user understanding on the product is also an important source of brand personality creation in the advertisement or any type of media communication. The communication represents the product's meanings - the claimed image of the product. Although the definition of advertising from a semiotic perspective states that the advertisement represents the actual product image, the advertisement represents the product only when there is harmony between the actual and the claimed image of the product. The spokesman or anchor in advertising provides the most direct way to build this relationship with consumers and bridge the brand and the mind of the consumer. This is the consumer-brand fusion process that leads to the brand behavior in the market in the short and long-run dynamics. The key function of advertising is to communicate the brand and the promise that can be delivered to the customers. The advertisement of a product has two dimensions- representing the core promise of the product and creating the consumer personality by transferring the personality traits. This process enhances the customer-brand relationship. Personification of brand through advertisement or market communication is actualized when there is match between the personality of the advertised product and of the customer.

A consumer-brand relationship becomes functional after the purchase is realized by the customer on an appropriate opportunity. The opportunity may be derived through the marketing constituents like availability, financial schemes for the buying and pre- and post-sales services. There are models that follow the same line of reasoning, that there is input, transformation, and output in the model. The input of the model refers to the advertising exposure, transformation refers to adverting processing, and output refers to advertising responses. Branding has to do with customer perceptions and their behaviors when buying; it is not a characteristic of a product, a graphic design, a company or a category. In branding the term 'media' refers to communication vehicles such as newspapers, magazines, radio, television, billboards and direct mail. Advertisers' use media to convey commercial messages to their target audiences, and the media depend to different degrees on advertising revenues to cover the cost of their operations. It has been observed that effective consumer-brand relationship can be established after the buyer realizes the purchase and simultaneously transfers the brand personality.

COMMUNICATION SENSITIVITY AND BRAND PERSONALITY

Brand-extension strategy in a competitive environment is comprises of two crucial strategic decisions: (i) *against which competitive brand* to position the new product, and (ii) *how to position* the new product. Hauser and Shugan (1983) discuss that the first decision that envisages the competitive-target decision requires an understanding of the competitive structure and an analysis of the opportunities and threats associated with selecting a certain position and the latter is concerned with the selection of product attributes or benefits that provide a differential advantage for the new product compared to the competitive offerings.[12] The positive advertising and communication help in building and nurturing the brand personality in the competitive situation in a market. The intimacy theory of communication builds the brand personality more effectively across varied consumer

12 Hausor John R. and Steven M. Shugan (1983) Defensive Marketing Strategy, *Marketing Science*, 27 (2), January, 319-360

situations than exchange or seduction theory. Drawing from psychology and social psychology, it presents intimacy attributes relevant to services marketing - the "five C's of communication, caring, commitment, comfort, and conflict resolution, which play a vital role in brand personality. The concept of sensitivity of communication maybe described as the brand personality is perceived by the consumers, when the advertisement is positive to their own personality and endorses the intimacy attributes with the communication.

Consumers expect to gain something from engaging in Word-Of Mouth (WOM) or that they indirectly satisfy a desire when providing personal opinion to others through WOM, regardless of the root of the motivation. Incentive programs may therefore work as an extrinsic motivator, and people may engage in more WOM behaviors when incentives are delivered, and this motivation may increase as the incentive increases. There is a positive relationship between the size of the brand and promise offered therein, and a consumer's likelihood to generate WOM. The development of message strategy is linked with an advertiser and media factor. It depends on what an advertiser needs and how the message for advertising can be carried on to the media effectively. A compromise to these factors would help in developing the most effective message idea, as a result of facts judged about products, markets, consumers and competitors. In this process, the strength of background information is the foundation of building message ideas. It has been argued that cognition and effect influence each other, and consequently can be seen as two components of one system. The underlying idea is that thoughts are not free of feelings and vice versa. Thus, advertising processing and response are a combination of both cognition and affect. Consumers use both their cognitive and affective systems to process advertising, and advertising responses can be both cognitive and affective.

COGNITIVE DIMENSIONS IN BRANDING

Cognition and emotion form a complex and inseparable relationship within higher-order human cognitive behavior. Higher-order image processing exists in emotions. In the central route of the elaboration likelihood model, emotions play a substantial role in understanding product features. From this perspective, understanding process of the advertisements may be considered as a higher order cognitive learning process on brands which includes not only reasonable understanding of functional benefit, but also an understanding of benefit based on user and usage imagery and brand personality. The processing of advertising comprises the sequence of cognitive variables and does not give importance to the constituents of it. Both impact on the consumer's attitude and behavior and the level of this impact do not depend on the order of the advertising processes. However, in case of advertising campaigns with multiple and different messages, the order effects may be important. Van Osselaer & Alba (2000) discuss that though the companies have full discretion in designing campaigns, it is all the more interesting to see if it makes a difference whether they start building brand personality by appealing to affective or cognitive reactions.[13] Therefore, the brand personality is influenced largely by the affective and cognitive attributes in the process of the advertising communication.

13 Van Osselaer Stijn M J and Alba Joseph W (2000) Consumer Learning and Brand Equity, *Journal of Consumer Research*, 27, June, 1-16

Cognitive response theory can be easily applied to marketing and advertising because it provides many important insights about persuasion variables and further more attempts to make predictions about variables such as distraction, repetition and issue involvement. Advertisers want the cognitive response that triggers something in the consumer's brain that gives them a favorable attitude about whatever is being advertised. One major reason cognitive responses are important to advertising is distracters. A distracter is a variable that inhibits the generation of cognitive responses. There are certain characteristics of the *stimulus* that *itself* may enhance or hamper the elaboration of the message. A second category of factors consists of the characteristics of the *individual* and finally the *situational factors* may be important. Several types of situational factors can be discerned. The environment of the subject at the time of exposure may influence message elaboration. Advertisements and point of purchase communications are frequently combined into clusters of messages, such as a commercial block on television, radio, or in a movie theatre. The *media context* can be an important situational factor. Media context is defined here as the characteristics of the content of the medium in which an ad is inserted as they are perceived by the individuals who are exposed to it. Media context is important. A message style that contrasts with the nature of the context may lead to positive advertising effects. This phenomenon may be explained by Meyers-Levy and Tybout (1997) as the *contrast effect* which explains that the novelty of advertising and the unexpectedness of the information given in its context often lead to increased attention, because the advertisements is perceived as innovative and interesting14. It has been observed that for the individuals with low product category involvement, advertising messages shown in a congruent media will lead to more positive attitudes towards the advertisement. The customers will tend to do more content analysis thereof and exercise the brand recall messages in reference to the communications that suite and vis-à-vis for the customer having high product category involvement. The comprehension to the customer on the brand and his response on the brand knowledge influence the creation of brand personality through marketing communications either by advertising or inter-personal communications such as word-of-mouth.

BRAND PORTFOLIO AND ADVERTISING

It is believed that the brand portfolio strategies will help in searching for the efficient frontier for the brand set - the boundary where brand managers can maximize their returns for any level of portfolio risk. However the scope of brand portfolio does not restrict membership to the brands owned by the company. The brand portfolio on the contrary, includes every brand that plays in the consumers' decision to buy. Brand portfolios connect the nature and identity of individual brands with the market categories they serve. These issues provide a company with the basis for building effective customer response, profitable growth involving market categories, and in some cases, for business innovation. Making a brand more valuable is a key business objective. However, this objective must be driven by more than marketing integration and commitment to the promise of brand experience. The competitive environment of the given company is characterized not only by interactions among different

14 Meyers-Levy and Tybout A. (1997). Context Effects at Encoding and Judgment in Compensation Setting: The Role of Cognitive Resources, *Journal of Consumer Research*, 24, June 1-14

companies within a given industry, but also by interactions among different brands produced by a single company. It is necessary to review the firm's advertising decisions under conditions of random and customer segment specific sales response to advertising within the context of multi-brand competition in order to diagnose the impact of advertising on the brand and customer portfolios thereof. Hence, the brand portfolio of a company is developed over the competing effective marketing communication as it influences the growth of sales and consumer decision in favour of the brands that are advertised close to the congruent media.

SELECTED READINGS

Aaker D. (1996). *Building Strong Brands*, New York, The Free Press

Baldinger A. and Robinson J. (1996). Brand Loyalty : The Link Between Attitude and Behaviour, *Journal of Advertising Research*, 36 (6), 22-35

Batra R. Lehmann D. and Singh D. (1993). The Brand Personality Component of Brand Goodwill : Some Antecedents and Consequences, in Aaker & Bie : *Brand Equity and Advertising : Advertising's Role in Building Strong Brands*, Hillsdale : Lawrence Erlbaum Associate Publishers, 83-95

Berry L. L. (2000). Cultivating Service Brand Equity, *Journal of the Academy of Marketing Science*, 28 (1), 79-83

Blackston M. (1992). Observations: Building Brand Equity by Managing the Brand's Relationship, *Journal of Advertising Research*, 32 (3), 79-83

Brassington F. and Pettitt S. (2001). *Principles of Marketing*, 3rd Edition, Pearson Education, Prentice Hall

Duncan T. and Moriarty S E (1998). A Communication Based Marketing Model for Managing Relationships, *Journal of Marketing*, 62, 1-13

Erdogan Z. and Baker M. (2000). Celebrity Endorsement: Advertising Agency Manager's Perspective, *The Cyber Journal of Sport Marketing*, 13, December, 1-15 (www.cjsm.com)

Fournier Susan (1998). Consumers and Their Brands: Developing Relationship Theory in Consumer Research, *Journal of Consumer Research*, 24 (March), 343-73

Hausor John R and Steven M. Shugan (1983). Defensive Marketing Strategy, *Marketing Science*, 27 (2), January, 319-360

Hill Sam and Lederer Chris (2001). *The Infinite Asset - Managing Brands to Build New Value*, Harvard Business School Press, Boston, 6-9

Jennifer L. Aaker (1997). Dimensions of Brand personality, *Journal of Marketing Research*, 34, August, 347-356

Meyers-Levy and Tybout A. (1997). Context Effects at Encoding and Judgment in Compensation Setting: The Role of Cognitive Resources, *Journal of Consumer Research*, 24, June 1-14

Redenbach A (2000). A Multiple Product Endorser Can be a Credible Source, *The Cyber Journal of Sport Marketing*, 13, December , 1-10

Tauber, Edward M.: Brand Leverage (1998). Strategy for Growth in a Cost-control World, *Journal of Advertising Research*, August-September

Van Osselaer Stijn M. J. and Alba Joseph W. (2000). Consumer Learning and Brand Equity, *Journal of Consumer Research*, 27, June, 1-16

Case 3.1

BMW: BUILDING BRAND THROUGH RELATIONSHIP NETWORKING[15]

"...Every automaker is critically involved with design. One of the ways we differentiate ourselves is through our different styling strategies. We are looking into the future, while we continue to be inspired by the great auto styles of the past..."

Hendrik von Kuenheim, President and CEO, BMW Group Canada

Quest for ensuring consumer satisfaction has been widely held as the key to corporate success. In the case of services, organizations must understand what their customers want because most services involve inter-person contacts, requiring greater, if not special, care and attention. While most firms are keen to provide good service, many do not know how to manage customer expectations effectively because of the inherently intangible nature that makes it difficult to define service quality.[16] Generally, a higher level of service quality is expected to lead to customer satisfaction and eventually to better customer loyalty and higher profits. It is intuitive that rendering quality in service means "satisfying customer's requirements" and firms that aspire to adopt this customer-oriented approach should identify and incorporate the customer requirements into the service design and capabilities. The focus should be on people and performance such that both customer loyalty and customer value are achieved. It is well known that customers judge actual quality according to their expectations.[17] This is best served by implementing all the essential service attributes that are capable of meeting, if not exceeding the expectations. BMW is embarking on a relationship marketing program to develop long-term ties with consumers by introducing a direct marketing template than can be rolled out across its range. Beginning in 1928 with the first BMW car, the company initiated mailing the product information to the prospective customers. The pack is intended to drive enquiries to the BMW Information Service free phone number, web site or customer's local dealer for more information or a request for a test drive.

Marketing communications is a creative subject and involves a range of marketing communications exchanges in cuboids of manufacturer, dealers and customers (existing and potential). The customers also engage in interpersonal exchange of opinions through the word-of mouth communication and

15 *This case has been written as the basis for class discussion rather than to illustrate either effective or ineffective handling of an administrative situation of the company.*
Author acknowledges the academic contribution of Mr Berezowsky Fernando Ms. Camacho Carolina and Cisneros Norma students of the course on markets and clients of Graduate Program 2002.

16 Hanser J.R. and Semister D.I. : Customer Satisfaction Incentives, *Marketing Science,* 13(4), Fall, 1994, pp 327 - 350

17 Peters VI : Total Service Quality Management, *Managing Service Quality,* 9 (1), 1999, pp 6-12

each group can provide communication feedback to every other group, especially through the marketing research and customer relationship activities of the company. Effective communication /promotion involve a number of activities. These include identifying the target audience and its characteristics such as individuals, groups, families, and businesses, and their socioeconomic profiles, personality, perceptions of risk, and stages in the buying process, etc. This is better understood in terms of buying roles within a household or family. These roles are typically: initiator someone who first suggests the idea of buying a particular good or service; influencer(s) - those who have implicit or explicit influence from within or outside the household; decider(s) - a person who decides on any component of a buying decision in relation to whether to buy, what to buy, what from, when, and how to pay; purchaser - the automobile purchasing agent or the prospect who goes into a shop; and user(s) - those who use or consume the product or service. Consumer buyer behavior is concerned with the process of buying and consuming goods and services. One can also consider consumer shopping behavior, i.e., visiting the retail shopping environment, which is characterized by various personal and social motives. Personal motives include: role playing, diversion, self-gratification, learning about new trends, physical activities and sensory stimulation. Social motives include social experience outside the home, communication with others having a similar interest, peer group attraction, status and authority, and pleasure of bargaining.

CUSTOMER PROSPECTING AND RETAINING TRENDS

Servicing products is an increasingly important part of the business. Manufacturers of everything from elevators and freezers to security systems and transportation equipment—products built to last—find that revenues from after-sales product installation, configuration, maintenance, and repairs are 30 percent or more of their total revenues, and the proportion is increasing. Some raise prices to achieve a quick boost in earnings without understanding the competitive implications and then watch as profits fall. Others introduce new offerings but fail to tailor the service-delivery model, only to see costs escalate and margins shrink. Part of the problem is that a services business is too often regarded as the poor stepchild of the core product group, so service managers aren't given the resources to develop the right systems, tools, and incentives to maximize returns. However, a handful of companies are now capturing tremendous value from their services businesses by taking a more careful, fact-based approach to designing and pricing services and by making the task a priority of senior management. The BMW is one among them in the automobile sector. Customers are segmented according to their service needs rather than their size, industry, or type of equipment. These companies then develop the pricing, contracting, and monitoring capabilities to support the cost-effective delivery of the services. When customers are segmented according to what they need—and not just industry or size—they tend to fall into one of at least three common categories. The "risk avoiders" are looking for coverage to avoid big bills but care less about other elements, such as response times. The "basic-needs customers" want a standard level of service with basic inspections and periodic maintenance. And the "hand-holders" need high levels of service, often with quick and reliable response times, and are willing to pay for the privilege. Customers that want maximum flexibility and a low financial commitment usually prefer time-and-materials billing: the company typically performs work as needed and charges an hourly rate for labor and a mark-up on parts and materials. While charges for time and-materials service are usually higher because service providers have no guarantee of consistent repeat business, local service competitors with lower overhead and labor costs usually exert some downward price pressure. With this type of package, service providers have little incentive to pursue productivity improvements that could lead to cost savings in the long run.

Customers that need greater predictability tend to demand full-coverage service contracts that work like extended warranties: they provide specific maintenance and repair services over a specified period, typically ranging from one to five years, for a specified price. For the service provider, this can be the most profitable pricing model, but it can also be the riskiest, especially, if it involves servicing a competitor's products. Not knowing the repair history and unique service requirements of equipment can cause costs to spiral upward. The age and condition of equipment matter a lot. In one case, the cost of servicing a seven-year-old supermarket refrigeration system was 30 percent more than the cost of servicing a three-year-old system. Several of the company's sales reps didn't consider the importance of the equipment's age and priced both service contracts at the same level. The companies that handle services most successfully have developed terms-and-conditions packages that share risk with the customer: clauses cover co-payments to reduce nuisance calls, deductibles on major repairs, and limits on covered consumables, such as fluids and batteries. Finally, every contract, wherever possible should include terms for automatic renewals, automatic annual price increases, and higher labor rates for overtime repairs.

BMW, Honda, and Toyota, among other companies, begin with a strong brand that imparts sales momentum to each model. Brands that are weak—because their products have acquired a reputation for shoddy workmanship, their designs are not evocative, or their models bear little relationship to one another—cannot pursue this top-down approach. But a company stands a good chance of selling more cars and, step by step, of rehabilitating the brand, if managers take pains to match each model to the consumer segments most likely to be interested in it, identify and overcome the obstacles that keep browsers from becoming purchasers, and emphasize both the functional and the process and relationship benefits of the model in question. BMW Direct is an initiative of BMW (GB) to help selected company car fleet buyers streamline their service for employees. BMW Direct is a web based, fully personalized, car configuration and ordering system for the purchase of new BMWs. This highly efficient rules based web application delivers a level of information previously unavailable outside of a showroom. The BMW Direct solution provides users with the ability to view details on all eligible cars online and then go on to configure them against a full menu of accessories. BMW Direct is truly 'CRM' compliant, providing two-way communication via automated alerts and e-mails and incorporating a Contact Centre to ensure immediate access to trained product advisors. Users can track online the status of their individual orders whether by web, phone, fax or email. The call centre functionality includes phone and e-campaign generation, customer enquiry handling and profiling to customised promotions. Post-sales support is delivered using a thin client solution, (using Citrix) to BMWs contact centre in Croydon and order management centre in Bracknell in UK.

BMW MILESTONES (1916-2001)

Bayerische Flugzeugwerke (BFW) is founded on 7th March 1916 and incorporates Otto-Werke. BMW acquires the BFW plant in 1922, but Bayerische Motoren Werke continues to date its foundation from the founding of BFW. Even its very first product, the aircraft engine IIIa, bore the stamp of innovation in 1917. Head engineer Max Friz constructed a high-altitude carburettor which allowed the air fuel mixture to adapt itself to its external surroundings. This counteracts the engine's impaired performance in thin air at high altitudes and gives it an edge over its competition. On 21st July, 1917, Rapp-Motorenwerke is renamed Bayerische Motoren Werke GmbH. The ongoing war means that the small company grows quickly. With expansion in mind, the firm builds a spacious plant right next to the Oberwiesenfeld airfield in Munich and continues to build engines for army planes until 1918. In 1918, BMW starts producing engines for use on and off road, including the first M 2 B 15 flat boxer engine. The neighbouring aircraft manufacturer, Bayerische Flugzeug-Werke, develops the "Flink", a light single-cylinder motorcycle, and the more powerful Helios with a longitudinal BMW engine. After relocating to the premises of Bayerische Flugzeug-Werke in 1922, BMW starts to redesign the motor bicycles. Its long experience with aircraft engines means the BMW AG foundry has an exceptional reputation at the start of the Twenties. Unsurpassed expertise in the field of light alloys is the key to the success of the R 37 and R 39 engines, the first standard-production engines with aluminum cylinder heads. Following on from the BMW 132 and the Bramo engines, series production of the BMW 801 aircraft engine starts in 1940. By the end of the war, over 20,000 of these 14-cylinder double radial engines will have been built in Munich, Allach, Berlin and Dürrerhof, all of which are fitted with a type of mechanical computer for automatic tuning.

BMW enters in the automobile manufacturing in 1951. A spacious sedan to match the highest expectations, the curvy, full-bodied design of the BMW 501 earns it the nickname of "Baroque angel". With the Eisenach plant now under Soviet control, it is also the first BMW automobile to be built completely in Munich. From 1954 onwards, it is joined by the 502, which possesses the world's first V8 light-alloy engine. The company designed in less than a year during 1956 the BMW 507, a very exclusive sports car: only a total of 252 are built. Most of the work is carried out by hand, customized to meet each buyer's wishes. Its timeless good looks, with a sleek silhouette, supple curves and expansive bonnet, guarantee that it remains the embodiment of the dream car to this day. In 1965, the preliminary contract of purchase for the Allach plant, concluded five years earlier by MAN, comes into effect and BMW Triebwerkbau GmbH is passed over to its new owner. BMW withdraws from jet engine construction for 25 years, focusing instead on car and motorcycle production. 1975 was the year of start for the manufacture of new series of luxury cars. Only a few 3 series models are initially launched, but over time the number grows to around thirty - from the 316g to the M3. The 3 Series is a global success - about seven million cars are sold worldwide over the coming twenty-five years. Each one combines compactness with exceptional handling and can, if desired, deliver power that is second to none.

1978 sees the launch of the R 45 and R 65 for first-time riders, with the R 100 RT topping off the BMW program. In 1980, the launch of the R 80 G/S is a global premiere for heavy touring endures. The BMW Monolever, a single swing-arm rear fork, causes a sensation. In 1981, a heavy-duty R 80 G/S wins the Paris - Dakar Rally, the most demanding race in the world. In 1985, the BMW K 75 is launched: a three-cylinder motorcycle with a horizontal 750 cc water-cooled engine. It bridges the gap between traditional two-cylinder boxers and the new four-cylinder engines. Around the world, these reliable three-cylinder models are the vehicle of choice for police authorities. A BMW off-road vehicle with four wheel drive existed as early as 1939, but the 325iX goes into production in 1985 as BMW's first four wheel drive automobile. The 5 Series follows this example soon after with the 525iX sedan and touring, establishing BMW in yet another market niche. The BMW X5 marks the initial high point of BMW's impressive four wheel drive creations. In the same year BMW Technik GmbH is founded as a think tank, free from the strictures of standard production. Independent of the company's day-to-day business, top BMW designers, engineers and technicians work here on new plans and ideas for the BMW vehicles of tomorrow. One of the first important projects BMW Technik GmbH embarks on is the Z1 roadster: small-scale production starts in 1988.

In the mid-1990s, BMW and Rolls-Royce plc set up the joint company BMW Rolls-Royce GmbH (BRR). Headquartered in Oberursel, this company soon employs a staff of 1,000 to work on gas turbines and aircraft engine components. BRR starts development work on a new generation of engines for short-haul aircraft. A car as suave as literature's smoothest spy - this is how cinema-goers are first introduced to the BMW Z3 in 1995. The classic principles of the two-seater roadster fuse with avant-garde sports car design, the ultimate in driving pleasure and a complete range of safety features. It is an irresistible combination: the Z3 becomes an international by-word for BMW's commitment to the art of car making. The BMW 5 Series is the first mass-produced car in the world to have a light alloy chassis. Front axle, multi-link integral rear suspension and brake calipers are all made of aluminum. Not only does it reduce weight, this material also offers the advantage of reduced unsuspended mass, another thing that leads to greater safety and improved driving comfort.

Keeping up with the new millennium, BMW is the first manufacturer to develop a navigation system exclusively for motorcycles, fitting it into the K 1200 LT. Twelve years after the first motorcycle ABS, BMW retains its lead in motorcycle safety standards with its latest innovation, the new integral braking system. The Z8 is a roadster for connoisseurs: its unitary aluminium spaceframe, high-performance V8 engine and brilliant design serve to make this homage to the BMW 507 a firm favourite without further ado. Capable of going from 0 to 100 km/h in less than just five seconds, the Z8 quickly assumes pole position in the top-of-the-range sports car market in the year 2000. In following year 2001 BMW chairman of the board, Prof. Joachim Milberg, officially opens the new Hams Hall engine plant near Birmingham. Considered to be one of the most modern in the world, the production unit is capable of building up to 400,000 four-cylinder engines a year.

MARKET PERFORMANCE OF BMW-2003

BMW Group continued its development during the first quarter 2003 amidst a difficult global economic and political climate. The focal point was the implementation of the product and market offensive which significantly affects the earnings of the Automobiles segment. The sales performance in the first quarter 2003 was marked by the effects of the product cycle of a number of BMW brand models. A total of 261,573 BMW, MINI and Rolls-Royce brand cars were sold during the quarter, 0.4% more than in the first quarter 2002. Total group revenues for the first quarter 2003 amounted to Euro 10,272 million, 4.6% below the record revenues recorded in the first quarter of the previous year. The profit from ordinary activities for the first quarter 2003 fell by 17.9% to Euro 830 million in line with expectations of the BMW Group. The decrease was attributable mainly to the continued high level of expenditure for the product, and market offensive and to the lower sales volume due to the current status of the product cycle of certain BMW models. The net profit of the BMW Group for the first quarter 2003 decreased by 19.3% to euro 510 million. The workforce increased to 102,637 employees at 31 March, 2003, 4.6% more than at the end of the first quarter 2002. The comparable number of employees at the end of the first quarter 2002 after adjusting for disposals and transfers of group companies was 97,905, so that the increase at 31 March, 2003 on a comparable basis was 4.8%.

As forecast, the number of BMW brand cars sold upto March 2003 fell by 7.3 %to 215,767 units (first quarter 2002:232,771 units).This was mainly attributable to the forthcoming BMW 5 series model change and model revisions of some BMW 3 Series versions. These changes resulted, as expected, in a volume decrease in advance of the new launches. Based on forecasts, the fall in sales volume during the first quarter will be more than compensated during the remainder of the year as a result of the launch of the new models. 139,053 BMW 3 Series vehicles were delivered to customers during the first quarter 2003,5.0 %less than in the equivalent period last year. The BMW 3 Series Limousine (73,936 units,+1.6 %) and the BMW 3 Series Touring (21,538 units,+1.3 %)both recorded slight growth. Sales of the BMW 3 Series Compact (–18.9%),the BMW 3 Series Coupé (–18.0%) and the BMW 3 Series Cabrio (–12.8%), however, all fell by comparison to the first quarter 2002.This development, in advance of the European launch of the revised versions in March 2003, was in line with forecasts. Sales of the BMW Z4,introduced in North America in autumn 2002,continued to perform well. During the first three months of 2003,a total of 6,331 Z4 Roadsters were sold. The BMW Z4 has also been available in Europe since the end of March 2003. The current BMW 5 Series is nearing the end of its product cycle. During the first three months of 2003,a total of 34,476 BMW 5 Series cars were delivered to customers, 25.1%less than in the same period last year and due to the product cycle of this model. The new 5 Series Limousine will be launched in July 2003 in line with plan. Sales of the BMW 7 Series also performed very well. The sales volume during the first quarter 2003 was 12,695 units, an increase of 10.8 % compared to the same period in 2002. Sales of the BMW X5 during the first quarter 2003 fell slightly.21,857 vehicles were sold, 4.7 %lower than the high volume recorded in the first quarter 2002. Since sales of this model were above expectations towards the end of 2002, the number of vehicles in inventories and transit fell sharply. Normal levels have now been built up again during the first quarter 2003. Production of the exclusive BMW Z8 will cease in June 2003. A total of 205 BMW Z8 Roadsters were delivered to customers during the first quarter 2003. The overall production and sales of the BMW automobiles is presented in Table 1.

"BMW is the brand people aspire to own. When people get to the point they can afford a luxury car, they buy a (BMW) 3 Series," says George Peterson, President of Auto Pacific Inc. in Tustin, Calif. BMW is also overtaking Toyota Motor Corp.'s luxury brand Lexus as the premium-car leader in the U.S. While the two rivals ended 2002 neck and neck, BMW has outsold Lexus for the first four months of 2003, a quantum leap compared with the early 1990s, when the Japanese took the U.S. market by storm. So far, BMW has steered its own redesign deftly. Despite a 53% increase in research and development and a 75% increase in capital expenditures over the past two years, BMW's net profit last year still rose 8.3%, to \$2.36 billion, while revenues climbed 9.9%, to \$49.5 billion. Operating margins, at 8% in 2002 and 8.7% in 2001- the heaviest years for investing- were

again among the highest in the industry. Lehman Brothers Inc. auto analyst Christopher Will expects the new-model push will generate a 20% rise in revenues next year.[18]

CONCEIVING CUSTOMER DELIGHT : THE VALUE CHAIN

Practicality and attention to customers' needs are the hallmarks of BMW's intelligent service. The Service Interval Display means that your car knows when it is ready for a check-up itself - no more inflexible service appointments. And every important item of information is easily accessible thanks to the KeyReader, which can scan information from every model dating from 2000 and later. All of which delivers even better service for our customers. All BMW models from the year 2000 or later store the most important service-related information on the key, and this automobile data can be transferred directly to a computer using the KeyReader. Both you, the owner, and your BMW dealer benefit from this new system, which does away with the routine questions and the risk of inaccuracies. And we've gone one better with the BMW 7 Series: the key is continually updated with all the maintenance-relevant information you can access under "Service" in the Control Display. The KeyReader system saves time, leaving you and your service professional to discuss your individual needs in greater detail. Helping customers establish a more intimate relationship with the brand is the objective of the Web site of BMW North America, Woodcliff Lake, N.J. In addition to serving as a market-research tool to understand customer needs, the site offers the opportunity to present vehicle features in an entertaining fashion. In a recent CyberDrive promotion, visitors could experience a balloon ride over the Napa Valley, a scenic drive through Europe, a race around the Nuerburgring course in Germany, a roller-coaster ride, and other exciting trips. Visitors chose different BMW vehicles to ride to their destinations-a 700 series luxury sedan for the European drive, a sporty 318i for the Nuerburgring track-and along the way were given demonstrations of new BMW product features such as all-season traction, park-distance control, and dynamic stability control. Cars could also be spun around inside and out to get 360-degree views of the interior and exterior.

"It goes beyond entertainment," says Carol Burrows, BMW North America's product-communications manager. "We try to establish an awareness of a brand personality and that we understand who our consumer is. For instance, we know you like excitement." During this promotion, the hit rate on the BMW site increased from 150,000 per day to 250,000 per day, where it has held since the program concluded at the end of July. With 70% of the visitors filling out a guest register, including plenty of lifestyle information, the BMW customer database doubled during the month long promotion. The **BMW Mexico** aims at providing lifetime guarantee to the client. The company initiated the customer relationship program through mass advertising campaign and created the data base of customers of BMW with all personal information containing members of family, date of birth, relationship with the customer, age, hobbies, contact address etc. The data was created for the household level with an objective to maintain direct and customized communication with each customers. In 1996 the company began to establish contact through the internet to the existing and prospective customers. The customer value chain governance at the BMW has been derived over

18 Business Week Online : BMW, June 09, 2003

the years since, 1950 in different states. The chronological evolution of the customer value chain process may be seen as below:

- Company built the brands through extensive mass advertising campaign (1950-2000)
- Customer database marketing has been implemented independent of the mass advertising campaign (1985-2000)
- Internet customer services on the interactive virtual platform in isolation without integrating with the existing customer database has been implemented (1996-2000)
- Company integrates the mass advertising campaign, customer database and virtual customer services through internet (2001)

The company has strong commitment to hold its brand promise on performance, value for money (VFM), safety, convergence technology and innovation in order to keep the customer satisfaction high and maintain the value chain impact on the brand. The customers make the decision to buy BMW automobiles on the following parameters:

- Usefulness of the products
- Perceived brand value (Which is created through the value chain process by the company to a large extent, besides the referrals and word of mouth impact)
- Value for money, and
- Pre and post sales services delivered by the company

Virtual call to the customers has really paid good returns to the brand globally. The Mini model of the company had bagged the credit of the car of the year in 2003. *"It has gone very, very well, especially in Internet sales. We share the revenue with our dealers on direct sales from the Web. This category has helped build our branding efforts and has added to Mini's brand awareness"* says Jack Pitney, general manager for the Mini division of BMW of North America LLC.

Company has secured its niche by intensive customer relationship and persuasion. The building of a robust existing and prospecting customer database in 2000 has given the company an added advantage to strengthen its brand in the market. BDR Consulting[19] was selected in September 2000 as system integrator and deployment project managers for the integrated business and IT solution for BMW direct because of their experience of multinational integrated web and call centre deployments. BDR were responsible for the initial scoping, requirements and design work, followed by the development and deployment of the completed system. BDR, though strictly vendor independent, worked with the BMW team to select 'best in class' tools –Vignette for content management, Clarify for the CRM and order management system. Through a password controlled, fully personalized web based front-end, users are able to view details on all eligible cars online and then go on to configure them against a full menu of allowable accessories. Additionally, they can build up a virtual 'garage' of configured cars, book test drives and request brochures before finally submitting their requested car for authorization by the Company Fleet and Contract Hire Company.

19 www.bdr-consulting.com

BMW Direct is truly 'CRM' compliant, providing two-way communication via automated alerts and e-mails and incorporating a contact centre to ensure immediate access to trained product advisors. Users can track online the status of their individual dealings whether by web, phone, fax or e-mail. Also available are web tools to enhance customer satisfaction, including a tax calculator, car comparator and residual value calculator. The contact centre functionality includes telephone account management, phone and e-campaign generation, customer enquiry handling, profiling to customize promotions, and post-sales support which is delivered using a thin client solution (using Citrix) to BMW's contact centre in Croydon and order management centre in Bracknell. In keeping with BMW's excellent brand image and customer expectations, the resultant solution delivered an excellent customer voyage when launched in April 2001 after a total project length of only 9 months, on time and to budget. Customers' expectations from BMW, a brand long-associated with quality, innovation and performance are of a high-level of accurate information and support. BMW Direct continues to exceed customer expectations and is setting standards for the rest of the industry to follow.

Top-Drive System Project of BMW

Traditional and Internet-based outbound communication channels can be used for the provision and management of CRM content for delivery to the customer. Increased efficiencies have been achieved through more efficient use of BMW customer service and relationship management personnel and the creation of new CRM standards in key areas of the organization, process costs were reduced significantly, while customer care quality has been raised by having access to a central integrated customer database. Increased frequency of direct contact between customers and BMW have been planned by way of personalizing the relations. Customers now have more contact options, dealer contacts are facilitated, and BMW has gained the ability to offer more complex products and services to its customers. CRM has been conceived by the company as a critical element behind an organization's ability to drive profitable and sustainable revenue growth, increase customer loyalty, and meet its overall corporate objectives. This program has been implemented in Germany and other European countries. BMW realized following key benefits of their CRM program:

- Ability to manage the customer through the application of different customer-centric processes while giving the customer the feeling of dealing with a single, interested, and intelligent entity.
- Multi-channel integration enables a closed communication cycle with the customer.
- Customers can pick the media of their choice and can expect the same quality in responses across all traditional and Internet-based channels.

CUSTOMER RELATIONSHIP TRACKING

Service is a technical skill while hospitality is an emotional skill and the combination of both the skills would bring the customer relationship memorable for ever. BMW believes in the retaining the customer for ever for a healthy customer-company relationship. Hence, the company banks on the technical and personal aspects of the services rendered to the customers. The company has built the robust data base for storing the information updates of the existing and potential customers with the following objectives:

- To provide a comprehensive view of the automobile and financial services to the BMW customers
- Deliver short term and money value packs information to the customers
- Augment customer loyalty through knowing the customer preferences and delivering the relevant and timely communications, and
- Online tracking of prospecting customers

Design of BMW customer database was aimed at providing information to the customers on comparative advantage of various automobile brands in the market. The tracking of the prospective customers is attended by the central system of measurement of the company. The report center monitors the communications and analyses the responses from the customers. The company is now able to view full shopper-owner path from the first point of contact, sales and till the automobile remains with the customer and also the variable required to frame his purchase decisions. The new marketing database contains a broad range of information pertaining to the BMW customer, that includes campaigns, short communications, corporate and product updates and financial services data. The tools of communication the company uses include welcome kit, loyalty program details, prost prioritization, BMW magazine, BMW owners circle, financial services programs and opportunities like "quick-win" program. The control group exercise of the company measures the effectiveness of programs in reference to mailed and non-mailed customer segments to assess the quick net returns. All customer relationship programs are built to the state-of the-art through effective interactive data base management focusing on the following issues:

- Providing reliable and additional information on owners and prospects than BMW has ever assembled before
- Render the communication program as a powerful tool to support BMW loyalty and prospect conversion programs
- Analyze the automated communication that supports the Owner Experience
- More information on owners and prospects than BMW has ever assembled before
- As an effective tool to support BMW loyalty and prospect conversion programs
- Generate automated communication that supports the Owner Experience to honor the customer.

Welcome kit reaches the customers within 30 days of the registration. It is a dialogue opener and an invitation to mark the BMW experience for one full year. The customer center makes periodic calls to restore the brand image of the company and this inherently fosters the personal information of the prospective customers. The kit provides the weekly update on the owner information, retrieve the solicited information by the customer and identifies the customer models, convergence to the loyalty program and build the buying activity log for the convenience of decision making to the prospecting customer. The company has strong determination on the loyalty of the customers to the BMW brand as it is reflected in their repeat purchase behaviour. The effectiveness of the customer relations program of the company is measured by the control and test group results. The company sends the newsletters to the prospecting and existing customer to facilitate their views on the brand performance, now the new BMW owners and acquaint with the accessories for different models.

Prospective customer relations are managed by a tailor-made strategy of the company to increase the prospect conversion to sell more BMW automobiles. The communications will be based on interactive opinion exchanges for better understanding the company, its products and services. The prospect conversion rate is measured on the basis of region, income and lifestyle of the customer. The new customers are prospected through tele-marketing, e-messaging, exhibitions and events managed by the company. The prospects are assessed by the sales personnel for rapid qualification and scores. The centers receive qualified leads for the prospects within 48 hours of the process. The leads are subjected to a tracking log and the lead prospects are contacted accordingly by the marketing staff of the company. The prospecting customers are tested through the scoring models that determine the priority of sales and customization. The test scores and anticipated response are adjusted and further client specific sales/ promotion program is chalked out. The cost of the prospecting program is audited by the company and an unsuccessful prospect is also retained for all relationship marketing communication on the database.

CHAPTER 4

PRICING STRATEGY

CHAPTER FOCUS

- *To acquaint with the pricing concepts and its relevance in the strategic marketing*
- *To know different pricing strategies and price-market relationships,*
- *To understand the issues associated with price leadership and non-price factors that influence the pricing decisions.*

Pricing goods and services is a critical job to maximize the profit of business organizations. Price is the one element of the marketing mix that generates revenue; the rest are costs. Many marketing executives exercise their best to increase prices to boost short-term profits. Stock markets in the United States, for example, are sensitive to quarterly earnings reports, and managers often raise the prices of cash cows to maintain earnings growth. Low prices can be used as a weapon to build market share. Prices that undercut competitors attract new customers and allow for greater utilization of facilities. However, low prices squeeze margins and often reduce net profits. Thus an ideal pricing strategy should be the one that balances the need for sales growth against market demand for profits. The selection of pricing objectives is determined by the decisions of business positioning. Many organizations need profit to satisfy the stakeholders and allocate resources for product development. The other objectives of the pricing strategy for a growing company may be maximizing the revenue, maximizing the market share and achieving the quality leadership. Several factors influence management's decisions about how price will be used in marketing strategy. An important concern is estimating how buyers will respond to alternative prices for a product or service. The cost of producing and distributing a product sets lower boundaries on the pricing decision. Costs affect an organization's ability to compete. The existing and potential competition in the market segments targeted by a company constrains the flexibility in selecting prices. Finally, legal and ethical constraints also create pressures on decision makers. Pricing plays a key role in the marketing strategy. Strategic choices about market targets, products, and distribution set guidelines for both price and promotion strategies. Product quality and features, type of distribution channel, end-users served, and the functions of intermediaries all help to establish a feasible price range. When an organization forms a new distribution network, selection of the channel and intermediaries may be driven by price strategy.

Pricing in markets is a controversial issue involving legal, economic, political factors both in the practice of differentiated pricing and uniform pricing. Some international marketers argue for uniform pricing while others, however, observe that the obvious differences in the markets of various countries favor the use of an internationally differentiated pricing policy. Conceptually, it is desirable on economic grounds to set different prices in different markets, because demand and supply differ from country to country. Such strategy of *differentiated pricing* may fit to any form of imperfect competition such as pure monopoly, oligopoly, and monopolistic competition. Thus, the multinational firms practice the varying prices in different markets. However, such pricing strategy may be risk averse as the firm may be charged with dumping allegations in the host country for selling at lower prices than the other countries. On the contrary, a firm essentially in a monopolistic or oligopolistic situation may price its products uniformly on global scale. For example, Airbus Industries Inc. sells a range of aircrafts and the company retains the same basic price for its planes everywhere excluding the taxes. At the introductory product stage the product is not highly diffused. Hence, a new product may be priced uniformly throughout the world. Further, if the diffusion process of an innovation has a similar pattern worldwide, standardized pricing would make sense for a foreign firm. However, the perspectives of local laws largely affect the decision on uniform versus differentiated pricing of multinational firms.

VALUE AND SKIMMING PRICING

Embryonic stage refers to such products that are newly introduced in the market and their recognition with the consumers is yet to be established. The value pricing may be an appropriate strategy to practice with the new products. It is also known as skimming the market. In this process, a high price is set for the product to 'cream off" all available demand. The price is maintained for some time, to allow the customers who regard the product as important to 'upgrade' them into the high price bracket. In a broad sense, it is the product segmentation. However, the value pricing approach would prove advantageous only when enough product awareness is created among the consumers through advertisements, demonstrations and effective consumer services. In the long run such an approach would create a specific group of customers or consumer segment for the product. For instance, the electronic products of some companies like BPL-Sanyo and Philips among the capital goods and some of the household consumable goods such as packed food and condiments coming form capital-intensive units constitute such consumers segments for their products.

Advantage of a high profit under the value pricing approach is anticipated in the long run when there is consumer segmentation for the product with a high recognition. However in this approach, the selling cost may shoot up reducing the profit margin low in the initial stages. In value pricing, another important factor to be considered is the territorial characteristics - low purchasing power or high purchasing power consumer segments or rural and urban. In the former, where the marginal propensity of consumption and income level of consumers are low, the value pricing, with a high product price and selling cost would not be a profitable approach. In such areas, where there are low-income group consumers, the product segmentation can be done formulating the 'dumping policy' at a low price. The price of the product can be raised to the maximum in coherence with the consumers' purchasing and paying capacity in the long run, after the product gets proper consumer recognition and makes headway in the market. Under such circumstances, the selling cost will however be lower as compared to the overhead costs.

It is possible to estimate the benefit of purchasing the product or service, if customer's economics is understood properly. Company management should be asking itself, "What is the highest price that can be charged such that the customer is better off after buying from us?" The value added pricing can be explained as a company provides transportation and disposal services for infectious medical waste from small generators, such as doctors and blood banks. As the regulatory and enforcement climates have stiffened, customers have become increasingly sensitive to the problems associated with proper disposal of this material. Unlike the competitors, who primarily price by the pound of material removed, the company may charge a fixed fee per container.

Skimming pricing is the strategy of establishing a high initial price for a product with a view to "skimming the cream off the market" at the upper end of the demand curve. It is accompanied by heavy expenditure on promotion. A skimming strategy may be recommended under the following business conditions:

- When the nature of demand is uncertain

Strategy Focus 4.1: Skimming Pricing Strategy- A Tool for Short-run Profit

A Company may implement the price-skimming strategy to take advantage of high short-term profits in view of the newness of the product and with reference to the effective market segmentation.

There are several advantages of price skimming

- A company may employ price-skimming strategy for an innovative or high technology-high value product which involves high research and development costs. This pricing strategy would also be suitable to the company where the costs of introducing the product to the market through sales, promotion, and advertising are relatively higher.
- A company can build a quality sensitive image for its product by charging high prices initially. This will initial allow the firm the scope of reducing price when the product becomes competitive. On the contrary, it would be difficult for a company to increase the price that has been set initially lower without taking risk of the loss of sales volume.
- Skimming can be an effective strategy in segmenting the market as a company may divide the market into a number of segments and reduce the price at different stages in each, thus acquiring maximum profit from each segment
- The practice of price-skimming is a right strategy tool, when a product is distributed through dealers. Since high prices are set by the company considering the margin-spread among suppliers, the skimming price is translated into high mark-ups for the dealer
- Practice of price skimming can be particularly successful for 'conspicuous' or 'prestige goods', as the buyer tends to be more egocentric in spending to buy such products. Similarly, where the quality differences between competing brands is perceived to be large, or for offerings where such differences are not easily judged, the skimming strategy can work well. An example of the latter would be for the manufacturers of 'designer-label' clothing.

- When a company has expended large sums of money on research and development for a new product
- When the competition is expected to develop and market a similar product in the near future, or
- When the product is very innovative and market is expected to mature very slowly.

Under these circumstances, a skimming strategy has several advantages. At the top of the demand curve, price elasticity is low. Besides, in the absence of any close substitute, cross-elasticity is also low. These factors, along with heavy emphasis on promotion, tend to help the product make significant inroads into the market. The high price also helps the segment market.

One may also turn to a penetration strategy with a view to achieving economies of scale. Savings in production costs alone may not be an important factor in setting low prices because, in the absence of price elasticity, it is difficult to generate sufficient sales. Finally, before adopting penetration pricing, one must make sure that the product fits into the lifestyles of the mass market. How low the penetration price should be differs from case to case. There are different types of prices used in penetration strategies: restrained elimination prices, promotional prices, and keep-out prices.

Dow Chemical Company stresses penetration pricing. It concentrates on lower-margin commodity products and low prices, builds dominant market share, and holds on for the long haul. Texas Instruments also practices penetration pricing. Texas Instruments starts by building a large plant capacity. By setting the price as low as possible, it hopes to penetrate fast and gain a large market share. Penetration pricing reflects a long-term perspective in which short-term profits are sacrificed in order to establish sustainable competitive advantage. Penetration policy usually leads to above-average long-run returns that fall in to a relatively narrow range. Price skimming, on the other hand, yields a wider range of lower average returns.

PRICING WITH DEMAND CURVE

This approach may be followed for pricing the products that already exist in the market and are mature with regard to sales realization in the open market condition. In this process, unlike getting customers to upgrade themselves and form segments, the pricing approach calls for widening the market and matching the product price with product demand. In this process, a high price may be set initially, but there is a sealing down of the price and mopping up of all available demand at each price level.

Likely demand at various price levels is difficult to estimate but, the implications pertaining to the results of sample survey can be used in pricing. The sales estimates may represent the demand schedule and in a firm, even with these points the curve can be drawn. Some preconditions may be reviewed to estimate the demand of the product such as (i) number of potential buyers (ii) propensity to purchase and of sales, and (iii) product attributes to attitude building. The demand curve has implications of these preconditions. If the price is changed there is a movement along with the demand curve and, if any of the preconditions of demand is changed, there is a scope of shift in the demand curve to the higher or lower side. In case the demand for the product is elastic, the price should not be kept high for any product. Pricing strategies are subject to the very nature of the product. If it is a core product made tangible without enough scorching expenditure, it can be priced at higher margins, as any close competitor does not encounter it. Marketing of such products depends on the pricing strategies suitable at every level of the distribution network.

PENETRATION PRICING

This policy may be adopted to penetrate the market as quickly as possible to secure cost advantages through pushing products in high volume. In case, new products of qualities similar to those already existing in the market, have to be introduced for crash sales in the market, the price may be derived in relation to its competitive products. The important issue to be kept in view is the anticipated selling cost and the volume of sales to determine the prices. The penetration price always needs to be little lower than the price of the existing products similar to it. The penetration price is conceptually an artificial pricing approach to push the product in the market. The real price may be fixed later in the process to assess the demand elasticity of the product in the primary and subsequent markets.

Penetration pricing is the strategy of entering the market with a low initial price so that a greater share of the market can be captured. The penetration strategy is used when an elite market does not exist and demand seems to be elastic over the entire demand curve, even during early stages of product introduction. High price elasticity of demand is probably the most important reason for adopting a penetration strategy. The penetration strategy is also used to discourage competitors from entering the market. When competitors seem to be encroaching on a market, an attempt is made to lure them away by means of penetration pricing, which yields lower margins. A competitor's costs play a decisive role in this pricing strategy because a cost advantage over the existing manufacturer might persuade another firm to enter the market, regardless of how low the margin former may be.

GEOGRAPHICAL PRICING

It is the strategy to exercise a discriminatory pricing policy across the various territorial market segments. The marketer who serves a number of distinct regions can adopt this policy without creating psychological barriers either to the customers or distributors in purchasing and selling the products.

Dual Standards

This strategy is largely backed by the concept of 'skimming in' and 'skimming off' price setting. A marketer can choose relatively a lower price for the product in the segments where the customer density is high but the purchasing power is low. On the contrary, a higher price may be fixed in the segments of high purchasing power where skimming off' strategy can be implemented. In setting up both the price standards, the marketing objective should remain intact and the overall orientation of the marketing managers has to remain the same.

CONSPICUOUS PRICING

Skimming approach implies in this pricing policy where the price of the product is kept higher than its substitutes in order to make it conspicuous, so the product may be recognised as a symbol of social status. An example of jewellery watches may be cited in this context that serve as a status product for the customers.

PSYCHOLOGICAL PRICING

This approach makes the customer feel that he is paying a relatively lower price for the product. To stimulate such a view the price is fixed in integral values very close to the round numeric values, e.g., prices of Bata shoes Rs.499/-, shirts in UK 3.99. Such a price structure gives the customer a materialistic satisfaction in buying the product.

VALUE-ADDED PRICING

In this price determining process, the company takes care of the value of its by-products in the principal product and prices them accordingly. Such approaches are generally applicable for evolving price strategies of semi-processed products like meat, oilseeds, milk, chemicals etc.

COMPLEMENTARY PRODUCT PRICING

Prices of the principal products are dependent on the pricing pattern of associated products, and vice-versa. It is logical that the prices of the complementary products should be lower e.g., film of camera, battery of camera etc. or else the customers may withdraw the principal product from use.

PRICE DISCOUNTS

This is one of the most popular strategies adopted by the private companies in order to attract the consumer towards their stocks and increase sales by offering a discount on the price of the products either on selected or all items in accordance with the business state of the organization. The discounts are offered in terms of cash, kind or discount vouchers, facilitating the customers to buy the products of the company for the amount discounted. The discounts offered by the government supported organizations include:

- Cash discounts
- Quantity discounts
- Discount in kind
- Trade discounts
- Seasonal discounts
- Institutional discounts
- Grant-in-aid discounts
- Allowances
- Stock clearing discounts.

A company may offer a discount either by making the customer pays less than the prescribed price of the product or set a strategy to provide additional quantity of products on the pre-set price.

Such transactions refer to cash and quantity discounts. For example the policy of discount of a firm in kind may be given to a customer, with high technology products for the principal product e.g. memory storage devise with the computer. The trade discounts are incentives to the distributors for the promotion of sales. The seasonal discounts on prices are related to the customers' demand for the product at a particular time. For example, during festivals, clothes are in high demand and are generally offered at seasonal discounts, to boost sales. The Handloom societies patronized by the Government of India, also offer seasonal discount subject to the availability of grant-in-aid for sales from the Government. On the bulk procurement of products, an institutional discount on the set price is offered by the companies to keep up the customer relationship. The company however may decide to offer a clearance sale discount on prices to ease inventory blockade and expenditure. It also helps an organization to refill the product-line with products or demand at par with fashion or time. The sales personnel of the company also get some benefit as a token or recognition for the service rendered in terms of price discount on selected products to keep their morale high in the future too.

DISCRIMINATE PRICING

A company modifies its pricing strategy for the products according to the customer-segments, product forms, product image, location and time. These approaches are to be decided on the basis of the competition prevailing in the market. However, a marketing manager has to keep his corporate objectives in view before discriminating the price in several forms stated above.

PROMOTIONAL PRICING

Under specific circumstances, companies will temporarily price their products below the list price to promote sales. In this process, sometimes, risk is taken by the companies to fix the price even below the cost. There are many forms of promotional pricing strategy. They are:

1. Loss leader pricing
2. Special event pricing and
3. Low financing

In this strategy, there always remains a threat of copying down by competitors. Thus, such a policy should not be recommended for a long period of time.

Pricing is a logical proposition keeping in view the competitive products in the market. A company has to determine the price on the basis of internal economics pertaining to business objectives, targets, marketing policies and profit targets and external forces like the demand and strategies of competitive products.

MARK-UP PRICING

It is an elementary pricing method that is exercised by adding mark-up standard to the cost of the product. There are considerable variations in mark-ups among the different products. Thus, this methodology is not considered to be scientific. However, mark-up pricing remains popular for several reasons (i) it is a cost plus exercise and appears to be fairer for both customers and sellers (ii) sellers opine that this approach is simple and (iii) price competition is minimised. The mark-up price may be calculated using the formula as below:

$$P_m = \frac{C_{pi}}{(1-S_r)} \quad ....(i)$$

Where, P_m = Mark-up price, C_{pi} = Unit cost price, S_r = Expected returns on sales

Unit cost of the product may be calculated from the following formula.

$$C_{pi} = V_c + \frac{F_c}{S_c} \quad ....(ii)$$

Where, V_c = Variable Cost, F_c = Fixed Cost and S_c = Unit Sales

Expected return price on sales may be computed from the projection stated in the following equation.

$$S_r = \frac{C_{pi} + T_r * Y_c}{S_c} \quad ....(iii)$$

$$S_c = \frac{C_{pi} + T_r * Y_c}{S_c}$$

Where T_r = Target Returns and Y_c =Capital investment in marketing

Mark-up price can be calculated substituting the values of unit cost and expected returns drawn from equation (ii) and (iii) in the equation (i).

PRICING FUNDAMENTALS

Fundamentals of global pricing are derived through the conventional practices followed in home markets. The basic determinants for the pricing of products and services are production costs, competitive factors, and break-even analysis and demand considerations. Domestic price is affected by the considerations on pricing objectives, cost, competition, customer, and state regulations. These considerations apply at home and in the host country. In addition to the conventional considerations on pricing, multiple currencies, trade barriers, and longer distribution channels make the pricing decision more difficult. The pricing objectives should be closely aligned to marketing objectives, which in turn need to be derived from overall corporate objectives. Essentially, the pricing objectives of a foreign firm intending to operate in the host country should be evolved in terms of profit or volume.

Cost factors play a significant role in determining the international prices of products and services. The mark-up on cost or price or a target returns on investment may constitute the profit objectives of pricing while anticipated volume of growth in sales may be considered towards the volume objectives of the international pricing. The standard pricing procedure for exporting consists of a cost-plus formula. The firm may evolve export prices by adding up the various costs involved in producing and shipping the product (which refers to cost-based pricing) and then adding a mark-up (that refers to the concept of "plus") to this amount to achieve a reasonable rate of return. The cost drivers of pricing include production costs, administrative costs, allocated research and development expenditures, selling costs, transport and warehousing charges, custom duties, and requisite fees towards documentation etc. paid through various facilitating agencies. In practice most firms seem to use full cost approach that includes direct costs and managerial costs in determining the international prices. However, the emphasis varies with the company strategy and the market situation. For an existing product entering a new market, direct costs tend to be a natural choice, since administrative or overhead costs are already covered at home and investments have been recouped. Fixed costs are those that do not vary with the scale of operations, such as number of units manufactured. Salaries of the managerial staff, office rent, and other office and factory overhead expenses are examples of fixed costs. On the other hand, variable costs include material and labor used in the manufacture of a product; bear a direct relationship to the level of operations. Some fixed, short-run costs are not necessarily fixed in the long run; therefore, the variable and fixed costs may be distinguished only in the short-run. For example the salaries of the marketing staff of a firm in the home country should be considered as fixed. Moreover, some costs that initially appear fixed may be viewed as variable when properly evaluated.

> Kimberly Clark's sales for the fourth quarter of 2002 faltered as its personal care business, mainly nappies, felt the pinch of a fierce price war, particularly strong in North America. Disappointing results followed the company's statement issued in December 2002. which warned that increasing competition in North America and adverse economic conditions in Latin America would impact 2002 revenues. Severe competition in nappies has been one of the most prominent features of the disposable paper products industry in the last decade, sparked by the two rival companies Procter & Gamble and Kimberly Clark. The impact of price competition was compounded by a gradual decline of sales due to consistently decreasing birth rates and the rise of improved private label offerings. In response to this trend Procter & Gamble undertook an aggressive price cut offensive in 2002, most notably in America. The strategy has been pursued on two fronts - through coupon campaigns, offering savings of up to US$5 per pack in the US, as well as the rationalization of their range in Europe, which saw the end of Pampers Premium and Sensitives sub-brands and the relaunch of Pampers Baby Dry. Such was the price pressure from its rival Procter & Gamble that Kimberly-Clark decided to abandon a planned price increase of its Huggies brand in 2002. While Kimberly Clark remained leader in North America, its market share dropped by 0.3 percentage points in 2002 compared to the gain made by its competitor of 1.4 percentage points. In Western Europe, there was a similar scenario with Procter & Gamble gaining 0.7 percentage points in share, while Kimberly-Clark's stake shrunk by the same amount. The declining pattern of birth rates in North America and Western Europe in the last three years has resulted in a drop of new born nappy sales by 5% and 1% respectively. On the other hand, a trend towards delaying toilet training has spurred sound demand for disposable pants. Procter & Gamble, which used to lead the nappies sector with its Pampers and Luvs brands, has started losing ground to Kimberly-Clark due to the increasingly popular training and swim pants recently introduced by the latter.[1]

---

1 Marzena Moglia : Nappies Feel the Pinch of Competitive Pricing, *The Euro Monitor International,* February 10, 2003, www.euromonitor.com

Impact of costs on pricing strategy can be studied by considering the ratio of fixed costs to variable costs, the economies of scale available to a firm, and the cost structure of a firm and competitors. If the fixed costs of a company in comparison with variable costs form the higher proportion of its total costs, adding sales volume will be a great help in increasing earnings. A foreign firm needs to consider the anticipated decline in costs while evolving the price for the goods and services, which may be described as the process of lowering the prices in order to gain higher market share in the long run. The concept of obtaining lower costs through economies of scale has often been referred to in the literature as experience effect, which explains that all costs go down as accumulated experience increases.

Titan Industries Ltd, a joint venture between the Tata group and Tamil Nadu Industrial Development Corporation (TIDCO), is faced with the first serious threat of competition since it started (in 1987), in the Indian Market for watches. The action began three years ago, when quantitative restrictions (QRs) on watch imports were lifted. Since then, swiss brands have entered at the prestige end, with Citizen just one rung below, even as Swatch, Espirit and others start wooing the youth. The Mid-priced zone has been less exciting :HMT and Maximal have been crawling along, while Timex struggles to recover. But as all the branded players have discovered, the real action is at the voluminous lower end – where the unorganized-sector and grey-market players have been having a blast. Smuggled Citizen movements, for instance, are hugely popular with tinted watch assemblers. In contrast, recognized brands have had it tough. Burdened by taxes, these account for less than half the total market, estimated at 45 million units in 2000-01 (including everything). And that was just the prologue: now comes the big monster. Chinese watches, at Rs 150-250 apiece, are here at half the price of local equivalents. And they threaten to crunch through the low-end. Perhaps even the middle. With sales of 6.9 million watches (estimate for 2000-01), Titan is still the undisputed leader of the Indian market. It is also India's most admired durables marketer. Yet, Titan is losing shelf space at the retail level. In fact, if equity analysts have ever worried about the firm's prospects, it is now. Aware that Titan's growth space is getting cramped from both ends, they are pouring over Titan's performance figures with grim diligence. Sales for the half year ended 30 September 2000 are up 18.6 percent to US$66.1 million, and PAT has more than doubled to US$2.16 million. But this includes the US$ 2.15 million Titan got for selling its share in RDI Print & Publishing. Of course, watches and jewellery are seasonal businesses, and the second-half will be much brighter, festive season and all. But that still doesn't reassure investors. Analysts have been wondering whether Titan would be better off offloading its watches business to some global player, and selling only jewelry. Though it's a high working-capital business, Tanishq is an unrivalled brand, and could see the company through. The brands Citizen, Omega and the like have been more visible than saleable. If anything at all, the Swiss brands' presence has helped create a segment of luxury watches for Titan. (This business may soon be brought under a new brand). People exposed to watches for US$2000 a piece are likely to find a Titan Insignia for US$ 220 or a solid gold Nebula for US$ 800 reasonable. Titan is also using smart new designs under Fastrack (for men and women) to counter Swatch and Esprit, which have undeniably won the admiration of the style – conscious Indian youngster.

As for the middle-market, Titan can count on its 'strong grip on distribution'. The retail network is a formidable barrier to competition."Its strength here has helped Sonata, a relatively low-priced brand (about US$10 apiece), achieve annual sales of almost 3 million units within just four years of launch. Indeed, it was because of this success that Titan needed to churn out 300,000 units more than the capacity of its Ho-sur plant (built in 1987 at an investment of US $100 million). Today, Titan sells in over 40 countries, and claims to be the 'world's sixth largest manufacturer watch brand', after Casio, Citizen, Timex, Swatch group and Seiko. The vision was always to be a globally significant player in watches and jewellery, adding that the company's core strength is its ability to anticipate change. The Chinese industry is tormented by overcapacity, and watch-makers are flailing their hands about for any high-volume deal. In fact, given that Titan is currently at full capacity, this is the best way to take volumes up (to 10 million units in a couple of years). Titan is more a marketer than a manufacturer. Where the watches actually come from is immaterial, so long as the brand stands guarantee. The strategy has theoretical backing: as products reach parity and people gain enough money to satisfy more than their basic needs, the most prized assets start shifting from manufacturing know-how and factory machines towards the consumer relationship section of the chain. This puts the emphasis on need-identifying, product designing and brand communication skills, with which there's greater scope to stand apart. Titan has already made some admirable breakthroughs in brand-building. As a brand, Titan sought ownership of the 'style' portion of the target consumer's mind. That may be fine at the upper-end, but what about the huge price-sensitive segment? The answer is brand sensitization. Anyhow, crushing costs is a Titan priority. Titan is highly cost-competitive on 'day' and 'date' movements. Watches are being redesigned with fewer parts (the quartz revolution cut the component count from 150 to 50, and now further reductions are being made) and gold-plating costs are being slashed. Meanwhile, an ERP system has reduced working-capital needs by some 20 percent this year, as lean processes deliver their magic, vaporizing inventories and speeding up the cycle. The average Titan that sells overseas is priced at $125, which is lower than Swiss brands but higher than the Japanese. However, what really counts is Europe, where Titan is striving hard to get past the 100,000-units mark. It must make some headway with the demanding European consumer before it can attain genuine global stature.

Titan was virtually unknown in Europe, but even here, Titan decided to use one monster to destroy another -by turning anonymity to its advantage. For, the flipside is that there is no nation with which anyone associates the brand. This gives it a chance to strike a truly global posture. Timex is American, Seiko is Japanese and Omega is Swiss. 'No one country could have made faces this beautiful' expresses the advertisement, juxtaposing a woman's face with an equally stunning watch dial, with the hands in perfect symmetry at 10 past 10. The idea is to show how the creative blending of diverse West Asian markets, where Titan is ranked either 2nd or 3rd position, accounts for more than half the figure. And the brand is doing fine in Myanmar, Sri Lanka and other markets under the Indian subcontinent's satellite-TV footprint. The crucial thing is that Titan is actually trying to build a global brand (an ad campaign was developed for the purpose some four years ago). It's obvious that on a dollar-to-dollar scale, the odds are stacked against Titan. And one might imagine that the depth of pockets is the issue. After all, what has worked to differentiate the brand in India is no big deal overseas. But brand building can be done cheaply too, so long as Titan is able to single-mindedly convey a point of differentiation that strikes the consumer. The general framework - Indian and Japanese can result in such extraordinary beauty. As an idea, it holds immense potential. The concept can be stretched to take Titan to a position of global uniqueness: a brand that knows how to bring information and ideas together from around the world, to fulfill human needs in novel ways. The campaign has a touch of classy understatement.

Use of a cost-based price has been observed as a common practice with the multinational firms after the concept of the *experience curve pricing* effect was regarded as an effective tool in pricing strategy. The experience curve describes the relative movement of unit cost and volume of production as how unit costs go down successively with the production of more units of a product. Through the "learning by doing" that comes from experience, the company's employees develop skills and capabilities that translate into lower costs. Hence, firm entering new foreign markets will gain in capabilities and economies of scale from accumulated production and market experience. In tune with the new market providing a chance for increased output and thus lower unit costs, the anticipated gains might be passed along to the customers in the form of low introductory prices or "penetration" prices in the introductory stage of the product life cycle. Whether the introductory price will be raised later or not depends directly on the correctness of the anticipated cost declines. Experience curve pricing has been adopted primarily by companies entering an existing market in the maturity stage. Many Japanese firms operate with this strategy, since it allows them to maintain a penetration price level in foreign markets. Companies habitually charge less than they could for new products, especially with revolutionary offers. Underestimating a product's value can be a costly mistake, since the introductory price often fixes its worth in the buyer's mind. Good pricing decisions take an expansive, rather than an incremental, approach to new products. Companies should construct a range of possible prices based on the new offer's value to customers and the competitive landscape.[1]

In determining the prices the nature of *competition* in each country also plays a key role. The competition in an industry can be analyzed with reference to such factors as the number of firms in the industry, product differentiation and ease of entry. In addition, competitive environment can be categorized as privileged position, leadership, chaotic, or stabilized competition. The competitive analysis should be done in order to reveal the global and domestic competitors in the particular market in reference to the price they charge for their products. These prices tend to set the "reservation" prices in the local market, that is, those limits beyond which the firm's product will not be considered and people will avoid buying. The analysis can go further and attempt to isolate the differential advantages that the firm's product might have over these existing offerings, so-called perceived value pricing.

It is necessary for a company to conduct *breakeven analysis* of the current or proposed business. A breakeven analysis examines the interaction among fixed costs, variable costs, prices, and unit volume to determine that combination of elements in which revenues and total costs are equal. Fixed costs are the expenses that must be made in business and are not impacted by sales. They will include such things as rent, basic telephone expenses and utilities, ages for core employees, loan or lease payments, and other necessary expenditures. A company should also include the wages as a fixed cost. Variable costs include those expenses that change as a result of sales volume. In a manufacturing business, the material cost of sales will be variable. Often utility expenses above some base rates increase sales, including gas or electricity charges in the factory or telephone expenses in the office. The labor component of production may be variable or fixed, depending upon the obligations to its employees. In some cases employees need only be paid for hours worked

---

2 Michael V. Marn, Eric V. Roegner, and Craig C. Zawada : *The Price Advantage,* John Wiley & Sons, 2004.

(variable expense), while in others, some minimum number of paid hours is required regardless of the number of hours actually worked (fixed expense). By reducing the company to these three factors for preliminary analysis, the company can avoid making serious mistakes and may discover significant opportunities. The management challenge will be to design and implement the programs necessary to achieve the desired results.

Another key factor in determining the price is *customer demand* for a product and it should be analyzed in view of the many influencing variables. The price of the product is one of the variables that influence the demand for the product. These considerations include the ability of customers to buy, their willingness to buy, propensity to consumer, the place of the product in the customer's lifestyle (whether a status symbol or a daily-consumption product), prices of substitute products, the potential market for the product (whether there is an unfulfilled demand in the market or if the market is saturated), the nature of non-price competition, consumer behavior in general, and consumer behavior in segments in the market. All these factors are interdependent, and it may not be easy to estimate their relationships accurately. The process of demand analysis also includes the forecast of relationship between price level and demand, simultaneously considering the effects of other variables on demand. The relationship between price and demand may be described as *elasticity of demand, or sensitivity of price*, which refers to the number of units of a product that would be demanded at different prices. The *industry demand* for a product may be considered as elastic, if it can be substantially increased by lowering prices. If lowering price has little effect on demand, it would be considered inelastic. In case of the total demand of an industry being highly elastic, the industry leader may take the initiative to lower prices. Environmental factors, which vary from country to country, have a direct influence on demand elasticity.

COST-PLUS PRICING

Cost-plus looks inwards and examines the company's cost and an expense structure to determine how much has to be added to the cost of a product to achieve a desired level of profitability. Most industries have rules of thumb that are often used to set prices. These rules of thumb are the cumulative results of the performance of many industry participants over time and should not be dismissed lightly. It is the rare company that can revolutionize the cost structure of a competitive market. Quite often these rules of thumb are expressed in terms of a profit margin (the "plus") to the cost of the goods being sold. For a high tech start up, 80% gross profit margins are often necessary. This means that if the product costs $20 to produce, the selling price for that product should be $100. It is imperative to find out what these rules of thumb are for the particular industry.

Activity-based costing (ABC), also referred to as activity-based accounting and transaction-based costing, is a concept that will probably be learned in a managerial accounting course and hear about it in a production and operations management course. Basically, it is a method of allocating costs to products and services. If ABC is used effectively, it is a great tool for planning and control. The advantages of the activity based costing in determining the pricing strategy is listed as under:

- Identify high overhead costs per unit and find ways to reduce the costs
- Avoid decreases in head counts due to inaccurate allocation of costs

- Measure profitability with higher accuracy than traditional costing that used only direct-labor hours as a cost driver
- Software packages can do simulations/calculations to see what are the costs for different types of activities
- Used with a strategic intent, ABC could help determine whether a new product/service should be added and/or an old product should be replaced
- Used in production planning, ABC could help to decide whether production should be outsourced or produced in-house
- Measure pricing and profitability

A company should identify, the major activities in a process/ department/ operation/system. Later, it may create cost pools, should groups of activities need to be allocated together. Selecting cost drivers should follow. The number of cost drivers used will probably rely on trade-offs. Too few may reduce accuracy while too many may increase complexity. After determining the cost drivers, the rate should be calculated. The Table 4.1 exhibits the activities and cost drivers planning to support the pricing decisions.

Table 4.1 Activity Based Costing

Activities	*Cost Drivers*	*Total Traceable Costs (USD)*	*Total Units*	*Rate (Overhead cost per unit in USD)*
Materials Handling	Number of Components	$ 100	50	$2/component
Machine Set-ups	Number of Set-ups	$ 200	100	$1/setup
Inspections	Hours of Quality Testing	$ 300	150	$2/hour
Administrative Activities	Number of Forms/Permits	$ 100	25	$4/form
Waste Disposal	Frequency of Disposal	$ 50	10	$5/occurrence

Rates are then applied to the respective cost drivers for each product/service that are under consideration. The overhead cost per unit can then be derived when the total product units divide the total cost for the product. The rates of the activities may be substituted accordingly to determine the cost of the products and services as exhibited in Table 4.2.

Table 4.2 Determining the Cost of the Product

Activities	*Rate (Overhead cost per unit in USD)*	*Product A*		*Product B*	
		Units	*Cost (USD)*	*Units*	*Cost (USD)*
Materials Handling	$2/component	30	$ 60	20	$ 40
Machine Setups	$1/setup	25	$ 25	75	$ 75
Inspections	$2/hour	50	$ 100	100	$ 200
Administrative Activities	$4/form	10	$ 40	15	$ 60
Waste Disposal	$5/occurrence	5	$ 25	5	$ 25

Foreign firms mainly follow the cost approach and the market approach towards the pricing orientation. The cost approach involves first computing all relevant costs and then adding a desired mark-up to arrive at the sales price of any products or services. The cost approach is commonly used by the multinational firms as it is simple to understand, apply and leads to fairly stable prices in the market. A conservative attitude would favor using full costs as the basis of pricing. On the one hand, an incremental-cost pricing could allow for seeking business otherwise lost. This method is an improvement over the pure cost-plus method since mark-up is derived more scientifically. Nonetheless, the determination of rate of return poses a problem. The percentage mark-up on cost of the product to determine the price may be calculated with the formula as given below:

$M_c = \left[\frac{\sum K}{Q_t}\right] Y_k$ where, M_c denotes percentage mark-up on costs, K represents the total invested capital, Q_t symbolizes the standard cost of annual normal production and Y_k exhibits the percentage desired returns on the invested capital.

On the contrary, the *market approach* of pricing proceeds in a reverse fashion. In this strategy of price determination estimation of the acceptable price in the target segment is made. Later, an analysis is performed to determine, if this price would meet the company's profit objective. The final price is based on the market rather than estimated production costs. Market approach is widely used in Japan which may be illustrated as a Japanese firm first examines the likely competitors and their products, and then estimates the unit cost necessary for viable entry into the market.

CUSTOMER EXPECTATION-BASED PRICING

Another approach is to price to the customer expectations. Experienced purchasers of products and services have general ranges and frames of reference for pricing expectations. Prices that are inconsistent with these expectations may be rejected without consideration. A low price may be associated with an inferior product or service, thereby being unacceptable to particular customers. A high price may be beyond what another buyer considers reasonable for his/her expectations of the product's benefits. Ultimately, prices should be set according to what the market will bear. This will be influenced by competitive actions, customer expectations, and the company's cost structure. No final pricing decisions should be made until a breakeven analysis has been performed which considers fixed costs, variable costs, and volume.

PRICING MODELS

Binomial Model

There are two main models used in the Australian market for pricing equity options: The Binomial Model and The Black Scholes Model. For most traders these two models will give accurate results. The binomial option pricing model was first proposed by Cox, Ross and Rubinstein in a paper published in 1979. This solution to pricing an option is probably the most common model used for equity calls and puts today. The model divides the time to an option's expiry into a large number of intervals, or steps. At each interval it calculates that the stock price will move either up or down with a given probability and also by an amount calculated with reference to the stock's volatility, the time to expiry and the risk free interest rate. A binomial distribution of prices for the underlying stock or index is thus produced. On expiry the option values for each possible stock price are known as they are equal to their intrinsic values. The model then works backwards through each time interval, calculating the value of the option at each step. At the point where a dividend is paid (or other capital adjustment is made) the model takes this into account. The final step is at the current time and stock price, where the current theoretical fair value of the option is calculated.

Black Scholes Model

First proposed by Black and Scholes in a paper published in 1973. This analytical solution to pricing a European option on a non-dividend paying asset formed the foundation for much theory in derivatives finance. The Black Scholes formula is a continuous time analogue of the binomial model. The Black Scholes formula uses the pricing inputs to analytically produce a theoretical fair value for an option. The model has many variations which attempt, with varying levels of accuracy, to incorporate dividends and American style exercise conditions. However with computing power these days the binomial solution is more widely used.

PRICE-MARKET RELATIONSHIP

Although the fair value may be close to where the market is trading, other pricing factors in the marketplace mean fair value is used mostly as an estimate of the option's value. Moreover, fair value will depend on the assumptions

Strategy Focus 4.2
Harley-Davidson Motorcycles – Pricing Strategy

Harley-Davidson, Inc. is the parent company for the group of companies doing business as Harley-Davidson Motor Company, Buell Motorcycle Company and Harley-Davidson Financial Services, Inc. Harley-Davidson Motor Company, the only major U.S.-based motorcycle manufacturer, produces heavyweight motorcycles and offers a complete line of motorcycle parts, accessories, apparel, and general merchandise. Buell Motorcycle Company produces sport and sport-touring motorcycles. Harley-Davidson Financial Services, Inc. provides wholesale and retail financing and insurance programs to Harley-Davidson dealers and customers. Harley-Davidson enjoyed a monopoly in the motorcycle industry for many decades. In the 1970's, Japanese manufacturers flooded the market with high quality, low priced bikes. From 1973 - 1983, Harley's market share went from 77.5% to 23.3% with Honda having 44% of the market by 1983. Harley-Davidson could not compete on price against the Japanese motorcycle producers, so it had to establish other market values and improve quality.

Harley-Davidson quickly learned it could not compete with the foreign manufacturers on cost. Not only did Honda have a low priced product, it was able to defeat Harley in advertising. Therefore, Harley developed a strategy of value over price. This was created through the development of mini-niches and the heavy construction of the parts. Japanese manufacturers used plastic while Harley used steel, which is able to be rebuilt and rebuke. Harley was careful not to exceed demand in production of their motorcycles. Currently, people must wait six to eighteen months for a new motorcycle and the price for a year-old Harley is 25% to 30% higher than a new one. By not being able to meet demands, an attitude of *must-have* has developed. Therefore, Harley has plans to double capacity to 200,000 motorcycles annually by 2003.

Retail sales of Harley-Davidson® motorcycles for the year 2003 grew 8.8 percent in the U.S., 6.7 percent in Europe, and 9.0 percent in Japan compared to 2002. Based on the information currently available, Harley-Davidson's full year market share for the 651cc and up segment is expected to grow in all of the Company's major markets.

Source: Harley-Davidson USA www.harley-davidson.com

regarding volatility levels, dividend payments and so on that are made by the person using the pricing model. Different expectations of volatility or dividends will alter the fair value result. This means that at any one time there may be many views held simultaneously on what the fair value of a particular option is. In practice, supply and demand will often dictate at what level an option is priced in the marketplace. Traders may have a fair value on an option to get an indication of whether the current market price is higher or lower than fair value, as part of the process of making a judgment about the market value of the option.

Volatility

Volatility figure input into an option-pricing model reflects the assumptions of the person using the pricing model. Volatility is defined technically in various ways, depending on assumptions made about the underlying asset's price distribution. For the regular option trader, it is sufficient to know that the volatility a trader assigns to a stock reflects expectations of how the stock price will fluctuate over a given period of time. Volatility is usually expressed in two ways: historical and implied. Historical volatility describes volatility observed in a stock over a given period of time. Price movements in the stock (or underlying asset) are recorded at fixed time intervals (for example every day, every week, or every month) over a given period. More data generally leads to more accuracy. Implied volatility relates to the current market for an option. Volatility is implied from the option's current price, using a standard option-pricing model. Keeping all other inputs constant, you can put the current market price of an option into any theoretical option price calculator and it will calculate the volatility implied by that option price.

PRICING STRATEGIES MANAGEMENT

Changes in the marketing environment may require a review of the prices of products already in the market. For example, an announcement by a large firm that it is going to lower its prices makes, it necessary for other firms in the industry to examine their prices. A review of pricing strategy may also become necessary because of shifts in demand. An examination of existing prices may lead to one of three strategic alternatives:

- Maintaining the price,
- Reducing the price, or
- Increasing the price.

If the market segment from which the company derives a big portion of its sales is not affected by changes in the environment, the company may decide not to initiate any change in its pricing strategy and maintain the status quo in the prices. The strategy of maintaining price is appropriate in circumstances where a price change may be desirable, but the magnitude of change is indeterminable. If the reaction of customers and competitors to a price change cannot be predicted, maintaining the present price level may be appropriate.

There are three main reasons for lowering the prices. Firstly, the prices as defensive measure may be cut in response to competition. To successfully compete in mature industries, many companies reduce prices following a strategy that is often called value pricing. For example, in view of the slipping profit margins and lower customer counts, McDonald's cut prices under pressure from major rival companies like Burger King, Wendy's, and Taco Bell. A second reason for lowering prices is offensive in nature. A company that follows this strategy is Home Depot; the largest home repair chain in USA. The policy of everyday low prices has enabled the company to grow into US$ 4 billion chain of 150 stores, mostly in the Sunbelt. Home Depot's goal is to go national with US $20 billion in sales at more than 350 locations by the year 2005. The recession in USA during the early 1990s caused consumers to tighten belts and to be more sensitive to prices. Sears, therefore, adopted a new pricing policy whereby prices on practically all products were permanently lowered. The company closed its 824 stores for two days to remark price tags and to implement its "everyday low pricing" strategy. A number of other companies, such as Wal-Mart and Toys "R" Us also pursue this strategy by keeping prices low year-round, avoiding the practice of marking them up and down. Consumers like year-round low prices because constantly changing sale prices makes, it hard to recognize a fair deal. Similarly, fast-food chains have started offering "value" menus of higher-priced items.

Last reason for price-cutting may be a response to customer need. If low prices are a prerequisite for inducing the market to grow, customer need may then become the pivot of a marketing strategy, all other aspects of the marketing mix being developed accordingly. An increase in price may be implemented for various reasons. First, in an inflationary economy, prices may need to be adjusted upward in order to maintain profitability. During inflation all types of costs go up and for adequate profits, an increase in price becomes necessary. How much the price should be increased is a matter of strategy that varies from case to case. Conceptually, the price should be increased to such a level that the profits before and after inflation are almost equal. An increase in the price should also take into account any decline in revenue caused by shifts in demand due to price increases. Strategically, the decision to minimize the effects of inflationary pressures on the company through price increases should be based on long-term implications in order to achieve a short-run advantage.

Downside of increasing price may be illustrated with reference to coffee. Let us say that there is a segment of customers who ardently drink Maxwell House coffee. In their minds, Maxwell House has something special. If the price of Maxwell House goes up (assuming that the prices of other brands remain unchanged), these coffee drinkers may continue to purchase it because the brand has a virtual monopoly over their coffee-drinking behaviour. There is a limit, however, to what these Maxwell House loyalists will pay for their favourite brand of coffee. Thus, if the price of Maxwell House is increased too much, these customers may shift their preference. The extent of the increase in price , however, depends on many factors. Each competitor has a different optimum price level for a given end product for a given customer group. It is rare that such optimum prices are the same for any two competitors. Each competitor has different options based on different cost components, capacity constraints, financial structure, product mix, customer mix, logistics, culture, and growth rate. The competitor with the lowest optimum price has the option of setting the common price; all others must follow or retreat. However, the continued existence of competitors depends on each firm retreating from competition when it is at a disadvantage until each competes primarily in a "competitive segment," a monopolistic situation where it has an advantage compared to all others.

This unique combination of characteristics, matched with differentials in the competitive environment, enables each firm to coexist and prosper in its chosen area (i.e., where it has monopolistic control).

Prices may also be increased to segment the market. A high priced soft drink company may launch its product for executives. This brand may be differentiated as one that provides stamina and invigoration without adding calories. To substantiate the brand's worth and make it appear different, the price may be set at double the price of existing soft drinks. Hewlett-Packard Company operates in the highly competitive pocket calculator industry, where the practice of price-cutting is quite common. Hewlett-Packard thrives by offering high-priced products to a select segment of the market. Strategic pricing is one of the most powerful sources of profits and growth. Yet, in recent years, it has been the least exploited driver of shareholder value. Few manufacturers review their pricing systematically. Most set prices reactively. Some extrapolate from history, and for others it's just a hunch. Today the need for strategic pricing is greater than ever. Pressures from price-sensitive consumers on one side, and a forceful and consolidating retail trade on the other, have resulted in significant price rollbacks on everything from cigarettes to cereal. Some claim the rollbacks have been good for business, but the net result has been considerable profit erosion. Pricing now is little more than a plug to make our plan numbers." The implementation of strategic pricing can provide following advantages.

- Boost total profitability by pricing based on consumers' long-term demand elasticity
- Increase sales of a company's most profitable products
- Improve the profitability of noncore businesses
- Stop price leaks by monitoring price concessions
- Create competitive advantage that is hard to imitate

Regaining control of prices, however, won't be easy. In most organizations, pricing power is diffused among many players making countless decisions across multiple functions and locations. Today no manager knows precisely what portion of any list price is actually realized. That means he or she can't position the product for the greatest return while making pricing decisions. It is necessary for the senior managers to rethink all aspects of pricing—strategies, tactics, processes, and capabilities—from the ground up. To succeed, the team must integrate four activities, as discussed below:

Product's Value Equation

Every product has an implied value equation, which takes into account the relationship between its quality, convenience, and price. This relationship will vary for different consumer segments. The team's first job is to analyze their products' value equations and benchmark them against the competitior's. The team should investigate

- Product positioning, which includes brand value, relative share position, and private-label development
- Competitive landscape, which includes the pricing supply curve, relative cost structure, and market discipline (leaders and followers)
- Consumer motivation, which includes segmentation of needs and benefits, long-term price elasticity, the impulse-buying dynamic, and life-cycle profitability in each segment

Objective is to ensure that the pricing structure supports the value equation as well as captures the full value of any advantages in cost, quality, or service. We call this "pricing to your sweet spot." If, for instance, the product is the only one of its kind to feature a warranty that consumers particularly value, it should be priced accordingly. Such a strategy goes beyond traditional pricing tactics to recognize the value of a product that can be realized in the marketplace.

Plug in the Price Leaks

Generic pricing often conceals differences in the cost of serving customers and can distort the net profitability delivered by channel, customer, and product. The SWAT team must discover the price leaks where profits are being lost. This involves tracking all the contractual and non contractual discounts, promotions, and other costs of serving customers (such as finance charges, warehousing and delivery costs, and administrative costs) that siphon off revenues.

Price leaks can be found throughout the company. Often, they are hidden in unexpected places or misperceived as the cost of doing business with customers. These "costs" should be examined with the same de-averaging tools that accountants and manufacturers use to examine product profitability. Once the team determines the true profitability of each account, opportunities for strategic pricing will surface. Companies that have systematically plugged their leaks have seen their profits increase by as much as 25 percent.

Negotiate Prices for Profits

Integrating the pieces of the pricing puzzle will also reveal opportunities to improve the productivity of promotions. In recent years, promotions have increased, and spending on off-invoice discounting, price exceptions, promotional allowances, merchandising funds, and rebates have grown dramatically. Too often, promotions amount to price leaks rather than investments. Although some promotions pay off, many merely transfer value to retailers and to consumers who forward-buy. Negotiating deals by using simplistic rules of thumb, such as number of cases shipped to retailers, can be misleading and expensive. Instead, negotiations and, for some retailers, payments should be based on true incremental volume actually sold to consumers. The company should review trade spending to determine the total return on investment. It also needs to determine its promotion strategy in the context of the retailer's pricing strategies. Differences in retailer pricing strategies (everyday low prices versus high-low pricing, for instance) and the margins that retailers take on various products will significantly affect a manufacturer's negotiating power and posture.

Process Streamlining

No pricing strategy will work for long without a well-managed process. The company should reach down in the organization, define clear roles and responsibilities, and make sure that the right information is always available to the people who need it. Several parts of the organization play a role in pricing, but it takes executive clout to synchronize all the levers, nail down the tactical side, and make the tough strategic decisions. A few companies have already moved in this direction by appointing a pricing board or council to integrate pricing data and streamline decisions. This doesn't centralize authority over pricing as much as manage the dissemination of information that others need in order to make the right decisions. The council monitors movement in the price of raw materials and analyses portfolio mix, account-pricing strategy, and profitability. Based on this information, the company redesigned its pricing structure and renegotiated its trade deals and rebate programs to focus on performance. It also established a new process for authorizing price exceptions. In addition to helping the company win back control over its prices, the streamlined process saved costs by eliminating rework and reducing administrative expenses. As a result, many companies increased its bottom line by several percentage points.

It's hard to believe, but Mercedes Benz is the only car maker to have introduced over six variants in India within a year. This makes one wonder what the size of the super-premium segment is. Estimates say, under 2,000 cars. Mercedes Benz, itself, sold 800 cars in the calendar year 2000, in India. Meanwhile, direct competitor BMW sold only about 100. The essential difference between the two is that BMW continues to import CBUs (completely built units) through its two dealers for India, a much longer process, (and therefore a limited service network), whereas Mercedes has had a manufacturing facility here for four years, set up with an investment of Rs 600 crore. Working in a market that is limited does not deter Jurgen Ziegler, managing director, Mercedes India: "The idea was to establish India as a quality manufacturing base for world markets. We never expected the Indian market for such luxury cars to be really big." Initially, the company focused on exporting CBUs from India to around 25 countries in the South African and East Asian markets. But in the last year, it has stopped exports of cars, and has instead developed its 20-odd local vendors to supply parts to its sister plants in Germany and the US. The company claims to have exported 200 million deutsche marks worth of parts so far. It now plans to supply components for the entire portfolio of Daimler products worldwide.

However, Mercedes now feels that it can bridge the gap between the premium luxury segment (where cars such as the Hyundai Sonata, Honda Accord, Opel Vectra and Skoda Octavia are likely to compete in therange of US$ 25000-35000 (approx.) and the super-premium segment (US$ 45000 plus). The recently launched C-class Mercedes is supposed to be the product. Mercedes feels that a customer would be willing to shell out an additional US$ 6500 (the range starts at US$ 46000) just for the lure of the 'three-pointer star'. The C-class comes in two trim levels of Classic and Elegance. The latter comes equipped with a multi-function steering wheel, alloy wheels and leather upholstery for a US$ 2000 more. It also has engine choices of petrol and diesel. To aid further differentiation amongst the differentiated, Mercedes will introduce the AMG range of body-styling kits to add on to the car. Of course, a Mercedes customer can then graduate up the value chain by moving from the C-class to the E-class (priced at around US$ 65000) and then all the way up to the S-class (priced at US$ 130,000). Others too are joining the game. It remains to be seen, however, if the Indian consumer can skip the D-segment entirely and move directly into the Mercedes segment. The pre-owned cars scheme (refurbished used Indian Mercedes cars) will definitely addict the consumer to the three-pointer star at prices as low as US$ 20000-22000 (approx.).

Ziegler, however, is not very happy with the Government's decision to raise the duties on imported cars to close to 110 percent. This puts a damper on Mercedes' plans to introduce a lot more imported models in the Indian market in CBU form. Presently, only the S-class from its stable is in CBU form (with just 20-per cent local content). The company claims that the C-class already has indigenous levels of over 50 percent, while the E-class (the oldest of the Mercedes series in India) has 70 per cent. Additionally, Mercedes hopes to sell a few M-class, SLK, CLK and other S-class imports as well. It also plans to market the Jeep range of vehicles in India, such as the Cherokee and Voyager from 2002 onward. The only stumbling block here is the 'homologation charges' that it has to pay per model of car that it brings in, which ranges from US$ 20000-22000, at the ARAI, Pune. Therefore, the reluctance of all car companies, in fact, to bring in their other international models; since volumes just won't justify investments.

Although most companies have focused on cost reduction, strategic pricing has a much more opportunity to boost profits by as much as 50 percent. These four questions can serve as a quick audit of your pricing capabilities:[3]

1. Do your competitors' pricing strategies seem irrational or inconsistent, or could they be part of a winning strategy?
2. Do you suspect price leaks, and if so, do you know where and how big they are?
3. Do you control all aspects of your pricing process?
4. Do you price by default or by design?

Strategic pricing is not a one-time tactic; it's a fundamental restructuring of all activities that affect pricing. That's why it offers long-term, sustainable value. And there's another, more subtle benefit. Because the restructuring occurs deep within the organization, it is nearly impossible for competitors to imitate.

PRICE CONTROL

Government rules and regulations pertaining to pricing should be considered while setting prices by the foreign firm in a host country. Legal requirements of both the host country and the administration of the host country must be satisfied. We have already discussed the legal aspects that affect marketing decisions of a foreign firm in Chapter 6. The firm need to consider the provisions of antitrust laws of the host country that would apply to any foreign pricing decision. A host country's laws concerning price setting may range from broad guidelines to product specific procedures for arriving at prices, amounting to virtual control over prices. However, government regulations evolved over time and may change during a firm's operation.

Consumer Information Act, 1978 of Ireland prohibits false or misleading indications of the price or the recommended price of goods, services or accommodation. The regulation on pricing in the country suggests that a consumer is expected to pay for the product or services what price he finds on it. The consumer should not have to pay any extra or 'hidden' charges. However, if a wrong price is marked on goods, the seller may be found guilty of giving a false price indication but the buyer does not have the right to demand that the goods be sold to them at the marked price. In other words a price ticket does not oblige the seller to sell at the price marked. The Act also makes it an offence to give a false or misleading indication of a previous price. If one price is stricken out and another has put in, the previous price must be accurate. In the absence of any indication to the contrary the goods in question must have been on sale in the same place at that previous price for at least

3 Michael Grindfors, Matthew A. Krentz and Henry M. Vogel , *Boston Consultancy Group*

> 28 successive days in the previous three months. The Irish law envisages that all prices must be indicated on or near the item or in such a position as to be easily read by the purchaser while he or she is at the place where the item is for sale and the prices given for goods or services must be stated as a single amount inclusive of tax. In the services marketing outlets a list of beverages, their measure and the corresponding price must be displayed both near the entrance and inside the premises as per the legal stipulations. Besides, where different prices are charged in different parts of the premises they must be displayed in the different parts of the premises.[4]

Different countries resolve different rates of inflation, some like Israel and Argentina in the past showing hyper-inflationary patterns by presenting the standard solution is selective price controls. The price controls may signal the global marketer that prices can not be changed frequently in the market and may pose a threat to normalize the profit of the firm in the situation of rising inflation. The currencies of such countries will continuously be losing their value against stronger currencies, while their governments will intervene in the workings of the financial system in order to bring some stability to prices. Under price controls, increases in prices usually need to be officially sanctioned. To obtain such sanction it is typically required that price increases be directly related to costs. Accordingly, companies with exemplary accounting records tend to have a much better chance of getting their requests for increases in price sanctioned. There are many types of price controls that are exercised in the developing countries to protect the consumers. Of these, mention may be made of *price ceilings,* which prevent prices from exceeding a certain maximum, and cause shortages. *Price floors,* which prohibit prices below a certain minimum, cause surpluses. Suppose the supply and demand for automobile tires are balanced at the current price, and that the government then fixes a lower ceiling price. The number of tires supplied will be reduced, but the number demanded will increase. The result will be excess demand and empty shelves. Although some consumers will be lucky enough to purchase tires at the lower price, others will be forced to do without. However, In terms of price discrimination, there are very few laws of the American Robinson-Patman type that prohibit discrimination unless justified by cost savings. The issue of bribery surfaces easily. The firm needs to get some legal advice on what is acceptable and what is not in the particular country.

BUILDING PRICING STRATEGIES

A firm's best opportunity lies in differentiating the product. A differentiated product offers more opportunity for increasing earnings through higher prices. Thus a company has to set-in the process of pricing strategy carefully analyzing its marketing-mix strategies in the host country. The first step in the process begins with determining the pricing objectives. This has to be done in reference to the strategy of selection followed in identifying the market segments. Since, pricing is one of the sensitive factors, the pricing objectives need to be carefully selected. Among many the major objectives helping in formulating the pricing strategy are as under:

4 For details on consumer protection regulation in Ireland see European Consumer Centre-Dublin at http://www.ecic.ie/consumer/misleading_info/mli_3.htm

- In the stiff competitive market scenario some of the companies functioning with over capacity and attempting to cater the shifting demands, often choose *survival* as the prime objective. The companies with this objective generally slash prices for operational reasons and do not look for any profit avenues. The company can survive with the price level as long as, it could recover the variable costs and some of the fixed costs. However, it would be difficult for the companies to get along with the survival pricing strategy in long-run.
- It has been a common organizational behavior of the business firms to augment their profit level to the maximum in a short span. The companies with such objective of *maximizing current profit* set their prices accordingly. In this process the companies assess the demand and costs associated with the alternative prices and formulate prices that generate maximum profit in short-run.
- *Some companies that reflect in their gross profit or revenue also choose maximum sales realization.* The maximization of revenue can be done by proper assessment of the demand of products of the company. It is assumed by many managers that the revenue generation is the only way for gaining more market share and so the high profit in long-run.
- Many companies will be of the favor to push the prices of their products upward with a view to skim the segmented markets. This strategy will help in building substantial buyers segments with reasonably high demand for the product and initial high-price does not allow more number of competitors to make entry. The high-price also helps the company to build-up the quality image of their product. The entry of *Kellogg's* in Indian market with their breakfast cereal product line has the same objective. It is a product positioned in the class market with high-price and skimming strategy. The high price added to the brand image of the products and its company. Similarly, *Surf Excel* the detergent from Hindustan Lever Limited, has adopted the market skimming strategy keeping the price comparatively higher. The consumers of the high purchasing power segment largely accept the product. The price of the product backed by the promotion wizards and quality added the high brand image in the market.
- Company may also achieve the product-quality leadership in the market by effective price intervention. The premium price strategy may earn high revenue for the company as well as help in brand positioning among the existing top bracket. This would in long run lead the company to become market leader.
- Besides, the manufacturing and marketing companies the price is also determined for the services. The social work organizations formulate the pricing strategy on the basis of the social price for the service. However most of the non-profit organizations fix-up the price for the services with a view to recover the full cost thereof.

Pricing takes its own dynamics in the market in the long run. The problem of pricing is observed generally when the firm is setting the price for the first time. This may happen when the company gets into the new business, acquiring products, distribution and expansion of the market area. Price has direct relationship with the product quality and brand image. Higher product quality and brand image would possess higher price. Such strategies are used for premium products while for the mass market price the price level is kept low and the quality of the product is medium. The company may place the products of medium quality and brand image in the average price bracket. Such pricing strategy would help to position the product for the consumer segment of middle level income category. In case the company desires to take its products to the mass market, it is necessary for the company to deliver the goods and services at the low price. However, the quality and the brand image would remain the same of medium quality. There exists the danger of all operations going sick in long term, if the company further tends to lower down the quality of the product in order to reduce the price. It may also hamper the brand image of the company to a large extent.

Company should also look into the price sensitivity factors associated with the price and demand of the product. In general the price sensitivity of the product would be higher provided the demand decreases in larger proposition to the increase in the price. This may happen when the product is close to the substitutes. Example may be cited of the edible oils as the brand switching is very fast and consumers are highly sensitive to the price rise. There happened 24 percent decrease in the demand of groundnut oil of *safal* brand in Karnataka in India in response to 6 percent increase in the oil price. On the contrary the consumers are less price sensitive in case of essential commodities like cereals, gas, petrol etc. Nagle[5] has identified some factors affecting the price sensitivity of the consumers. The consumers are less sensitive to the price of the products, (i) which have rare availability and unique value (ii) when they have inadequate knowledge of the substitutes (iii) when it is not possible to distinguish the attributes and quality of the product with the competing products (iv) when the expenditure is lower to their income (v) when the total cost incurred to the end product by the buyers will be less (vi) when the cost of the product is borne by the third party (vii) when the product is of high quality, status and is exclusive, and (viii) when the buyer can not store the products for long run at low prices viz., Fruits and vegetables, milk etc.

Company may look for the strategic options in determining the price of the product. Under the circumstances of high customer loyalty and the possibility of losing good percentage of them to the competitors, the company need not make any changes in the price and rather maintain the existing price level. The company may gradually prune the consumer segments and increase the price. However, in exigencies the company may raise the price to cover the rising cost but simultaneously ensure quality improvement in the product. Such strategic option may lead the company for smaller market shares and maintained profitability. The company may choose the strategy to maintain the price and increase the quality of the products in view of long term increase in the profitability. It is cheaper to maintain the price and increase the perceived quality of goods and services. The company may also opt for cutting the price partly and increasing the perceived quality for maintaining the existing market share. It is needed to offer high value for the goods and services by reducing the price to some extent. This would help the company to win the confidence of the consumers and keep

5 Nagle Thomas T: *The Strategy and Tactics Pricing*, Prentice-Hall, Englewood Cliffs, New Jersey, Chapter III, 1987.

its market share intact. The above discussed situations are some of the probable market situations which require strategic pricing for the mutual gains of the company and consumers.

Company can always protect its price and market share by various means. In case of escalating costs of the resources, process, inputs, packaging and other components the company can strategically respond to the high costs or increasing demand without raising the prices of its goods and services. As such the company may look into the following possibilities:

- Shrinking the volume of the product
- Substituting low cost material in packaging
- Rationalizing the product process
- Reducing overheads and curtsey promotion
- Creating new economy brands of the goods and services

Best response to the market situations varies largely. Hence, a company should always develop alternative strategies and analyze the marketing-mix in detail. The bundling pricing strategy is also an important strategy being used by many companies in the competitive environment. This strategy may be defined as an inclusion of extra margin in the price to cover a variety of cascading price functions and services which are required to sell and maintain the products in the long run in the spatial and temporal markets. This pricing strategy may be implemented to generate extra revenues to cover the anticipated expenses of providing services and maintaining the product and to generate revenues for supporting after-sales service personnel. The price bundling strategy also helps to establish a contingency fund for unanticipated happenings and developing an ongoing relationship with the customer.

This strategy is ideally suited for technologically sophisticated products that are susceptible to rapid technological obsolescence because these products are generally sold in systems and usually require the following:

- Extra technical sales assistance,
- Custom design and engineering concept for the customer,
- Peripheral equipment and applications,
- Training of the customer's personnel, and
- A strong service/maintenance department offering prompt responses and solutions to customer problems.

Implementation of this strategy would yield results in keeping the asset in an acceptable condition for resale or release and generate positive cash flow. The price bundling strategy would provide instant information on changing customer needs and also helps in increasing the sales due to "total package" concept of selling because customers feel they are getting their money's worth.

OTHER PRICING MODALITIES

Export pricing is affected by the price destination which determines as who will pay the price-the final consumer, independent distributors, a wholly owned subsidiary, a joint venture organization or someone else. The nature of the product whether it is raw or semi-processed material, components, finished or largely finished products or services or intangible property like patents, trademarks, formulas etc. also affect the export pricing in a country. Besides, the export pricing in a country is affected by the currency used for billing which reveals the currency of the purchaser's county, the seller's home country currency, or a leading international currency. The price destination is an important consideration since different destinations present different opportunities and problems. For example, pricing to sell to a government may require special procedures and concessions not necessary in pricing to other customers.

Determination of transfer prices in multinational companies is an important issue because a substantial proportion of international exchanges consists of transactions between a parent corporation and its affiliates. The *transfer pricing refers* to the pricing of goods or services among units within the corporation. It serves as a measure of the economic performance of profit centers within the enterprise. It differs from market price, which measures exchanges between a company and the outside world, for the net effect of transfer pricing is borne by the same organization. There has to be a price paid for the products shipped between units of the same organization when the shipment crosses national borders so that the correct duties and related fees can be paid. However, since the transfer prices directly affect the amount of purchases in the cost accounting of a foreign subsidiary, they have a direct influence on the subsidiary's financial performance.

STRATEGY FOR PRICE LEADERSHIP

Price-leadership strategy prevails in competitive market environment. The leading firm then makes pricing moves that are duly acknowledged by other members of the industry. Thus, this strategy places the burden of making critical pricing decisions on the leading firm; others simply follow the leader. The leader is expected to be careful in making pricing decisions. A faulty decision could cost the firm its leadership because other members of the industry would then stop following its footsteps. For example, if in increasing prices, the leader is motivated only by self-interest; its price leadership will not be emulated. Ultimately the leader will be forced to withdraw the increase in price. The price-leadership strategy is a static concept. The major factors that influence the price leadership include:

- Substantial share of the industry's production capacity
- Large market share of the products and brands in the market
- Domination in the product class or consumer segment
- Cost effective production and distribution strategy
- Strong distribution system, perhaps including captive wholesale outlets
- Good customer relations
- An effective market information system that provides analysis of the realities of supply and demand
- Sensitivity to the price and profit needs of the rest of the industry

- A sense of timing to know when price changes should be made, and
- Effective product line financial controls, which are needed to make sound price leadership decisions

In an environment where growth opportunities are adequate, companies would rather maintain stability than fight each other by means of price wars. Thus, the leadership concept works out well in this case. In the auto industry, General Motors is the leader, based on market share. Usually, the leader is the company with the largest market share. The leadership strategy is designed to stave off price wars and "predatory" competition that tend to force down prices and hurt all parties. The leaders chastise companies that deviate from this form through discounting or shaving. Price deviation is quickly disciplined.

NON-PRICE FACTORS

Factors other than price may be important in analyzing buying situations. Buyers may be willing to pay a premium price to gain other advantages or, be willing to forgo certain advantages for lower prices. Other important factors besides price that may be important are quality, uniqueness, availability, convenience, service, and warranty. In an attempt to recover from intense price competition, fast food chains are marketing value menus of higher-priced items. These value strategies include the quality of the food, user friendly service, and attractive dining facilities. For example, McDonald's advertising message, "What you want is what you get," emphasizes the concept of value. Value mapping is a useful technique for analyzing how buyers perceive the offerings of different brands. One approach is to first develop the map based on managers' opinions, followed by obtaining value perceptions from a sample of consumers.

Certain buying situations may reduce the importance of price in the buyer's choice process. The price of the product may be a minor factor when the amount is small compared to the importance of the use. Examples include infrequently purchased electric parts for home entertainment equipment, batteries for appliances, and health and beauty aids during a vacation. The need for important but relatively inexpensive parts for industrial equipment is another situation that reduces the role of price in the buyer's purchase decision. Maintenance personnel to repair production equipment use quick metal, an adhesive produced by Loctite Corporation. At less than $20 a tube, the price is not a major concern since, one tube will keep an expensive production line operating until a new part is installed.

AN OVERVIEW ON PRICING STRATEGY

Pricing strategy is of high importance to the functional and policy management levels of a company. Pricing decisions are primarily affected by factors, such as pricing objectives, cost, competition, and demand that are difficult to articulate and analyze. There are two principal pricing strategies for new products, skimming and penetration. Skimming is a high-price strategy; penetration strategy sets a initial price to generate volume. Three strategies for established products were discussed about maintaining the price, reducing the price, and increasing the price. A flexible pricing strategy provides leverage to the company in terms of borrowing the time and commitment both from market to market and from product to product line-pricing strategy, which is directed toward maintaining a balance among products offered. The leasing strategy constitutes an alternative to outright sale of the product. The bundling strategy is concerned with aging products and associated services together. Price-leadership strategy is required in competitive market environment to outperform the rivals, where one company in an industry emerges as a leader and sets the pricing strategy to build market share.

REFERENCES

Rajagopal, "*Marketing Management: Text and Cases,*" Delhi, Vikas Publishing House, 2000.

Simon, Hermann, and Martin Fasfnacht : "Price Bundling," *European Management Journal,* Vol.11, December 1993, pp. 403-411.

Simon, Hermann, and Eckhard Kughe :, "The European Pricing Time Bomb," *European Management* Journal, Vol.10, June 1992, pp. 136-145.

Gijbrechts, Els : "Prices and Pricing Research in Consumer Marketing: Some Recent Developments," *International Journal of Research in Marketing,* Vol. 10, No.2, June 1993, pp. 115-151.

Monroe, Kent B. : *Pricing: Making Profitable Decisions,* New York McGraw-Hill, 1990.

Nagle, Thomas T. : *The Strategy and Tactics of Pricing,* Englewood Cliffs, NJ: Prentice-Hall, 1987.

Rao, Vithala. "Pricing Models in Marketing ," in *Handbooks in Operation Research and Management Science: Marketing,* Joshua Eliashberg and Gary L. Lilien, eds. Amsterdam: North-Holland, 1993, pp. 517-552.

Simon, Hermann : *Price Management,* Amsterdam: North-Holland, 1989.

Haywood Klien : "Illinois Bell Faces New Environment as Era of Competitive Pricing Nears," *The Wall Street Journal,* 31 December 1981: Vol. 9.

Robert J. Dolan : *"How Do You Know When the Price is Right?"* Harvard Business Review, September-October 1995: 174-183.

Stuart U. Rich : "Price Leaders: Large Strong but Cautious about Conspiracy," *Marketing News,* 25 June 1982: Vol. 11.

Case 4.1

THE AIR CARGO COMPETITION

The Runway

DHL was commissioned in 1969 to serve American Exporters with cost effective and quick delivery of documents across the countries in the world. It had first started sending documents by air to Honolulu from San Francisco. Over the years the DHL has spread its wings in 223 countries having its headquarters at Brussels. The DHL operates in India as the Express Division of Airfright Ltd. (AFL) established in 1945, having about US$ 90 million turnover[6] in the international market. AFL is knows as leader shipment services in the US$ 89 million organized sector express industry, of which the international business segment is estimated to be US$ 58 million while the rest belongs to the domestic market. DHL has invested about US$27 million in information and communication, infrastructure, and manpower during the past four years in India to set-up its roots with a vision to capture the growing international business in the country. In this service marketing sector the DHL has laid greater emphasis on infrastructure and logistics management in India for improving the service conditions of the company. Despite some operational odds the DHL stands first in the country among the existing cargo operators. It has marked a growth of 30 percent in the Indian market on an average per annum since 1992-93 and has marked the turnover of US$ 48 million during 1995-96. The closest competitors of DHL which stand at the second and third positions in the market are Blue Dart with a turnover of US$ 25.6 million and Elbee with a turnover of US$ 21.8 million respectively.[7] AFL was commissioned to serve to the import needs of TATA for expanding industrial network in India. In 1978 AFL and DHL were in the international alley by signing the contract for 10 years and later renewed it in 1988 for an indefinite period.

Taking Off

Business move of DHL has been designed to cater a special category of exporters in India. This courier company began selling services and later shifted its focus on packages with the development of fax and e-mail devices to international destinations. This category may be explicitly called as small exporters operating in large number. DHL spends about US$ 490 million annually on air freighting of goods weighing nearly 3,00,000 tones of each 500 kilogram consignment on an average to and from India. Of this the potential express fright segment estimated about ten thousand tones assembled of about 2,00,000 pieces of 50 Kilogram each in the *jumbo* packs. The jumbo box was later designed lighter to weigh 25 kilogram as it was an ideal weight for an individual to lift without exerting himself.

---

6 The financial data originally reported in the company documents are in Indian currency and accounting system. These figures have been converted into the US dollars for the convenience of understanding. Such conversions may give the approximate values.

7 Kohli Vanita : The Flying Elephant, *Advertising and Marketing,* 8 (12), September 30, 1996, p 36

Obviously, the data reveals that the DHL serves to the businessmen of small and medium category looking for an international market link. The idea of jumbo packaging boxes was conceived from an Australian experience but had been branded as jumbo by the office of DHL located at Singapore and could establish its brand identity in the market. Further in view of the need of Indian cargo customers, the jumbo junior boxes weighing up to 10 kilograms were introduced in May 1996 and their booking has been doubled as compared to the jumbos. However, in international markets the smaller packaging makes handling slightly complex due to time constraints and custom formalities. The DHL observed that the Indian parcel market is highly segmented and needs a down the line business approach at low cost.

Competitive Strategy

Courier services are more time loyal than brand loyal. In fact the price is paid for the time and guarantee of delivery of the goods and documents than any other consideration. The DHL saw the need of Indian exporters for dispatching samples, small shipments, time and fashion sensitive goods and found that if they were not delivered on time the business hand in distress. Hence the price was the consideration but DHL took in view of high volume low margin to hook-up the Indian courier market. DHL has put the service charges reasonably lower as compared to the other international courier agencies. The profit margin of DHL is realized from two areas- firstly, from the old customers and secondly from the volume of cargo. The US based DHL office uses the same infrastructure to move a packet of 100 kilogram as it would do for sending a document. Hence, the packets weighing 500 gm and above have the built-in cost of infrastructure and handling. DHL's focus area is South-East Asia while there are other courier services existing for the European countries and USA.

In terms of size and network the DHL India is ahead of competitors but its revenues are lower as compared to its counterparts in the international market. DHL operates in 223 countries while FedEx (Federal Express, international partner of Blue Dart Express) does its business in 211 countries of Europe and the US. Similarly the UPS, a division of Elbee operates in 200 countries with major focus in the US. The revenue is highest of UPS $21 billion followed by FedEx ($9.4 billion) and DHL ($4 billion) in 1995. The employee turnover of DHL is about $ 3.68 million as compared to $2.36 million of Elbee. DHL believes in wider area of operation to establish brand image and business roots in the international market. The right price is the price which no competitors can cross down. The DHL strategy is based on service efficiency at lower expenses in the international market. The door delivery service is another advantage which added to the performance of the company and the Jumbo Box became a high value brand in India.

Perspectives

There are two prominent areas to be developed in the cargo and courier services- door delivery and uninterrupted logistics. The communication network should be built strongly through the latest available techniques like internet and super highways. DHL pools the need of warehousing for smooth distribution of cargo to the individual destinations and provides logistic support through its Express Logistics Centers (ELCs). It would be possible in developing nations because of availability of labor at low cost for the logistics functions like assembling, sorting, billing and delivery. However, a different strategy needs to be looked for the developed countries due to high labor costs. In the context of liberalization, there exists greater threat of new entrants in this field by 2000 AD. Hence, the strong concept selling in the target markets would help growing the brand image and public opinion.

Issues for Discussion

Above case illustrates the international portfolio of a company, which has segmented its market and clientele. It has been enjoying the significant market share within its area of operation but is not far away from the threat of international giants in the field of service marketing. Despite the efforts of DHL to be the first in the row of cargo and courier companies, there remain some issues for discussion in-depth. They are:

- Is the pricing strategy adopted by DHL sustainable in long run ?
- What should be the strategy-mix for expanding the market to other customer segments spread over globally?
- What should be the size of cargo and documents for global delivery approach?
- Why should DHL operate in domestic market in India when it could exploit more opportunities in the international market?
- What should be strategy for concept selling and mass advertisement?
- How can DHL become the brand leader in the international market?
- How can the communication and logistics networking are done? Can this type of strategic alliance work efficiently?

A manager should also think of the prolific areas of investing money in future from the corporate angle. The time and cost involvement in handling more global accounts and its impact on the profit bowl are the major concerns before the company.

Case 4.2

'CRIMSON NECTAR' BLOWS-UP IN BOARDROOM :

A Case of Building Marketing Policy of a New Generation Product[8]

Innovation by definition will not be accepted at first. It takes repeated attempts, endless demonstrations, monotonous rehearsals before innovation can be accepted and internalized by an organization. This requires "courageous patience."

Warren Bennis

Decision to develop new products and push them in the market is usually based on either ambition or anxiety. Ambitious companies note that sales of solutions win fatter margins than sales of products and generate longer and more lucrative customer contracts, provide access to new markets, and even help procure a more favorable press. Anxious ones fear rapidly commoditizing core-product markets, pricing pressure from increasingly savvy buyers, and the appearance of aggressive new intermediaries. The companies need to look more carefully before leaping into solutions. They ought to be sure that what they are offering really is a solution—that they have correctly assessed the degree of integration, customization, or both, required to turn a bundle of products into a truly integrated package. These two elements—customization and integration—are more than just the glue that holds the package together: the way the elements are integrated and the extent of customization define the added value for buyers and earn the added financial benefits for sellers. The health drink like Crimson Nectar may achieve commercial integration but offers no more than some incremental convenience to the customer, and certainly not the customization or the technical integration needed to deliver value beyond what is to be had by purchasing a hamburger, fries, and a soft drink individually. The restaurant thus can't charge a premium for its offering; on the contrary, it must provide a discount. Setting up a new business unit to provide a growth strategy for this new market lengthened the sales cycle and was expensive: selling, general, and administrative costs may rise to 14 percent, from 9 percent. Is it a healthy sign for a company to go ahead with the new products? This case discusses further on this issue.

---

8 This case has been developed by Dr. Rajagopal, Professor of Marketing, Business Division, ITESM, Mexico City Campus, Mexico 14380 DF (E-mail : rajagopal@itesm.mx)
This case has been written as the basis for class discussion rather than to illustrate either effective or ineffective handling of an administrative situation of the company. November 2003.

CONSUMPTION TRENDS OF NON-ALCOHOLIC BEVERAGES

Despite comprising 20% of the non-alcoholic beverage market, fruit juices and juice drinks lag behind carbonated beverages and bottled water. Those two segments, however, are facing changes themselves, changes that could propel the fruit juice and juice drinks category. Water and fruit juices have the perception of healthfulness. Recent bottled waters have incorporated new flavors and functions, blurring the line between fruit juices, isotonic and water beverages. The growth in bottled water segment and decline in carbonated beverages segments could mean a promising future for juices. Common wisdom has led the bottled water segment to new heights, as consumers have embraced the message of drinking eight 8-oz. servings of water daily. An extension of this philosophy could easily boost the juice and juice drinks market.[9] Nonetheless, sales of fruit juices and juice drinks dropped 2%—from US $10.8 billion in 2001 to US $10.5 billion in 2002. Juices account for 60% of sales, the remainder going to juice drinks. They have a high penetration of the U.S. consumer market, so the potential for future growth appears to be limited. In fact, Mintel projects less than 1% growth from 2002 to 2007, though this could be higher by "increasing per capita value" through more product introductions, and convincing consumers that juices are a convenient beverage. Heineken, the world's No.3 brewer, with US $11 billion a year in sales, can no longer take for granted the strengths that have made its squat green bottle the envy of the business. It has been observed that the US $367 billion world beer market is changing. Beer consumption is declining in the USA and Europe. Advertising and packaging are becoming more daring, in a bid to capture the young 20's segment. However, in the times of changing preference to the non-alcoholic beverages the success of enhancing the scope of alcoholic beverages like beer is no longer guaranteed.

Consumers having preference for carbonates beverages across the globe are moving to healthier drinks such as bottled water and fruit/vegetable juices and manufacturers are looking into other alternatives to sustain growth in carbonates. Non-cola carbonates are perceived as healthier than cola variants, and flavoured non-cola carbonates sourced from local fruits such as Guaraná (one of the Brazilian exotic fruits) have become a growth point for major manufacturers in Latin America. Investment in developing and marketing exotic fruit flavoured drinks has been the natural move for soft drinks manufacturers, already constricted by the dominance of Coca-Cola and PepsiCo within the cola carbonates market. While the Brazilians are crazy about Guaraná, the Venezuelans' own local non-cola carbonates success story is a carbonated malt drink. Venezuelans consume a "malta", or malt, as an alternative to other cold beverages - malts are considered as nutritious and refreshing option since their main ingredients are derived from plants. Total malt carbonates brands together account for more than 70% of off-trade sales of other non-cola carbonates in Venezuela. Malt products are mainly produced by local beer producers. Domestic beer companies manufacture malts because they are able to produce and distribute these products with significant economies of scale using the same umbrella brands for both their beer and malt offerings. Furthermore, as advertising of alcoholic drinks is not allowed on broadcast media such as radio and public television, beer producers tend to use malta as a way to increase recognition and awareness of their beer brands. Malta brands

9 *Mintel International Group :* Report on "Fruit Juice & Juice Drinks Market", Chicago, 2002 Web site: www.mintel.com

have logos similar to beer, but as it is a soft drink, these can be advertised on public TV channels and on the radio. Flavoured non-cola carbonates are expected to continue to provide the momentum for growth in the non-cola carbonates category in the foreseeable future. Consumers will increasingly demand diversity of drinks, which will help spur sales in this category, whilst the ample supply of tropical fruits will provide a good platform for manufacturers. It is predicted that growth in flavoured non-cola carbonates will largely outperform the growth in carbonates as a whole in major countries in Latin America, growing by some 12% in volume terms between 2002-07, compared to just over 7% for non-cola carbonates in the same period.[10]

Traditional beverages from Latin America and other regions of the world offer good opportunities in the development of new and exotic beverages. Those beverages are prepared by using both native and non-native crops. In some cases traditional processing techniques involve fermentation. Long before the Spanish were able to produce a beverage using cocoa beans, the Mayas and the Aztecs of Mexico and Central America used cocoa in foods and beverages. Natives of Paraguay consumed Yerba Mate before the Europeans arrived in South America. In the 17th century, Jesuit missionaries expanded the use of Yerba Mate to other parts of the world. The industry based on this beverage is now a US $350 million industry that employs more than 400,000 people in Argentina, Brazil and Paraguay. Yerba Mate tea is now consumed in the United States and Europe where products such as carbonated beverages have been produced using extracts. Guaraná is a creeping shrub native to the Brazilian Amazon. Natives use a traditional method of preparation by drying and roasting the seeds and mixing them with water to form a paste. Local tribes used Guaraná to prepare foods, drinks and medicines. The Brazilian soft drink industry has produced carbonated beverages using Guaraná for years and now some companies in the U.S. are also producing drinks with Guaraná.[11] Pulque is a Mexican drink made by fermenting the sap of the undeveloped flowering stem of Agave. The fermented juice of the fruit of the Nopal[12] is consumed as a beer called Colonche. Chicha is a fermented beverage made with corn in some Latin American countries.

In 2002, the major soft drink companies launched many products in the recently opened niche market of energy drinks in Mexico. International companies such as Red Bull and Coca-Cola want to gain consumer acceptance by supporting events and promoting their products all over Mexico. Although the introductory price of such drinks in the country is considered high, the market is expected to develop at a respectable rate. Flavored water was very dynamic at the end of the review period. Companies are catering to those individuals who are tired of carbonated soft drinks and are looking for something healthier and pure. This new niche market, opened by Sabritas (a company owned by PepsiCo), is experiencing the emergence of new competitors with different capabilities. The amazing growth rates in volume terms proved that the product has potential in the Mexican soft drinks market. Certainly the market will become more dynamic with more players and different product presentations. Flavored water is a special sub-sector to watch closely in the following years.

10 Euromonitor : Local Flavours Spur Sales of Non-cola Cabonates in Latin America, *Euromonitor International,* 11 March 2003. Website : www.euromonitor.com/article/

11 Sancho Madriz, M. :*Traditional Beverages of Latin America,* California State Polytechnic University

12 Nopal is a edibal cactus, popularly used by Mexicans.

EXOTIC FRUIT NECTARS- INDUSTRY DIMENSIONS[13]

Pepsi's FruitWorks continued to outperform Coke's Fruitopia, registering a gain of 5.0% in 2002. However, this is a big change from the 405.0% increase recorded as recently as 2000 and reflects a maturation of the brand. The Sunny D. brand of Procter & Gamble grew slightly in 2002, after two years of sizeable declines. The company has put more emphasis on "chilled" single-serve Sunny D. of late, helping to counteract the declines in shelf-stable Sunny D. In 2002, Fruitopia suffered a 20% - plus decline for the second straight year. The Coca-Cola brand thus dropped below US $100 million in wholesale sales for the first time since 1997. This was enough to push market share from 3.4% in 2001 to 2.2% in 2002. After two years at 2.7%, Odwalla ended up with 2.9% of the market in 2002. Continuing a multi-year downward trend, Mistic lost 18.4% in 2002 to fall to US $ 55.9 million. The brand has lost more than half its market share since 1998, skidding from 3.9% to 1.8%. Consolidation and a growing presence of mega beverage companies characterize the fruit beverage market in general and the single-serve fruit beverage segment in particular. All three major carbonated soft drink (CSD) purveyors have added fruit beverage holdings in the new millennium.

In 2000, Cadbury Schweppes gained a more substantial single-serve fruit beverage presence with the acquisition of Snapple and Mistic from Triarc Companies. It added Nantucket Nectars in 2002. Pepsi added SoBe to its line-up, which also includes FruitWorks, Tropicana and Dole in 2001. In the same reference period. Coke expanded its presence in the single-serve juice segment with the purchase of Mad River Traders, a supplier of New Age teas, fruit drinks and sodas and Odwalla, which focuses mainly on fresh packaged juices. The latter runs under existing management as an independent part of the company's Minute Maid division. Coca-Cola also owns Fruitopia.

Advertising expenditures have grown as bottled water has become less of a "commodity" and more of a branded item. In 2002, bottled water ad dollars grew by 8.0% to US $ 84.2 million. However, bottled water's share of ad expenditures fell by one percentage point to 13.1% during the year. Energy drinks, led by Red Bull, increased ad dollars by 57.9% in 2002. The segment, which started in the U.S. only in 1997, surpassed redy-to-drink (RTD) tea in 2001, to become the fifth most advertised wellness and functional beverage segment. In 2002, enhanced water came into its own in terms of sales and ad expenditures. More was spent on enhanced water during the year than even RTD tea. This product of late noticed a turnaround in advertising support and after 42.6% decline in expenditures in 2001, RTD tea marketers planned for spending more than double budget in 2002.

In 2002, the top ten advertisers grew advertising expenditure by 19.0% to US $ 453.7 million. This represented 70.4% of all wellness and functional beverage expenditures, up from 69.0% in 2001. Gatorade remained the top advertiser by far despite only a 2.4% increase in expenditures. Two generic advertisers were among the top three advertisers in 2001. Representing the milk industry, Dairy Management Inc. and the Milk Industry Foundation combined for about US $ 103 million in expenditures, down from $117.5 million in 2001. Another generic advertiser, Florida Department of

13 This section of the notes have been submitted by the Company Secretary as background paper to the board meeting on introducing the new product in the Latin American market.

Citrus, came sixth with $38.2 million in expenditures. The agenda for the board meeting of the company is exhibited in Appendix 1.

IDEA CHAIN MANAGEMENT

Companies today rely heavily on their extended enterprise network to create value in their products and services. Beyond the immediate boundaries of the company, providers, partners, distributors, and customers hold critical expertise and knowledge on their areas of activity. There is tremendous potential among the competing companies in the fruit beverages sector to innovate and improve continuously by collecting and exploiting ideas from each specialized company in the value chain. The US has long research on the sources of ideas that steer innovation that indicate the scale of this potential for new product development. Idea Chain leverages this potential by selectively involving relevant external stakeholders in focused Idea Management initiatives across the extended enterprise network. By actively using the innovative power of business partners and customers, companies can significantly improve their products and processes. Improving the business through innovative ideas is in the mutual interest of every element of the value chain: suppliers, wholesalers, service partners and retailers. Idea chain is a process of bottom-up innovation process that involves the employees of the company, consumers, packaging organizations, distributors and retailers. Idea Chain can be used as a centralized hub to capture potential improvements suggested anywhere in the value chain. By sharing these suggestions and acting upon them fast, products, services and processes can be improved seamlessly, enabling companies to stay ahead of the competition.

With marketing, and particularly in new product development, doing things differently can also pay big dividends. Yet, most of those in new products use the same tactics-the same development and research tools-in very similar ways. The New product developers should inject creativity into the process, and use their methods and tools in different ways in order to manage the change. The brainstorming anonymously using an online web connectivity may be identified as "ideation chat room" to get some new dimensions and refinement tips. The idea chain is a contemporary concept and is used by many companies offering the customer solutions. *Many ideas grow better when transplanted into another mind than in the one where they sprang up* said Alma Garcia , the Marketing Vice President of the United Spirits Mexico SA de CV.

BOARD ROOM DISCUSSIONS

Board meeting began citing the reference of IBM Chief tabled by Mr Robert Green, CEO of United Sprits Mexico.

> *"With every business being swept along by the e-business revolution, there has never been a higher premium on the ability to innovate. I do not know how any company competes today without a thriving research and technical capability..."*
>
> ***Lou Gerstner, Chairman and CEO IBM***

Everybody remembered the 1994 launch. Amidst pirouetting belly dancers and firecrackers that lit the sky, was born the exotic fruit product "Crimson Nectar"- the nectar of red ripe cherries with malt and sugar. The product may be used as juice following the recommended dilution, toping application on ice-creams, cakes and pastries and as a substitute of red wine. This is non-alcoholic fruit beverage proposed to position as a strong natural and nutritive substitute of red wine and beer. The marketing team couldn't stop talking about the brand's many 'firsts'-the tamper-proof guala-cap, the unbreakable flexi-bottle, and the richly embossed label (the first for an exotic juice in the popular price band). It looked world class. For the Mexican division of Universal Spirits (US), the company behind the brand, it was a strategically bold move. A domestic brand priced at US $4 for 750 ml, a mere $ 6 Pesos premium over the country's largest selling brand Macduff, Crimson Nectar was intended to fetch US handsome volumes in the regular exotic juice segment (18 million cases a year). And with an ad campaign crafted to lead the consumer up the self-destiny-defining curve, Arturo Hernandez, the then CEO of US' Mexico unit,[14] was sure it would be a winner.

So, it was selling an amazing 2 million cases in 2001-02. That was less than half what No. 1 Macduff did (over 5 million cases), and less than two other brands that were older, but it was still "one helluva lot", as Mr. Hernandez saw it. At the moment, Crimson Nectar was up for sale. The company's UK headquarters wanted it to be sold. Its reasoning: as a global company, it no longer wished to sell a local brand, that too at the lower end of the market. That was not the only change at US. Mr. Hernandez was no longer chief of the Mexico arm. Yet, he was somehow still attached to the brand that had been his career's biggest success. Attached enough to float his own firm and make his own bid for it.

Now, here he was, at the office of Rockport Frapp, the investment banker appointed by US to evaluate the brand, wondering what was taking so long. Executives from US, who were also present, were ready to do most of the talking. "It's been awhile, hasn't it?" asked Mr. Hernandez, "Any second thoughts?" Ms. Dulce Flores, Chief Investment Analyst, Rockport Frapp, looked distinctly uncomfortable. Ms. Alma Garcia , Vice President (Marketing), US, shot a glance at his CEO, Robert Green, and then replied: "It's not an easy evaluation exercise, and since building a liquor brand in a restricted market is such a gruelling task, we have very few guideposts to go by." "There's Flags," said Mr. Hernandez, referring to the sale some years ago of another regular exotic juice brand, "which does about 3.5 million cases." Mr. Green spoke next. "Mr. Hernandez," he began, "we've seen that data, and you know better than us that we invested more in terms of both money and effort, in creating Crimson Nectar. The brand also has higher long-term potential than Flags. Given the requisite inputs, Crimson Nectar could even overtake Macduff for segment leadership. Had US not wanted to play only at the upper-end of the liquor market, it would be a terrific asset."

Asset, it certainly was. An asset that existed in people's heads. In US, occupying a well-defined portion of the consumer's mind was non-negotiable. Its vodka, Dostoevsky, was selling transparency, while its well-recognized Scotch brand, Adam Hume, was selling forward mobility. Crimson Nectar had also lodged itself neatly in its target's mind space. "Crimson Nectar is profitable," added Ms.

14 Mr. Arturo Fernandez is currently holding the position of Marketing Advisor and Member of the Board of Directors of United Spirits Mexico SA de CV

Flores, "and that is because the consumer remains in sync with the brand proposition of 'success'." This was getting awkward for Mr. Hernandez, who didn't want to underplay the brand success, but he wanted the best bargain he could get. Paying a 'sentiment surplus' was not good business. Plus, there were other Mexico marketers in the running for Crimson Nectar too. Most of these companies had better production and distribution capabilities, and deeper pockets than Mr. Hernandez's company. Yet, he saw himself as the rightful steward of the brand, the one best placed to help it evolve. Given his limited resources, much depended on the brand's perceived value amongst a handful of bidders-something that could be influenced by the auction's floor price.

Mr. Hernandez was aware of the likelihood that rival bidders could be dissuaded. The industry grapevine had been whispering that Crimson Nectar was actually a loss-making brand, since the payments to the 12 third-party manufacturers were just too high for such a low-realization brand. The packaging was overly expensive too, and cost-cutting could take some of the sheen off the brand. Mr. Green, however, was confident of attracting impressive bids from almost every liquor marketer in Mexico. Kiddo Mexico, a subsidiary of Kiddo International, had indicated that it was open to local acquisitions to augment its organic global brand-led growth. Others in the fray included Highlands, Bernard Wyss and Raspsons.

Ms. Garcia, who was watching the meeting unfold quietly all this while, finally decided to address Mr. Hernandez's key concerns. "It will take another week," she said, "since we're still studying the market's prospects. But, off the record, the floor price of US$ 3.6 mentioned in the press may be an under-estimate. That is what the discounted future cash-flow method indicates, by our preliminary calculations. And we don't want frivolous bids from non-players. Also, with clamps on brand communication getting tighter, the replacement cost of the brand is higher than before. Take that into account as well. It is not a normally competitive market, but if there's a boom later, the brand will be ready to capitalize on it. Current figures are not the only consideration."

"Precisely," interjected Mr. Green, "and at the end, I know that US will listen to business sense. If we find that the brand is significantly worth more than $ 200 Million Pesos, then maybe disposing it off isn't such a good idea. The asset still has scope to appreciate, and maybe we can even have a cut-off of US $ 30 million." "I'm not sure about appreciation," responded Mr. Hernandez, "given the advertising restrictions you spoke of. Also, don't forget the problem with Crimson Nectar mineral-water, it didn't do very much for the brand, as market research showed." "Yes," smiled Ms. Flores, "but the brand's gene code remains with US, and it is a matter of finding creative expression. The brand's growth curve hasn't plotted yet. By 2007, we could be No 1. Investors would pay anything for a market leader in such a difficult category."

"Really?" asked Mr. Hernandez, a little hot around the collars by now. "Then why don't you fight headquarters to keep Crimson Nectar? If the world's biggest brand can keep a local cola, then why not you? Ah, because it just won't get due attention, and won't reach No 1. This could happen with any acquirer- the bigger it is, the lesser attention it gets. It is in your interest to see that the buyer is able to extract the best value from the brand. Why price yourself out of the range of small bidders?" It was Ms. Garcia's turn to intervene. "The US does not want to narrow the field-but it does not want to sell Crimson Nectar short either, as simple as that. It's a good brand, and deserves a high floor price as a signal of its worth. This isn't a distress sale, you know." "But you don't have much room in your portfolio to keep it," said Mr. Hernandez, "So, if nobody matches your minimum bid, you'll have a lot of explaining to do to your global headquarters. I won't recommend taking that risk."

EXPERT VOICE IN BOARD ROOM

Before Mr. David Abraham was strangled with the questions of board members, he put this statement re-arranging his bow "...*Without ambition one starts nothing. Without work one finishes nothing. The prize will not be sent to you. You have to win it. The man who knows will always have a job. The man who also knows why will always be his boss. As to methods there may be a million and then some, but principles are few. The man who grasps principles can successfully select his own methods. The man who tries methods, ignoring principles, is sure to have trouble...*"

Should US' Mexico arm go for a high or low floor price for Crimson Nectar's auction? Any kind of auction is really a process to get the highest price for a product. To achieve that, one has to attract many suitors, and to attract suitors, one has to look both desirable as well as gettable. Putting a high floor price that is not in line with real brand value is more likely to dissuade bidders, since most bidders actually assume that the real price will anyway be above the floor price Mr David Abraham of MRC, California consulting firm said further. On the other hand, it is true that though a low floor price may attract many bidders, all bids could also fall short of US' expectation. Hence, it is important to set the floor price in such a way that while still looking commercially good to attract many bidders, it remains close to the actual worth of the brand. The worth of the brand is essentially the sum total of assured brand earnings in perpetuity. This is determined by the discounted cash flow (DCF) over the next 10 years and thereafter on terminal value. This is the real value of the brand and should be the floor price. The arguments of Ms. Garcia and Mr. Green for a higher floor price on account of other intangible assets are not really valid, because these intangibles are already reflected in the DCF measure. Also, let's not forget that the future works both ways. There is no zero-risk environment, and ideally the discounted cash flow should be adjusted for risk factors on the basis of the brand strength as determined by measures such as current market share, stability, nature of industry, geographic spread, support, trademark protection etcetera.

In most valuation methods, the lowest discount rate is 3-3.5 percent, which is applicable to near-zero risk investments such as Government bonds. Given the uncertainties related to the alcohol industry in Mexico, if you put Crimson Nectar against the brand strength parameters mentioned above, it's not difficult to see that there could well be a risk discount on the expected cash flow, in addition to the regular present-value-determining discount, which I would estimate as high as 10-12 percent. Hence, if the discounted cash flow, after adjusting for charge on capital employed, taxes and inflation, indicates a price of $ 36 Pesos, go ahead and offer that as the floor price. This is consistent with the current value of the brand. Any price above this is really a premium paid by the buyer for strategic reasons, and is a windfall to US. There is indeed a risk that a failed auction will erode the brand's perceived value. Remember that the key to good auctioneering lies in making bidders believe that a profitable deal is just on the edge of their reach, and if they 'stretch' a little, they've got it! Take it too far, you lose both bidder and the bid.

Universal spirits is at a strategic fork, in choosing its future course in an evolving market. Headquarters may have embarked on a corporate vision to drive growth only through global brands, but in Mexico, the group appears to be in an enviable position, with the choice of combining a successful local business with an international portfolio in a market that is not just evolving, but doing so dynamically, Mr Roberto Vargas Gonzales a Mexican business consultant appointed by the US Inc. said in his analysis report. Would selling a large-volume brand in Mexico, where restrictions on brand building in the spirits market tend to only increase, be a wise move? In addressing this question, US Mexico may see Crimson Nectar as a one-off opportunity that should not be let go so easily, but it will still have to weight the option of keeping the brand against the strategic course the company wants to embark on from here. What are US' broad strategic goals for the market? Can Crimson Nectar contribute? The alternative, as outlined, is to go the corporate way, with laser focus on its core global brands. This means selling Crimson Nectar. As circumstances have it, there are a number of contestants with their own agenda for the brand and a bid representing the price they're willing to pay. From an ex-manager who has his signature on the brand's success, to the company that wants to get a minimum fair value if not higher, to the competition that may or may not be in the race for tactical reasons, to the investment bankers who want to ensure that they get 'fair value' for themselves. As the owner of the brand and the business it is, I believe that, it is the US group that must set a clear strategic direction the company wants to take. From there on, only these strategic compulsions should drive the valuation exercise, with a minimum condition being that a fair value be paid, if the company opts to divest itself of the brand.

Trying to gain higher value for Crimson Nectar by throwing in various future scenarios when it is not the strategic intent of the company to pursue Crimson Nectar's growth, could not be of any benefit to US. Over time, this could probably even erode the value of the brand. If its future strategic course is to sell Crimson Nectar, then US should arrive at a realistic minimum floor price for the brand, without muddling the picture with talk of what it could have done with the brand (or how far it could grow). That's irrelevant to the evaluation exercise. Crimson Nectar's future would be up to the buyer, which would be free to set new goals for the brand and pursue a course quite different from the strategy envisaged by US. That does not mean that US' managers stop thinking about Crimson Nectar's evolution as a brand. In fact, it would be advisable for US to have a well-defined fallback plan on how it will maintain and sustain the brand equity of Crimson Nectar, if it is not able to sell it immediately at the desired minimum floor valuation.

It must be said at the outset that there is an embarrassment in this case arising out of the former CEO himself being one of the interested parties in Crimson Nectar. The people discussing the brand's value with him now were probably his juniors reporting to him just a short while ago. There is, therefore, a human dimension to this already problematic decision that we must recognize. Mr. Hernandez, of course, is interested in the lowest possible price as a potential buyer, so his views are hardly to be taken into account as objective, in answer to the question posed at the end of the case. Nonetheless, given the price range talked about (US $ 20 million is mentioned), it is doubtful that he is hoping to buy the brand with just his personal resources. Clearly, there must be some other agency or financier group or banker who would have to be rationally persuaded that at that price, the brand Crimson Nectar is a good buy. The valuation of a brand is fraught with a lot of nonsense and confusion, but is ultimately a matter of bargaining between intending buyers and the seller, no matter what the theories say. In conceptual terms, I divide the theories into three simple, broad types. The first is what may be termed as "the past method" and could be based on some calculation of the aggregate investment already made on building the brand. This is really irrelevant because brand loyalties are relatively fickle in such a category (that is, low-end exotic juice); and there is no reason to believe that the brand would somehow 'reimburse' the cost of the seller's prior efforts.

Second is a 'what the traffic can bear' approach (or the current reality method), which draws a parallel with similar products sold by someone else. This is all right for regular products that you and I buy, but not for assets such as brands, for which there isn't a large volume of trade to go by as precedent. So that too, at best, could only be a guideline. The third is the approach (the discounted future method) popular with finance professionals, and takes a discounted cash flow or some modified form of an asset-pricing model. If you pay US $20 million for Crimson Nectar, how much can you expect to earn back over its reasonable economic life? Considering that its current annual sales are at US $ 30 million Pesos, and assume that it earns say 12 percent a year, pre-tax. Does this seem a good rate of return? Only someone with knowledge of liquor industry margins could tell. The hunch is it may be okay, if one can presume that the market performance of the brand would continue to be as impressive in the face of competition. Frankly, in this case, signaling is of little consequence, because by now most people who matter would know the brand is on the block because the foreign owner has lost interest. So I would just go ahead and sell it at a price that takes a fairly short time horizon (say five to seven years) for discounting purposes, and get rid of the brand. "Once the money is such that you can get a greater return from it in your rationalized product line, take the money and run" would be my advice. Auctioning is hardly the right mode for such a sale. It has to be based on closed bids and detailed negotiations thereafter.

CUSTOMER VALUE AND RE-ENGINEERING PROCESS

Further to the discussion on the strategies suggested by David Abraham and Roberto Vargas, the CEO of the company Robert Green presented his ideas on the customer value chain and the business re-engineering process for the new generation products of the company especially Crimson Nectar. In the era of global competition, regardless of whether the company operates in FMCG, industrial goods or services, leading organizations around the world are being driven to rethink their business strategies and reorient towards process change for reaching higher efficiency levels. In order to engineer their process change, it is essential to consider the customer value criteria based on the attributes of four major business determinants - quality, service, cost and time . The customer value metrics is detailed in Table 1.

Table 1 Re-engineering Customer Value

Quality	*Service*	*Cost*	*Cycle time*
• Customer relationship • Useful applications • Minimum variance • Process integrity • Minimizing waste • Regular improvement	• Customer support • Flexibility in meeting customer demands • Delivery and service • Information flow • Value assessment	• Innovation • Quality assurance • Logistics • Staffing • Materials management	• Market preparation • Lead time • Ordering and delivery • Response analysis

Among various attributes of quality the companies must look for continuous improvement in the products deliverables and minimize the variances. The customer support in terms of product and price should be prioritized for achieving competitive excellence. The cost factors, may need very important consideration, in the processes re-engineering as the quality improvement efforts, would lead to price rise due to design improvement, quality assurance, restructuring the distribution and logistics strategies, inventory and staffing. The customer value largely depends on the cost of time involved in the change process. Re-engineering forces the companies to quantify the business efforts by way of quality, service and cycle time reducing the cost to the customer at the same time increasing the speed of innovation and new-product development. The time required for market preparation includes the concept selling, pre-positioning advertising and information for market initialization. The lead time is the time taken for stabilizing the sales and customer response to the changes engineered in order to outwit, outmaneuver and outperform the competitors in the market. In the process of re-engineering the business strategies, it is essential for the companies to analyze the customer response to the innovation and modify the entire process, accordingly before finally setting the changes in the market.

ADJOURNMENT

Chairman of the Board has adjourned the meeting for the date to be communicated to the members and concerned staff, after concluding the fruitful discussion that enlightened the marketing strategy makers to decide over the pricing conflict of Crimson Nectar. The decision that were drafted today were on setting-up of a floor price for the product to support the consumer decision to accept the change to the non-alcoholic beverages like Crimson Nectar.

Penetration pricing strategy has been condensed from the discussions and has been advocated to be used when an elite market does not exist for the new products and demand seems to be elastic over the entire demand curve, even during early stages of product introduction. High price elasticity of demand is probably the most important reason for adopting a penetration strategy. The penetration strategy is also used to discourage competitors from entering the market. When competitors seem to be encroaching on a market, an attempt is made to lure them away by means of penetration pricing, which yields lower margins. A competitor's costs play a decisive role in this pricing strategy because a cost advantage over the existing manufacturer might persuade another firm to enter the market, regardless of how low the margin former may be.

All customers are not equally profitable. To maximize profits, customers must be segmented and viewed as unique sales opportunities. Value-based segmentation evaluates customer needs and then segments into value categories. This gives salespeople a better focus for their efforts and better tools to meet the needs of customers who demand lower prices. The result is to change the focus of customer negotiations from their price to the company's value! The best strategy to ensure profitability is to maintain a strong price structure that lets your company maintain higher prices and limit the impact of aggressive customer price negotiations. An effective price structure includes value-based price metrics, relative price levels, and a predefined criteria for discounting. Developing such a structure involves understanding the value-needs of customers and devising techniques such as segmenting, bundling / unbundling features and services and developing a better understanding of product costs. When customers negotiate for lower prices (are there any that do not?) the company will know how to address their needs while maintaining its profits.

Demand for environmentally preferable products (EPPs) in export markets can represent important trading opportunities for developing countries. For example, heightened consumer concerns in the area of food safety and quality has generated increased demand for organic food. In addition, there is a certain demand for "Fair Trade" products, aimed at facilitating the marketing of products made by small producers in developing countries. The Crimson Nectar can also be positioned as the EPP that would attract additional strength for the product against the alcoholic beverages. The company can also attempt for getting the eco-label for the Crimson Nectar. This new trend has been encouraged largely by consumer awareness-building campaigns led by environmental NGOs, consumer groups and the media, particularly in Northern European countries. In response to consumer pressure as well as for competitiveness reasons, producers, manufacturers and retailers took into account serious environmental considerations relating to the production process.

Mr. Robert Green thanked the board members and executives of the company for their cooperation in the making it convenient to attend the meeting and also for putting their best efforts to drive the new product through the corners of competition and all segments of the consumers. He quoted the words of Aristotle "*Excellence is an art won by training and habituation. We do not act rightly because we have virtue or excellence, but we rather have those because we have acted rightly. We are what we repeatedly do. Excellence, then, is not an act but a habit...*" and bid a good bye to all the esteemed members and executives.

REFERENCES

Blundell, Richard: Consumer Behaviour: Theory and Empirical Evidence—a Survey, *Economic Journal,* Vol 98, March 1988, 16-65

Heien, Dale : Habit, Seasonality, and Time Aggregation in Consumer Behaviour, *Applied Economics,* 33 (13), October, 2001, 1649-1653

Lähteenmäki, Liisa, Nielsen, Niels A., Poulsen, Jacob B, Ueland Oydis and Åström Annika : *Consumer perception of food products involving genetic modification: Results from a qualitative study in four Nordic countries,* Aarhus School of Business, The MAPP Centre, Working Paper # 72, July 2000, 1-105

Molina, Jose Alberto : Is Spanish Consumer Behaviour Consistent with the Utility Maximization? A Non-parametric Response, Applied Economic Letter, *Taylor and Francis Journals,* 3 (4), April, 1996, 273-241

Appendix I : Specimen

Meeting of the Board of Directors, Universal Spirits Mexico SA de CV
Agenda

I. Call to Order

II. Items for Discussion/Possible Action

#1 Report on September 5-6, 2003, Board Retreat [Ms Angelica Segura, Company Secretary] *(Estimated Time: 5 minutes)*

#2 Report – Exotic Fruit Nectars-Industry Dimensions [Dulce Flores/Alma Garcia]*(Estimated Time: 5 minutes)*

#3 Renewal of Resolution on Advisory Committee for Finance and Budget [Ben Ferrell]*(Estimated Time: 3 minutes)*

#4 Report on Consumer Behaviour of Non-alcoholic Beverages [(Robert Green)*(Estimated Time: 3 minutes)*

#5 Competitor Analysis and Advertising Trends (Phil Ames-Market Research manager) *(Estimated Time: 5 minutes)*

#6 Budgeting for New Launch [Ben Ferrell – Accounts Manager]*(Estimated Time: 5 minutes)*

#7 Discussion on the marketing activities of Crimson Nectar *(Estimated Time: 20 minutes)*

#8 Revisions to marketing Policy/Marketing Strategy 2*(Estimated Time: 5 minutes)*

#9 Report on action points on marketing of Crimson Nectar [Alma Garcia]*(Estimated Time: 10 minutes)*

#10 Report on retailing of the product/ supply chain management (Functional Managers) *(Estimated Time: 30 minutes)*

#11 Market penetration and repositioning strategy in the weak markets (Dulce Flores, Alma Garcia, Arturo Henandez)*(Estimated Time: 45 minutes)*

III. Executive Session

Consultants' opinion on the marketing strategies of the Crimson Nectar in the Latin American markets. Mr David Abraham and Roberto Vergas to highlight their reports on the marketing strategies as per the contract agreement of the consultation.

IV. Reconvene

V. Announcements

VI. Quick Meeting Evaluation

VII. Adjournment

Board will announce, it will go into Executive Session, if necessary . The Board of Trustees may also announce, it will go into Executive Session, if necessary, to receive advice from Business Legal Counsel regarding any item on this agenda.

Case 4.3

BLOCKBUSTER ENTERTAINMENT CORPORATION: CROSS PROMOTION AND PRICING STRATEGY

Blockbuster's corporate objective was to provide customers with entertainment, instructional, and cultural videos in pleasant, family-oriented, and spacious surroundings. Blockbuster had developed the "superstore" concept on the premise of large title selection and convenience, with rental rates as a less important factor. The typical store had 8,000 to 10,000 square feet of selling space and stocked an average of 10,000 tapes. The videocassettes were arranged alphabetically within more than 30 categories. The facing of the films also encouraged customers to pick up more than one film as they browsed through the selections. Since, the actual movies were displayed with their descriptive boxes on the showroom floor, the customer knew immediately, if the selection was available for rental. This helped the sales personnel by not making them search for the titles behind the counter or in the back room. Once the customer made the selection, proprietary computer software allowed store personnel to process transactions rapidly. Customers received free membership. When applying for membership, their general preferences and other demographic information were put into the database. Blockbuster developed a laser barcode scanner system, which sped up the transaction time while also providing management with a database on customer addresses, customers' buying habits, rental activity by tape, and so on. This database allowed Blockbuster to develop more effective marketing/promotional activities. In 1990, there were 12 million members in the Blockbuster system, and this number grew at a rate of 300,000 new members per month.

In addition to broad title selection and convenience factors, all Blockbuster Superstores conformed to standardized design specifications and operating procedures, much like the McDonald's chain. Blockbuster's tag line was "Arnerica's Family Video Store". All Blockbuster Superstores offered extended business hours from 10 in the morning till midnight, seven days a week. Most stores were highly visible, located in free-standing structures or at the end of strip shopping centers, and had plenty of free parking. They were designed to be destination points and did not rely on traffic drawn by neighbouring stores. In keeping with its emphasis on customer service, many stores had exterior drop-off boxes, provided a child's play area, and sold movie-oriented food products.

Franchise Development

Blockbuster believed that the penetration of available markets in a short period of time was a critical success factor in competing in the videocassette market; therefore, they employed a strategy of franchise development. The ratio between corporate-owned and franchise locations was 50:50. Blockbuster aimed to run the operations in major markets while franchising out those locations in smaller, less dominant markets. By the end of 1995, the company hoped to reduce this 50 : 50 ratio to

40:60 as Blockbuster expanded further into the smaller markets. Opening a Blockbuster Video Superstore generally required between $ 425,000 and $ 700,000, exclusive of any franchise fee or development fee. In many cases, the ability of a prospective franchise owner to meet these large financial requirements was contingent on the availability of outside financing. Each franchise owner had the sole responsibility for all financial commitments relating to the opening and operation of superstores in the franchised territory, including rent, utilities, payroll, and other relevant expenses. The typical franchise agreement called for a $ 55,000 initial fee for the right to operate under the Blockbuster Video name, a fee in the amount of up to $ 30,000 for the required proprietary software, and a continuing monthly payment of $ 650 for the maintenance of the software. Additionally, the franchisee had to pay (1) a continuing royalty and service fee equal to a certain percentage of gross sales, ranging from 3 percent to 8 percent, (2) a percentage of gross revenue for national advertising and marketing programs, approximately 0.5 percent, and (3) an additional percentage of revenue for local advertising.

Franchise owners were generally required to have an opening inventory of 5,000 to 7,000 tapes. They were not required to purchase their initial inventories from the company (used tapes could usually be purchased at lower prices) but, because of barcoding and packaging requirements, many chose to do so, because it was much easier and more efficient. The company priced videocassettes competitively with major cassette distributors and charged a packaging and handling fee. Franchisees were not allowed to place any tape in inventory that had not been previously approved by the company. The company's franchise agreement required the franchise owner to participate actively in the operation of the franchise. To assist its franchisees, the company offered a wide range of services including site selection and lease negotiation assistance, construction assistance, employee training, and computer hardware and software support on a fee basis. All franchise owners and managers, in typical McDonald's fashion, had to attend a program at Blockbuster University that trained them in the standard operating procedures and practices of the company.

Pricing

Average videocassette cost Blockbuster $ 40 to purchase, package, and deliver to its store locations. Blockbuster, then charged customers for each tape. which they were allowed to keep for three evenings. The pricing structure was used to encourage multiple rentals per visit by the customer, as Blockbuster customers averaged two tapes per visit. This liberal three-day policy could be disastrous, though, because the big hits were rarely available for Friday or Saturday rental. "Whenever I go to Blockbuster they don't have the movies I want," said a customer in Atlanta. Company officials stood by the policy for customer convenience and marketing reasons. Though the $3 pricing structure was above the industry average of $ 2 per night, Blockbuster believed that the consumer was willing to pay the premium for the services and selection.

Distribution

Blockbuster operated an 80,000 square feet distribution center in Dallas, Texas and other states of USA and Mexico through, which it supplied new stores with videocassettes and other necessities. The facility had storage capacity of 400,000 cassettes and was used for shipping, receiving, and packaging rental videocassettes according to the company's uniform standards. This process involved removing each rental from its original carton. applying barcode labels to the video, and placing the cassette into its hard plastic case The display carton was created for each cassette by inserting a foam device into the original carton and shrink wrapping it. The end result of this process was a shipment that arrived at the store alphabetically sorted within categories and ready to be placed on display shelves. All stores received their initial titles from a pre-selected inventory compiled by this facility, alleviating the store manager from the tedious task of selecting 8,000 titles. This system at Blockbuster greatly contributed to the efficiency of videocassette selection and distribution nationwide.

Advertising and Promotion

Company advertised the Blockbuster Video Superstore on television, radio, newspapers, and billboards and through direct mail. Blockbuster's corporate marketing department, with the assistance of national advertising agencies, developed advertising campaigns were implementation through out the Blockbuster system. Along with its explosive store growth, Blockbuster's advertising expenditures increased from US $25 million in 1989. to US$560 million in 1990, to over US $90 million in 1991. One of Blockbuster's marketing themes. "WOW! What A Difference," incorporated the competitive standing of the company. Blockbuster believed it offered a combination of variety, convenience, and service that no other firm could provide. In response to this belief and the consumer's perception of these attributes, Blockbuster expressed, "WOW! What A Difference."

As part of their marketing program, Blockbuster began running McDonald's-like promotions. In 1990, they launched the Blockbuster Video $10 million game which was the largest promotional event ever in the video industry. The game utilized game pieces and a variety of prizes ranging from free rentals to $100,000 in cash. Plans called for another such promotion in the summer of 1991. The company also sponsored a college football game in 1990, with the introduction of the Blockbuster Bowl, the sixth largest college bowl game. Both programs were expected to be repeated in future periods. Blockbuster's advertising and promotions were founded on the belief that an effective advertising umbrella would increase store sales by a significant amount. Additionally, the marketing clout established by Blockbuster offered those advantages and economies of scale over competitors on a national basis.

CHAPTER 5

DISTRIBUTION STRATEGY

CHAPTER FOCUS

- *To build knowledge on fundamentals of distribution and supply chain management,*
- *To develop management skills in developing the distribution and logistics strategies,*
- *To learn about the functional excellence in the distribution management, and*
- *To understand the concepts of distribution planning and management issues in contemporary perspective.*

Marketing is defined as an exchange process. Distribution strategies are concerned with the channels that a company may engage to make its goods and services available to consumers. Channels are the organized structures of buyers and sellers that bridge the gap of time and space between manufacturer and the customer. There are hundreds of ways goods and services can be distributed to customer. These may be identified from direct bulk shipments in railcars or pipelines to the use of complex arrangements of brokers, wholesalers, and retailers. No single distribution satisfies the needs of every firm, and many organizations use several channels to reach different market segments. A paper mill, for example may contact large users directly, whereas independent wholesalers service smaller customers. Distribution channels help conquer the time and distance intervals that divide users from the merchandise they need. Channel members initiate and complete many of the following vital activities:

- Communication: Dispense product information to customers and report on market potentials, competitors, and market conditions
- Bargaining: Negotiate agreements on prices and terms with potential
- Reordering: Transmit orders for merchandising back to manufacturers
- Financing: Acquire funds to finance inventories and distribution facilities

- Maintain inventories: Assume the risk of storage and movement of the channel.
- Cash settlements: Collect money from buyers and deliver it to sellers.
- Ownership: Transfer title for goods and services from one firm to another

Some of these activities flow forward (title, inventories) and some move backward (ordering, market data). All of them need to be performed by someone who does the work of distribution depending on the costs different channels and the efficiencies of specialization. If the manufacturer assumes these functions, the selling prices must be adjusted to cover the costs. The cost of incurred to the manufacturer declines whenever, the functions are shifted to intermediaries, but such shift increases the cost at the dealer's end. Sometimes distribution activities are transferred to the consumer (like self service gasoline) and prices to the buyer are lowered. The distribution planning may invariably be based on the market survey carried out at the time of preparing the business plan. The distribution planning should be to make the products available to a larger number of consumers at lower marketing costs. To reduce the cost of marketing, it is required to determine the most feasible channel. The product characteristics and the operational area are the major factors to be considered while selecting a distribution channel. In any channel, different distribution approaches can be adopted to deliver the products more economically to the ultimate user. The important factor to be assessed in this process is the cost-effectiveness. It is observed that, the longer the chain of intermediaries in product distribution, higher is the cost of marketing. Since cost is one of the determinants of profit, it should also be viewed from the angle of product distribution. The exclusive distribution approach is always confined to an area. Such a distribution plan can be useful in the areas (i) where the demand concentration for the product is low (ii) which are located at a distance from the high concentration areas i.e., urban places (iii) the storage, transportation and other overhead costs are higher and (iv) the competition is absent or very low. In the urban areas where the market competition for the product is high and the retailing is at large-scale, a selective distribution policy would be more useful. However, retailers and consumers in rural areas and in the location, where the purchasing power of the consumers is low but a large number of retailers are in a business fray, regard the approach of extensive distribution of products. In other words, such an approach would help the market condition. The following seven factors should be considered while developing the products distribution policy.

- Product - characteristics and consumer recognition
- Size and value of sales - extent of sales realization
- Market area - consumer coverage, retailers and other traders
- Existing methods of distribution - impact, problems, and
- Needed efforts - consumer approachability, appealing to distributors, cost-effectiveness and sales realization

PROFILE OF PRINCIPAL DISTRIBUTION STRATEGIES

Channel structure strategy is about using perspectives of intermediaries in the flow of goods from manufacturers to customers. Distribution may be either direct from manufacturer to retailer or from manufacturer to customer or indirect involving the use of one or more intermediaries, such as wholesalers or agents, to reach the customer. The channel structure strategy is aimed at reaching the optimal number of consumers in a given time schedule at the lowest possible cost while maintaining the desired degree of control. In implementing this distribution strategy the company should make the comparison of direct versus indirect distribution on the basis of the following parameters:

- Cost,
- Product characteristics,
- Degree of control, and
- Other factors.

Cost variable includes distribution costs, opportunity costs which incurs during the non-availability of the product inventory costs and shipping costs. The product attributes may be measured in terms of replacement rate, gross margin, service requirements and the time involved in search thereof. The degree of control is generally greater when direct distribution is followed. The factors other than above are adaptability, technological changes and social/cultural values. The effective implementation of channel structure strategy may result effectively in performing the direct distribution. However this may result into the high marketing costs and needs a large degree of control. The foreign firms need to consider the following issues for channel selection for effective distribution:

- Market access
- Multiple markets, seasonality, safety, channel length
- Value added competencies
- Resources, logistics and control, competitive skills
- Financial consideration
- Building distribution network, revenue-cost implications, operating capital requirements
- Flexibility and control conditions

Strategy Focus 5.1: Radio Frequency Identification Technology in Distribution Management

Wireless identification and tracking with Radio Frequency identification (RFID) technology represents a new way to conduct operations, which creates new benefits and challenges. This technology operates with a reader that identifies the product tag in the warehouse and sends the signal about its movement through a computer based tracking tool. The identification is accomplished by an interrogator, also called a reader or "master," and a tag, also called a transponder or "slave" that has a unique identification code. Data is exchanged between tags and readers using radio waves between the tag and interrogator, and no direct line of sight is required for the transaction. The interrogator asks the tag for the code, or processes the signal being broadcast by the tag, decodes the transmission and transfers the data to a computer. The computer, in turn, may simply record the reading, or look up the tag identification in a database to direct further action, and may also direct the interrogator to write additional information to the tag. The latest generation of RFID allows the dozens of individual objects within a group to be uniquely identified at the same time. This is in contrast to bar codes, which must be read one by one, and can be very advantageous in high-speed reading, sorting and material handling applications.

The low-cost tags generally are have limited data storage capacity, typically 32 to 128 bits, which are read-only (not rewriteable) like bar codes, and have limited read range. On the contrary, high-cost tags are available for many more complicated longer read applications. They often have their own power source for managing large storage databases. RFID systems are available in a wide range of frequencies to suit various performance needs. Frequency is an important factor in transmission range and speed. This is an important consideration when planning logistics and supply chain applications. Most RFID technology used in warehousing and distribution operates at 13.56 MHz (high frequency), 860-930MHz (ultrahigh frequency, or UHF) or the 2.45GHz (microwave) band.

Wal-Mart has already begun its RFID pilot with selected distributors in 2006 while other eight suppliers that started shipping a handful of RFID-enabled pallets were Gillette, Hewlett-Packard, Johnson & Johnson, Kimberly-Clark, Kraft Foods, Nestle Purina PetCare, and Procter & Gamble.

- Channel network and participation, procedural control
- Channel strategy illustration
- Sales forecasting, selling approaches, cost factors, promotion and creativity, control

Customers receive comprehensive information about the product, company and distribution channel in this strategy and acquire strong image of the product and brand. This strategy would also help in building the indirect distribution vice-versa at lower marketing costs, less control and limited channel management responsibilities. The channel-strategy decisions include deciding to manage or coordinate operations in the channel of distribution, becoming a member of a vertically co-ordinated channel, or becoming a member of a conventional channel system. The following factors need to be assessed in the choice of the channel strategy:

- Market Access
- Value-Added Competencies
- Financial Considerations
- Flexibility and Control Considerations

Decision on market targeting needs to be closely co-ordinated with channel strategy, since the channel connects products and end-users. The channel selected should offer the most favorable combination of value-added competencies. Making this assessment requires looking at the competencies of each participant and the trade-offs concerning financial flexibility and control factors. The financial consideration in selecting the channels is to be done in reference to status of resources available for launching the proposed strategy and evaluating the revenue-cost impact of alterative channel strategies. Management should decide the extent of flexibility to be provided to the channel. The legal and regulatory measures also affect the channel selection.

DISTRIBUTION STRATEGIES

Distribution scope strategy is advantageous for establishing the distribution of goods and services effective with the target customers. The company may choose to implement the exclusive distribution strategy wherein one retailer is granted sole rights in serving a given area or intensive distribution approach in which a product is made available at all possible retail outlets. The company can also prefer to have the selective distribution approach to serve many customers but not through all the retail outlets in a given area that distribute the product. This strategy should be followed with the objective to serve chosen markets at a minimal cost while maintaining the desired product image. Of many core issues associated with the international distribution channels, following are listed as below:

- Market considerations
- Selling capabilities
- Product know-how
- Credit Worthiness
- Business image or personality
- Geographical coverage

- Strategy building ability
- Inventory handling
- Customer service
- Successful track record

Company needs to assess the consumer buying habits, gross margin/turnover rate, capability of dealer to provide service, capability of dealer to carry the full product line, and product styling in order to implement the distribution scope strategy effectively. This strategy may result into all categories of distribution such as exclusive, selective and intensive distribution. The distribution scope strategy provides the opportunity for strong dealer, high degree of control, good forecasting capability, sales promotion assistance from manufacturer, possible loss in sales volume, and possible antitrust violation during the implementation of exclusive distribution approach. The competition in marketplace, price discounting, and pressure from channel members to reduce number of outlets may emerge, if selective distribution is followed in the process of implementing the distribution scope strategy. However, the distribution scope strategy would result into low degree of control, higher sales volume, wide customer recognition, high turnover and price discounting when applied to the intensive distribution environment.

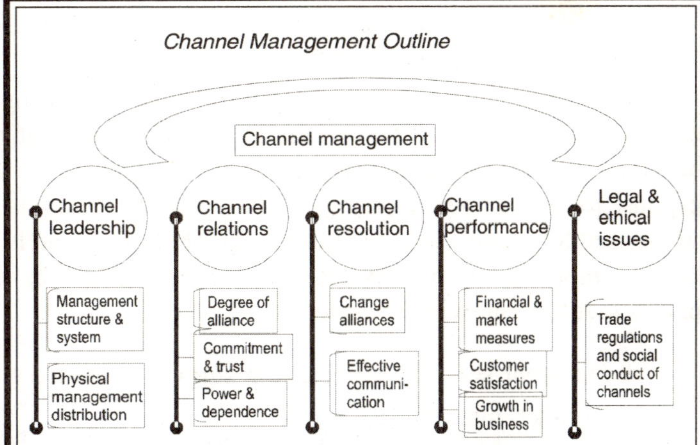

Figure 5.1 Distribution management

Multiple channel strategy employs two or more different channels for distribution of goods and services. Multiple-channel distribution has two basic categories - complementary and competitive. In complementary approach each channel handles a different non-competing product or market segment and two different and competing channels sell the same product in the competitive type of the multiple channel distribution strategy. This strategy may be followed to achieve optimal access to each individual market segment in order to increase business. Complementary channels are used to reach market segments otherwise left un-served, while the competitive channels are used with the hope of increasing sales. The requirements for implementing this distribution strategy are market segmentation and cost/benefit analysis.

> Ericsson Enterprise Systems (EES) has redesigned, its distribution and sales strategy addressing the enterprise market. The business unit Enterprise Systems will now move the sales and distribution of its products and systems to selected partners who are considered to be value added dealers and distributors, system integrators, and operators. This strategy will enable the company to serve our customers in a more competitive way, offering a greater

choice of channels, a more efficient way of purchasing and combining solutions, services and products, and secure fast delivery of products. As part of the new multi channel strategy, EES has set up Ericsson regional offices and expand its current indirect channel by establishing business relationships with value-added dealers, resellers, integrators, operators and ISPs (Internet Service Providers). The product portfolio of EES includes PBX systems, integrated global communication networks, cordless solutions, wireless LAN systems, computer telephony integration (CTI) applications, IP based switches, data communication products, and contact centres.

Complementary channels may be promoted by assessing geographic considerations, volume of business, need to distribute non-competing items, and saturation of traditional distribution channels in the given operational area of the company. However, the use of competitive channels can be a response to environmental changes. The Figure 5.1 exhibits the channel management strategy that can be used for identifying the multiple distribution channels and developing a balanced strategy for effective implementation of distribution. The expected results of implementing this distribution strategy may include the following advantages:

- Different services, prices, and support provided to different segments
- Broader market base
- Increased sales
- Possible dealer resentment
- Control problems, and
- Possible over-extension.

However, over-extension can result in decrease in quality/service and may have negative effects on long-run profitability. It is necessary to properly configure the channel for optimum goal realization. The major issues required for configuring the channel appropriately have been detailed as below:

- Distribution intensity
  Number of client accounts, periodicity and extent of reordering, services and satisfaction
- End user configuration
  Market segments, product information, company profile, guiding skills for decision making
- Product attributes
  Product line, life cycle, application and value added qualities
- Manufacturer's capabilities and resources
  Brand strength, bargains, terms and conditions
- Service functions
  Services offered, inventory and retail management
- Skills of intermediaries
  Managing trade offs, business correspondence, communication skills, developing effective sales plans

In case the channels, so configured are not responding to the distribution needs of the market, they may be modified. The channel modification strategy introduces a change in the existing distribution arrangements on the basis of evaluation and critical review in order to maintain an optimal distribution system given a changing environment. Evaluation of internal/ external environmental shifts is required to implement changes in consumer markets and buying habits, changes in the retail life cycle, changes in the manufacturer's financial strength, and changes in the product life cycle. One of the requirements of the channel modification strategy is continuous evaluation of existing channels, cost/benefit analysis, consideration of the effect of the modified channels on other aspects of the marketing mix and ability of management to adapt to modified plan. This strategy may reveal results towards maintenance of an optimal distribution system for dealers and customer with effect to suggested changes.

An important step in selecting the distribution strategy is deciding, how many levels of organizations need to be included in the vertical channel and the specific kinds of intermediaries to be selected at each level. The measurement of distribution intensity in the selected markets helps in deciding how many channel levels to use and what types of intermediaries to select. An industrial products manufacturer may choose either distributors or sales agents, which are independent organizations that receive commissions on sales to contact industrial buyers. It is important to know where the targeted end-users might be expected to purchase the products of interest. The selected intermediaries that are should provide an avenue to the market segments targeted by the producer. Analysis of buyer characteristics and preferences provides important information for selecting firms patronized by end-users. This in turn guides decisions concerning additional channel levels, such as the middlemen selling to the retailers that contact the market target customers. The complexity of the product, special application requirements, and servicing needs are useful in guiding the choice of intermediaries. Looking at how the competing products are distributed may suggest possible types of intermediaries. The breadth and depth of the products to be distributed are also important considerations because intermediaries may want full lines of products.

Large producers with extensive capabilities and resources have a lot of flexibility in choosing intermediaries. These producers also have a great deal of bargaining power with the middlemen, and they may be willing or capable to perform certain distribution functions. Such options are more limited for small producers with capability and resource constraints. The functions required to be performed in moving products from producer to end-user include various channel activities such as storage, servicing, and transportation. Studying these functions is useful in choosing the types of intermediaries that are appropriate for a particular product or service. Evaluation of the experience, capabilities, and motivation of the intermediaries and channel membership is also important in configuring the channels. The companies in particular or within the same industry often vary in skills and experience. The more complex the channel network, the more challenging, it is to complete various distribution functions. The selected channel configuration typically takes into account several important trade-offs. However, the agents make it necessary for the manufacturer to perform several functions, such as inventory stocking, invoicing, and service.

Administration by a member of the channel structure in order to establish control of the channel and provide a centrally organized effort to achieve common goals may be defined as the channel control strategy. This strategy has the core objectives to increase control, to correct inefficiencies, to realize cost effectiveness through experience curves and to gain efficiencies of scale. Commitment and resources to fulfill leadership obligations is the major requirement to implement this strategy for distribution. Typically, the channel controller is a large firm with market leadership /influence; however, it is not always observed. The implementation of channel audit is also one of the necessary tools for exercising the channel control. The cores elements of channel audit include distribution and logistics, delivery cost, channel profit, selling capabilities, competitive strategies etc. The successful implementation of this strategy would result in increased control, professional management, maximizing market impact and elimination of internal and external inefficiencies. The channel control strategy would also help in central programming and achieving the operating economies for increased profitability. It has been observed that multinational companies largely depend on industrial distributors to sell their products. Products suitable for distributors usually are those which have a large potential customer base and can be stored. Also distributors are attracted towards the products, which can be sold in small quantities, bought by people who are at low levels in their organizations, and promise rapid delivery and service. Companies should select distributors that serve the market segment, not just the geographic area, and are suited to where the product is in its life cycle.[1]

Conflict management strategy would help in resolving conflict among channel members. This strategy may be followed to devise a solution acceptable to the conflicting members so that they will co-operate to make it work. The choice of a strategy for solving the conflict needs reasonable bargaining with the affected parties and adopt give-and-take attitude. The bottom line must be favorable enough to both parties to induce them to accept the terms of the bargain. This strategy would however, provide scope for frequent formal interactions with the other party to develop an appreciation of each other's perspectives and willingness to interact to solve problems. Sometimes, it is required to bring a neutral third party into the conflict to resolve the matter by means of conciliation, mediation, or arbitration (compulsory or voluntary). The effective implementation of this strategy of distribution would provide a clean platform for business by elimination of snags in the channel and revealing results that are mutually beneficial to the parties involved. However, the need for management of time and effort and increase in costs also results while implementing this strategy. The strategy for developing effective distribution system is to focus on Collaborative Planning, Forecasting and Replenishment (CPFR) approach. This strategy may be developed in association with the leading distribution agencies and suppliers in the region. The company developing the CPFR with another distribution company should agree on the scope of collaboration and develop a joint business plan. It is preferable to work out a single forecast on the product and consumer demand in the operational market area. In this process the company may identify and resolve the exceptions related with the consumer forecast and develop single order forecast. The company may generate orders finally on the basis of constrained order forecast.

A research study[2] found that in USA many retailers wanted to adopt a Collaborative Planning Forecasting and Replenishment (CPFR) strategy. 36 percent of the respondents said they had planned

1 Hlavacek James D. and Tommy McCuistion J. (1983), Industrial Distributors-When, Who and How, *Harvard Business Review*, March

2 Retailers want import management, not ERP systems, *Logistics Management Distribution Report*, Issue: August 31, 1999

to implement a CPFR program within two years. Under such a program, suppliers and retailers share data to determine stock replenishment jointly. Respondents preferred supply chain software; 24 percent said they already had installed it and 16 percent said an installation was in progress. Some 88 percent of respondents said they would use supply chain software for merchandise planning, while 81 percent said they would use it for replenishment.

INTERNATIONAL CHANNEL SELECTION

There are two forms of international distribution - direct and indirect, which are being practiced by the multinational firms. The direct distribution channel may appear to be more effective, in practice it is better only, if the customers are geographically homogeneous, have similar buying habits, and are limited in number. Indirect channel is used by the companies preferably in the regions where customers segments and their buying habits are heterogeneous.[3] A foreign company may go through either one or multiple agents or merchant intermediaries in a host country. The major difference between these intermediaries may be described in terms of the legal ownership of goods. An agent, without taking title to the goods, distributes them on behalf of the principal, the manufacturer. Merchant intermediaries do business in their own names and hold title to the goods they deal in. The different types of indirect distributors, who operate in the overseas market include:

- Export management company
- Manufacturer's export agent
- Foreign freight forwarders
- Commission agents, and
- Country-controlled buying agents

Besides these categories of intermediaries, the export merchants, cooperating exporters and export vendors constitute the forms of merchant middleman involved in the operation of distribution of goods and services. The above types of intermediaries do not take title, they do take possession of goods. However, they have different duties in respect to continuation of relationship with the principal (long-term versus temporary); degree of control maintained by the principal (complete versus slight versus none); pricing authority accorded to the agent (full versus partial versus advisory), affiliation with buyer or seller; number of principals served at a time (few versus many); involvement or non-involvement with shipping or handling of competitive lines; provision of promotional support (continuous versus one-time versus none); extension of credit to the principal (regularly versus occasionally versus rarely versus never); and provision of market information (good versus fair versus poor).

Indirect Distribution Channels

An *export management company* (EMC) may be defined as an independent export organization that serves different companies in their export endeavors. The relationship of EMC with exporter is of a client and not of an employer. The EMC operates under the client's name for all international

3 Bruce Seifert : Export Distribution Channels, *Columbia Journal of World Business*, Summer , 1989, pp 15-22

communications. However, the scale of the operations of EMCs would vary in different countries. An EMC may appear just as a person or as an organization and manages all export activities of the client overseas. The large export management firms often maintain international offices in strategic locations. The export management companies generate their income either from commissions or from discounts on goods they buy for resale overseas as these organizations also undertake exporting more effectively and generally at a lower cost than other channels. The Manufacturer's Export Agent (MEA) is another type of indirect distributor, who provides services similar to those of EMC, but the MEA covers limited markets and the contractual relationship is short-term. An exporter may offer a contract for performing a particular transaction and the MEA would act using own names while following the procedural requirements and receive a commission for services. A Webb-Pomerene Association may be described as one of the organizations undertaking international distribution services indirectly in United States of America. This association is formed among competing U.S. manufacturers especially and exclusively for the purpose of exports according to the Act of 1918 of USA. The members of a Webb-Pomerene association can engage in different international marketing activities to their mutual advantage. These associations can determine prices, combine shipments, jointly undertake marketing research, or share information with each other, and allocate orders among different members of the association within the operational area as stipulated by US law. The *foreign freight forwarder* specializes in handling overseas shipping arrangements and their services can be utilized for handling goods from the port of exporters' location to the foreign port of entry. A foreign freight forwarder receives a discount or fees from the shipping company. However, freight forwarders undertake extra services such as packing covering an additional cost.

Commission agents also anchor as the distribution channel in the overseas markets. Foreign customers interested in buying overseas products are represented by commission agents. They serve as so-called finders of desired goods at the lowest price for their principals. The commission agents receive their commission from their overseas clients. The *country-controlled buying agent* may be defined as a procurement operator of a foreign government, seeking to buy designated goods for his country. Many developing countries have entrusted these agents with the task of procuring different goods for them. There is another channel for distribution of the products and services overseas, which may be described as *export merchants*. They buy directly from manufacturers according to their specifications, taking title to the goods. These merchants generally have contacts with the overseas agents through whom the goods are sold either to the wholesalers or retailers. The export merchants assume all possible risks associated with the products they purchase from the manufacturers and sell in their own names. Their compensation consists of a mark-up percentage based on market conditions. In general, export merchants may be considered alike domestic wholesalers. On the contrary the *export vendors* are the organizations, which specialize in buying inferior quality and overproduced goods in a country for distribution in overseas markets. These companies procure the sub-standard goods outright, taking title to them and ship the goods to one or more countries for selling therein through their established contacts.

Many companies develop their alliance with other companies to establish the distribution network or form a joint venture with other companies in order to manage distribution of their products and services in international markets. For example, the Colgate-Palmolive company distributed, Wilkinson

Sword men's toiletries in selected overseas markets, Whirlpool used Sony in Japan and Breck Shampoo used Schick in Germany to be the distributor for their product. This system of distribution is known as *co-operative exporter*. A co-operative exporter may be any company that has an established system of handling exports for its own goods and distributes products overseas for other manufacturers on contract basis. These co-operative arrangements are also termed as *piggybacking*. The piggybacking consists of two players - the carrier and the rider. The firm actually engaged in exporting is usually the larger firm with established export facilities and foreign distribution and, it may described as the carrier while the rider may be determined as the company using the exporting company to carry its products to the foreign countries By piggybacking, companies can please foreign distributors by giving them a more complete line of products. This distribution channel also intends to offer extra customer convenience by providing related products. For example, Singer sells fabrics, patterns, and sewing accessories in addition to sewing machines. Finally, firms with seasonal sales may piggyback to keep their export operation working at full capacity throughout the year. However, piggybacking is a sale of know-how and services rather than a sale of products from the point of view of the carrier firm.

Uni-Channel Distribution Management - A Case of Fertilizer Marketing

There are many ways of distribution management. The cost effective distribution would be through zero channel approach where manufacturer or marketer has direct access to consumer without using any intermediate channels. The mono-channel distribution system solely depends on one channel and attempts to market its products. On the contrary, multi-channel distribution system consists of long chain of intermediaries to reach the product to the end-user. Indian Farmers fertilizer Co-operative Ltd (IFFCO) is a giant fertilizer manufacturing company in India which produces over 50 lac MTs of nitrogenous and complex fertilizer. By virtue of co-operative principle, IFFCO has emerged as largest mono-channel fertilizer distributor in the country. The marketing channel at the grassroots of IFFCO fertilizer is the primary marketing societies (PMS) for distribution of fertilizer to its members. However, the PMS behaves like a consumer and prioritises sales according to the brand preference of the farmers. It is not mandatory for the PMS to sell the products of fertilizer companies of the cooperative sector. Hence, it is not an exclusive dealer to the IFFCO or Krishak Bharati Fetilizer Co-operative Ltd (KRIBHCO) fertilizers but operates as an authorised dealer, which trades with other brands also simultaneously. Since the PMS are of third level organisation in the cooperative hierarchy in the state, a fixed ratio of marketing margin statutorily goes to the district society and state federation or apex society. Such arrangement of margin distribution often is felt by the PMS as parting the marketing margin to the intermediate level organisations without any transparency of their role in trading or product promotion process. Hence, there is a need to use PMS channel by appropriate management techniques to promote sales at the grassroots.

Primary and district societies may be directly approached for distribution of fertilizers to make the marketing operations more dynamic. It is often found difficult to transport the fertilizer from the centrally located warehouses to the PMSs, due to interruptions in transport services, road links and transit risks. Thus, it would be appropriate to look for some service storage facilities in PMS located in central villages to cater short distance supplies. This would enable to distribute fertilizers in short-time and at reasonable cost. The staff of PMS may be provided high motivation in terms of

Strategy Focus 5.2:
Balanced Distribution Plan of Apple Computer

Apple Computer Inc. has announced a new U.S. product distribution strategy that will reduce channel inventory, increase Apple advocacy, and streamline channel operations. The Company will leverage long-standing relationships with Ingram Micro Inc. and MicroAge, Inc. to more effectively manage inventory and secure products to resellers and therefore customers faster than ever before. "We're working with distributors who have made a sizable investment and commitment to Apple and are focused on helping us get our products into the channel faster," said Mitch Mandich, senior vice president. "Ingram Micro and MicroAge are both increasing the number of resources they dedicate to Apple and improving their advocacy of our products."

"Ingram Micro and MicroAge offer the perfect balance of volume distribution and customization that is required to most effectively bring our products to our key customers," Mandich added. This move compliments Apple's changing product sales and channel strategy and is designed to streamline inventory management, improve the customer experience, and increase advocacy for Apple and its products among its key distributors. "This move is good news for the channel. As Apple's largest distributor in the world and long time authorized distributor, we have always supported Apple and their customers, and will continue to do so. We fully support their effort to streamline distribution and better manage channel inventory," said Jeff Rodek, worldwide president and chief operating officer, Ingram Micro. "Ingram Micro was the first distributor to start a division dedicated exclusively to Macintosh, which we continue to invest in. We also continue to support our Apple resellers and VARs, as well as our 500 vendors who supply Mac-related products."

"As an Apple distributor for over 15 years, we're delighted to be an integral part of Apple's success," said Bob O'Malley, president of MicroAge. "Apple has designed a program that will benefit everyone in the supply chain, especially our customers, while simultaneously contributing to the bottom line." This announcement applies to Apple's product distribution policy in the United States only, and has become effective on Dec. 1, 1997. Apple Computer, Inc. ignited the personal computer revolution in the 1970s with the Apple II, and reinvented the personal computer in the 1980s with the Macintosh. Apple is now recommitted to its original mission - to bring the best personal computing products and support to students, educators, designers, scientists, engineers, businesspersons and consumers in over 140 countries around the world.

Source: Apple Computers Inc., Press release information, website: http://www.apple.com/source/

behavioural inputs as well as in terms of monetary incentive on sales of fertilizer of above a cut-off limit. Similarly a farmer consumes highest quantity of IFFCO fertilizer in an agricultural season may be felicitated and rewarded. Such approach would boost the morale of farmers and help the building the product image positively.

Schick Company for its safety razors tried piggybacking after encountering difficulty in the distribution in German market, and established a temporary alliance with another consumer goods company. Later the company has set up its own sales subsidiary in Germany to distribute the wide range of its products. However, in some international markets where distribution is complex or customer requirements are highly personalized, the company might choose to engage in a distribution alliance with a competitor. The Ricoh Company of Japan which is original equipment manufacturer of photocopier machines allowed its competitor, the Savin Company to sell their copiers in the United States in order to gain quick market penetration.

Direct Distribution Channels

Manufacturing company overseas performs the international marketing largely by proxy, wherein the products are distributed through another firm that carries its products overseas. The overseas manufacturing companies gain the international marketing know-how and achieve the sales targets through the indirect approaches, however, are limited. The firm can commit itself to its performance in the host country, further by direct exporting in which the manufacturer firm undertakes the export task rather than delegating it to others. The manufacturing company then takes-up the tasks of market contact, market research, physical distribution, export documentation, pricing, promotion and other strategic functions. It has been observed that direct exporting activity generally generate more sales than indirect exporting. The advantages of direct distribution are reflected not only in augmenting the sales but also in exercising increased control, better market information, and development of expertise in international marketing. The direct exporting may have higher costs as they are borne by the manufacturing or exporting firm, whereas they are shared in the process of indirect exports. A Firm may choose the direct distribution for its products through agents, which include sales representatives, purchasing agents and export broker.

Sales representatives may be described as the sales representatives or a person in-charge distributing the products and services of a manufacturing company, similar to the USA. A manufacturer supplies the sales representatives with literature and with literature and samples to conduct sales in a pre-designated territory. These representatives usually work on a mission basis, undertake no risk or responsibility, and operate in reference to a stipulated contract for a fixed tenure. They may also choose to operate on either exclusive or non-exclusive basis, and serve as a good source of market information. The purchasing agent is also referred to as a buyer for export or an export commission house. Such agents operate in may developed countries including markets in North America, seeking goods of interest to their foreign principals. Their product quality and price demand is determined according to the requirements of their principal business houses. The *export brokers* are another form of direct agents who play a significant role when firms choose to get their products distributed in overseas markets. An export broker brings the home country seller and foreign buyer together on the negotiating platform. The export brokers receive a commission from the seller for their services. In the process of transaction the brokers take neither title nor possession of goods and assume no financial responsibility relative to the export transaction. Export brokers who are popularly engaged in international transaction of agricultural products like grains, cotton etc are rarely involved in the export of manufactured goods.

Another type of distribution process through direct export agent firms involve *foreign merchant intermediaries,* who generally take title to the goods and arrange to sell them under their own name. The foreign merchant intermediaries offer services similar to a domestic wholesaler. The important types of foreign merchant intermediaries include export distributors, foreign retailers, export jobbers, and trading companies. Of these, an *export distributor* procures products from a manufacturer in the home country at the greatest possible discount and resells them for a predetermined profit by him. Such intermediaries get active in distributing products that require periodic servicing as they are committed to provide adequate service to the customers through carrying a sufficient quantity of spares and parts, maintaining facilities, and providing technicians to perform all normal servicing operations. Export distributors procure the products in their own names and usually maintain an ongoing relationship with the exporter in the home country. They acquire exclusive sales rights in a host country or region and receive easy terms of payback from exporters. However, sometimes the manufacturers of a home country prefer to deal directly with *foreign retailers,* particularly in the case of consumer goods like cookies, and other confectionary products. In some countries, reputed and large retailers dealing in general merchandise or specific range of products like textile, photo goods, electronics etc. perform dual roles in terms of selling the products directly to consumers through their own outlets and also distributing imported goods to smaller retailers. Thus, it is observed that exports handled by the retailer generally receive wide coverage. On the contrary, the *export jobbers* determine customer needs overseas and provide them by making purchases in the home country. Some jobbers reverse the process, catering to the needs of home country customers by supplying imported products. The jobbers mainly deal in staple groceries and freely traded products under open general license for which brand names have little importance.

DISTRIBUTION IN GRAY MARKET

Gray market refers to distribution through unauthorized channels. The pipeline in a gray market is legal, but somewhat controversial. Many consider it unethical while others argue that it is economically unsound because it often involves purchasing goods and selling them at a profit without adding any value. In a gray-market a broker buys goods from a distributor overseas, where wholesale prices are low, then diverts them to the home country market and sells the goods at higher prices. The transactions in the gray market are usually direct from a manufacturer or exporter to a distributor located in the home country. In the process, the distributor diverts the shipment to another storage site, where it is either held or transported to a free trade port (such as Panama) where the discount retailers learn of the stored products through brokers and purchase large quantities of stored goods at the lower international wholesale prices. The gray markets are especially prevalent in the trading of luxury goods such as jewels, upscale clothing, perfumes and high-tech goods like computer accessories and chips. The gray market may also appear in the international market, when a company manufactures in several nations and sells its products in many countries, the same product might appear in the market in different countries at widely different prices. This can be due to "parallel" imports, unauthorized middlemen importing the identical products and brands from countries whose prices are lower because of exchange rates. These imports are also called *"gray trade."*

LOGISTICS MANAGEMENT

Concept of logistics is understood as the integrated management of forecasting, inventory control, transportation, warehousing, and order entry and customer service product planning functions by a large number of companies in the recent business environment. Logistics and the supply chain management is an art of management of flow of materials and products from the source of production to the end user. This system includes the total flow of material right from the stage of acquisition of raw materials to the delivery of finished products to the customers. The function of physical distribution is a component of the logistics system, that involves the outward movement of the goods and services from the company or the source of production or supplies. On the contrary the physical supply refers to the portion of the logistics system concerned with the inward movement of the goods and services to the delivery points. The function of distribution is the combination of activities associated with advertising, sales and physical transfer of the goods and services to the retail and wholesale delivery points. Hence, the logistics management is an important function to be handled in the marketing process. The effective logistics management can improve both cost and customer service performance of the company. The components of integrated logistics management are exhibited in Table 5.1.

Table 5.1 Logistics Management: The Integrated Pipeline

Supply	*Operations*	*Distribution*
• Production/Source • Purchasing • Inward transportation • Raw material and ad-hoc inventory	• Production planning • Scheduling • Ad-hoc inventory for production	• Forecasting • Customer service • Finished goods inventory • Warehousing • Outward transport

In the growing competitive market-most of the companies are looking at streamlining their operations in an integrated manner to manage the flow of materials from the production point to the outlet of end users. The integrated concept to manage the supply chain is proving to be analytical and able to transcend internal operational problems. The implementations of the integrated pipeline of the logistics variables help achieve a quantum leap in functional integration and operational effectiveness. It is also necessary for developing an appropriate supply chain. The managers have to think about their supplies, operations and distribution activities as a pipeline and as inter-related. The inter-functional linkages in the logistics management have further implications on the cost, service and time. The cost factor refers to the full cost of processing and moving goods from the source of production to the distribution points. The efficiency in the delivery of goods is a function of reliability, quick replenishment of stocks, minimizing the transit and storage losses and maintaining the lead-time delivery of the goods to the use points. Time is an important factor in the management of logistics pipeline that may be viewed from the point of total consumption of time in moving the goods from the source of production to the end user passing through the pipeline. The pipeline approach provides a mechanism for analyzing the impact of operational policy of the each function, identifying the conflicts and inconsistencies thereof. The advantages of the pipeline concept of logistics management are many, of these the benefits that may provide the managers efficient means for determining the logistics and distribution strategies are as under:

- Determining the long term production lead time on the system inventory,
- Impact on marketing promotions on the operating costs and effective net margins,
- Budgeting transport operations – net cost and savings, and
- Storage and warehousing cost estimation for the movement of goods – buffer stocking, retail stores and transit distribution sheds.

Pipeline analysis provides the potential benefits of lower costs, better service and effective time management for the movement of goods and services. The process of decision making in providing better logistic support begins from the stage of raw material supply required for production. The second stage in the process is managing the inventory at the manufacturing point and facilitating the outward movement of goods. The movement of goods to the intermediate storage points and retail points are also the functions that require appropriate logistic decisions. The logistics management has greater bearing on Just In Time (JIT) system that requires a close coordination of various backward and forward functions. The companies through the supply chain management can improve the efficiency of logistics operations. The supply chain needs to be managed for effective delivery of goods and services to all channel members including suppliers, manufacturers, distributors and customers. The benefit of supply chain management is that all the above entities in the system behave as, if they are part of the same company and attempt to enhance performance significantly across the board. The Supply Chain Manager of the company should understand the following seven principles for its effective execution in the market:

1. Manager should understand the customer values and requirement. He should know that any information seeker of the goods and services of the company is a customer and in this process a wholesaler or carrying & forwarding agent is a customer of manufacturer, a retailer is a customer of wholesalers and an end user of the goods and services is a customer of retailer as well as of the manufacturer. The requirement of the customers may be assessed in terms of delivery of the goods, merchandising support and value added services.
2. Effective logistic planning can be done by the manager of the company on comprehensive mapping of the logistics assets across the operational area and not just in the company. The information on locations of distributors, storage and warehousing facilities, transporters, railway rake points, shipment and cargo movement points, intermediate outlets, retail outlets, franchisees or vendor managed outlets would be helpful for making decisions on inventory deployment, distribution scheduling, transport and storage and other infrastructure facilities.
3. It is necessary for the manager to organize customers for easy flow of goods and information. This task requires aligning supplier's needs with the customer's buying process. This may be defined as single window policy of logistics management and can be pursued by the companies by providing electronic connectivity. The excellent example may be cited of the Torrent Pharmaceuticals Ltd., which has a wide distribution network at regional, area and district levels for the distribution of the medicines through the regional sales agents, area stockiest and retail druggists and chemists. The regional sale manager in consultation with the area and district sales managers collects information of the stock replenishment requirement to various channels. The orders are placed with the company through electronic mail or fax that helps the fast movement of goods to the destinations. The electronic network helps the Torrent Pharmaceuticals Ltd, not only to process the orders quickly but also to monitor the inventory at various points.

4. Manager should work for establishing more responsive supply chain through integrated sales and operational planning strategies. This task requires sharing real time demand and forecast information both within the company and across the supply chain. Information is one corporate resource that would enable the managers to make positive decisions. Information sharing helps in managing supply chain, sourcing and procurement and customer service. Such information inflow and dissemination will also provide opportunity improvement in design and engineering aspects, research and development, exploration of new business areas, new product development and all marketing functions.
5. Company should consider leverage manufacturing and sourcing for flexible and efficient supply chain operations. Leverage manufacturing concept may be explained with an example of postponement or slow down production process to reduce the inventory at the source of production or developing multiple stock keeping points for storage in the lean season. The physical distribution in these units may be activated when it is required. Automatic replenishment programs may be linked to the production sources and the stocking points. The companies can also use the demand signals such as point of sales data as a yardstick for market place activity.
6. Companies must develop customer driven alliances and relationship management across all channels and customer segments. Such action strengthens the strategic partnership and supply chain management operations.
7. Companies must puruse to develop the customer driven performance measures to drive the behavior of all channel members and customers. This would help in tracking the economic performance and extended supply chain to the new areas.

It is essential for the companies to manage the demand chain for their product along the supply chain management. The rationalization of the product line, new product development, pricing, promotion and comparative advantages over the competing brands need to be taken up before starting the production and commercialization. The customers need to segment according to product and tailor made marketing policies. The value additions in the distribution of the goods need factors such as product priorities, finance, display, point of purchase material, retailer's schemes etc. to be assessed by the company to make the channel members pro-active. This process would integrate the supply chain management with the demand chain management. It requires collaboration between manufacturers, distributors, retailers to build demand through the effective consumer marketing and merchandising.

Manufacturers and suppliers are abandoning their traditional adversarial relationships characterized by price haggling and hedging bets on product orders in favour of a collaborative-commerce model designed to be mutually beneficial. In order to bridge the path for new alliances, vendors are rolling out enhanced supply-chain planning and forecasting tools and Supplier Relationship Management (SRM) technologies that provide real-time access to the demand, inventory, price, sourcing, and production data to be shared by manufacturers and their suppliers. Some companies have started collaborative effort with appliance vendors, but they plan to implement the system with other vendors.

Ford Motor, in Dearborn, Michigan, USA is using supply-chain planning software from SynQuest to determine delivery-route schemes for each auto part at the lowest overall

> transportation cost while supporting just-in-time manufacturing requirements at Ford assembly plants. The software is designed to model Ford's complex inbound network, which includes transportation routes, cross docks, and plant and supplier operations. Ford has 46 manufacturing and assembly plants in North America and 500 suppliers, says Frank Taylor, Ford's vice president of material planning and logistics. The software allows Ford to simultaneously evaluate multiple sets of variables including transportation mode, frequency, and freight costs to orchestrate inbound parts movement. As a result of the deployment, Ford's inbound network has reduced errors such as missing a part at a plant, from thousands per million to single-digit errors per million. The suppliers of Ford Motors also benefit from this system.

Collaborative-commerce technology is designed to encompass a product's life from cradle to grave including product design, sourcing, procurement, supplier negotiation, demand planning and forecasting, and price and revenue optimization. These leading-edge applications can bring suppliers into the product design process and work in real time to support inventory levels for just-in-time manufacturing. The SAP and ERP applications use advanced-planning macros to enable collaborative planning, forecasting, and replenishment. Through collaborative planning, a company can communicate to the suppliers about inventory on a common site. Through such way suppliers know what is coming down the pike and can change production. An enterprise does not have to communicate with each supplier. On the sales side, collaborative commerce helps manufacturers co-ordinate products from different business units and make better forecasts. For instance, a PC vendor could use collaborative commerce to build a purchase order, orchestrating all of the different purchase-order components out of different divisions.

CHANNEL MANAGEMENT

A firm needs to carefully examine the patter of distribution that fits competitively to the market environment of the host country. Intensive distribution is an attempt to reach the mass market, and it requires broad-based channel structure where as selective distribution refers to distributing through a few so-called elite outlets located in the premium market segments. The exclusive distribution refers letting a designated channel undertake distribution on a monopoly basis such as the task of distributing a company's exclusive products. Host country trade practices concerning the distribution of a particular product are other influential variables to be examined by the foreign firm during the process of developing the channel management strategies.

> Characteristics of the product and the market target to be served often suggest particular distribution intensity. Different degrees of distribution intensity can be implemented. Selective distribution falls between the two extremes. Rolex watches and Coach leather goods are distributed on a selective basis. For example, an expensive product, such as a Toyota Lexus luxury automobile, does not require intensive distribution to make contact with potential buyers. Moreover, several dealers in a trading area could not generate enough sales and profits due to the luxury car's limited sales potential. Similarly, Escada's management, in choosing to serve the middle to upper price-quality segment of the apparel market, essentially preempted consideration of an intensive distribution strategy. In contrast, Kodak film needs to be widely available in the marketplace. The distribution intensity should correspond to

the marketing strategy management selects. Strategic requirements, management's preferences, and other constraints help determine the distribution intensity that offers the best strategic fit and performance potential. The requirements of intermediaries are considered, along with management's desire to co-ordinate and motivate them.

Choosing the right distribution intensity depends on management's targeting and positioning strategies and product and market characteristics. The major issues in deciding distribution intensity are:

- Identifying which distribution intensities are feasible, taking into account the size and characteristics of the market target, the product, and the requirements likely to be imposed by prospective intermediaries.
- Selecting the alternatives that are compatible with the proposed market target and marketing program positioning strategy.
- Choosing the alternative that (1) offers the best strategic fit, (2) meets management's financial performance expectations, and (3) is sufficiently attractive so that intermediaries will be motivated to perform their assigned functions.

DEVELOPING LOGISTICS STRATEGY

Strategy building for effective logistics management is a multi-functional concept and needs inter-disciplinary approach. This involves physical distribution, services, cost and customer care in an integrated manner. The number of locations of distribution points, warehouses, mode of transport, cost-service factors, carrier selection, inventory positioning, inventory levels, order–entry and processing, delivery information, transit loss management, soiled stock replacement, replenishment schedule, time management, delivery and remittance collection schedule and so forth are the various function associated with the logistics strategy planning.

Cost-service curve of logistics strategy exhibited in Figure 5.2 reveals that a company may select a high service position (A) by providing a network of warehouses, use of premium transport mode that is safer and faster as compared to the existing modes, higher inventory levels and also high service. On the contrary a company may select low–cost positioning (B) with minimum infrastructure support. However, most of the companies do not operate at maximum efficiency and they are positioned at the lower end of the curve. Such companies must develop, suitable strategies for efficient delivery of goods and services at optimal cost.

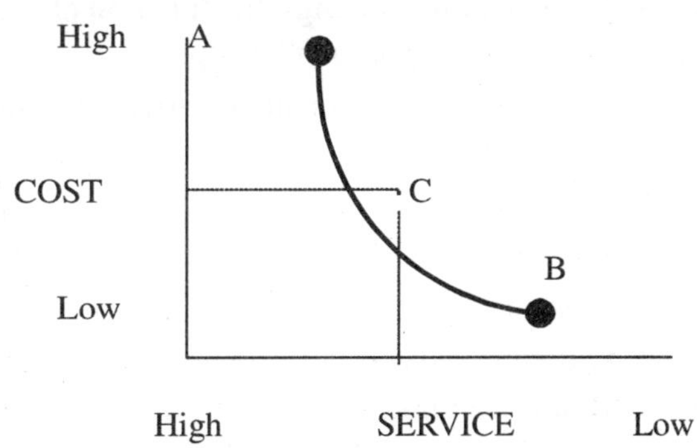

Figure 5.2 Cost–service curve in logistics

Logistics has greater role to perform in contributing the value proposition to the customer of a company. The customer value can be increased by reducing the amount of inventories by way of continuous replenishment of stock at every level to keep the distribution chain active and moving. The structural decisions in developing the logistics strategy needs to think of the suitable channel policy as to route the goods and services through the routine channels or to reaches the customers directly. Some of the companies do not have the distributors, for example Eureka Forbes Ltd. dealing in vacuum cleaners and water purifiers reach its products and services directly to the customer through its sales personnel. This helps the company in reducing the cost of distribution, and analyzing the customer requirements more closely to augment the customer value. On the contrary the companies that are associated with multi-brands and wide operational area look for a distributor network. Such decisions are taken as structural plans in the companies. The structural decisions are very complex and require careful examination. However, amidst new technologies and new operating options available to the companies, these structural decisions provide opportunities to the companies to achieve more at less cost and create value in the whole process of logistics management. The logistics strategies also require the functional efficiency in transportation, warehousing and materials management. The implementation of logistics strategy involves adequate data base, information flow, appropriate policies and procedures, organizational system and change management. The logistics managers thus, need to co-ordinate with various section personnel in the organization to prepare for better decision-making.

PHYSICAL DISTRIBUTION

As stated in the pre-text physical distribution is one of the components of the supply chain management but plays a significant role in the process of the marketing management in general and comprises three major constituents of the distribution management system- transportation, warehousing and inventory management. This function involves planning, implementing and controlling the physical flow of raw material and final goods from the points of use to cater to the customer needs at a moderate rate of profit. The physical distribution involves several activities enchained with each other as stated below:

- Sales forecasting
- Distribution planning- this function also involves the activities of production planning and materials procurement for production or manufacturing
- Inventory management includes operations of order processing, receiving and inbound transportation
- Packaging
- In-plant or in-company stocking or warehousing
- Shipping
- Outward transportation
- Retail warehousing, and
- Customer service

Many cost conscious companies state their objective of physical distribution to provide right products to the right outlets at the right time with minimum expenditure. In fact, the main aim of the physical distribution should be to achieve maximum customer satisfaction at low cost. It is essential to plan distribution management in concurrence with the marketing objective of the company. For example, Pepsi Foods Ltd. in India has delineated the strategy of providing Pepsi and its sister brands to the customers at *an arm's length* and hence, it has done close networking of retailers and distributors. It is therefore necessary to identify the area of operation and the strength of dealer-retailer to develop appropriate distribution strategy. The physical distribution is a function of freight cost, total fixed warehouse cost, variable warehouse cost including inventory and the total cost of lost sales due to average delivery delay.

Process of physical distribution begins with complying with the customer orders. The shorter the process of realizing the customer order the faster would be the distribution of goods to the selected points. The key need of most of the companies today is to shorten chain of intermediaries in the whole distribution system. This chain involves various steps including transmission of the order by the salesperson, order entry and customer credit check, inventory and production scheduling, order and invoice shipment and receipt of payment. If this chain is longer the process time will be longer and the customer satisfaction would be lower. This would also affect the profitability of the company. The functions of distribution are taken as supportive mechanism by many companies in the developing markets like India and suffer from the long run strategic planning.

Inventory management is concerned with stocking inventory to fill customer orders. It involves two decisions-how often to order in a given period and how much to order. The expenditure involved with these decisions is inversely related. If too many orders are placed in a year with a firm, the ordering costs will increase accordingly. On the other hand, if large quantities are ordered at a time, the total number of orders is reduced and hence the total ordering cost. However, the costs of carrying large purchases go up. Thus, an optimum number of orders and the size of each order need to determined to gain cost effectiveness in the distribution process. This optimum point can be figured by using different forms of informational inputs and an appropriate mathematical formula. The transport management is a major function of international physical distribution and transportation decision mainly involves the choice of a mode of transportation for shipping the goods both internationally and locally within a foreign nation. Such decisions are influenced by the availability of transportation, nature of product, shipment, and passage distance, type of demand and cost of different shipping alternatives.

DISTRIBUTION PLANNING

There are three basic elements: (i) product recognition, (ii) price structure and (iii) the distribution planning which are required to develop an effective marketing mix. The relative importance of these three elements varies from product to product and from time to time. Distribution is often the key to a successful sales and marketing policy. The synchronization process for the distribution planning is discussed as below:

- Product - Attributes and consumer recognition.
- Size and value of sales - Extent of sales realisation.
- Market area – Consumer segments, coverage, channel length.

- Existing methods of distribution - Impact, problems and prospects.
- Needed efforts - Customer value, Value added distribution, cost effectiveness
- Overhead costs - Operational expenses, personnel management, and,
- Monitoring- Information flow, schedule of distribution, cash flow and payments.

> **Strategy Focus 5.3: Distribution Strategy of Reckitt & Colman of India Ltd.**
>
> Almost 70 percent of Reckitt's sales came from towns with population greater than 100 thousand. But only 20 per cent of its distributors accounted for 70 percent of the company's turnover. Expanding coverage through these distributors simply pushed up costs (freight, salesmen). "We had to keep subsidising the distributor till he achieved proper coverage and volumes, states the general manager, RCI. Today, Reckitts rural thrust is being built around a new approach: use the low-cost super-stockist channel, and to make it viable, generate enough demand by creating the right product formats for these markets. (Mortein coil's pricing – Rs 3.50 for a pack of two – is at par with the loose coils that sell in rural markets. This year, the company will launch three new Dettol extensions tailored specifically for the rural buyers.) Reckitt has adopted the super-stockist system in Tamil Nadu, and plans to take go national by next year. The company has plans to cover a million outlets in the next three years.

Objective of distribution planning is to make the product available to the consumers at a more convenient outlet. The distribution planning for products should be considered with prime importance to withstand the market competition. It is because, if a competitive product is available at approachable outlets or at low price, there are all chances of foregoing the sale. Therefore, to deal under such competitive market situation a systematic planning for delivering the product to the consumers through different distribution channels, need to be determined. The time and distance factor for the delivery of goods normally influences the buying decisions where the manufacturing of products is subject to consumer order, occasional demands and door to door delivery promises. In this regard the planning needs to be done evolving different methods for efficient product distribution through identified channels. In this process, there is a need to look into the infrastructure factors viz. transport, road, communication etc in support of the channel efficiency. In fact the consumer is only interested in getting the product but a lot of responsibility lies with the marketing personnel in delivering the product at appropriate time and place.

Large number of pharmaceutical companies in India does not consider the distribution as one of the main functions in the marketing process. The distribution cost structure of this industry is higher as compared to other industries. The countrywide optimal distribution system requires an in-depth financial service analysis of the system such as carrying and forwarding agents, depots and super stockist. The financial load on the companies in regard to distribution chain was found very heavy when it came to adhere to the Drug Price Control Order (DCPO) of 1995 announced by the Government of India enforcing the minimum 16 percent retail trade margins for all formulation on the maximum retail price (MRP) and would be exclusive of the excise duty for the controlled category of products and 20 percent for the decontrolled category of products. This additional financial load has made the pharmaceutical companies rationalize their distribution network. These products go through a few more stages than typical products. They start from factory and reach the final customer, the patient, through the medical professional. However, the value chain satisfaction is a debatable issue in this industry. The benefits are generally two-way. Fewer carrying and forwarding agents handling larger volumes, for instance could save transportation cost. Agents will be satisfied with their space utilization so long as orders keep coming in. However, at every level of the distribution hierarchy an active sales force is seen to be playing an important role in pushing the orders in the pipeline that keeps their spirit up. In all, it can be stated that it is the logistics that makes the distribution network profitable for the company. The Usha International Ltd. (UIL) , the company known for the sewing machines, also has the marketing arm of US $ 300 million Siel Group selling the industrial and farm equipments as well as appliances. The company had a rapid growth between 1987-88 and 1996-97 which changed other consumer durables' marketer beyond recognition. The sale of UIL grew from US $29 million4 to US$ 69 million[4] with a compound rate of growth of over 7 percent per annum. The company has a wide distribution network which includes Divisional Offices (15), Warehouses (26), Company owned retail outlets (50), Exclusive sales and service centers and multi-brand outlets (5000), and Centralized spare parts facility centers for small appliances (8). The UIL has a strong network of distribution channels and the products are made available to the customer at the low cost with higher extent of satisfaction as compared to the other companies. The distribution of 5000 sales and service center of the company provides better access to the retailers and customers.

Distribution planning may invariably be based on the market survey carried out at the time of preparing the business plan. The distribution planning should be to make the products available to the larger number of consumers at lower marketing costs. To reduce the cost of marketing, it is required to determine the most feasible channel. The product characteristics and the operational area are the major factors to be considered while selecting a distribution channel. In any channel different distribution approach can be adopted to get the products more economically to the ultimate user. The important factor to be assessed in this process is the cost effectiveness. It is observed that, longer the chain of intermediaries in product distribution, higher is the cost of marketing. Since cost is one of the determinants of profit, it should also be viewed from the angle of product distribution. The exclusive distribution approach is always confined to an area. Such distribution plan can be useful in the areas (i) where the demand concentration for the product is low (ii) which are located at distance from the high concentration areas i.e. urban places (iii) the storage, transportation and other overhead costs are higher and (iv) the competition is absent or very low. In urban areas where market competition for the product is high and the retailing is at large scale, selective distribution policy would be more useful. However, retailers and consumers in areas where the purchasing power of consumers is low but a large number of retailers are in business fray feel the approach of extensive distribution of products. In other words, such approach would help the market condition.

These factors are inter-related and affect the whole network of product distribution. The distribution chain or network may be long or wide; there is a need for effective control without which the entire business plan may break mid-way. Distribution policy needs to be developed in accordance to the product characteristics and its segmented market. Ethically, in business short path of distribution network leads to minimization of risks and maximization of profit. An ideal network of distribution would be two-tier between manufacturer and end user.

4 Exchange rate US $1 = INR 45.85 (Average trend of last week of July 2001)

Coca-Cola uses an intensive distribution strategy, which means the company attempts to push its products through as many wholesalers and retailers as possible. In addition, Coca-Cola is using a decade-old strategy by investing in international bottlers to improve local operations in countries with increased sales. As a result, Coca-Cola spent during the past three years an average of $ 900 million a year to beef up its bottlers in emerging countries. For example, Coca-Cola and its bottling partners spent $ 500 million in China and $1 billion in Mexico in the past five years. Coca-Cola also announced plans to spend $ 2 billion in Brazil and Latin American bottlers.(14) Another strength of Coca-Cola's distribution strategy is that it takes into account the different distribution attitudes of the countries. As a result, Coca-Cola does not have a global distribution policy. In other words, the distribution systems differ from country to country. This is one reason why Coca-Cola is still the leading beverage company in the world, because PepsiCo could not overtake Coca-Cola with its global strategy. The most important way for Coca-Cola to distribute its products is by working together with international bottlers. These bottlers are as involved in the distribution system as franchisees. This relationship works in a way, that Coca-Cola supplies the franchisees with the syrup, and allows them to mix it with the necessary, additional supplements like carbonated water. Finally, the bottlers manufacture the end product and distribute it. It's useful to have a close relationship with these companies, because their performance will reflect in sales and profits of Coca-Cola. Therefore, Coca-Colas tries to gain influence on these bottlers by buying shares or acquiring former independent bottlers. This strategy is another part of Coca-Cola's success over the past decades. Over the years, Coca-Cola has built a global network of such relationships. Coca-Cola's choice of its distributors is very important. The attributes a distributor has to have are experience and expertise in production, marketing and certainly distribution of soft drinks. The choice of the bottling partner in the increasing market of Poland is one example of this. Coca-Cola was searching for a partner for a $30 million joint venture for a state-of-the-art bottling plant. Coca-Cola decided to choose Ringnes, a Norwegian company, because of the company's more than 50 years experience and expertise in the soft drink market. Coca-Cola still has a good relationship with the company.

An important aspect of the choice of Coca-Cola's distributors is, as mentioned before, having a high degree of control over them. Coca-Cola chooses large wholesalers for distribution because this strategy will decrease the number of distributors for Coca-Cola. This is helpful to involve as less companies as possible to keep its secrets from getting public. Coca-Cola's successful distribution network offers Coca-Cola more opportunities for additional alliances. This network is important for developing new products or to enter new markets. The joint venture between the world's largest food company, Nestle S.A.[5], and Coca-Cola, is one example of this. Both companies were looking for a possibility to increase their sales in the coffee (Coca-Cola) and tea (Nestle S.A.) market. Coca-Cola had the distribution system, but not the right trademark to put on a coffee product or ultimately a tea product, Nestle had. By combining their strengths, consisting of excellent bottling/distribution system and technological expertise, both the companies were able to formulate ready-to-drink coffee, tea and chocolate beverages. In addition, the joint venture was able to leverage on established brand names, like Nescafe, and Nestea (Nestle S.A.). Not only Coca-Cola benefited from the

5 Nestlé SA refers to the Nestlé Mexico SA

joint venture. Nestle also got benefited from Coca-Cola's distribution system because Coca-Cola already had access to 800,000 vending machines in the Japanese coffee market as opposed to Nestle's access to 100,000. In recent years, the importance of fountain locations such as convenience stores and gas station has increased, but still the largest distribution parts are the restaurants, which make up over 80 percent of all fountain sales. The above mentioned market share of all the US fountain (65 percent) is a result of contracts with McDonald's and other chains. Coca-Cola is the exclusive cola supplier in more than 90 percent of the fountain locations. Market research shows the importance of being a leading fountain supplier. Coca-Cola's distribution system is very flexible in coping with political barriers and trade barriers. First, Coca-Cola arranged the development of new plants as a joint venture with the Chinese Ministry of Light Industry. In fact, Coca-Cola built its first plant in China in 1927, but had to leave the country after the Communists took over in the late 1940s. Second, Coca-Cola announced a $ 48.8 million joint venture in Southern Vietnam. This move was the first in Southern Vietnam involving US funds since diplomatic ties were restored with USA. After years of trying, Coca-Cola has signed a deal to re-enter India, the world's second most populous country, where its soft drinks haven't been bottled since 1977. This re-entry was only possible because Coca-Cola had previously formed a joint venture with an Indian company.

FUNCTIONAL EXCELLENCE IN DISTRIBUTION PLANNING

Companies must draw separate plans for the distribution resources and distribution requirements. It is beneficial for two reasons. Firstly, such planning yields excellent results in a given supply chain from manufacturers to the customers for replenishing products in time and secondly the traditional logistic chain can be modified by way of building linkages and quick responses for continuous replenishment of stock and keeping the channel partnership intact. The continuous replenishment helps the companies in shifting the administrative burden for inventory management and replenishment at the customer's warehouse back to the manufacturer. This however, involves higher transportation costs but also offers benefits to the manufacturer. The companies should look for the following three approaches for quick replenishment of the goods to the outlets:

- Customer specified approach that may be followed by the companies as the simplest tool in the process of stock replenishment process. The customers may be asked to provide minimum and maximum inventory re-order at the points of convenience and its periodicity.
- Manufacturer may alternatively maintain more active management of customer inventory levels, generally using classic re-ordering indicating the point of convenience and its frequency.
- Channel distribution planning is the most comprehensive approach for continuous replenishment. It involves setting up each of the company's customer warehouses as nodal points in the distribution planning system and activating the replenishment to these nodes.

Warehousing function is one of the important activities in the distribution management. The companies must decide on a desirable number of stocking locations. The increase in number of outlets should not slow down the process of distribution. The number of stocking locations must strike a balance between customer-service levels and distribution costs.The supply chain management has been an integrated component of the implementation, control and evaluation of the marketing program in the companies. Today, with lean and healthy operations as their foundation, progressive companies are focusing intensely on growing revenues, thereby breaking the downsizing death spiral. Instead of merely striving to meet annual cost-reduction targets, managers at these leading companies are repositioning the supply chain as an enabler of growth. Logistics professionals played key roles in improving the cost competitiveness of their operations across the supply chain by adopting new strategies, closing warehouses, trimming inventories, outsourcing non-essential services, and installing powerful forecasting and material-control systems. Successful growth companies often follow one or more of three key growth strategies: customer franchise management, new product development, and channel management. Each of these growth strategies depends on supply chain innovations

Logistics and the supply chain management is an art of management of flow of materials and products from the source of production to the end user. As a primary interface point with the customer, supply chain management can offer value in the form of competitively superior delivery and value-added services, as defined by customers. In this way, the value foundation translates to customer-service excellence. In parallel with the downsizing and engineering efforts of the past decade, customer service re-emerged as a key management priority for a wide range of manufacturers. But for many companies, meeting basic service requirements and achieving customer satisfaction are still the primary goals. The integrated concept to manage the supply chain is proving to be analytical and able to transcend internal operational problems. The implementations of the integrated pipeline of the logistics variables help achieve a quantum leap in functional integration and operational effectiveness. Companies such as Procter & Gamble and Newell, both manufacturers of a variety of consumer products, understood early on the growth ambitions and strategies of Wal-Mart. By tailoring their logistics to support the retailer's growth, they have grown as well. Notably, a major component of Wal-Mart's growth strategy has been superior economics, including a low-cost, highly efficient merchandise supply chain. The retailer backs up this strategy with significant investments in state-of-the-art logistics, information systems, and communications technology.

SELECTED READINGS

Robert E. Weigand, "Fit Products and Channels to Your Market," *Harvard Business Review* January-February 1977): 95-105.

Donald V. Fifties, "Make Your Dealers Your Partners," *Harvard Business Review* (March-April 1996): 84-96.

Philip Kotler, *Marketing Management,* 7th ed. Englewood Cliffs, NJ: Prentice-Hall, 1994.

Louis W. Stern, Adel I. El-Ansary, and James R. Brown, *Management in Marketing Channels,* Englewood Cliffs, NJ: Prentice-Hall, 1989.

Alan R. Raedels : *Value Focused Supply Chain Management,* Irwin Inc, New York, 1995.

David Frederick Ross : *Competing Through Supply Chain Management,* Chapman & Hall, New York1998.

David Simchi-Levi, Philip Kaminsky, Edith Simchi-Levi : *Designing And Managing The Supply Chain,* McGraw-Hill Companies, Inc., Irwin McGraw-Hill Higher Education, 2000.

John T. Mentzer, editor : *Supply Chain Management,* Sage Publications, Inc., Thousand Oaks, 1998.

Kern, G. and Guerrero, H., "A Conceptual Model for Demand Management in the Assemble-to-Order Environment", *Journal of Operations Management,* 9(1), 65-84, 1990.

Lee, H. and Billington, C.: "Managing Supply Chain Inventory: Pitfalls and Opportunities", *Sloan Management Review,* pp. 65 -73, Spring, 1992

Lee, H. and Billington, C.: "Material Management in Decentralized Supply Chains", *Operations Research,* vol. 41, no. 5, 1993.

Case 5.1

DOMINO'S PIZZA DISTRIBUTION PLAN[6]

Domino's Pizza Distribution (DPD) is the primary source for food service and Equipment and supply (E&S) distribution for Domino's mainland U.S. pizza stores. Through a network of 18 distribution centers—all of which manufacture fresh dough—DPD regularly supplies over 4,300 stores with more than 250 products. These items range from all food items (except soft drinks) to pizza boxes, napkins, forms, and cleaning supplies. All of the food products that the stores buy from DPD are shipped from one of their distribution centers on their private truck fleet. E&S supplies stores with everything from ovens and signs to pizza cutters and uniforms from two distribution points (and in some cases, they drop ship directly from their suppliers). Their International Division manages similar operations to support Domino's stores in Canada, Alaska, Hawaii, and Puerto Rico. From private fleet and delivery and service specialists to their customer-service representatives and field managers, each distribution center acts as a key part of the support channel for the pizza stores it services. The DPD Division started to grow in earnest in the early 1980s as Domino's store growth began taking off. In the mid-1980s, when nearly 1,000 stores were hidded in a single year, the DPD network grew to its most expansive distribution structure. Their distribution centers historically have acted autonomously, focusing intensely on excellent customer service. Each center had developed methods and procedures tailored to support its assigned market.

It was during the late 1980s that their existing core-information systems were put into place. At the time, these UNIX-based, customized systems employed leading technology. Back then, functionality was fairly limited to transaction process management. After a period of limited change in the early 1990s, Domino's Pizza Distribution started to re-assess its strategic vision. In 1995, the current vision for DPD started to take form. The core guiding principles of their strategy are to:

- Achieve Customer Satisfaction and Success
- Impress customers and help their business succeed.
- Perfect the Supply Chain
- Focus on delivery systems—from the farmer's field to the consumer's front door.
- Develop Individuals and Teams and
- Find, develop, and keep the best people.

Over the past couple of years, DPD has aggressively pursued this strategic direction and has been doing the groundwork required to support this vision. DPD now is in the midst of implementing

6 This case has been written as the basis for class discussion rather than to illustrate either effective or ineffective handling of an administrative situation of the company.

advanced technology and operational solutions that will allow them to perfect their supply chain. Although Domino's Pizza stores are not required to use DPD as a source for product or equipment, 96.5 percent do source through them. Their aim is to build an operation that ensures their continued position as the leading distributor/manufacturer servicing the pizza stores.

LEADERSHIP STRATEGY

Domino's Pizza Distribution has determined that its supply chain will play a key strategic role in supporting the operations and growth of Domino's Pizza stores by providing excellent service and quality products at the best available price. Their goal in perfecting the supply chain is two fold: (1) Streamline the supply chain and eliminate non-value-added activities and (2) Reduce or eliminate the order-fulfillment and logistics activities that their stores need to perform. DPD is, and will continue to be, best suited to provide this value. They will invest in the most appropriate assets that maximize their effectiveness and efficiency, while providing the best return to their principal stakeholders—the more than 1,200 franchisees. Importantly, DPD has a unique profit-sharing philosophy with these stakeholders. The arrangement dictates that they create a balance between value-added service and least-cost distribution that provides their customers with excellent service and a highly profitable business opportunity. They strongly believe that their commitment to provide excellent service to their stores, to help them reduce the challenges of operating in a difficult and competitive market, and to do everything possible to enhance their profitability makes them the best sourcing alternative. Therefore, it is critical that they be the best in the business. Their strategic vision would lead them to that goal.

Operational Vision: Maximize Quality and Service

If they look at the activities—both value-added and non-value-added—within the entire supply chain, it becomes clear that different supply chain participants are best suited to perform specific tasks. DPD is positioning itself to provide the following services :

- Overall management of and planning for inventory of food products, store equipment, and supplies.
- Control of the physical flow of products all the way to the picking locations within the back room of the store.
- Manufacturing and delivery of fresh, ready-to-use dough products.
- Sourcing of the best pizza ingredients for their stores.
- Sourcing of the best equipment and supplies for their stores.
- Management of the store order process, including determination of what should be delivered and when.
- Ownership of inventory from the point of Domino's possession to the time of use by the stores.

Much of DPD's supply chain is not complex. They have comparatively few SKUs. They have known Customers, accessible demand information, and relatively small distribution centers. The complexity comes from the high-velocity, high-volume, synchronous processes required to plan, process, manufacture dough to order, route, pick, load, and deliver more than 10,000 deliveries per week. DPD's current and planned operations are highly service focused. They typically have a 10- to 15-hour order cycle from initial order entry to dispatch. Actual delivery time varies from two to 24 hours. They do not have an order cut-off. In fact, they accept add-ons after the truck has left, either sending another shipment or meeting the truck with the additional product. They strive for a minimal number of service errors and currently ship over 98 percent of their deliveries 100 percent correct. (This is a measure of order-fulfillment effectiveness and does not incorporate product-quality issues that would not be apparent from the package. They also are working with their suppliers to maximize quality product at the stores.) At present, they're managing this service level with more than 50 inventory turns a year. The most critical failure occurs when a store is unable to sell pizzas to its customers—a "store closing." A store closing counts no matter how little time the store is out of operation, and no matter what challenges nature has dealt. For Domino's Pizza stores, bad weather brings opportunity. Many consumers rely on fresh, hot delivered pizza while they are dealing with weather problems. Bad weather, coupled with unpredictable peaks in demand, provides unique challenges for DPD. Normally, they have fewer than 15 store closings per year.

One particularly innovative operational objective is to better manage the age of the four million pounds of dough that they produce and deliver to stores every week. This "living" product performs differently throughout its shelf life. Dough that is too young or too old should not be used. Their delivery cycle allows for the stores to have very little old dough remaining at the end of shelf life. Their goal is to sequence the production of their dozens of dough SKUs, so that the product at the time of delivery is aged correctly to meet the stores' needs. For example, if the store will have a fair amount of dough in stock when the delivery is made, they should ship dough that will be younger at the time of arrival. Their information-systems solution will provide a planning engine that allows them to perform this kind of dynamic product planning.

THE INFORMATION TECHNOLOGY SOLUTION

Domino's now is implementing an entire suite of operational and financial information-technology solutions that will provide them with advanced support for their business. In weighing the benefits of various best-of-breed operational solutions, they felt that the most critical functionality was the ability to have a fully integrated, work-flow-driven order-fulfillment process. This would allow complete, real-time visibility to the entire portion of the supply chain that they manage. The need for advanced functionality to manage each individual process is limited given the simplicity of many of their processes. For example, in their dough-manufacturing process, they blend ingredients, mix, cut, form, cool, and package the dough product. There are no by products. All of their facilities are under 60,000 square feet, so warehouse functionality is not required to deal with distance-related zone optimization. Overall co-ordination of the integrated processes clearly is their competitive advantage in achieving high levels of flexible customer service at a low cost. In evaluating information-technology options, they sought a solution that fit their business model and provided the tools and information team members needed to enhance business performance. This would allow them to build around the inherent functionality of the software instead of designing heavy modifications.

From a technology point of view, the new systems needed to provide a flexible technical infrastructure to support changing business requirements. In a distributed operation, it was important that hardware and software configuration not constrain where they chose to put systems functionality. With their large number of sites, they also wanted to ensure that a highly reliable technical infrastructure was inherent in the solution. This would provide an environment that minimized downtime risks and provided for high availability of all systems. The selection process incorporated the modern approach of paring down the pack to eight vendors using 20 to 30 key decision criteria. Later the company developed a demonstration script, building on their knowledge of what they saw in their operational vision as well as insights gained from standard product demonstrations of leading packages. In order to perform a two-day scripted demonstration four vendors were invited. Each of these demos was attended by more than 60 Domino's team members from the selection team and from the end-user community. The whole process to identify a supply chain IT solution took a relatively short five months.

A central data warehouse and multi-dimensional analysis tools has been implemented, and have been viewing their operations from an activity-based management perspective for about a year. Although posing quite a cultural change for most of their team members, these new broad operational measures have been key in driving operational change. However, the availability of analysis and decision-support information from their new technology solution far surpasses, what they have to work with today. The PeopleSoft/Essbase/Cognos solution provides both excellent accessibility to information and the tools for end-users to analyze that information effectively.

RE-ENGINEERING FOR CROSS-FUNCTIONAL EXCELLENCE

Upon analysis, they determined that their current procedures and processes, though adequate for today's operations, would not leverage the advanced technological solution they had chosen. Therefore, they are designing their new core processes around the inherent functionality of their new IT solution. Their re-engineering efforts will surely cause some system functionality modifications. Yet, they certainly will try to limit these so that future upgrades and integrations are easier to accomplish. Since, the PeopleSoft solution allows them to manage entire processes, they have eliminated functional or department thinking from their design process. This has taken a bit of effort since Domino's as a corporation, including DPD, historically has been functionally aligned. Interestingly, the breakthrough really came during the scripted demos when team members had to sit through the functionality presentations of other departments. The core supply chain process relates to the flow of inventory and its parallel flow of dollars. This process is called *Forecast to Cash.* Within this process are several sub-processes. Notice in the exhibit that the corresponding systems' modules tend to relate to typical, current departmental definitions. Although focusing on modules will benefit their design team when dealing with the IT implementation, it confuses supply chain process re-engineering. To assure proper design and implementation, the supply chain has been selected as both an entire process and as sub-processes. As they look at the entire process, different users may be involved in different portions, and different divisions may use certain portions of the entire process. There also are processes that are relatively unrelated to this core Forecast-to-Cash process. These include budgeting, treasury, asset management, item management, maintenance, project management, and

Administration of travel/expenses. The overall integrated view, however, assures that they can create a completely integrated supply chain solution that also considers these other processes.

In order to accomplish this integrated supply chain re-engineering, their project team is structured to promote cross-functional process design and team interaction. Each of the sub-processes will be developed using the same methodology. From a reengineering standpoint, the processes will be designed in parallel with overall Forecast-to-Cash process oversight. From a technical development and modification perspective, IT configuration and modification will be structured around the system architecture. The goal is to simplify the solution by establishing consistent core processes throughout their divisions and functions. For example, several of their divisions process purchase orders. On the surface, Distribution's PO process looks much different from that of the Corporate Home Office. However, if they look deeper, they see that Distribution places different types of POs: food; store equipment and supplies; office supplies; and capital assets. The team believes that it makes sense for the whole corporation to buy supplies and capital assets using the same process, even if it is somewhat different from how Distribution purchases food. This approach will facilitate support of the continuous improvement to both their processes and the supporting systems.

PHASED APPROACH TO IMPLEMENTATION

Phased implementation approach has been developed for their supply chain solution. The first phase implements core transactional functionality that will allow the end-users to see and control the entire core set of processes. Some planning functionality and basic decision support will be included. The second phase will add greater functionality depth to many of their sub-processes to improve their efficiency and effectiveness. Sophisticated integrated planning and advanced decision support will be incorporated. They expect to continually improve upon their solution with additional enhancements and new releases from their software solution providers. The design of Phase 2 is planned to overlap the implementation of Phase 1.

Team has struggled over this phased implementation approach. Different constituencies have their own needs and agendas—for example, minimizing the need to work on two systems at the same time, putting a solution in quickly, getting a fair amount of additional functionality (over and above current) in the first phase. To complicate matters, certain technology architecture attributes make some solutions easier to implement than others. After a couple of months of debate, they reached a consensus on at least the functionality goals of the phasing approach. There are still technical issues to resolve. The large number of sites within their system complicates rollout of the phases. Their current plans are to first pilot the complete Forecast-to-Cash process at one distribution center. In parallel with this, they will implement the core financials functionality at their Corporate and Distribution Home Offices. Once all of these locations have been tested and the interface issues resolved, they will begin rollout to other distribution centers. Because of the impact on their team, they will probably limit rollout to no more than five distribution centers at a time. Their equipment and supply operations will be rolled out in a similar process once they have established control over the distribution-center implementation. This phased implementation approach will provide a large increase in competitive functionality early on, while assuring high acceptance and minimizing risk. It leads them to a fully configured system with well-documented procedures and incorporates the user-supported re-engineering efforts of the design phase. The target date for the Phase 1 implementation startup is May 1998. They expect full rollout of Phase 1 to take a year. The Phase 2 rollout could possibly overlap the end of the Phase 1 rollout.

TEAM-DEVELOPMENT INITIATIVES

Many aspects of Domino's re-engineering and information-technology solution involve implementation risks. And these largely center on their end-user team members' acceptance and understanding of the solution. They have several initiatives planned or under way to minimize this risk.

Communication of Their Operational Vision

Through communication programs, their team members are beginning to understand two important principles of this process. First, this solution is a core requirement for DPD to successfully achieve their mission in the future. Second, it makes sense to leap-frog several levels of systems solutions to take advantage of the latest supply chain solutions and technologies. This means that their process transitions cannot be gradual. In reality, many of their processes will change dramatically. It is important for team members to realize that the radical nature of the change is not because they have been performing poorly; they have, in fact, been providing service to their customers at levels that far exceed industry standard. Instead, they are making the leap purely to take advantage of the best tools now available to meet their mission statement. As a result of this communication, most team members have embraced the need to implement the level of change required. Discussions throughout the organization following the scripted demos raised the level of excitement as people began to get a glimpse of the potential tools that will be brought to the operations. Most team members, however, still are not fully aware of the magnitude of the change—and the profound impact, it will have on their day-to-day activities.

Functional Training

Many of the new processes that will be incorporated in their solution involve methods never before used at Domino's. Some of these methods are fairly complex. Thus, it's important for their team members to understand the underlying principles prior to using the system tools. For example, their managers and team leaders needed to really understand the principles of activity-based management before they could utilize this information for decision making. If they do not build the fundamental skills, they run the risk of a chaotic implementation because the users have neither visibility over nor understanding of the decisions made by the system.

Involvement in the Design and Implementation Process

Ownership is key in their strongly entrepreneurial environment. At Domino's, as in most companies, solutions forced down upon the end-users are resisted—no matter how good they are. Although it is impossible to have all 1,100 of their DPD team members involved in the design process, they can and will be involved in the implementation. To ensure that they do not miss anything during the design process, they will incorporate a diverse group of team members from all of their processes to ensure appropriate design, buy-in, and grass-roots communication on how the new solutions will work.

Advanced Systems End-User Training

Their team members are used to computer-based training. And they plan to leverage this experience through integral PeopleSoft training tools as well as CD-ROM and intranet solutions. PeopleSoft's on-line work-flow support provides new users with excellent information on how their process works and interacts with other processes.

Technology Support

System must operate reliably and technical issues and concerns must be addressed quickly. They are transitioning to an environment, where IT tools will support nearly all of their activities. Although they have not yet determined exactly how their systems will be supported, they recognize that placing the burden of technical support on the end-user community will only cause frustration and encourage inappropriate quick fixes.

ACHIEVING THE VISION

To sum up, Domino's Pizza Distribution's strategy is to support the operations and growth of Domino's Pizza stores by providing excellent service and quality products at the best available price. They need to make significant technology investments and undergo substantial process changes in order for DPD to provide the best return to their stakeholders, the franchisees. DPD should continue to be responsible for the core value-added processes within their supply chain. New systems tools will allow them to significantly enhance their already excellent service capabilities. Advance planning and scheduling in their dough-manufacturing process will allow them to improve the consistency and quality of this critical pizza ingredient. Even though many of their core processes are relatively simple, their role as planner, just-in-time manufacturer, and distributor uniquely positions them to coordinate and synchronize the entire flow of product and cash. Domino's has selected PeopleSoft's ERP solution as the core of their future systems direction. They will incorporate advanced work-flow-supported client server/network computing technologies while leveraging their corporate intranet. They believe this highly flexible solution will provide them with a close functional match that minimizes the need for dramatic systems modification. During this whole effort, they cannot neglect their most important resource—their team members. Through communication, involvement, skills enhancement, training, and technical support, they can assure a successful implementation of this new technology and achieve the strategic supply chain vision.

Team Play

Team structure has been in place at Domino's since the inception of the company—long before the concept had become fashionable. Domino's Pizza Distribution's organization has both line operations teams (executive leadership, distribution center leadership, and departmental leadership) and support or special project teams. The re-engineering and information technology team structures are critical to the success of the process to perfect the supply chain. The design and implementation teams has been built to develop a cross-functional perspective, leveraging internal and external expertise. Every function of DPD is represented on the teams, both at a technical resource and end-user level. In addition, several members of the team represent corporate functions. During the development and implementation process, they also will include representation from their other supply chain participants—the suppliers and stores.

DOMINO'S MISSION: GLOBAL LEADERSHIP

Domino's Pizza has been dedicated to quality service, product, and delivery excellence for more than 35 years. Its mission: To be the leader in off-premise pizza convenience to consumers around the world. Domino's was founded in 1960 by Thomas S. Monaghan and owes its success to a few simple precepts: A limited menu offered through carryout and delivery. Domino's delivers quality products with a Total Satisfaction Guarantee: Any customer not completely satisfied with the Domino's Pizza experience will be offered a replacement pizza or a refund. Tom Monaghan's philosophy guides the entire corporation in how it accomplishes its corporate and divisional mission statements:

- Being fanatical about product quality and service consistency.
- Providing product variety to meet all customer needs.
- Placing team-member and customer safety and security above all other concerns.
- Creating an environment in which all team members feel valued, because they are.
- Building and maintaining trusting relationships that reward franchisees and other partners for their Contributions.

Domino's Pizza Inc.'s sales in 1996 reached $ 2.8 billion, marking the fourth consecutive year of increased sales. Domino's Pizza has over 1,200 franchisees, and operates more than 5,700 stores throughout the United States and in 57 international markets.

CHAPTER 6

PROMOTION STRATEGIES

CHAPTER FOCUS

- *To learn the process of creating commercials using effective message strategy, creative mix, copy writing, campaign and media plan for international marketing,*
- *To develop skills on advertising research, Internet advertising and direct response advertising, and*
- *To understand the sales promotion strategies and contemporary retailing approaches.*

Promotion strategies are concerned with the planning, implementation, and control of persuasive communication with customers. Promotion includes advertising, personal selling, sales promotion, and publicity of goods and services. Advertising refers to the corporate-sponsored messages transmitted through the mass media channels including electronic and print media and static communication sources like billboards, wall paintings etc. Personal selling involves strategies of establishing person-to-person business relations with the customers. The sales promotion encompasses different techniques (for example, samples, trading stamps, point-of-purchase motion, coupons, contests, gifts, allowances, and displays) that support and complement advertising and personal selling. Publicity includes seeking favorable comments on product or service and/or the firm itself through a write-up or presentation in mass for which the sponsor is not charged. These strategies may be designed around advertising, personal selling, sales promotion, or any combination of functions of these. Global advertising is largely uniform across many countries, however, uniformity may not be necessarily in media vehicles with similar global reach. In many cases complete uniformity is unobtainable because of linguistic and regulatory differences between nations or differences in media availability, but with regard to products and services, the localized advertising can still be considered as uniform in a given region. In contrast, multidomestic advertising is a type of international advertising adapted to particular markets and audiences.

One of the major strategic issues associated with the development of effective promotion strategy is the availability of financial resources for a specific product/market. The distribution of the notional budget among advertising, personal selling, and sales promotion is another strategic matter. The formulation of strategies dealing with these determines the role that each type of promotion plays in a particular situation. Promotion strategy consists of planning, implementing and controlling communications from an organization to its customers and other target audiences. The function of promotion in the marketing program is to achieve various communications objectives in the market segment. An important marketing responsibility is to plan and co-ordinate an integrated promotion strategy and to select the specific strategies for the promotion components. It is important to recognize that word-of-mouth communications among buyers and the communications of other organizations, may also influence the target audience of the company. The promotion-mix has the following components:

- Advertising
- Personal Selling
- Sales Promotion
- Direct Marketing, and
- Publicity

Advertising may be defined as the strategy of communicating, a sales message to potential customers. Advertising plays a crucial role in international business worldwide and it is the critical factor in achieving sales goals under tough competitive environment. It has been observed that in the globalization era, the national and multinational companies are increasingly considering successful advertising as a prerequisite to profitable global operations. Advertising is one segment of a well-organized, continuous marketing plan. Effective advertising is a cumulative process that maintains current customers, attracts new customers and establishes a favorable position for the business with competitors. Advertising will not cure slow business growth or low profits, nor will it create a better business person or a well-organized business. Advertising offers specified benefits to a specific or target audience. As part of a sound marketing plan, advertising becomes an investment in the future of the business, instead of one more expense. An effective advertisement is based on a careful analysis of the situation before money is spent. Advertising as a percentage of GNP rise in many countries as their in marketing practices move increasingly in directions pursued in the U.S. In China the advertising industry has been growing at a rate of 50 percent per annum.

Implementing an advertising and promotions plan best carries out Advertising and promotions. Many products or services have failed in the market, not because of their quality, packaging or pricing, but because the potential customers didn't know they were there, and if they did, they didn't know what those were or how to use them. In order to sell your product or service you must promote it. One effective method of promotion is advertising. The goals of the plan should very much depend on the overall goals and strategies of the organization, and the results of the marketing analysis, including the positioning statement. The plan usually includes what target markets you want to reach, what features and benefits you want to convey to them, how you will convey it to them (this is often called your advertising campaign), who is responsible to carry the various activities in the plan and how much money is budgeted for this effort. Successful advertising depends on knowing the preferred methods and styles of communications of the target markets that you want to reach with your ads. A media plan and calendar can be very useful, which specify what advertising methods are to be used and when.

> Over a period of time, the Cancer Society of India observed that enough awareness about the cancer has not been generated in the society and consequently the cancer check out patients departments (OPDs) in the hospitals had very low turnout. The Society realized the need for launching an effective campaign for the cancer check and decided to provide free check-up facilities. The leading advertising agency Ogilvy, Benson and Matter (OBM), Mumbai was the chosen for this campaign. The Cancer Society of India and OBM felt to assess the level of awareness of the people and their perception about the disease and its symptoms. The research study conducted on the sample of 600 existing and anticipated patients revealed that the awareness of the cancer disease was very high (96%) but people had no specific knowledge of the disease, people associated very low chances of survival with cancer and as a result of fear of death the tendency of confining the disease to oneself largely prevailed, patients also thought, it would be very expensive to get the treatment for the cancer. However, the attitude of the patients of lower income group towards the disease was fatalistic and the patients of middle income group were pessimistic. The hope was only for the patients who come from high-income group and could afford the treatment. The findings of the research the campaign by the OBM highlighted on the confidence building and awareness aspects. The campaign in the print media was largely educational describing the myth and reality of the disease. The perceived causes, symptoms, likelihood of getting the cancer, cure and medical support have been the major themes of the campaign. The body of the text of advertisement also brought out the top of the mind reactions of the patient and his family members and attempted to build the confidence by wiping out the fear of death from the minds of the patients. The focus of advertising was on bringing the attitudinal change, social acceptability. Building mental strength and motivating for free check-up at Indian Cancer Society Centers (ICS). The basic problem that emerged in the campaign was the co-ordination of information and professional support. The free check-ups were not the cure for the disease and it discouraged patients, as the economics of treatment seemed to be very high. The campaign in the print media did not make a marketable dent in the rural areas, as it would not have been backed with the strong word of mouth support.[1]

Fashion Advertisements (FAds) and strategies building for optimum sales realization are prominent among various sales promotion tools. As discussed earlier, the FAds have a greater impact on the elite clientele group as compared to other measures used for raising the sales. The product branding and packaging technology is the core input for FAds. Attractive packaging and popular branding have a significant role in the market expansion and product promotion. In a competitive market economy, the brands are hired by the manufactures for product marketing. In this system, new product managers have to face an uphill task. In marketing new products, it is essential to take potential as well as existing customers into confidence through an effective communication management. In the absence of building up such awareness, the new product manager gets fringe benefits while the brand owner gets a higher share in the consumers' rupee. As such, these companies

---

1 Cancer Society of India: Cancer Awareness Programs, *Evaluation documents,* CSI, Mumbai, 2000 Web site: http://www.indiancancersociety.org/activities/activities.htm

may not be in a position to establish their own brand due to many weaknesses pertaining to capital, technical know-how and market guidance. The future threat in this regard can be visualized in the light of selling their product. In the long run their identity will be only as a manufacturing unit, but not as a product seller. Packaging in the competitive product market is an important determinant as far as the buyer's behavior is concerned. The more attractive and durable the packaging of any product, the greater would be the product resistance and market demand. 'The New packs' may be the hard core of some FAds which could be more appealing to the target customers. It requires enough capital to invest in the packaging technology.

Advertising, direct marketing and public relations are the important tools for the promoting international marketing. The process of advertising in an international business begins with a market situation analysis conducted to assess marketing opportunities for the product in the existing market. On identifying market environment the marketing strategies are formulated and supported by communication linkages. Advertising strategies are developed in accordance with the marketing plan and advertisements are released according to the media plan. Hence, commercial advertisements seen by the consumer are like the tip of an iceberg emerging from a situation analysis, trade goals and strategies that have been evolved by the marketing and advertising managers. However, it is difficult to establish whether advertising is the first or the last component in the entire process of marketing. Despite numerous research efforts on the function of advertising, a unified theory has not yet emerged.

DEVELOPING ADVERTISING STRATEGY

Advertising is a key instrument in promoting the products and services in the international markets. However, the rationale of advertising and media communication strategy has regional variations and among industries. A advertising carries the corporate, products and services communication among the consumer segments without any limits, it is risk avers towards cultural conflicts and deceptive information for gain rapid market share. Hence, many firms have ethics codes for advertising. Advertising has significant contribution in international business as it involves a commitment of funds. Though the cost of effective and ineffective advertising varies, both incur high expenses. An effective advertising campaign represents a tangible resource and is transferable internationally from one market to another. Further advertising is regarded as the sole representative by many international companies in establishing and maintaining a desired position of products in the international market. Once a desired position for a product or service has been achieved through advertising, any local market interventions such as price or promotion related effects, make low impact. Thus, global advertising needs certain degree of centralization in terms of controlling the expenditure and carrying the sustainable impact of communication in the markets world over.

> Advertising expenditures in Singapore grew 29 percent during in 2000 to the top S $1.0 billion, with strong growth momentum generated by industry deregulation and keen competition. Newspaper remained the key advertising medium, registering expenditures of S$545.4 million and a 27 percent growth. Advertising in the Straits Times, the main paper of newspaper giant Singapore Press Holdings (SPH), accounted for more than 65 percent of the total newspaper expenditures. While newspapers take up almost 50 percent

of the advertising dollar, TV is close behind with a 34 percent share, accounting for S $ 377.8 million after a strong growth of 35 percent, with Channel 8 and Channel 5 attracting most of the advertising for TCS. ACNielsen AdEx monitors gross advertising expenditures in major media at published rate card values, giving an indication of the state of the industry. Consequent upon full deregulation in force since April, the telecommunications sector has entrenched itself as the top advertising product category, posting a staggering 132 percent growth year-on-year to S $115.9 million in the first nine months. Singtel, Starhub and M1 remained the 3 leading players, together accounting for a fringe share of S $ 93.9 million.

Banking and investment was the second fastest-growing category during the first three quarters, registering S $46.3 million, up 51 percent over the same period in 1999. Key players included Bank of Singapore, DBS and Standard Chartered Bank. Bank of Singapore spent most of the money on promoting its financial portal, finatiq.com, but it was DBS that made it into the top 10 advertisers with monitored expenditures of over S $12 million, mainly used to promote the DBS American Express Credit Card and 'Eight' investment fund. On the other hand, Standard Chartered Bank featured aggressively its 'Best of Breed' booklet, a special compilation that offered a thorough list of top-performing unit trusts in Singapore, prominently in TV commercials and newspapers. Among all brands, McDonald's remained the most advertised brand with S $12.4 million worth of advertising, up 34 percent. The bulk of advertisements went on TV, which accounted for over 70 percent of the total value.[2]

Multinational companies may derive important strategic decisions for international advertising to make their brand image stronger. The concept of an advertising campaign developed at home can be transferred to other countries by translating them into local languages or there is a need to customize the advertising as per the socio-cultural and market requirements in different countries. Many firms strongly believe that a successful advertising concept has no geographic boundaries and may do well anywhere. Critics of standardization in advertising argue however, that cultural differences require a campaign to be tailored to each country. However, customization of advertising for a particular country may be justified on the plea of cultural differences and public communication regulations among countries. A standardized advertising approach seems particularly unsuited in developing countries where exist differences in lifestyle, per capita income, market structure, and various aspects of the environment as compared with developed countries.

Nike is a champion brand builder. Its advertising slogans *Just Do It*, *There Is no Finish Line* have moved beyond advertising into popular expression. Nike's athletic footwear and clothing has become a commonly talked product of America and its brand name is as well known around the world as Honda and Federal Express. Consumers know Nike for attention-grabbing commercials that feature athletes like Bo Jackson and Michael Jordan. They anxiously await the debut of new Nike advertising, and are equally enthusiastic in their response. "Nike's advertising is laden with the solitary, self-involved spirit some associate with jogging". Bo knows advertising. Wieden &

2 Source : AC Nielson : AdEx Monitor, 2000 http://www.acnielsen.com.hk/news

> Kennedy's Nike ads, multi-talented baseball and football star Bo Jackson, stretched the boundaries of jock worship and neatly crossed the bridge from sports marketing into pop culture. The eight spots helped build a Bo Jackson myth, then deconstructed that legend and found humour in chastising those who got caught up in it, all the while peddling high-tech, cross-training shoes. The first Jackson ads were part of the 1988 debut of Nike's famous tagline, "Just do it." A trio of light hearted spots showed Jackson cycling, running and playing basketball. An advertisement shows a radiant woman running past two clogged lanes of suffocating traffic, the drivers gray and faceless. Under the title, "Man vs. Machine," the text notes that machines have "put our bodies out of a job". A series of posters shows a solitary runner in a majestic natural scene over the headline, "There Is No Finish Line." Nike expands in the text: "Sooner or later the serious runner goes through a special, very personal experience that is unknown to most people. Some call it euphoria. Others say it's a new kind of mystical experience..." and so on. TV advertising is a large part of Nike's marketing success. Originally, Nike became a billion dollar company without television. For years Nike relied on the athletes to wear their shoes, and ran a limited number of print ads in specialized magazines like Runner's World. They did not complete the advertising spectrum until 1987 when they used television for the first time.[3]

It is a complex issue for the multinational companies to opt for the advertising strategy between the standardization and localization. Among many factors that help the firms to decide on the type of advertising strategy to be adapted, the analysis choice criteria, advertising transferability and organizational support may be useful. The choice criteria comprises of the factors associated with environmental factors, advertising objectives of the company and target market where the advertisement needs to be delivered. A range of environmental variables affect advertising transferability across national boundaries. Of these some are listed as below:

Rate of economic growth of country

- Per capita income and distribution of income
- Average size of household
- Level of education
- Level of nationalistic feeling among the consumers
- Attitudes towards work and leisure
- Attitudes toward wealth and returns on investment
- Assessment of satisfaction towards spending
- Ethical and moral standards
- Availability of time on commercial broadcast media

3 for detailed discussion on Nike please see Robert J Dolan : Nike Inc, in 1990's : The New Directions, *Harvard Business School Case,* Harvard Business School, April 1995; also see official web site of Nike Inc. www.nike.com

Strategy Focus 6.1:
Earnings by Selling Media Rights for Sports Events

The global economic downturn intensified the competition with other forms of entertainment. Not surprisingly, sports that have been traditionally popular in the United States or Europe which are the most lucrative television-advertising markets enjoy an inherent advantage and are grabbing the biggest slices of a competitive pie. Soccer and US football together take more than a third of the revenues in the global TV sports market (exhibit). But commercial success isn't just about popularity. The sports industry's core sources of revenue can be divided into three main categories: broadcast rights, sponsorships (including licensing and merchandising), and ticketing and hospitality (such as entertainment and catering in sports venues). Each category accounts for roughly one-third of the industry's revenues, and each has enjoyed strong growth. Total revenues from television rights are particularly important because of the exposure television generates for a sport and its sponsors rose by 14 percent a year from 1997 to 2001. The advertising revenues of the US networks couldn't match the amount they had paid to acquire broadcast rights at the business cycle's peak, so they lost an estimated $ 4 billion from sports programming that year. When sports rights holders renegotiate their television contracts, prices are unlikely to go on rising sharply. Golf and tennis are major sports but not huge to be regarded as global sports. Their audiences consist largely of affluent people who often play tennis or golf themselves. Such characteristics make the audience not only attractive targets for advertisers but also potential purchasers of goods licensed by the governing bodies of the two sports or by event organizers. Yet golf has been more successful than tennis has in exploiting this high-income niche.

The decline of consumer interest is another sobering, and more structural, development. In Europe, the number of sports-TV viewers fell by 15 percent from 1996 to 2001 as other forms of entertainment programming, such as reality TV, came into fashion. In the United States, even the traditionally popular Monday Night Football game of the National Football League (NFL) has lost 17 percent of its TV viewers since 1999. And fewer amateur athletes are playing certain major sports—the number of participants in US baseball games dropped by 10 percent from 1991 to 2001, for example. This decline potentially reduces the level of interest in watching these sports on TV and in spending money on them over the longer term. Consequently, in some areas the sports business is becoming a buyer's market in which broadcasters and sponsors not only resist any increase in price but also insist that games be tailored to their needs

Source : Tekla V. Back, Philippe Blatter, and Jacques R. Bughin: Playing to Win in the Business of Sports, The McKinsey Quarterly, Internet Edition, July 2004

- Adequacy of coverage of market by broadcast media
- Availability of satisfactory electronic, print and outdoor media
- Extent of Independence of media
- Government control on public and commercial communications
- Import/export perspectives
- Legal restraints on advertising within the country
- Import duties and quotas in the country

It has been observed that advertising objectives vary in each country. Though, advertising of products and services do not lead directly to sales, it can be for transferring the customer from one phase to the next. Advertising only attempts to bridge the gap between unawareness of a product or service-to awareness among the consumers, which further leads to comprehension, conviction and finally action towards buying the products. The advertising objectives for the products in the developing countries are largely oriented towards perceived benefits, value for money and better quality. For example, a DVD player manufacturer's advertising objectives for India would have to be different from those for the UK and USA, as in these countries the DVD player market has attained its maturity in the product life cycle, while in India it is in its growth stage. Hence, the major focus of advertising in India may be to comprehend the customer about the values associated with the product whereas in the developed countries like UK and USA the advertisements may focus on moving the consumers from conviction to action. Thus, the advertising concepts for marketing DVD playerss would not be effective in India. The advertising strategy also depends on the *target market* in the host country. If the proposed advertising campaign for another country is aimed towards a segment that is more or less similar in nature to the segment served in the home country, standardized advertising would appear satisfactory. Further, the attributes of a product involve also determines whether such advertising is appropriate. The product attributes include buying and usage patterns, psychological attributes and cultural factors. The *media availability* and the *cost benefit relationship* are other factors that determine the nature of advertising to be implemented in the host country. If the cost of adoption of advertising to the local conditions exceeds the benefits that an adaptation might provide, it would be wise for a firm to choose standardization of advertising contents.

Transferability of a commercial advertisement has various barriers comprising the cultural, communication styles, legislative, competitive and implementation factors. The cultural barriers also carry the social and cultural limitations laid by the religion. The local phonetics for the standardized advertisement that may provide an awful sense sometime hinder the free transferability of commercials. The competition for a product varies from one country to another country and some time requires changing the viewpoint for its proper positioning. The legislative barriers may be those imposed under the public laws in a country like child and gender abuse. However, some companies develop the global prototypes which are developed considering all possible barriers in other country and can be easily transferred. Such global prototypes comprise the facilities of voice-over and the provisions of visual change to avoid language and cultural problems. These advertisements may also be re-shot with local spokespeople but using the same visualization. Drakkar Noir, a man's fragrance, in an Arab print advertisement shows a woman's hand caressing a man's hand holding the product; in the United States the same hand grasps the man's wrist. Colgate-Palmolive, Proctor & Gamble, Nestlé and Coca-Cola often use prototypes of actual commercial and advertisement samples that demonstrate, what headquarters want in the advertisements with specific written guidelines for acceptable deviations from the prototypes in terms of story and message (usually limited flexibility) and creative aspects (layout, color, symbols-usually more flexibility), with suggestions for appropriate media.

ADVERTISING ENVIRONMENT

As with the marketing environment, advertising also works in an environment that may be understood by studying the conditions under which it function. The environmental factors affecting the advertising are given below:

- Social and cultural factors
- market competition related factors
- legal factor
- economic factors related to business and consumer

These factors nurture advertising as well as other related environments like marketing. The environment helps planners asses the extent of the investment needed and to accordingly decide the advertising strategies. Environmental conditions provide a base for formulating the advertising policy and to provide magnitude and direction. The contemporary advertising system is an example of a "free enterprise" environment.

S ocio-cultural environment comprises of shared beliefs, social values, customs, life styles, ethics and community behavior. These components play a major role in shaping the behavior of consumer. Thus advertising should keep to the social cultural standards and if failing to do so, the consumer should resolve not to buy the advertised product. A competitive environment provides more options to influence the consumer. Hence, to plan strategies for effective advertising, there is a need to look into the product policies, distribution approaches, pricing mechanism and promotional strategies with reference to competitive products and their sustainability in the market. The legal environment consists of enforced regulation under which advertising has to be developed and exposed. Business fluctuations, the broad economic framework for establishing business at the embryonic stage, prospects and political stability form the economic environment for developing advertising plans. Thus, it is difficult for any advertiser to ignore these factors while planning advertising within the given economy of the country or region.

There are many other factors which have stake in the advertising environment and play a significant role in determining policies for effective advertising as a communication and marketing tool. These factors are:

- Technology development
- Growth in per capita income
- Increase in disposable income
- Higher purchasing power of consumer
- Growth of popular consumer clusters
- Development of infrastructure
- Increase in education standards of consumer
- Specialization in advertising techniques
- Use of research and development results

- Growth of brands and variety of trade
- Growth of service sector
- Growth in marketing finance

Scope of the advertising is very wide and leads to an integrated impact on the planning process.

THE ADVERTISING PROCESS

As stated earlier, advertising is closely associated with marketing variables. Hence, the process of advertising depends largely on the market environment. The marketing plan enables the advertiser to set objectives, the advertising budget and the time plan for scheduling the advertisement. In an advertising process the important determinants are communication strategy and media strategy. The strategy for communication includes the type of message to be released, its length, contents, audience interest, product characteristics and frequency of message dissemination. The message tactics also need to be developed in accordance with the media and media watchers. An appropriate media strategy needs to be selected by a firm analyzing media responses carefully. Upon selection of an appropriate media, the firms should work out an operational plan of putting the advertisements to cater the market objectives. The process of advertising is illustrated in figure 6.1.

Whole advertising process, results in the exposure of the advertising product as an output which

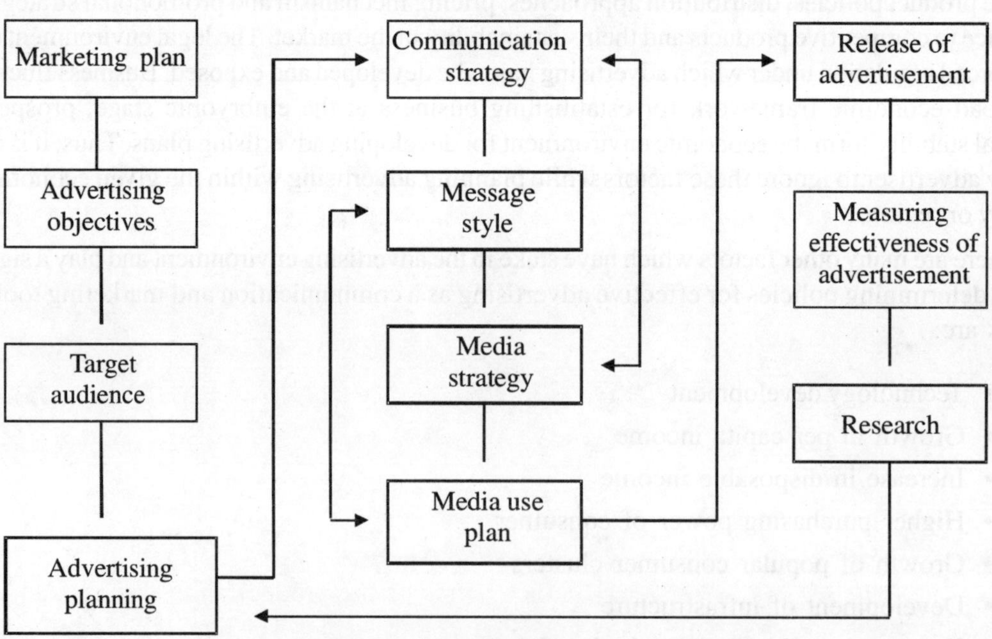

Figure 6.1 Advertising process model

needs to be evaluated for its effectiveness in a given marketing situation. The media consultants, media representatives, and advertising agencies form the organizational structure and within its frame the process of advertising is made functional. The response analysis of advertisement shows mixed impacts. Sometimes, the advertisements receive a very positive response from consumer augmenting the market, for the product while at the same time negative responses also distort the product market. Such cases need to be further subject to research on the improved communication styles and the media vehicle in order to recharge the advertising planning process with new inputs.

ADVERTISING CATEGORIES

Advertising is a creative task and varies according to the need and taste of the target group. It can be categorized into audiences, types of advertiser, mass media and functions. There are three sets of audience in advertising-business, professionals and consumers. The *business-to-business advertising* is directed towards processors, wholesalers and professionals. An advertisement carrying a message for raw materials, business machines or services to the manufacturing units are categorically of a business-to-business nature and can be termed as *industrial advertising*. Similarly when an advertisement is directed towards a group of professional like engineers, doctors, it is called *professional advertising*. The advertising audience may also be categorised as a mass or a class. An example of advertising for biscuits may be planned for the mass audience while a rich processed and canned food may be directed towards high class audience.

Volume of the business of a company and the geographical coverage of the product would be another consideration for classifying advertising strategies. The countrywide coverage of a product such as automobiles, television sets, refrigerators and the like is called as *general advertising*. Advertising for a product limited to regional markets for local consumption is defined as *local advertising*. Advertising can be also classified with reference to the medium used to deliver the message like national TV network, cable TV network, radio, news paper and magazines of national and regional status.

Functional classifications of advertising are of an illustrative and symbolic nature. The advertising classification according to functions is given under:

- Product advertising
- Non-product or institutional advertising
- Primary advertising
- Selective advertising
- Direct action advertising
- Indirect action advertising

Product advertising emphasizes the characteristics of the product and other related issues while the institutional image is build up by *non-product advertising*. The brand of the company, its public relation aspects and regulations is based on the theme of the advertising in this category. For example, we have the Tata steel company which prefers institutional advertising highlighting the biographical excerpts of the founder veteran or emphasizing the development nurtured by the company in rural housing, education, health and sports. Such advertising mentions the product of company as a secondary message.

Primary advertising attempts to promote a market for indigenous products which are largely unbranded while selective advertising is done for the products that are branded or that fall in line with related brands. Selective advertisement is used by individual companies to stimulate a market for their products after the demand has been established. Direct action advertising generates instant demand for the product and is found to be an effective stimulus for short-run sale campaigns. The art of abstract communication is called indirect advertising, which does not seek immediate attention of the mass audience. However, this type of advertising is appreciated by the class audience to some extent.

ADVERTISING AND BUYER PERCEPTION

Advertising of a product or services has direct concern with the buyers. The communication that reaches buyers has varied response depending on the time span of advertising, the type of message and the intensity of the exposure. Thus, its essential for an advertiser to map consumer perceptions on an advertised product or service to increase its effectiveness. A study of the consumer's state of mind and market segmentation would supplement the creativeness in developing the messages exposure style, media use and related matters. The perceptual mapping of consumer needs to be done considering many human factors for effective advertising. These factors are:

- Structural factors
- Mind set
- Expectations
- Previous experience
- Latent needs
- Role
- Social status
- State of mind
- Perceptual consistency
- Selectivity
- Retrieval and action
- Cultural and group factors

An advertising strategy needs to be developed in close association with the social status and cultural factors of the consumers. Perceptions are built depending upon the role of an individual in conceiving and understanding communication. His state of mind, latent expectations, his consistency in perceiving the message and other related factors substantially contribute to advertising strategies.

STRATEGIES IN ADVERTISING

Advertising strategies for a product for an agency and in the media are different in the long term as compared to short term perspectives as the objectives of organizations also vary. However, theoretically, an effective advertising strategy needs to comprise of the creative use of media, budget, message strategy, exposure strategy research and public relations. The right message to the right audience at right time is the fundamental principle of advertising and strategies need to be formulated accordingly.

ADVERTISING STYLES

Different styles of advertising are an art form and can not be limited to theoretical boundaries. The advertising manager is always at liberty to design the message in an appropriate manner for achieving the best results. However, some common techniques are observed in the product advertising. They are:

- Comprehensive advertisement
- Positive advertisement
- Negative advertisement
- Social theme based techniques
- Future project base techniques
- Entertaining and family oriented
- Gender sensitive
- Product-customer age cohesive
- High frequency insertion - drive
- Average frequency insertion cue
- Scientific message
- Abstract message
- Indicative and symbolic for segment customer
- Influence leader oriented
- Comparative product profit oriented

These techniques change according to the behavioral changes in the customers towards products. All techniques may not be appealing but are equally expensive. Hence, an advertising manager should be very selective in adopting the appropriate technique, as the advertisement / communication expenditure also reflects in the total cost of a product. The message strategy should match with any of the four advertising objectives - psychological pull, action, marketing and institutional oriented. The application of any of these objectives would help in generating messages ideas. These ideas however, need to be tested with different components of the 'creative – mix'. This mix consists of verbal and non-verbal elements. Table 6.1 exhibits the components of 'creative-mix' in advertising.

Table 6.1 Creative-mix in Advertising

Verbal elements	*Non-Verbal elements*
• Copy writing	• Visuals and Illustration
• Headlines	• Layout
• Slogans	• Typography
• Brand names	• Trade mark
• Performance statements	• Colour combination
• Institution reports	• Dynamics
	• Music
	• Special effects

Decision making in the "creative-mix" is based on the advertising objective and the audience. In developing an advertisement, thinking feeling has a high importance among other behavioral variables. An advertising objective for long lasting effectiveness should posses the following characteristics:

- Continuity : For a hierarchical order of advertising
- Precision : To educate the consumer in a short time span
- Measurability : Enabling the performance of the monitoring exercise and feed back analysis effectively
- Realism : Presenting the facts and market experience of the product or a firm
- Flexibility : Convenient for all ethnic groups, age, class and literate groups to understand and retrieve
- Impression : Should possess symbiosis of product and company with consumer

Advertising objects should have three determinants of product. They are dissemination of message; decision making and the evaluation of the advertisement or advertising strategy.

DEVELOPING A MEDIA PLAN

Media Planning

Media planning is an essential exercise to be performed in advertising management. In developing a media plan, five basic dimensions need to be assessed. They are - (i) media objectives (ii) target market (iii) media types (iv) media vehicle and (v) media scheduling . Besides these factors, continuity is also an important indicator which relates to time scheduling of messages on media. At the introductory stage, it is necessary to allocate an advertising budget for higher media time that can be gradually reduced as per the stand of merchandise as the market advances. However, the life cycle of the merchandise also needs to be considered while setting objectives.

Setting Target Markets

It is necessary to take the help of a media specialist in identifying target markets for the merchandise to be identified and the type of advertisement required thereof. Market segmentation principles have to be considered deciding upon a target market for the physical distribution of merchandise and accordingly, the type of media has to be selected.

Media Selection and Budgeting

Data on effective media response has to be analyzed for the selection of a particular media. The cost of advertising on media is worked out on the basis of frequency and continuity that need to be set for allocating an advertising budget. While selecting media for advertising the following factor combinations have to be ensured by the advertising agency:

- Perfect match of media type to target market
- Perfect match of media type of advertising objectives
- Match of media type to advertising budget, and
- Match of selected media to competing advertisement

It is necessary to make substantial budgetary provisions in the media plan, if the advertising has to be done in more than one media type. However, the relative weights of the media have to be decided upon on the basis of analyzing the "efficiency indicators" for the media in particular.

MEDIA SCHEDULING

An advertising planner has to decide the scheduling of advertisements in the media with reference to its periodicity in a day, hour, month and year. When an advertisement, should be aired on the media and during which hour on the day should be planned audience considering behavior while watching the media and the nature of the product. For example, breakfast foods are scheduled to be advertised during the breakfast hours to have an effective impact. Scheduling advertising with respect to media time, periodicity in a month and the number of months in a year would be helpful in allocating resources in advertising budgeting and for media buying. The advertising planner needs to develop a media time, flowchart once the scheduling exercise is completed. Although the media schedule plan is not a permanent document as some elements like type of merchandise, style of copy, media policy are subject to change without notice, the flowchart would be the right guiding bird's-eye-view for the planner.

DIRECT RESPONSE ADVERTISING

Media advertising largely attempts to generate an indirect response towards the merchandise or services advertised. Direct response advertising includes mail-media advertising, catalogues, departmental store's advertising yellow pages, handouts, and window displays. Media marketing is an effective buyer-seller interactive system in which the merchandise advertised is brought close to the buyer using one or more advertising styles, and the response is measured with reference to the location and volume of transaction. Mail-media advertising involves promoting the merchandise market by establishing contact with potential and existing consumer through mail orders, publicity materials and telephone service. In this process no personal selling is performed. Direct mail advertising has many advantages. It attempts to build goodwill between sellers and buyers. Hence, mail advertising is often identified as productive advertising technique.

Numerous advantages of this system are listed below:

- It is highly selective
- This form of advertising is elastic as retailer can add or delete the name of consumer at his discretion
- A wide variety of merchandise or services can be advertised to the same consumer
- Privacy on consumer preference/order can be maintained
- Market competition can be avoided instantly
- Direct mail advertising is personal specific
- Home delivery of goods and service can be assured
- Performance of merchandise/service sales can be monitored and evaluated

Despite the many advantages of the direct mail advertising, there exist some demerits also. The most commonly observed problem in mailing business orders is the high expenditure involved in the process. The periodical updating of the mailing list is a major task in direct-mail advertising and consumes large business time. Besides these advantages, it sometimes becomes disinteresting and irritable to the persons addressed and they feel offended as the 'copy' the mail-order may not match with the profile of person to whom it is sent. The different types of mail-order advertising comprise of a comprehensive text and a visual copy which attempts to make the interesting reading. The various types of mail-order advertising are:

- Business reply mail with pre-paid postage fee
- Information enclosures, circulars etc
- Postal cards without an order form
- Self-mailing folders and
- Booklets and catalogues

Mail-order advertising is a quantitative exercise and requires the systematic processing of data. Hence, computerization is the basic requirement to handle the data with reference to classifying consumers, sorting types of orders, making a record of compliance to order and other functions.

DISPLAY ADVERTISING

Window display is the most prominent style of direct response advertising as it establishes ready information, product impression, and impulse of buying that helps in decision making. Display advertising can be indoor and outdoor. Indoor display advertising consists of showcase advertising and indoor displays in departmental stores. There are some common kinds of *indoor display* of merchandise. They are :

- Display of merchandise in showcase of departmental stores
- Display of merchandise in a decorative style in the showcase/window

- Display of prestige copy under a simulated environment
- Display of merchandise on a dummy
- Theme display and
- Demonstration of the use of the merchandise

Outdoor display of merchandise or services may be done in the form of sign boards, commercial hoardings, posters, neon signs, vehicle sign boards, train posters, electronic sign boards, balloons, fibre optical billboard and other special effects. Merchandise advertising on vehicles is called transit advertising which carries the message from place to place. It is a good way to reach specific markets and can be tailored according to the geographical market segmentation.

Advocacy advertising on the other hand, attempts to highlight contemporary arguments directed at specific general clients like political activists, consumer groups, and media and government agencies. Advocacy advertising consist of:

- Ideological advertising which is principle oriented and attempts to highlight the ethics of an institution
- Defense advertising which argues to protect the image of institution against contemporary controversies.
- Reply bound advertising seeking quick and ready response to issues highlighted in the advertisement
- Position taking advertising emphasizing the point of view of an institute of and thus an emerging issue with a strong arguments to seek public acceptance or a referendum
- Ally recruitment advertising asking interested persons to present their views in support of the ethics of an institution in order to strengthen its position before their joining a position in the institute

Advocacy advertising has the advantage of exhibiting the message in a controlled situation, which then helps in dealing with complex issues. An institution can plan a series of advertisements for a campaign, supporting its views and an image building simultaneously among the clientele group. Institutional advertisements are generally released on multi-media and cover a substantially larger segment of the target audience. Table 6.2 has categorically listed out all the details that need to be checked by both advertiser and the client company before launching into product promotion in international markets.

BRAND POSITIONING AND ADVERTISING EVALUATION

Positioning of a brand or product is an art. This involves selecting the best selling propositions that help in realizing sales targets to a large extent. The position of a brand and its perception among the target consumers is based on functional advantages and the emotional association of the buyer with the product of a specific brand. Hence, a brand manager should look into these behavioral aspects while considering brand positioning in the market. Brand positioning is using the consumer preferences backed by a strong psychographic logic regarding branded products of similar nature. It is essential

Table 6.2 The Advertising Checklist

Checklist for International Market Promotion	
• Advertising restriction	• Check legal environment
• Collaboration	• Check the support given by distributors / manufactures
• Direct mail	• Check response level
• Distribution	• Check guarantee of the product well before distribution and then advertising the product
• Franchising	• Select a right brand for business contract for franchising
• Global brands	• Assess their response
• Language and literacy	• A common language is beneficial to generate brand image across the countries. Right translation of the message needs to be ensured .
	• Use universal names
	• Attractive and cost effective
• Names	• Local language is always preferable with
• Packaging	• emphasis on vital life style variables
• Public relation	• Guard against such marketing evils
• Rumor / defamation	• Choose the right time and the right vehicle in the right media at the right place
• Media planning	• Right interpretion of cultural signs in advertisements
	• Simple and effective
	• Broad customer networking for direct trading
• Semiotics in advertising	
• Message style	
• Telemarketing	

to measure the intensity of the brand impact of close substitute brands in the market. Broadly, brand positioning constitutes the framework of market structure. There are four major components having an integrated impact on brand positioning. They are:

- structure of the market where the brand has to be positioned
- characteristics of consumer segmentation
- consumer perception on competing brands and the one that is to be introduced and
- benefits offered by the brand that suits the perception of consumer

These components, closely associated with one an other , need to be studied in an integrated manner while considering brand positioning. Market segmentation and positioning strategies are to be planned simultaneously as both factors are involved in either process. However , it can be stated that the success of brand positioning is based on the differential advantage offers of competing brands in the market. Brand positioning theory specifies that distances among competing brands and product differentiation are the dynamic factors that develop clarity in consumer perception and help the positioning of product brands successfully in the market.

POSITIONING METHODS

Brand positioning is an important activity in advertising management as it provides a platform on which to develop advertising and media strategies. There are some logical approaches used in positioning brands in the market. They are :

- Using corporate identity
- By brand endorsement
- Category-related positioning
- Advantage-related positioning
- Time related positioning and
- Price quality positioning

Corporate identity oriented positioning would be identical to that of the company over a considerable period which has been recognized by the consumer. The brands are endorsed by the identity of the company for each of new product-entry following a success of the previous product. Example may cited of toilet soaps of the same company - Hindustan Lever, with product names such as Lux, Lesancy etc. These products are endorsed as - "A quality product from Hindustan lever". Such endorsements of brands would help in positioning the products effectively in the market.

Category-related brand positioning refers to the physical product in different incarnations. One product in different physical designs is promoted through advertising in the market all at the same time. A brand manager is required to modify the functional features of existing brands to make it close to the category related positioning exercise. *Advantage-related positioning* usually decides where products can provide multiple benefits to the consumers. Hence, a brand manager has scope for differentiation of similar products based on the benefits extended. The *time-related brand positioning* exercise is based on the promotion of merchandise with reference to time and age. This is another factor that decides another differentiating strategy to establish brand identity. For instance, a mosquito repellent is used at night while room freshener is sprayed in the morning hours. These characteristics can be used for devising an advertising strategy to help positioning the brand of merchandise. The *price -quality positioning* approach is simple and effective for oligopolistic market conditions. The satisfaction of consumers is the principal indicator in positioning a brand of merchandise based on the relative satisfaction ratio of the price and quality of the brands.

There are some other approaches of brand positioning based on factors like product line, technology and research. The major scientific brand positioning methods are stated below:

- Product line brand positioning
- Performance oriented brand positioning
- End-use based brand positioning
- Technology based brand positioning
- Research based brand positioning

Brands of merchandise can also be positioned in the competitive market considering the various aspects of market segmentation. Of these the more prominent indicators are:

- Demographic factors comprising age, income, sex, occupation, education, location variables and the like
- Behavioral factors with reference to the variable of consumer satisfaction, taste, touch, appearance, etc., related to the product
- Additional benefits in terms of multiple usage, health improvement, energy and the like
- Psychographic factors determining personality, social status and life style

Brand positioning can also be determined taking into consideration the unique features of the merchandise. Packaging may be one of the attributes e.g. Brooke Bond's ' stand pack ' of green label coffee has a distinctive packaging among other existing brands in the market. Another approach of brand positioning is selling a challenge for the close competitor linking marketing strategy to warfare. Such an approach is called as *brand positioning by the competitor.*

CONCEPT OF PROMOTION MIX

Personal selling consists of verbal communication between a salesperson or selling team and one or more prospective purchasers with the objective of making or influencing a sale. Many companies feel that the personal selling is better strategy to manage the interface of buyer and seller and therefore annual expenditures on personal selling are larger than advertising. However, advertising and personal selling strategies share some common features, including creating awareness of the product, transmitting information, and persuading people to buy. The personal selling is an expensive way of persuading the buyers as compared to various ways of advertising. Salespeople can interact with buyers to answer questions and overcome objections, they can target buyers, and they have the capacity to accumulate market knowledge and provide feedback. *Sales promotion* consists of various promotional activities, including trade shows, contests, samples, point-of-purchase displays, trade incentives, and coupons. Sales promotion expenditures are substantially greater than the amount spent on advertising. *Direct marketing* includes the various communication channels that enable companies to make direct contact with individual buyers. The common direct marketing techniques are catalogues, direct mail, telemarketing, television commercials, radio, magazine, newspaper, electronic shopping and kiosk shopping etc. The distinguishing feature of direct marketing is the opportunity for the marketer to gain direct access to the buyer. Direct marketing expenditures account for a large portion of promotion expenditures. Electronic shopping is one of the newer forms of direct marketing. *Publicity or public relations* for a company's product, service, or idea involves communications placed commercially in the media. The objective of public relations is to encourage the media to include company-released information in media communication.

Table 6.3 Criteria for Determining Promotion Mix

Product factors	*Market factors*	*Customer factors*	*Budget Factors*	*Marketing mix factors*
• Nature of product • Perceived risk • Durable versus non-durable • Typical purchase amount	• Position in its life cycle • Market share • Industry concentration • Intensity of competition • Demand perspectives	• Household versus business customers • Number of customers • Concentration of customers	• Financial resources of the organization • Traditional promotional perspectives	• Relative price/relative quality • Distribution strategy • Brand life cycle • Geographic scope of the market

A variety of factors should be considered to determine the correct promotion mix in a particular product/market situation. These factors may be classified as product factors, market factors, customer factors, budget factors, marketing mix factors etc. as outlined in the Table 6.3. Development of an optimum promotion mix is by no means easy. Many companies often undermine the roles of advertising, personal selling, and sales promotion in a given product or market situation. Decisions about the promotional mix are often diffused among the decision makers, impeding the formation of a unified promotion strategy.

Recent research conducted by the Strategic Planning Institute for Cahners Publishing Co. identified the following decision rules that can be used in formulating ad budgets. These rules may be helpful in finalizing promotion mix decisions.[4]

- Market share - A company that has a higher market share must generally spend more on advertising to maintain its share.
- Sales from new products-If a company has a high percentage of its sales resulting from new products, it must spend more on advertising compared to companies that have well-established products.
- Market growth-Companies competing in fast-growing markets should spend comparatively more on advertising.
- Plant capacity-If a company has a lot of unused plant capacity, it should spend more on advertising to stimulate sales and production.
- Unit price (per sales transaction)-The lower the unit price of a company's products, the more it should spend on advertising because of the greater likelihood of brand switching.
- Importance of product to customers (in relation to their total purchases)- Products that constitute a lower proportion of customers' purchases generally require higher advertising expenditures.

4 *Refer Workbook for Estimating your Advertising Budget* : Cahners Publishing Co., Boston, 1984

- Product price-Both very high-priced (or premium) products and very low priced (or discount) products require higher ad expenditures because in both the cases, price is an important factor in the buying decision and the buyer must be convinced (through advertising) that the product is a good value.
- Product quality- Higher-quality products require a greater advertising effort because of the need to convince the consumer that the product is unique.
- Breadth of product line-Companies with a broad line of products must spend more on advertising compared to companies with specialized product lines.
- Degree of standardization-Standardized products produced in large quantities should be backed by higher advertising outlays because they are likely to have more competition in the market.

Expansion of product market largely depends on the way the product sales are organized. There are many techniques adopted in organizing effective sales. They are- departmental stores, supermarkets, mobile sale units, emporia, exhibitions and fun sales. Among these systems, the departmental stores and supermarkets have received considerable attention in towns, urban and semi-urban areas, while the mobile shops and fun sales have induced the buyers in the rural areas. The fun sales are organized in less developed areas through the entertainment program. Such a system is being observed in different Asian countries. In future more flexible methods of sales may appear to cover a larger consumer segments under product market.

ADVERTISING OBJECTIVES

It is necessary to pinpoint the objectives to build a good advertising program of the ad campaign. It would be wrong to assume that all advertising leads directly to sales. Sales is a multiphase phenomenon, and advertising can be used to transfer the customer from one phase to the next: from unawareness of a product or service, to awareness, to comprehension, to conviction, to action. The objectives of advertising may be defined by any one of the following approaches: inventory approach, hierarchy approach, or attitudinal approach.

A number of scholars have articulated functions performed by advertising. The objectives of an ad campaign may be defined from an inventory based on a firm's overall marketing perspective. The *inventory approach* to set-up objectives of the advertising may be set considering many aspects as presented in Table 6.4.

Inventory approach is helpful in emphasizing different objectives in advertising. These advertising objectives may be selected with reference to the overall marketing plan. This approach helps the advertiser choose a better functional platform for projecting the advertisement.

In *hierarchy approach,* the objectives of advertising should be stated in an action oriented psychological form. Accordingly, the objectives of advertising may be defined as (i) gaining customers' initial attention, perception, continued favorable attention, and interest; or (ii) affecting customers' comprehension, feeling, emotion, motivation, belief, intentions, decision, imagery, association, recall, and recognition. The concept of this approach is that customers move from one psychological state to another before actually buying a product. The purpose of advertising should be to change the

Table 6.4: Setting Advertising Objectives – Inventory Approach

Areas of Influence	*Attributes*
Increase sales	• Encouraging potential purchasers to visit the company or its dealers • Obtaining leads • Inducing professional people (e.g., doctors, architects) to recommend the product • Securing new distributors • Prompting immediate purchases through announcements of special sales and contests
Creating awareness	• Informing potential customers about product features • Announcing new models • Highlighting the unique features of the product • Informing customers about product availability • Announcing price changes • Demonstrating the product in use

customers from the state of indifference or negative to the positive approach and ultimately towards purchasing the product. The *attitudinal approach* of advertising is instrumental in producing changes in attitudes; therefore, advertising goals should be defined to influence attitudinal structures. This strategy is helpful in developing a positive consumer attitude towards the company, brand, product class and attributes, competitive advantages and post sales services. The attitudinal approach is an improvement over the hierarchical approach because it attempts to relate advertising objectives to product/market objectives.

A person completely familiar with all product/market perspectives should define advertising objectives. A good definition of objectives aids in the writing of appropriate ad copy and in selecting the right media. It should be recognized that different ad campaigns for the same product can have varied objectives.

ADVERTISING STYLES

It is an art and can not be limited to the theoretical boundaries. The advertising manager always stays at liberty to design the message in the most appropriate manner to insert in a popular media for achieving best results. However, some common techniques are observed in the product advertising. They are:

- Comprehensive advertisement
- Positive advertisement
- Negative advertisement
- Social theme based techniques
- Future project base techniques
- Entertaining and family oriented

- Gender sensitive
- Product-customer age cohesive
- High frequency insertion - Drive
- Average frequency insertion- Cue
- Reorienting Consumers- Flanker
- Scientific message
- Abstract message
- Indicative and symbolic for segment customers
- Influence leader oriented
- Comparative product profit oriented

These techniques change according to the behavioural changes in the customers towards the products. All techniques may not be appealing but are equally expensive. Hence, an advertising manager should be very selective in adopting an appropriate technique, as the advertisement/ communication expenditure also reflects in total cost of the product and also affects the pricing structure.

MESSAGE STRATEGY

Development of message strategy is linked to an advertiser and media factor. It depends on what an advertiser needs and how the message for advertising can be carried on the media effectively. A compromise to these factors would help in developing the most effective message idea, as a result of facts judged about products, markets consumers and competitors. In this process the strength of background information is the foundation of building message ideas. The copy writers, artists and creative advertising personnel of advertising agency should know the pulse of generating effective message ideas. There are two basic sources of idea stimuli - (i) intuition drawn on the basis of acquaintance with the product or service and (ii) scientifically collected data on the product and its marketing plans. The data can be collected in two ways as stated below:

- By administering primary investigation tools
- By obtaining secondary information supplied by authentic sources.

Message strategy should match with any of the four advertising objectives comprising psychological pull, action, marketing and institution oriented. The application of any of these objectives would help in generation of message ideas. However, it needs to be tested on different components of 'creative-mix'. This mix consists of verbal and non-verbal elements.

> They say love never grows stale. At least Oswal Woollen Mills believes it is true. The 60-seconds advertisement for its Monte Carlo brand of winter wear, featuring Lisa Ray and Dino Morea (models of India), aims to add a fresh, contemporary dimension to this core value. The film opens in a western-style departmental store all decked up for Christmas. As Ray's character travels up the escalator, Morea's travels down, and of course they don't notice each other. Finally, both girl and boy land up at the same store, leaving identical Monte Carlo bags at the entrance.

Box 6.1: Monte Carlo—advertising concept and strategy

Girl has a tiff on the cell phone with someone and stomps off in high dudgeon... with the wrong bag. Boy is left with his mouth hanging open, having failed to stop her. Back home, girl excitedly pulls a red pullover out of the bag and slips into it. Only to discover it's about five sizes too big. Bemused at first, she figures out the mix-up and starts fooling around, enjoying the sensation of being lost in the enveloping warmth. The doorbell interrupts her fun. The girl answers door to discover the boy outside, holding up her bag. A little talk and the glimmerings of a romance before he departs, leaving the pullover with her along with the memory of 'the way you make me feel'. This Television campaign has significant non-verbal signals that convey the product and consumer relationship. The rich red wool, sparkling eyes and flickering firelight create an island of warmth and human bonding in the midst of a frosty winter.

Company is trying to achieve and maintain its leadership position by giving the brand a chic edge in the face of a plethora of competing brands. The predictable success is anything to go by, the storyline should appeal to the young Indian.

CREATIVE-MIX

Decision making in creative-mix is to be based on the advertising objective and audience. In developing an advertisement, thinking and feeling sets high importance among other behavioral variables. An advertising objective for its long lasting effectiveness should possess the following characteristics as exhibited in the Table 6.5.

Table 6.5 Creative-mix in Advertising

Verbal elements	*Non-verbal elements*
• Copywriting Illustrations	• Visuals
• Headlines	• Layout
• Slogans	• Typography
• Brand names	• Trade mark
• Performance statements combination	• Color and Special Effects
• Institution reports	• Dynamics
	• Music

STRATEGIES TO DEVELOP WORD-OF-MOUTH ADVERTISING[5]

Word-of-mouth advertising has been called the world's best kept marketing secret. No matter how much money the movie industry spends on advertising, we still consult our friends about which movies to see. And our friends and relatives are the number one source of information about places to visit. Some categories are more dependent than others on word-of-mouth referrals. Topping the list, for example, are decisions about choosing a doctor, a mechanic or lawyer. The companies and advertising agencies believe that consumers tend to rely less on word-of-mouth, however, in choosing where to buy a car, obtain a personal loan or get a haircut. Word-of-mouth exists because it is impossible for consumers to know everything about everything. When a product is complex and difficult to evaluate and when there is risk involved in the decision - as is the case with the purchase of many services - consumers often look to others for advice.

Consumers look at the people they know, or those with whom they have strong ties. And if their advice is good, they regard these people as expert sources in the future. Word-of-mouth has many benefits for companies. Leads attracted to the business via word-of-mouth cost less and such sales are easier to close. As well, referrals tend to generate better quality customers in terms of profitability and loyalty compared with those attracted via price promotions in advertising campaigns. Marketing consultants Mercier Gray found that 60 percent of consumers purchased products solely through personal recommendation and that only 29 percent had ever bought a product as a result of seeing it in a TV advertisement. Although word-of-mouth is an extremely effective tool, few people know how to develop it. The best word-of-mouth advertising programs happen by design, not by chance. Word-of-mouth can be managed. Here are some tips to help the managers do just this.

1. ***Memorable service***

   Word-of-mouth does not happen overnight. It ultimately depends on the quality of your customer service. This is rarely based on one thing you do. Rather it is the result of hundreds of little things you consistently do a little bit better than your competitor. Things like exceeding customer expectations and delivering on your promises. People often remember your customer service more distinctly than your product, so focus on making the experience memorable. Absolutely nothing will help you to generate referred business, if your company cannot deliver a superior experience.

2. ***Be positive***

   Train your employees never to say anything negative about your company to customers or to friends. Reward those who speak positively. It is also good policy not to badmouth the competition. If your organization uses volunteers, ensure they also understand their roles as ambassadors. Train them the same way you would train the employees.

3. ***Talk to customers***

   Ensure your customers know how important referrals are to your business and let them know how much you appreciate them. It is necessary to plant word-of-mouth seeds. When

5 *The Record,* February 21, 2001

clients express their satisfaction with your goods and services, acknowledge their kind words with a sincere thank you. Then, take it a step further and let them know how much of your business is as a result of referrals from satisfied customers like them.

4. ***Incentive programs***

   Some organizations use incentive programs to generate referrals. Tactics such as paying cash for referrals may work. However, too often they smack of a bribe in exchange for a list of names of your friends. Instead, offer free samples that let you introduce clients to products or services they might not have otherwise tried. You could also give discounts against future purchases, memberships or other gifts.

5. ***Maintain a presence***

   One of the best things you can do is to simply stay top of mind with your customers. Ensure your company maintains a presence by sending a quarterly newsletter, or by inviting them to special events, if appropriate.

6. ***Network***

   Another key to building a word-of-mouth referrals is networking. The only people who are going to give referrals to you consistently are people who know and trust you. You need to spend time with the right people in structured professional environments, building friendships and lasting professional relationships.

7. ***Help others***

   Referrals are like boomerangs. What goes around comes around. So be sure to remember those who have sent you referrals when you are asked for the name of someone who can help.

Advertising objectives should serve three key determinants of product. They are -dissemination of message; decision making and evaluation of the advertisement or advertising strategy. The Table 6.6 exhibits the attributed that are required for developing the good advertising.

Table 6.6: Attributes of Good Advertising

Attributes	*Reason*
Continuity	For hierarchical order of advertising
Precise	To educate the consumer in short span
Measurable	Enabling to perform monitoring exercise and feed back analysis effectively.
Realistic	Presenting the facts and market experience of the product or institution
Flexible	Convenient for all ethnic groups, age, class and literate groups to understand and retrieve.
Impressionistic	Should possess long term symbiosis of product and company with consumers

COPYWRITING

Copy refers to the content of an advertisement. In the advertising industry, the term is sometimes used in a broad sense to include the words, pictures, symbols colors, layout, and other ingredients of an ad. Copywriting is a creative job, and its quality depends to a large extent on the creative ability of writers in the advertising agency or in the company. However, creativity alone may not produce good advertising copy. A marketing strategist needs to have his or her own perspectives incorporated in the copy such as the following basic parameters what to say, how to say it, and to whom to say it. The copy of an advertisement should address information on advertising objectives, product, target customers, competitive activity and ethical and legal considerations. Although copywriting may be the outcome of a flash of inspiration on the part of an advertising genius, it must rest on a systematic, logical, step-by -step presentation of ideas.

Copy of the commercial of Hong Kong and Shanghai Banking Corporation (HSBC) shows how financial institutions invariably appeal to the consumer's emotions through their advertising when money matters are supposed to strictly involve head-over-heart decisions. The television commercial film, conceptualized by Lowe Lintas, HSBC Group's global creative agency is part of an international series being run in the print and electronic media, based on the same tagline. The film is a part of HSBC's ongoing image campaign which seeks to drive home the brand attributes of trust, integrity, reliability and excellent customer service. What we are trying to show is that every HSBC employee is willing to go that extra mile for the customer, beyond the call of duty.

In advertising terminology copywriting refers to "studying of text" or "body of the text" to be put in an advertisement and devising its "Headline" or caption. In broad sense 'copy' refers to writing of a message of an advertisement, including the headline and text. It is believed that an advertisement is complete

Is it like kissing a girl ?

Strategy Focus 6.2: Delivering the Product Objectives: The Coca-Cola Way

The Atlanta-based soft drink giant Coca-Cola has always emphasized a strong role for advertising to sell its soft drinks. In its various advertising campaigns in recent years, Coca-Cola utilized such major themes as 'things go better with Coke', 'Coke is it', 'Always Coca-Cola', and others to sell its products. A brand can be a badge, an emblem, a global symbol that can bestow credibility, and attract instant attention in a new country, a new category, a new industry. The Atlanta-based soft drink giant, one of the world's biggest advertisers, relies heavily on sports-related advertising to boost worldwide sales, particularly for Coke Classic (during its sponsorship of the 1994 soccer World Cup, Coca-Cola saw double-digit sales increases in Mexico and Argentina). The Olympics represent Coca-Cola's biggest 1996 marketing thrust. In the summer of 1996, the company spent more than US $200 million in Games-related marketing, including the Olympic city park and approximately 70 billboards lining the streets of metro Atlanta. It's Atlanta, Coke's hometown, and it was the 100th anniversary of the Olympics. The Olympic Games contributed to increased brand awareness because every visitor was exposed to the advertising of the Coca-Cola company. In addition the advertising campaign had been seen in many different countries.

Source : Adapted from various sources, The Business Week, The Euro Monitor, 2003, 2004

when visuals are supported by words i.e. copy, though visual advertising makes an in-depth impact, the value of text can not be ignored. An exclusive non-verbal creative-mix cannot convey the message in isolation. Hence the importance of copy writing is invariably considered by advertising agencies.

However, contrary to this notion, some advertising agencies feel that the consumers make buying decisions from the visual illustrations and price line information because of the impact of "copy". Yet, in the field of advertising both believes are honored and integrated for effective response. Copywriting in advertising depends on the four conditions. They are: desired response for copy writing, inducement offered for advertisement and an approach for copy writing adopted by the advertising agency. These conditions are inter-related. An institutional copy and a promotional copy of the advertisement may be categorised on the basis of desired response. A set of inspirations which endeavors to have an institution 'copy' lies in (i) selling the idea (ii) acquainting consumers with products and (iii) attracting long range patronage for the product from consumers. A "Service copy" is required for product canvassing in retail stores while a "prestige copy" is taken to build reputation of the product advertised and its company. Unlike 'service copy', the 'prestige copy' offers the merchandise to build its image and utility. A 'promotional copy' is used for generating instant sales in the retail stores. The details of the product in fashion and its stand in the market are provided to the consumer for reference in the 'fashion copy'. It presents and interprets facts graphically with glamorous visuals and the exposure styles which are commonly accepted by the consumers. The advertising of household application products or direct utility merchandise is dealt in 'Utility Copy' to educate the consumers of usage of such products.

DEVELOPING MEDIA PLAN

Media planning is an essential exercise to be performed in advertising management. In developing a media plan, five basic dimensions need to be assessed. They are (i) media objectives (ii) target market (ii) media types (iv) media vehicle and (v) media scheduling. Besides these factors, continuity is also an important indicators which relates to time scheduling of messages on media. At the introductory stage it is required to allocate advertising budget for higher media time that can be gradually reduced as the stand of merchandise in the market advances. However, the life cycle of the merchandise also needs to be considered while setting the objectives.

Setting Target Markets

It is required to take the help of media specialist in identifying target markets for the merchandise to be identified and the type of advertisement required thereof. The market segmentation principles have to be considered for setting target market for physical distribution of merchandise and media has to be selected accordingly.

Media Selection and Budgeting

Data on effective media responses has to be analyzed for selection of the particular media. The cost of advertising on media on the basis of the frequency and continuity needs to be set for allocating advertising budget. Besides, while selecting advertising media the following factor combinations have to be ensured by the advertising agency:

- Perfect match of media type to target markets
- Perfect match of media type to advertising objectives
- Match of media type to advertising budget, and
- Match of selected media to competing advertisements.

It is required to make substantial budgetary provisions in the media plan, if the advertising have to be done in more than one media type. However, the relative weights of the media have to be decided on the basis of analyzing the "efficiency indicators" for the media in particular. Companies typically plan and execute their advertising through five strategic factors - developing the budget, planning the advertising, copy development approval, execution, and monitoring response. Media may be defined as those channels through which messages concerning a product or service are transmitted to targets. The media available to advertisers are newspapers, magazines, television, radio, outdoor advertising, transit advertising, direct mail and the Internet. The factors such as the product or service itself, the target market, the extent and type of distribution the type of message to be communicated, the budget and competitors' advertising strategies influence selection of an advertising medium. Except the advertising perspectives employed by the competition, information on most of these factors is presumably available inside the company. It may be necessary to undertake a marketing research project to find out what sorts of advertising strategies the competitors have used in the past and what might be expected of them in the future.

Media selection calls for two managerial decisions- the selection of medium to be used and e specific vehicles to be chosen within a given medium. The *cost-per-thousand-contacts comparison* has traditionally been the most popular method of media selection but it has many limitations. This method is based on measuring the impact of advertisement on contacts (persons) and the approach can be highly misleading if one considers the way in which advertisers define the term exposure. According to the media definition, exposure occurs as soon as an advertisement is inserted in the magazine but its impact is never considered. This method also fails to consider editorial images and the impact power of different channels of a medium. An alternative approach to media selection is *matching of audience and media characteristics* to specify the target audience and match its characteristics to a particular medium. This approach should be applied considering the following stages:

- Build a profile of consumers in reference to their location, accessibility and demographic composition.
- Study media profiles for audience coverage, reach and frequency of viewing.
- Match consumer profiles to media profiles. The consumer characteristics for a product should be matched to the audience characteristics of different media. This comparison should lead to the preliminary selection of a medium, based primarily on its coverage in terms of either readership or viewership.
- The preliminary selection should be examined further with regards to product and cost considerations. Cost is one of the major concerns in media selections. Cost should be balanced against the benefit expected from the campaign under consideration.

- Finally, the total budget should be allocated to different media and to various media vehicles. The final selection of a medium should maximize the achievement of media objectives.

To sum up, it may be stated that two types of information are required for media selection-customer profile and media characteristics. The advertiser should build a consumer profile for his or her product/market. Each medium, however, presents the information in a way that makes it look the best. It is desirable, therefore, to validate the audience information supplied by media owners with data from bureaus that audit various media. However, as money is committed to a selected medium, it is ' desirable to review the medium's viability against evaluation criteria.

Scheduling

An advertising planner has to decide scheduling of advertisements on media with reference to its periodicity in a day, hour, month and year. During which hour of the day an advertisement should be exposed on media has to be planned considering the human behavior of watching media and the nature of product. An example may be mentioned of scheduling an advertisement of breakfast foods during the breakfast hours on media, which would have an effective impact than releasing, it in late height slot of the media. Scheduling the advertising in respect of media time, periodicity in month and number of months in a year would be helpful in allocating resources in advertising budgeting exercise for media buying. Scheduling should be done in width and length of media buying. The advertising planner needs to develop a media time flowchart once the scheduling exercise is completed. Although, media schedule plan is not a permanent document as some elements such as type of merchandise, style of copy, media policy are subject to change without notice, the flow chart would be the right guiding tool for planner.

DIRECT RESPONSE ADVERTISING

Media advertising largely attempts to generate indirect response of the merchandise or services advertised. The direct response advertising includes mail-media advertising, catalogues, departmental store's advertising, yellow pages, handouts, and window displays.

Direct Mail Advertising

Direct marketing is an effective buyer-seller interactive system in which merchandise under advertisement is brought close to buyer using one or more advertising styles, and the response is measured in reference to location and volume of transactions. The mail-media advertising involves promoting merchandise market by establishing contact with potential and existing consumers through mail orders, publicity materials and telephone service. In this process, no personal selling is performed.

Direct mail advertising has many advantages. It attempts to build goodwill between seller and buyers. Hence, mail advertising is often identified as productive advertising technique. The numerous advantages of this system are listed below:

- It is highly selective
- This form of advertising is elastic as the retailer can add or delete the name of consumers at his discretion

- Wide variety of merchandise or service can be advertised to the same consumer
- Privacy on consumer preference/order can be maintained
- Market competition can be avoided instantly
- Direct mail advertising is personal and specific home delivery of goods and services can be assured
- Performance of merchandise/service sales can be monitored and evaluated.

Despite many advantages of the direct mail advertising, there exist some demerits also. The most commonly observed problem in mailing business orders is high expenditure involvement in the process. The periodical up-dating of mailing list is major task in direct-mail advertising which consumes large business time. Besides these disadvantages, sometime it becomes disinteresting and irritable to the persons addressed and they feel offensive as the 'copy' of mail-order is not matched with the profile of persons to whom it is sent.

Different types of mail-order advertising comprise comprehensive text and visual copy of advertisement, which attempts to make the readership interesting. The various types of mail-order advertising are as below:

- Business reply mail with pre-paid postage fee
- Information enclosures, circulars etc.
- Postal cards without order form
- Self-mailing folders, and
- Booklets and catalogues.

Mail-order advertising is a quantitative exercise and requires systematic processing of data. Hence, computerization is the basic requirement to handle the data, in reference to classifying consumers, sorting types of orders, record of compliance to orders and other functions.

Display Advertising

Window display is the most prominent style of direct response advertising as it establishes ready information, product impression, and impulse of buying that helps in decision making. Display advertising has many ways of performance - indoor and outdoor. The indoor display advertising consists of showcase advertising and indoor displays in departmental stores. There are some common kinds of indoor display of merchandise. They are:

- Display of merchandise in showcases of departmental stores with an abstract and combination.
- Display of merchandise in decorative style in show case/window
- Display of prestige copy under simulated environment
- Display of merchandise on dummy theme display, and demonstration of use of merchandise

Outdoor display of merchandise or services may be done in the form of sign boards, commercial hoardings, posters, neon signs, vehicle sign boards, train posters, electronic sign boards, balloons, fibre optical billboard and other special effects. The merchandise advertising on vehicle is called transit advertising which carries message from place to place. It is a good way to reach specific markets and can be tailored to the need of geographical market segmentation.

ADVERTISING CAMPAIGN

This strategy is adopted by advertisers when the merchandise or service has to 'gate-crashed' in the market and marketed with horizontal expansion policy. Campaign advertising is primarily concerned with achieving quick sales response in target markets through clearance advertising and regular price-line advertising. Such campaigns are of short duration but possess similarity in copy writing and continuity in releasing exposures. Hence, campaign is a series of advertisements exposed in a given time at regular intervals in the same media, or medium. The advertising campaigns are of natural and local level and have institutional patronage. The advertising campaigns are planned in advance and are set orderly.

This approach is beneficial to gain regular consumers as well as occasional buyers, as a series of advertisements leave an impression on the consumers and are early identifiable. It is observed that such advertising campaigns not only build consumer strength but also bring prestige to retail sales, institution and advertising agency. However, in planning advertising campaigns and putting it through media care should be taken in its continuity, message dissemination and periodicity as in absence of such regulation, the impact of campaign may not be achieved to the mark.

INSTITUTIONAL ADVERTISING

It is a form of public relations performed through communicating message to the target audience directly related with the institution. It is not necessary that an institution developing advertising message should strictly be of commercial nature. The strategy for institutional advertising needs to be selected matching the objective of institution and clientele. For example a business company may develop institutional advertisement for distributors in the employees of a company, an association of medicos may release message of social health awareness, government can do so for generating awareness of franchising during elections and so on. Institutional advertising involves non-personal mass-media communication by an identified institution to accomplish its goals. There are various type of institutional advertising practices observed, of which some major kinds are released through the following messages:-

- Social awareness about civil rights, health, population etc.
- Promotion of a public service
- Generating awareness about innovation, achievement, new facts of development
- Improved or added market value of products
- Employees, welfare and image of institution

- Placement advertisements with profile of company's achievements.
- Opening debate on controversial issues.

Institutional advertising thus, can be of commercial and non-commercial nature. Functionally, institutional advertising can be classified into two categories - image advertising and advocacy advertising. Image advertising is designed to mobilize opinion about the institution and create an image through its merits. So, it can be stated that an image advertising exhibits the human face of an advertiser. Image advertising is of four types and they are:

- Institution identification advertisements
- Goodwill advertisements
- Civil rights and responsibilities advertisements
- Public service advertisements.

Such advertisements are non-argumentative and non-controversial as most of the themes are of public interest such as, population control, crime prevention, water, food and energy conservation, campaign against drug abuse and the like. On the contrary, advocacy advertising attempts to highlight contemporary arguments directed either at specific general clients like political activists, consumer groups, media and government agencies. *Advocacy advertising* consists of following forms:

- Ideological advertisement, which is principle oriented and attempts to highlight the ethics of an institution.
- Defense advertisement which argues to protect the image of the institution against contemporary controversies.
- Reply bound advertisements seeking responses to the issues highlighted in the advertisement.
- Position taking advertisement emphasising the viewpoint of an institute of issue thereof with strong argument to seek public acceptance or referendum.
- All recruitment advertisement asking interested persons to present their views in support of the ethics of institutions in view to strengthen its logic prior to their joining position in the institute.

An advocacy advertising has an advantage of exhibiting message under controlled situation of advertiser which helps in dealing with complex issues through corporate focus. An institution can plan a series of advertisements as campaign supporting its views and building image simultaneously among the clientele group. Institutional advertisements are generally released on multi-media and cover substantially larger segment of target audience.

ADVERTISING APPROPRIATION

Advertising appropriation is an essential management approach to control the advertising expenditure and gain optimum response at reasonable level of investment. The common method of appropriation will be on the basis of the net sales per annum. The advertising appropriation can also be done on the change of turnover of the company over the previous year. This method is also known as returns on investment of the company in a given time. The advertising activity can be appropriated on the basis of developing an advertisement, campaign, direct advertising, buyer-seller relationship and image building. The advertising budget, which is the principal tool of appropriation, consists of the expenditure related to the selected category of goods and services and media for advertising. The advertising expenditure needs to be appropriated also in reference to different sales regions in respect of goods and services, media and consumer preference. The expenditure variables in production of advertising include the insertion charges of the commissioned media, art work, mechanical production, talent, non-media promotion expenditure like point of purchase sale promotion, displays, exhibits etc. Besides the client service charges of the advertising agency, administrative costs and overheads also need to be considered in advertising appropriation.

ADVERTISING RESEARCH

Advertising research is a prerequisite for developing advertisement as well as assessment of effectiveness of the advertisement. It is necessary to understand thoroughly, the product profile in terms of its physical properties and composition to enable to develop a meaningful and factual copy. The organizational profile needs to be understood clearly for linking the product with the organization and its brand. It is a must to conduct buyer behavior survey to know the perceptions of the viewers and the potential response. The advertisement pre-testing results also needs to be analyzed and used for modifying the copy and presentation style.

Media effectiveness may be studied for any advertisement by conducting the veiwership survey, media vehicle response, advertisement scheduling results, frequency and reach assessment and the impact of the previous advertisement. The effectiveness of any advertisement can be measured at two different levels – pre-insertion and post-insertion of the advertisement in the media. The concept of the advertisement can be measured in a pre-testing campaign, by viewing or presenting to sample viewers and getting free association of the consumers and merchants while developing the same. The specific and non-specific themes may be tested with specially identified viewers. The reach and status of the media is to be assessed before insertion of the advertisement. The copy research can be assessed using the following approaches:

- Consumer Jury
- Matched samples
- Portfolio test or message recall efficiency
- Storyboard test or image retention through video clipping
- Other mechanical devices.

Assessment of the effectiveness of the advertisement in the post-insertion stage needs to be done on the basis of audience exposure, attitude and change.

Table 6.7 Advertising Research: Dimensions to Understand

Area	*Advertiser's decision*	*What is to be measured*	*Method of measurement*	*Research goal*	*Advertiser's goal*
Motivation Research	What to say	Consumer behaviour	Unstructured Focus Group	Low cost research	New appeals
Copy Research	How to say	Credibility of message and recall	Pre-testing Mailing questionnaire	Significant data sets	Good recall of advertisement
Visual Research	How to show	Response to visuals	Video Devices	Ranking	High Impact
Media Research	Where to show	Media effectiveness	Viewership survey	Ranking	Best Ad-Media Recall
Public Opinion	Target audience/ consumers	Level of impact	Personal interviews	Represen -tative groups	Optimum impact
Operations Research	Economics of advertising	Financial effectiveness	Statistical tests	Advertising appropriation	Satisfactory client service and revenue generation

in attitude and turnover effect in terms of sales volume. The controlled field experiments may also be conducted to assess the attention on the advertisement, comprehensiveness of the message, technical execution of the advertisement and the overall impact. The programming of the advertising research is exhibited in the Table 6.7.

EFFECTIVENESS IN ADVERTISING

Print advertising tends to work more slowly than television or radio, typically. Therefore, an especially long period of time (or an especially heavy media schedule) is required to fully evaluate the total effects of print advertising. Advertising for new products is more effective than advertising for established products. It's easier to create effective advertising for new products, in other words, than it is for established products. The inherent "news value" of new products is the principal reason new product advertising is more effective. Given the greater effectiveness of new product advertising, one of the most common marketing mistakes is failure to take advantage of this inherent advantage (i.e., to under-spend on introductory advertising for new products).

Persistently high advertising failure rate results primarily from lack of an accurate feedback mechanism, a lack of testing and evaluation. If an agency doesn't know when it is advertising is bad or why it's bad, how the agency can possibly improve it is advertising. Marketing research can provide this feedback, but it is too expensive for the typical advertisement or commercial. The degree of sales effectiveness can vary greatly from one commercial to the next. One commercial might be several times more effective than another. This indicates that the quality of advertising tends to be more important than the quantity of advertising. Nevertheless, the quantity of advertising (i.e., the media weight) must achieve a threshold level for the advertising to have any positive effects. Limited telephone tracking research (and this can be done with small budgets) can monitor the cumulative effects of advertising upon awareness, brand image, and consumer attitudes, and is one of the simplest and most effective ways to make sure that advertising is doing its job. Message recall is a positive factor, but its importance should not be overstated. Brand registration, however, is always important (as opposed to message/element recall). If consumers don't remember the brand name, the effectiveness of the advertising is correspondingly reduced. Failure to register the brand name is one of the most common weaknesses of the commercials.

Advertising effectiveness cannot be determined by any one measure, such as persuasion or recall. Recall is a good measure for some commercials, but not for others. Persuasion scores don't work very well for brands with high market shares, and cannot be relied upon for brands in poorly defined product categories. Purchase intent works reasonably well for new products, but poorly for established products. A large number of important variables must be examined to judge the potential effectiveness of advertising. The commercials on AM/FM radio can be as effective or more than effective television commercials on the basis of sales return per dollar of media. Typically, radio production budgets are much less than television and radio commercials are rarely submitted to the rigors of marketing research evaluation.

WEB ADVERTISING AND PROMOTION

Internet is the fastest growing medium in the 90's with 25 million users and with an average estimated growth of 10-20% per month. It has great potential as an advertising medium. Its feedback and interaction possibilities enable advertisers and Internet users to customize and differentiate the advertisement to meet the user's own requirements. Internet advertising is becoming part of some companies' marketing strategy. However, it requires new strategies and thinking. The benefits of Internet advertising are its ability to cover all promotional objectives from awareness to action by leveraging all 5 elements in the promotion mix. Online advertising has been increasingly booming and had reached about $ 2 billion in 1998. Internet advertising offers a variety of advantages. It offers an exceptional ability to target specific customers. Besides, it blurs the division between content and advertising, which the traditional media regard as sacred. If the money is right, many online publishers are willing to strike whatever sort of partnerships an advertiser might want. The Internet is also a highly selective, cost effective media with greater measurability than any other media. Despite higher global reach Internet is not a local mainstream media yet. Traditional advertising is consumed passively, yet on the Internet, the users have to actively select an advertisement. These changes the way advertisers generate and re-train customers. To persuade visitors to revisit and spend time on the web site the advertisers must fulfill real customer needs on continuous basis. This requires clear objectives and targeting. Informative quality content, advertisement with interesting entertainment or direct sales possibilities can add value to the customer. Internet implementation requires understanding, commitment and resource allocation from corporate management to operate successfully. The marketing department should be responsible in conjunction with advice from a competent advertising agency for Internet strategy development and implementation.

Interactive Internet could be the solution to advertisers' requirements. But new advertising strategies are needed in this medium. The Internet is a two-way interpersonal communication flow. The key distinguishing features are the interpersonal feedback and this interaction process provides relevant customer information in order to serve them more effectively in the future. Users can also interact with the Internet medium itself through machine interactivity. As compared to traditional media the user is fully in charge of the information pull. Internet is a hybrid medium that can combine all the three identified communication strategies including mass communication, interpersonal communication and machine interactivity communication. Internet allows advertisers to utilize all the five elements in the promotion mix. It therefore, provides the means of covering all promotional objectives from awareness to action.

Internet advertising will increase and become easier to measure, and the gap between this new precise, interactive marketing capability and conventional "fuzzy" passive media will widen. The following reasons are advanced for the growing popularity of Internet advertising:

- Web presents great advertising opportunities for marketers because of its continuing growth, its user demographics, its effectiveness, and its cost competitiveness.
- Overall Web population is reaching critical mass. Marketers pursuing certain segments of the population are finding the Internet increasingly useful.
- Internet is reasonably good at achieving standard advertising objectives, such as shaping attitudes. However, it also has capabilities that the traditional media cannot match. Features that make the Internet a superior medium include its ability to address, its interactivity, and its scope for customization.
- In terms of advertising economics, the Internet can already compete with existing media, both in response as measured by click-through and in exposure as measured by cost per thousand. Moreover the economics of internet provide better effects when a target consumer segment is defined.
- Like traditional media, the Internet needs consistent matrices and auditing in order to gain broad acceptance from marketers. Both are emerging slowly, driven by old players such as Nielsen and new ones such as Web Track.
- Advertisers and agencies cannot afford to produce a different advertisement and negotiate a different price for every site. Standards for size, position, content, and pricing are needed for positioning an advertisement.

Success Factors

Advertiser must assess what he wants to achieve through an Internet presence. Initially this calls for an evaluation of how well the advertisers' target audience and product portfolio suit the Internet. Companies targeting well educated, innovative, affluent males or students have great potential for success as their segments are found highly represented on the Internet. Products and services with high information intensity and high buyer involvement are also found suitable for Internet promotion due to its ability to carry large customized information at low costs. Mail order companies can also take advantage of Internet purchase facilitation. Low product fit or low audience fit companies can still take advantage of building or reinforcing a brand image or getting a learning experience with interactive media. Traditional advertising is consumed passively. On the Internet, users have to do something actively to select an advertisement. This alters the way advertisers generate and retrain customers. Banner ads, malls, search engines, word-of-mouth combined with use of conventional media can generate visitors to a web site. Since, users are in charge of the navigation, advertisers must persuade users to revisit and spend time on the web site by fulfilling real customer needs. This requires clear objectives and targeting to add value on a continuous basis while retaining the user. Informative quality content, innovative advertisement or direct sales possibilities can add value to the user's site visit. Internet advertising demands management understanding and commitment for success. Management must determine Internet objectives and strategies to allocate efficient resources such as capital, equipment and people.

REFERENCES

Allen, Alistair and Joan Hoverstadt, *The History of Printed Scraps.* London: New Cavendish Books, 1983.

Alter, Stewart. T*ruth Well Told: McCann-Erickson and the pioneering of global advertising.* McCann-Erickson Worldwide, 1995.

Atwan, Robert. *Edsels, Luckies, and Frigidaires: advertising the American way.* New York: Dell Publishing Co., 1979.

Craven David W.: *Strategic Marketing,* McGraw Hill, New York , 1999

Dalrymple Douglas J. and Pearson Leonard J. : *Marketing Management* : *Text and Cases,* John Wiley and Sons, New York, 1995

Herbert Jack Rotfeld: Misplaced marketing The social harm of public service advertising, *Journal of Consumer Marketing,* 19 (6), 2002, pp 465-467

Jeffrey Durgee: Qualitative Methods for Developing Advertising That Makes Consumers Feel, ''Hey, That's Right For Me'', *Journal of Consumer Marketing,* 7 (1), 1990

Jain Subhash C: *Marketing Strategy,* South Western College Publishing, Ohio, 1999

Kathleen Mortimer: Services advertising: the agency viewpoint, *Journal of Services Marketing,* 15(2), 2001, pp 131-146

Kotler Philip : *Marketing Management : Analysis, Planning, Implementation and control ,* Prentice Hall, New Delhi , 1995, p. 684-713

Laird, Pamela Walker. *Advertising progress: American business and the rise of consumer marketing.* Baltimore: Johns Hopkins University Press, 1998.

Lamoreaux, Naomi R. *The Great Merger Movement in American Business,* 1895-1904. Cambridge: Cambridge University Press, 1985.

Shengliang Deng and Jing Zhao : Evolution and evaluation of export advertising in China, *The Journal of Business and Industrial Marketing,* 10 (5), 1995, pp 38-49

Storholm Gordon R : *Sales Management,* Prentice Hall, Englewood cliffs, NJ, 1982, pp. 38-66

Stuart C Rogers: How to create advertising that works, *The Journal of Business and Industrial Marketing,* 10 (2), 1995, 20-33

Uta Werner; John McDermott and Greg Rotz : Retailers at the crossroads: how to develop profitable new growth strategies, *Journal of Business Strategy,* 25 (2), 2004, pp 10-17

Case 6.1

PENETRATING MEDIA MARKET ACROSS THE BOUNDARIES: THE STRATEGY OF AZTECA AMERICA[6]

"........ One by one, the men of extravagant vision and exaggerated showmanship have been toppled from the upper ranks of the world's media giants. This trooping of grey faces into the unruly media world marks a distinct change of mood. Talk of "vision", "synergy" or "new paradigms" is out; the daily grind of evaluating and improving operating performance is paramount. The need to return to the basics of the business...."

Peter Chernin, The News Corporation

TV Azteca is one of the world's two largest producers of Spanish-language television programming. It operates two national television networks through 554 transmitters across the country: the family-driven Azteca 13 and the youth-focused Azteca 7, covering 97% and 95% of Mexican households, respectively. TV Azteca also operates two international networks: Azteca International, which reaches 13 countries in Central and South America; and Azteca America, the fastest growing Hispanic television network in the United States, covering more than 70% of the US Hispanic population. In 2003, TV Azteca celebrated its tenth anniversary. TV Azteca's mission is to create shareholder value by producing and distributing the best Spanish-language television content in the world. In 2002, the company produced 8,110 hours of television programming in proven formats-popular stories/soaps, entertainment, sports, reality shows and newscasts. The quality of TV Azteca's programming is evidenced by its steadily growing share of the Mexican audience and its equal success abroad. TV Azteca's most successful popular stories/soaps, which are distributed to about 90 countries, now capture 60% audience share in the Philippines, and 30% in Spain.

---

6 The case has been developed by Rajagopal, Professor of Marketing, *Business Division*, ITESM-CCM, Mexico City Campus, Mexico City 14380 DF (E-mail : *rajagopal@itesm.mx*)

This case has been written as the basis for class discussion rather than to illustrate either effective or ineffective handling of an administrative situation of the company.

Author acknowledges the academic contribution of Mr Jorge Arturo Rodriguez N, student of the course on Advanced Selling System and marketing executive of Television Azteca, Mexico; Gabriela Gomez, Angelica Ramirez and Angela Segura of the above course in conducting the investigation and presenting the case as a part fulfilment of the course in the January-April 2003 trimester of Graduate Program of ITESM-CCM.

INTERNATIONAL TREND OF TELEVISION INDUSTRY

Fourth Estate has been growing very fast and the print and television industry has been regarded as the pivot of contemporary business economics. The television media entertainment companies have increased manifold in two broad categories-TV channels and cable operating companies across the countries with intense competition. In the May sweeps, Nielsen's numbers showed that for the first time, more folks were watching cable TV in prime time than were tuned to the four largest networks. The cable guys increased their audience to 49%, while viewership for the major four US television companies - ABC, CBS, Fox, and NBC slipped to just 47% of the overall audience.[7] Entertainment companies therefore, need certain qualities like readiness to take big risks, laser-quick reactions to fickle changes of taste, and a supreme confidence in their own gut instincts—all virtue. "Show business doesn't attract leaders, who know how to listen properly or leave people alone," comments Roger Fransecky, head of the Apogee Group, which advises many media bosses. "But when you manage creative people, you must intrude carefully." The HBO company shows that it is possible even for a vast corporation to retain an edgy creative outfit that achieves both critical and commercial success.[8] The secret has been twofold: the creation of a small boutique-like identity within a huge corporate institution; and the granting of creative independence within a tightly controlled operation. The television industry in US seems to be promising as the advertising recovery has been observed at fast pace. The results look promising, with U.S. ad sales projected to rise 5.3% in 2003, more than double the prior year's 2.6% hike.[9] Despite the slump in overall ad spending, agencies that target Hispanic consumers are scrambling to keep up with ever-growing campaigns.

A large number of advertisement buyers are moaning that advertising budgets for the big guys, including auto makers and financial institutions, are being slashed by as much as 20%. The free-spending dot-coms are no longer in business, the ad folks say, so fewer dollars are chasing TV commercials. "It is an ad recession," says Andrew Donchin, senior vice-president of Carat USA, an advertising agency whose clients include New Line Cinema, Midas Muffler, and RadioShack. He predicts the amount being bought in the upfront season will be off 6% to 10%. Hispanic Americans constitute a bigger, more widely dispersed, and more affluent market. The survey showed that the number of U.S. Hispanics grew by 58% in the past decade, to 35.3 million. Moreover, Hispanics' buying power increased 118%, to $ 452 billion, from 1990 and 2001, according to the University of Georgia's Selig Center for Economic Growth. That far outpaced the 68% growth in non-Hispanic buying power, to $ 6.6 trillion.[10] Advertisers take little solace in the fact that they get "make goods" — free ads in other parts of the network schedule to compensate for ratings below what the networks promised. That's one reason why advertisers have been lapping up cable TV in recent years, increasing their upfront spending by 24%, to $ 5 billion, for prime-time spots on cable in 2000. People still pay for cable because they get better reception, but without ads cable probably wouldn't be very profitable.

7 Nielsen Universal Estimates, 2002 quoted in Get Set for Nights.., *Business Week,* May 29, 2002

8 How to Manage the Dream Factory, *The Economist* (print edition), Jan 16th 2003

9 *Business Week,* December 30, 2002

10 Aixa M. Pascual and Gerry Khermouch : No Ad Recession for Hispanic Marketers, *Business Week,* February 19, 2002

The e-business portals, internet search engines and virtual entertainment shops have been becoming the potential threats to the TV companies in fetching earning from advertising agencies. The positive reinforcement of traditional media and online media consumption reflects both the power of cross media marketing, and the fact that the Internet is a logical channel for TV/Print/Radio prompted transactions.

Mergers and acquisitions in the media industry seems likely to accelerate following a US court decision removing the rule prohibiting media companies from owning cable systems and local broadcasters in the same market. More than 100 media companies around the world have upward of $1 billion in revenues, and the entertainment and media businesses are still fragmented compared with other industries such as pharmaceuticals and aerospace.[11]

COMPANY BACKGROUND AND TIME LINE

Azteca America is the wholly-owned subsidiary of TV Azteca's Spanish-language broadcasting network for the US Hispanic market. The network supplies the best of TV Azteca's programming content to U.S. affiliates from different top Hispanic genres –popular stories/soaps, news, sports and entertainment, talk shows, etc.- 24 hours a day, seven days a week as well as network and national spot sales. The Azteca America Network's current affiliates include KAZA-TV (Channel 54) in Los Angeles, CA; KUVR-TV (Channel 68) in Reno, NV; KTNC-TV (Channel 42) which covers the markets of San Francisco, Oakland, San Jose, Sacramento, Stockton and Modesto, CA; KAZH-TV (Channel 57) in Houston, TX. Each affiliate directs its efforts on local market sales and distribution. Azteca America Network also holds an equity interest in some of its strategic affiliates; that helps to ensure a seamless interaction with, and knowledge of, local markets. Through these affiliates, Azteca America can now bring its programming to roughly 28% of the U.S. Hispanic audience, estimated to be in excess of 35 million. Azteca America will continue pursuing affiliations, acquisitions and lease-management agreements in order to grow its coverage of the US Hispanic market. To date, audience results, in the key markets it has entered, have been encouraging. Azteca America supplies the best of TV Azteca's programming content to U.S. affiliates from different genres

TV Azteca, the second private TV network of importance in Mexico in November 1997, made an offer to acquire Telemundo, an important television network in the Hispanic US market. But Telemundo was sold to a company formed by Sony, Liberty, Bastión and Apollo for 776 US million dollars. By April 1998, in Las Vegas, Ricardo B. Salinas Pliego, the owner of TV Azteca and Salinas Group, met Harry Pappas, from the Pappas Telecasting Group. They signed a proposal document to conform a new company and create a Spanish Network Television for the USA. TV Azteca, along with Pappas Telecasting Group, further proposed to acquire Telemundo during mid 1999, which could not be materialized. Therefore, the new society organized by TV Azteca and the Pappa's Group decided to continue on planning the launch of the new Spanish Television Network. In March, 1999, the TV Azteca signed an agreement with Echostar that allowed this company to broadcast Mexico's channel 13 signal in the USA. Thus, the first image of TV Azteca arrived in USA and

11 Media Mergers: The Wave Rolls On, *The McKinsey Quarterly,* No.2, 2002

people began to recognize the new signal. This partnership deal has set the gateway for expansion of the media and entertainment industry across boundaries. The deal reflected that the TV Azteca would get in exchange of the new channel's telecast of programs, a 20% of the new company's capital. The marketing of new programs, generating sales through advertisement are the principal resources for generating capital in the new company, which was named as *Azteca America.* Mr. Luis Echarte took over as CEO of the company to meet the challenge thereof.

Pappas group proposed to acquire some television stations in the principal Hispanic markets in America on the basis of financial credibility of the company. In June 2001, the original agreements came into force that envisaged that the TV Azteca would own the company while Pappas group would retain the property of the television stations. In order to establish the alliances with the television stations, the company decided that every station would be able to receive the transmission signals of Azteca America under the agreement of revenue sharing of 50 percent from each party. Finally, Azteca America commissioned its transmission in Los Angeles and California during December 2001. Later the transmission was extended to Reno and Navada areas also. In May –June 2002, the first non-Pappa's group television stations were merged into the network of Azteca.

HISPANIC MARKET IN THE US

US Hispanic Market is an important market. If it could be compared with a country, it would represent the largest economy in Latin America with over $560 billion in purchasing power and over 38 million people at the close of 2001. This market is huge, both in terms of population and economic power. The largest minority group in the US is also the fastest growing one. Between 1990 and 2000, the Hispanic population increased by 58%, about eight times the average growth of the rest of the US population. Within this period, Hispanics accounted for 40% of total US Hispanic growth. The rest of the growth is explained by immigration factors. The Hispanic population is also highly metropolitan, an easy group to reach – if you speak the language, and know the culture. Of the population, 15 cities concentrate two thirds of all Hispanics, and 25 cities represent more than three quarters. Of the top 15 and 25 cities, Azteca America has a coverage of eight and seven, respectively. The major Hispanic markets in USA are exhibited in Box 1. Demography of the Hispanic population has a phenomenal standing in US. Hispanic households are younger in age and larger in number. The typical

Box 1: Major Hispanic markets in USA

Ten Largest Hispanic Business Markets in the U.S.	Ten Largest Hispanic Business Markets in Texas
Los Angeles, CA	Houston
New York, NY	San Antonio
Houston, TX	El Paso
Miami, FL	Dallas
San Antonio, TX	Corpus Christi
El Paso, TX	Laredo
Dallas / Fort Worth, TX	Austin
Hialeah, FL	Brownsville
Chicago,IL	McAllen
San Diego, CA	Forth Worth

Source: U.S. Department of Commerce 1990 Census Report. 1992 Economic Census, and 1994 Census Project Survey.

Hispanic household is roughly 40% larger than the average US household. According to 2000 census data, 36% of Hispanic were under 18 years old, versus 24% for Caucasians. The median age of Hispanics is 26 years, versus 38 years for Caucasians and 30 years for African-Americans. The typical Hispanic household has nearly twice as many children under age 18, and 50% fewer persons over 65 years old compared to average US households.

Established Hispanic markets like New York, Los Angeles, Miami, and Chicago are still posting the largest absolute gains in Hispanics. But the fastest growth is happening in what the Pew Study calls "New Latino Destinations" - markets like Atlanta, Orlando, and Broward County (Ft. Lauderdale PMSA). In fact, an astonishing 61 of the top 100 markets fell into this category: i.e., markets with a relatively small base of Hispanics, but explosive growth between 1990 and 2000. Some of the other 61 "New Latino Destinations" with the most dramatic increases in Hispanic share are:

- Bergen-Passaic, NJ PMSA (11% Hispanics in 1990 to 17% in 2000)
- Fort Worth-Arlington, TX PMSA (11% to 18%)
- Las Vegas, NV MSA (10% to 21%)
- Nassau-Suffolk, NY PMSA (6% to 10%)
- New Haven, CT PMSA (6% to 10%)
- Salt Lake City, UT MSA (6% to 11%)
- Raleigh-Durham, NC MSA (1% to 6%)
- Springfield, MA MSA (8% to 13%)
- Washington, D.C. PMSA (5% to 9%)
- West Palm Beach, FL MSA (8% to 12%)

These newer markets often pose special challenges for advertisers and publishers since, accompanying this growth in Hispanic population. Here again, South Florida illustrates the point. Whereas Miami-Dade's Hispanic market has traditionally been mainly Cuban (although this has declined dramatically from 91% Cuban in 1970 to 53% in 2000), Broward County is a new kind of market with no clear dominant Hispanic group: Puerto Ricans (21%) and Cubans (20%) account for a roughly equal share. But political and economic unrest has led to the fastest growth of population coming from South America: Argentina, Colombia, and Venezuela in recent years. South Americans account for more than a third (34%) of Broward Hispanics.[12] The purchasing power of Hispanic population has more than doubled from $223 billion in 1990, and has grown by 18% since 2000, alone ($491 billion). Hispanic buying power is growing at a much more rapid pace than buying power of either total non-Hispanic or any other racial or ethnic group. In 2002, the ten states with the highest aggregate Hispanic buying power are exhibited in Box 2. Hispanic market trends have shown the fast-growing consumers' purchasing power. It is estimated that this figure represents a 144% growth over the 1990 value, which is 2.1 times the non-Hispanic growth rate. In 1999, annual expenditures for Hispanic households averaged US $29,333, which was 15.8%

12 CarlosPelay : Hispanic Market Growth: Dispersion and Diversity, *Media Economics Group*, HispanicAd.com, September 4, 2002

lower than the general population's. And their expenditures in some categories is higher than average. Hispanics spent 12.3% of their income on food at home, as compared to the general market which spends only 8.3%. Hispanics spend US$102.6 at the grocery store per week, or 23.9% more than the general market does. This buying power could build the competitive edge for companies that successfully harness this market.

EXPANSION IN HISPANIC AMERICAN REGIONS

Azteca America had planned to launch the new Network by October 2000, with the signal broadcasted in Miami, Houston, Corpus Christi, Las Vegas and Laredo, although the official announcement would be done by April 2001. In July 2001, Azteca America starts broadcasting in Los Angeles, CA. through KAZA's Channel 54.

Box 6.2: Hispanic buying power: top ten cities in USA in 2002

(In US Billion Dollars)

California ($170.7 billion)	Texas ($93.7b)
Florida ($52.4b)	New York ($48.1b)
Illinois (25.6b)	New Jersey ($22.3b)
Arizona ($17.5b)	Colorado ($13.0b)
Georgia ($11.3b)	New Mexico ($11.0b)

Source : Carlos Pelay, Hispanic Magazine Monitor, Media Economics Group, July 24, 2002

"We're very excited about the opportunity that this operation will bring to our distribution network. This is an important step for us as we continue to build our dynamic network and brand equity. The scale of our commitment to Hispanic viewers is further demonstrated by this major opportunity," said Luis J. Echarte, CEO of Azteca America.

Azteca America, which will also be responsible for promotional activities, will provide programming to the Los Angeles station 24 hours daily and manage the sales team that will be responsible for local and national spot sales. By December 2001, Reno and Nevada were included. Eventually 25% of Pappas' Houston and San Francisco stations were bought by TV Azteca and in January, 2002 this two stations started broadcasting the Azteca America's programming too. In May and June, 2002, the first non-Pappas Group TV Stations became part of Azteca America's Network: The Salt Lake City, a Univision former station, Orlando, which began broadcasting from Universal Studios, Las Vegas and Santa Barbara. The network of Azteca America in USA serving the Hispanic population is exhibited in Figure1.

Affiliation process with other regional channels further persuaded by the Azteca America during the above reference period in getting stations like Albuquerque, Austin and Palm Springs. In November 2002, the Aza Gazette , the magazine that updates the information on the Azteca America's entertainment activities in the Hispanic market of the America, was launched. The Aza Gazette has the also the focus of maintaining the corporate information of Azteca America's partners involved and informed in reference to their growth, success, and achievements. By December, stations like New York, Miami, Fresno, Bakersfield, Wichita and West Palm Beach get incorporated to the Network. By this time Azteca America had a 53% of the Hispanic Population Coverage in the US and it started to be considered as a real Television Network since then. In January, 2003, the last acquisitions were

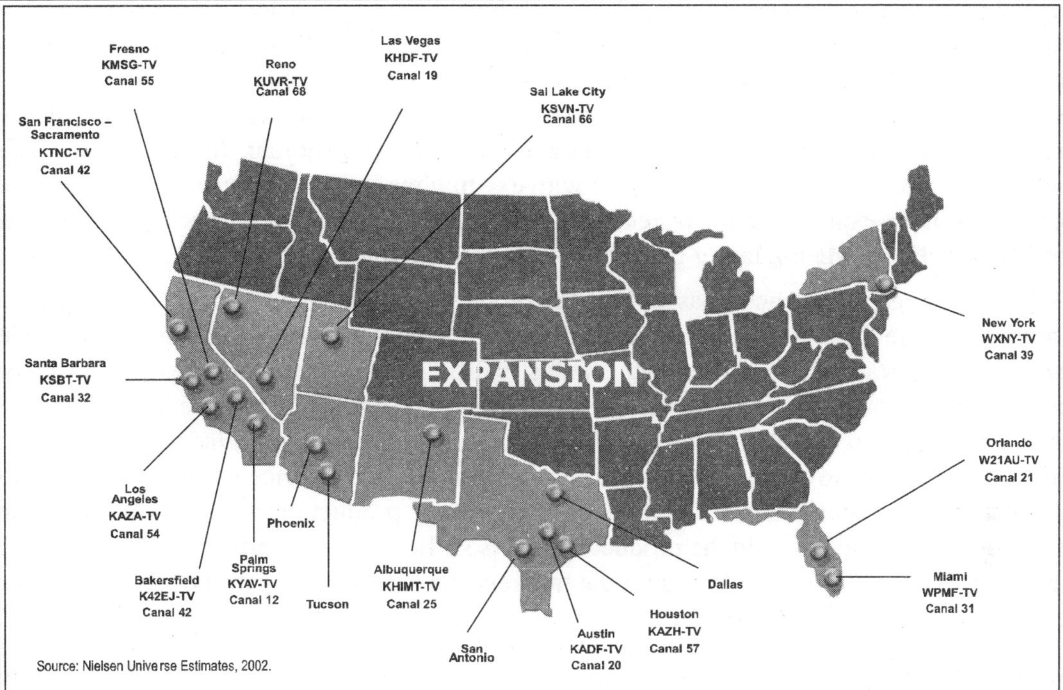

Figure 1: Expansion network of Azteca America Television to cater to the entertainment of Hispanic population

made. Stations like San Antonio, San Diego, Phoenix, Tucson, Dallas, El Paso and Victoria, TX, become part of the family.The first Azteca America Affiliation's Convention was held on February 6 and 7, 2003 and was a complete success due to the participation of all of the Stations.

Azteca America broadcasting network focused on the U.S. Hispanic market, affiliated two new stations in Arizona, KPSW Channel 43 in Phoenix and KQBN Channel 14 in Tucson during July 2003. Azteca America reaches 26 markets, covering 63% of U.S. Hispanic households, introducing its programming to the ninth and twenty-fourth largest Hispanic markets in the United States, respectively. As a result, Azteca America now covers 12 of the top 15 Hispanic markets. It is estimated that by the end of 2003, Azteca America will have a coverage of about 74% of the US Hispanic Population as exhibited in Appendix 'A'.

ADVERTISING ISSUES

Internet advertising has emerged as one of the competitors for the television industry to get sponsors for the programs, general merchandise and event advertisers. If the money is right, many online publishers are willing to strike whatever sort of partnerships an advertiser might want. The Internet is also a highly selective, cost effective media with greater measurability than any other media. Despite higher global reach Internet is not a local mainstream media yet. Traditional advertising is consumed passively, yet on the Internet, the users have to actively select an advertisement. This changes the way advertisers generate and re-train customers. To persuade visitors to revisit and spend time on the web site the advertisers must fulfill real customer needs on continuous basis. This requires clear objectives and targeting. Informative quality content, advertisement with interesting entertainment or direct sales possibilities can add value to the customer. In terms of advertising economics, the Internet can already compete with existing media, both in response as measured by click-through and in exposure as measured by cost per thousand. Moreover the economics of internet provide better effects when a target consumer segment is defined.

TV-advertising market encompasses both the product markets and the market for TV programs. It is argued that the TV industry has several idiosyncratic characteristics that need to be modeled, and show that the strategic interaction in this industry differs from other industries in many respects. It has been found that a move from a TV monopoly to a TV duopoly may reduce both the total number of viewers and the total amount of TV advertising. A softening of price competition in each product market results in more investment in programming, higher price per advertising slot, and more advertising. A reduction in the number of firms in each product market may have the opposite effect, if the price competition in the product market is sufficiently soft initially. It may be observed that even small asymmetries between product markets can cause large asymmetries with respect to which producers buy advertising on TV.[13]

"Probably in a year we pruned to raise; in another one, to lower, but the great opportunity for us is to give a jump to the United States", said Luis Echarte, president and CEO of Azteca America.

TV Azteca has 40% of the televising market in Mexico. The existing production does not cost much to take the best successes there. The Association of Hispanic Agencies of Publicity (AHAA) has estimated that the total the advertising cost to the announcements in Spanish would be 3.2 % of the total advertising costs. The performance of TV Azteca in terms of production of programs during 1998-2002 is exhibited in Figure 2. It is committed to provide programs to the American company until 2017, in exchange for 15% of shareholder. TV Azteca paid to Pappas Telecasting Group $116 million dollars to buy 25% of three stations and to form a television network that would affiliate more local TV stations, as stated before. After affiliating 17 stations affiliated, the

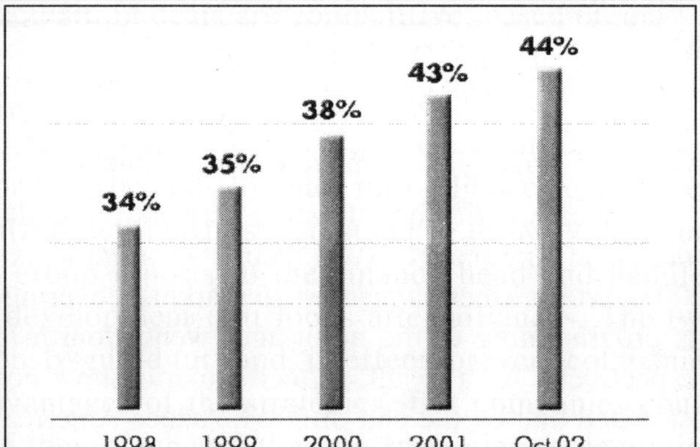

Figure 2 Production of programs by TV Azteca

13 Nilssen, T, Sorgard, L.: TV Advertising, Programming Investments, and Product-Market Oligopoly, Norwegian School of Economics and Business Administration, *Working Paper* # 6, 2000, pp 1-46

size of the National Group would be big enough to sell advertising campaigns hopefully by 2004 according to Echarte, the President and CEO of Azteca America. But reaching only 56 percent of the population Azteca America is far from competing with Univision that reaches at 97% from the Hispanics with a rating of between 77% and 84%, and 120 advertisers.

Plan of Azteca is to gain 20% of the market in four years. Ingrid Smart, President of the AHAA describes the goal as "aggressive". NBC, the new owner of Telemundo, second television transmitter of the Hispanic market, have money to invest. Also three other chains of Spanish language by cable television exist and about 10 or 15 independent channels exist in the market.

Traditional advertising-break consists of a number of short video sequences (commercial-spots) that have been inserted in the broadcast stream from the transmission point. Every single household within the broadcast footprint watches the same spots, in the same sequence at the same time. Media planners acknowledge the fact that a large percentage of the viewers do not belong to their target group. Showing irrelevant advertising to people that may neither be interested in the suggested offerings, nor be of interest to the advertiser, has become the norm in the broadcasting and advertising industry. However, successful in financing the media industry, the traditional mass communication model of advertising is growing inadequate to provide a relevant experience to television viewers. Television advertising is irritating to a lot of people-research has shown that as much as 30% of people zap during the advertising-break.

For many years production companies have specialized in syndicating "generic" or "tagged" television commercials for specific businesses such as automobile dealers, banks, etc. There have always been two major problems with these syndicated commercials. One, they always have a non-localized "canned" look; and two; the production and marketing expenses have kept prices high and unaffordable. Product placement, advertising seamlessly integrated into movie or television productions, is a common way of partially financing media projects. So is product licensing, where television programs and movies are vehicles for marketing products associated with them. Cross-marketing, a growing phenomenon, has made media advertising to children particularly insidious.

SALES FORCE DEPLOYMENT OF THE COMPANY

Sales Force is conformed by 3 persons in the US. They have to prospect, visit and close sales of the prospective clients for advertising in the Network channel. On the other hand, in Mexico, TV Azteca's Sales Department has more structured sales strategy. There is a Manager and a Sales Representative in charge of prospecting possible clients to advertise in the US Hispanic market, usually to clients that are already clients of TV Azteca having products that might be advertised and sold in the US market. Most of the few firms that have closed some of their advertising budget to do it, are worldwide companies which have products in the US as well as Mexico, and have the distribution coverage as well. The organization of sales force of the company is exhibited in Figure 3. The Manager is supported by the entire Sales Force of TV Azteca., which is divided into two divisions: National Sales and Local Sales. National Sales is formed by 40 persons, distributed as follows:

- 4 Directors
- 12 Managers
- 24 Sales Representatives

Local Sales, has a team of about 30 persons, which are divided into five regions:

- North
- Center
- South-Pacific
- South
- Mexico City

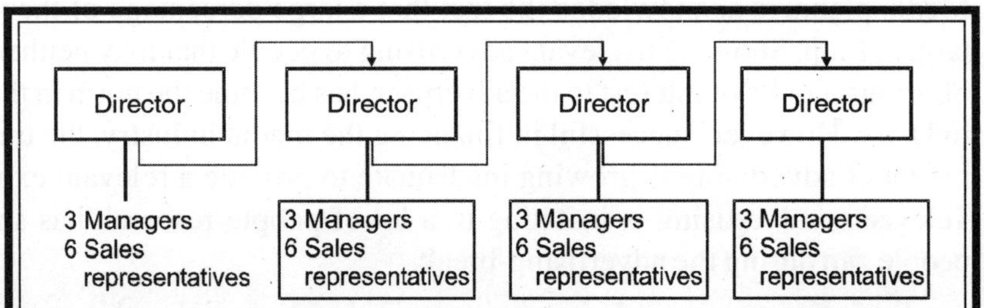

Figure 3: Organization of sales force of Azteca America

Their regional clients are usually small companies with a reduced budget for advertising that don't have enough money to advertise nationwide. Unfortunately, the Sales Force is dedicated to attend more than 700 clients which advertise in Mexico's TV media, therefore there isn't much time and compensation for them to dedicate part of their time to attend US sales goals. Moreover, to the fact that US Sales Force is unlimited to fulfill US Industry market that could be a prospect to advertise their products in Azteca America makes it really hard to achieve Azteca America's goal of sales and growth.

PERFORMANCE IN HISPANIC AMERICAN MARKET

TV AZTECA spends around $250 million dollars in production per year and over 8,000 hours of original programming with 8 new popular stories/soaps (over 1,000 hours of original stories/soaps programs) per annum. Programming is distributed in Mexico, Central and South America and throughout Europe. Working hand in hand with TV Azteca to bring U.S. Hispanics the best entertainment, news, and sports programming in the language they prefer:

- Reaching an upscale audience and growing.
- Providing creative advertising and marketing platforms for advertisers.
- Serving the Hispanic community.
- By the Hispanics and for the Hispanics, Azteca America... (Es Tu Casa[14])

14 It is your home

- Innovative and Passionate Popular stories/soaps
  - Created for a family audience
  - Real-life, contemporary scenarios
  - Urban settings
  - Contemporary issues
  - Oriented to youth as well as adults

In the beginning of 1999, to get established in the USA Hispanic market, TV Azteca had 3 possible strategies to choose from:

- Keep selling individually produced shows to the USA television companies.
- Look for an strategic alliance with Telemundo to obtain the value added programming for the programs it produced.
- Create the third Spanish Television Network in US throughout signing long term contracts with small independent groups of local TV stations owners, and/or acquiring TV stations with a financial partner.

Entertainment programs of Azteca America has emerged as bouquet of variety and carrying the original ideas that had successful telecast in the Mexican TV network. The programs carried the psychological tint of acceptance as they were woven around the Hispanic talks, comedy, leisure and gender issues. The core concepts of the entertainment programs of Azteca America may be delineated as under:

- Talk, comedy, game, women's magazines, reality
- Newest emerging Spanish-language network
- 100% owned by TV Azteca, premier Mexican TV network
- TV Azteca… a brand associated with high quality programming throughout the Spanish-speaking world
  - Owns and operates two networks and over 540 stations in Mexico
- Effective advertising solutions
  - Only US Spanish-language network to fully own its content
  - Allows for creative marketing strategies and platforms
- Community-driven
  - Providing a voice for the Hispanic community

Programs were aimed at a high quality entertainment for the Hispanic population as the TV Azteca owns and operates two networks and over 540 stations in Mexico. The Azteca America, as a media company has been positioned as a community driven organization and operates through the creative marketing strategies. The company has identified four segments of the viewers- households, youth, children and executives. The programs for the youth viewers include informed commentary on the athletic events that the Hispanics are thrilled of, has been brought to viewers with cutting-edge technology and production capabilities. The programs for company to develop some social programs that create social benefits to the Hispanic society. The volume and variety of the programs produced by the principal company TV Azteca in Mexico is exhibited in Figure 3.

Vive Sin Drogas (Drugs Free Life)

This program is made throughout public service announcements warning teens of the dangers of illegal drugs. This program coveys with the help of community leaders, drug de-addiction experts and those with first hand experience, through live coverage of schools and communities envisaging the message to stay off from drugs. This program was launched in Los Angeles in November 2002.

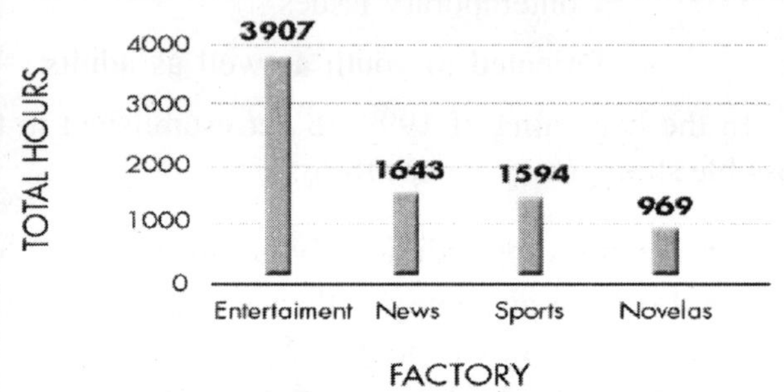

Figure 3: Production of programs by TV Azteca (until October 2002)

El Juguetón

During the holiday season, Azteca America's talent urges viewers to donate toys to needy children and families. In 2001, El Juguetón's 6th anniversary in Mexico, TV Azteca presented 1,600,000 toys to children who would otherwise have no gifts. By 2003, it accounted for more than 3 million toys. This program was also launched in Los Angeles in Christmas 2002.

STRATEGY PERSPECTIVES FOR FUTURE

To survive, a company must no longer trust existing trends or "strong signals;" instead, it needs to identify "weak signals" - those which announce future changes in their strategic landscape. Shifts occur at the point where an industry or an environment is about to change dramatically and where the rules for playing the game are being transformed into drastically different ones. This needs to be analysed from the point of view of competing media companies, cable networks and DVD marketers in the Hispanic customer segment in America. A key success factor in screening trends is to develop a solid filter to be used to sifter through the immense mass of information available. This filter can be much broader than just observing competitors or technology trends. It usually includes the notion of ideas and competencies. The process of screening trends is especially developed in companies which have understood that, often the answers about the future are already here, but need to be uncovered. Further, benchmarking consists in comparing your company or industry to the "Best-in-class" to understand which areas to develop or competencies to acquire.

".......Customers want more of everything they value. If they value low cost they want it lower. If they value convenience they want it easier and faster. If they look for state of the art they want it first and want to push the envelope. If they need expert advice they want more time and dedicated effort and investment".[15] Under such circumstances what should the entertainment company do to

15 Rajagopal : Marketing Governance: A Conceptual Analysis, *Working Paper,* ASCI, India, 2000

be the market leader in the given segment? One of the approaches gaining the competitive advantage may be to improve the position of the business within the industry by way of acquisitions and augmenting the market share enhancing the scale of operations and competitive positioning. The media companies have to be innovative and create new opportunities - new products, services, and markets.

Developments in information technology, affect the performance of marketing decision-makers through different routes. Advances in information technology enhance the possibilities to collect data and to generate information for supporting marketing decision-making. Potentially, this will have a positive impact on decision-making performance. Managerial expertise will favour the transformation of data into market insights. However, as the cognitive capabilities of marketing managers are limited, increasing amounts of data may also increase the complexity of the decision-making context. In turn, increased complexity enhances the probability of biased decision processes (e.g., the inappropriate use of heuristics) thereby negatively affecting the decision-making performance. Marketing management support systems, also being the result of advances in information technology, are the tools that can help marketers to benefit from the data explosion. These systems are able to increase the value of data and, at the same time, make decision-makers less vulnerable to biased decision processes. One of the research analysis leads to the expectation that the combination of marketing data, managerial judgment, and marketing management support systems will be a powerful factor for improving marketing management.[16]

Among many other strategies built around the competitive and survival situations in the media business for overpowering the market, Adrian J. Slywotzky[17] said that "*Think about it a bit. Let it stew. Play with the ideas and continually refocus on the implications for your organization. Make notes. Discuss with colleagues and customers.....*"

---

16 G.H. van Bruggen, A. Smidts and B. Wierenga : *The Powerful Triangle of Marketing Data, Managerial Judgment, and Marketing Management Support Systems,* Erasmus Research Institute of Management (ERIM), Erasmus University Rotterdam, Discussion Paper 35, 2000

17 Adrian J. Slywotzky : *The Art of Profitablity,* Warren Books Inc, September 2002

REFERENCES

Bass, Frank M. Pessemier E. A. Tigert, D J.: A Taxonomy of Magazine Readership Applied to Problems in Marketing Strategy and Media Selection, *Journal of Business,* 42 (3), 1969, 337-63

Häckner, Jonas & Nyberg, Sten, 2000 : *Price Competition, Advertising and Media Market Concentration,* Research Papers in Economics 2000:3, Stockholm University, Department of Economics

Masih, Rumi : An Empirical Analysis of the Demand for Commercial Television Advertising, *Applied Economics,* 31 (2), 1999, pp 149-163

Shachar, Ron, Anand, Bharat N. : The Effectiveness and Targeting of Television Advertising, *Journal of Economics & Management Strategy,* 7 (3), 1998, pp 363-396

Spence, A. Michael & Owen, Bruce, 1977. Television Programming, Monopolistic Competition, and Welfare, *The Quarterly Journal of Economics,* Vol. 91 (1) pp. 103-26.

APPENDIX 'A'

Coverage of Television Network in the Hispanic Market in USA by the Aize of Households

Hips. TV HH Market Rank	*Market*	*Hispanic TV HH Coverage*	*Hispanic TV HH (000)*
1	Los Angeles	16.30%	1,585
4	Houston	4.10%	399
8	SF–Oakland–SJ	3.26%	317
15	Sacram-Stock-Modesto	1.87%	182
55	Reno	0.25%	25
33	Salt Lake City	0.56%	55
19	Orlando	1.20%	117
25	Las Vegas	0.93%	91
11	Ablbuquerque	2.13%	207
21	Austin	1.07%	104
52	Wichita	0.30%	29
43	Palm Springs (19 Cable)	0.38%	37
3	Miami	5.66%	550
2	New York	11.31%	1,100
31	West Palm Beach–Ft. Pierce	0.58%	56
30	Bakersfield	0.62%	60
38	Santa Barbara	0.43%	42
14	Fresno–Visalia	1.94%	189
84	Victoria	0.10%	10
6	Dallas	3.33%	324
7	San Antonio	3.27%	318
9	Phoenix	2.53%	246
24	Tucson	0.98%	95
12	San Diego	1.98%	192
13	El Diego	1.96%	191
5	Chicago	3.95%	384
26	Altanta	0.89%	86
10	Harlingen–Wsclo–Brnsvl–McA	2.39%	232
	Total	**74.25%**	**7,223**

Source: *Nielsen Estimates on Television Industry, 2002*

CHAPTER 7

MARKETING RESEARCH

CHAPTER FOCUS

- *To understand the tools and techniques of marketing research and their application in assessing the marketing functions in a competitive environment,*
- *To develop skills on qualitative marketing research and developing the market research proposals, focus group analysis, questionnaires and analysis of observation, and*
- *To learn designing marketing research projects, data collection, quantitative analysis techniques and reporting.*

Today, there is increasing competition in the markets. It has therefore become necessary to understand the internal and external dynamics that consist of an inter-product and inter-organization marketing-mix strategy in optimizing profit and the volume of sales. The consumer oriented factors constitute the external dynamics of marketing. A marketing manager has to explore all possibilities of developing an effective plan for launching and sustaining the product in the market and in doing, so he needs a clear perspective based on the information analyzed. This necessary step of information collection for important decision-making variables and an explorative analysis forms the core of marketing research. It is a tool used in formulating marketing strategies and for reforming plans based on the extensive feedbacks. Marketing research, hence, may be defined a as systematic gathering, recording and analyzing of data on the variables of marketing goods and services.

SCOPE OF MARKETING RESEARCH

Marketing research is concerned with the factors, that are directly involved in marketing of goods and services, and it includes the study of the effectiveness of the marketing-mix, advertising strategies, competition and consumer behavior. It not only helps in formulating strategies suitable for market intervention but also guides in perspective planning by analyzing formation for future projections.

Marketing research is largely carried out on the basis of a consumer market survey, that is, conducted by administering structured schedules or questionnaires in person or mailing them to sample respondents, organizing syndicate discussions, pilot tests, etc. All medium and large scale companies engaged in consumer products marketing invariably allocate 0.5% to 2% of their net sales resources for conducting marketing research for future planning. Most capital goods oriented companies invest a larger share in conducting marketing research. There are many decisions that are based on marketing research (analyzed via quantified data collected on vital market indicators). These are:

Product - Market Decisions

1. Identifying market characteristics
2. Product-mix research
3. Determining product sustainability
4. Innovative product range
5. Preferential and profitable positioning of products
6. Distribution analysis
7. Pricing strategies impact analysis
8. Product testing - pilot studies
9. Market share analysis
10. Short and long range forecasting for price and demand of the product
11. Sales trend analysis
12. Competition pattern
13. Consumer-behavior analysis in reference to price, product-mix and comparative advantages over other products
14. Assessment of impact advertising and
15. Analysis of gender preferences of products, etc.

Country Decision (For international marketing)

1. Entry Decision
2. Financial Risk
3. Legal risk
4. Opportunities
5. Production and marketing costs

Marketing research is conducted scientifically using effective statistical techniques, today. An effective information system would make the marketing research a more analytical, fact finding and prolific decision-making exercise. The scope for marketing research is very wide and experimented with identifying potential markets as well as determining the marketing-mix. There are many typologies, argued upon the marketing research scholars. However, the generally accepted framework details the scope of marketing research on both markets and the marketing-mix. However, marketing research orientation shifts according to different typologies. Motivational research is very significant, and it studies the psychographics or qualitative perspectives of customer life style. This is a continuum of new skills and ideas that are accredited to marketing research concepts and practices. Marketing research thus makes important contributions to the management by supporting decision-making to set objectives, developing an action plan, executing the plan and controlling its performance.

MARKETING RESEARCH PROCESS

Marketing research has two distinct dimensions that are governed by the exploratory, descriptive and casual approaches. Exploratory studies are based on primary data pertaining to identified samples focusing on a set of objectives. Such studies are generally woven around a hypothesis and attempt to generate new ideas to serve the objectives of the research. Descriptive marketing research tries to describe the magnitude and direction of the problem and brings out the output for a logical debate on the marketing managers' floor. A research plan determining data sources, methodology, tools, and sample design and data collection methods needs to be formulated after setting objectives. The data collection process has to be initiated from primary or secondary or both sources administering a checklist and questionnaire. The data should then be subjected to an appropriate analysis in view of the set objectives and its findings are to be presented in a draft report. International marketing research is processed in the following steps:

Step 1

Determine Management Level

Corporate

Regional

Local

Step 2

Determine Type of Marketing Research

Decision

Strategic

Tartical

Step 3

Determine Information Requirements

Primary

Secondary

Paricipatory

Step 6

Collect Data

Personal interviews

Mail questionnaires

Focul groups

Step 7

Update Data Bank

Revalidate data

Collect most recent data

Prune obsolete information

Step 8

Analyze Data

Use statistical analysis

Test results

Adjust to models

Step 4

Develop Research Design

Indentify problem

Evolve Sampling Design

Identify Variables

Designing Reasearch Instrument

Step 5

Examine Data Bands

Pooled categorized sources

Generic sources

Commercial soruices

Step 9

Present Report

Derive most appropriate inferences

Illustrate the analysis results

Exhibit results from visuals

Develop executive summary, and

List action points for managers

Step 10

Integrate Results and Recommendations into management decision–making

It is necessary for a firm to have a clear perception on the research objectives as it is the guiding tool for the entire process of market research. Let us assume a multinational marketer is interested in finding out the potential market for a brand of yogurt in England and Thailand, The problem definition in the two countries will have to be stated differently. In the United Kingdom, the yogurt might be primarily perceived by the consumers as a healthful and relaxing product to be used prior to retiring. In Thailand, the research would determine, if yogurt would be considered mainly as energy food to start the day. After the problem has been defined, the necessary information may be found and method to obtain, it must be determined. In some cases, the study may be confined to secondary data, that is, published information that has been collected elsewhere. Such data may be available free (for example, government statistics), for a price (for example, syndicated research findings), or through restricted distribution sources (for example, trade association statistics). Making decisions about operating a business in any country specifically requires information pertaining to political, financial and legal indicators. Besides these, data related to infrastructure, duty and taxes and general economic variables of the country are also required to be analyzed. The risk factors associated with operating a country specific business in the international order are also a prerequisite of international marketing research. The product specific data is required to assess the market potential and profitability with reference to a specific country or region. The primary data is collected from the earmarked sample that also administers a questionnaire in person or through mail. However, it has been observed that mailing responses are often discouraging and do not exceed 20 percent of the sample size. The secondary sources of data are the published statistics in internal reports, government publications, periodicals, books and commercial sources (like reports of the chamber of commerce, trade associations, quoted data from earlier research work, etc.) The methodology of study comprises of identifying data sources, research approaches, tools, sampling design and data collection methods. This part forms the principal component of a research plan.

Rise in consumer health awareness is driving innovation in the global cosmetics and toiletries industry, over the last five years, consumer health awareness has increased significantly,

> around the world due to a growing focus on health issues in the media and an increasing investment in health initiatives on the part of governments, according to the research from Euromonitor International. While it is clear that increasing consumer concerns for health and wellness have obvious repercussions for markets such as packaged food and Over-The-Counter (OTC) healthcare, the study has also found that, it has become an increasingly influential factor in the cosmetics and toiletries market. Things went a step further last year when L'Oréal and Procter & Gamble forged joint ventures with Nestlé and Pharmavite respectively to expand into OTC dietary supplements, encouraged by trends indicating that consumers are increasingly keen to co-ordinate health regimens with beauty practices. The Nestlé/L'Oréal joint venture heralded the launch of Innéov Fermeté (an anti-ageing formula), while Procter & Gamble and Pharmavite jointly launched Olay Vitamins. More recently roles were reversed somewhat as Healthspan, a Guernsey-based mail order vitamin supplier for the UK market, launched a dedicated range of make-up and skin care products which target women aged between 45 and 60. The research shows that the trend is widespread in the US market, as US consumers are becoming increasingly convinced that beauty starts with "wellness". Retailers are increasingly linking their beauty lines to non-beauty products, positioning health products, like vitamins, in close proximity to cosmetics. Manufacturers for their part are introducing cosmetic lines that tout claims often found in OTC products, like Sally Hansen's Healing Beauty Fast and Flawless make-up line, with products featuring anti-wrinkling and acne-fighting ingredients. The market is clearly strong for cosmetics and toiletries products that associate themselves with wellness, with many lines now routinely infused with vitamins and increasingly with natural and herbal extracts.[1]

Observation research approach is commonly used for formulating descriptive marketing research plans. The focus-group and participatory approaches are useful exercises for exploratory marketing research that does not have complete perspective results. The survey method has proved to be an effective research approach for exploratory studies for analyzing data. This makes use of quantitative methods leading to a distinctive analysis of factors and future projections. Experimental research attempts to studying the impact on the control group through different applications of business models, checks, reformative goals and qualitative/quantitative analysis methods to draw results. This approach is identified as one of the most scientific methods in relating a research approach with its results. However, a good marketing research approach needs to be characterized by the following qualities:

1. Scientific method
2. Originality and creativity
3. Potential to use multiple methods for cross checking the emerging results
4. Interdependence on analytical models and data sets
5. Cost of research

A marketing research plan should comprise of these qualities for drawing effective results and for preparing a useful document to be used for optimizing business propositions in and any situation.

1 Leonie Tait : Increasing interest in health and wellness drives innovation in cosmetics and toiletries, *Euromonitor International,* 11 January 2005. Web site: www.euromonitor.com

SAMPLING TECHNIQUES

Effectiveness of marketing research largely depends upon the formulation of an appropriate research design consisting of—adequate sample size, variables and proper tools—for data collection suitable to the problem given. A researcher has to collect substantial background material to conceptualize the research study before heading towards the formulation of a research design for the problem concerned. The nature of problems varies in consumer marketing research. There are many design conflicts encountered by the researcher in evolving a suitable research design. They are:

1. The sample size (Quantitative)
2. Respondents (Classified)
3. Information to be sought (Issue specific)
4. Time frame (Schedule for completion, class-intervals of time to be reserved) and
5. Tools for information collection (Interview, Mail, Telephone, etc.)

It is essential, for a marketing researcher to determine the sample size in terms of the number of respondents, regions, products, firms, etc. to be studied and the type of respondents to be covered under study. The classification of respondents, according to their income levels, locality, gender, etc. needs to be formulated prior to deciding what questions are to be asked to them. A synchronized list of issues embodying the questionnaire to be administered should be drafted with the aim of retrieving information from the sample respondents. In conducting any research, time management has considerable importance and hence, the time schedule for information retrieval should be decided. In this context, the cutting-edge of time, class-intervals, and time series issues need to be decided by the researcher. On completing the designing process, the tool(s) for data collection need to be selected. The tools of primary data collection include interviewing, mailing questionnaires, telephone conversations, etc. An integration of all these components makes a perfect research design. The details of each component are discussed as follows:

Sampling

Sampling process should begin with identifying the area of the study with reference to the section of the population to be interviewed and the spatial distribution of the respondents. This step sets the demographic and geographic boundaries of the sample design. A researcher cannot develop the sample design until the universe (area) of the study is defined. The size of the sample should be determined carefully through the medium of the questionnaire. To do this, a researcher has to find the answer for two questions in deciding an appropriate sample size. They are— (I) how large should the sample be and (ii) how the respondents should be selected. Statistically, a minimum number of 30 respondents of a homogeneous group is generally significant, whereas, the size of the heterogeneous group needs to be decided upon qualitative considerations of the sample—viz. purchasing power, the volume of products in demand, behavioral dimensions etc. in context of a consumer product. Two kinds of anticipated errors in the sampling process which often occur are:

(i) Administrative errors in carrying out the survey design. These include communication errors, flaws in the interviewing schedule, irrelevance of framed questions, etc.

(ii) Sampling errors due to the misrepresented samples, faulty selection of the universe for study and the like.

Hence, sampling needs to be done scientifically taking all error possibilities into consideration.

Sampling Techniques

There are many techniques for sampling used in marketing research. However, the correctness of the technique is subject to the nature of the problem identified for the study and to the objectives set for the same. The various sampling techniques are detailed below:

Simple Random Samplin: This method is very flexible. It is not restricted to any one type of respondents, gender, income levels and other variables. The technique allows the researcher to pick sample respondents from the universe of study irrespective of class barriers. However, the minimum and maximum sample size needs to be defined.

Multi-stage Random Sampling: This technique is a more complex form of simple random sampling which prescribes that a researcher divide the universe of the study based on selected variables such as customers by age, customers by income level, customers by sex, etc. and select the samples randomly within the categories formed. However, the minimum and maximum sample size needs to be kept in view while sampling under various categories.

Cluster Sample Design: To make the information collection effective, a researcher can group the respondents into a group or cluster. This can be done demographically or geographically or both depending upon the intensity of the data collection and the time schedule thereof.

Stratified Sampling: In this process, the respondents clusters are made in hierarchical order and sample size is determined on a proportionate basis in each stratum. For example, the sample size of customers needs to be selected with reference to different age groups. In this exercise, the customers have to be classified, according to different age-groups, and their population ascertained and proportionately sampled out using a parameter (say 5 percent). In this technique, the sample size is mostly adjusted within the strata.

Purposive Sampling: This technique is administered, according to the choice of the researcher of area, population and related variables. However, it is necessary to look into the thrust of the research for a sample design to be evolved accordingly. In this method a researcher should logically set the universe of the study and sample variables with reference to the research problem.

Quota Sampling: This is a term for representative sampling in which a researcher prescribes a quota of individuals, product, etc. to be studied and which considerably represents the segments of universe. In this technique, a common error may occur while allotting correct quota to get a significant representation of the sample for the study.

Structuring a Questionnaire

A questionnaire is defined as a set of questions related to the research problem that are used for interviewing a sample respondent. The questionnaire is generally prepared in a structured form with many types of questions. A questionnaire may include the following sets of questions:

1. Long descriptive questions
2. Two questions in one
3. Multiple choice questions
4. Closed and open-ended questions
5. Indirect questions
6. Direct questions and
7. Attitudinal questions

The open-ended questions are difficult to codify for analysis. However, they could generate a substantial input for formulating descriptive cases and observatory analysis. The multiple choice questions have the advantage of easy coding and computerized analysis but at the same time, they limit the scope of response. The direct questions are posed to respondents to get to know their view points exclusively while indirect questions attempt to measure the logical framing of responses and in cross-examining the responses of the respondents.

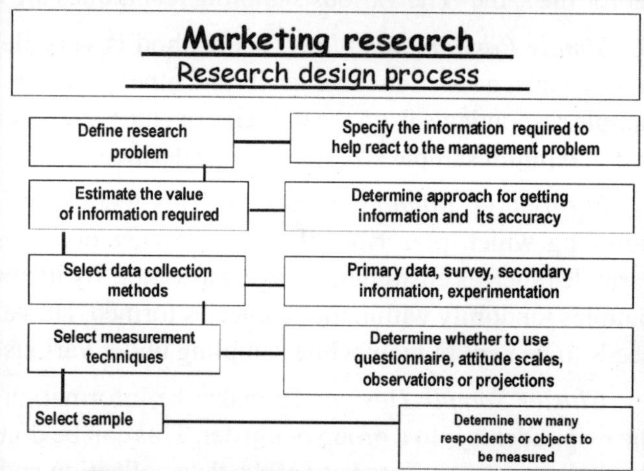

Figure 7.1 (A) Research design process

TOOLS OF DATA COLLECTION

Research tools play an important role in managing information during field work. Data collection is a process which encounters many problems while administering the questionnaire to potential respondents. Hence, a wise researcher should always pretest the questionnaire designed in a pilot survey. Data collection may be carried out through the following tools in order to ensure substantial information flow into the research. They are:

1. Personal interview
2. Mail survey
3. Telephone interview
4. Permanent mail panels, and
5. Observation

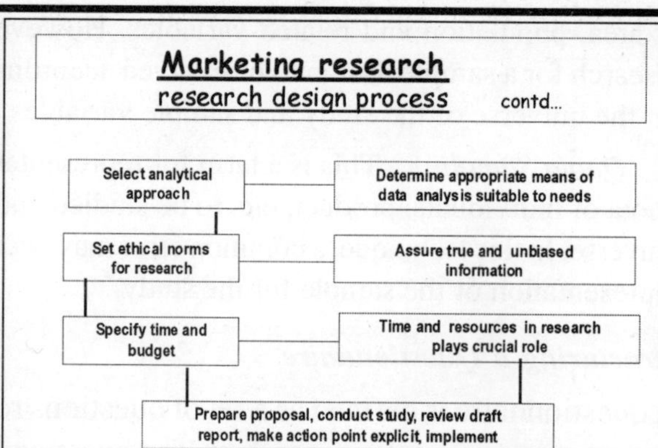

Figure 7.1 (B) marketing research

A substantial data flow can be generated in field research through personal interviews as this facilitates the documentation of expanded responses to questions posed, thus providing scope for more detailed information for analysis. On the contrary, telephone interviews are time bound and one is often left with short answers, and with codes which pose a problem in the analysis of information. Such conversations are not cost effective and cannot be applied for marketing research of consumer or popular goods and services. This tool may prove effective to contact those customers who are not easily available. Interviewing has to be managed within a short span of time. The market research design process is exhibited in Figure 7.1.

Survey conducted via mailing questionnaires needs a long time for information collection and the turn out of response is also found to be limited. However, it may be considered by the researcher as one way of placing the informer on the company's permanent mailing list for a time series information inflow scheduled for long run. Such a tool is useful in collecting time series data with flexible sample size and long term research schedules. The example of a company may be cited which was willing to monitor washing machines or water filters or Xerox machines as major products of the users through permanent mailing panels at the company office. It also helps in building up the buyer-seller relationship.

DATA PREPARATION

Data collected in the field work needs to be prepared for analysis and then summarized. This exercise helps in arranging data sets and classifying clusters for analysis. The data preparation process involves the editing of data, the coding of responses categorically, tabulation of responses into frequencies or analysis tables, graphical representation of data and analytical results and summary statements highlighting the main findings of analysis in different data sets. Editing of data involves the examination of raw data to ensure the accuracy of information and its presentation in usable form. Initial surveying of data needs to be done keeping the following issues in mind:

1. Are responses consistent?
2. Consistency of responses
3. Are the responses complete?
4. Are responses containing doubtful motives, and
5. Whether any indirect responses?

Such screening is necessary for the answers of open-ended questions. They need to be carefully classified for clustering input for analysis. However, multiple choice data formats are easy for loading and preparing sets. Editing of data also requires checking the consistency of responses to related queries. The responses have to be cross checked and a researcher should get a satisfactory presentation of information. Incomplete responses need to be sorted out and attempts should be made to extract the relevant parts of the response from the indirect phrases for presenting information effectively. In order to increase the efficacy of information desk editing, it is essential to edit the administered questionnaires at the end of the day during the field work. It helps in recapitulating the interviews held and the discussions thereof before undertaking editing work.

Coding is another exercise to be carried out in the process of data preparation. It is generally done to numerically codify the responses of open-ended questions and classifying them appropriately. The codified data is used for statistical analysis. The pre-coded questionnaires are also used for interviewing but they have a imitation in terms of restricted response options. Such formats are useful for handling large data analysis through computers. Tabulation is the process of arranging data into an illustrative form pertaining to different variables of a factor. This exhibition of cross tabulation is self explanatory to a large extent. However, the presentation of analysis results or raw data can also be done through simple tabulation techniques. Cross tabulation is one of the most popular designs for summarizing marketing research data. A researcher can identify, the statistical relationship between variables and their significance by looking at the cross tables.

DATA ANALYSIS APPROACHES

Data in an original form remains raw at any source. It needs to be fabricated to fit into the analytical design of the study. This task may be determined, according to the need that arises in usage of data for the analytical model. There are different procedures for data analysis for extracting information from a given data set. They are as follows:

Regression Analysis

This method is used to identify, the trend using a time series data of one or more variables. A researcher distinguishes the variables as dependent and independent in nature. The analysis highlights the contribution of variables to variations in the dependent variable. The analysis, if carried by two or more independent variables, is termed as multiple regression. One prerequisite for such analysis is a time-series data of the variables identified.

Discriminate Function Analysis

This method is used to determine the impact of particular variables(s) on the dependent variable. This statistical process helps in finding the discriminating variables which could be combined in a forecasting equation to lead better for the group cluster. This analysis has been used to identify and develop criteria for market segmentation, and also to examine consumer behavior with reference to brand choice.

Factor Analysis

The use of the approaches earlier discussed tended to give biased results on dependent variables due to high inter-correlations among the explanatory variables. The factor analysis attempts to provide an explanation for the correlations of a larger set of variables. This analysis may be useful to determine the attitudes of customers towards the products of a company in a given situation.

Cluster Analysis

This process is helpful in obtaining segregated results for a group of variables of a homogeneous nature. In marketing research, it is essential to set sub-groups like consumer goods, capital goods, (in product) range, people, place, income levels, etc. Analysis is done keeping in view the clustered data as one segment or factor in the statistical process.

Conjoint Analysis

This method is used for exploring the possibilities of designing and launching a new product that can attract customers. Customers are asked to rank some hypothetical products, this information is put through composite indexing and the final ranks are computed. This method is commonly used for psychometric tests and measurements in determining behavior. It is a popular approach for ranking the performance of the product as well as the company in the market. These analytical approaches support the study of identifying factors, variable correlations and interdependence in a given situation. Models help the marketing manager to come to an appropriate decision on the basis of the logical interpretation of analytical results.

The link between the dependent variable and its determinants is specified in the micro-dynamic model. The impact of product promotion activities on the volume of sales can be explained by studying the links between advertising expenditure, the number of media message insertions, the level of product awareness, usage rate, etc. through this model. The micro behavioral model hypothetically analyzes independent variables like consumers, dealers, etc. who interact and produce a report of behavior. The queuing model provides a logical base for making, such decisions in the area of time-run sales or marketing whether to make the customer wait for the product or to alter the policy in view of competitive threats. This model can be effectively used in supermarkets, transport organizations, etc. The decision making models comprise of mathematical techniques, decision theories and probability models, which are calculus and theory oriented. The game theory is also an important approach in the decision making exercise. It draws attention to the identification of alternative decisions, uncertain variables and value of different results[10].

Approaches other than those discussed above are specific to the problem. For instance, the focus group analysis based on qualitative information may be done for determining product policy. The related research and analytical approaches are as exhibited in Table 7.1

Table 7.1 Research Tools for Different Types of Analysis

Analysis areas	*Research tools*
Product Policy Decision	• Focus group
	• Survey of developing new product
	• Concept testing/test marketing
	• Product attitude data
Pricing	• Price sensitivity approaches
Distribution Decision	• Data on shopping patterns and
	• Consumer behavior
	• Distributors attitude and policy
	• Data on performance of store different store types
Advertising Decision	• Concept pre-testing
	• Evaluation and feedback analysis
	• Surveys on media habits
Sales Decisions	• Analysis of response in terms of revenue
	• Profit and image of promotional strategies

It is, however, advised in the case of international marketing research that a greater use of qualitative research techniques may be made at the initial stages of market entry in order to familiarize one set with the international environment. Further, a concrete research process can be developed, more complex if possible, and administered in different countries having a varied social, economical, political and legal environment.

MARKET INFORMATION MANAGEMENT

Market environment varies from country to country, hence the type of market information required to conduct a marketing study may vary accordingly. Under such situation it may be described that wherever a marketer is free to set prices based on competition, a detailed analysis of competition should be made. However, in a country where the price is set by the government, information on governmental cost analysis would be of greater importance. Indeed, the market environment determines the kind of information needed to do the international marketing research. Such efforts determine the different approach towards accessing the market information from domestic marketing research work. Market research for a foreign firm may be aimed for testing, entering, or leaving a market and deals with market performance, market shares, and sales analysis and forecasting. The marketing performance research broadly includes the market measurements, either to compare a company's performance against the predetermined targets or to project the possible changes in the future. The market shares of rival companies provide important information to analyze the marketing strategy for a new company. The research towards measuring the market share of a company may be conducted in reference to a company's proportion of total sales in an industry during a stipulated time, which remains usually a year. The competitor with a respectable market share will have a cost advantage over its rivals. This cost advantage can be passed on to the customers through lower prices, which in turn strengthen the company's hold on the market. The sales forecast is the single most important information to be analyzed by a company for preparing appropriate budgets.

> Monsanto has the largest market share amounting to 75 percent of the glyphosate market in Mexico and its flagship brand Faena has about 80 percent of the total market share. Faena and other glyphosates are used by the corn and other pre-plant (nursery) growers as well as citrus and other perennial crop growers in Mexico. The emergence of the private brands and generic compounds has posed significant threats to the Monsanto brands. Hence, the company is planning to re-launch an improved product Faena Full (New Faena) in a counter-move to the private brands by deploying the New Faena as a premium line extension brand to the Faena and release the New Faena along with Faena (existing). The company sought an independent market research to be conducted based on the primary investigation focusing the pricing and positioning decisions for New Faena brand of Monsanto, the most attractive herbicide for the corn and citrus crops in Mexico. The study was conducted with the following objectives:

- To identify the relative market size and potential for glyphosates in Mexico,
- To analyze the price elasticity of Faena and New Faena of Monsanto,
- To analyze the market share, volume and revenues of Faena and New Faena under the different pricing strategies of the company,

- To assess the optimal price-range for both the brands in the same product line of the company,
- To document the growers' perceptions on the factors of marketing-mix associated with the glyphosates and the Monsanto Brands, and
- To discuss analytically the perceived strengths and weaknesses of the Faena and the New Faena of Monsanto.

Furthermore, the Mexican market is broadly segmented into two sets of growers in both the crop types. The first segment consists of those growers who pay a discounted price around $52 Pesos per litre (anti-generic buyers) and the other segment of the buyers who pay the list price of $ 75 Pesos per litre. This price differentiation issue has been the principal factor to divide the users segments and product portfolios. The corporate objective of this study is to offer strategic solutions to the company on deploying the New Faena as a premium line extension brand or replacement brand for the Faena (existing) and determining the optimal pricing and appropriate positioning. The primary data has been collected from 551 growers actively using the herbicide with generic compound glyphosate for the corn and citrus crops. The data was collected through the dealers of Monsanto located in Mexico City and adjacent states by administering a short and purposeful questionnaire. The informal opinion of the dealers on the brands of Monsanto has also been documented.[2]

A company operating overseas must often decide which product lines it should add, drop, or rejuvenate. These decisions require a variety of information towards conducting both product-line research and individual product research. A firm may also seek marketing research on an individual product in reference to its movements through the life cycle, since different marketing programs must be developed for every stage. It is important to identify the existing stage of a product so as to choose the appropriate marketing program. Marketing research can be of real value for an international firm in identifying a product's life cycle in different countries. The multinational companies generally consult promotion research in order to select appropriate advertising copy and make the best media selection in the host country. Promotion research is designed specifically for application in advertising and personal selling. Besides, the firm should also look for knowing appropriate channel for distributing the products and services. The distribution research consists of channel research and location research which provides information on the availability of channels and their relative desirability. The location research may be helpful in determining the decisions about warehousing, inventory, and transportation. Another important area of research for the foreign firm is on pricing as, it is necessary to know the prevailing competitor's strategies in order to set appropriate prices. A strong market research towards information about the ability of consumers to pay, about dealer reaction, and about the effect of price on demand is necessary to determine the competitive pricing strategies for firm in the host country. Such studies that measure the public perception of a product's quality in relation to price also help in making pricing decisions and a company sets the prices of its products to meet both short-term and long-term objectives accordingly.

2 Rajagopal: Product Portfolio Management and Pricing Strategy of Faena : The Monsanto Experience in Mexico, ITESM, *Discussion Paper*, 2003

MONITORING AND EVALUATION RESEARCH IN MARKETING

Monitoring and Evaluation in marketing is a new discipline, which may broadly be classified as a component of development planning. It is an important tool for assessing, the physical and financial progress of product marketing in developing markets where the product is relatively new and yet to make customers familiar with its usage. Though 'monitoring' is an old concept, the 'evaluation' approach began with the new experiments in production and technology extension in the areas of modern consumer products and services. Monitoring and evaluation studies helps us understand the status of the product in the market and the prospect of cultivating better ways and means of distribution, pricing, promotion and product-mix strategies for a company on the basis of the consumer feedback. The monitoring and evaluation analysis helps in determining the trend of consumer behavior, volume of sales and related variables. Behaviorally, monitoring and evaluation may be defined as learning dynamics in the planning and management of marketing development projects. Much of it is still undergoing the process of 'trial and error'. Global concern for business development has led to close competition of product standards and administering customer-oriented strategies for accrediting the product and the company with the welfare business theory. In attempting to establish such theories, one of the important factors to be considered is evolving an efficient marketing-mix system which is a complex and important parameter that determines growth in business. Thus, monitoring and evaluation studies have vital role to play in reconciling the business administrative tasks within a competitive environment.

> It has been observed through the market research studies[3] that value sales of toilet paper increased by 1% in 2003, after experiencing five years of decline and despite Japan not having recovered from the more than decade long recession. This growth was primarily due to a price increase by the major manufacturers in autumn 2002. Although consumers spent less on toilet paper during the economic downturn, it is difficult to minimize usage, thus value sales rose. Most standard and luxury toilet papers also come in scented rolls. Aromatherapy is a popular fashion in the home, encompassing bath and shower products, body moisturizers and scented toilet paper. Manufacturers are also adding prints to toilet paper, which consumers can use to brighten up their bathrooms. The Elleair range of toilet paper from Daio is available in a number of different prints, such as rose or lavender, to match the scents. Standard toilet rolls are also available in different colors, so that consumers can match the color schemes of their bathrooms. It has been forecast that toilet paper value sales will increase by 9% in real terms between 2003 and 2008. Major manufacturers raised toilet paper prices in autumn 2002, and it is possible that further rises may follow before 2008.

Another major impetus to the growing interest in monitoring and evaluation is based on development concerns in marketing management. It is used as a tool to probe the failure and success factors that are responsible for successful/unsuccessful strategies. The flows in decision-making can be understood from the marketing evaluation reports, which would help to draw lessons for the future and to build-up appropriate alternative strategies. Marketing management is an interdisciplinary concept which

3 Leonie Tait : Luxury toilet paper growth in Japan, *Euromonitor International,* 22 October, 2004.

needs integration, as very often, several distinct components are administered by separate agencies. Monitoring and evaluation play a crucial role in the co-ordination of the marketing plan implementation. Lessons drawn from monitoring and evaluation help in identifying the gaps in the existing approach and aid the designing of alternative projects.

Structural Components

Monitoring and evaluation are the analytical methods applied to relevant data and information in order to get feedback reports of the existing implementation pattern of the project or scheme. It is sometimes essential to have a monitoring and evaluation unit, at various distribution points to monitor demand and supply status, customer orientation and other behavior issues. The specific tasks of the monitoring and evaluation unit are given below:

(i) To monitor the flow of goods and services to the terminals from production centers via the established backward and forward linkages

(ii) To evolve accuracy in data and information flow to analyze the feedback and

(iii) To evaluate the marketing project and to study the impact thereof on the target group to build up alternative approaches for better implementation and outcome.

Ideally, in a company, the monitoring and evaluation structure (with reference to marketing management) should be situated at marketing regions under the charge of a monitoring and evaluation manager vested with the task of periodical monitoring of demand, supply, pricing, quality, retailing and other related matters. He should be assisted by a statistical assistant. However, this structure is subject to the turnover and marketing research potential of the company. This unit is, by and large, concerned with the data pertaining to physical and financial targets and achievement. However, the feedback on marketing is also to be considered at the same time. Thus, a monitoring and evaluation unit in a potential company would be very helpful to developing marketing plans for indigenous products of the region, through effective monitoring and evaluation research. The monitoring and evaluation unit in such agencies can be relatively small depending on the area of operation and of location in the administrative hierarchy. In fact, the monitoring and evaluation unit should form an integral part of the marketing research unit set up and should also serve as the Marketing Planning Secretariat of the companies, individually or in a cluster. A small and compact team is preferable in most cases when compared to large units as supervision would become a problem in the long run. The monitoring and evaluation head should preferably be a senior-level manager in the management hierarchy. The task of designing a monitoring and evaluation system for a marketing project should start in the embryonic stage itself.

SWOT ANALYSIS

It is observed that no product marketing is effective in the long run unless the modifications in marketing approaches are properly carried out. There is a need to develop self-appraisal mechanisms within the product - marketing system to acquaint oneself with the existing strength, weakness; opportunities and threats (SWOT) of the product in the market. Such analysis has to be done with reference to prevailing market conditions for the product. The Table 7.2 explains the areas of SWOT analysis for achieving better marketing efficiency. The companies may restructure the production and marketing design for their products on the basis of weaknesses and threats in order to explore better opportunities and to achieve more strength in the product market.

Table 7.2 Areas of SWOT Analysis

Strength	*Weakness*	*Opportunities*	*Threats*
• Production recognition	• Product Recognition	• Uninterrupted entry	• Neck competition
• Long standing in market	• Short span	• Weak competition	• Fashion advertisements
• Consistency in price, quality and supply	• Pricing mismatch	• Substitutes and complementary products	• Contemporary marketing mechanism
• Effective distribution network	• Product design	• Access for MIS and CAS	• Frequent shifts in demand
• Strong Market Information System (MIS) and Consumer Awareness System (CAS)	• Product transformation system	• High density marketing area	• High cost of marketing
	• Risk		• Political and technological threats
	• Low market investment		
	• Poor accessibility to market		

Product marketing has a tertiary environment comprising of the Social, Technological, Economic and Political sectors (STEP) which affect the marketing of products indirectly. These factors together with vested interests provide scope for developing a capitalist environment by interrupting the inflow of products to potential markets which in turn provides an opening for the products to capture these markets through the STEP approaches. The STEP effect is common for the new product entries that put the customers into indecisiveness often. The power structure of capitalist industries operates with a strong resistance in competitive markets and even dilutes state intervention to a large extent. It would help to protect the consumer system within the framework of STEP to avoid marketing interruption at the premature and mature stage of product cycle.

QUALITATIVE MARKET RESEARCH

There are many forms of conducting qualitative research in marketing. Of these, focus group analysis and exploratory research are commonly used by the international market research firms. In foreign markets, focus groups have the advantage of being relatively inexpensive, can be completed quickly, and can reach local pockets of the total market. Unfortunately, they can also constitute a non-representative sample because the typical screening criteria are incorrect in the new environment or are not implemented correctly. Generally the non-random sample sizes of focus groups are best fit to discuss the issues of common interests. The participants of the focus groups are paid for their time investment, usually a small amount. The compensation to the focus groups participants are typically US $2.5 in the United States, about the same in Europe. However, the amount varies by city and by respondents' occupation, more than by country. It is necessary to provide all freedom to the participants of the focus group during the process of discussion on the predetermined issues and the role of moderator should be minimized. Such open house situation would provide an unbiased environment to the participants for holding discussion on the given issue. A French company sent the videotapes of five focus groups to a Latin American client, who was surprised to observe the dominating attitude of the moderator toward his respondents. The moderator, not without pride, explained to the perplexed sponsor that he usually dealt with corporate customers for industrial products, not teenagers discussing audio tape design.

There are many cultural aspects affecting the application of the kind of direct questioning involved in the typical consumer survey. In high context cultures the idea that one can understand consumers from their responses to a formal survey is naive. Open ended questions are often left blank by respondents in hierarchical cultures who are not used to explaining their reasoning or are afraid of being too transparent. The response pattern and the data reliability factor vary in many countries as the way respondents generally behave indifferently to a stranger (interviewer). Another type of qualitative research may be conducting a *general survey* through an open ended questionnaire and make a contents analysis at the end of the survey. Surveys of relatively large random samples drawn from a sampling frame of representative product users constitute the "meat and potatoes" on descriptive market research. Whether administered by mail, phone, or in person, such surveys are used for a variety of marketing purposes, including segmentation and positioning, concept testing, and customer satisfaction and competitive product evaluation. But the problems with survey research methods in certain markets have been well documented. A major problem associated with surveys may be towards the attitude of the respondents toward the study. In Latin American and East-Asian societies, there will be prospective respondents who refuse to divulge any opinions simply because they "do not want to be taken advantage of," distrusting the function of market research. In more risky cases people will consent to participate only to fake their responses so as to distort findings. To handle these problems of the non-cooperation of respondents, the firm needs to thoroughly understand the general sentiments of the respondents in the local market and frame the questionnaire accordingly. However, it is also a good idea to monitor the process by observing some pilot interviews if at all possible.

> World Bank research project[4] was aimed at studying the Vietnam's recent success in promoting economic growth, reducing poverty, and raising living standards with the aim of providing policy lessons for other low-income countries. Most economists and other social scientists would agree that economic growth is essential for improving household welfare and that the form of that growth has important implications for poverty reduction. Yet this consensus still leaves many questions unanswered. Two stand out: What policies promote broad-based economic growth? And what policies should countries adopt to ensure that economic growth quickly reduces poverty—both raising income and consumption and improving other

4 The World Bank : Economic Growth and Household Welfare in Vietnam-*Policy Lessons from Vietnam,* World Bank, 2001

indicators of living standards? These questions are difficult ones, and more empirical evidence is needed to provide recommendations sufficiently precise to guide policymakers. A recent example of success is Vietnam and the World Bank attempted to address the following questions:

- What policies led to Vietnam's high rate of economic growth and allowed it to continue that growth (though at a lower rate) during the recent economic crises in East Asia and elsewhere?
- Which Vietnamese households experienced growth in their incomes and expenditures, and which components of their incomes increased most quickly? What public policies brought about these changes in household incomes?
- How have increases in income affected other aspects of living standards in Vietnam, such as child nutrition, school enrollment, adult health, fertility, child labor, and infant and child mortality? What has played a more important role in these socioeconomic outcomes towards income or the more direct affects of such public policies as social safety nets?

Growth in Vietnam has averaged about 8 percent a year since around 1988, while the incidence of poverty declined from about 75 percent in 1988 to 55 percent in 1993 and 37 percent in 1998. The research addresses the first question by using macroeconomic data and cross-country data analysis, and the second and third by using data from the 1992–93 and 1997–98 Vietnam Living Standards Surveys.

Faster, cost effective and most commonly used method for learning about customers in a market is to do a *trade survey*, interviewing people in the distribution channels and trade associations. In the trade surveys type of buyers, the type of buying processes used, and the sources of buyer information are clearly defined. These professional market research firms can also provide a solution to the multinational companies seeking trade surveys as who should be the respondents, when to administer the questionnaires, what should be the nature of questions and the number of questions to be used in the trade surveys. These market research firms provide a good starting point for further data gathering and analysis. The market research also involves *direct observation* on customers buying and using this method to know the consumer behavior towards existing products can be very beneficial. The behavior of consumers towards the existing products gives important clues to customer preferences, especially in mature markets. In markets where access is free and the customers have well-developed preferences, the sales records of the various products constitute, in fact, a shortcut to understanding customer preferences. This method is very useful during the pre-launch stage for the foreign firms to develop an appropriate launch of their products in the segmented markets. The method of observation also faces some practical difficulties if certain assumptions are made to interpret the observed issues. A firm may assume that current products reflect customer preferences and such assumption is likely to hold only in mature markets with no entry barriers. However, where customers have been deprived of products because of trade barriers, consumer preferences might well display a desire for something different. Such latent preferences can't be uncovered through observation. On the other hand, the *causal marketing research* involves experimental methods of research and causal models. The aim of such research may be to determine the extent to which a causal variable such as price or advertising has an effect on variables such as brand preference or purchase. There are typical research designs that may be used in such experimental methods and towards the estimation of links in causal models. The problems addressed in the casual market researches tend to be about the fine-tuning of price levels, testing of alternative advertising copy and visuals, and the link between post-sales service and customer satisfaction. The basic notion underlying the research is that a multinational company needs to understand precisely, which of the contemplated marketing activities will have an appropriate bearing on the results.

SELECTED READINGS

Arnold E Amstunz, *Computer Simulation of Competitive Market Response,* Mot Press, Cambridge, 1967, also see Kotler Philip, op cit, p. 124 – 128

Breen, George Edward, *Do it yourself Marketing Research*, McGraw-Hill, New York, 1977.

Buell Victor P. *Handbook of Marketing Management*, McGraw-Hill, New York, 1986, p. 32 - 2 to 39-12.

Crisp R.D. 'Marketing Research Organization and Operation, Research Study 35', American Marketing Association, 1958, pp. 39-47, quoted in Tom Cannon: *Basic Marketing Principles and Practices*, Holt, Rinehart and Winston, London, 1980, p. 62.

Kotler Philip, *Marketing Management: Analysis, Planning, Implementation and Control*, Practice Hall, New Delhi, 1988

Rajagopal, *Project Formulation and Analysis*: Participative Constraints, Working Paper, National Institute of Rural Development, Hyderabad, 1992.

Rajagopal, *Organizing Rural Business: Policy, Planning and Management*, Sage, New Delhi, Chapter 4, 1995.

Ralph S. Alexander, *Marketing Definitions,* The American Marketing Association. Chicago, 1960, p. 16.

Weiers, Ronald M. *Marketing Research*, Practice Hall, Englewood Chiffs, New Jersey, 1984, p. 278 - 288.

William R. Dillon, Matthew Goldstein and Leon G Schittman, Appropriateness of Linear Discriminent and Methodological Classification Analysis of Marketing Research, *Journal of Marketing Research*, Feb. 1978, p. 103 - 112.

Susan P. Douglas and Samuel Craig C. *International Marketing Research*, Prentice Hall, New Jersy, 1983.

Case 7.1

CADBURY SCHWEPPES : POSITIONING IN LATIN AMERICA[5]

Jean Jacob Schweppes, a German born Swiss entrepreneur had started commercial production of synthetic carbonated water in 1783, following the method devised by J B Priestly, an English scientist in Geneva. In 1792, Schweppes shifted hid fuzzy water business to England and built the brand on his name considering the poetic touch in its pronunciation (the first three letter of his brand name schw…e gives the sound of bottle being uncapped). In 1969, this soft drink manufacturing company merged with a leading confectionery of UK Cadbury and became Cadbury Schweppes plc. This company has put together a pointed portfolio of beverage brands to emerge as the global leader for non-cola drinks. This company with its base in London has earned revenue of 4 billion by its world-wide sales claiming thus to be the undisputed global leader in non-cola soft drinks.

THE PRODUCT LINE

J Schweppes and Co.'s aerated water made instant success in British markets right from its beginning in 1972. The company launched its next product Schweppes Aerated Lemonade in 1835 followed by a product Indian tonic water, a drink which was used as a diluting agent for Gin and Vodka. From this originated the British habit of mixing quinine with water to prevent malaria in the tropical climate of India during the colonial period. This product had a slight bitter taste which appealed to its western consumer. Later the company, in 1870 added ginger to its product ginger ale using the technology developed for extracting flavor from the fruits and vegetables. In 1900, the company had gone public and launched series of fruit beverages. During 1955-62, the company diversified its product line and spent 5 million dollars for entering into global market with processed fruits and vegetables products like marmalades, jams, canned fruits. However, these product were given-up by the company in latter years. It concentrated again on soft drinks and ventured into expanding its market for soft drinks by prominent brands tie-ups. In 1969, the Schweppes & Co. merged with Cadbury but did not make any significant changes in the soft drink product line. In order to expand its market in US, it bought Canada Dry in 1986 and in 1993 the company introduced low sugar citrus drinks to suit to the tastes of American buyers. The merger with Cadbury in 1969, has enabled Schweppes & Co. to diversify its product line to confectionery products also. In 1994, it became the third major player for confectionery products in the world market.

---

5 Professor of Marketing, Business Division, ITESM, Mexico City Campus, Mexico 14380 DF (E-mail : *rajagopal@itesm.mx*)
This case has been written as the basis for class discussion rather than to illustrate either effective or ineffective handling of an administrative situation of the company.

MODES OF ENTRY

For long time Schweppes plc. had operated in the market with its headquarters at London for its manufacturing distribution and marketing activities. During the late 18th century, the company entered the international marketing avenue by setting-up its subsidiaries and bottling plants across Africa, Australia, North and Latin America, New Zealand and the European mainland. Despite other companies entering the international markets, Cadbury Schweppes Plc. claims that it has set-up bottling operations in 15 countries apart from licensees in 85 countries. The confectionery division which market chocolates and assorted candies has manufacturing plants in 23 countries and marketing offices in more than 100 countries. The company has entered the Indian market by setting-up Cadbury Schweppes Beverages India Pvt Ltd. (CSBIL), a total subsidary of Cadbury Schweppes plc in 1994. The popular brand of the company in the carbonated beverages is Crush.

BRAND MANAGEMENT

Schweppes & Co. has reserved its brand, since its inception, on all the products it has manufactured and marketed internationally. The brand game began after the company had a shock and had to withdraw its diversified fruit-processed product during the early sixties. The big merger happened in 1969 with the UK based major confectionery player Cadbury plc. The idea after such a merger was more to use both strong brands for enhancing the marketing horizon of American and Australian markets. The company bought Canada Dry in 1986, in order to enter the American markets. The competition however, increased in the late 80's with other US based soft drinks like Red Cheek Mott's apple juice and Crush International and the English goodies labeled Basset foods. In 1993, the company brought A&W Brands Inc., the US based manufacturer of A&W root beer and Squirt - a long sugar citrus fruit drink. Schweppes acquired Dr Pepper/Seven up Inc., America biggest non-cola soft drinks by investing 2.5 billion in 1994. CSBIL has already launched Crush, Canada Dry, Soda Water, Bitter Lemonade and Schweppes Tonic Water in the Indian market. Even though other brands have come up in the international market, Cadbury Schweppes plc has acquired enough consumer strength to sustain itself in the global brand race where soft drinks and confectionery products are concerned.

CORPORATE GROWTH

Cadbury Schweppes plc has accounted for 55 percent turnover in total beverages sale in the UK with sales of 2.2 billion during 1994 (up by 7 percent compared to its performance in 1993). The company in the US market leaped from 5 to 16.5 percent augmenting its overall beverages volumes by 75 percent more than the pre-acquisition figures of the big US brands Dr Pepper and Seven Up. The combined statistics for beverages and confectionery during 1994, for the company account for 42 percent of sales in UK, 19 percent in North America and 13.5 percent from Australia and Asia. Dr Pepper and Seven Up brands have higher sales in north America when compared to any other market. The company stood at 11.2 percent in world-wide sales in 1994.

BRAND PROMOTION

Schweppes name flavored the brand to expand geographically even though production was clamped during the second world-war period. The brand's humorous one liners made the consumers recall the brand often. This paid off well after the war was over. The creative language used throughout the global market was very convincing, emotional and promising. "Thirsty, take the necessary Schweppes " was a memorable phrase in the UK media. The direct marketing advertisement made " Schweppes essence" a common household term in the whole England. Later the brand's characteristic " Schhh.... " was exploited by advertising agencies for launching a mass campaign. It was woven around the mystery of the sound of the first three letters of the brand - " the secret of schhh". The brand was defined as a way of life " Schwepping " and as a series of legends set in an imaginary English country called " Schweppshire ".

BUSINESS THREATS

Major marketing challenge before the company was to expand the non-cola segment, to replace the major international cola drink players like Pepsi, Coke and Thumps-up (Indian Market). The aggressive marketing of cola based companies have overshadowed, the market for non-cola drinks simply because of their strict quality check, their stronghold in the distribution network and their effective monitoring of market trends. Coca-cola, the US based soft drinks company has emerged as a major competitor for Cadbury Schweppes & Co. with its performance in 195 countries generating a gross revenue of 16.2 billion and profit worth 2.6 billion during 1994. In the international market, Coca-Cola has acquired 46 percent share of cola drinks. It has become the second top international company in the soft drinks market. This company has about a hundred brands in its portfolio, of which Coke, Diet Coke, Fanta and Sprite account for the major share in sales among the other brands of the company.

ISSUES OF CONCERN

Majority of international marketing companies dealing with consumer products keep watch on the spatial expansion of the business of Cadbury's Schweppes. In order to implement such an expansion strategically the companies make an entry into the selected country as a distribution agency or as a production firm. However, in business economy the mode of entry for an international marketing firm has always been a debatable issue on account of the cost of production versus the cost of marketing. Further, the optimum product line to be handled to sustain the company in the international brand race markets has also become a prime concern for developing firms with indigenous product brands. International business decisions are by take independently by any firm or through its strategic alignments. The viability of owning a large number of subsidiaries, joint ventures and production units in different countries needs to be assessed on the scale of economy for an international marketing or production company. Above all, effective advertising and publicity tops the concern of an international marketer in order to realize higher revenues and profit from the sales of the product. In this process, owning an universal brand and using a multi-lingual advertising and publicity approach may prove worthy in the long run. However, in a developing country, a specific or regional brand and promotional strategies may also prove as the best decentralized strategy. Nonetheless, the international marketing of consumer goods is a total management game.

REFERENCES

Fahe Liam: *Competitors: Outwitting, Outmaneuvering and Outperforming,* John Wiley and Sons Canada, 1999.

Peter Senge: *The Fifth Discipline,* Doubleday/Currency, New York, 1990.

John J. McGonagle *et.al.*: *A New Archetype for Competitive Intelligence,* Quorum Books, Westport, CT, 1996.

CHAPTER 8

SALES MANAGEMENT

CHAPTER FOCUS

- *To understand the concept and overview of sales management in a business environment of the company,*
- *To acquire skills for formulating the strategic sales program, implementation, evaluation and control of sales program, and*
- *To practice the application of sales management techniques through analysis of cases and diagnosing the live environment.*

Selling is an art largely associated with the behavioral skills of the sale personnel of a sales organization. Today, selling is performed using scientific methods of product presentation, advertising and various approaches drawn to take the customer into confidence. A foreign firm begins to sell their products to export markets by switching from domestic market and launches new product lines or services to gain competitive advantage. Sales personnel in international business can be classified in two ways - by performance or by their nationality. In regard to the task they perform, there are three categories of selling tasks - sales generation, sales support, and missionary work. Sales generation is the creative task of helping the customer to make a purchase decision. It is concerned with after-sale service. Missionary work is undertaken by a salesperson to stimulate demand to help the distributors. There are four categories of sales which include every type of sales position, as given below:

- Consultative sales
- Technical sales
- Commercial sales and
- Direct sales

The sales people may be categorized by nationality as expatriates and natives. The expatriates are home-country employees on deputation in the host country while the natives are employees who belong to the host country. The efficiency of sales, depends up on the type of sales person and the techniques used in selling goods or services. The consumers are the decision makers in buying the goods and services proposed for sales and hence play key role in the sales process. These selling categories require a specific management approach to deal with the market.

CONSULTATIVE SALES

Consultative sales may be defined as the selling of specific goods or services to technical organizations. The consultative type of companies keep accounts of their clients and assign the sales force to attend to specific client accounts. Computer systems management, structural planning of factories, human resources management, capital market services and the like may be listed in the category of consultative sales.

Since performing sales for goods and services of this category demand high skills, they require a low-key, low-pressure approach by the sales personnel. Consultative sales require comprehensive knowledge of the product or services and the user orientation. A successful salesperson in this field needs to have great confidence and an experience of successes achieved periodically. Of all sales types, the consultative sales person is probably the most professional and demands the highest compensation for his skills and abilities.

TECHNICAL SALES

Product knowledge, its application, relevance to contemporary technological development and sales skills are the essential characteristics needed to be present in salespeople engaged in the sale of goods and services of technical products. The dominant industries in this field are electronics, engineering products of all branches, medical equipments and the like. The buying influence is generally drawn from a professional manager. The personal sales in this category are limited. However, organizational sales of technical goods and services are higher compared to the former. The compensation given to the sales force of this category is often linked with performance apart from a low salary.

COMMERCIAL SALES AND DIRECT SALES

A large sales force is engaged in the commercial sales of consumer goods and services. These sales are very much individual-consumer oriented. The sales personnel operate as sales representatives of the company or as facilitators of an in-house retail store. The major task of the sales representatives is to collect orders from consumers or organizations. In performing direct sales, the representatives attempt to generate an emotional appeal and this motivates the buyer. It has been observed that the turnover rate in direct sales require a strong persuasive ability and skills to identify a customer's buying motives. Direct salespeople receive compensation in terms of commission on the volume of sales.

ORGANIZING THE SALES FORCE

Sales force can be organized in many ways subject to the product type, coverage and buyers prospects. The different ways of organizing the sales force are stated below:

- Region based sales force (territorial)
- Product based sales force
- Market based sales force

Region based sales force may be organized for vertical and horizontal coverage of different areas spread across the operational area. The vertical hierarchy of sales force may be at the central level, zonal level, and area level and down to the markets located in the various towns. The horizontal area of operation may in a given area across the towns or villages. The size of the sales force depends on the geographical spread of the sales operation, volume of sales and the density of buyers.

Product based sales force generally belongs to a company and functions as a team to promote the sales of the product in the given area. Examples may be cited of automobile company. The sales force needs to be specifically organized the product to be in tune with the functional requirements of the market. Examples may be cited of the service for computer industries products in the market. To market such a device, a group of professional sales and service engineers are required to boost-up the market for the principle product as well as for the service packages of the ancillary unit. The major steps for effective selling in any category of the sales organization are listed below:

- *Prospecting and qualifying* - collecting basic information about consumers, references, joining a prospect's organization, initiating communication
- *Negotiation* - about the orders, delivery, pre and post sales service, organizational benefits and the like
- *Approach* - the sales package

Strategy Focus 8.1: Go-to-Market Strategy to Deliver Better Customer Value

Go-to-market strategy (GTM) encompasses the channels that a company uses to connect with its customers and the organizational processes it develops to guide customer interactions from initial contact through fulfilment. The right go-to-market strategy has a significant impact on a company's ability to cost-effectively deliver its value proposition to each of its target segments. Growth in technology and the proliferation of channel options have certainly played a role as business firms are becoming increasingly focused and sophisticated in the way in which they compete to create superior customer value. GTM strategy may be administered successfully by considering the following process path:

- Understanding customers' needs, expectation and behavior

  Products, Channels, Value Proposition and Markets
- Aggressive use of low cost channels

  Short run market penetration, profit maximization
- Fit between selling approach and selling contents

  Product-Channel Fit, Process Fit, Value Fit
- Trade-off between market coverage and control

  Reaching the range of potential customers

  Exercising control on sales relationship and deliveries

  Market expansion and new channel partners

As companies tailor their value propositions to better address, customer needs beyond product specifications and to better align their cost of sales and fulfilment relative to those needs, go-to-market strategy plays a central role. To compensate for less-frequent product launches and a focus on integrated solutions rather than specific products, Microsoft now organizes its marketing efforts around annual GTM campaigns. GTMs focus Microsoft and its partners on short-term strategic challenges and provide consistent marketing approaches for most of its business products. GTMs address the lack of new product releases on which to hang marketing campaigns by identifying a strategic issue facing Microsoft and constructing a framework for addressing, it with broad-reach advertising, sales tools for partners and the Microsoft field sales force, and customer and partner incentives.

- *Presentation and Demonstration* - convincing the buyer
- *Problem solving* - resolving conflicts pertaining to all Ps and As
- *Delivering* - closing the deal by satisfying the consumer
- *Follow-up*- post-sales service and maintaining of relationship

RETAILING

Retailing is a set of activities performed in selling the goods and services directly to the end users. The goods and services sold to the consumers are meant for their personal use and not for resale or business activity. Retailing is the last activity, conducted in the chain of product distribution. In principle, retailing is a business activity which involves the sales of goods and services to a large number of consumer spread over a large area. There are different forms of retailing. Many of the forms keep emerging, according to the convenience of the buyers and the retailers. In large towns, retailing is organized and mostly performed through stores and automatic vending machines. However, in the rural areas the retailing of goods and services are conducted through the traditional pattern of displaying the goods in the mobile van, carts and on footpaths.

For understanding the types of retailers and their function, we can classify the retailing network into two broad categories - (i) store retailing and (ii) non-store retailing . Like the growth cycle of business firms, the retailing activity also passes through 4 stages embryonic, growth, maturity and decline. A retail store observes the period of accelerated growth, reaches the stage of maturity and then starts declining. It has been observed that the old fashioned retail stores took more than five decades to reach the stage of maturity in terms of volume of sales, coverage of consumers and expansion of chain of retail stores. However, modern retail store types reach their maturity very fast due to organized retailing management. Some of the major store, retailers are briefly described here:

- Departmental store
- Exclusive retail store or specialty store
- Super markets
- Convenience store
- Supermarkets, hyper-store
- Discount store
- Non-franchise or catalogue store

DEPARTMENTAL STORE

A departmental store offers a wide range of products in an organized fashion and is easily accessible by the consumer. The product line of departmental stores is substantially long.

Departmental stores provide better amenities to consumers for shopping by virtue of having adequate infrastructure for parking, leisure activities and hobbies. Departmental stores provide the consumer services of honoring the product guarantee, warranty, post sale services and the latest technical information. Departmental stores also organize educational program for the benefit of the consumer on the various aspects of products use and other related matters.

EXCLUSIVE RETAIL STORES

Exclusive or specialty retail stores are unlike departmental stores and do not have a long product line. These stores are narrow in their product lines and are largely confined to the product line of a specific company. They present a varied assortment within that product line. Examples can be drawn from many consumer goods companies promoting exclusive retail stores like Phillips for a range of electrical, audio and video household gadgets; Raymond's for textiles; Bata for shoes and leather goods, and so on. Exclusive stores can be further classified with a narrow distinction as stated below:

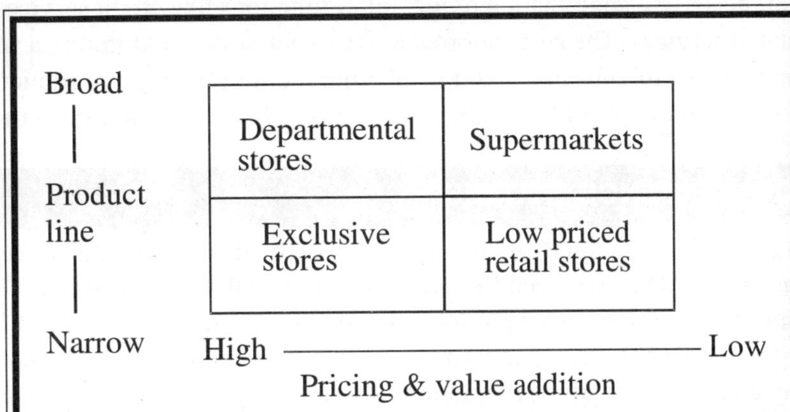

Figure 8.1 Categorical map of retail stores

- Single line stores
- Limited line stores
- Super specialty stores

Single line stores may be identified as the retail stores selling only one product like textiles. ***Limited line stores*** may be defined as the shops having micro specialization based on goods and services, gender and age, like exclusive Men's wear retail stores, *Kids Shoppe* for garments etc. The retail stores engaged in selling products scientifically designed for a particular purpose may be categorized as ***Super specialty stores,*** e.g. surgical equipments stores, sports accessories; fashion garments stores and the like. The classification of retail stores and their functions may be well understood through the retail position map plotted in figure 8.1.

SUPER MARKETS

Super markets are a type of organized retail stores that handle a relatively large volume of goods and services at a low cost - the high margin principle of retailing. Consumers are provided franchise in the super markets and there are largely organized as self- service outlets. Super markets exhibit a long range of product line of various consumer needs like grocery, household appliances, entertainment, toys, garments etc. It has been observed that super markets earn an operating profit of 1-2% on their sales and 10-15% of their net worth. Super markets also provide consumer conveniences like in-shop entertainment, pantry, home delivery service, opinion survey and consumer education. Super markets have chain retailing in many countries like Woolworth's in the UK and Europe. There is a marginal difference between a super market and a hyper-store. The latter category of stores operates on a larger area (approximately 100-200 thousand square feet) with a wide range of products. These markets have a combination of all retail functions like credit services, discounts, finance and other related services. The basic approach of a hyper-store is exhibiting a wide range of assorted products for all types of consumers and displaying them in bulk. The product handling costs in such stores would be minimal and they also function as the sole distributors to the convenience stores.

CONVENIENCE STORES

These stores are small retail outlets located near residential areas for the convenience of the consumers. They are open for long hours and all through the week. This category of stores carries a limited line of consumer products. Convenience stores operate at a high turnover and a relatively higher profit basis compared to any of the other retail stores. The consumer seems to be willing to pay a higher price to the retailers for the convenience provided to them at their door steps.

DISCOUNT STORES

In principle, a discount store should sell all types of merchandise, offering largely reputed brands at lower prices but not inferior goods. Recently, some consumer products manufacturing companies have started owning discount retail stores to sell products earmarked as second grade by their quality control division. Hence, discount retail stores have moved from general stores down to specialty merchandise stores such as discount sporting goods stores, garments, shoes, electronic, book stores and the like.

CATALOGUE SHOWROOM

Catalogue store is a new generation super store which deals with a variety of goods and services of a wide range. Such stores conduct retailing operation for all types of goods including interiors, construction material, mechanical gadgets, electronics, and many more. Consumers buying goods from catalogue shops have to ask for or indent specific goods as per the inventory specification in the catalogue. The consumers wait in the designated place for the delivery of the goods and at times the stores even arrange a home delivery for heavy products. Catalogue stores provide a return facility to consumer within a stipulated period. The goods can be returned to the stores without any reasons, if the consumers are not satisfied.

NON-STORE RETAILING

Besides on-store retailing the direct selling approach has emerged in the recent past as an effective sales instrument. Direct selling is one of the most popular non-store retailing activities, particularly for consumer goods. The sales representatives of the company / distributors canvass the product on a door to door basis and contribute in augmenting sales. Automatic vending machines for selling consumer products like chilled beverages, etc. are also making use of non-store retailing approaches. The specific non-store retailing types are given below:

- Direct marketing
- Automatic vending machines
- Business by mail orders
- Tele-shopping or Net-shopping
- Mobile retailing

Multi-level retailing stores, chain-retailing stores, co-operatives network and merchandise conglomerates are the new forms of retailing emerged in the recent past.

DECISION MAKING IN RETAILING

Retailing is considered to be one scientific, grassroots level selling approach in the twentieth century. Hence, a retailer has to make the right decision at the right time to promote his retail business. The specific areas that need to be planned properly are (i) choice of place (ii) choice of products - assorted or exclusive (iii) price level (iv) tools of retailing and (v) consumer services. The decision regarding the choice of place and product are inter-related e.g., in a high income locality, a retailer should plan for high price assorted - product stores and vice versa in a low income consumer locality.

TOOLS OF RETAILING

Retailing is an art. Retail stores play a vital role in product promotion as they are directly associated with consumer. A successful retailer tries to get the consumer involved in the trade by providing a good reception, good facilities and individual attention. However, a retailer follows a variety of approaches to make his retailing a success. Some of the tools used by the retailers for promoting their business are listed below:

(i) retailers dealing with similar products form an association to jointly carry promotional activities such as advertising, pricing and other related matters

(ii) retailers do pre-ticketing by placing price tags on those products indicating all the required information such as the date of manufacture, size, volume, name of the manufacturer, date of expiry, product code of the manufacturer as well as that of the retailer for any complaints or reordering

(iii) retailers also help the consumer in re-indenting the products by sending them reminders and catalogs of the products

(iv) retailers also introduce special prices during the peak seasons for storewide promotion

(v) consumers enjoy the privilege of returning or exchanging damaged goods without paying any additional price and

(vi) distributors and company representatives get the sponsorship of the retailer for demonstrating their products in his store

There are many methods that foreign company adopt to promote the sales of its products. The common approaches may be the cross selling, price discounts, volume packs etc. However, there are many advanced ideas, which are used by the multinational companies as described below:

- Coupons – Assuring benefit
- Bonus pack- more product for regular price
- In-pack, On-pack, Near-pack
- Specialty Container – Value added benefits
- Continuity program- rewards system for multiple buying
- Refund- Price draw-back
- Sweepstakes- Random chance of winning
- Contests
- Mail premium – Post-purchase benefits
- Sampling
- Price-off-discounts
- Trade deal- Incentives to retailers
- Cause marketing- social benefit oriented (like soliciting contribution to UNICEF)

Besides these services, retail stores provide many pre- and post-purchase services to satisfy the customers. The *pre-purchase services* include accepting orders via telephone and by mail, in-store and outside store advertising, interior and window display, consumer convenience, fitting rooms, shopping hours, organizing consumer entertainment like the integrated cable TV, fashion shows, recipe contest, baby shows etc. The retailers provide selected *post-purchase* services to consumer such as - home delivery of goods, gift packaging, returns and exchanges, tailoring, installation, demonstrations, accepting credit transactions and cheques. In addition to the services listed large and chain retail stores provide leisure and general amenities to the consumers like rest rooms for consumers, baby sitters, restaurants, etc.

DISTRIBUTION

Distribution is an activity where in goods and services are supplied to the agencies for reselling. In other words, distribution includes all the activities involved in selling goods and services to the retailers or the activities in any intermediate channel between consumer and distributors. Distributors perform a key function in selling goods and services to the retailers. The major functions of distributors are listed below:

- Sales and product promotion
- Counseling retailers for assortment building
- Bulk breaking and small packaging
- Warehousing
- Financing
- Risk bearing and
- Providing market information

Distributors on one hand supply finished goods and services to the retailers and on the other, their also engage them-selves in procuring raw products for processors. Thus it can be stated that a large category of distributors play a dual role in procurement and distribution. The various types of distributors may be classified as given under:

- Exclusive wholesale distributors
- Wholesale procurers and distributors
- Industrial distributors
- Mail-order distributors
- Commission agents

It has been observed that most distributors use their proprietary brands to get recognition with retailers for the goods and services provided by them. Nowadays, distributors provide value added services to their clients such as up-dated market information, computerized indenting and billing, and forward and backward integration of services. Sales forecasting is the process of organizing and analyzing information in a way that makes, it possible to estimate the sales growth. This document outlines some simple methods of forecasting sales using easy to find data.

INFORMATION ON SALES

Get out on the street and study competitors. Visit their stores or the locations where their products are offered. Analyze the location, customer volumes, traffic patterns, hours of operation, busy periods, prices, quality of their goods and services, product lines carried, promotional techniques, positioning, product catalogues and other handouts. The sales executives of company should know the customers and update business information. The principal sources of market information include:

- Competitors
- Neighboring Businesses
- Trade suppliers
- Downtown business associations
- Trade associations
- Trade publications
- Trade directories

It is important for the company to consider, how well competition satisfies the needs of potential customers in the selected markets. Also to determine the best fit of the firm's strategies in the determined market segment or niche. Should the firm offer a better location, convenience, better price, later hours, better quality, and better service, may be the further interest of the firm to gain the competitive advantage.

Conversation with suppliers can help the firm a great deal about how industry works and what trends are taking place in the market. They may be able to give valuable information about pricing techniques and mark ups, about the fastest moving lines, objectives of selling activities, and why some competitors are successful. Conversation with the customers or potential customers can give insight into what their needs are. They can indicate what they look for in industry, what they think of competition, what price they might pay and what level of service they like.

> Now more than ever, companies see the power of a strong brand. At a time, when battered investors, customers, and employees are questioning whom they can trust, the ability of a familiar brand to deliver proven value flows straight to the bottom line. The BMW holds the bottom line of customers to make decision on the best brand for satisfying the highest value for money. The company spends hundreds of millions on aggressive communications and upgrades the range of accessories that bear the AT&T-BMW name in order to shed its stodgy me too image. The objective of BMW Mexico is to offer the life time guarantee to the client, the one who enjoys the pleasure to lead. In order to obtain this goal, the company not only puts all efforts offering automobiles of high technology, but also delivers the customized services on the lines of the corporate policy. The company's office in Mexico offers 2 years of guarantee without any mileage restrictions and 6 years of guarantee against corrosion of the body, whenever the automobile is registered with the authorized network BMW Mexico. Besides, 2 years of guarantee is offered to the buyer in original spare parts of BMW without any mileage limitations. All the vehicles and motorcycles of BMW are being sold in the authorized BMW showrooms in Mexico from November 2001. A BMW not only allows the buyer to enjoy the technology as he leads in the life but also brings him the updated technological innovations at the reasonable costs of maintenance. The BMW Mexico offers the driver's safety course for the owners of BMW. Thousands of participants confirm every year that this initiative of BMW for greater security and sovereignty in the traffic is a great success. The PEGASO, Center of Training in Private Security and its Instructors certified by BMW guarantee that the highly skilled methods and techniques are imparted to the clients by the professional mechanical engineers of the company. In order to offer, the highest level of professionalism in the training courses, PEGASO facilities, Center of Training in Deprived Security, are established in important places which allows optimum learning and enhance the driving skills.[1]

Surveys and Focus Groups represent more formal ways of getting insight from customers. If there are specific information requirements for an identified target group, it is likely that the firm can undertake a useful survey. A focus group involves getting feedback from a specially picked group using controlled interview techniques. However, designing an unbiased questionnaire may require attention to detail. The process usually allows the participants to provide their opinions,

1 For details refer BMW Mexico information page at www.bme.com.mx

Strategy Focus 8.2: Team Selling Strategy for High Value Products

The growth of team selling is changing conventional ideas about sales and customer service. Team selling, also known as cross-functional selling, involves the efforts of different people from different areas within an organization working together to sell to and service a customer. This strategy of selling began in early '70s when sales teams were formed in high-technology organizations such as IBM to service the complex needs of their larger customers. It was observed necessary to have, along with a salesperson, technical support people and application specialists involved in *e.g.* inventory control, manufacturing and production planning. Besides IBM, General Motors adapted the team selling strategy and developed as part of the culture of the company. Executives of the company felt that organizing a sales team is a major task to sell the high technology-high value products. The sales team should necessary have a technical and finance person and likewise others. Interestingly what's happened with team selling is that over the years it's filtered into less-technology-oriented businesses such as advertising, consumer packaged goods, and financial services. Several issues may emerge before they are formally addressed as the sales teams generally start to form naturally and informally. Communication among team members is difficult to establish, but is one of the keys to the effectiveness of this approach. There are many reasons for a company to choose team selling because this strategy:

- Provides strategic advantage.
- Meets the needs of demanding, global customers more effectively.
- Establishes long-term, quality relationships with clients.
- Provides competitive advantage through a different kind of customer interface strategy.
- Increases flexibility in terms of how customers are served.
- Increases sales and potential profitability.
- Forces resource allocation decisions at the field level.
- Generates better input to new product and services development.

Team selling effectiveness also depends on selection and training. Training to back up the appropriate selection is so important, in fact, that IBM sends their team leaders to a customized executive development program on how to be an effective key account executive. It's a tough, rigorous program and in addition, IBM requires recertification every few years. Also at the organizational level, in order for a team selling approach to be successful, the supplier organization must have a strong market orientation as part of its organizational culture.

come up with new ideas and brainstorm. This is valuable for generating new concepts, getting feedback on proposed advertising or gaining insight into attitudes and opinions about a new product. Focus groups require a skilled interviewer and hand picked participants and professional firms can handle such projects in an efficient way.

SELLING AND BUYING PROCESS

There are three types of buying situations among the consumers in the international markets and they need to be managed carefully by the foreign firms. These buying situations include straight re-buy, modified re-buy and new task buy. The least complex buying situation is the straight re-buy buying situation, wherein the customer has considerable experience in using the product and is satisfied with the current purchase arrangements. In this case, the buyer is merely reordering from the current supplier and engaging in routine response behavior. A modified re-buy buying situation exists when the customer has previously purchased and used the product. Although the customer has information and experience with the product, it will usually want to collect additional information and may make a change when purchasing a replacement product. A new task buying situation, in which the organization is purchasing a product for the first time, poses the biggest problems for the buyer. Because the account has little knowledge or experience as a basis for making the purchase decision, it will typically use a lengthy process to collect and evaluate purchase information. The decision-making process in this type of situation is often called extensive problem solving. The salesperson must first gather information about (1) the prospective customer's operations to determine whether there is a need for the products or services he or she has to offer and (2) the concerns of various personnel within the customer organization who might influence the final purchase. Then, many low-key sales calls may be necessary to educate the various purchase influencers about the seller's offerings and to establish credibility within the customer's organization. Even after a sale is made, the representative or other members of an account management team-may have a lot of work to do supervising the installation of the product, training the customer's personnel to use it, and providing other post-sale services to ensure the customer will be satisfied and to increase the chances for future sales.

Since different employees of a customer's organization may be active at different stages of the purchase process, an important part of sales planning involves trying to determine who the salesperson should contact, when each contact should be made, and what kinds of information and appeals each participant is likely to find most useful and persuasive. In many cases, however, the roles played by various members of the buying center are sufficiently consistent across similar types of firms that a company can establish policies to guide its salespeople. A widely recognized framework identifies seven steps that organizational buyers take in making purchase decisions:

- Anticipation or recognition of a problem or need,
- Determination and description of the characteristics and the quantity of the needed item,
- Search for and qualification of potential suppliers,
- Acquisition and analysis of proposals or bids,
- Evaluation of proposals and selection of suppliers,
- Selection of an order routine, and
- Performance evaluation and feedback.

Customers' buying centers are likely to involve a wider variety of participants, when they are considering the purchase of technically complex, expensive products such as a computer system-than when the purchase involves a simpler or less expensive product. Consequently, firms that sell technically complex capital equipment sometimes organize their salespeople into sales teams or utilize multilevel selling, with different salespeople calling on different members of the customer's buying center to reach as many decision participants as possible and to give each participant the kinds of information that person will find most relevant. It is necessary for the foreign firm to review periodically, the policies or organizational structures to guide its salespeople in dealing with customers' buying centers.

In view of the rapid escalation of selling costs the multinational companies are using new technologies to reduce the selling cost and increase sales efficiency. The automation of sales force is one of new technologies that are being used by the multinational companies. Such technologically advanced sales strategies help the companies in reallocating sales effort to customer retention, minimizing the non-selling tasks increase the efficiency of the sale persons. Most salespeople are employed in various kinds of retail selling. These jobs involve selling goods and services to ultimate consumers for their own personal use, like door-to-door selling agents, insurance agents, real estate brokers, and retail store clerks do. A much larger volume of sales, however, is accounted for by industrial selling - the sale of goods and services at the wholesale level. Industrial selling activity includes sales to resellers, sales to business users (such as when a manufacturer sells materials or parts to another manufacturer, who uses them to produce another product or when a Xerox salesperson sells a law firm a copier to be used in conducting the firm's business) and sales to institutions. The activities involved in both retail and industrial selling, and managing sales forces for these types of sales activities, are very similar. Success in either type of selling requires interpersonal and communications skills, solid knowledge of the products being sold, an ability to discover the customer's needs and problems, and the creativity necessary to show the customer how a particular product or service can help satisfy those needs and offer solutions to the problems. While globalization makes the organization of the sales force more complicated, firms tend to resolve organizational issues in international markets in largely the same way as they do in the developed countries. The situational and strategic factors that influence firms' organizational decisions appear to be similar in both types of markets, and those factors seem to affect organizational choices in similar ways both at home and abroad. However, a good coordination of sales and marketing activities is important for a firm to service its customers and compete effectively, observations indicate that many organizations do not assign responsibility for all their marketing activities to a single unit.

MEASURING SALES PERFORMANCE

Basic objective of salesperson performance evaluations determine how well individual salespeople have performed. However, the results of salespersons' performance evaluations are used by the foreign firms for various sales management purposes as under:

- To ensure that compensation and other reward disbursements are consistent actual salesperson performance
- To identify, salespeople who might be promoted
- To identify, salespeople whose employment should be terminated and to sup evidence to support the need for termination
- To determine the specific training and counseling needs of individual salespersons and the overall sales force

- To provide information, for effective human resource planning
- To identify, criteria that can be used to recruit and select salespeople in the future
- To advise salespeople of work expectations
- To motivate salespeople
- To help salespeople set career goals, and
- To improve salesperson performance.

These diverse purposes affect all aspects of the performance evaluation process. Performance evaluations for the purpose of identifying salespeople for promotion into sales management positions should focus on criteria related to potential effectiveness as a sales manager and not just current performance as a salesperson. One of the methods that is workable and effective, discusses the development sales benchmarking to perform competitively in the market. Some managers find it difficult to measure the performance of sales representatives because of the variations in the attitudes of sales representatives, customers and business conditions. However, a few questions as stated below may be put forth to the managers before getting started with the evaluation process:

- Volume of sales in national currency/US Dollars
- Amount of time spent in office
- Personal appearance: for example, clothes, hair, cleanliness and neatness
- Number of calls made on existing accounts
- Number of new accounts opened
- Completeness and accuracy of sales orders
- Promptness in submitting reports
- Amount spent in entertaining customers
- Extent to which sales representative sells the company
- Accuracy in quoting prices and deliveries to customers
- Knowledge of the business
- Planning and routing of calls.

Usually managers evaluate their sales representatives primarily on the basis of sales volume, they rely too much on the number of sales calls made by each of their sales representatives, compare each sales representative's present sales results with past sales for a corresponding period, expect their sales representatives to follow explicitly the selling methods that worked for them when they were selling or they give their sales representatives too much freedom. Although, it is impossible to determine with precision all the performance evaluation approaches used by sales organizations, several studies have produced sufficiently consistent information to warrant some general conclusions. Most sales organizations evaluate salespersons performance annually, although firms conduct evaluations semi-annually or quarterly. Relatively few firms evaluate salesperson performance more often than quarterly. It has also been observed that a large number of multinational companies engaged in selling their consumer goods use combinations of input and output criteria that are evaluated by quantitative and qualitative measures. However, emphasis seems to be placed on outputs, with evaluations of sales volume results being most popular. Besides, the sales organizations, which set performance standards or quotas tend to enlist the aid of salespeople in establishing these objectives. The degree of salesperson input and involvement does, however, appear to vary across firms. The multinational pharmaceutical companies generally assign weights to different performance objectives and incorporate territory data when establishing these objectives while most salesperson performance evaluations are conducted by the field sales manager who supervises the salesperson. However, some firms involve the manager above the field sales manager in the salespersons performance appraisal. Also some foreign firms use more than one source of information in evaluating salespersons performance. Computer printouts, call reports, supervisory calls, sales itineraries, prospect and customer files, and client and peer feedback are some of the common sources of information. Although performance appraisal continues to be primarily a top-down process, in some companies it leads to the implementation of a broader assessment process. An increasingly popular assessment technique, dubbed 360° feedback involves performance assessment from multiple scorers, including sales and external customers, team members, and even salespeople themselves.

SALES COMPENSATION

Developing an equitable and functional compensation plan that combines balance, consistent motivation, and flexibility is extremely challenging in international operations. This is especially true when a company operates in a number of countries, when it has individuals who work in a number of countries, or when the sales force is composed of expatriate and local personnel. Fringe benefits play a major role in many countries.[2] The expatriates working in high-tax countries prefer liberal expense accounts and fringe benefits that are non-taxable instead of direct income subject to high taxes. A successful sales commission plan should possess three characteristics as given below:

- The plan should offer an immediate positive reward to the salesperson for his achievements.
- The compensation plan linked to the career path should be clear and simple to understand.
- It should be relatively free of influence from factors outside the salesperson's control.

A sales commission plan based on these three principles, will reward the company by doing what it is supposed to do and encourage the profitable selling efforts by the sales force. Sales people operate under the gun most of the time. They're pressured to produce by the company, by their families, and by their own egos. Paying salespeople a straight salary is uncommon. Such plans are well suited for paying sales support personnel and sales trainees. Sales support personnel, including missionaries and prospectors, are involved in situations in which, it is difficult to determine who really makes the sale. Because missionaries and prospectors are concerned primarily with dissemination of information rather than direct solicitation of orders, a salary can equitably compensate for effort. Compensation based on sales results might not be fair. Salaries can provide control over salespeople's

2 Richard B. Peterson, Nancy K. Napier, and Won Shul-Shim, "Expatriate Management: A Comparison of MNCs across Four Parent Countries," *Thunderbird International Business Review*, March-April 2000, 42(2), pp. 145-166.

activities, and reassigning salespeople and changing sales territories is less a problem with salary plans than with other financial compensation plans. Salary plans also make it easier to encourage teamwork and customer service. The other methods used by the multinational companies include straight commission and a combination of salary and commission plan. The Table 8.1 exhibits the reasons for adapting the specific compensation plans:

Table 8.1 Compensation Plans for Sales Persons

Components	*Needs*
Salary	• Motivate effort on non-selling activitiesn
	• Adjust for differences in territory potentialn
	• Reward experience and competence
Commissions	• Motivate a high level of selling effortn
	• Encourage sales success
Incentive payments	• Direct effort toward strategic objectivesn
	• Provide additional rewards for top (bonus) performersn
	• Encourage sales success
Sales contests	• Stimulate additional effort targeted at specific short-term objectives
Personal benefits	• Satisfy salespeople's security needsn
	• Match competitive offers

1. Straight commission offers strong financial incentives to the sales persons to maximize performance. However, they also limit the control of the sales force. Some industries like real estate, insurance, automobiles, and securities traditionally pay the salespeople straight commission. In these industries, the primary responsibility of salespeople is simply to close sales; non-selling activities are less important to the employer than in some other industries. The huge direct-sales industry, including such companies as Mary Kay Cosmetics, Tupperware, and Avon, also pays by straight commission.

SELECTED READINGS

Barton A. Weitz, Stephen B. Castleberry, John F. Tanner: *Selling: Building Partnerships,* 5th Edition, McGraw Hill, 2003

Cron, William L., and Michael Levy: Sales Management Performance Evaluation: A Residual Income Perspective, *Journal of Personal Selling & Sales Management,* August, 1987, pp 57-66.

Chang, Julia: Born to Sell, *Sales and Marketing Management,* Vol. 155, No. 7, July, 2003, pp 34-38.

Cummings, Betsy: *Coaching Clinic, Sales and Marketing Management,* Vol. 155, No. 12, December, 2003, pp 39-42.

Day, George: Managing Market Relationships, *Journal of the Academy of Marketing Science,* Vol. 28, No. 1, winter, 2000, pp 24-30.

Honeycutt Jr, Earl D., Kiran Karande, Ashraf Attia and Steven D. Maurer: A Utility Based Framework for Evaluating the Financial Impact of Sales Force Training, *Journal of Personal Selling & Sales Management,* Vol. , No. , Summer, 2001, pp 229-238.

Honeycutt Earl D, Ford John B and Simintiras Antonis : *Sales Management- A Global Perspective,* Routledge, 2003

Michael T. Bosworth: *Solution Selling- Creating Buyers in Difficult Selling Markets,* McGraw Hill, 1994

Moon, Mark, and John Mentzler: Improving Sales Force Forecasting, *Journal of Business Forecasting,* Summer, 1999, pps 7-12.

Mishory, Jordana: *Frequency Matters, Sales & Marketing Management,* Vol. 156, No. 7, July, 2004, pp 36-38.

Sharma, Arun: Customer Satisfaction-Based Incentive Systems: Some Managerial and Salesperson Considerations, *Journal of Personal Selling and Sales Management,,* Vol. ?, No. 2, Spring, 1997, pp 61-70.

Thomas N. Ingram, Raymond W. LaForge, Ramon A. Avila, Jr., Charles H. Schwepker, and Michael R. Williams: *Sales Management – Analysis and Decision Making,* South-Western College Publication, 2003

Case 8.1

CANON IN MEXICAN BUSINESS ENVIRONMENT[3]

Canon started out as a company with a handful of employees and a burning passion. That company soon became a world-renowned camera maker and is now a global multimedia corporation. However, the origin on their success remain unchanged: the passion of early years of the early years of the company and technological expertise amassed over more than 60 years. Canon pioneered the world's first digital full-color copying machine, and the company has continued to introduce the latest innovations in true color reproduction and high-speed output. Small-diameter toner particles and the four-drum system are just two revolutionary advances in this arena. To stay competitive in today's fast-paced, borderless business world, the company is now stressing compatibility with the newest Windows operating systems and localization around the world for all printing conveniences. Canon has also deployed its strengths in optical and precision technologies to create leading-edge systems and components for the broadcasting, medical, semiconductor production and related industries. Products incorporating key Canon components and technologies are leading the way for industries in the digital era.

CORPORATE PHILOSOPHY

Corporate philosophy of Canon is kyosei. A concise definition of this word would be "Living and working together for the common good," but our definition is broader: "All people, regardless of race, religion or culture, harmoniously living and working together into the future." Unfortunately, the presence of imbalance in our world -in areas such as trade, income levels and the environment- hinders the achievement of *kyosei.* Addressing these imbalances is an ongoing mission, and Canon is doing its part by actively pursuing *kyosei.* True global companies must foster good relations, not only with their customers and the communities in which they operate, but also with nations and the environment. They must also bear the responsibility for the impact of their activities on society. For this reason, Canon's goal is to contribute to the prosperity of the world and the happiness of humanity, which will lead to continuing growth and bring the world closer to achieving *kyosei.* To help attaining sustainable, recycling-oriented societies and fulfil its responsibilities as a good corporate citizen, Canon is realizing the concept of environmentally conscious management. The corporate philosophy

3 This case has been prepared by Dr. Rajagoapl, Professor of *Marketing, Business Division,* ITESM-CCM, Mexico City Campus, Mexico City 14380 DF (E-mail : rajagopal@itesm.mx)
This case has been written as the basis for class discussion rather than to illustrate either effective or ineffective handling of an administrative situation of the company.
Author acknowledges the academic contribution of Ms. Olga Garcia (ITESM-CCM 00372979) student of the course on Advanced Selling System and marketing executive of Canon Mexico; Maria Carmen Vega and Eduardo Tamson of the above course in conducting the investigation and presenting the case as a part fulfilment of the course in the January-April 2003 trimester of Graduate Program of ITESM-CCM.

of *kyosei* remains as the guiding tool for the employees of the company in their quest to build a group of companies that are appreciated and respected around the world. Canon has pursued diversification and laid a solid base for growth well into the future through one of the world's most comprehensive corporate R&D efforts and with a global network of R&D facilities capitalizing on expertise in each region, Canon is building the future.

KEY AREAS OF CANON IN MEXICAN MARKET

Canon delivers innovative digital business solutions to ensure that its customers achieve and maintain the information edge. The increasingly competitive global marketplace, and the fact that the organizations must store, process and share immense volumes of information with both speed and accuracy have been the key areas of the company to penetrate in the territorial gateways like Mexico for Latin American market. The company functions with four key areas in Mexican market that include marketing, logistics, sales and services operations. The marketing activities of the company consist of planning and budgeting, pricing, forecasting, purchases, marketing research and developing promotional strategies. The company is also engaged in developing attractive media –mix and advertising campaigns and launches the loyalty programs for its major brands. The virtual shopping network is also a major part of the marketing functions performed by the company in the country. The company feels that the loyal, ongoing customers are the backbone of every business and in the prevailing highly competitive environment, these shoppers cannot be ignored or else they may be won over by competitors. The repeat customers are more apt to buy a full range of merchandise, not merely items that are under promotional programs. This means that the dealers and retailers of the company can reach profit margin goals. The logistics functions of the company is largely international trade oriented, as the Canon Mexico is a part of Canon USA and many products of the company are acquired from its USA counterpart as inbound logistics. The import process has been one of the major activities of the company in Mexico. The logistics of the company further involves the key activities of transport, inventory management and developing appropriate overseas trade and information strategies.

Services of equipments, periodic maintenance of the canon products with the accounts, administering the warranties, and call centre control functions constitute the major part the services network activities of the company. The call centre has the responsibility to attend on the customer complaints, suggestions and design the conflict resolution strategies. The compliance with the NOM procedures has been another principal activity of the company, that is considered as part of the services functions. All Mexican products in the market must comply with Mexican Mandatory Standards (NOMs) and their similar imported products too, and they can be called to demonstrate the accomplishment in the customs office before the entry to Mexico. The Certificate of Conformance with NOM is the only legal document accepted in Mexico to demonstrate compliance, when issued by an accredited and authorized product certification body. The sales activities comprise prospecting, managing dealers accounts, customer and dealer support, quota compliance and developing area based strategies for augmenting the sales. Each sales area has been identified, as a profit centre and is expected to thrive its best in achieving the targets.

BUYER BEHAVIOUR AND DISTRIBUTION

Each different product market consists of buyers, and buyers are all different in one way or another. They may differ in their wants, resources, locations, buying attitudes and buying practices. Because buyers have unique needs and wants, each buyer is potentially a separate market. For example, in the health supplements market, the seller identifies market segments, and develops different health supplements products and marketing mixes tailored to each needs and wants. The market for some products like health supplements and formal clothing appeal to many buyers irrespective of the age, income levels, price and other competitive factors associated thereof. The consumers might have bought such products many times in their life or some might have purchased at least once in life time. There is no single way to segment a market. The Canon Mexico analyses the buyer behavior as exhibited in Figure 8.2. The most important factors influencing a consumer's involvement level are their perceived risks. The purchase of any product involves a certain amount of risk, which may include:

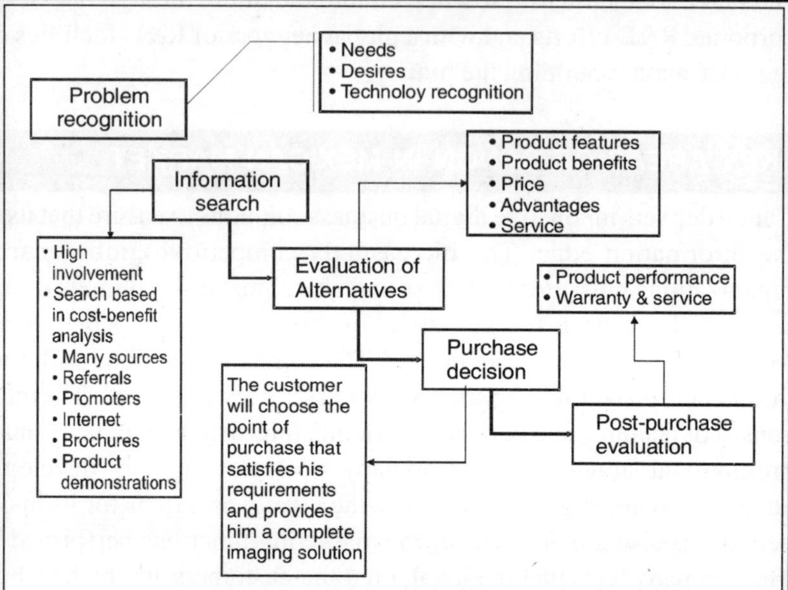

Figure 8.2 Managing buyer behaviour: Canon way

- Product Failure – risk that the product will not perform as expected. (e.g., will the health supplements make me feel better and prevent me from diseases?)
- Financial – risk that the outcome will harm the consumer financially (e.g., will buying a formal suit cause me financial hardship?),
- Operational – risk that consists of alternative means of performing the operation or meeting the need (e.g., is there any maintenance required for the ball dress?)
- Social – risk friends or acquaintances will decide the purchase (e.g., what will my friends think of me in this dress?)
- Psychological – risk that the product will lower the consumer's self-image (e.g., will I look stupid, if I wear this dress?)
- Personal – risk that the product will physically harm the buyer (e.g., is this health tablet meant to do me any good? Will it perform as it claims or will it ruin my health instead?)

In a high degree of perceived risk, decisions in this case may require significant financial commitments and involve social or psychological implications.

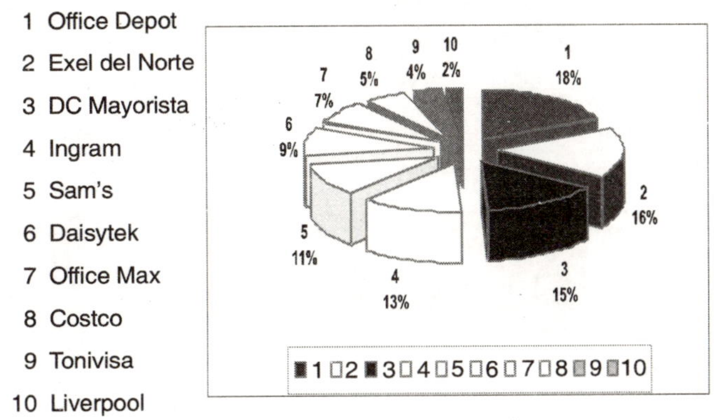

Figrue 8.3 Retail sales of Canon products by channels in Mexican market

Sales force the company is trained to understand the consumer behaviour and develop their strategies accordingly. The needs, desires and the technology preference for the better perceived use value of the products are slated by the staff of the company and necessary information and supports are pooled through high involvement in the subject, cost-benefit ratio of the product purchase, referrals and available point of purchase sources with the dealers. The alternatives are evaluated to frame the customer focussed decision on the basis of the product attribute analysis and comparative advantages in reference to price, quality and services of the products of the company. The purchase decisions of the buyers is stimulated by providing the point of purchase of their choice that satisfies their requirements and optimizes the level of satisfaction in terms of personal attention and product handling. The post-purchase evaluation is done in reference to the product performance, warranty administration and customer services by the call centre division of the company. The purchase decision for a Canon product takes 1-7 days on an average.

PRODUCT DISTRIBUTION AND SALES

Distribution strategy is considered to be the pivot of marketing functions that involves channels of marketing, point of purchase options and focuses on the customer relationship management. The strength of the distributor might include profits and cash flow, products and technologies, vendor arrangements, intellectual property, consistent sales, brand recognition, and access to capital. It is in the interest of the company to identify and use such strengths of the channel may be the wholesalers, large or small retailers, to establish core competencies. This allows the company to find a niche, where the firm can stand out as a recognized market leader. The product distribution system of Canon involves distribution centre that manages the logistics operations with retailers and wholesalers. The retail channels consist of specialised electronic stores, office equipment depots and superstores. The performance of the top dealers in Mexico, inclusive of the superstores and office equipment depots is exhibited in Figure 8.3. The maximum sales is contributed by the Office Depot (18%)

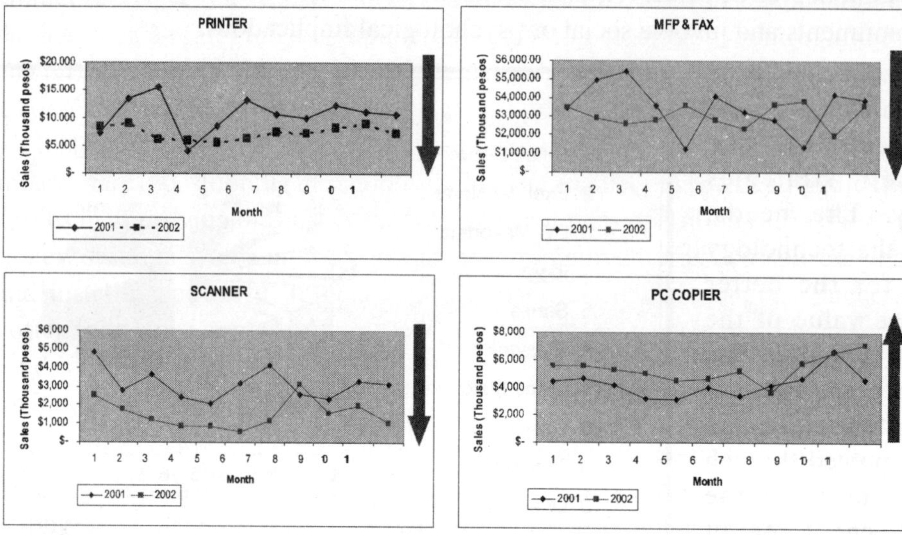

Figure 8.4 Sales performance of Canon products in Mexican market (2001–2002)

followed by Exel del Norte (16%) and DC Mayorista (15%). The large super markets who may also be considered as the bulk distributors, such as Costco and Sam's Club contribute 5 percent and 11 percent to the total for the Canon products of wide range sales in Mexico.

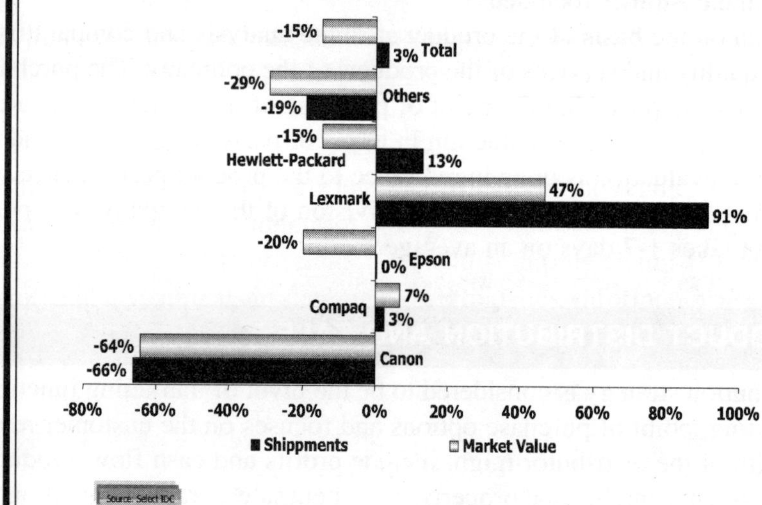

Figure 8.5 Shipment and mark value relationship across principal brands in Mexican market (2001–2002)

Sales performance of different Canon products during 2001-2002, has been exhibited in Figure 8.4 that delineates the trends in the sales in specific product categories.

Sales of the printers and scanners of Canon have shown the declining trend in 2002 as compared to the previous year. The printer market had faced greater competition as compared to the scanner markets as it remained below $15 Million Pesos all through the year 2002. The sales of the scanners had also shown a declining trend and remained below $ 3 Million pesos during 2002 against its sales performance in 2001. The sales performance was also not very encouraging for the MFP/Fax machines during the above referred period. However, the sales had shown an upward trend for the PC Copier equipments that touched the sales revenue of about $7 Million pesos during 2002, as compared to the previous year.

Company was loosing the gross profit in office equipments due to flaws in the management, the product market, strong prospecting and efficient servicing. Besides the problems of inventory, increasing competition and unfocussed promotion, approaches lead the causes for decline in the overall sales of office equipment products. This situation had a significant impact on the reduction of the market share of the company products in office equipments category and piling losses in the stock keeping units (SKUs). During this period the Canon Mexico received instruction from its controlling counterpart Canon USA either to relinquish the office equipments division in Mexico or merge the same with photo and video division. The company had increasing dependency on the Canon USA for supplying office equipments in Mexican market. The prices were higher for the Canon products as compared to its close competing brands and that situation had reflected also in Mexican market, when indented from the company's USA counterpart. The delivery of the products suffered inordinate delays due to the shipment problems at the USA and Canada ports. The decline in the market value had caused 64 percent negative growth to the company in reference to the inkjet printers due to the delay in shipment. The Figure 8.5 exhibits the status of market value and shipment of office equipments in Mexican markets during 2001-2002, across the principal brands. In the above referred period the market value in general also did not grow favourably and the overall industry share for the office equipment products marked only to 3 percent in the Mexican market. The most advantageous brand during the reference period was Lexmark as it retain 47 percent of the market value against 91 percent of its product shipments to the country. The high price of the products posed many marketing problems including their positioning against the competing brands. Under the given conditions the company could not position the Cannon products in Mexican market on the basis of price advantage, which is one of the sensitive tools to hold consumer behaviour in favour of the brand. However, the company had positioned the office equipments in the high price bracket on the basis of

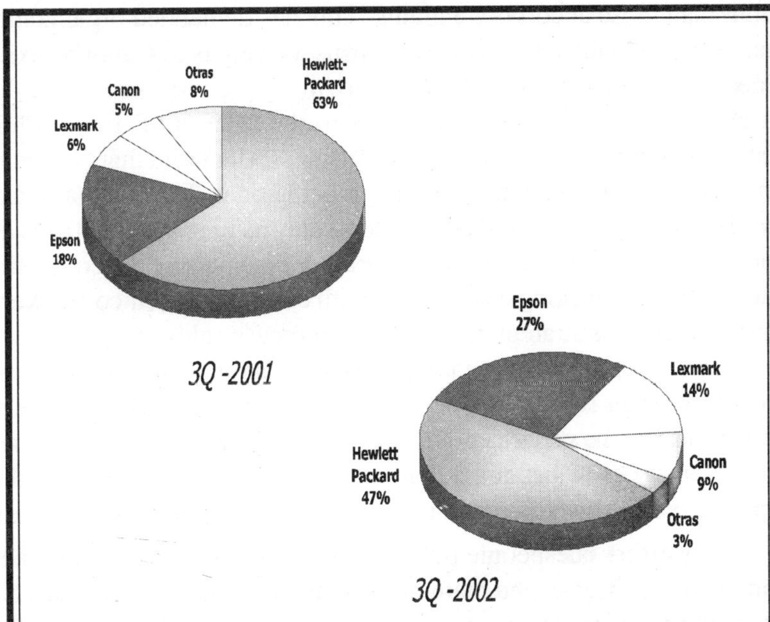

Figure 8.6 The inkjet printer market share (2001–2002)

the attributes and long term use values. This strategy with all sales force dynamics in the market could not truly pull the sales graph upwards against its competing brands during 2002. In the third quarter of 2001, Canon held 5 percent market share in inkjet printers in the country which was augmented to 9 percent in the same quarter of 2002. The inkjet printer market share in Mexican market during 2001-2002 is exhibited in Figure 11.6. Hewlett Packard remained the largest market participant with 63 and 47 percent of market share during 2001 and 2002 respectively. However the market share of HP had declined in 2002 against the previous year and all the other principal brands gained the market share during the referred period. Epson was found to be the second leading brand capturing 27 percent of the market share in inkjet printers during 2002.

Among variety of problems responsible for the low turnover of the Canon office equipment products in Mexican market, the inadequate knowledge of the product and dealers is also significant. This made the sales people underachieve their monthly quotas. The customer visit schedule of the sales representatives and support services integration are interrelated and play key role in improving the overall performance. The sales representatives of photo and video products express that there is lack of adequate demand for the office equipment products while the sales representatives of the office equipments division find that there is no adequate market for the photo and video products of Canon. The sales staff of either division of the company had enough time to refresh themselves with contemporary skills and update their action points for improving the sales performance in the market.

ORGANIZATIONAL RESTRUCTURING

Recession has resulted in layoffs everywhere. But employees at small outfits may have less to worry about than those at corporate giants. This has demanded organizational re-structuring for sales and marketing in many large corporate firms as well as in Canon Mexico. The reorganization has been tuned in the company with reference to hiring process, responsive departmental network, integrated coordination and financial incentives to the sales staff. Bruce Phillips, a senior economist at the National Federation of Independent Business, USA said that "If you went industry by industry, you'd find that more small firms are hiring than big ones. That's always true in recessions. Large firms are more labour-intensive, and people don't stay as long at small firms as they do at big ones." Selling is not a competition, it's a connection. Rather than putting the competitive instinct in overdrive, devote your energies to making connections with customers, their co-workers, the people in the organization, and beyond. This strategy will not only increase sales and profits, it will speed up the sales cycle. It is necessary for the large organizations like Canon to optimize their staff strength and prune, the low productive sales resources. Too many salespeople, especially those new to the profession, rush right into discussing the specifications, financing, or advantages of their wares. On the contrary the seasoned professionals know better the markets and clients. They establish the personal, professional or both types of contacts well before the sales conversation moves on to the details and get to close the deal.

More effort salespeople put into analyzing the competition, the less time they will have left to understand, cultivate, and maintain connections with customers. This can be a fatal mistake, since it opens the door to the very competitors they were worried about in the first place! Never forget, your customers are your competitors' prospects.[4] Some companies require their salespeople to make a

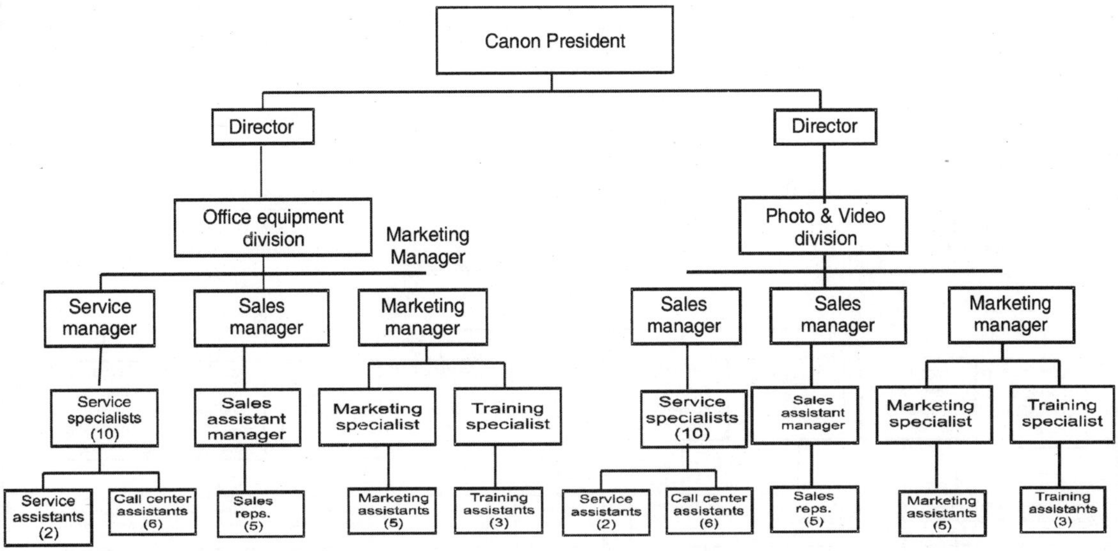

Figure 8.7 (a) Sales organizational structure of Canon Mexico before merger

minimum quota of outbound phone calls every day. Unless you have an unbelievably well-targeted list to work from, chances are that telemarketing will produce a very low return on the time invested. The re-structuring the sales organization of Canon has been proposed to maximize the per capita productivity.

This has been considered simply as an arrangement of activities involving the group of people recharged with improved goals and coordinated activities. The office equipment division and photo and video division have been merged and the sales re-organization was brought into force. The Figure 8.7(a) exhibits the sales organizational structure before the merger of its office equipments and photo and video divisions. The Figure 8.7(b) shows the re-structured organization of the sales department of the company integrating the above referred two divisions. The re-organization has been brought into force as Consumer Imaging Group (CIG) with three distinctive departments – marketing, sales and service. This reorganization had aimed at inculcating the new staff, styles and shared values for better understanding of the market situations and building consensus on the marketing and sales strategies. The culture as a product has also been focussed on the role of sales people for benchmarking their individual business goals as high as of the competitors.

Products handled by the consumer imaging group include bubble jet printer, laser beam printers, printer consumables, image scanners, fax machines, multi-functional printers, personal copier and

4 Michelle Nichols : The Seven Deadly Myths of Selling, *Business Week Online,* April 18, 2003

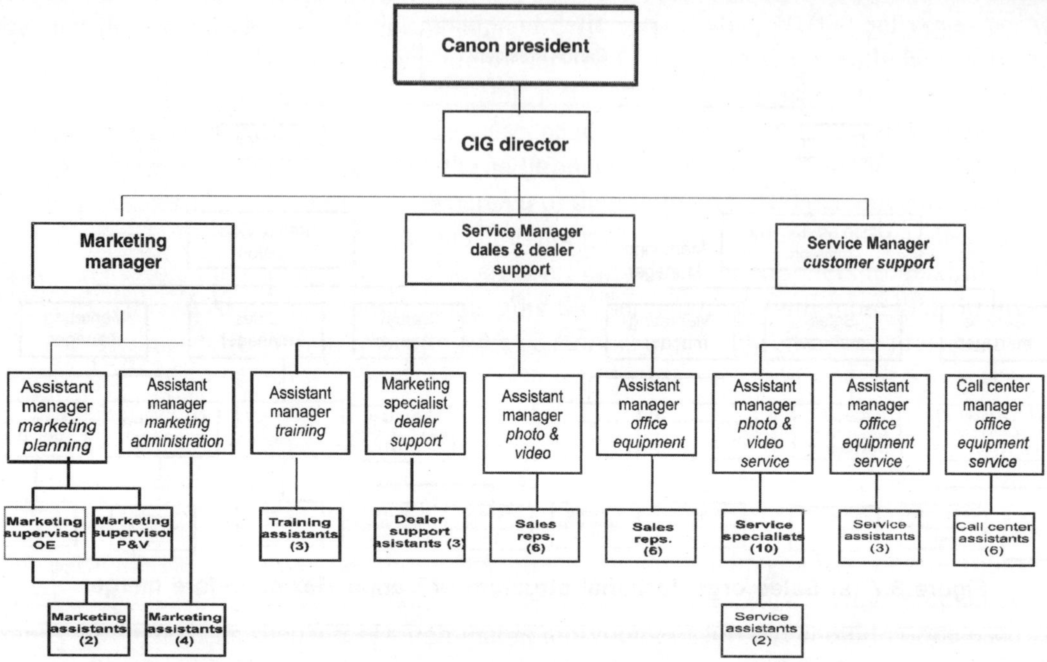

Figure 8.7 (b) Sales organizational structure of Canon Mexico after merger: consumer imaging group

calculators in the range of office equipments. The photo and video products constituted the compact cameras, SLR and digital cameras, lenses, camcorders, binoculars and projectors.

COMPENSATION PROGRAM

Compensating sales people by commission is a simple proposition made difficult by many companies. While commission-based compensation isn't the only–or even necessarily the best–way to compensate a sale force, it is predominant in most industries that rely on a direct personal sales force to market their products or services. The basic problem with many of these commission plans is that they are expected to encourage the sales person to produce, as well as to shape other behaviors. And that's where the problems lie. There are three basic issues to be considered while developing the compensation plan for the sales force:

- Plan should offer an immediate positive reward to the salesperson for doing well the things you want done well.
- It should be clear and simple to understand.
- It should be relatively free of influence from factors outside the salesperson's control.

A sales commission plan based on these three principles will reward the company by encouraging profitable selling efforts by the sales force. The financial incentives to the sales force of the company was revised on the following line:

- Sales contests
- Incentive payments for enhanced market coverage
- Commissions, Salary and
- Periodical benefits to the sales personnel over the basic or fixed pay.

Focus group[5] interviews with the employees of the company, revealed a new sales commission plan aimed at providing more income to the sales staff with higher degree of motivation. It has been felt by the group that the incentives plan needs to be of broader perspective and should also be able to motivate the sales people who have poor performance. The discussion of the focus group discussions envisaged that higher commissions need to be awarded to that sales staffs who over-achieves the given quotas. The changes in the new compensation plan were suggested towards the mix of salary and commission to the sales people.

Table 8.2 Plan of Recommended Incentives

Quota achievement	*VMC* Entitlement (percent)	*Trimester bonus* Entitlement (percent)
200 percent or more	200	300
175-199		250
150-174		200
125-149	150	150
110-124	125	125
100-109		100
90-99		80
80-89	50	60
60-79		40
Less than 59	40	No Bonus

Source. Focus Group

Salary component was suggested to constitute 60 percent of the total compensation offer and 40 percent should be earned by the employee towards the variable monthly compensation(VMC) spread into trimester bonus and monthly commission of 20 percent in each period. The formula suggested that the monthly commission may be fixed in the range of 50-200 percent and the trimester bonus should have maximum 300 percent entitlement on the quota achieved during the given period by the

5 Given the situation of the company a focus group discussion was conducted by the students of the course on Advanced Selling System covering 12 marketing and sales personnel. The discussion of the focus group was informally recorded and analysed to know the emerging solutions to most of the issues raised in the cases. The issue of compensation is one among them to be addressed.

sales person. The Table 11.2, discusses the plan of monthly commission and trimester bonus as emerged from the focus group discussion. The group also suggested that the trimester bonus should be made recoverable and not lapsable. In case of under achievement of the targets by the sales persons in any month of the trimester, the trimester bonus should be calculated on the basis of the total achievement. The following example shown in Table 8.3 explains the calculations of the trimester bonus:

Table 8.3 Bonus Calculation Table

Period	*Quota*	*Achievement*	*Bonus Entitlement*
January	110	150	73
February	130	160	81
March	260	190 #	137
Semester	500	500	**100**

 # Under Achievement

Group suggested that the trimester bonus may be paid on the sales achievement on the selected products like Powershot S-100 of the company. The employee may opt for either monthly variable commission or the semester bonus which has the advantage of recovering the lost bonus in the stipulated period unlike the monthly commission.

It has been broadly agreed during the discussions that the reward system for the sales persons should also be positive, not negative, in nature. Be sure that the compensation system adds to the salesperson's income when he or she succeeds. A structure which instead removes income for failure to produce also removes all incentives except fear. And fear is a short-lived motivator with ultimate negative results for the company. On the contrary a group of discussants argued that a frequently-encountered commission system which violates all of these rules is the one basing the commission rate on achievement of a budget or quota set by management rather than the sales person. Shortening the quota period to move the reward closer to the sale would seem to be the logical answer to this problem, but since it's impossible to figure out what an individual sale earns before the sales person works on it, the commission plan can't have a positive effect on their efforts.

FUTURE PERSPECTIVES: BEYOND CUSTOMER SATISFACTION

A satisfied Canon customer is the one who is likely to choose Canon again in the future. This is why customer satisfaction is an integral marketing priority, and why the company continues to devote significant resources to this end. The Canon support desk, responds swiftly to myriad customer queries via telephone, facsimile, e-mail and other means. It also collects and analyzes people's opinions and provides valuable feedback to individual product divisions for future product developments and services. Canon is expanding its solutions business on a worldwide basis, helping customers improve their ability to conduct business on the Web while raising their productivity. The company is pursuing absolute customer satisfaction by making performance, operability, design and other modifications as requested by customers. The reach of the company towards building customer loyalty by creating trust on the brand would be the most significant philosophy. The Appendix 'A' explains the categorical discussion on building the trust among the customer segments in fray of competition of the corporate giants.

REFERENCES

Bresnahan, Timothy F, Reiss, Peter C. : Entry and Competition in the Concentrated Markets, *Journal of Political Economy,* 99 (5), 1991, 997-1005

Canon Inc. : *Annual Report,* 2003

Elie Ofek : *Customer Profitability and Lifetime Value,* Harvard Business School Publications, January 2002, 1-7

Internet sources : www.canon.mx, www.businessweek.com

Kimberly D. Elsbach : How to Pitch a Brilliant Idea, *Harvard Business Review,* September 2003, 1-9

Mitchell Colin : Selling the Brand Inside, *Harvard Business Review,* January 2002, 5-11

Robert J. Frank, Elizabeth A. Mihas, Laxman Narasimhan, Stacey Rauch : *Competing in a Value Driven World,* McKinsey & Company, 2003, 1.14

Varian, Hal R. : A Model of Sales, *American Economic Review,* 70 (4), 1980, 651-659

APPENDIX A

Explanation for the strategies reaching beyond customer satisfaction

T - Truth

Trust and solid relationships are built on telling the truth. Companies must maintain this principle both with internal and external customers. It is imperative that this value is represented in everything a company does. We have seen how the lack of solid ethics can crumble even the largest of companies.

R - Responsibility

Trust is built when everyone within an organization realizes what their responsibilities are and that they are held accountable for them. Choose to schedule reviews quarterly for every member of the company to make sure they are aware of their responsibilities. Take ownership of mistakes and be diligent to find ways to make corrections.

U - Unselfishness

Trust is built when employees devote their time and talent in the workplace and do it, unselfishly. Customers appreciate the employee who goes out of their way to satisfy the customer. Customers don't appreciate hearing how badly the employee wants to go home, or how they didn't get a break, or how awful their schedule is.

S - Security

Trust is built on a feeling of security. Good lighting in the parking lot and store entrance, rooms fitted with doors that lock, employees that handle ringing up a sale with accuracy, and alarm systems that are visible are all ways to make the customer feel safe in your place of business. Employees want to feel a sense of job security and that they are appreciated for the job they do.

T - Teamwork

Trust is built when everyone within the organization feels a sense of ownership. How well do your employees work together? Are they willing to go out of their way to help each other out? Do the managers roll up their sleeves to help when the workload is overwhelming? Is there a reward system in place that encourages employees to want to excel? Most importantly, are there cheerleaders within the organization to keep the momentum going when times are tough?

CHAPTER 9

STRATEGIC MARKETING

CHAPTER FOCUS

- *To understand the concept of marketing strategy,*
- *To acquaint with the marketing screening process and strategic marketing planning, and*
- *Building comprehension on the issues of strategic marketing and marketing management.*

Strategy can be defined as a rational set of time-sequenced actions aimed at gaining a sustainable advantage over competition and improving position with customers. Strategy answers *what and where* questions concerning your business. It is a shared vision describing what the organization should be in the future and where it is going, not how it will get there. Strategy is the framework managing the "how" choices which determine the future nature and direction of the organization. It focuses on accomplishing maximum and enduring positive differentiation as opposed to the competition in meeting customer values. The choices guided by strategy relate to the entire range of the organization's products or services, market, principal capabilities, growth rate, return from and allocation of resources. Perhaps most importantly, strategies identify critical issues that are the changes, modifications and additions to the organization's structure and systems, to its capabilities and resources'. to its information needs and management that result from setting strategy.

Strategic marketing is a bridge between the marketing management and marketing and interplays with three forces in the markets-customer, competition and corporate entities. The marketing strategy synchronizes the functional activities among the 3Cs and helps in building the distinctive strengths in the corporate houses to deliver better customer values. An effective marketing strategy should include a clear definition of market, an appropriate match between the corporate strengths and market needs and competitive performance. A good balance of these attributes would build a successful marketing strategy and justifies the role of marketing in an organization. The Table 9.1 exhibits the marketing interplays at various levels in the business environment.

Table 9.1 Role of Marketing in Different Levels of Organizations

Level of organization	*Basic roles*	*Identification*
Product/Market	Formulate, implement control and evaluate specific marketing programs	Marketing management
Corporate	Provide interplay between customer and competitive perspective for developing an effective blend of strategy	Corporate marketing
Business Unit	Develop need based approaches to direct the present and future course of marketing activity for the unit	Strategic marketing

Marketing strategy in terms of the three Cs is an endeavor to satisfy the customer needs in a given business environment by building the corporate strengths and competitive advantages. The strategy is oriented towards long terms goals and perceived as a tool to develop relationship between the corporate and customer ends. Marketing strategy is to achieve maximum positive competitive differentiation that is other than the rival activities to satisfy the customer needs.

> Concept of marketing strategy may be illustrated with reference to the case of Emerson Company. Emerson makes basic products essential to a variety of industries, such as refrigerator compressors, pressure gauges, and garbage disposals. What distinguishes this St. Louis, MO Company from the herd is its dazzling record of 36 uninterrupted years of increased earnings, without significant price increases, since the mid 1980s. During the highly competitive 1980s, Emerson staunchly endured the challenges of low-cost Brazilian, Korean, and Japanese competitors.
>
> Several factors contributed to Emerson's success: (1) Management recognized early that low-cost, aggressive competitors would remain permanent part of the global scene and would intensify into the next decade. (2) Management exerted the discipline to secure cost-efficient operations at every level of the organization. (3) Management demonstrated the flexibility to focus on growth markets and exit those segments with little chance of turning a profit, such as defense and construction, and niche businesses such as gardening tools. (4) It realized that cost cutting was only one part of the success equation to sustain growth; the other, that strategic marketing planning should function as the operating system for managing both long-term objectives and day-to-day operations. To make the planning system work, Emerson company has followed the following strategy:

- Periodically surveys all employees to assure input and participation from every functional area of the business. Such input permits additional strategy options to surface that can be evaluated, refined, and implemented.
- Identifies customer's problems early, while they are still manageable, enameling marketing and sales to take immediate action.

- Keeps vigilant watch on troublesome competitors so that managers loose no time in redirecting their efforts where needed.
- Tracks sales growth, new product development, and market expansion as the benchmarks to monitor the plan.

A single example sums up Emerson's accomplishments: ten years ago a Japanese plant could offer temperature sensors for washing machines for 20%below Emerson's price. Today, Emerson's costs are below the Japanese, and the company has regained the market shares. Rigorous planning, then, is at the heart of Emerson's system for managing growth.

FOCUS OF STRATEGIC MARKETING

A large number of the rapid growth firms present written business plans[1] for strategy implementation. The written plans enable CEOs to manage more critical business functions, grow faster and achieve a higher proportion of revenue from new products and services than those whose plans are unwritten. Additionally, written business plan helps growing firms to increase their revenues faster over their competitors than those without a written plan. The major advantages and issues associated with strategic marketing planning are as under:

- Strategy is a major focus for higher revenues and profits- and to hatch new products, expand existing business, and create new markets.
- Business strategy is the single most important management issue and will remain so for the next five years.
- Democratize the strategy process by handing it over to teams of line and staff managers from different disciplines.
- Create networks of relationships with customers, suppliers, and rivals to gain greater competitive advantage.

A company may use strategic marketing planning to identify long-term opportunities and manage day-to-day operations. Strategic marketing planning is an essential instrument to grow present markets, spot growth markets, recognize new product innovation, and stay alert to new opportunities. The Figure 9.1 exhibits the key areas of strategic management and the process thereof.

Situation Analysis

Marketing plan process begins with a *situation analysis* of a specific product or market. Whereas the strategies plans look ahead three to five years, the situation analysis requires that you look back three to five years to obtain a historical perspective of business. The situation analysis is divided into three parts: marketing mix analysis, market background, and competitor analysis. For *marketing mix analysis,* objectively and factually write sales and unit volume by product, analyze pricing and access promotion and distribution. *Market background* deals with the nature of audience, human factor, the image you convey, what customers think of product, and the frequency of its use. The examination of

1 According to Cooper & Lybrand's 1998 Trendsetters Barometer survey about two-thirds of the fast growing companies had written marketing plans.

the background permits you to think extensively about marketplace and customers. The third part also permits you to *analyze competitors* in detail.

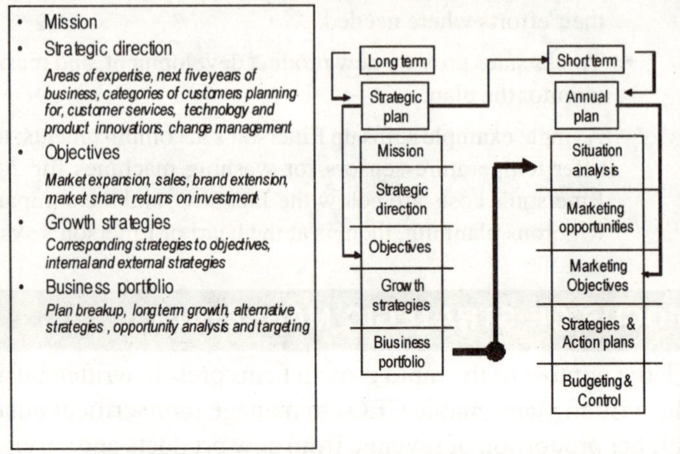

Figure 9.1 Paradigm of strategic marketing management

Marketing Opportunities

After you have analyzed the situation, the next step is to evaluate opportunities. Surprisingly, managers often neglect this part of the process. This planning step is exceedingly important, since the whole purpose of conducting the situational analysis is to expose opportunities. Opportunities are voids or gaps in a product, a market, or a service that can be filled to satisfy customer needs and wants. This stage of marketing plan is best achieved by incorporating the input of various functional managers from manufacturing, R&D, product development, finance and sales. Brainstorming is a useful technique for identifying opportunities. For example, consider the features and benefits of product. Study the situation analysis, including competitive intelligence, and allow the ideas to flow. Do not attempt to judge them- just record them as they emerge. The probability is that you will record 90% to 95% of them, form a new product, or render a new service.

Marketing Objectives

Third step in the marketing plan is to work out primary and functional marketing objective. First, develop *primary quantitative objective*, such as sales in dollars and units, market shares, gross margins, return on investment, return on assets, and any other quantitative information required by the organization. Second, develop *functional objectives* as they pertain to product, packaging, services, pricing, promotion, and distribution. These functional areas are commonly referred to as the *marketing mix* . It should be evident that the marketing mix is a key part of the marketing plan in that it represents the controllable factors you can employ to achieve the primary financial and volume objectives. The marketing mix also helps you identify sources of competitive problems and, in turn, suggests possible solutions or strategies.

Strategies and Action Plans

On the basis of marketing objectives, you can now develop the strategies and action plans that translate those objectives into action. Unless you can support objectives with firm action plans, they are useless. They are no more than good intentions until you develop the strategies and tactics that will make them happen. Thus, for each objective, develop a strategy and a tactic action plan. Further, each strategy should include details about what is going to happen, when it is going to happen, and who is responsible for carrying out the action.

Financial Controls and Budgets

This step in financial plan involves the financial controls, budgets, and variance reports that translate into numbers for the actions that you have stated in the previous steps (see chapter 3, under Financial Resources Analysis).

Combinations of the long-term strategic and annual marketing plans form a total strategic marketing plan for any level of an organization, from corporate management down to product line manager. Further, for every major product and market described in the business portfolio, you should develop a specific annual tactical marketing plan. Thus, you combine a long-term strategic viewpoint with a one-year tactical framework to create action- something that the strategic plan by itself could not accomplish and for which the marketing plan alone is too narrow a perspective for today's competitive environment.

STRATEGIC MARKETING SCREENING PROCESS

The following screening process will help the managers to zero-in on visible prospects for growth. Once identified and prioritized it can be converted into long-term and short-term marketing objectives, strategies, and tactics.

1. *Present Markets*: To identify the best opportunities for expanding present markets, it is necessary to investigate the emerging businesses or acquire new users for product. Determining how to displace competition should be thought of which is particularly significant move in no-growth markets. Increase product usage by current customers and redefine market segments where there are changes in customers buying patterns. Work jointly with customers on innovation ideas to reformulate or repackage the product according to their specific need. Identify new uses (applications) of the products and services and reposition the product to create a more favorable perception over rival products. The investigation should be carried where to expand into new or unserved market riches.
2. *Customers:* The distribution channels need to be assessed to identify the best opportunities for expanding, improvement or expansion in the customer base. Refine the product pricing policies to match market share objectives. Enrich communications, including advertising, sales promotion and publicity and deploy the sales force to target new customers with high potential. Enhance customer service, including technical services and complaint handling. Identifying the changes in trade buying practices, where the buying process may have shifted from manufacturer to distributor or to end-user makes the marketing strategy good for effective implementation.
3. *Growth Markets*: Targeting the key geographic locations, specifying which markets or user groups represent, the greatest long-term potential is required to identify the major growth markets.
4. *New product Development*: To give priority to "hot" candidates for new product and services development that will impact on immediate and long-range opportunities, the

company should focus on new products that can be differentiated and that have the potential for an extended life cycle. Search for ways to diversify into new or related products, product lines, and/or new items or features. The techniques to modify products by customer groups, distribution outlets, or individual customer applications should be examined and initiate the work on improving packaging to conform to customer's specifications and to distinguish product from rivals. Simultaneously there is a need to establish new value-added services.

5. *Targets of opportunity*: Innovative attitude and entrepreneurial thinking would develop the focus on areas outside current market segment or production line not included in the other categories. However, strategic directions or mission statements need to be referred as a guideline to assess how far a company can realistically diversify from its core business and still retain its vitality.

STRATEGIC DIRECTIONS

To begin with the strategic marketing planning process the managers should think of strategic direction as the mission or vision statement of the company, business unit, product line, or individual product. It is the long-range philosophy of a business unit. It reflects a strategic vision of what product or business can become in the long run. Strategic directions may be considered by a firm in reference to the following issues.

- What are distinctive areas of expertise?
- What business should you be in over the next three to five years or long term?
- What types of categories of customers will you serve?
- What customer functions are you likely to satisfy as you see the market evolve?
- What technologies will you see to satisfy customer/ market needs?
- What changes are taking place in the markets, consumer behavior, competition, environment, culture and the economy?

Point of this exercise is that the responsibility for defining a strategic direction no longer belongs only to the upper management. Managers from various departments- marketing, product development, manufacturing, finance and sales – contribute to the overall strategic direction of a business by asking, "What business should I be in for my individual product?" The major work in this area of strategic thinking is attributed to Theodore Levitt, of the Harvard Business School, in his classic article, "Marketing Myopia". Using the railroad as a prime example, Levitt shows how the railway system declined in use as technology advanced, because managers defined their product too narrowly. He explains that to continue growing, companies must determine customer's needs and wants and not rely simply on the longevity of their products. According to Levitt, a myopic view is based on the following four beliefs that begin in a manager's mind and permeate an organization: (1) growth is guaranteed by an expanding and affluent population; (2) there is no competitive substitute for the company's major products; (3) excessive belief in mass production and rapidly declining units coats as output rises; (4) preoccupation with a product that lends itself to experimentation, manufacturing cost improvement. The Figure 9.1 illustrates the strategic marketing planning process for an organization. A strategic direction for one of Dow Chemicals agriculture herbicide products formally reads, "Chemical control of brush on right-of- way." This product driven orientation was too "myopic" and came across more as a product definition than a strategic vision. When revised to reflect a border market driven focus that would drive future product and market development, it reads

> *Provide high-quality products and services to meet vegetation management goals on right-of-way, industrial, municipality and aquatic /wetland sites at a profit. Products and services may include chemical, mechanical, application, distribution, consultation and establishment of desirable vegetation.*

Analyze how expansive the statement is and how it defines potential and product/markets development. In other words, it summarizes a vision. In another example, Becton Dickinson, a health care firm, originally described the strategic direction for one of its hypodermic needles as, "Our strategic direction is to be the leading manufacturer of hypodermic products for the health care field." Here, too, this narrow focus of good intentions was broadened to provide a forward-looking orientation. The revamped statement read as - *Our strategic direction is to meet the needs of consumers and health care providers for drug-delivery devices by offering a full line of hypodermic products and products systems. Our leadership position will be maintained through acquisition to provide alternative administration and monitoring systems.*

Guided by such a statement, managers could expand their vision and direct the product line into innovative product systems, technologies, and ultimately expand their holds on existing markets and launch into new markets. Four critical planning steps for managers to observe in this process area are as follows:

Step1: Strategic Direction

It is necessary to define the scope of company, business unit and product line. In order to establish the strategic direction the competency of business unit, profile of customers to be served in future, required technology and competition need to be reviewed be the firm.

Step 2: Objectives and Goals

As illustrated in the auto parts and the electric utility cases, indicate the performance expectations such as sales, profits and other quantitative objectives. Also managers need to list non-quantitative objectives, including upgrading distribution channels, building specialty products, upgrading field services, and launching new or upgrading old products.

Step 3: Growth Strategies

Select strategies to reach objectives. These relate to product positioning, product quality, distribution, pricing, packaging, value-added services, and customer/technical services.

Step 4: Business Portfolio

Based on the previous three sections, develop a product and market portfolio strategy that defines the following:

- Existing products into existing markets.
- Existing products into new markets (Westinghouse focused on law enforcement markets).
- New products into existing markets.
- New products into new markets.

Strategy on product marketing may be developed in many ways to better position existing products in the prevailing markets. Development of such strategies may be categorically described as:

- Market penetration to position existing products in new markets
- Market development to introduce new products into existing markets.
- Product development to introduce at new products for new markets, and

Diversification as a guideline for sustainable market growth for ling term.

STRATEGIC MANAGEMENT

Strategic marketing delineates 3Rs emphasizing the right products for right growth markets at right time. These issues are also highlighted in the marketing management but from a different perspective. The resources of the firm are identified as uncontrollable variables of the marketing mix in the process of marketing management while the strategic marketing systematically defines all the variables and examines its necessary inputs to maximize the corporate performance. Strategic marketing is a plan of all aspects of the strategy of an organization in the market place unlike a simple marketing plan that deals with so-called marketing-mix.[2] Strategic marketing differs from marketing management, in many areas like orientation, core philosophy, approach, and relationship of business organization with various environmental variables. One of the prominent differences between the strategic marketing and marketing management is the temporal framework. This process deals with long range planning and the decisions thereof would have long-term implications. The inductive and intuitive attributes dominate the strategic marketing process while marketing management is largely oriented towards analytical examination of the associated marketing factors and its implementation. The strategic marketing advocates the democratic decision making process which is defined as bottom-up approach while in the marketing management, the flow of directions are from top-down to make decisions. The Figure 9.2 exhibits many points of differences between the strategic management and marketing management. In the strategic management process environment is considered as ever changing and dynamic. On the contrary the marketing management assumes that the environment is constant for effective implementation. However, occasional changes are noted in the marketing management. The continuous search of

2 Derek F Abell and John S. Hammond: *Strategic Market Planning,* Prentice-Hall, Englewood Cliffs, New Jersey, 1979 PP 1-16

opportunities is one of the major focuses of strategic marketing and is aimed to explore the opportunities for optimizing its businèss goals in the long run. However, an ad-hoc search is conducted in the marketing management process to find new opportunities. The marketing management has a narrow profit center approach, while the strategic marketing pursues broad objectives of achieving synergy between different components of organization, both horizontally and vertically. The strategic marketing activity requires high degree of creativity and originality in the approach.

Marketing management	Strategic marketing
▪ Action oriented ▪ Existing opprtunities ▪ Non-product variables ▪ Stable environment ▪ Reactive behaviour ▪ Day-to-day management ▪ Marketing department ▪ Low diversification ▪ Profit objective	▪ Analysis oriented ▪ New opportunities ▪ Product -market ▪ Dynamic environment ▪ Pro-active behaviour ▪ Long -range management ▪ Cross functional organization ▪ High diversification ▪ Customer satisfaction

Figure 9.2: Major difference between strategic marketing and marketing manageemnt

The implementation, control and monitoring skills are preferred in the marketing management activity unlike the strategic marketing. Strategic marketing needs a proactive perspective, and the marketing management requires the reactive perspectives for effective leadership .

A division of Cargill Corp. developed its strategic direction that would take it from a commodity type business of egg production to a value-added, broader definition:

> *We will be a leading marketer of quality, value-added egg based food products serving primarily the food service industry. We will be a least-cost producer and a leader in developing and implementing innovative products and processes to meet the needs of an evolving marketplace.*

Statement reflects a clear and pragmatic vision that moved the division away from its orientation of just dealing with fresh egg production to one of going to the next step by preparing and packaging ready-to-use egg-based products for all types of institutions. These statements are no more word play. Rather they have a practical application in creating a workable mental set whereby managers can envision how a product line or business might expand over the next three to five years. In turn, the statements help shape objectives, strategies, and a portfolio of products and markets. If you view the basic product as railroad cars traveling on parallel tracks down a path, the result is a short-sighted business condition that, in turn, confines products, services, and market development on a narrow dimensions. Redefined as a transportation company, however, the strategic vision includes transportation of all types- air, water, space, and diverse forms of transportation still unknown. Since railroads company owns land on either side of the tracks, a transportation viewpoint can conceivably include laying underground pipe to transport food, fluids, chemicals, and power lines.

This type of expansive strategic thinking is not limited to the private sector of profit-making corporations. It applies equally well to the public sector. Consider the March of Dimes Defect Foundation, an organization that was originally dedicated to the cure of Polio. Fortunately, polio is no longer a serious threat. Dose that situation mean that March of Dimes is out of business and can serve no useful functions? Not at all. By redefining its mission, or strategic direction as *birth defects,* the organization is alive and well, using its skills and resources in a broader mandate to serve societies needs. Even companies with strong positions in the market place and with profitable businesses are redefining mission statements to embrace the inevitable movement towards new technologies. For example, consider GTE Directories Corp., the producer of the familiar telephone directories known as Yellow Pages. Its basic business consists of selling advertising space, the volumes, and distributing the directories. At one point GTE defined its business purpose and developed the following mission:

> *A worldwide integrated and marketing corporation of directional hard copy and electronic advertising media and informational services.*

Does the mission specifically state that the company is the producer of the Yellow pages? Not at all. Does the statement include that product? Yes, by using the phrase" directional hard copy" , it includes the product line of Yellow Pages. Yet the clear implication is that the manager can think expansively of new products that may take different forms. Now consider the phrase " electronic advertising media". Taking into account the evolving use of the Internet and the yet-to-be developed technology, GTE can link up to new media that can augment its Yellow Pages or, in time, even displace it. This portion of the mission permits managers at all levels of the company to open their minds to new possibilities, while still remaining consistent with GTE's basic business. Finally, the phrase "Information services" opens the window into expansion areas as developed countries move increasingly towards service economies and information transfer, thus building "a worldwide integrated publishing and marketing corporation". Yet, how far should thinking go towards a market-driven orientation? It is the best to initially think as far toward that orientation as possible, and then come back to a more comfortable position somewhere between the two extremes of a product-driven and a market-driven orientation. That position is usually based on the following factors:

- Culture of the organization, with the broad range of behaviors exhibited as conservative to aggressive.
- Availability of human, material, and financial resources for maintaining existing business functions and for investing in future growth.
- Amount of risk that the management is willing to assume in going into debt.
- Degree of environmental change that is anticipated in market behavior.
- Threat of competitive activities and their impact on survival and growth.

On the other hand, staying rooted to a product-driven orientation is observed in stage of business and further. The responsibility for conceptualizing a mission or strategic direction is considered to be largely an individual effort regardless of level in the organization. Since strategic direction is a collective process in a firm, an individual manager is no longer a victim of a narrow focus that ends up with mature products, price wars, and other competitive conflicts. A broader market-drived viewpoint allows thinking more expansively about business, market, and customer needs beyond products and services of a business firm.

Primary guideline when developing objectives and goals is that they have a strategic focus. That is, they broadly impact business, in keeping with the score of strategic direction, and that the objective covers a time frame from three to five years. This time period is reasonable for most businesses short enough to be realistic and achievable in an increasingly volatile market place, yet long enough to be visionary about the impact of new technologies, changing behavioral patterns, the global market place, emerging competitors, and changing demographics. Specifically, objectives and goals can be classified as quantitative and non-quantitative. For example, in quantitative statements, you include performance expectations such as sales growth (dollars, units), market shares, return to investment (ROI), and other quantitative measurements that are usually standard requirements of general management or financial department. Non-quantitative objectives and goals cover areas such as upgrading the dealer organization, expanding secondary distribution, improving marketing intelligence system, building new specialty product lines, repositioning older commodity products, and reorganizing to become a market-driven business.

Diverse examples of two actual companies- an auto parts manufacturer and an electric utility company- illustrate specific ways in which quantitative and non-quantitative objectives and goals are stated. Because of the confidential nature of these statements, the names of these two companies are omitted and the numbers have been altered. Furthermore, these objectives are only a sampling. The actual number of objectives ranged from 15 to 25 for each company. Other, less complex companies could realistically have as few as 5 to 10 objectives.

Although some managers resist the use of non-quantitative objectives, there are long-term market conditions or internal obstacles that need to be overcome, and numbers cannot always be attached to the objectives.

GROWTH STRATEGIES

While objectives and goals indicate what you want to accomplish, growth strategies deal with how, or what actions you are going to take to achieve those objectives. The major guideline is this: Each objective must have a corresponding strategy. Strategies are divided into two categories: internal and external. *Internal strategies* relate to marketing, manufacturing, R&D, distribution, and pricing, as well as to existing, and new products, market research, packaging, customer services, credit, finance, sales activities, and organizational changes. *External strategies* refer to such possibilities as joint ventures, licensing agreements, new distribution network, emerging market segments, and any opportunities for diversification, if that diversification fits the company's strategic direction.

Examples of the some companies on their internal and external strategy processing would help in understanding the application of strategic marketing. The issues of internal and external strategies of the companies are discussed as under:

Auto Parts Manufacturer

Internal Strategies

- Install an internal computerized program that links the top 80 distributors inventories with independent repair shops ordering requirements.
- Complete the upgrade of Memphis, TN depot, and launch just in time delivery service to distribute within 125 miles of the facility.

- Execute a new warranty administration program that is equitable to the company, distributors, and end-user customer, with a timing of 15 days for the claims disposition, compared with the current 21 days.
- Implement a quality improvement program consisting of continuing education programs, and establish indices of performance levels in accordance with new corporate objectives.

External Strategies

- Establish quality teams at distributors to review causes of errors and recommend corrective actions.
- Form joint venture with (name of company) to increase total market shares in selected fuel and cooling systems components, resulting in sales of $ 17 million and 22% market share.
- Establish an image for high-performance parts in the after-market by establishing 125 new performance center dealers in key segments of the U.S. and Canada.
- Establish teleconferencing broadcasting sessions to the field to maintain competitive advantage.

Electric Utility Company

Internal Strategies

- Establish a corporate lighting group to plan marketing programs and serve as technical support for all lighting activities.
- Establish a central promoting group to develop and produce literature and sales aids; plan and coordinate trade show activities; develop advertising themes and positioning strategies; and coordinate public campaigns.
- Operate an ongoing training activity to introduce product and share information with company employees, contractors, dealers, retailers, and customers on equipment features, applications, benefits, sales, and service techniques. Develop a performance-type housing construction rating system to certify and endorse properly insulated and weatherized homes.

External Strategies

- Construct and manage a network of insulation, westernization materials, and electric heating equipment distributors to support builder design and construction activities.
- Develop and invent an active call program targeted at key builders in prime market areas identified for long-term urban redevelopment.
- Develop joint working relationships with electric equipment manufacturers to work on applications involving high temperature and environmental concerns.

It is also appropriate here to distinguish between a strategy and a tactic. A strategy is a long-term objective, with wider implications for company than does a tactic. A strategy usually affects the function of organization such as manufacturing, product development, and finance. It concerns the broader aspects of new markets and distribution systems. On the other hand, a tactic is a shorter-term action to achieve a short-term objective. It is a subset of a strategy and is usually concerned with local issues of more limited impact, such as a single product being launched in a target market segment with specific promotional activities. In practice, a single objective could be accomplished through four or five strategies and with six to ten related tactics.

A business portfolio contains a listing of all existing markets and products, and all potential new markets and products that are feasible within the next three to five years and matching company's strategic direction. The central guideline is that strategic direction has tangible meaning only, if it translates into viable markets and products. The following case illustrates the usefulness of a business portfolio plan to balance short-term earnings with long-term growth, still maintaining a competitive advantage.

The case of Foster Beer in India would reveal the business portfolio issues associated with the strategic marketing. Australians and their supposed lifestyle shot to fame only after Foster's came along. At least that's the image of Australia that Foster's is trying to project as a typical beer-drinking country. 'How to speak Australian,' the television campaign's sign off; 'Foster's. Australian for beer', tries to equate Australia with Foster's. The Managing Director, Foster's India Ltd, says that "This is what we've been looking at as step one in our strategy, and have been consciously focused on from day one." Last year, Foster's chalked up sales of Rs 250 Million and sold 1.58 million cases in India, making it a significant player in the Indian market for beer.Foster's entered India in July 1998, amidst much fanfare. The objective of the company is to create the segment of international beer in India. Just as five years ago, vodka brands co-existed in the domestic market till Smirnoff came along and similarly, rum brands till Bacardi came in, Foster's is looking at creating a new up market segment. Pre-launch, Foster's sponsored the Aussie cricket team's tour of India to build hype for the brand.However, creating a category, especially in liquor, is not an easy job, more so in an environment where there is restricted advertising and other communication platforms. Added to that, beer consumption in India is a minuscule 0.5 liters per capita, per annum. Compare this with neighboring China, where it's at 16 liters per capita, per annum. Among developed countries, the consumption is much higher, with the Czech Republic topping the list at 156 liters per capita, per annum. Even Vietnam is about eight liters per capita.

Foster's is banking on the trend that more people will move to beer from hard liquor on one hand, while some will graduate from soft drinks to viewing beer as a soft drink on the other. In fact, India is one of the few markets where beer is actually classified under 'alcohol' and faces the same level of taxes and excise duty as other spirits. The size of the beer market and the size of the spirits market is almost the same in India. However, the market dynamics are slowly changing. The distribution of alcohol is a State-controlled activity. So much so, that the taxes and duties vary significantly from state to state, making it virtually impossible to follow a uniform strategy.Currently, Foster's is strong in Maharashtra, with an 80-percent coverage of the 5,000 retail outlets in the state. In Delhi, a market it just entered, it covers about 80-odd retail outlets. Pondicherry and Hyderabad are the other markets in India where it is present. The company feels to plan and execute a slightly different strategy for each state. That is the next step of the strategy, to move into other metros as well, with tailor-made strategies. Meanwhile, Foster's is looking to consolidate its presence in its existing markets

STRATEGIC MARKETING PLANNING

Planning is the approach to making decisions concerning systematic allocation of resources. It is worth emphasizing that planning is a process, not an event. It is organic and ongoing and it is a key element of the overall management process. Planning is a way of defining your own future and if you don't like what you see, you are able to change your plan. With the above in mind, it is possible to define a strategic plan as a formal written document of what you intend your firm to become, the vision of its future position and value. A strategic plan is a detailed, specific declaration of your intentions with regard to customers, competitors, suppliers, investors, equipment, location, employees and the future of your firm. It is a way of getting commitment from management, key employees and other key persons associated with your firm. Strategic planning is systematic way of making the firm successful through the discipline of strategic thinking and vision used as a framework for all other decisions in the firm. Strategic planning requires an honest evaluation of the company's current situation and where it has been in the past. Finally, strategic planning demands the commitment of the owner/CEO for it to be successful. It requires commitment of resources, both financial and personnel, for its development. It demands complete follow up. A plan that is not carried out due to lack of leadership or the required tools needed for completion is a total failure and a waste of time and money.

Common Problems

- Failure to develop an understanding of what strategic planning really is.
- Failure to accept and balance interrelationships among intuition, judgment, managerial values, and the formality of the planning system.
- Failure to encourage managers to do effective strategic planning through an appropriate rewards system.
- Failure to tailor and design the strategic planning system to the unique characteristics of the company.
- Failure of top management to spend sufficient time on the strategic process.
- Failure to modify the strategic planning system as conditions within the company change.
- Failure to mesh properly the process of strategic planning from the highest levels of management to its complete implementation.
- Failure to keep the planning system simple.
- Failure to secure within the company a climate for strategic planning.
- Failure to link the major elements of strategic planning and the implementation process.

Core Activities in Strategic Marketing Process

o Force an integrated look at total commitments.

o Generate new data about the future.

o Extend time horizons being considered by managers.

o Involve more people in longer-term thinking.

o Develop a systematic method for communication about the future.

- o Provide a valuable framework within which to evaluate individual proposals and budget options.
- o Allow more effective management of operations.
- o Establish mutually agreed-upon commitments.
- o Contain sufficient information to lend credibility to its promise.
- o Maintain strategic focus.
- o Foster awareness of options and their likely consequences.
- o Identify critical issues, choices and priorities on which management attention must be focused.
- o Provide linkage to the system for allocating and committing capital funds.
- o Keep paperwork manageable.
- o Accommodate a plurality of managerial and planning styles.
- o Become woven into the fabric of the organization to become a natural part of getting the job done.
- o Most importantly the process can be effectively used to:
- o Generate critical information in an orderly and timely manner.
- o Identify issues and possible crisis points.
- o Improve communications.
- o Reinforce teamwork
- o Enhance decision-making.

Structure of Marketing Plan

- o Mission Statement/Objectives
- o Product-Service/Market Matrix
- o Industry Attractiveness and Market Structure
    - ▪ Market/Customer Group Analysis*
- o Business Segment Analysis
    - ▪ Business Segment Performance Analysis
    - ▪ Business Segment Contribution Margin Analysis
    - ▪ Generic Competitive Strategies
    - ▪ Business Segment Competitive Analysis
    - ▪ Detailed Individual Competitor Strategies *
    - ▪ Competitive Analysis - Major Competitor Summary *
    - ▪ Competitive Analysis - Points of Sale/Contact
    - ▪ Business Segment Strategic Plans
    - ▪ Detailed Product/Service Analysis

- Product/Service Line Review
- Product Life Cycle
- New Product Evaluation Matrix
- Product/Services Competitive Analysis

o Technology Plan

o Human Resource Planning

o Organizational Chart

- Time Allocation *
- Function Reassignment Plan *
- Management Depth Chart *
- Personnel Plan Summary
- Personal Goals*

o Management System Analysis

o Benchmarking/Continuous Improvement *

o Strategic Financial Data

o Financial Pro-Forms

o APPENDIX

- Company History
- Company Profile
- Key Corporate Values

Major thrust of the strategic marketing is to identify the markets, understand the competition therein and plan for sustainable approaches for survival of business. The marketing process is complex and emerges from the interplay of three forces – customer, competition and corporation in a given business environment. The formation of a successful marketing strategy requires varieties of information from the internal and external sources. The internal information is sourced from top management policies and activities market operations. The external information pertains to social, technological, economic and political (STEP) and product market environment. The effectiveness of the marketing perspectives of the corporation is another input to the strategic marketing.

DEVELOPING ACTIVITY SCHEDULE

Marketing is one of the pre-requisites of the economy irrespective of its status - developed or developing in different parts of the world. In rural areas of the developing countries the marketing activity has a major role to perform in generating employment and income among the manufacturing and marketing firms. However, it is found through reviewing the contemporary literature on rural marketing that there exists a gulf between the ethics and logistics of business in true sense. It has been observed over the period that marketing is a complex phenomenon and need a planned effort to venture into the various vital issues of the business. Indeed, it is a synchronized approach of buying and selling for the sake of the economic interest of the producers as well as the traders - may be an individual or an institution.

Consumption System

Activity Scheduling

Step 1: Conduct market survey of existing consumption patterns with reference to competitor's products and their attributes, production potential,actual quantity produced, trade channels, distribution and logistics, pricing methods , infrastructure, gross earnings , net profit and the related economic issues.

Step 2: Identify demand for your product, supply gap, scope for penetration, Networking retail and carrying and forwarding agents, factors influencing trade channels.

Step 3: Analyse logistics,I dentify prospective traders, draft plan for linkages with respect to credit, production, designing, skill development and extension services.

Step 4: Discuss with strategic business partners, get consensus, official approvals, work-out competitive international brand alliance, if the competitor is very strong, schedule the firm and commodity for marketing purposes, provide designs, market requirements, assist in availing inputs, watch production and competitors' moves.

Step 5: Schedule plans for production and operations management, generate confidence among the partners and stake holders in the business.

Identifying Business Opportunities

Since the entire marketing opportunities, depend on obtaining favourable buying decisions from different segments of prospective consumers, It is essential to well acquaint with the opportunities existing in the given spatial and business conditions. The activities in this connection need to be scheduled as under:

Activity Scheduling

Step 1: Appraise market situation in terms of consumer segmentation, with reference to the aspects of demography, product design and purchasing power (income groups). Penetrate the product and services in both competitors segment, and the new segment exclusively selected for launching.

Step 2: Appraise market situation in terms of product acceptability, product design and appearance, response to quality, reliability, price, substitution attitude.

Step 3: Appraise market situation in terms of mode of buying to analyse attitude of payments for purchases made viz. cash, credit, monetary instruments (cheques, drafts, credit cards etc.). Provide relatively better services to the customers as compared to the competitor.

Step 4: Appraise the market situation to find available, distribution network, delivery points, suitability for the type of trade (retailing, wholesaling, exports etc.) and season of demand, replenishment schedule and inventory management.

Step 5: Appraise the market situation to find out the scope of sales promotion and the facilities for advertisement, media response, coverage and the comparative advantages of similar products in the operational area of market.

Step 6: Do scaling of operations for time and quantity for procurement, sales and turnover at the present prices.

Step 7: Analyse the prospects of business through planning distribution network, procurement scheduling and sales.

***Step 8*:** Workout price brackets, managerial costs, price spread, marketing margins and costs of communication. Offer competitive margins to the trade channels and have long terms goal of operating on volume.

Step 9 : Prepare draft business plan, analyze marketing budget, discuss at various managerial levels and finalize.

Step 10 : Review the plan, get plan approved and draw interim implementation plan for venturing into business.

Step 11 : Allocate tasks to personnel, schedule time spread implement a pilot business, observe the business pulse.

Step 12: Draw conclusions, complete business infrastructure and do periodical monitoring of business outlets and consumer preferences.

Market Segmentation

Aspects of product distribution and market segmentation have close coherence with each other.Markets are segmented for two broad reasons - product accessibility to the consumers and selecting better approaches for the product sales. We need to perform a set of activities scheduled as below :

Activity Scheduling

Step 1 : Make decision on marketing approach basing on consumer segmentation done according to the demographic density and purchasing power.

Step 2 : Make decision on having the type of business viz. exclusive retail outlet, wholesale, mixed outlets, etc franchisees etc. Find suitable name for the outlets e.g. Opera, Heritage etc. which could always be on the top of the mind of customers.

Step 3: Set locations for business, demarcate operational area, ensure transport, parking and communication facilities at the outlets for the customers.

Step 4: Develop business infrastructure, consumer amenities viz. parlors, kids corner etc. for making the customers ore comfortable while transacting the business.

Step 5: Identify feasible distribution approaches viz. self management, regional distributors, dealers etc., fix-up security- turnover ratios and sales - margin ratios with the distributors. Appoint supply chain managers to look into these aspects more technically.

Step 6: Plan product indenting approaches for the outlets, plan contemporary and appealing product displaying styles at outlets, approachable sites of customers, dealers and distributors.

Step 7: Schedule product delivery time, check complaints, define delivery route, plan transport for intensive and extensive distribution.

Step 8: Select aggressive sales approach in the introductory state and later gradually turn to defensive mechanism retaining the customers , use quality products in the outlets, provide incentives to consumers.

Step 9: Plan for periodical sales monitoring, contact consumers periodically through structured checklists and provide incentives to the dealers viz.cash awards,certificates etc.in long - run performance.

Step 10: Analysing the long run performance of the business and consumers' acceptability of products or specific product plan for product segmentation to create specialised market.

Product Pricing

There are three principal ways of product pricing, namely (i) value pricing (ii) pricing with the demand trend and (iii) penetration pricing. It is required to understand the pricing concepts well before venturing into the product marketing. The activities which need to be scheduled during this operation are detailed as below :

Activity Scheduling

Step 1: Identify demand for the products to be launched in the market, review the price structure of the similar products.

Step 2**:** Decide the pricing approach, keep near to the competitor's prices, consider the customer inclination in final price structure.

Step 3: Follow methodological approach in pricing, keep tentative price and term it as inaugural offer, launch the product, watch the price response on consumers, set it for a gradual increase, fix the price at an optimum point.

Step 4: Watch market reaction ,reserve decisions, experience value pricing approach in high income and economy approach in middle income brackets.

Step 5: Watch competitive breakthroughs and breakdowns, reserve alternate prices, to gain accreditation of consumers go for dumping price, give short span for fluctuation.

Step 6: Stabilise prices. get consumers' accreditation and introduce periodical innovations in products with five percent change in previous prices.

Step 7: Do periodical evaluation of price strategy, renew consumer's accreditation for new products ,continue cycle of such pricing mechanism in the market.

Organisation Building

There are some important steps to be considered for building up a sales organisation within the limits of working capital.

Activity Scheduling

Step 1: Set-up directive levels, line of function and answerable levels, decide the structure of organisation-vertical or horizontal.

Step 2: Allocate tasks, define functional lines, keep informality in business dealings, earmark competent authority for specific tasks and delegate powers.

Step 3: Develop market information system - manual or computerized, streamline policy directives and actions.

Step 4: Keep minimum hierarchical tiers in decision making, conduct self-appraisal tests for individual monitoring, avoid personal conflicts in business, draw consensus in problem solving.

Step 5: Develop local expertise, provide service opportunities for local people to induct loyalty in the organisation, restrict budget on personnel expenditure at the embryonic stage of the business firm.

Step 6: Identify new resources for business expansion, prepare action plans, monitor the progress periodically.

Step 7: Workout the efficiency of leasing out some of the supporting activities viz. security, maintenance of outlets, packaging, delivery system etc.

Step 8: If it is a co-operative set-up involve members in manage decisions, policy issues and monitoring activities. The member's control in management is essential.

Sales Management

It is technique to improve the positions of sales realisation and acquire efficiency in the business by minimising the risk and maximising the profit. The steps to be followed in the function are as under:

Activity Scheduling

Step 1: Identify the sale points, position the products, provide wide local publicity, offer inaugural subsidy in price. Relatively high investment in advetising and publicity is essential in the early stages of market capturing.

Step 2: Workout the sales cost, manpower-sales ratio, managerial costs and recurring costs.

Step 3: Draw line of effective communication, distribute visuals to dealers and outlet managers, devise and use triangulates and hangers for advertisements. Aggressive communication strategy to be worked out for the first phase of business performance.

Step 4: Gear up product sales , re-launch the products if necessary, take consumer opinion, consider qualitative aspects for product improvement. Advertise through the flanker communication approach.

Step 5: Identify bulk markets, establish co-ordination with the government departments, public sector undertakings etc, do good liaison ,schedule consignment deliveries and keep direct links.

Step 6:

Identify seasons for marketing, provide festive offers to the consumers, show demonstrations on product manufacturing, if feasible.

Step 7: Visualize the scope of future product market, plan to enhance the business activities, look for the scope of diversifying the activities in related fields.

Step 8: Workout marketing budgeting, anlayse price spread, review profit and chalkout plans for prolific reinvestment in diversified field of business.

Advertising Management

The activity of sales promotion largely depends on the advertising techniques that are followed in the product marketing. There are some fundamental steps for the media planning. However, it is to remember that each media has its own positive and negative dimensions.

Activity Scheduling

Step 1: Define target audience, product type, the spatial and temporal aspects of demand for the product(s).

Step 2: Select the most appropriate type of media, inter and intra-cost structure and range of exposure.

Step 3: Workout a balance between appreciation and frequency of media advertisement, popularise good phrases in association to the product dominant in the market. Have memorable punch line for the product, do also authentic comparison to convince customers, use celebrities and popular anchors.

Step 4: Select the popular approach of communication, draw positive- negative ways to finger attention on the concept of product through the selected media, draw final stress on the merits of the products.

Step 5: Use folk culture methods to popularise the product in urban and rural markets, organize free show on specific occasions.

Step 6: Decide for continuous advertising or 'bursts', adopt the pattern of Drive, Cue and Flanker at subsequent states of the product promotion. Achieve state of art in product advertising.

Step 7: Design short visual advertisements (approximately 10-15 seconds) and insert at high frequency for a limited period, increase the intervals of insertion, keep in mind the consumers' attention, interest desire and action towards the product.

Packaging and Branding

In the contemporary era the packaging and branding device plays an important role in mobilizing the products in the potential markets and help in acquiring the consumer recognition. In this aspect a synchronized efforts needs to be made to use the packaging and branding parameters effectively.

Activity Scheduling

Step 1: Use the less expensive but hygienic material for packaging, provide attractive designs, look for uniqueness.

Step 2: Introduce periodic changes in the packaging pattern, popularize aesthetic touch in the packing, introduce at different levels.

Step 3: Use memorable symbols for branding, develop popular brand, in case of dynamic product hire brands of good companies, make long-run brand switch for operation.

Step 4: Do not change the brand or logo frequently, do consider a brand representing emotional importance to customer, get copyright.

It is essential for any firm entering into a competitive market environment to assess the strength, weakness, opportunity and threat at every stage of business planning. Such exercise would help in reforming the policies for the subsequent stages. The activities discussed above form the core issues for effective business planning in an effective manner.

REFERENCES

Armstrong Scott J. (1988), Review on Alfie Kohn's Book, *Journal of Marketing*, 52, October, 131-132

Bissey Marie-Edith, Canegallo Claudia, Ortona Guido and Scacciati, Francesco (2003), *Competition vs. Co-operation: An Experimental Enquiry*, Department of Public Policy and Public Choice, POLIS, Italy, December, pp 1-26 (Available with http://ideas.repec.org)

Cetindamar Dilek, Catay Bülent and Basmaci O. Serdar (2005), Competition through Collaboration-Insights from an Initiative in the Turkish Textile Supply Chain, Supply *Chain Management -An International Journal*, 10 (4), April, 238-240

Charlesworth W. R. (1996), Co-operation and Competition: Contributions to an Evolutionary and Developmental Model, *International Journal of Behavioral Development*, 19 (1), March 1996, 25-38

Christian Arnsperger and Philippe Villé (2004), Can Competition Ever be Fair: Challenging the Standard Prejudice, *Ethical Theory and Moral Practice*, 7 (4), August, 433-451

Craig, C. Samuel and Douglas Susan P.: Responding to the Challenges of Global Markets: Change, Complexity, Competition and Conscience, *Columbia Journal of World Business*, 31, 1996, 6-18.

Davies Andrew (2004), Moving Base into High-value Integrated Solutions: A Value Stream Approach, *Industrial and Corporate Change*, 13(5), October, pp 727-756.

Daghfous A. (2004), Organizational Learning, Knowledge and Technology Transfer-A Case Study, *The Learning Organization: An International Journal*, 11 (1), January, 67-83

Dempster N, Freakley M. and Parry L (2001), The Ethical Climate of Public Schooling under New Public Management, *International Journal of Leadership in Education*, 4 (1), January, 1-12

Drucker Peter F. (2005), Managing Oneself, *Harvard Business Review*, 83 (1), January, 100-109

Dubey Jayshree and Patel Rajani P. (2004), Small Wonders of the Indian Market, *Journal of Consumer Behaviour*, 4 (2), December, 145-151

Encaoua David and Hollander Abraham (2002), Competition Policy and Innovation, *Oxford Review of Economic Policy*, 18 (1), Spring, 63-79

Keller, L. Kevin: *Strategic Brand Management – Building, Measuring and Managing Brand Equity*, New Jersey: Prentice Hall, 2003, 409-411

Kapferer, Jean-Noel: *Strategic Brand Management*, Second edition, London, Kogan Press, 2000, 125-140

Rajagopal and Sanchez R. (2004), Conceptual Analysis of Brand Architecture and Relations within Product Categories, *Journal of Brand Management*, 11 (3), pp 233-247

Rust R. Zeithaml V. and Lemon K. (2000), *Driving Customer Equity*, New York, The Free Press

Sam Hill and Chris Lederer : *The Infinite Asset - Managing Brands to Build New Value*, Harvard Business School Press, Boston, 2001, 6-9

Sharp B. (1995), Brand Equity and Market Based Assets of Professional Service Firms, *Journal of Professional Services Marketing*, 13 (1), 3-13

Tauber, Edward M.: Brand Leverage: Strategy for Growth in a Cost-control World, *Journal of Advertising Research*, August-September, 1998.

Wartick S. L. (1992), The Relationship Between Intense Media Exposure and Change in Corporate Reputation, *Business and Society*, 31, 33-49

Yoo B. and Donthu N. (2001), Developing and Validating a Multidimensional Consumer Based Brand Equity Scale, *Journal of Business Research*, 52, 1-14

Case 9.1

TROPICANA FRUIT BEVERAGE IN INDIA

Focus of the strategic marketing may be well explained in the case of Tropicana Beverages Company, a unit of Pepsi, when it planned to enter the Indian market. Broadly the focus of the strategy of the company delineated on the market place where to compete. The strategy further focused as how to compete and when to compete determining the strategy of means and time of business strategy. Tropicana Beverages Company (TBC), a global Pepsi Co unit that entered India in 1998, wants to shift the market towards packaged fruit juices. Its brand, Tropicana, is a brand of pure fruit juices. Fruit-based drinks are different. Any beverage containing a fruit content of less than 20 percent is a 'fruit drink' (Frooti, Slice). More than 20 but less than 85 percent fruit content could be termed a 'nectar' (Dabur Real). More than 85-percent fruit content qualifies a drink to be a 'pure fruit juice'. Tropicana began its foray by test launching a juices brand called Dole in Bangalore. The attempt was to understand the Indian consumer. The feedback was encouraging. Not only did customers have the ability to pay, but there was also a clear need for a good-quality product in the category. The main brand, Tropicana, was launched in June 1999, in Delhi. By September, it moved to Bangalore. The second phase of expansion saw the brand hit Mumbai and Pune.

Tropicana now sells in 18 cities, though only at select retail outlets. In a tropical country, the way fruit juice is transported and stored is of paramount importance. Exposure to sunlight and heat bears the risk of ruining the product. Tropicana, being a 100-percent natural product without any additives and preservatives, strategy of distribution is largely controlled. Expand to the necessary limit, so that it is readily accessible, and then entice these consumers to drink more." This insures its promise of quality, which is what will place the brand securely in consumer mind space as a trusted symbol. It's not an easy game. Enkay's Onjus, an overnight success that expanded rapidly, has dropped out of the business. "The category itself defines the strategy," says the country Director, "and so, by choice, we are available at just 20,000 retail stores."

Core strategy of the brand is to first raise off-take in the specific areas by ensuring frequent distribution service, and then expand the overall market by simultaneously playing up the health benefits and overcoming people's resistance to packaged juices. The Indian consumer, having been cheated on quality for years, sees health value only in freshly squeezed juices (done before her eyes). This is a misperception, says Tropicana, and it hopes to counter it by emphasizing product quality. According to TBC, if the juice's quality can be trusted, modern packaging adds value. It allows the consistent delivery of the world's most nutritious and tasty fruits, in a contamination-resistant form that is both light and convenient. To reduce 'thermal shock', Tropicana comes in Tetrapaks, made of a six-layer material that insulates the liquid from heat. The threat of exposure rules out PET and glass bottles, despite the visual appeal of transparency.

In Tetrapaks, though, the domination of Frooti, Parle Agro's mango-based drink, is near total in India. This dissuaded TBC from launching a mango flavoured variant. But would there be any demand for any other flavour? After all, Parle Agro and Godrej Jumpin' found that mango was the only viable fruit flavour in India. "Mango has become a preferred choice because it is the only choice," explains Manglik, adding that mangoes are easy to procure and process. But differentiation was needed to make the brand stand out. Ignoring conventional wisdom, TBC decided to offer a new set of flavours namely spate orange (pure orange), sweet orange (a blend of orange and white grape), pineapple, apple and red grape.

Sweet orange is specially blended to satisfy the Indian sweet tooth. TBC is even toying with the idea of tomato and mixed fruit juices. Tropicana has been a success, with a claimed 35-percent share of the branded-fruit-juice market, placed at Rs 100 crore in 2000-01. The other major player is Dabur Real, which has an equivalent share. In volume terms, Tropicana has logged sales of 500,000 cases (12 litres each) for the year, a figure it wants to double in 2001-02 (and every year thereafter). TBC's three-tier distribution structure is made up of 15-16 C&F (carrying & forwarding) agents, 150 distributors and 20,000 retailers. TBC transports its juices in refrigerated vehicles from the factory to distributors.

Price-wise, Tropicana is about 85 percent more expensive than fizzy drinks. Till 1998, importing fruit concentrate was not even permitted by India. Since then, things seem to be moving in the right direction. The 2001-02 Union Budget has reduced excise duty by 16 percent. Customs duty has also been scaled down, from 38.5 to 35 percent. The Frooti drinker will have to be given a reason to spend extra money. Dabur Real, though, has similar prices, along with the advantage of Dabur's widespread distribution network (it sells in 55 towns). Dabur has been around longer, in India, and is higher up the learning curve on consumer insights and demand patterns. The only problem, according to an ex-Dabur executive, is that Dabur is used to operating in monopoly markets, and may not be able to handle MNC competition. At posh outlets in the metros, Tropicana claims to outsell Real by a good margin. And those are outlets that also tend to stock imported juices from Australia and West Asia. Berri's, for example, is a juices brand that is selling in India at fairly competitive prices. Coca-Cola's Minute Maid is also expected to enter the Indian market.

Advertising is low-key. The brand's tagline, devised by FCB Ulka: 'The taste of good health'. As things stand, Tropicana has taken on the onus of market expansion. A recent attitude study shows that as people get older, they look for value additions, moving to more nutritious drinks. Also, parents are keen that their children drink liquids that are healthful, instead of all those fizzies. Tropicana offers convenience, standardized quality and perennial availability, compared to squeezed-at-home juice, and hygiene for the fruit-juice-stall customer. But the shift to packaged fruit juices still remains a leap of faith for the Indian consumer. What the market needs is the sort of attention that cola-style brand warfare attracts.

Strategic plan is defined as the managerial process of developing and maintaining a strategic fit between the organizations and changing market opportunities. It relies on developing (1) a strategic direction or mission statement (2) objectives and goals (3) a growth strategy and, (4) business portfolio plans.

CHAPTER 10

Innovative Marketing Strategies

CHAPTER FOCUS

- *To understand the contemporary marketing strategies developed by global companies and applied in varied marketing environments,*
- *To develop creative thinking and strategy building skills on market entry, profit impact on marketing and business negotiations, and*
- *To gain knowledge on social marketing concepts, its applications and corporate strategies.*

Growing internationalization of business induces changes in the positioning of competitors and appropriate competitive strategies. As the companies attain gradual success in geographically expanding their business and effectively performing international operations, they reach at critical point and would be able to synchronize the proximity to the overseas markets and customer needs. The global companies at this point blue print their successful business systems in the emerging markets by creating relatively decentralized operations in production, marketing and sales. Business-to-business marketing refers to the marketing of products and services to organizations rather than to households or ultimate consumers. The implied alternative is consumer marketing, although the distinction between the two areas is not entirely clear-cut. Business-to-business marketing has also been termed as industrial marketing, commercial marketing, and institutional marketing. Although many of the same products will be bought by both business and consumers, it is possible to identify a number of ways in which the emphasis of business-to-business marketing differs from that of consumer marketing. These differences are seen to have considerable implications for the manner in which business-to-business marketing is undertaken.

Market structure is the first of these, with business markets tending to have a greater concentration of both buyers and sellers in comparison to consumer markets. Derived demand is another feature, with the demand for business products and services said to be dependent to an extent on the level of activity the buying organization generates in its own markets, although this will clearly not always be the case. The scale of business purchases is often seen as greater than that for consumers and products are generally held to be more technologically complex although both of these factors are relative and something of broad generalizations[1] (Chrisnall, 1989).The manner in which purchase decisions are made is another area in which businesses are said to differ from consumers. Many organizations employ professional purchasers, or have a purchasing department, although it has been noted that the purchasing department is often not the most powerful influence on supplier choice. Purchases are generally made not for self gratification but to achieve organizational objectives and are therefore often held to be based more on "rational," "economic" or "task " considerations such as price, quality, and delivery criteria, than the purchases of consumers. However, it is widely recognized that business buying is more likely than consumer buying to be guided, at least, by formalized rules, evaluation criteria, or procedures.

Business purchase decisions are also typically seen as a more complex process than those of consumers, involving several people, frequently from different departments. Various different organizational purchasing roles include "users" of the product or service in question; "gatekeepers," who control information to be received by other members of the buying centre; "deciders," who actually make the purchase decision, whether or not they have the formal authority to do so; and "buyers," those who do have formal authority for supplier selection, but whose influence is often usurped by more powerful members of the buying centre.

Importance of long-term, relatively stable relationships between buyers and sellers has been emphasized, which has led to the development of the interaction and *network* approaches to business-to-business marketing, where the role of *marketing management* is seen in terms of the management of a range of individual buyer-seller relationships in the context of a broader network of interconnected supplier, buyer, and competitor organizations. The various differences in emphasis between business-to-business marketing and consumer marketing have led to attempts to develop the scope of the *marketing concept* and to reappraise such marketing tools as the *marketing mix*, which is seen as inappropriate in its traditional form.

ECONOMIC VALUE-ADDED (EVA) CONCEPT

Economic value-added (EVA) is the after-tax cash flow generated by a business minus the cost of the capital it has deployed to generate that cash flow. Representing real profit versus paper profit, EVA underlies shareholder value, increasingly the main target of leading companies' strategies. Shareholders are the players who provide the firm with its capital; they invest to gain a return on that capital. The concept of EVA is well established in financial theory, but only recently has the term moved into the mainstream of corporate finance, as more and more firms adopt it as the base for business planning and performance monitoring. There is growing evidence that EVA, not earnings, determines the value of a firm. The chairman of AT&T stated that the firm had found an almost perfect correlation over the past five years between its market value and EVA. Effective use of capital is the key to value; that message applies to business processes, too.

1 Chrisnall, P.M. (1989), *Strategic Industrial Marketing*, 2nd ed., Prentice-Hall

Main differences between EVA, earnings per share, return on assets, and discounted cash flow, the most common calculations, as a measure of performance are as follows: Earnings per share tells nothing about the cost of generating those profits. If the cost of capital (loans, bonds, equity) is, say, 15 percent, then a 14 percent earning is actually a reduction, not a gain, in economic value. Profits also increase taxes, thereby reducing cash flow, so that engineering profits through accounting tricks can drain economic value. As Bennett Stewart, the leading authority on EVA, comments, the real earnings are the equivalent of the money that owners of a well-run mom-and-pop business stash away in the cigar box. Renowned investor Warren Buffet calls these "owner's earnings": real cash flow after all taxes, interest, and other obligations have been paid.

> Return on assets is a more realistic measure of economic performance, but it ignores the cost of capital. In its most profitable year, for instance, IBM's return on assets was over 11 percent, but its cost of capital was almost 13 percent. Leading firms can obtain capital at low costs, via favourable interest rates and high stock prices, which they can then invest in their operations at decent rates of return on assets. That tempts them to expand without paying attention to the real return, economic value-added. Discounted cash flow is very close to economic value-added, with the discount rate being the cost of capital. Determining a firm's cost of capital requires making two calculations, one simple and one complex. The simple one figures the cost of debt, which is the after-tax interest rate on loans and bonds. The more complex one estimates the cost of equity and involves analysing shareholders' expected return implicit in the price they have paid to buy or hold their shares. Investors have the choice of buying risk-free Treasury bonds or investing in other, riskier securities. They obviously expect a higher return for higher risk. To attract investors, weak firms must offer a premium in the form of a lower stock price than stronger firms can command. This lower price amounts to the equivalent of a higher interest rate on loans and bonds; the investor's premium increases the firm's cost of capital.

Cash flow and the cost of capital employed to generate that flow have become the key determinants of business performance, with earnings per share increasingly a misleading or even damaging target for strategy and investment. When a firm switches from FIFO (first in, first out) to LIFO (last in, first out), its cost of goods assumes the price of the most recent purchases of materials in inventory. This typically reduces its profits because the older purchases cost less than the more recent ones. Yet the firm's stock price will rise, even though its reported profits drop, because it pays less in taxes, thus increasing its after-tax cash flow. The money spent to acquire the goods in inventory is exactly the same regardless of which method is used, but LIFO increases economic value-added.

> How do you measure the capital invested in assets in place? Many firms use the book value of capital invested as their measure of capital invested. To the degree that book value reflects accounting choices made over time, this may not be true. In cases where firms alter their capital invested through their operating decisions (for example, by using operating leases), the capital and the after-tax operating income have to be adjusted to reflect true capital invested. How do you measure return on capital? Again, the accounting definition of return

on capital may not reflect the economic return on capital. In particular, the operating income has to be cleansed of any expenses that are really capital expenses (in the sense that they create future value). One example would be R& D. The operating income also has to be cleansed of any cosmetic or temporary effects. How do you estimate cost of capital? Discounted Cash Flow (DCF) valuation assumes that cost of capital is calculated using market values of debt and equity. If it assumed that both assets in place and future growth are financed using the market value mix, the EVA should also be calculated using the market value. If instead, the entire debt is assumed to be carried by assets in place, the book value debt ratio will be used to calculate cost of capital. Implicit then is the assumption that as the firm grows, its debt ratio will approach its book value debt ratio.

One of the key business processes of the firm is managing capital and resources, which is obscured by accounting system on various expenses. Salaries, software development, rent, training, and, and other ongoing costs constitute the process capability of a firm. The cost of displacing workers towards process reengineering, downsizing and the like may appear as an "extraordinary item" on the balance sheet of a firm. By treating processes as capital assets or liabilities, firms may ensure that they directly contribute to the added economic value. Both EVA and DCF valuation should provide us with the same estimate for the value of a firm. Information that is required for both approaches is expected cash flows overtime and costs of capital over time.

Firms are often evaluated based upon year-to-year changes in EVA rather than the present value of EVA over time. The advantage of this comparison is that it is simple and does not require the making of forecasts about future earnings potential. Another advantage is that it can be broken down by any unit - person, division etc., as long as one is willing to assign capital and allocate earnings across these same units. While it is simpler than DCF valuation, using year-by-year EVA changes comes at a cost. In particular, it is entirely possible that a firm which focuses on increasing EVA on a year-to-year basis may end up being less valuable. Advantages of economic value additions may be observed as:

1. EVA is related to Net Present Value (NPV). It is closest in spirit to corporate finance theory that argues that the value of the firm will increase, if you take positive NPV projects.
2. It avoids the problems associated with approaches that focus on percentage spreads– between Returns on Equity (ROE) in association Cost of Equity and Returns on Change (ROC) in reference to Cost of Capital These approaches may lead firms with high ROE and ROC to turn away good projects to avoid lowering their percentage spreads.
3. It makes top managers responsible for a measure that they have more control over - the return on capital and the cost of capital are affected by their decisions - rather than one that they feel they cannot control as well - the market price per share.
4. It is influenced by all of the decisions that managers have to make within a firm - the investment decisions and dividend decisions affect the return on capital (the dividend decisions affect it indirectly through the cash balance) and the financing decision affects the cost of capital.

Relationship between EVA and Market Value Added is more complicated than the one between EVA and Firm Value. The market value of a firm reflects not only the Expected EVA of Assets in Place but also the Expected EVA from Future Projects, To the extent that the actual economic value added is smaller than the expected EVA the market value can decrease even though the EVA is higher. This does not imply that increasing EVA is bad from a corporate finance standpoint. In fact, given a choice between delivering a "below-expectation" EVA and no EVA at all, the firm should deliver the "below-expectation" EVA. It does suggest that the correlation between increasing year-to-year EVA and market value will be weaker for firms with high anticipated growth (and excess returns) than for firms with low or no anticipated growth. It does suggest also that "investment strategies" based upon EVA have to be carefully constructed, especially for firms where there is an expectation built into prices of "high" surplus returns.

When focusing on year-to-year EVA changes have least side effects:

1. Most or all of the assets of the firm are already in place; i.e., very little or none of the value of the firm is expected to come from future growth. [This minimizes the risk that increases in current EVA come at the expense of future EVA]
2. The leverage is stable and the cost of capital cannot be altered easily by the investment decisions made by the firm. [This minimizes the risk that the higher EVA is accompanied by an increase in the cost of capital]

Strategy Focus 10.1: Packaged Food: Changing Consumer Needs in India

The consumer preferences are shifting from traditional home-made delicacy to the packaged foods in India. Although Indian consumers are becoming more sensitive with regard to the food they purchase, convenience packaged food products are affordable only to certain consumer groups. Indian consumers are price-sensitive for the packaged food products especially as the average Indian household does not consider most packaged food essential. Middle and upper-middle income segments are thus the major targets for value-added food products, such as ready to serve, semi-cooked and frozen foods. The majority of households still prefer fresh foodstuffs, which are readily available at affordable prices. Freshly prepared food is also overwhelmingly preferred, and achieves high sales through the huge number of eating establishments. The unorganized segment, in the form of cottage industries producing mostly unbranded and often unpackaged food products, also remains important in the Indian landscape. *Euro-monitor* projects current value growth of just over 8% for the packaged foods market in 2003. Similar to the preceding year, a combination of price discounts and small packaging sizes is expected to allow leading packaged food manufacturers in India to increase product penetration into rural areas, as well as entice repeated purchases.

Despite the various catch-up strategies deployed by Hindustan Lever and other regional players within confectionery, ice cream, dairy and oils and fats, the Gujarat Co-op. Milk Marketing Federation Ltd. (GCMMF) further extends its market during 2001-2003 with frequent product launches and re-launches. Its brand presence especially at the mass level, an excellent distribution network spanning all urban areas, and continued expansion into rural areas added values to the customers preferences. More importantly, while Britannia Industries enjoyed good realization within bakery products, Hindustan Lever suffered from the continued poor performance of its ice cream operations. The retailing scene in India is evolving, and the emergence of these modern retail stores is gradually shaping changes in the shopping habits of the Indian population. The outlook for packaged food in India will, however, be pale in comparison with countries on a similar path of economic progress, such as China, Indonesia and Vietnam.

3. The firm is in a sector where investors anticipate little or not surplus returns; i.e., firms in this sector are expected to earn their cost of capital. [This minimizes the risk that the increase in EVA is less than what the market expected it to be, leading to a drop in the market price.]

While focusing on year-to-year EVA changes can be dangerous in view of the following threats:

1. High growth firms, where the bulk of the value can be attributed to future growth.
2. Firms, where neither the leverage not the risk profile of the firm is stable, and can be changed by actions taken by the firm.
3. Firms where the current market value has imputed in it expectations of significant surplus value or excess return projects in the future.

These problems can be avoided if the objective is restated as maximizing the present value of EVA over time. However, while doing so some of the perceived advantages of EVA such as its simplicity and absorbability may disappear.

MARKET ENTRY STRATEGIES

Type of market entry strategy chosen depends upon a number of factors, including the following: amount of available investment capital; degree of risk one is willing to assume; knowledge of foreign markets; knowledge of working with diverse cultures; knowledge of export/Import transactions; available distribution systems; time commitment; ability to handle stress and uncertainty; potential profit; and a number of other factors as well. The following lists some of the more common market entry strategies.

1 *Assembly operations* - An organization sends parts for a product to a foreign plant for final assembly. The products are then sold in the foreign market or exported to other countries. Assembly plants may allow a company to take advantage of low cost labour in the most labour-intensive portion of production. There may also be lower duties and other taxes, because unfinished products are imported, instead of finished products. Assembly, plants also allow a foreign manufacturer to meet host country requests for more domestic production, while at the same time allowing the manufacturer to maintain control over production by using its own sub products as supplies and materials for the foreign assembly plant. A potential problem, especially with plants located to pacify foreign governments needs for domestic production, is that the foreign government may institute quotas on the amount of foreign parts, which may be used in the host country.

2 *Contract manufacturing* - Some companies use manufacturers in foreign countries to make (or assemble) their product, and distribute them through the foreign manufacturer's existing marketing channels. Thus, entry to the country is achieved with the assistance of local companies using proven marketing channels. Although the cost of this type of method is usually a substantial portion of the product revenues, it allows a company to test the market for its goods and become more familiar with doing business overseas.

3 *Exporting* - This is one of the simplest methods of foreign market entry. The product is exported to a buyer who then distributes it to the foreign market. Market entry of the

product is achieved without considerable investment of either time or capital. The key to exporting is knowing the components of the export transaction very well. If knowledge is not present there are a number of export agents available to assist the exporter of products.

4 *Joint venturing* - A joint venture is an agreement between two companies to co-produce and distribute a product. A separate entity is commonly established to handle a joint-venture arrangement. Joint ventures normally involve a foreign company and a host country company. Some countries require some local equity participation in all companies operating within their borders. A joint venture is a way of meeting equity participation requirements. One of the major problems associated with joint ventures (in addition to usually high capital investment needs) is obtaining the right joint-venture partner. If partners are not compatible, do not understand each other's cultures, do not have a common language, or do not share basic intentions regarding the outcome of the joint venture, the chances of the arrangement succeeding are reduced.

5 *Franchise agreement* - This is an agreement in which a company holding the rights to a product, trademark, process, etc. allows another company to make and distribute the product or use the trademark under a contractual agreement. The franchise agreement spells out the details, which usually Include the geographic area in which the franchise is good, the fees to be paid to the franchiser, as well as any other requirements the franchiser is able to place in the contract. A franchise agreement is a method of entering a foreign market by having a local business, (hopefully an established and highly reputable business) distributes and/or produces a foreign firm's product. This builds name recognition and provides a good foundation from which to add more foreign franchises or to begin owned operations overseas.

6 *Licensing* - Licensing provides the right to, a foreign company to use trademarks, patents, and other protected property rights in return for a licensing fee. The company holding the property rights is able to obtain distribution through an established business in a foreign country, and avoid the problems with high capital outlays and competing in a country in which it is relatively unknown. Licensing may also be a way of gaining some protection from pirating or other invasion of intellectual property rights because it sells these rights to an existing foreign company, which is more likely to be able to protect them in the host country. Licensing also allows a company to enter a market in which foreign entry restrictions are high or currency convertibility problems exist. A license fee flows out of the country as an expense of the local business, instead of a repatriation of profits to a foreign parent company.

7 *Management contracting* - A firm can enter foreign markets under a contract to manage a new or existing commercial operation in those markets. For example, a manufacturer has a proven record of aggressive and efficient management in its home country. The manufacturer may be approached not to provide product but instead management expertise for a operation having problems in a foreign country. This places, the management of the original manufacturer into a foreign 'operaticn in which international experience may be

gained success in one management contract may lead to additional contracts and eventually equity ownership in foreign firms. The only real problems associated with management contracts is that, they remove top management from the home country operation are normally temporary, and may incur the blame, for a problem which previously existed in a foreign company.

8 *Manufacturing* - This mode of entry may be considered as developing capability to produce goods in a foreign country. This method allows the greatest control of the overseas operation but also the greatest investment in capital, management time, and effort. Often direct investment in facilities is achieved through the purchase of an existing company's assets in a foreign country but many large companies build new facilities when they expand. The decision to purchase or build a manufacturing plant in another country may be forced upon a company by competition or foreign government demands for local representation.

9 *Piggyback exporting* - Piggyback exporting describes a situation in which one company markets its products through the distribution channels of a second company. Two major reasons for piggyback marketing are: (1) a local company desires to enter multinational markets but lacks the money, experience or possibly the inclination to learn what is necessary to be successful in the international marketplace; (2) an existing multinational company is seeking to fill out its product lines to stay competitive overseas. Piggy backing involves products which compliment one another instead of competing. This method of exporting is one of the least problematic of all of the methods of entering foreign markets. Of course, success is dependent upon who the partners are and the commitment to making the partnership function effectively.

10 *Wholly owned subsidiaries* - This form of market entry provides a company full control over its foreign operations. This method of market entry requires large capital investment, commitment of time and effort, and normally a willingness of some employees/ management to travel to and live in a foreign country. Fully owned subsidiaries are commonly existing businesses acquired by the company. If this is so, the investment in management and expatriate time and effort may not be as significant as with a start-up operation.

DEVELOPING ENTRY PLAN

An international marketing plan is prepared considering various factors that determine marketing functions across various countries. However, the marketing plan primarily needs to be designed considering the principal business components as stated below:

- Commitment on decisions taken by the marketing firm
- Selection of country or cluster of countries (trade region)
- Mode of entry in the market
- Appropriate marketing strategy in tune to the marketing environment of the identified country or region.
- Building effective marketing organization

Selection of a country is a critical exercise that involves the examination of all the above variables besides undertaking the demand analysis and financial estimates. The commitment of the firm to its trading decisions in the selected country, cost-benefit ratio study, and market operational methods largely determine the mode of entry of the firm into the international marketing avenue. The marketing strategy needs to be evolved assessing the objectives of the firm in the local markets in order to acquire differential advantage. Once the marketing-mix is critically analyzed, an implementation strategy can be formulated by the marketing firm. However, to ensure effective implementation of marketing policies, the marketing organization needs to be strengthened first. The decentralized organizational structure at regional levels would be appropriate for a marketing firm, when planning for international marketing in more than one country. Such an organizational set-up would facilitate monitoring of demand, supply, price trend and political interventions more comprehensively. The centralized set-up would be of greater cost, but less effective in exercising the marketing implementation and control measures.

A two stage selection process is required for the firm in identifying the product, market and services for international marketing. In this process, first, potential international markets need to be explored. Secondly, comparison of the domestic market of the firm with those abroad needs to be carried out in order to ensure that marketing at the international level has co-operative advantages over the domestic market.[2] Identifying a marketing region is always better than restricting to an individual country for the purpose of cost effective distribution networking. In addition, the tariff walls at the border countries need to be studied carefully. The firm involved in the international marketing should also make efforts to develop export markets in the initial stage. This would help in product specialization. International business firms have found that exporting is cheaper than manufacturing in overseas markets. There still remain some basic issues to be examined by the firm engaged in international marketing. These are:

- Size and growth
- Marketing potential of a country or region
- Similarities in host countries
- Free trade area, customs, common market
- Economic and political unions
- Appropriate economies of scale in managing business
- Accessibility, infrastructure and its cost
- Possibilities of decentralizing business activities
- Geographical boundaries of the markets
- Long run market segmentation

Exporting firms should understand that the export operations are subordinate to the domestic market policies and that the policy of the business firm to market the surplus home produce in the international market, would largely be determined by the opportunities offered by the host country or regional markets. However, the considerations on —(i) the firm's extent of awareness on varying requirements of consumers (ii) market response to the design and packaging of the product (iii) the impact of the pre-launch promotion among the focus groups and (iv) the size of the market which influences the adaptation process of goods and services at the international markets level.

---

2 Rajagopal (2004), Conceptual Analysis of Brand Architecture and Relationships within Product Category, *Journal of Brand Management*, 11(3), 233-247

> Roche is a pharmaceutical research, technology and market-driven company, whose unique portfolio of products and services creates superior value for the customers. The products of the company are delivered through its affiliates located all over the world. Affiliates or regional representations are direct link to the customers and local markets of the company. Roche Diagnostics integrates its own know-how with that of selected partners from a wide range of specialized areas. With this objective in mind, Roche Diagnostic's strategic alliances and collaborative partnerships are aimed at combining potential with an innovative and ambitious approach. Best known examples of successful and long lasting partnerships are the global alliances with Hitachi (since 1978) for clinical chemistry and immunoassay systems, with Sysmex (since 1998) for hematology systems and with Stago (since 1973) in selected countries for coagulation systems. Roche Centralized Diagnostics (formerly Roche Laboratory Systems) directs its products and services at private labs, laboratory associations and central hospital laboratories, offering high-performance analysis systems to measure hundreds of different parameters in clinical specimens as well as programs to optimize lab processes, from sample down to result management. In co-operation with its partners Hitachi, Sysmex and Stago, Roche Centralized Diagnostics offers a full line of solutions for laboratories of all workloads. Roche Centralized Diagnostics' ultimate goal is to improve patients' health through the application of modern laboratory diagnostics as an integrated part of health management systems. In another alliance, Roche-Syntex Mexico is engaged in selling the diagnostic reagents and equipments to the government and private clinics. The company also provides the diagnostic equipments to these health institutions and hospitals on lease. The business environment of the diagnostic market in Mexico is highly competitive and distributor oriented. The laboratory diagnostics supplier base in Mexico is confined to the selected suppliers dominating 80% of the total market.[3]

A strong economic information system would help the firms in preparing international marketing plans more effectively. The synthesis of these inputs for planning is essential in pursuing global strategies. Thus integration of information of competing companies is a pre-requisite for developing sound plans. The selection of a market place at international level is a critical process and is required to be filtered at many intermediate levels to select the core business country.

Franchise Planning

Franchising is not a business itself, but a way of doing business. It is essentially a marketing concept introducing an innovative method of manufacturing and distributing goods and services. Franchising is a business relationship in which the franchisor (the owner of the business providing the product or service) assigns to independent entrepreneur (the franchisee) the legal right to manufacture, market and distribute the franchisor's goods or service using the brand name for an agreed period of time. The International Franchise Association defines franchising as a continuing relationship in which the franchisor provides a licensed privilege to do business, plus assistance in organizing training, merchandising and management in return for a consideration from the franchisee. Franchising has become popular because it allows a much greater degree of control over the marketing efforts in the foreign country. In franchising, product lines and customer service are standardized, two important

3 Rajagopal (2003), *Sales Force Re-organization for Maintaining Profitable Growth: A Case of Roche Diagnostics Mexico (A),* Discussion case, ITESM, Mexico City Campus, 1-19

features from a marketing perspective though cultural differences might require adaptation. Franchising can offer people looking at self-employment a greater chance of success than starting their own businesses, but, it is a path that many people are not aware is open to them. A franchisor's main ongoing commitment to his franchisees is to provide support. A support program should be well defined prior to joining a given franchise group and is likely to cover areas such as staff issues, marketing and system compliance. There are four possible models of franchising as discussed below :

- Manufacturer-Retailer: Where the retailer as franchisee sells the franchisor's product directly to the public. (*e.g.* Automobile dealerships).
- Manufacturer-Wholesaler: Where the franchisee under license manufactures and distributes the franchisor's product (*e.g.* Soft drink bottling arrangements).
- Wholesaler-Retailer: Where the retailer as franchisee purchases products for retail sale from a franchisor wholesaler. (*e.g.* Hardware equipments and automotive product stores)
- Retailer-Retailer: Where the franchisor markets a service, or a product, under a common name and standardized system, through a network of franchisees.

First two categories cited above are often referred to as product and trade name franchises. These include arrangements in which franchisees are granted the right to distribute a manufacturer's product within a specified territory or at a specific location, generally with the use of the manufacturer's identifying name or trademark, in exchange for fees or royalties. The business format franchise, however, differs from product and trade name franchises through the use of a format, or a comprehensive system for the conduct of the business, including such elements as business planning, management system, location, appearance and image, and quality of goods.

> Papa John's has recently expanded its business in Edinburgh and Glasgow (UK). Its new-look stores compete with more established names like Pizza Hut and Domino's Pizza. The competition in the fast food market is fierce and challenging for potential franchisees. Papa John's operates a comprehensive marketing and public relation campaign for all stores. Launch events typically include a 'grand opening' day with entertainment, free pizzas and visits from local dignitaries. It also runs national marketing campaigns and special offers, backed up by a marketing team to help franchisees promote their stores at a local level. Franchisees can expect to pay extra for those services. The prospective franchisees need to undergo three stages, interview process which include an initial telephone, interview to ascertain suitability and solvency of applicants, an informal meeting and presentation of factual details including an outline of potential working hours and staffing requirements and a more formal gathering to discuss site positioning and to release paperwork, including a legal/franchise agreement and a business plan template to present to the bank. The company has proposed a 5 percent royalty fee on the store's weekly net sales figures, and a 4 percent marketing fee is also charged on its weekly net sales.[4]

4 For details on the case study please see Case Study *:Papa John's,* New Business.Com http://www.newbusiness.co.uk/cgi-bin/showArticle.pl?id=3562

There are many benefits of becoming a franchisee of which major ones are listed as under:

- Franchisor provides detailed consultation and training in operating the business as well as choosing locations for the business.
- Franchisee benefits from operating under the established brand image and reputation of the franchisor .
- Franchisees usually need less capital than they would, if they were setting up a business independently because the franchisors, through their pilot operations and buying power, will have eliminated unnecessary expenses.
- Franchisor helps the franchisee obtain occupation rights to the trading location, comply with planning (zoning) laws, prepare plans for layouts, plans ergonomics and refurbishment, and provide general assistance in calculating the correct level and mix of stock for the opening launch of the business.
- Franchisee taps into the bulk purchasing power and negotiating capacity made available by the franchisor by reason of the size of the franchised network.
- Franchisee has access to use of the franchisor's patents, trade marks, copyrights, trade secrets, and any secret processes or formulae.
- Franchisee has the benefit of the franchisor's continuous research and development programs, which are designed to improve the business and keep it up-to-date and competitive.

One of the drawbacks of franchising is the need for careful and continuous quality control. Such close supervision of the various aspects of distant operations requires well-developed global management systems and labor-intensive monitoring. Inevitably, the relationship between the franchisor and franchisee must involve the imposition of controls. These controls will regulate the quality of the service or products to be provided or sold by the franchisee to the consumer. As the effective managerial skills are required, international franchising has become successful largely among those enterprises which have long experience with franchising at home, before venturing out in international markets.

Planning for Strategic Alliance

A strategic alliance for international marketing is developed by pooling resources directly in collaboration. This strategy is more advantageous than joint venture. In this process, the business partners bring together the specific skills of production, marketing and control in order to maximize their profit and have a major stake in the international business scenario. Many organizations have come to rely on alliances with key players in the marketplace as strategic ventures for maintaining a competitive advantage. These key relationships can help foster organizational learning, thus giving an edge over the competition. This serves as a primary motivation for alliance formation. A new trend of collaborative strategy in international business has gained popularity based on strategic alliance through which leading firms, particularly in high-tech industries gain mutual benefit. Strategic alliances are partial merger, but have comprehensive impact on the performance of the firm. They involve mutual dependence and shared decision making between two or more separate firms. Strategic alliances differ from joint ventures as they encompass selected activities within time limits. Strategic goals pursued through strategic alliances are product exchange or supply alliances, learning alliances in research and development and market positioning alliances.[5] There are some important types of alliance that can be set-up for optimizing the business. They are:

- Technology based alliances
- Production based alliances
- Distribution based alliances
- Resource based alliances

One way for a firm to enter into a foreign market is to create a strategic alliance. A global strategic alliance is an agreement among two or more independent firms to co-operate for the purpose of achieving common goals such as a competitive advantage or customer value creation. Strategic partnerships may emerge in many forms including research and development consortium, co-production alliance, co-marketing partnerships, cross-licensing and cross-equity arrangements. Such alliances do not result in formation of a separate corporate entity but equity joint ventures form new strategic allies as legal entities to do specified business. The emergence of strategic alliances in Canada and other industrialized countries are related to economies of scale or scope, resource pooling, and risk and cost sharing among alliance partners. They include globalization of the world economy, systemic technological change, and the growing acceptance of the view that competition, by itself, does not necessarily ensure optimum, innovation-led growth. While international alliances provide firms with strategic flexibility, enabling them to respond to changing market conditions, they can also be effective paths for achieving global scale in enterprise operations along with mergers and acquisitions and green field investment. The driving forces behind international strategic alliances include cost economizing in production, research and development, strengthening market presence, and accessing intangible assets.[6] In the recent trends of globalization, the practice of entering the international market through such alliances seems to be gearing up along with political support from developing countries. However, the companies having a larger share in the international market still reserve the right to entertain or not, any such alliances. Strategic alliances offer many advantages in business, of which some significant ones are as indicated below:

- Organizational efficiency will be improved with the flexibility and informality in strategic alliances.
- Alliances developed strategically offer access to new markets and technologies.
- Risk and expenses are shared among the allies reducing the impact of risk on the participating members.
- Alliance would help the partners build their independent brand and manage retailing of goods and services.
- Alliances can take various forms, from simple research and development deals to heavy budget projects.

---

5 Schoenmakers, Wilfred and Duysters, Geert (2006), Learning in Strategic Technological Alliances, *Technology Analysis and Strategic Management*, 18 (2), 245-264

6 Nam-Hoon Kang and Kentaro Sakai (2005), International Strategic Alliances: Their Role in Industrial Globalisation; OECD, *STI Working Paper* # 2000/5

Strategic alliances are especially useful for seeking entry into emerging markets. Foreign firms in emerging markets seek to optimize the market performance in global economy, and strategic alliances appear to be the obvious solution for mutual benefit.

Planning for Joint Ventures

A joint venture involves partnership between two or more business firms interested in pooling their resources and expertise to achieve a common goal. The risks and rewards of the enterprise are also shared. The reasons for forming a joint venture may include business expansion, development of new products or moving into new markets, particularly overseas. The joint venture may offer more resources, increased capacity of production, enhanced technical expertise and established markets and distribution channels. Entry into an international market would be possible either as a wholly owned subsidiary of any firm or as a joint venture. Joint ventures provide the best partner-like manner of obtaining foreign trade income the firm chooses to begin a business relationship with a firm in the host country. These two partners could agree upon a contract setting out the terms and conditions of how this will work. Alternatively, joint ventures may be set up as a separate joint venture business, possibly a new company. A joint venture company can be a very flexible option wherein partners own substantial resources in the company, and agree on a managing strategy. Firms of any size can use joint ventures to strengthen long-term relationships or to collaborate on short-term projects. A successful joint venture can offer:

- Access to new markets and distribution networks
- Increase in production capacity
- Risk sharing and control process policies among business partners
- Working with specialized staff and technology

However, partnering in business may also be complex. It may consume time and effort to build the right relationship, while operational problems may grow with the following ideological and functional discrepancies:

- Objectives of the venture are not clear and communicated among the partnering firms
- There exists an imbalance in levels of expertise, investment or assets set into the venture by the different business partners
- Coordination problems of cross- cultural issues and management styles affecting the functional integration and workplace co-operation
- Lack of sufficient leadership and support in the early stages

Success in a joint venture depends on thorough research and analysis of aims and objectives. This should be followed up with effective communication of the business plan to everyone involved. International joint ventures are used in a wide variety of manufacturing, mining, and service industries and frequently involve technology licensing. The company looking for a joint venture invites foreign firms by issuing by a regional or global invitation to share stock ownership in the new unit. However, the control of the unit will rest with the companies accepting either a minority or a majority position. Largely, multi-national companies prefer wholly owned subsidiaries for effective control. A major potential drawback of joint ventures, especially in countries that limit foreign companies to minority participation, is the loss of effective managerial control. This can result in reduced profits, increased operating costs, inferior product quality, exposure to product liability, and environmental litigation and fines. When firms decide to create a joint venture, the terms and conditions need to set out in a written agreement. This will help prevent any misunderstandings once the joint venture is up and running. A written agreement should cover:

- Structure of the joint venture
- Objectives of the joint venture
- Financial contributions, liabilities, distribution of profit, and other matters related to corporate finance and accounts
- Protocol on transfer assets or employees in or out of the joint venture
- Ownership of intellectual property created by the joint venture
- Management and control of operational issues
- Responsibilities, tasks and processes to be followed in production and operations activities
- Protocol on managing liabilities, sharing of profits and losses
- Policy and process of disputes settlement between the partnering firms in the joint venture, and
- Exit policies to being the joint venture to an end and cause and effect management at post-closure.

Ranbaxy Laboratories Limited (Ranbaxy) has raised its equity stake in Nihon Pharmaceutical Industry Co., Ltd. (NPI), a Joint Venture between Ranbaxy and Nippon Chemiphar Co. Ltd. (NC), from the present 10% to 50%. With this enhancement, NPI will become a 50:50 Joint Venture between Ranbaxy and NC. Ranbaxy and NC have signed the agreement on November 11, 2005. The increasing financial stakes of Ranbaxy in the shareholding of the joint venture reinforces the Company's strong commitment to the Japanese market. Further, the new structure recognizes the equal commitment of both partners and their intent to grow the generics business in Japan, in a collaborative manner. Ranbaxy and NPI have had a successful relationship. This logical move by Ranbaxy to enhance its stake flows from the increased comfort level of both partners and take the business to higher levels of performance. The 50:50 JV exemplifies the synergy and the strengths, which the respective companies bring to the Joint Venture. In Japanese ethical pharmaceutical industry, NC is one of the first companies to recognize the importance of generics and to make the generic business a pillar of the company's business. NC intends to be a leading company in Japan's generics market. Both partners have a complementary role to play. NC provides the regulatory know how and in-depth knowledge of the Japanese market, while Ranbaxy brings to the table, its diversified and rich generics product pipeline along with its astute understanding of the global generics business.[7]

7 Ranbaxy Laboratorios Ltd. : Ranbaxy Consolidates Relationship with Japan JV Partner Nippon Chemiphar, *Rainbaxy Press Release*, November 11, 2005 http://www.ranbaxy.com/newsroom

Smaller firms often want to access a larger partner's resources such as a strong distribution network, specialist employees, and financial resources. The larger company might benefit from working with a more flexible, innovative partner or simply from access to new products or intellectual property (IP). Joint ventures offer mutual advantages for domestic and foreign firms to operate in a global competitive business environment sharing both capital and risk and by making use of mutual technical potentials. Japanese companies, for example, prefer entering into joint ventures with American firms as such arrangements help them to ensure against possible trade barriers.

CONTROL MANAGEMENT

A control feedback system is one of the core components of international marketing management and it serves to assess performance. Monitoring is one of the tools to measure the degree of the success of international marketing and needs to be incorporated in the plan itself. The marketing plans need to specify the periodicity of the control exercises and its prime objective. The monitoring calendar for international marketing firms may be designed keeping the following checks in mind:

- Budgetary control
- Plan implementation
- Performance of marketing functions (11Ps) which include product, price, place, promotion, packaging, pace, people, performance, psychodynamics, posture and proliferation
- Periodical appraisals of marketing information
- Social, cultural and political changes

Overall objective of these checks and controls is to determine the achievement of targeted results on time. These points need to be administered from the corporate office of the business firm in a centralized manner in order to enable effective planning and execution process. The standardization of marketing-mix is usually centralized to ensure the quality of all the components of the mix across the markets in the operational region. Besides, it is important to provide a common business language across markets which would help in understanding local markets more analytically. The checks need to be exercised at different levels of the marketing plan execution and to build-up a strong communication and information system. A consolidated document of the target group index (TGI) may be an appropriate tool for information processing and analysis. The variables which need to be covered in the TGI include consumer goods, industrial goods, services, spatial and temporal trend of demand and price, distribution patterns, marketing budgets, response to advertising, communication services and the like. International marketing research needs to be conducted on specific issues of interest and inferences may be tagged along with the Monitoring and Evaluation (M&E) process. Nevertheless, M&E should be conducted periodically as a tool of control.

PROFIT IMPACT ON MARKETING STRATEGY

In developing strategy, both corporate and business unit management need to be able to realistically appraise the level of performance that should be expected for a given business, and to be clear as to what factors explain variations in performance between businesses, and within a business over time.

Important guidelines that help address these questions have been developed from the Profit Impact of Market Strategy (PIMS) program.[8]

Background to the PIMS Methodology

At the heart of the PIMS program is a business unit research database that captures the real-life experiences of over 3,000 businesses. Each business is a division, product line, or profit centre within its parent company, selling a distinct set of products and/or services to an identifiable group of customers, in competition with a well defined set of competitors, for which meaningful separation can be made of revenue, operating costs, investment, and strategic plans. The business's served market is defined as the segment of the total potential market that it is seriously targeting by offering suitable products and/or services and toward which it is making specific marketing efforts. On this basis each business reports, in standardized format, over 300 items of data, much of it for at least four years of operations. ROI is defined as follows: pre-tax after deduction of corporate expenses but prior to interest charges divided by average investment where this is equivalent to the historic net book value of plant and equipment plus working capital (i.e., total assets less current liabilities). Note that four year averages are used for all figures. The information collected covers, *inter alia*, the market environment, competitive situation, internal cost and asset structure, and profit performance of the business. A full listing of the information captured by the PIMS database is given by The Strategic Planning, Institute's PIMS data manual.[9]

Businesses in the database have been drawn from some 500 corporations, spanning a wide variety of industry settings. These corporations are based for the most part in North America and Europe. An understanding of why one business should be loss making while another achieves premium returns lies at the heart of strategy formulation. To explain this variance, cross-sectional analysis is carried out on the database to uncover the general patterns or relationships that account for these profit differentials. The fundamental proposition that underpins this approach is that the name of a business has no bearing on its level of performance. Research on the database has identified some 30 factors that are statistically significant at the 95 percent probability level or better in explaining the variance in profitability across businesses. These factors, which operate in a highly interactive way, collectively explain nearly 80 percent of the variance in ROI across the database. The more powerful factors are listed in Table 10.1 under four categories: marketplace standing, market environment, and differentiation production structure. It should be noted at the outset that part of the explanation of variance is definitional. This comes about because some of the profit-explaining variables, such as investment/sales revenue, contain elements, which are also present in the construction of the dependent variable, ROL However; the emphasis is on behavioural relationships. Definitional elements are included in the independent variables only when it is impossible to separate out the behavioural and definitional effects of a particular factor.

---

8 Schoeffier S. Buzzell, R. D. and Heany D. F. (1974), Impact of strategic planning on profit performance, *Harvard Business Review*, 52 (2), 137-45

9 Buzzell R. D. and Gale B. T. (1987), *The PIMS principles*, New York, The Free Press

Table 10.1 Key-determinants of ROL in the PIMS Database

Category of factor	*Impact on ROI as factor increases*
Marketplace standing	+
Market share	+
Relative market share	+
Served market concentration	
Market environment	+
Real Market growth	+
Selling price inflation	+
Market differentiation	–
Purchase amount immediate customers	–
Importance of purchase to end user	
Differentiation from competitors	+
Relative product quality	+
Relative price	–
Relative direct cost	–
% Sales new products	–
Marketing/sales revenue	–
R&D/sales revenue	
Capital and production structure	–
Investment/ sales revenue	–
Investment/ value added	–
Receivables/ investment	+
Fixed capital /investment	–
Capacity utilization	+
Unionization	–
Labor effectiveness*	+

MARKETPLACE STANDING

There are several measures of a business's marketplace standing: market share (the business's sales expressed as a percentage of total sales made within the served market), market share rank., and relative market share (,the business's market share divided by the sum of the shares of its three leading competitors). Whichever measure is adopted, a strong positive correlation between marketplace strength and profitability is observed. Figure 10.1 shows the relationship

Figure 10.1 Market share and profitability

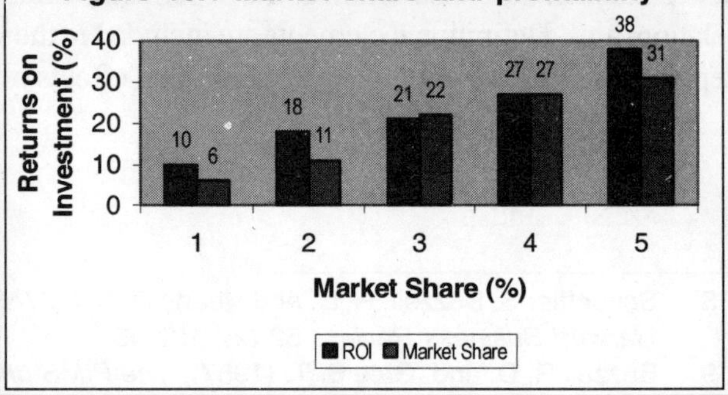

between market share and profitability. Businesses with strong market share (above 38 percent in the upper quintile of the distribution) achieve on average a 38 percent ROI, compared to only 10 percent for their low-share counterparts (below 8 percent in the lower quintile of the distribution). While the data exhibited in the above figure shows that strength of marketplace standing and profitability are strongly related, the question remains as to why we observe the effect. The numbers are a fact, but hypothesis and further examination are required to explain the relationships. It should be remembered that market share in and of itself is not important: it is an output measure which reflects a business's historic and potential ability, to gain substantive competitive advantages within its activities and in the marketplace.[10] Factors, which explain the underlying reasons why share may help profitability, are shown in Table 2.

Table 10.2 Potential Benefits of Strong Market Standing

* "Experience curve" and "learning curve" benefits

Widely publicized by the Boston Consulting Group, the experience curve effect sees cost per unit come down in a fairly predictable manner as cumulative volume doubles.

* Economics of scale and scope

Can drive down cost per unit throughout the cost structure of a business as well as benefiting balance sheet productivity. Key areas for potential benefit are seen to be:

- Purchases: stronger negotiating stance with suppliers leads to preferential terms
- Manufacturing: plant scale and run length
- Distribution: drop size and drop density
- Marketing/R&D: spreading fixed cost component over a larger number of units
- Investment productivity
- • Improved asset utilization
- • Improved ability to control all current asset components and extend current liabilities

* Relative perceived quality

Higher market visibility offering the "low-risk" option for buyers in many instances. Scale benefits should give ability to establish stronger brand and better control distribution.

* Competitive ability

- Potential to act as "Industry statesman"
- Opportunities to set and administer prices
- Size may deter competitive attack
- Size will heighten ability to control the chain from supplier to customers
- Better ability to spread risk and explore more competitive avenues

Powerful as these factors are, the fact remains there is nothing inevitable about the relationship between share and profitability. Over 30 percent of the businesses in the database with market

10 Buzzell R. D. Gale B T and Sultan R. G. M. (1975), Market share - a key to profitability, *Harvard Business Review,* 53 (1), 97-106

shares above 40 percent have ROL's below the average of 22 percent. These businesses have often become victims of their own success, wedded to historic investment decisions and burdened with complexity costs.

What the PIMS data highlight is the danger of low market share in an environment that is either marketing- or R&D-intensive. This is because both marketing and R&D have many of the characteristics of a fixed cost. Businesses with small market shares often find that they have to spend as much as their larger competitors on these activities, but do not have the same volume over which to spread the costs. The result is that they are trapped in the low-profit cells. The value-for-money in a business is a critical determinant of gaining competitive advantage. PIMS assesses this position by judging a business's relative competitive standing in terms of quality and price. It then examines, how that offer is supported by new product activity, marketing, and R&D expenditure and the extent to which price is underpinned by the relative direct cost position of the business. "Relative perceived quality" is seen as the key driver of business performance under this category of factor. Quality in the MIS database is defined from the perspective of the external marketplace. Customers evaluate the total benefit bundle of products and services offered by the business and rank it relative to leading competitors as being superior, equivalent, or inferior. The "relative perceived quality" measure used by PIMS is then computed by subtracting the percentage of product and service attributes that are judged as being superior to competitors from the percentage, which is judged as inferior. Relative perceived quality has a major positive impact on profitability. Businesses whose offer is judged as clearly superior to that of competitors on average achieve more than twice the ROI of businesses whose offer is judged as inferior. Not only is the relationship between quality and return one of the key determinants of performance in the database, but it is extremely robust in all types of business and marketplace situations. Businesses that achieve a significant quality advantage relative to their competitors can choose to benefit in one of two ways: either they can charge premium prices or grow market share at competitive pricing levels, or some combination of both. Relative perceived quality is closely related to profitability. The implications appear to be that high-share businesses that offer poor quality weaken in position, while weak-share businesses that offer high quality strengthen in position - both extremes may be transitory in nature.

Capital and Production Structure

Within this category of factor, the most powerful of the PIMS findings relates to investment intensity. The definition of investment in this context is fixed capital, measured on an historic basis as the net book value of plant and equipment, plus working capital, defined as current assets less current liabilities. Investment intensity itself is measured in two ways: first, investment is rationed to sales revenue in the conventional manner; and, second, investment is rationed to the value added actually generated by the business (where value added is defined as net sales revenue less all outside suppliers' inputs). Both measures are simultaneously employed to assess investment intensity, as many businesses have low levels of investment to sales (turn their asset base frequently) but because of a high bought-in component have high levels of investment to value added, Having cautioned that a balanced view on the overall investment intensity of a business is only achieved by using both measures in combination, on an individual basis each measure is similarly related to profit performance in the PIMS data base, and here the more familiar investment/ sales revenue ratio is employed to illustrate the investment intensity effect.

As the investment intensity in a business rises, so the ROI that it achieves falls dramatically. This finding is the most powerful negative relationship in the database, with ROI's averaging only 8 percent for investment intensive businesses, compared to 38 percent for low investment intensity businesses. The finding is consistent with the experiences of many businesses in sectors such is airlines, shipbuilding, base chemicals, low alloy steel, refining, smelting, and commodity pulp and paper, which in large degree achieve at best modest rates of return. Part of the reason for the relationship is definitional. As the investment level in a business increases, it simultaneously increases the denominator of the ROI ratio, hence dragging down the value of the ratio. That there is a behavioural element to the investment intensity effect is vividly illustrated, if the return on sales (ROS) achieved at different levels of investment is considered. If a business is to hold ROI as investment intensity increases, ROS should increase smoothly. In practice, ROS is at best flat, and in fact starts to tail off at higher levels of investment intensity. Moreover, it should be remembered that return has been taken pre-tax and pre-interest, with no financial charge made on the amount of investment used in the business. If even a modest capital charge rate is applied to a business's returns to reflect its investment, the relationship would start to turn sharply down. If businesses were sufficient to offset the level of investment that they need to sustain their sales, there is indeed a powerful behavioural element to the ROI/investment intensity finding.

At the start, it was observed that profit performance varies enormously from business to business and within a business over time. Several of the key research findings arising from the PIMS database that help to explain this variance in performance have been discussed. Care must be cautioned in interpretation. Comprehensive insight is not obtained by examining one or two factors at a time: it requires a multifactor approach in order to start to capture the complexities and tradeoffs in business. To this end, PIMS researchers have developed several models that help assess the level of ROI, cash flow, productivity, and so forth that should be expected for a business, given its structural make-up. Once these benchmarks have been established, attention can be focused on the next stage of strategy formulation; that of managing change. It can be extremely misleading to use the general findings presented for this purpose. That market share is generally closely related to profitability is observable; but that is not to argue, of course, that a business should try to grow share in all instances - the feasibility and cost-benefit trade-off of such a move needs close examination. To this end, other modelling techniques and the database itself, via matched sample, analysis, provide important empirical vehicles for the identification and evaluation of particular strategy moves by researchers and practitioners alike.

MARKET UNCERTAINTIES AND ENTRY DECISIONS

In turbulent markets the competitive strategy provides the conceptual magnitude that integrates various functional activities and marketing programs for sustaining the competitive threats. The effective competitive strategies have a direct bearing on possessing the relative market share and growth of the business organization. The strategies are the directional statements and need to be converted into the step-by-step plan of action for effective plan implementation. The strategic directions have four options that can be expressed by 4As - arena, advantage, access and activities. The arena may be defined as serving the targeted market segment through an appropriate scale of operations and scope of activities to be performed for competitive advantage. The advantages in the process, consist of positioning the products theme that differentiates the business from competitors. The access may be referred to the communication and distribution channels used to reach the market in the uncertain business conditions. These activities are interdependent and are affected by the change in any of the factors. The arena of the market largely dictates the customers, to be served by the company, the competitors to by-passes and the key success factors to be considered upon. Each market has distinctive profile of key success factors developed by the attributes of the market. The recent development of corporate strategies shows that many multi-national companies are considering their choice of the market arena based on the following factors:

- There is an increasing trend of market fragmentation. New segments with specific needs are emerging and are being served by the specialist competitors by offering tailor made goods and services.
- Traditional market boundaries are disappearing as a consequence of the rush of substitutes emerging due to the technological growth..
- Transformation of existing self-contained regional and national markets into global markets.

In the above discussed situations the challenge for the corporate sector management may be observed as to find the right balance of global reach and standardization of the activities versus the traditional strategies or local adaptation. The companies need to find out the competitive advantages within the chosen arena of business. The core issue associated with the competitive advantage is positioning of the theme, that sets a business apart from the rivals in the way that is meaningful to target the customers. It is necessary for the companies to move aggressively against the competitors to retain their market territories and build a strong defense. Thus, Kodak asserted itself in the film market against the strategies of Fuji in American market. The supply gluts also put pressure on advantages. The markets for the pharmaceuticals, electronics and automobiles suffer chronic global overcapacity to the extent of 15-40 percent. Such problem situation demands the companies to develop the strategies of competitive advantage to hold the key success factors and become the market leader. Such strategies are required as there are too many firms competing and the customers may back integrate by their marketing requirement rather than buying them. This situation reduces the volume of market demand relative to supply and the customers may sell their excess capacity on competition with their one-time supplier.

Need for the competitively advantageous strategies may further be justified as a large number of firms are increasingly productive in reference to the rapid diffusion of the technologies. The customers' bargaining power also works out to be an instrument to either broaden or narrow the differences between the competitors. The companies that use intermediaries are often encountered with balancing the power of distribution and delivery of services. In consumer markets, the retail trade is forcing major concessions on the multi-national brands. Such strategies hold the access to the retail network through a long chain of channels. Conventionally the choice of appropriate scale in business and scope thereof were guided by the concepts of *the bigger is better* and *umbrella control of activities*. In the current era of globalization, the decentralization of activities and production sharing have become more effective tools in marketing. The profit centre approach (PCA), control circles and total quality management practices has endorsed the success of small integrated units operating in a well defined market. In view to promote the PCA concepts and maintain the control circles, the large companies are increasingly creating the autonomous, small and entrepreneurial units to find responsive solutions to the customer problems in the well defined market niches.[11] Corporate structures are

[11] Frederick E. Webster Jr.: It's 1990- Do you know where your marketing is?, *Mass Marketing Science Institute*, Cambridge 1989.

changing in order to accommodate the concept of PCA and control circles and are exploring for the long term advantages by way of heavy investment to develop the core competencies.

> BMW, Honda, and Toyota, among other companies, begin with a strong brand that imparts sales momentum to each model. Brands that are weak—because their products have acquired a reputation for shoddy workmanship, their designs are not evocative, or their models bear little relationship to one another—cannot pursue this top-down approach. But a company stands a good chance of selling more cars and, step by step, of rehabilitating the brand, if managers take pains to match each model to the consumer segments most likely to be interested in it, identify and overcome the obstacles that keep browsers from becoming purchasers, and emphasize both the functional and the process and relationship benefits of the model in question. BMW Direct is an initiative of BMW (GB) to help selected company car fleet buyers streamline their service for employees. BMW Direct is a web based, fully personalized, car configuration and ordering system for the purchase of new BMWs. This highly efficient rules based web application delivers a level of information previously unavailable outside of a showroom. The BMW Direct solution provides users with the ability to view details on all eligible cars online and then go on to configure them against a full menu of accessories. BMW Direct is truly 'CRM' compliant, providing two-way communication via automated alerts and e-mails and incorporating a Contact Centre to ensure immediate access to trained product advisors. Users can track online the status of their individual orders whether by web, phone, fax or email. The call centre functionality includes phone and e-campaign generation, customer enquiry handling and profiling to customised promotions.[12] Post-sales support is delivered using a thin client solution, (using Citrix) to BMWs contact centre in Croydon and order management centre in Bracknell in UK.

Technological changes are the main impetus behind new market opportunities. The extent of such change may be explained from super technologies to the appropriate and intermediate technologies. The strategic choices have wide ranging ripple effects through the organization that determine the key success factors and growth performance. Some companies would be making right strategic choices by improving the implementation process of competitive advantages. These companies are guided by the shared strategic vision and are driven by the responsive attitude towards the market requirements. They emphasize the continuous strive to satisfy the customers. A strategic vision in managing markets may be understood as the guiding theme that explains the nature of business and the future projections thereof. These projections or business intentions depend on the collective analysis of the environment that determines the need for the new developments or diversifications. The vision should be commissioned on a concrete understanding of the business and the ability to foresee the impact of market forces on the growth of business. The vision will motivate the organization for collaborative business planning and implementation. The powerful visions are also the statements of intent that create on obsession with winning thorough out the organization.[13] The business strategy broadly incorporates the following dimensions:

- Customer needs
- Consumer segments

12 Rajagopal (2003), *Building Customer Loyalty Through Relationship Networking : A Case of BMW Mexico, Discussion Case*, ITESM, Mexico City Campus, 1-16

13 Day Geogr. S. (1990), *Market Driven Strategy: Process for Creating Value*, The Free Press, New York, 10-18

- Technology and resources
- Activities in the value added chain

Strategic thrust has a significant magnitude and direction in sailing the business though the turbulent situation. The factors associated with the competitive advantage and business investments uphold the strategic thrust to achieve the business objectives though the positive channel efforts. The competitive advantage may be assessed in reference to the superior customer value and lowest delivered cost. Such combination of the strategies may be termed as competitive superiority, that explains cost effective delivery strategy to enhance the customer value. An overall edge is gained by performing most of the activities at a lower cost than competitors. This would enable the company to optimize its cost of delivery of the new products and simultaneously enhance the value of customer value to up-hold the strategic thrust of the company.

> Canon delivers innovative digital business solutions to ensure that its customers achieve and maintain the information edge. The increasingly competitive global marketplace, and the fact that the organizations must store, process and share immense volumes of information with both speed and accuracy have been the key areas of the company to penetrate in the territorial gateways, like Mexico for Latin American market. The company functions with four key areas in Mexican market that include marketing, logistics, sales and services operations. The marketing activities of the company consist of planning and budgeting, pricing, forecasting, purchases, marketing research and developing promotional strategies. The company is also engaged in developing attractive media –mix and advertising campaigns and launches the loyalty programs for its major brands. The virtual shopping network is also a major part of the marketing functions performed by the company in the country. The company feels that the loyal, ongoing customers are the backbone of every business and in the prevailing highly competitive environment, these shoppers cannot be ignored, or else they may be won over by competitors. The consumers might have bought such products many times in their life or some might have purchased at least once in life time. There is no single way to segment a market. The most important factors influencing a consumer's involvement level are their perceived risks. The purchase of any product involves a certain amount of risk, which may include product failure, financial, operational, social, personal and psychological. The repeat customers are more apt to buy a full range of merchandise, not merely items that are under promotional programs. This means that the dealers and retailers of the company can reach profit margin goals. The logistics functions of the company is largely international trade oriented as the Canon Mexico is a part of Canon USA and many products of the company are acquired from its USA counterpart as inbound logistics. The import process has been one of the major activities of the company in Mexico. The logistics of the company further involves the key activities of transport, inventory management and developing appropriate overseas trade and information strategies.[14]

There are major types of strategies catalogued and given various names by different authors. Often these strategies and tactics are so bold and innovative that they "change the rules of the game." Leaders are increasingly being advised to seek that objective in planning and executing their

---

14 Rajagopal (2003), *Striving with Competition in Global Imaging Market : Canon in Mexican Business Environment*, ITESM, Mexico City Campus, 1-22

strategies. The pace of change today is dizzying with new technological breakthroughs occurring at shorter intervals, and global competition putting the heat on. Mergers and acquisitions change the competitive landscape unexpectedly, and strategic alliances develop even among the companies that were, or still are, competitors. The concept of "*Hyper-competition* explains the highly aggressive form of competition that characterizes hi-tech industries today. Hyper-competition is said to be increasingly making its way into other industries as well. They speak in terms of surprise, speed and mobility, terms suggestive of the military approach. Not that aggressive action is new in business so much so as the level, intent and severity of business "combat" have changed dramatically. It is necessary to build the strategic business mindset to outwit the competitors and gain competitive advantages over the segmented markets. The following factors need to be considered for achieving the strategic business leadership:

- A clear sense of desired outcomes before acting. Develop a plan capable of delivering outcomes that will add significant value to a state of affairs.
- Explore possibilities outwards to capture the larger context, to see how the pieces fit together.
- Adaptive to realities and flexible in choice of tactics. Recognize that once action begins the "game board" is fluid offering both new threats and new opportunities.
- Wherever possible, attempt to achieve multiple objectives through singular actions.
- Plan a couple of steps ahead of competition.
- Anticipate the actions of business rival and strategically rehearse next responses should those contingencies arise.
- Core discipline to observe the market moves and rival reactions.
- Capitalize on business crises or behavioural change in the markets in order to turn them to advantage.
- Stay future-focused.
- Plan the business strategy implementation in both sequential and parallel direction to accomplish goals and sustain the impact thereof.
- Develop negotiations with the business intermediaries on win-win platform at an acceptable cost.
- Supplement actions with those of others (allies, partners, joint ventures.)
- Be patient, with a good sense of timing.
- Be able to scrap or alter plans when information indicates actions are not attaining their intended results.
- Develop alternate strategies for contingencies
- Use speed and surprise to gain advantage.
- Form alliances with opponents of his opponents in business.
- Learn the strengths and weaknesses of rivals.
- Be aggressive in pursuing goals, cordon the moves and ready to take on to the next.
- Assure that everyone in the company knows one's role and is equipped with the resources to contribute.

- Monitor activities in the operating environment.
- Use "what if" speculation to stretch thinking in the direction of opportunities and possibilities.
- Study the logic of the opponent's tactics with an eye toward determining what their ultimate end purposes may be.

These are some tested aspects of thinking employed by leaders to gain and hold strategic advantage. They can serve as a checklist when responsibilities include thinking strategically. Customers want more of everything they value. If they value low cost they want it lower. If they value convenience they want it easier and faster. If they look for state of the art they want it first and want to push the envelope. If they need expert advice they want more time and dedicated effort and investment. By raising the level of value that customers can expect from everyone, leading companies are driving the market and driving their competitors out of business, or at least into a malaise of mediocrity. Here are a few options for managerial consideration:

- Alter the industry structure to change the basis of competition. Reconfigure the value chain - retailers become wholesalers and suppliers, insurers takeover brokerages, banks move into insurance, etc.
- Improve the position of the business within the industry by way of acquisitions and market share. Alter the playing field to achieve an enhanced scale of operations and competitive positioning.
- Innovate and create new opportunities - new products, services, and markets.
- Employ barriers to entry in terms of significant capital investment, proprietary technology, or in the magnitude of resources required to compete effectively.
- Increase the dependence of customers for products and services in terms of the total value for customers or higher costs of switching to alternates.
- Change and enhance supplier relationships to obtain cost and quality improvements, reduced cycle times, and integrated processes.
- Change the basis of competition by creating a service relationship and differentiation. Move away from price to service, software, and customer relationships.
- Centralize into high volume, low cost, automated, 'focused factories', to achieve the lowest cost operations in support of customer value.
- Decentralize into custom, low volume, flexible factories, quick to market, responsive, and able to customize products to specific customer requirements.

Controls may be considered as checkpoints used to verify performance progress by comparison with some standard in a given competitive environment. Generally, the business standards are established by top management in the planning process. The control and analysis process need to be revised with the growing size of the firm and its business operations. Controls must go along with the expansion process and tight control should ensure consistency in product and marketing performance. Since, multinational companies typically have several foreign subsidiaries in different parts of the world, a good control system is important to ensure that these subsidiaries move together toward a common goal, spelled out by the corporate strategic plan to meet any market uncertainties. These issues need to be considered in anticipation by the international firms while deciding the entry strategies in foreign markets.

MANAGING SOCIAL MARKETING

Fundamental activities of marketing are fairly straightforward, though not always easy. First, the market (target audience) must be defined according to the goals of the program. Finding out what those in the market want, or will at least accept, and grouping them into categories based on this and other characteristics, is a major task of research. The organization must then select the consumer categories whose wants and needs they can meet. Based on this information, they determine the product that will be offered to meet those wants, and make the product available. Next, prospective consumers must be informed about the offering and how to get it. Throughout this process, the organization must continually evaluate each element of the marketing mix to best serve the consumer. The actual process for developing, a social marketing program can be divided into four research-based, systematic stages:

An effective social marketing strategy must be built on the foundation of solid research. This may include both reviewing secondary research sources and conducting primary research, such as surveys, focus groups or in-depth interviews.

Secondary Research Review

When beginning a program, the crucial first step is to find any available information that is applicable to the marketing effort. Secondary data is information that has already been collected for another purpose—in journals, popular media, computer databases or other sources. A secondary research review can help to provide preliminary answers to questions about the scope of the public health or social problem, previous attempts to address the problem, who the probable target audience is, who the "competition" is (non-adoption of the "product" may be the main competitor) and information about potential media vehicles. In social marketing, key sources of information include technical and professional journals; national public opinion polls, health and consumer surveys; past coverage of the issue in newspapers, trade journals and consumer magazines; census statistics and other demographic surveys; government health departments; radio and television stations and local advertising agencies and market research firms. Each can provide different types of information, so it is desirable to be as thorough as possible in the research review. This method of information-gathering can be a relatively quick and inexpensive way to become familiar with the market and identify areas requiring further primary research. However, data from these sources may not always be current or accurate. In addition, the questions investigated in someone else's study may not be relevant to the program.

Focus Groups

Focus groups are an excellent method for obtaining information about the target audience's perceptions, beliefs and language regarding a particular topic. It is a qualitative method, which probes into the reasons that people feel and act the way they do. Focus groups give more depth of information than do surveys or other quantitative methods. By bringing together a group of similar people, a forum is provided for them to discuss a particular issue and react to each other's comments in a directed way that is not possible through individual interviews or participant observation. Focus groups are used often throughout the social marketing process, from the planning stages to development and refinement of the message and materials. In situations, where time and cost are important considerations, focus groups may be the most efficient method of data collection. Among their many uses are: generating ideas about services or products, and pre-testing product positioning, message concepts or pre finished communication materials.

A focus group generally consists of eight to ten unacquainted participants, who are fairly similar to each other in terms of sex, age, ethnic background, risk factors and other relevant characteristics related to the target audience. A trained moderator, who poses open-ended questions from a discussion outline and tries to involve everyone in the discussion, leads the group. This occurs in a comfortable, non-threatening environment where participants are encouraged to speak what's on their minds, especially if it is different than what other people are saying. The discussion is usually recorded on audio or video tape, and lasts one to two hours. Although focus groups are an excellent technique for obtaining qualitative information from several respondents at once, there are some disadvantages to the method. First, people may be reticent to discuss sensitive subjects, such as sexual behaviour, in front of a group. For certain topics, it may be more appropriate to conduct individual in-depth interviews, which use the qualitative probing questions of focus groups, but afford more privacy to the respondent. Another disadvantage is that focus group results are not directly to be projected back to the target population. However, after hearing the same thing from a number of participants, it is likely that their views are common to many in the target audience. The qualitative nature of the research and small sample sizes preclude the use of focus group results as baseline data for program evaluation.

Baseline KAP Study

Based upon the information unearthed by the secondary research review and/or focus groups, it should be possible to narrow down the scope of the problem. Prior to the implementation of a program, data are needed regarding audience awareness, knowledge, attitudes and behaviours related to the program issue. In order to guide the development of the marketing strategy and to provide a baseline from which to determine whether the program accomplishes its goals, a KAP (knowledge, attitudes and practices) study should be conducted. Using the preliminary research, the survey is drafted and pre-tested in order to evaluate its validity, reliability and to identify any other problems with its design. As with any survey, the interviewers must be trained, interviews must be conducted and data must be entered and analyzed. This can be an expensive and time-consuming task. However, this type of survey can be very useful for identifying and understanding the audience better in terms of their demographics, psychographics and individual behaviours. Depending upon the validity of the technique used, the survey can help estimate how many in the population are "users" of the product (e.g., how many practice safer sex), identify their attitudes toward the product and learn other quantitative information on the attributes of users and non-users.

Many other important facts can be determined from the results of the KAP study. A crucial issue is the consumer's readiness to adopt the product. Within the population, there are many segments of people who have different levels of awareness, knowledge or adoption of the behavior. In Prochaska's "Stages of Change" model, consumers are thought to move along a "readiness continuum," consisting of different stages—from being unaware to aware, to knowledgeable, interested, motivated, ready-to-try, users, and then possibly non-users. The strategy that will be used for the program depends upon the point on the continuum at which the majority of the target audience is located. For example, gay males in San Francisco who may need help in maintaining their safer sex behavior would merit a much different approach than that used to create awareness among heterosexual females in the Midwest. Depending upon the extensiveness of the study, other factors which can be identified may include the level of consumer demand for the social marketing product, insight into how to position the product, benefits and barriers to use of the product and the media habits of the target audience.

A thorough qualitative analysis of the potential target audience should be conducted either as part of the development of the KAP survey or to further explore issues that arose from the survey. Once the target audience has been identified, the next step is to learn as much about them as possible. If this is done before the KAP questionnaire is developed, the information can be used to make the survey even more useful by giving insight into the consumers' lives, determining the language used by the target audience about the topic and identifying key issues, which the researchers might not have recognized themselves. The most common methods used to gather this qualitative information are focus groups and marketing databases.

Marketing Databases

In addition to information about attitudes and behaviours related to a particular topic, social marketers need to know about their target audience's other habits in order to reach them most effectively and efficiently. Once the target audience has been identified, the database can be used to provide additional information about those people. In some cases, social marketers may want to better understand other groups who may influence those in the target audience. These may include spouses, parents, in-laws, doctors, policymakers or other influential in their lives. For example, the parents of asthmatic children or husbands of women with breast cancer may be just as important to understand and target. This can be done through any of the methodologies described above.

Media Analysis

If the social marketing campaign will be using mass media to promote the message (as most will), it is crucial to identify the optimal media channels for placement efforts. Media planning and analysis are an important investment, even if relying upon stations to run public service announcements. If messages miss the target audience, the effort is wasted and will not be successful. Two ways to increase the chances of reaching the target audience are: first, identifying the appropriate media vehicles and second, understanding the media "gatekeepers" who control the content and flow of information that reaches the target audience. In order to plan a successful media campaign, social marketers must know how best to reach the target audience. There are many sources of information on consumer media habits. Among these are the aforementioned marketing databases, which provide information on demographics and media habits: television viewing, radio listening, magazines and newspapers read. These services can help to compare which types of media, and specifically which vehicles, are used most by the target audience. Based upon the cost of each, and the estimated gross impressions for the target audience (how many people it will reach), the most effective and efficient vehicles for the campaign can be determined.

All of these databases vary, however, in terms of geographic breakdown, income levels sampled and information beyond bare demographics. There are a couple of sources that focus on minority media habits, such as the US Hispanic Market, from Strategy Research Corporation. After identifying the key media vehicles for the campaign, social marketers must research and understand the media gatekeepers at these vehicles, who are most important to their program. Ideally, a survey should be conducted to determine their awareness, knowledge and attitudes on the issue, their interest in the topic and their perceptions of how their audience views the topic. A gatekeeper audit aids in predicting how these influential people will react to the social marketing program, allowing proactive strategizing. Combining the information gleaned from all of the sources in the planning stages will produce a strong foundation for building an effective program.

Development of Social Marketing Program

Second phase of the social marketing program involves development of the message and materials. Based upon the results of the research conducted in the planning stages of the program, concepts and materials are created and pre-tested with members of the target audience. This testing and refinement process is one of the essential elements of a social marketing program. There are a number of different ways of evaluating the effectiveness of the product positioning, packaging, name and promotional materials, but all involve getting feedback from the consumer directly.

Concept/Positioning Testing

Prior to actually producing materials, positioning concepts must be developed and evaluated by members of the target audience. "Positioning" refers to the way the product is perceived by the target audience relative to other similar products. Generally, the positioning is based upon the key selling point of the product. Product positioning may be derived from the attributes or product features (e.g., electronically tested condoms), product benefits (e.g., "for a happy family"), user image (e.g., "for the man who takes charge of his life"), product use (how or when it is to be used—e.g., "with the woman you love"), or category (e.g., to prevent AIDS versus to prevent pregnancy). Selecting the best positioning statement is often based upon testing of a few different concepts in focus groups or in-depth interviews. The objectives of testing the positioning concepts are to determine the level of interest in the product, what the concept statement communicates to the audience, whether consumers feel it is relevant to their lives, perceptions of uniqueness, importance and credibility of the statement, perceived benefits and barriers to use, reasons why they would use the product, its overall appeal and the image of the brand and its users. Research participants are shown each concept statement, one at a time, and asked to respond. At this point, the testing is to determine what to say, not how to say it. Determination of a name for the product or campaign may also occur during this process. The strongest concept is chosen based upon the research findings and the marketing strategy and objectives. This pre-testing helps to clear up confusing language, provide insights to help refine and strengthen further work, decide the most meaningful feature or benefit of the product and generate ideas for development of the advertising message.

Materials Testing

Before taking the final concept statement and beginning mass production of the communications materials and package (if a physical product), still more research is necessary. Using the information obtained from the concept testing, materials are created, and then tested using pre-finished executions. These may include theme lines, posters, news clips, videotapes, brochures, public service announcements and product packaging. These materials should be evaluated in terms of memorising capability, impact, communication, comprehension, believability, acceptability, image, persuasion and other key attributes. Although focus groups and in-depth interviews are often used at this stage, there are additional methods of testing materials as well. One of these research methodologies is the central-site intercept interview. Interviewers are stationed at a location commonly visited by the target audience, such as a shopping mall. The interviewers then select and screen subjects who appear to fit the target audience definition and ask them to answer a questionnaire, after exposure to a near-finished version of the social marketing messages or materials. This method is neither statistically representative to be projected to the entire target audience, but it can reach a large number of people quickly and inexpensively. Other, more sophisticated means exist to assess the effectiveness of campaign materials, especially those made for television. Several syndicated copy testing services exist, which offer two general types of methodologies—forced exposure and natural exposure testing. Forced exposure, such as theater testing, involves the recruitment of people to a central location to ostensibly preview and evaluate new television programs. During the session, respondents see a television program along with a "clutter" of advertisements for various products and services, either once or a number of times. They then are asked to remember and write down the products or brands, for which they saw ads and the commercial message for each. They may also fill out a pre/post brand choice questionnaire. This method can also be used to test public service announcements. Both theatre-style testing and day-after recall tests can be done with radio ads as well. Print testing uses a modified type of theatre test, in which the advertisement is presented along with other ads in a magazine format and tested for its retention, communication and persuasion. All of these methods, however, can be very expensive, especially if done by a testing service.

Readability Testing

With printed materials, the readability of the text is crucial, particularly for lower SES audiences, who are more likely to have lower reading levels than the general population. The readability of printed text may be assessed, either by hand or using a computer program, by using standard formulas, such as SMOG or FOG, that analyze sentence length and number of polysyllabic words. Longer sentences and more syllables mean that a higher reading level is needed by the intended audience in order to fully understand the material. Readability testing is generally recommended for materials that have a lot of text, such as longer print ads, brochures or information kits.

Professional Review

In addition, to testing the materials with the target audience, it is often helpful to have health communication peers and representatives of intermediary organizations review them as well. The professional reviewers evaluate the pre-finished materials, and comment on appropriateness, clarity, design and comprehensiveness. This may be done over the phone or through a written questionnaire.

Test Market

Best way to gauge potential success of the social marketing program is the test market. By bringing together all of the elements of the marketing mix in a real situation, the test market provides a "dress rehearsal" before launching the program everywhere. A key to the projection of the results is in the selection of the location for the test market. The findings may be different, based upon variables such as race, ethnicity and size of the area, and this must be accounted for. Using an experimental design, with one or more control markets, may help to reduce some of these uncertainties. The test market can help to diagnose strengths and weaknesses of the program, so that each element can be fine-tuned. It will allow the staff to become experienced in operating the program and to measure real-life costs. In addition, it can be invaluable in identifying any social, political or cultural problems that may be encountered.

Before the program is introduced to the test market, certain benchmark measures should be assessed. These include consumer awareness, knowledge and use of the product, or other indicators, such as condom sales or number of calls to a toll-free hotline. The test market generally lasts three months to a year, or until a steady performance level (e.g., awareness or behaviour) is achieved. The measurements should be taken often, in order to determine how people are reacting at each phase of the product's lifecycle. Although, this is the best way to predict how the program will do when rolled out nationwide, test markets do have disadvantages. First, they can be very costly and time consuming, especially if the program is not successful. Second, by the time the program moves from the test market to full placement, certain variables in the environment may have changed that impact upon the success of the program. The test market is the ultimate evaluation of all of the elements of the program, and even with the best of research in the beginning, it may not always succeed.

Implementation of Social Marketing Program

Once each element of the social marketing mix is considered ready to go, the full program is put into effect and monitored to assure that it stays on target. It is essential, that feedback systems are in place in order to catch any problems, especially those that could escalate into major ones. These indicators of implementation success may include media monitoring and analysis, evaluation of program activities and issues/marketing monitoring.

Media Monitoring/Analysis

When marketing programs seek mass media coverage for their promotional activities—whether public relations efforts (e.g., press conferences, community events) or public service announcements—they need to be able to evaluate the success of these activities. The next step is for the researcher to analyze the clips qualitatively, assessing the messages each contains and the accuracy or desirability of those messages. Ideally, all of the available information about each clip should be entered into a database, from which a statistical analysis can be drawn. This analysis should include information about placement volume, target audience impressions, message content and quality measures. If a communications strategy was devised prior to the activity, this analysis can help to assess its effectiveness. The results can provide implications for placement activities in the future.

Activities Evaluation

In addition to mass media placement, the program must evaluate the impact of its activities upon the people who participate in them or see the coverage. These components might include special events, community events, speakers programs, retail promotions, direct mail, collateral materials or other outreach efforts. When these activities will be repeated a number of times, evaluation allows revision and improvement. Indicators of success in program activities may include the number of media placements, number of people trained, and number of posters produced and distributed, responses to direct mail or calls to a toll-free number. This monitoring can be done inexpensively and rapidly, and can help to keep the program on target.

Issues/Market Monitoring

In order to stay on top of trends and developments in the field, the social marketing program should track changes and events that have strategic implications. This may include monitoring media coverage, attitude surveys, legislative initiatives or other important developments. This may be done easily, though not cheaply, through news and information databases, such as the AP wire, Nexis/Lexis, and legislative tracking systems such as Washington Alert. This and the other elements of research and evaluation in the implementation stage are designed to keep the program on track through revisions and improvements.

Assessment

Purpose of a social marketing program is to effect some change in the target audience's attitudes and behaviors. The true test of the effectiveness of the program is not the number of PSAs which were aired, but whether it contributed to improving people's health and lives. However, there are a number of distinct levels to evaluation of the program, and each is important for different reasons. These can be divided into three basic types: process, outcome and impact evaluation. Process evaluation determines whether the intended target audience was reached. If so, outcome evaluation looks at whether they engaged in the desired behavior after being exposed to the message. Finally, impact evaluation judges whether performing the behavior induced the desired change (i.e., a reduction in related mortality and/or morbidity).

Process Evaluation

While the social marketing program is in effect, process evaluation should take place intermittently in each part of the program. As detailed in the implementation phase, it includes media monitoring and analysis, as well as evaluation of program activities. The first wave of tracking should occur six months to a year after the product introduction, and ideally should be conducted at least annually. If possible, the methodology and wording of the questions should be identical to the first survey in order to maintain comparability of the results. The key measurement areas to track include awareness of the product, advertising awareness and recall, knowledge level, attitudes and perceptions, images of product and users, experience with the product, and behaviors (trial and repeat). The new questions should be very specific about the particular product or campaign, in addition to the earlier, more general questions about attitudes and behaviors regarding the topic.

Based upon the standards set in the program objectives, the results should focus on levels of awareness, trial and continued/repeat usage. The interpretation of these measures provides direction for improvements and areas upon which to concentrate in the future. If the survey indicates low levels of awareness of the product or campaign, the program should investigate whether the media vehicles are, in fact, reaching the target audience effectively and appropriately, and whether the communications materials are memorable, understandable and consistent with the program objectives. If there is high awareness, but low trial, this indicates that the message is reaching the audience, but other elements of the mix may be weak. These problems may be with the distribution system, price, product image or packaging, poorly conceived promotion activities or competition from other sources. Finally, both awareness and trial may be high, but the target audience does not sustain the behavior. In this case, there may be problems with the product itself, or consumers may be unmotivated to continue usage. This type of process evaluation can be very helpful in diagnosing problems or indicating success.

Outcome Evaluation

Follow-up survey will help to identify the extent of attitude and behavior change in the target population, and tie it to their exposure to the campaign or use of the product. A "user profile" can be compiled, either from the KAP survey or from additional studies of users and non-users. For example, those who use condoms can be compared with those who do not on a number of attributes. These would include demographics, contraceptive history, lifestyle factors, sexual behavior, brand use, advertising awareness and attitudes toward the particular social marketing product. Evaluation efforts can also utilize secondary sources to determine changes in behavioural measures. These include the annual National Health Interview Survey (NHIS) and the state-based Behavioural Risk Factor Surveillance System (BRFS) conducted by the Centers for Disease Control. However, these general studies do not necessarily contain the information that is relevant to a particular social marketing program. If the organization is a government agency, it may be possible to add one or two relevant questions to the surveys.

Impact Evaluation

Actual impact of the social marketing program is often difficult to assess accurately. Educational efforts are relatively transient, and gone long before changes can be seen. Because campaigns change so quickly, it is impossible to determine the effect of a particular spot on overall trends. However, we can at least compare mortality and morbidity rates before and after implementation of the program in many cases. The most effective way of establishing a cause-and-effect relationship between health marketing efforts and the changes in behavior and health outcomes is to conduct an intervention study in one or more communities, with matched communities as controls. Assuming that there are no significant differences between the intervention and control communities, marketing activities may be linked to changes in the communities with precision and reliability. If conducting the study in a number of communities, the effectiveness of various elements of the program can be tested by including the factors responsible for holding the functional dependence.Whenever marketing behavior changes, it is imperative to acknowledge the need for responsibility and accountability to the people in the target audience. Although in the end, the results of the program are the final measure of success, the means to that end are just as important. People should never be coerced into a behavior, even though it may be "for their own good." Programs may also have side effects and unintended consequences, which can be harmful in the long run. For example, a program intended to empower minority women to use condoms resulted in a number of beatings by their male partners, who perceived their insistence on condoms as an insult. Programs, which offer incentives for behavior change, may encourage materialistic values and a disinclination to do anything without an extrinsic reward. Ethical criteria must be considered from the beginning in selecting the target audience, designing research and determining a social marketing mix, and must also be used in evaluation throughout a program to make sure that it "does no harm." Every element of the program must be ethically sound.

COMPREHENSIVE BRANDING

Comprehensive branding (CB) may be defined as the management of both the manufacturing and marketing process chain for ensuring the customer perceptions of the products of a company. In other words the company chooses to establish the brand image that is as close as possible to the opinion of the customer, that the gathers from the available resources and actually experiences with the product with lowest variation. The concept of comprehensive branding encompasses two components of *total quality management* and *integrated marketing communications*. There is a parallel process to these two programs driven by the creation of delivery of references, that the consumer uses in making purchase decisions and utilizing the key tools of benchmarking, specifications and process control. The inputs fro the specifications are provided to the company for design manufacturing process for product and message image by the consultants and suppliers. In turn, the message is passed to the agencies by the consultants and suppliers do the same to their employees. The message is carried by the media from the agencies and distributors act as the carriers of product. Both media and distributors deliver the message and products to the customers for setting specifications for the products and message. The actions processed through the consultants, agencies and media constitute the *Integrated Marketing Communication (IMC)* which communicates a consistent message to consumers through alignment of the agencies and media with vision of the company, and he image of the brand. The component of *Total Quality Management (TQM)t* is experienced in the comprehensive branding process through the inputs delivered by the suppliers, employees and distributors about the product and services. The TQM helps in communicating the corporate vision to ensure that every step of the product path, form manufacturing to the consumer delivery, maintains the integrity of the brand image. The synergy of IMC and TQM make the company to present the comprehensive branding strategy in the market. In this process, the company ensures that all communications and the product paths have total compatibility with the specifications and perceptions of the brand image of the company that has been chosen to portray and as perceived by the customers.

A company's advertising, promotion, changes in name, new logo design or other activities will not successfully build a brand unless there are certain well-defined values which are consistently communicated and demonstrated by the company which are recognised and appreciated by customers. Once brand values have been identified, they should drive all other activities impacting on customers and be used to achieve consistency, which is so meaningful to consumers. All aspects of marketing and communications should reflect the brand values, as should company employees in demonstrating those values in their behaviour to customers .Building a brand is a corporate strategic issue and not a short-term tactical activity. For companies wanting to satisfy the needs of consumers and beat the competition, then building a brand provides an opportunity which, if realised, could do not only this but also defy the test of time - for brands have no limit to their life expectancy. Many brands established in the 1930s are still the top brands in the late '90s. From Coca-Cola to Colgate, Kelloggs to Kodak, we see many examples of the big brands successfully having defended their number one position in their chosen markets and they, along with other famous names, have become synonymous with their industries.

Brand loyalty also means that companies achieve a greater consistency of demand through customer retention. Over time, good brand strategies generate the production volume which gives the economies of scale necessary to have a favourable impact in unit costs. In turn, this allows companies to achieve higher margins, putting them in a winning situation. Brand resilience can help companies ride out stormy weather, as with Mercedes in 1982, when other car manufacturers around the world suffered disastrous sales, apart from Mercedes which continued to sell well: often up to 50 percent more than other European competitors. And, because of the magnetic influence they have over purchasing behaviour, successful brands allow companies to charge premium prices for their products and services, which of course generate higher profits. Surveys indicate that brand leaders can return a margin four to six times that of the closest competitors. Brands can even assist moves across industries to penetrate new markets. Dunhill is an excellent example of this. Formerly based in the declining-image industry of Tobacco, Dunhill is now firmly established internationally in upmarket clothing, toiletries and fashion accessories.

A firm, which would like to involve itself in the international business, may look for its entry into international marketing in many possible ways including exporting, licensing, franchising, or as a production firm with multi-national plant locations. However, at any level of market entry the managerial trade-off lies between extent of risk and operational control. The low intensity modes of entry minimize risk *e.g.* contracting with a local distributor requires no investment in the destination country market as the local distributors may own offices, distribution facilities, sales personnel, or marketing campaigns. Under the normal arrangement, whereby the distributor takes title to the goods or purchases them as they leave the production facility of the international company, there is not even a credit risk, assuming that the distributor has offered a letter of credit from his bank. At the same time such arrangement to enter a destination country may minimize control along with the risk factor. In many cases, low-intensity modes of market participation cut off the international firm with information network while operational controls can only be obtained through higher-intensity modes of market participation, involving investments in local executives, distribution, and marketing programs.

> Breakfast cereal, a relatively new introduction to the Bulgarian market, is the fastest growing sector in the Bulgarian bakery products market. According to a research study,[15] ready-to-eat breakfast cereals grew by 90 percent in value terms during 2000-2005 and the market grew by approximately 14 percent just in 2005. Despite this impressive growth, cereal consumption in Bulgaria is low compared to other countries, which illustrates the immaturity of the market and its potential for the future. Besides the "novelty" of breakfast cereals, a key reason for the success of breakfast cereals in Bulgaria is their healthy image, which manufacturers have carefully created by illustrating that their products are part of a balanced diet. Although the concept of health and wellness is growing in popularity in Bulgaria, consumers still need additional education on the subject. The foreign cereal manufacturing companies like Nestle, Kraft, Kellogg and General Mills etc. have therefore, invested heavily in radio and television advertising to promote a healthy image for their products and attract health conscious consumers. These companies have also set up demonstrations in supermarkets that are designed to educate consumers on the health benefits of breakfast cereals. By using samples and other promotional materials, manufacturers have tried to inspire trials and eventually repeat purchases of their products. These campaigns mainly targeted the bigger cities, where consumers are generally more willing to try new products. The entry of foreign brands in the breakfast cereals in Bulgaria is further moved ahead by the fast expansion of supermarkets and the development of this distribution channel over the next several years will play a crucial role in making breakfast cereals more widely available.[16]

15 Euromonitor (2006): Breakfast Cereals Boom in Bulgaria, January

16 *Ibid*

Many companies begin their internationalization opportunistically through a variety of arrangements that may be described as "piggybacking," because they all involve taking advantage of a channel to an international market rather than selecting the country-market in a more conventional manner. Piggybacking is an interesting development. The method means that organizations with little exporting skill may use the services of one that has. Another form is the consolidation of orders by a number of companies in order to take advantage of bulk buying. Normally these would be geographically adjacent or able to be served, say, on an air route. The fertilizer manufacturers of Zimbabwe, for example, could piggyback with the South Africans, who both import potassium from outside their respective countries. Such practices may be noticed as American breakfast cereal products like Post from the owners of the leading US brand, which entered in the Mexican market via their subsidiary Kraft rather than direct from USA, thus leading to the rather bizarre situation of packs of breakfast cereals with English language packaging covered with stickers in Spanish. The most common form of piggybacking is to internationalize by serving a customer who is more international than the vendor firm. Thus, a customer requests an order, delivery, or service in more than one country, and the supplier starts selling internationally in order to retain the customer and increases its penetration of the account. This is particularly common in the case of business-to-business companies and technology-oriented start-ups.[17] The innovative concept of market entry strategy is based on moving with *consumer space* which indicates that foreign firms enter the destination market by developing adequate consumer awareness on the products and services prior to launch. This strategy is followed largely by the fast moving consumer goods manufacturing companies and such practice is termed as go-to-market strategy. Go-to-market planning enables the firm to achieve higher margins, accelerated revenue growth and increased customer satisfaction through existing sales channels. An effective go-to-market strategy aligns products & services, processes, and partners with customers and markets to deliver brand promise, the desired customer experience, and tangible value. Go-to-market strategy services help technology suppliers overcome market challenges.

> Anti-ageing products are driving growth in Hong Kong's skin care market, on the back of increasing consumer interest in premium products and the development of consumer-focused cosmetics retailing. Consumer interest in premium products has been spurred, in part, by recent media reports on the safety of chemicals present in some skin care products. Catching on to this consumer trend, manufacturers have been introducing more premium anti-ageing products containing rare ingredients, and products benefiting from more advanced technology, to the market. This has generated greater consumer interest in premium quality products and has provided a further boost to the market. Guerlain, for example, is expected to launch a new skin care cream in 2006, which is based on a rare orchid extract and is expected to retail for more than US $350. Further, a recent entrant to Hong Kong's skin care market, Sulwhasoo which is a premium herbal based brand from Amore Pacific of Korea, that draws on Oriental medicine by using a unique compound of five herbs to deliver a range of products targeted at women over 35. The value driver of growth in the anti-ageing products market in Hong

17 David Arnold (2003): *The Mirage of Global Marketing: How Globalizing Companies can Succeed as Markets Localize*, Financial Times Prentice Hall, Upper Saddle River, NJ, 24-65

Kong is the trend towards concept stores and beauty boutiques, which are retail outlets designed to emphasize the experiential aspects of premium cosmetic products. Developed to attract new customers and gain their loyalty in Hong Kong's increasingly competitive market, these brand-specific beauty salons and spas, not only engage in a highly personalized product sales process, but also provide make-up and skin care services. Since 2004, major players, such as Kose, L'Oréal, H_2O and cult brand Aesop, have set up concept stores around the city, in the hopes of developing a loyal customer base.[18] Such retail strategy where concept of the product is delivered with practical experience on it establishes the go-to-market strategy on consumer space.

Some firms who are aggressive have clearly defined plans and strategy, including product, price, promotion, and distribution and research elements. Passiveness versus aggressiveness depends on the motivation to export. In countries like Tanzania and Zambia, which have embarked on structural adjustment programs, organizations are being encouraged to export, motivated by foreign exchange earnings potential, saturated domestic markets, growth and expansion objectives, and the need to repay debts incurred by the borrowings to finance the programs. The type of export response is dependent on how the pressures are perceived by the decision maker. The degree of involvement in foreign operations depends on "endogenous versus exogenous" motivating factors, that is, whether the motivations were a result of active or aggressive behavior based on the firm's internal situation (endogenous) or a result of reactive environmental changes (exogenous).[19] There is certainly no single strategy that fits all firms, products and markets. The competitive strategy for an established firm to start a new venture and launch a new product must be shaped by the characteristics of the firm, the market, and other environmental factors. Market entry through expansion of the company draws many challenges to firms considering new business options. Capitalizing on overseas markets often opens doors to new levels of top and bottom line growth. Moreover, introducing a new product or service into a new market is an even bigger strategic challenge. A successful entry strategy may conceptualize and implement well structured entry processes to drive future growth, explore diversified stream of revenues and augment profit margins. It also addresses new competitors, customers, partners, suppliers and other market dynamics. However, there are five major modes which a foreign firm may apply to enter in the international markets. These modes of entry include exporting, contractual agreement, joint venture, strategic alliance.

---

18 Olivier Hofmann (2006), Anti-ageing Skin Cream Booms in Hong Kong, *Euromonitor*, May (online edition)

19 Piercy, N (1982), Company Internationalization: Active and Reactive Exporting". *European Journal of Marketing,* 15 (3), 26-40.

SELECTED READING

Aaker, D. (1996). *Building Strong Brands,* New York, The Free Press.

Baldinger, A. and Robinson, J. (1996). Brand Loyalty: The Link Between Attitude and Behaviour, *Journal of Advertising Research,* 36 (6).22-35.

Brassington, F. and Pettitt, S. (2001). *Principles of Marketing,* 3rd Edition, Pearson Education, Prentice Hall.

Hausor John, R. and Steven, M. Shugan (1983). Defensive Marketing Strategy, *Marketing Science,* 27 (2), January, 319-360.

Morgan, R.M. Hunt, S.D. (1994), *"The Commitment-Trust Theory of Relationship Marketing",* Journal of Marketing Vol. 58, No.3, pp.20-38.

Morris, M. H. David, D. L. Allen, J. W. Avila, R. A. and Chapman, J. (1991),Assessing the relationship between performance measures, managerial practices, and satisfaction when evaluating the sales force, *Journal of Personal Selling and Sales Management,* 11, Summer, 25-35.

Ofek Elie, (2002), *Customer Profitability and Lifetime Value,* Harvard Business School, Note, August, 1-9 (Publication reference 9503-019).

Oliver, R. L. and Anderson, E. (1994), An empirical test of the consequences of behavior- and outcome-based control systems, *Journal of Marketing,* 58(4), 53-57.

Ouchi, W. Z. (1979), A conceptual framework for the design of organizational control mechanisms. *Management Science,* 25, September, 833-847.

Rajagopal, (2005), Measuring Variability Factors in Consumer Values for Profit Optimization in a Firm - A Framework for Analysis, *Journal of Economics and Management,* 1(1),85-103.

Rajagopal, (2006), Measuring Customer Value and Market Dynamics for New Products of a Firm: An Analytical Construct for Gaining Competitive Advantage, *Global Business and Economics Review,* 8 (3-4), 187-204.

Rajagopal, (2006), Measuring Customer Value Gaps: An Empirical Study in Mexican Retail Markets, *Economic Issues,* 11(1), 19-40 Samiee S and Roth K (1992), The influence of global marketing standardization on performance, *Journal of Marketing,* 56 (2), 1-16. Sekaran U (1983), Methodological and theoretical issues and advancements in cross-cultural research, *Journal of International Business Studies,* 14 (2), 61-73.

Tauber, Edward M., Brand Leverage (1998). Strategy for Growth in a Cost-control World, *Journal of Advertising Research,* August-September.

Case 10.1

DELL TAKES A DIFFERENT TACK IN CHINA

American computer giant Dell is trying hard to crack the Chinese market, and it's willing to depart from some of its tried-and-true business methods to do so. With industry experts predicting that Chinese demand for PCs will continue growing at around 20 percent next year, the market is clearly going to be even more crucial for Dell and other multinationals looking to offset the effects of the global recession. It is easy to see why. Although China is the world's biggest country, with over 1.3 billion people, not many folks own computers — fewer than 30% of residents in the wealthiest cities, including Beijing, Shanghai, and Guangzhou, according to a Nov. 30 article in the *People's Daily*. For the country as a whole, PC penetration is "no more than 10%," the newspaper reported. What's more, just 2% of large and midsize Chinese businesses have set up their own intranets. The country's current total market for computers, software, and information services amounts to about $29 billion, according to industry estimates. As the Chinese economy develops; Dell is counting on those numbers to improve. It's already trumpeting success in China. Having entered the market in the late '90s, many years behind rivals like Compaq and IBM, Dell is now China's No. 4 PC seller. No. 1, of course, is local powerhouse Legend, followed by two other Chinese companies, Founder and Tongfang. That makes Dell the leading foreign brand. To get to that position, Dell has been doing some things differently.

Goal, is to bring down the cost of a PC and make it more attractive for the 85% of the Chinese urban population that don't have one, but can afford it. Dell won't reveal revenue numbers for the Smart PC, but the company credits the model as one reason sales have been growing — 16% in the third quarter, giving Dell a 4.9% market share. So far, it's buying the Smart PC from Taiwanese contractors that assemble the machines in China. But next year, Dell will begin producing the Smart PC at its own, 350,000-square-foot factory in Xiamen, a coastal city in southeastern Fujian province. The Xiamen plant opened in November, 2000, and is one of Dell's biggest factories. Dell has also adjusted to the Chinese market's demands by focusing more on consumers, figuring they're the fuel for market growth. Half of Dell's PCs in China go to individuals. But reaching them isn't easy, especially given their inexperience with the direct-purchase model Dell uses so well elsewhere. So, Dell has been sending sales teams to shopping malls in China's big cities, giving consumers a chance to "see and touch" the Smart PCs, and make them less worried about buying by phone.

Once Dell makes the sale, it faces another challenge: getting paid. Not many Chinese use credit cards, something that has forced Dell to come up with alternatives. One is payment on delivery, although that has obvious shortcomings, since some buyers may not have the money when the PCs arrive. To provide a more secure method, Dell has started working with Chinese banks. Now, a customer in Beijing or Shanghai can call up Dell, order a PC, and then walk down to his neighbourhood bank and pay for it there. Dell faces many other obstacles in China. While Beijing's upcoming entry into the World Trade Organization should make it easier for foreign multinationals to do business in the country, local outfits like Legend still enjoy a lot of advantages in marketing and distribution. And when it comes to making sales to government-backed companies or state ministries, Legend and other locals already have government connections. Dell could play a trump card of its own. The company buys over $1 billion in parts from China, and that's likely to grow dramatically as more of its Taiwanese suppliers expand their operations in the mainland.

REFERENCES

Albrinck J, Hornery J, Kletter D and Neilson G (2001), Adventures in Corporate Venturing, *Strategy and Business*, 22, pp 119-129

Biggadyke R. (1979), The Risky Business Diversification, *Harvard Business Review*, 57, pp 103-111

Frost P. J. and Egri CP (1990), Influence of Political Action on Innovation: Part I , *Leadership and Organization Development Journal*, 11(1), pp 17-25

Ghemawat P. (1991), *Commitment: The Dynamics of Strategy*, New York, Free Press

Ligos, Melinda, Andy Cohen & Jennifer Gilbert (2004), Extreme Makeovers, *Sales and Marketing Management*, Vol. 156, No. 5, May, 36-43

Suarez Feranando F. and Lanzolla Gianvito (2005), The Half Truth of First Mover Advantage, *Harvard Business Review*, April, pp 1-8 (Ref R 0504J)

Tushman M. and Nadler D. (1986), Organizing for Innovation, *California Management Review*, 3(1), pp 73-84

Zahra S. A. (1993), Environment, Corporate Entrepreneurship and Financial Performance: A Taxonomic Approach, *Journal of Business Venturing*, 8(4), pp 319-340

Zahra S. A. (1996), Governance, Ownership and Corporate Entrepreneurship: The Moderating Impact of Industry's Technological Opportunities, *Academy of Management Journal*, 39(6), pp 1713-1735

Zimmerman, Eilene (2004), Motivation on Any Budget, *Sales & Marketing Management*, Vol. 156, No. 1, January, 37-44.

Case 10.2

CONSUMER PREFERENCES ON BUYING AUTOMOBILES

In recent years, the number of car makes and models has grown in every product segment. At the same time, the once vast gaps in quality, performance, safety, fuel efficiency, and amenities have all closed significantly. Although variations in quality and performance persist, the remaining possibilities for differentiating products, and thus achieving competitive advantage, revolve around styling and other intangibles and the emotional benefits, they confer on the customer. Marketers have long understood that consumers are influenced by the emotional connections, they form with products-and with manufacturers, dealers, and other owners. The consumers attach significantly greater importance to relationship and emotional benefits than to a car's functional attributes, at least when they meet minimum standards or don't fall far short of the competition's. Nevertheless, those intangible benefits are the weakest links in the automakers' performance ratings.[20] Customers view tends to reflect the conventional wisdom in product design. The perceived value is created when companies use customers as a sounding board for their own ideas. As the auto critiques have opined that few customers would have been able to articulate the minivan concept beyond vague musings and now as the case may be with the PT Cruiser of Chrysler which append the idea of vintage look and modern comforts together with the car.

Box 1: PT Cruiser: a blend of ideas and technology

An automotive company must understand the factors that affect the performance of a network to restructure it effectively. Of these the first and foremost is geographic distribution: outlets must be close to customers but not too close to one another. In reality, neither condition is met. The once robust networks of the Big Three—GM, Ford, and DaimlerChrysler—were built largely in the 1920s, 1930s, and 1950s, for example, and haven't been adapted to demographic shifts: these networks are too tightly clustered in urban areas and too sparse in the suburbs. The second factor is the skill of the dealers, for some are much better at running their businesses than others are. Indeed, the experience of one major manufacturer suggests that, adjusting for market size and location, dealers in the top quartile sell three to four times as many vehicles as dealers in the bottom quartile.

Power and profit in the supply chain is still maintained by the major automobile manufacturers like the U.S. "Big Three" (Ford, GM, DaimlerChrysler), as well as foreign competition like Honda,

20 Anjan Chatterjee, Matthew E. Jauchius, Hans-Werner Kaas, and Aurobind Satpathy : *Revving-up Auto Branding,* The McKinsey Quarterly, Number 1, 2002

Toyota, and Nissan, to name a few. Even smaller manufacturing companies, which control very little of the global market share of car manufacturers, still dominate their own supply chains. The market leaders for 2002 are listed in Table 1 as below.[21]

Table 1: Automobile Industry Leaders in 2002

Industry leaders	*Home country*	*Worldwide market share (%)*	*Sales in 2002 (million $)*	*Change in sales (%)*
General Motors	USA	17.03	186763	5.4
Ford Motor Co.	USA	14.82	162586	1.1
Daimler Chrysler	*USA*	*14.30*	*156838*	*15.3*
Toyota Moto Corp.	Japan	9.80	107443	1.3
Honda Motor Co. Ltd.	Japan	5.86	64305	23.5
Fiat Spa	Italy	4.77	52314	-6.2
Nissan Motor Co. Ltd.	Japan	4.48	49110	-12.9

Source: S & P Market Insight 2003

Movement in the car manufacturing industry is taking place on various levels. Consolidation, supply chain integration and globalization are reconfiguring the automotive landscape, while mobility problems are pushing the car industry into rethinking the very existence of the business and the concept of transport. Numerous trends on various levels are currently reshaping the automotive industry. Some trends will have a lasting impact. Other trends will be short lived. The source of many of these trends is the changing environment in which the car is operating. Changing world demographics, newly emerging economies, increasing environmental legislation, diminishing protectionism and shifting subsidies are at the origin of many trends as the car manufacturers are forced to adapt to the profoundly changing surroundings. Challenges within the car companies themselves, such as declining profitability and mounting over-capacity are also a contributory factor.

CHRONOLOGY OF GROWTH

In the history of automobiles the firm Benz & Cie. In 1900, delivers 603 auto-mobiles, 341 of them abroad, making it the world's biggest automobile manufacturer. The Chrysler Corporation came into existence in 1924. In New York, Walter P. Chysler unveils, while still head of Maxwell, his ZSB car, a vehicle bearing the Chrysler name. Denied access to the New York Auto Show because the new car was not actually available for sale, Walter P. Chrysler displays the "Chrysler Six" in the lobby of the nearby Hotel Commodore, causing a media and industry sensation. The Daimler-Motoren-Gesellschaft and Benz & Cie. merge as Daimler-Benz AG in 1926. The head office of the company is in Berlin, organization of the central administration begins in Untertürk-heim. With the final assembly

21 Efraim, Levy. *Standard & Poor's Industry Survey: Autos & Auto Parts*. December 26, 2002. *Standard and Poor's Market Insight* website: http://umi.compustat.com/cgi-mi-auth/mihome.cgi

of the first 170 V (W 136 I) vehicles in van, delivery, and ambulance versions, Daimler-Benz AG resumes postwar production. A total of 214 units are produced in 1946. Daimler-Benz AG gets a foothold in the North American car market through an agency agreement with Maximilian Hoffman. 253 cars are sold in 1952.

DaimlerChrysler is one of the world's leading automotive companies. Its passenger car brands include Maybach, Mercedes-Benz, Chrysler, Jeep®, Dodge and smart. Commercial vehicle brands include Mercedes-Benz, Freightliner, Sterling, Western Star and Setra. It offers financial and other automotive services through DaimlerChrysler Services. With 365,600 employees, DaimlerChrysler achieved revenues of EUR 149.6 billion ($158.8 billion) in 2002. DaimlerChrysler has a global workforce, a global shareholder base, globally known brands and a global outlook. DaimlerChrysler's strategy rests on four pillars: Global Presence, Strong Brands, Broad Product Range, and Technology Leadership.

RECENT PERFORMANCE

Daimler Chrysler achieved an operating profit of EUR 0.6 billion for the second quarter (Q2 2002: EUR 1.7 billion). The operating profit for the second quarter of 2002 included a charge of EUR 257 million as the balance of several one-time effects. The Mercedes Car Group division increased its operating profit by 2% to 1861 million, primarily due to the full availability of the new E-Class and the CLK coupe. Chrysler Group posted a second-quarter operating loss of 1948 million (Q2 2002: operating profit of EUR 414 million including a restructuring charge of EUR 374 million). The deterioration is due to lower shipments and increased incentives, including higher provisions for marketing costs related to dealer inventories and for guaranteed residual values. At Commercial Vehicles, further progress with the implementation of efficiency-enhancing programs meant that the division's result improved from an operating loss of EUR 7 million in Q2 2002 (including restructuring expenses of EUR 39 million) to an operating profit of EUR 211 million. The Services division also improved its operating profit, by 47% to EUR 334 million due to more favorable refinancing conditions, higher margins and better risk management.

Daimler Chrysler sold a total of 1.2 million vehicles during the second quarter of this year (Q2 2002: 1.3 million). Mercedes Car Group sold 318,000 passenger cars, nearly equaling the very high prior-year figure, despite the weakness of markets in Western Europe, which are very important for this division. A decrease for the Mercedes-Benz brand (-5%) was offset by an increase for the smart brand (+7%). There was a very good market response to the new E-Class, the new CLK convertible, and the new smart roadster and roadster-coupe. Chrysler Group recorded unit sales (shipments to dealers) of 721,900 passenger cars and light trucks, 12% lower than the 816,000 vehicles recorded for Q2 2002. Higher deliveries of the Jeep® Liberty and deliveries of the new Chrysler Pacifica were more than offset by lower deliveries of other vehicles, particularly passenger cars and minivans.

Sales of 125,700 units by the Commercial Vehicles division were close to the level of Q2 2002, despite the start up of the Actros and the launch of the Viano and the new Vito, deliveries of which will not begin until September. The market has responded very positively to these new vehicles.

Freightliner achieved a slight increase in unit sales despite the very low level of demand in the United States. Group revenues for the second quarter decreased from EUR 39.3 billion to EUR 34.3 billion, primarily due to the appreciation of the euro against the US dollar, but also as a result of lower unit sales in the second quarter. Adjusted to exclude currency translation effects, the decrease amounts to 2%.

At the end of the second quarter of 2003, DaimlerChrysler employed 372,100 people worldwide (June 30, 2002: 374,100). Despite the first consolidation of the New Venture Gear Inc. with some 3,800 employees, the size of the Chrysler Group workforce decreased to 97,100 people (-6%). This was due to the measures taken to reduce costs and increase efficiency, as well as the sale of Eurostar Graz with around 2,000 employees in Q3 2002. The number of people employed by the Mercedes-Benz sales organizations for passenger cars and commercial vehicles increased by 10% to 43,700 as a result of acquiring dealerships within the framework of the Metropolitan strategy.

PT CRUISER : PERFORMANCE APPRAISAL

Box 2: PT Cruiser: transmission

To set all that power into motion, choose from a 5-speed manual transaxle or an optional 4-speed automatic.

The standard 5-speed manual transaxle has ratios spaced to give optimum performance and fuel efficiency from the standard 2.4-liter engine. A heavy-duty Getrag 5-speed manual is on GT and Dream Cruiser Series 3. The four-speed automatic is an electronic, fully adaptive transaxle, and is included with the 180-horsepower turbocharged engine. This transaxle is available on GT (shown) and Dream Cruiser Series 3 with the AutoStick® shifter. AutoStick allows you to change gears without a clutch, or ignore shifting altogether and let the transaxle shift for you.

Pick up the pace with PT Cruiser's High Output 2.4-liter turbocharged engine. It creates 220 horsepower at 5000 rpm and 245 lb.-ft. of peak torque available from 2400 to 4400 rpm. This engine is included on GT and Dream Cruiser Series 3. A new turbocharged 2.4-liter DOHC 16-valve four-cylinder engine producing 180 horsepower and 210 lb.-ft. of torque is available on Touring and Limited and included on Platinum Series. PT Cruiser's standard 2.4-liter DOHC 16-valve four-cylinder power plant offers 150 horsepower at 5,100 rpm and 162 pound-feet of torque at 4,000 rpm. You'll appreciate those numbers when you step on the gas pedal to climb a hill or pass another vehicle. Interior amenities like leather-trimmed seats with real suede accents and a leather-wrapped steering wheel are all standard on PT Limited. In fact, the interior styling of every PT Cruiser is luxurious, refined and designed to fit the customer's preferences. Interior amenities like leather-trimmed seats with real suede accents and a leather-wrapped steering wheel are standard on PT Limited. The air conditioning, power windows, rear windshield wiper/washer, rear defrost, and an AM/FM stereo radio with CD player and six speakers standard are also part the interior excellence. The car has many customization options for colours and wheels. The PT Cruiser experience includes a reassuring sense of protection. That's because we've included some of the most up-to-date safety features like Next Generation driver and passenger front air bags. The available supplemental side air bags (standard on Limited, Platinum Series, GT, and Dream Cruiser Series 3) for front occupants offer additional protection for driver and front-outboard passenger in the event of a collision. PT Cruiser's front disc and rear drum brakes provide smooth operation and good pedal feel. Large-diameter front rotors ensure ample stopping ability and heat resistance. Standard drum-type rear brakes have stamped steel hub sections and cast iron friction surfaces. Sentry Key engine immobilizer is standard on all PT Cruiser models, and prevents the engine from running without a properly encoded key, to help shut out thieves. The available Remote Keyless Entry controls door and lift-gate locks, and includes a panic alarm for extra security.

SLUMP IN CHRYSLER'S MARKET

DaimlerChrysler's picture continues to grow gloomier. Chrysler sales slumped 15%, dragged down by weakness across its entire lineup. Jeep Grand Cherokee sales were up 9%, but every other Chrysler, Dodge, and Jeep model was flat or down for the month, except for the newly arrived Chrysler Crossfire and Pacifica, for which no year-over-year comparison can be made. Chrysler sold 578 of its sporty Crossfire roadsters. And the daily sales rate for the Pacifica, a minivan-SUV blend that got off to a poor start in March, increased 15% from August to September.[22] Daimler Benz CEO Jürgen E. Schrempp carried out a $36 billion fusion with Chrysler Corp., his promise of creating the world's most profitable carmaker is a financial blowout. After an unexpected $1 billion loss in the second quarter, Chrysler may end 2003, in the red, despite Schrempp's boast a year ago that the unit would earn $2 billion this year. That wipes out the gains of 2002, and follows on the heels of the $5.8 billion loss in 2001. Survey revealed embarrassing quality deficiencies at Mercedes itself, raising questions about whether the drain on management from Chrysler was affecting the classiest of German marques. Mitsubishi Motor Corp., another troubled imperial possession that was supposed to boost profits through cost savings from shared engineering and purchasing, has warned of a $683 million first-half loss and has slashed its full-year earnings forecast by 75%, as U.S. sales plunge.[23]

Toughest challenge may be the relentless downward pressure on pricing in the U.S. In an effort to maintain share and cash flow, General Motors Corp. has continued the incentives war it launched in late 2001, changing the face of American auto retailing. Consumers considered the price tag steep for a Chrysler, especially one sharing showrooms with drastically marked-down alternatives. Little wonder the Pacifica got off to a dismal start and needed a $1,000 rebate to juice sales.

THE TIME AHEAD

Worldwide upswing that had been hoped for in the mid of 2003 did not materialize. In the euro zone, economic expectations were further dampened by the very significant appreciation of the euro against the US dollar. Sales of automobiles in the United States in the second quarter were lower than in second quarter of 2002. Even lower unit sales were only avoided by offering customers higher incentives. Demand also declined in the automotive markets of Western Europe.

22 Business Week Online : Decent Zip fro Auto Sales, News Analysis, *BW Online*, October 02, 2003
23 Gail Edmondson and Kathleen Kerwin : Daimler Chrysler Stalled, *BW Online*, September 29, 2003

However, in the recent weeks, important leading indicators indicated a potential towards an improvement in economic prospects. On this basis we expect a gradual stabilization in demand for passenger cars and light trucks in the United States, during the second half of the year. In Western Europe, however, we expect demand for passenger cars to remain at a low level for some time. Also in the market for medium and heavy trucks, we still see no signs of a sustainable upturn. Mercedes Car Group expects to attain in 2003, similar high levels of the previous year in terms of unit sales, revenues and earnings, despite the continuation of difficult market conditions. Chrysler Group has taken further steps to improve and stabilize its earnings in the second half of the year, particularly in the areas of marketing and sales, and has implemented substantial additional cost savings. For the year as a whole, Chrysler Group is still striving to achieve a slightly positive operating profit on an ongoing basis. However, there are substantial risks due to the potential development of the competitive environment in the United States.

Commercial Vehicles division expects to achieve a significant improvement in its operating profit compared with 2002, as a result of new attractive models and the effects of the ongoing efficiency-improving activities. The Services division plans that the operating profit from its ongoing business for the full year will be higher than in 2002, partly due to more favorable refinancing conditions. With the current difficult market conditions particularly in Japan and the United States, we cannot expect the same contribution from MMC to our results as in the last year. MMC will continue to implement its turnaround and will push forward with new initiatives to improve sales. The Daimler Chrysler Group is looking ahead to generate revenues of approximately EUR 135 billion in full-year 2003, lower than last year (2002: EUR 149.6 billion), primarily due to the appreciation of the euro against the US dollar but also as a result of lower unit sales.

INDEX

A

Activity Based Costing, 155-156
Activity Scheduling, 356
Advertising environment, 237
  process, 238
  categories, 239
  styles, 241
  research, 263

B

BMW, 19,131
Brand architecture, 116, 121
Brand driver, 110,125
  equity, 105, 107
  hierarchy, 118
  leverage, 108
  map, 109
  personality, 126
  positioning
Branding comprehensive, 401
Break-even analysis, 154
Breakthrough products, 9

C

Cadbury Schweppes, 305
Campaign, 232
Canon Mexico, 326
Cash flow, 369
Channel selection, 201
Chinese millers, 13
Coca-cola, 217
Collaborative
  planning, forecasting and replenishment, 200
Competition, 2, 5
Competency, 34
Competitive intelligence, 16
Competitor learning, 10
Conflict management, 200
Consumer preference, 409
Consultative sales, 310
Control management, 382
Copywriting, 256

D

Data analysis, 294
  collection, 292
Dell, 21, 406
DHL, 173
Distribution planning, 194
  physical, 212
  strategy, 196
Direct distribution, 205

E

Economic value addition, 368
EID Parry, 48

F

Flanking attack, 28
Franchise planning, 376
Frontal attack, 27

G

Gatekeeper, 368
Growth strategy, 351

H

Harley Davidson, 158
Hindustan Lever Limited, 17, 139
Hewlett Packard, 89

K

KAP Strategy, 394
Kimberly Clark, 151

L

LG Electronics, 35
Logistics management, 207
L'Oreal Netherlands, 96

M

Monopsony, 372
Market entry, 372
Market information, 296
Market place, 21
Market research decision, 286
    process, 287
Market uncertainties, 387
Marketing plan, 355
Mark-up, 149-150
Media plan, 257
Media scheduling, 243

N

New product development, 75
Niche strategy, 6

O

OECD, 18

P

Personal selling, 248
Price control, 164
Price leadership, 169
Proctor & Gamble, 22
Product design, 72
    life cycle, 74
    line, 68
    planning, 81
    portfolio, 83
    strategy, 85, 89
Profit impact on marketing strategy, 383

Q

Qualitative market research, 300

R

Reengineering, business process, 41-44
Retailing, 312

S

Sales performance, 321
    Compensation, 323
Sampling techniques, 290
Screening process, in strategic marketing, 345
Skimming, pricing strategy, 144
Social marketing, 393
Strategic direction, 346
SWOT analysis, 299

T

Titan industries, 152
Tropicana, 365

W

Wal-Mart, 53
Web advertising, 265
World Bank, 302